Psychology's Interpretive Turn

Psychology's Interpretive Turn ❦

The Search for Truth and Agency in
Theoretical and Philosophical Psychology

Barbara S. Held

American Psychological Association
Washington, DC

Published by
American Psychological Association
750 First Street, NE
Washington, DC 20002
www.apa.org

To order
APA Order Department
P.O. Box 92984
Washington, DC 20090-2984
Tel: (800) 374-2721; Direct: (202) 336-5510
Fax: (202) 336-5502; TDD/TTY: (202) 336-6123
Online: www.apa.org/books/
E-mail: order@apa.org

In the U.K., Europe, Africa, and the Middle East, copies may be ordered from
American Psychological Association
3 Henrietta Street
Covent Garden, London
WC2E 8LU England

Typeset in Goudy by Stephen McDougal, Mechanicsville, MD

Printer: Book-mart Press, Inc., North Bergen, NJ
Cover Designer: Naylor Design, Washington, DC
Technical/Production Editor: Tiffany L. Klaff

The opinions and statements published are the responsibility of the authors, and such opinions and statements do not necessarily represent the policies of the American Psychological Association.

Library of Congress Cataloging-in-Publication Data

Held, Barbara S.
  Psychology's interpretive turn : the search for truth and agency in theoretical and philosophical psychology / Barbara S. Held. — 1st ed.
      p. cm.
  Includes bibliographical references and index.
  ISBN-13: 978-1-59147-925-3
  ISBN-10: 1-59147-925-8
  1. Psychology—Philosophy. I. Title.

  BF38.H448 2007
  150.1—dc22   2006102168

British Library Cataloguing-in-Publication Data
A CIP record is available from the British Library.

Printed in the United States of America
First Edition

To the memory of Edward Pols, philosopher and poet

CONTENTS

PREFACE

With the publication of *Back to Reality* in 1995, I thought I had said all that I had to say about the antirealist epistemology, or the postmodern "linguistic turn," that had impacted psychotherapy theory and practice by the late 1980s. As it turns out, I was wrong.

At the 1997 annual convention of the American Psychological Association (APA) in Chicago, I was encouraged to join APA's Division 24 (Society for Theoretical and Philosophical Psychology) by its soon-to-be president Brent Slife. He had read *Back to Reality* appreciatively and thought I might overcome the isolation of teaching at a small college in Maine by joining a group of scholars with similar interests. He was right, although at the time I could not foresee the implications of his thoughtful invitation.

Brent was the first of several scholars in the Society to suggest that although *Back to Reality* made a good case against the excesses of postmodern antirealism, there were important matters that had been overlooked. In particular, these scholars said that whereas postmodernism had indeed shortchanged psychological inquiry by depriving it of a realist epistemology, modern objectivism had also shortchanged psychological inquiry by depriving it of an agentic ontology. Interpretation, or the "interpretive turn," is the answer to the shortcomings—or excesses, depending on how you interpret them—of both postmodern and modern approaches to psychology, these scholars maintained, and they themselves had written much about just that issue. Those individuals most keen to help me expand my horizons of understanding were—in addition to Brent Slife—Blaine Fowers and Frank Richardson, and I am grateful to all three of them for sending me their papers, encouraging me to read their books, and welcoming me into their interpretive fold. That was in 1998, the year I started to read what had been recommended by them.

By 1999 I realized that there were common themes among these and other scholars, themes that I found intriguing yet not quite satisfying. What impressed me most was their attempt to moderate or avoid the perceived extremes of both postmodern and modern approaches to psychology—and by 2000 I realized that I had conceived another book, owing to the sophisticated, nuanced, and provocative arguments of these important scholars. This time, however, I would not limit myself to psychotherapy but would consider questions that pertained to the philosophy of psychology as a whole. Moreover, I would expand my analysis to include ontological as well as epistemological matters. And so *Psychology's Interpretive Turn* was born.

Other scholars in the Society, and some who are not, deserve credit for helping me to think with greater breadth and depth. Ronald Miller and Daniel Fishman, for inviting me to comment critically on their own philosophies of psychology, both on their panels and in their journal. M. Brewster Smith, Alan Tjeltveit, Hank Stam, James Coyne, David Livingstone Smith, David Jopling, Benjamin Folkman, and Daniel Robinson, for encouraging me to swim upstream against the tide of antiobjectivism that has come to dominate the philosophy of those who seek an agentic psychology. Last, but certainly not least, Joseph Rychlak and Stan Messer, for their efforts in bringing *Back to Reality* to the broadest possible readership, which will no doubt have consequence for this new volume. My heartfelt thanks to them all.

Of no lesser importance are the several scholars in the Philosophy Department at the University of Miami in Coral Gables, Florida, who, in giving me a visiting scholar position in the Spring 2001 term, also gave me the knowledge I would need to strengthen my analysis. Conversations and courses with Edward Erwin, Harvey Siegel (department chair), Susan Haack, and Charles Siewert were invaluable. I owe my greatest debt of gratitude to Amie Thomasson, whose own philosophy turned out to be the most important gift of all. Without her seminal "upstream" work in the ontology of human and other kinds, my book's core would have been considerably less substantial. That she later read and commented critically on the entire book manuscript, and gave me countless hours of clarifying discussion, made her my most crucial resource.

My thanks also to my colleagues in the Psychology Department at Bowdoin College in Brunswick, Maine, for putting up with my leaves while I wrote; to my husband, David Bellows, and my friends and colleagues David Page, Jeff Nagle, Peter Doan, and the late Peter Trumper, all from Bowdoin's Chemistry Department, for their unfailing support; to the students in my advanced seminar, who asked all the right, hard questions; and to Bowdoin College for the funding that made my time at the University of Miami possible. I am especially grateful to my former student Timothy McIntyre and to my colleague Richmond Thompson, of Bowdoin's Psychology Department, for their helpful comments on the manuscript. Thanks also to psychology majors Luke ("Luciano") Monahan, Alexa Ogata, Sarah Clark, Sara Afienko, and Hande Ozergin for their help in preparing the manuscript for publication; to Eliot Werner of Eliot Werner Publications for his keen editorial eye; and to Susan Reynolds of APA Books for swimming upstream with this "salmon" author by taking a chance on an unusual book and Emily Leonard and Tiffany Klaff of APA Books for turning my manuscript into a book.

Though he is now gone, I again owe everything to my dear friend, colleague, and mentor Edward Pols, who taught me how to think philosophically, both in individual tutorial and by personal example. It is to him that this volume is dedicated.

I

INTRODUCTION
AND ORIGINS

.

1

INTRODUCTION

Truth is always in the middle. A demonstrably false maxim, yet perenni-
ally appealing to those who like to see themselves as balanced and moderate judges. If this maxim were true, then the truth must lie at B midway
between A and C; but then it is also and incompatibly at the midpoints
between B and A and B and C.
  —Antony Flew, A Dictionary of Philosophy: Revised Second Edition

Psychologists and philosophers have long challenged the application of
philosophies (of being and knowing) devised for inquiry in the natural sciences to inquiry in the social sciences, including the psychological inquiry
that is the subject of my analysis. In more recent years, many have proposed
alternative philosophies of what are frequently called the human sciences,
which are defined in distinction to the natural sciences. The distinction rests
especially on the desire to preserve the human agency, or a broadly conceived capacity for self-determination,[1] that many believe disappeared in the
(mechanistically)[2] deterministic shuffle of natural science methodology.

For over 25 years, the most visible and popular of these alternative philosophies has been embodied in the postmodern movement, which—in all
its diverse incarnations[3]—propounds some form of antirealist or antiobjectivist

---

I am indebted to Charles Siewert for bringing the quotation that opens this chapter to my attention.
[1]I have much more to say about the definitions of *agency* that abound, especially in chapter 6.
[2]Because the agentic notion of self-determination implies a kind of determinism, I distinguish it from
nonagentic determinism by use of the term *mechanistic/nonagentic determinism* or simply *mechanistic
determinism.*
[3]See Rosenau (1992) and Fishman (1999), who distinguish various forms of postmodernism, some of
which are more extreme than others. For example, Rosenau distinguishes "affirmative" postmodernists
from their more extreme "skeptical" comrades.

epistemology (or theory of knowledge): that knowers make or construct in language, rather than discover, social or psychological reality. The postmodern movement embraces both social constructionist (e.g., Gergen, 1985, 1994) and constructivist (e.g., Neimeyer & Mahoney, 1995; Rosen & Kuehlwein, 1996) doctrines.[4] And it aims especially to "liberate" humans from the seemingly oppressive, reductionistic forces of the mechanistically deterministic causality that postmodernists find in modern/conventional psychology, where a realist or objectivist epistemology prevails. The postmodern movement is therefore said to advance human agency, or self-determination, in virtue of its antirealist/antiobjectivist philosophy. According to that philosophy, we are free to become what we subjectively interpret or linguistically construct ourselves to be. About this, more in due course (Held, 1995, 1998a, 2001, 2002a, 2002b).

In the past decade, growing disenchantment with postmodernism has been expressed not only by those antagonistic to the very idea of postmodernism but also by those who have some degree of sympathy with it. A prominent sign of the latter group's disenchantment can be found within the writings of philosophically minded theorists who strive to avoid the (for them) unacceptable extremes of both the postmodernist and the modernist philosophies of psychology with which they nonetheless share certain commonalities. In advancing their more nuanced philosophical arguments, adherents of this proliferating "new-wave" alternative therefore seek a middle ground between what are variously called (a) the antirealist, antiobjectivist, antiessentialist, antifoundationalist, antideterministic, antiuniversalist, and ultimately *nihilist* doctrines of the more radical or bona fide postmodernists, on the one hand, and what are variously called (b) the scientistic, positivistic, objectivist, essentialist, absolutistic, deterministic, universalist, foundationalist and ultimately *reductionistic* doctrines of modern/conventional psychological scientists, on the other. Because many of these new-wave theorists speak expressly of seeking a middle-ground philosophy of psychology, I call them "middle-ground theorists" (or MGTs)—although this is not what they call themselves, perhaps because collectively they cover a range of philosophical views and because they sometimes prefer to speak of transcendence in addition to moderation or mediation. About these terminological matters, more later in this chapter and in chapter 3.

In light of their philosophical diversity and the fact that these theorists do not organize themselves as middle-ground theorists (MGTs), it would be wrong to think of them as constituting a movement proper, at least in any

---

[4]For distinctions (and similarities) between the doctrines of social constructionism and constructivism, see Held (1995, pp. 102–105), Neimeyer (1998), and Stam (1998). Just here note that the differences in the two doctrines (which have dissipated over the years) originated in the question of whether humans construct reality individually (constructivism) or collectively, as a function of local discursive or social contexts (social constructionism).

conventional or explicit sense. However, because they all commit themselves—in one way or another—to locating a middle-ground or moderating alternative to both modernist and (radical) postmodernist philosophies of psychology, I find in them a commonality that merits our consideration. Indeed, if MGTs were to found a bona fide scientific approach to psychological inquiry that avoids both the nihilism they find in (radical) postmodern psychology and the reductionism they find in modern/conventional psychology, they would no doubt become the collective object of considerable scholarly attention. After all, their numbers are growing and their ambitious "common" pursuit of a philosophical middle ground may well be on its way to replacing "conventional" postmodernism as the stronger—or at least more complex—challenge to modern or mainstream approaches to psychology. Moreover, they arrive on the scene as concerns about psychology's fragmentation mount and attempts at unification proliferate (e.g., Henriques, 2003; Sternberg, 2005).

Yet to date there exists no comprehensive, systematic consideration of these theorists' views, especially of their answers to two of psychology's most fundamental philosophical questions. First, an *epistemological* question: Is objective psychological knowledge possible? Second, an *ontological* question: How does that possibility (or its absence) pertain to human agency (or freedom)? In this volume I analyze their answers to those two questions about knowing/knowledge (or epistemology) and being/existence (or ontology), and in so doing I suggest some answers that depart considerably from theirs.

In expressly seeking an innovative philosophy of psychology, these theorists' criticisms of both modern/conventional and (radical) postmodern approaches to psychology have recently become even more penetrating, incisive, and provocative. It therefore seems odd that so far no comprehensive assessment of their mounting arguments has appeared. There may be compelling reasons for this paucity of critical response. One is that the postmodern movement within psychology is itself so very broad that it covers many disparate factions under its huge umbrella (see Fishman, 1999; Held, 1995; Rosenau, 1992). For that reason MGTs may not be seen as distinct enough from (radical or bona fide) postmodernists to constitute their own movement—although I hope to demonstrate in this volume just why that belief would be mistaken. Moreover, the postmodern movement within psychology is still fairly young, and those who criticize that movement (including MGTs) are relative newcomers to the scene as members of an identifiable group. After all, MGTs do not indicate that they perceive themselves as members of a movement, and—as we shall see—they sometimes put forth disparate views about what it means to locate a philosophical middle ground for psychology.

Whatever the reasons for the dearth of critical response to MGTs as an identifiable entity, there is much to be gained from considering them a coherent movement. In seeking middle-ground answers to the two fundamental philosophical questions (about the nature of psychological knowledge and its relation to human agency), these theorists share a common commitment to what some have called the "interpretive turn" in the social or human sciences. This is a turn in which conventional views about the "foundations of knowledge" and the nature of the "knowing subject" (Bohman, Hiley, & Shusterman, 1991, p. 1) are called into question.[5] In making the interpretive turn, these scholars take the (contextualized) interpretive or meaning-making powers and acts of human agents to be fundamental both to human (social and psychological) *existence* (an ontological matter) and to *inquiry* about that existence (an epistemological matter). They also, in their efforts to transform the discipline of psychology, commit themselves to acknowledging and advancing "human freedom, agency, and power" in ways that those who have not taken the interpretive turn, such as modern/conventional psychologists, are said not to have committed themselves. Bohman et al. (1991) expressed this succinctly.

> From the point of view of the human sciences, the claim of the uniqueness of interpretive methods not only protected them from the imperialism of natural scientific method but also involved important ontological, moral, and political convictions having to do with human freedom, agency, and power. (p. 4)

Manifestations of the interpretive turn taken with a moderating or mediating impulse and attention to human agency can be seen in many seminal writings of the past 2 decades, though it is in the past decade that they have begun to proliferate. Here, arranged chronologically, are some of the books that exemplify this trend: Bernstein's (1983) *Beyond Objectivism and Relativism*; Polkinghorne's (1983) *Methodology for the Human Sciences*; Howard's (1986) *Dare We Develop a Human Science?*; Messer, Sass, and Woolfolk's (1988a) *Hermeneutics and Psychological Theory*; Faulconer and Williams's (1990b) *Reconsidering Psychology*; Hiley, Bohman, and Shusterman's (1991) *The Interpretive Turn*; Freeman's (1993) *Rewriting the Self*; Slife and Williams's (1995) *What's Behind the Research?*; Harré and Stearns's (1995) *Discursive Psychology in Practice*; Harré's (1998) *The Singular Self*; Martin and Sugarman's (1999a) *The Psychology of Human Possibility and Constraint*; Fishman's (1999) *The Case for Pragmatic Psychology*; Richardson, Fowers, and Guignon's (1999) *Re-Envisioning Psychology*; Martin, Sugarman, and Thompson's (2003) *Psychology and the Question of Agency*; Hersch's (2003) *From Philosophy to Psychotherapy*; Slife, Reber, and Richardson's (2005) *Critical Thinking About Psychology*; and Fowers's (2005) *Virtue and Psychology*.

---

[5]In *The Interpretive Turn*, Bohman et al. (1991) draw a distinction between philosophy's "linguistic turn," which concerned the "structure of language, word-world relationships, and the analysis of meaning" and the "interpretive turn," which has, in a variety of interpretive disciplines, called into question "views about the foundations of knowledge and the knowing subject" (p. 1).

Although all in search of a philosophical middle ground for the "human sciences" have taken the interpretive turn in one way or another, not all who have taken the interpretive turn are in search of a middle ground. Indeed, the radical postmodernists, who represent one pole or extreme against which MGTs have defined their positions, may also be said to have taken the interpretive turn, albeit in a less moderate way. In my previous volume *Back to Reality* (Held, 1995), I criticized the impact of the (radical) postmodern movement on psychotherapy, especially as it pertained to the unique particularity of therapy patients. In this volume I attend to the important ontological and epistemological questions that occupy MGTs, who seek to revise the discipline of psychology as a whole (i.e., including most if not all of its subdisciplines)[6] but with a moderating philosophical impulse. Their revisionist efforts are therefore broad in scope, and their answers to the two fundamental philosophical questions (about psychological knowing and being) that I have already set forth are indeed more subtle and nuanced (and so in some ways more difficult to challenge) than those of bona fide postmodernists. This of course only adds to their importance.

I do not aim to cover the entire range of alternatives to conventional/ modernist and radical postmodernist philosophies of psychology that abound and proliferate as I write. Rather, my goals are more modest. In addressing two of psychology's core philosophical questions (about the possibility of objective psychological knowledge and its relation to human agency), I set my sights on those who—in taking the interpretive turn—have expressed their aim to locate a middle ground between, or moderation of, the two perceived extremes. And they seek a middle ground that integrates, reconciles, avoids, and/or transcends those perceived extremes for nothing short of the purpose of revising our understanding of human psychological existence (ontology) and in consequence transforming our approach to psychological inquiry (epistemology).

At this point I find the common message propounded by MGTs to be far more important than the message of bona fide or radical (i.e., non-middle-

---

[6]For example, Richardson et al. (1999) state the following:

> There are areas of psychological investigation that may be best served by naturalistic, straightforwardly scientific methods, such as neuropsychology or basic sensory psychology. These domains of study are not as likely to be influenced by the interpretive capacity of humans as, say, applied social or clinical psychology . . . . The naturalistic model is appropriate to studies of the physical infrastructure of human action. (p. 278)

Similarly, Miller (2004) states the following:

> Although physiological psychology; the study of psychophysics; and, possibly, some aspects of sensation, perception, and learning do lend themselves to causal analysis, the problems of developmental, social, personality, and abnormal clinical psychology are biographical and do not lend themselves to causal analysis in the traditional sense. (p. 141)

However, Slife and Hopkins (2005) argue on behalf of "an alternative interpretive framework" (p. 143) for neuroscience research. See Miller (2006a, 2006b) and Held (2006a, 2006b) for elaboration of Miller's views.

ground-seeking) postmodernists, even though the latter—unlike the former—enjoy the (promotional) benefits of working within an explicitly labeled movement. I proclaim the greater importance of the MGTs not only because of a pervasive disenchantment with and compelling critique of postmodernism across the academic landscape (e.g., Gross, Levitt, & Lewis, 1996; Norris, 1990; Patai & Corral, 2005) but also because MGTs are unique in their complex efforts to reconcile what have generally been viewed as the irreconcilable, opposing philosophies of modern and postmodern psychologies.

Thus the MGTs' common message leads them (and us) to reconsider fundamental questions about (a) the nature of psychological existence, especially regarding agency and causality, and (b) the best way to conduct psychological inquiry to attain truth or knowledge, given the nature of psychological existence. The mission that guides their efforts may therefore embody greater potential for disciplinary psychology. For that reason, and because MGTs (unlike bona fide postmodernists) do not cast their common message within the confines of a self-labeled movement, I quote them liberally. Using their own words surely gives a fuller sense of their distinct arguments as individual theorists, which in turn allows differences as well as commonalities in their views to be appreciated. Moreover, extensive quotation also gives evidence that I have not merely (linguistically) constructed either them or their common message. To the contrary, both the theorists themselves and their common message exist independently of my own notice and (interpretive) discussion of them, so they may be said to have an objective existence, though I have of course constructed the term *middle-ground theorists* (and its acronym, MGTs) to characterize them and their common aspirations.

A TWO-PRONGED MISSION: TRUTH AND AGENCY

Let us begin now to flesh out the two-pronged mission at which I have only just hinted in more explicit terms and as MGTs themselves express it: (a) to defend the realism denied by the antirealism that radical postmodernists propound in the name of agency or freedom and (b) to defend the agency denied by the mechanistically deterministic theory of causality that MGTs find in the objectivism of modern/conventional psychology. Put differently, MGTs argue that (a) radical postmodern psychologists, in making their interpretive (or linguistic/conceptual) turn, have taken their antirealist philosophies too far. In so doing, they have compromised psychology's ability to be a truth-tracking enterprise, one that can provide realist knowledge about human psychological existence. MGTs also argue that (b) modern/conventional psychologists have failed to make any interpretive turn owing to their objectivist philosophies. Their objectivism is said to necessitate a mechanistically deterministic and reductionistic ontology (or theory of causality), which has compromised psychology's ability to acknowledge the agency, freedom, or self-determination that we enjoy by way of our interpretive or meaning-making powers.

Later in this chapter, and in chapters 2 through 3, I elaborate just how a realist or an objectivist theory of knowledge (i.e., epistemology)—realism/objectivism that I equate but which MGTs do not[7]—came to be linked by radical postmodernists to an antiagentic (or mechanistically deterministic and reductionistic) theory of human psychological existence (i.e., ontology). I also explain how MGTs, in accepting that link, have tried to maintain a *realist*, but not *objectivist*, epistemology without relinquishing human agency or the (ontological) capacity for self-determination. After all, it is not immediately obvious how either a realist/objectivist or an antirealist/antiobjectivist *epistemology* should have any bearing whatsoever on the *ontological* matter of human agency in particular and the nature of causality (deterministic or otherwise) in general. Making this link more obvious will therefore be a recurring theme throughout this volume. Indeed, in addressing the two questions that guide my analysis, I do find an important link between the ontological matter of agency, on the one hand, and the epistemological matter of warranted knowing, on the other. But mine is not the link that radical postmodernists or even MGTs suppose. Moreover, the MGTs' attempt to reconstrue that link (between agency and knowing) in more realist terms has substantial consequence for psychology nonetheless. That consequence can be seen especially in the MGTs' reconstrual of what the subject matter of psychological inquiry should properly be.

In my analysis I assess whether any of these MGTs are succeeding in their mission. Have they indeed found a valid philosophical middle ground, both ontologically and epistemologically, between modern objectivist and postmodern antirealist approaches to psychology? Or are they merely a manifestation of one or the other, cloaked in new terminology? If they do succeed in their intended mission, then they may well affect our view of psychological existence (i.e., our ontology) and, consequently, our approach to psychological inquiry (i.e., our epistemology) in ways not attained or even envisioned by radical postmodernists—who, owing to their more extreme positions, have indeed made themselves vulnerable to extensive critique across the academic landscape (e.g., Cheney, 1995; Crews, 2001; D'Souza, 1991; Ellis, 1989; Farber & Sherry, 1997; Glass, 1993; Gross, Levitt, & Lewis, 1996; Himmelfarb, 1994; Kimball, 1990; Koertge, 1998; Lehman, 1991; Norris, 1990; Patai & Corral, 2005; Windschuttle, 1996).

Although the MGTs' philosophical positions are (to be sure) more moderate and subtle, and so less vulnerable to immediate defeat, than those of radical postmodernists, their mission is revolutionary nonetheless. They seek nothing short of a transformation of the discipline of psychology as a

---

[7]In chapters 8 to 9, I explore critically and in detail how MGTs claim to have attained a realist epistemology that is not objectivist.

whole (see note 6), in the name of attaining psychological truth or knowledge and maintaining human agency. It is time, then, to assess whether their ontological and epistemological arguments and recommendations are sound and justified: Would psychology indeed benefit from their interpretation-based vision of overhaul?

Here I should add that it may be a bit misleading to entitle this volume *Psychology's Interpretive Turn*. After all, the so-called "turn" is one that some psychologists have taken, but many—probably most—psychologists have not. Both postmodernists and their more moderate, middle-ground-seeking colleagues hold out hope that the interpretive turn will become ubiquitous, or taken for granted, as the correct(ive) philosophy for the human (or social) sciences in general and psychological science in particular. As Bohman, Hiley, and Shusterman (1991) put it, "'Hermeneutic universalism' [is] the claim that interpretation is a universal and ubiquitous feature of all human activity" (p. 7). MGTs surely accept this claim, albeit with different implications for psychology than those envisioned by radical postmodernists. But are they right to do so? It depends on what is meant by "interpretation," and Bohman et al. (1991) say there is no consensus about that: "The more philosophy and the interpretive disciplines [e.g., literary criticism, cultural anthropology, jurisprudence, historiography, feminist theory] proclaim the importance of interpretation in all inquiry, the less there is agreement about what it is, what interpretive practices presuppose, and how to judge interpretive successes and failures" (p. 1). This assertion does not bode well for those who seek consensus about interpretation in the human sciences, for the attainment of either (a) evidential criteria about what constitutes valid or true interpretations, in the hope of avoiding "nihilistic," "relativistic," "ethnocentric," or authoritarian interpretive practices (Bohman et al., 1991, p. 2), or (b) a strong revisionary impact on the human sciences.

BETWEEN MODERN AND POSTMODERN PSYCHOLOGIES

This volume, then, gives my analysis of current views about the nature of psychological truth/knowledge and its relationship to human agency. I conduct my analysis with express attention to the efforts of recently fashionable psychologists and philosophers who have attempted to steer a middle course between what they perceive to be two opposing philosophical extremes. Let us now begin to sketch the two perceived extremes with the broadest strokes possible. This I follow with further explication of the twin goals (or two-pronged mission) of the MGTs.

1. Modern/Conventional Psychology

On the one hand, there are the greatly sought virtues of objectivity and realism that underlie much if not all of modern/conventional psychological inquiry. These philosophical allegiances (about which more in this chapter and chapter 3) are seen to provide a basis for discovering the objective, deterministic, and general (if not universal) causal laws that govern human psychological existence. Owing to their very governing nature (and failing any successful compatibilist formulation),[8] these laws are thought by many to deprive humans of agentic action (or self-determination/freedom) in any conventional or traditional sense. After all, if we exist psychologically according to mechanistically deterministic causal laws that function independently of our beliefs about their nature (this is why the laws are said to be objective), then how can we be said to act agentically—that is, with purpose or intention derived from some degree of autonomy or freedom of will?

2. Postmodern Psychology

On the other hand, there are the much celebrated "virtues" of subjectivity[9] and antirealism that have propelled what can now be fairly called (radical) postmodern psychological inquiry. Postmodernist inquiry in psychology typically takes human agency or self-determination to be one of its foundational assumptions, especially in its emphasis on the purposive but epistemically subjective act of human interpretation of all experience. In a nutshell, if objective (psychological) knowledge is itself merely illusory—a wish born of "Cartesian Anxiety" over epistemic uncertainty (Bernstein, 1983, p. 19)—we are then seemingly free to be whatever we "agentically" choose (subjectively) to interpret, narrate, believe, or desire ourselves to be. This is of course especially the case if there are no (objective) mechanistically deterministic causal laws that govern or constrain our psychological existence and that can thus in principle be discovered, in the first place. Therefore the antiobjectivist/subjectivist (or antirealist) epistemology of radical postmodernism becomes linked to its antideterministic, or "agentic," ontology (more about these philosophical views and the specific radical postmodernist theorists and therapists who propound them in chap. 2).

---

[8]See Erwin (1997, pp. 1–19) for a discussion of the compatibilist possibility of having "autonomy" and "free choice" within the confines of a "lawful" or deterministic science of psychotherapy. He rests this possibility on the distinction between what he calls "metaphysical autonomy," which he says "presupposes the freedom needed for moral responsibility" and which may "always remain beyond our reach" (p. 17), and "inner autonomy," which he says includes (a) "the capacity to reflect on one's preferences, wishes, and values, and to change them" based on rational deliberation; (b) "eliminating one's defective desires, wishes, and values"; and (c) "increasing the capacity for self-control" (p. 18).

[9]Here I use the term *subjectivity* to refer to an epistemological doctrine in distinction to objectivity. The term *subjectivity* is problematic for postmodernists, owing to the denial of a coherent subject or self in radical postmodernist ontologies. Of course if there is no subject or self, postmodernists are left with the problem of how they can defend their subjectivist epistemologies. See Held (1995, pp. 15–20) for elaboration, and chapters 3 and 8 of this volume for more on the objective/subjective distinction.

3. The Middle Ground: A Two-Pronged Mission

The protagonists in my analysis are the MGTs themselves. In seeking to reconcile the two perceived extremes, MGTs aim for an approach to psychological inquiry that does justice to their view of our agentic human nature. This view especially emphasizes our (rational) capacity for the interpretation or meaning making that they say guides our actions in ways that are not mechanistic or reductionistic. This is an agency that they (unlike radical postmodernists) seek without relinquishing realism, in either ontological or epistemological terms. It is sought, that is, without relinquishing the attainment of the most complete and true (i.e., realist) account of human psychological existence possible. Thus the *twin goals* (or two-pronged mission) of the MGTs parallel the *two fundamental philosophical questions* that guide my analysis. The two-pronged mission is (a) to attain a truth-tracking (or realist) form of psychological inquiry that (b) does justice to the realities of human agency. As we shall see in chapter 2, the first goal (a) was abandoned from the start by radical or bona fide postmodernists, who purchased "agency" (or freedom) at the expense of realist inquiry of any sort. Again, I believe this difference puts MGTs in a stronger position—or at least a more defensible one—than their postmodernist colleagues.

In short, MGTs claim to work between two opposing forces: (a) the Scylla of modern/conventional psychology that, they argue, does not even try to give human agency its due because it allegedly denies the existence of that agency in virtue of its objective, mechanistically deterministic causal laws and (b) the Charybdis of postmodern psychology that, MGTs argue, cannot give human agency its due—despite its intention to do just that in making its now famous linguistic turn—owing to its unconstrained antirealism and relativism. Although they often use the metaphor of the middle ground to describe their quest, MGTs sometimes speak of transcending the two perceived extremes to attain a "ground" that is at once loftier and more inclusive than either or both of them (see chap. 3). However, I adhere to the metaphor of the middle ground throughout my account and analysis, because I think it best captures that to which MGTs aspire.

I have already suggested that there is diversity within the ranks of those whom I consider MGTs. Indeed, they descend from a variety of theoretical schools within psychology and philosophy, including what has been called (neo)hermeneutics (e.g., Freeman, 1993; Hersch, 2003; Martin & Sugarman, 1999a; Richardson, Fowers, & Guignon, 1999; Woolfolk, 1998), (moderate) social or discursive constructionism (e.g., Edley, 2001; Freeman, 1993; Harré, 2002; Liebrucks, 2001), and (neo)pragmatism (e.g., Fishman, 1999; Miller, 2004).[10]

---

[10]Although he advocates pragmatism to some extent in the form of the "'pragmatic case study' approach" (p. 210) that Fishman propounds, Miller (2004) seems to lean more toward a narrative framework when he offers a "comprehensive narrative psychotherapy case study" approach (p. 211).

And yet their nuanced views about psychological existence and knowledge about that existence tend to overlap. This is seen not least in their ubiquitous allegiance to interpretation (or active knowing) *within* an interpretive context, which for them constitutes a core feature of psychological existence or agency (chaps. 4–7) as well as an epistemic condition (chaps. 8–9). They are therefore committed to taking an interpretive turn in one way or another, and always with their eyes on the ball of moderating radical postmodernist and conventional/modernist philosophies of psychology. Because their theoretical and philosophical allegiances overlap, it is difficult to classify them along clear ideological lines.

For example, Freeman (1993, pp. 15–16) seems to adopt hermeneutics as his framework, but he nonetheless fuses the language of Gadamerian hermeneutics with social constructionism when he seeks to

> bring these ideas together . . . by saying that just as narrators tell about their lives in ways that are circumscribed by the social world in which they live—hence the "social construction of narrative"—so too do readers read, bringing their respective horizons of expectation with them. (p. 200)

Fishman (1999, 2001) calls himself a pragmatist, yet he (2001) says, "The pragmatic psychology view can be characterized as a 'moderate' constructionist position that also falls in the middle of the realist versus constructionist continuum" (p. 279). He also says that the "moderate constructionism" he adopts has "its basis in 'pragmatic relativism'" (pp. 279–280). "Moderate constructionism is consistent with pragmatism's de-emphasis on ontological issues of what is real" (p. 280). Neimeyer (1995, 1998), a decidedly radical constructivist who calls himself an *"arealist"* by claiming to be "only vaguely interested in the ontological question of whether a real world exists in any meaningful sense beyond our construction of it" (1995, pp. 341–342), also says that social constructionism and constructivism both endorse a "neopragmatic theory of truth" (1998, p. 141).

Moreover, as we shall see, some MGTs regularly cite each other with approbation; this suggests at least an informal bond among them. Of prime importance, most if not all the MGTs whom I review propound a pragmatic epistemology that gives their antiobjectivism common ground (chap. 9). However, it is their two-pronged mission—their quest for a psychology that (a) gives a truth-tracking or realist (but not objectivist) account of human psychological existence and yet (b) does not deprive humans of their agentic (interpretive) capacities—that ultimately unites them in middle-ground philosophical territory. In short, they want all the realism of modern/

That he and Fishman have joined forces in editing the online journal *Pragmatic Case Studies in Psychotherapy* suggests that the two frameworks are not incompatible, and so I will continue to place Miller with Fishman in the pragmatic camp, though he may see himself as quasi-pragmatic at best (see chap. 3, note 12).

conventional psychology, but without its attendant objectivism, which they problematically equate with mechanistic determinism and reductionism; they want all the "agency" of postmodernism, but without its attendant antirealism and extreme relativism. The attainment of realism without objectivism, then, lies at the heart of the mission they set for themselves. I therefore give considerable attention to that (daunting) goal, beginning with the next two sections of this chapter. Despite this common aspiration (to attain realism without objectivism), I nonetheless introduce individual MGTs in chapter 3 by way of the three "traditions" in which they work, to demonstrate just how much their middle-ground quests—and the middle-ground language in which they express those quests—overlap.

GOALS OF THIS VOLUME

A Critique With New Philosophical Voices

In contributing to the existing discourse about the quest for a truth-tracking psychology that gives agency its due, I present in some detail the work of philosophers whose views have not heretofore been represented in the writings of MGTs—this despite the fact that these views are highly relevant to the MGTs' ontological and epistemological arguments. Thus in the course of responding to the two philosophical questions that guide my analysis—again: (a) is objective psychological knowledge possible? and (b) how does that possibility (or its absence) pertain to human agency?—I hold specific goals of my own. First, I set forth in a systematic way the approaches to human psychology proposed by MGTs for their self-proclaimed (dual) purposes, so that their nuanced arguments about psychological truth and agency can then be seen as constituting an identifiable position in which common guiding philosophical assumptions and disciplinary aspirations prevail. Second, I subject that identifiable position about psychological truth and agency to critical analysis, with the help of those profoundly relevant philosophical voices that have gone unheard by MGTs and their radical postmodern colleagues. These voices are especially relevant to my own answers to the two philosophical questions that guide my analysis.

In the course of my critique, then, I aim to broaden the discourse about the two perceived philosophical extremes to which MGTs respond in their mediating or moderating quest—not least by questioning the extent to which certain assumptions about each of the perceived extremes are warranted. I give particular attention to problematic assumptions made by MGTs about (a) the nature of epistemic objectivity and (b) the consequences of their understanding of objective (psychological) knowledge for psychological existence or agency as well as psychological inquiry. These consequences are said by MGTs (as well as bona fide postmodernists) to follow (logically) from adopting an objectivist epistemology as they understand it; these consequences therefore constitute some of the MGTs' (as well as bona fide postmodernists') primary reasons for rejecting conventional objectivist approaches to psychology. It is time, then, to set forth in a preliminary way the ontological and epistemological definitions of objectivity that I will use throughout my analysis. Here recall again that whereas I equate objectivism and realism, MGTs do not. It is only with this distinction in mind that we can begin to appreciate how MGTs attempt to defend realism while repudiating objectivism in pursuing their revisionist goals for psychology.

Preliminary Definitions of Ontological and Epistemological Objectivity

That the meanings of the terms *objectivity*, *realist*, *subjectivity*, and *antirealist* as well as their many variants (e.g., *objectivism*, *realism*, *subjectivism*, *antirealism*) have themselves been the object of much contention complicates my account. After all, these terms have both ontological and epistemological meanings—that is, they make reference to philosophies of being and knowing, respectively—and which meaning is in play at any given moment, and in any given text, is not always obvious. Moreover, postmodernists have typically embraced subjectivity in an epistemic sense to deny the possibility of objective (or realist) knowledge, while at the same time denying the existence of a coherent ontological subject (see note 9). This complicates matters further, as does the MGTs' desire to embrace the *realist epistemology* that bona fide or radical postmodernists deny, while simultaneously rejecting the possibility of objective knowledge and knowing (i.e., an *objectivist epistemology*). Accordingly, I address these definitional problems in a preliminary way here and in chapter 2, and again with considerable elaboration in chapter 3. Throughout my account I attempt to be as clear as possible about the ways in which I am using these terms, as well as others (such as *relativism*) that are central to the arguments of MGTs.

For now, let us begin with these preliminary definitions: An objectivist or realist *ontology* grants that there is a way that the world is, and that this way is independent of anyone's beliefs about how the world is. This is so even if beliefs about the nature of the world, including especially the human world, can and sometimes do change the way the world is. An objectivist or realist *epistemology* grants that the truth of a claim about (some aspect of) the world is independent of anyone's beliefs about the truth of that claim. I call these two definitions preliminary, because how they can obtain when the aspect of the world under consideration is mind-dependent—which psychological entities, kinds, or phenomena of course are—is a matter that calls for more distinctions. These I offer in chapters 3, 5, 8, and 9.

Not surprising, the term *agency* also suffers from a similar plurality of meaning. Consider this statement: "At this point in the history of inquiry, traditional notions of agency are dead or dying, and their replacements have yet to be born or yet to reach maturity" (Davies, 2005). I take up the matter of agency in detail in chapter 6, where I set forth the various ways in which MGTs use and define this term to emphasize the freedom and transcendence that allegedly follow from our *interpretive* agentic powers. Just here I continue to use more commonsense notions of agency, such as the autonomy, self-determination, or freedom thought by many to be expressed in purposive or intentional action (e.g., Pols, 1998; Rychlak, 1997). However, I emphasize one meaning or another throughout the volume, depending on my intended emphasis.

THE TWO-PRONGED MISSION REVISITED: REALISM VERSUS OBJECTIVISM?

The two-pronged mission of MGTs—(a) the attainment of a truth-tracking/realist (but not objectivist!) form of inquiry about human psychological existence that (b) champions the agentic nature of that existence—is central to my analysis for two reasons: first, because these goals parallel the two foundational philosophical questions (about the possibility of objective psychological knowledge and its pertinence to agency) that I address in this volume; second, because these goals appear to motivate much of what MGTs have contributed to the discourse about those two foundational questions. Moreover, depending on how the term *truth* is defined in psychological inquiry (chap. 5), these twin goals can be construed as nothing short of a bona fide version of the problem of the compatibility of determinism and free will (see note 8).

That last point is not obvious; let me therefore make it a bit differently. MGTs (as well as radical postmodernists) claim that in modern/conventional (i.e., objectivist) psychological inquiry, truth or knowledge consists in the discovery of universal, deterministic causal laws that (a) govern psychological existence mechanistically and that (b) are deemed objective in virtue of their operation independently of our beliefs about their existence and nature. How then, MGTs pointedly ask, can that (objectivist) inquiry possibly credit such mechanistically determined beings with the agentic powers of self-determination that they seem (so obviously)[11] to have? Either the mechanistically deterministic psychological laws that are supposed to be known objectively or the insistence on an ontology of human agency or self-determination would have to be relinquished. Because for MGTs agency cannot be abandoned—it is what fuels their campaign—we are left with epistemic

---

[11]In asking "What Kind of Agent Are We?" Davies (2005) challenges the tendency to hold tight to "traditional notions of agency" and uses that tendency as evidence of what he calls "conceptual conservatism," if not "conceptual imperialism." He argues that neither is acceptable in bona fide scientific inquiry, in which we must always be ready to give up even our most dearly held concepts and beliefs.

objectivity (i.e., objective psychological knowledge) as the dispensable doctrine. To put this the other way around: If one starts with the inviolable assumption of an agentic psychological ontology and one equates an objectivist epistemology (or objective psychological knowledge) with the discovery of mechanistically deterministic causal laws, then one cannot compatibly hold an objectivist epistemology—unless, that is, a compatibilist middle-ground solution is worked out (chap. 9). More typically, MGTs have sought to fulfill their two-pronged mission—to achieve their twin goals—by changing the conventional meaning of the term *realism* (or *realist*), so as to distinguish it from the "objectivism" (or "objectivity") that they denounce (chap. 5).

I contend that this (MGT) formulation of the problem of conducting truth-tracking/realist (but not objectivist) psychological inquiry—and thus attaining true/realist (but not objective) psychological knowledge—without relinquishing (the truth/reality of) human agency unnecessarily conflates epistemic objectivity (or the possibility of attaining objective psychological knowledge) with a mechanistically deterministic ontology (or theory of causality). I find this conflation both in the formulations of MGTs and their radical postmodern colleagues. In their attempts to exalt human agency, both groups seek to banish from psychological inquiry the search for (mechanistically) deterministic causal laws, which laws they problematically equate with epistemic objectivity.

Throughout my analysis I therefore give considerable attention to this conflation in the hope of demonstrating its illogic. The logical (and negative) point is this: The attainment of objectively true (psychological) knowledge (or epistemic objectivity) does not (logically) depend on, require, or necessitate mechanistic determinism—certainly not in everyday, common-sense inquiry and, depending on the type of knowledge that psychological science can legitimately be said to provide, not even in scientific inquiry. After all, it is in principle possible to have objective scientific knowledge of the fact that there exist no mechanistically deterministic causal laws in a certain area of inquiry!

By contrast, the positive point I advance is that agentic being—especially the rational interpretation-based agency that MGTs propound—does depend fully and necessarily on the possibility of objective (psychological) knowing and knowledge (i.e., epistemic objectivity). Thus any approach to inquiry of any sort that deprives us of our capacity for objective knowing and knowledge (including objective knowledge of human social or psychological existence) also deprives us of our capacity for a *rationally* agentic existence. This line of argument, rather than any express attempt to resolve the tension between determinism and agency or free will, will direct my analysis, although I address aspects of that tension in the course of my analysis.

In questioning some of their guiding assumptions, I inevitably take different stands than do MGTs on the relation between epistemic and ontological matters—that is, between matters of knowing and being, respectively, at least within psychology. Of prime importance is my defense of the possibility of objective psychological inquiry, a possibility rejected by MGTs and radical postmodernists owing to (a) objectivity's perceived incompatibility with human agency and (b) the mind dependence of psychological phenomena. In my prior volume *Back to Reality* (Held, 1995), I critically assessed the postmodernist rejection of a realist or objectivist epistemology, a position that defined the postmodern narrative therapy movement. There I argued that a realist or objectivist epistemology has been wrongly thought to undermine the unique particularity of therapy clients[12] (see Held, 1995, chap. 3, 1998b, 2001). In the present book I defend the possibility of objective psychological knowledge in all its many forms—that is, I defend that possibility for psychology in general rather than only within the confines of a particular therapy movement. This broad-based defense is important, in that objectivist philosophies continue to be seen by many theorists as problematic for most—if not all—areas of psychological inquiry. This is so even for those who have taken the interpretive turn in more moderate ways than have radical postmodernists, in virtue of their advocacy of the realist epistemology that radical postmodernists reject. Recall, however, that whereas MGTs think there can be a realist epistemology that is not objectivist, I do not. And because that difference between us constitutes a significant difference, I give considerable attention to it in chapters 8 to 9.

In extending my defense of objectivity to psychology in general, I also for the first time give detailed consideration of ontological—as well as epistemological—matters of objectivity (and subjectivity): After all, ontological positions have logical consequences for epistemic positions, and vice versa. I accomplish this extension by examining the deep relation between knowing and being, including especially the agentic being that both radical postmodernists and MGTs take to be foundational in their proposed ways of acquiring knowledge about human psychological existence. Thus in this volume I take a logical, important, and large next step, by reaching down to the philosophical core of psychology to reconsider the nature of (a) psychological existence or agency, (b) psychological knowledge or truth, and (c) the relationship between (a) and (b).

The aphorism that begins this volume gives away its conclusion, which I now make explicit: Although the middle ground is a tempting place to be—after all, Aristotle himself found great virtue in the "golden mean"—I argue that locating it in both ontological and epistemological (as opposed to

---

[12]In *Back to Reality*, I argued that it is the extent to which the system of therapy used to guide practice provides predetermined content, and not whether the therapist relies on a system of therapy premised on a realist/objectivist or an antirealist/antiobjectivist epistemology, that determines the extent to which the practice of therapy would be individualized (vs. systematic). In short, the more "complete" the system of therapy, the more the content of practice would be predetermined, and so the more systematic—or less individualized—a practice based on such a system of therapy would be (Held, 1995, p. 76).

ethical) terms is not without its problems. In short, the middle ground is neither feasible nor desirable in all matters; it is at least not feasible or desirable in seeking a philosophical grounding for a true or realist account of human psychological existence that successfully preserves our capacity for agentic functioning on rational (interpretive) grounds.

A PREVIEW OF THE CHAPTERS

Part I: Introduction and Origins

This volume is divided into four sections. In Part I (chaps. 1–2), I make a brief foray into the intellectual context in which the MGTs emerged: the postmodern/constructionist movement in psychology. I have argued that this movement devotes itself to the liberation of the individual by way of a thoroughgoing antirealist or antiobjectivist philosophy, in which the constraints imposed by (objective) reality—including the findings of modern/conventional psychological science—have been happily denied or dismissed (see Held, 1995, 1998a, 1998b, 2001, 2002a, 2002b). In chapter 2, I begin my exploration of the postmodernist assumption that objective knowing and knowledge (i.e., an objectivist epistemology), both in everyday, commonsense inquiry and in formal scientific inquiry, are incompatible with human agency. Epistemic objectivity is therefore thought to be incompatible with the freedom or autonomy needed for self-determination, including the capacity to transcend or overcome undesirable circumstances. As we shall see, in many ways the (radical) postmodernist quest for an "emancipatory" psychology is not incompatible with the middle-ground quest for an agentic psychology—though the latter, unlike the former, admits of the real (and so, by my lights but not theirs, objective) existence of constraints on both being and knowing. These constraints are said by MGTs to limit the extent of the liberation from (or the transcendence or overcoming of) undesirable circumstances that we can reasonably hope to attain; this is just the sort of limiting factor that gives MGTs their middle-ground status in both ontological and epistemological terms.

Indeed, some radical postmodernists not only reject what they would surely see as a "retreat" to any such constraining middle-ground philosophy; they also advance ever more extreme forms of antirealist/antiobjectivist philosophies in the service of unlimited freedom. Noting the self-refutational problem of making realist or objective (truth or knowledge) claims about human psychological existence in the context of denying the possibility of realist or objective truth or knowledge, these more radical radicals "resolve" the impending contradiction by trying to eliminate any such claims altogether. (One is then left to wonder about what their psychological knowledge/expertise consists in.) This most extreme reaction in turn contextualizes the efforts of MGTs to locate a more modest and realistic—if not conventionally realist/objectivist—solution to the problem of discerning the true nature of human psychological functioning while defending the agency (and capacity for transcendence) on whose behalf they labor vigorously.

Part II: The Interpretive Turn in Moderation: Ontology

In Part II (chaps. 3–7), I present the claims made by MGTs about the nature of human psychological existence, namely, their "ontology of personhood." Then, in Part III (chaps. 8–9), I consider the antiobjectivist epistemic consequences for psychological inquiry that on their view follow from that ontology of personhood. In these two sections, I assess whether any of the MGTs' proposals for a psychological discipline that avoids the ontological and epistemological "excesses" they find in modern and postmodern psychologies succeed in their intended mission. I therefore ask whether any of them have achieved their two-pronged mission of (a) defining a truth-tracking or realist (but not objectivist) form of psychological inquiry (i.e., a realist epistemology) that nonetheless (b) takes human agency (i.e., an agentic ontology) seriously.

I begin by laying a terminological foundation in chapter 3. There I discuss three sets of distinctions that are used regularly in both modern and postmodern circles to set forth binary oppositions, or polarities, to which MGTs respond: the objective/subjective distinction, the realist/antirealist distinction, and the objectivist/relativist distinction. In the rest of chapter 3, I provide evidence of the MGTs' attempts to locate a philosophical middle ground—both ontologically and epistemologically—between the perceived extremes of modern and postmodern philosophies, by demonstrating how they reconstrue these sets of polarities in terms of the (neo)hermeneutic, social or discursive constructionist, and (neo)pragmatic traditions from which they originate. My evidence consists in many quotations that illustrate MGTs' express use of the "middle-ground" language of reconciliation, integration, mediation, and moderation (and sometimes the language of avoidance or transcendence/overcoming) to characterize their search for a proper philosophy of psychology, one that navigates between (or sometimes beyond) the polarized extremes to which they respond.

In chapters 4–7, I explore the four core ontological claims made by MGTs. In chapter 4, I contextualize the four claims by contrasting the self-proclaimed "ontological mutism" of some radical postmodernists/constructionists with the MGTs' commitment to articulating as fully as possible a proper ontology of psychological existence. There I also present the first of their four ontological commitments: their case for our ontology of "being in the world." This consists in their appeal to the local, situated nature of our (psychological) existence, in which we are often said by them to be historical or cultural (and hence historically or culturally interpretive) "all the way down." Thus psychological universals are said by MGTs to be problematic; they always require some form of contextualist qualification.

In chapter 5, I set forth the second of the four ontological commitments made by MGTs: their case for the realist (but not objectivist) nature of our situated (psychological) existence. They make their case primarily by attempting to obliterate the objective/subjective distinction and, in some cases, the objectivist/relativist distinction. Here I discuss the self-reflexive (or self-determining) nature of what MGTs profess to be a realist ontology, one in which humans are in some ways what they interpret themselves to be within their cultural or discursive contexts. About this claim I am especially critical. Most important here is that because MGTs claim we do not exist psychologically independently of our (culturally based) beliefs about (or interpretations of) the nature of our psychological existence, the realist status of that existence (which they wish to defend despite their antiobjectivism) can and should be called into question. Related to this, I give their alternative, unconventional definitions of the terms *truth* and *real*; these are definitions by which they purport to explain how they can (consistently) propound truth and realism while rejecting an objectivist philosophy of human social or psychological being (ontology) and knowing about that being (epistemology). I also explore their views about the nature of the dependence of our psychological existence on mind or knowing processes—for example, is it a logical or causal dependence that they propound? The answer to that last question has important implications not only for the agency that MGTs defend but also for their version of (ontological) realism. Regarding the latter, I rely on the work of certain philosophers (especially Thomasson, 2003, 2007) to explain how there can be a realist ontology about human social or psychological (i.e., mind-dependent) entities that in principle permits the objectivist inquiry (or epistemology) that MGTs reject.

Chapter 6 is devoted to the third of the four ontological commitments: the MGTs' case for our agentic psychological nature. This includes most profoundly the capacity to transcend or overcome our local, situated social/psychological existence by means of our rationally interpretive or meaning-making powers. These powers are themselves said to be constrained by the local discursive or interpretive contexts in which they emerge and function. Here I contrast two competing bases (given by certain MGTs) for the possibility of such transcendence: (a) one that exists externally to each individual, in the (local) nature of the cultural context in which we each reside, and (b) one that exists internally to each individual, in the (universal) nature of mind or rationality itself. To elaborate, (a) refers to the pluralistic or "multivocal" nature of all cultural contexts, in which a welter of competing beliefs or interpretations always coexists and so presumably allows—and even perhaps ensures—our capacity to transcend or overcome (to some extent) what now exists in any given context. By contrast, (b) refers to the universal rational, imaginative, and dialectical nature of mind, which allows and even perhaps ensures our capacity to transcend or overcome (to some extent) what now exists in any given context.

Chapter 7 concludes the section on ontology with the fourth of the four ontological commitments: the MGTs' case for the fluidity of our social/psychological existence owing to our self-reflexive (or self-determining) interpretive agentic powers. The fluidity of that existence—or what I and others refer to as an "ontology of flux and flow" within the social/psychological world—seemingly affords the opportunity for transcendence of, or change in, that world in the first place. Nonetheless, the flux is not seen by MGTs to be so infinitely chaotic or ephemeral as to preclude the stability or constraint on which ontological realism (and thus realist inquiry) ultimately depends. Here I discuss the ontological relativism that MGTs attempt to minimize if not eliminate, in the service of their commitment to "realism."

Part III: The Interpretive Turn in Moderation: Epistemology

After presenting the four ontological claims, in Part III (chaps. 8–9), I turn my attention to the epistemological consequences that, on the MGTs' view, follow from their middle-ground realist, agentic, and fluid ontology of "being in the world." In this section I examine the MGTs' case for a "situated" form of knowing, a form of knowing that is for them dependent on their ontology of being in the world, and so in which the particularities of our local, situated (psychological) being/existence play no minor role. It is not trivial, then, that for MGTs situated knowing not only depends on situated being but also is constitutive of that being—of our very being/existence as psychological agents—by way of the self-reflexive (self-determining) impact of our knowing or interpretive powers on that existence. Hence the obliteration of the distinction between the knowing subject and the object to be known (in psychology and other human sciences), which prepares us for the obliteration of the objective/subjective distinction altogether—or so MGTs seem to suppose.

Not surprising, this obliteration leads straight to their antiobjectivist epistemology, which they express in three claims that also abound in radical postmodernist writings and that I examine carefully in chapter 8. First, there is no distinction between the knowing subject and object to be known; therefore there can be no objective (psychological) knowing and knowledge. Second, our situated, culturally value-laden existence implies we cannot have "a view from nowhere"; therefore, there can be no objective or value-neutral (psychological) knowing and knowledge. Third, our human ontology of "flux and flow" affords no stable causal psychological laws; therefore, there can be no objective (psychological) knowing and knowledge. In subjecting these claims to critical scrutiny, I also demonstrate how MGTs (like their radical postmodern colleagues) create what I call a "straw man of objectivity" that contributes substantially to their problematic epistemic assertions.

No epistemological critique can avoid discussion of what is core to any epistemological doctrine: the standards of warrant that *should* be used to justify knowledge claims. In chapter 9, I assess the epistemic standards for psychological inquiry advanced by MGTs. More specifically, I ask whether the MGTs' (locally) "perspectival," "pragmatic," and "value-laden" forms of (naturally occurring or "naturalized") warrant manage to avoid the strong epistemic relativism for which they take radical postmodernists to task. And if those forms of warrant do so manage, then can the weak(er) form of relativism that some MGTs propound still be shielded under the realist epistemological umbrella they claim to hold? Moreover, in either case what kinds of empirical questions can be asked legitimately within what MGTs consider a proper form of psychological inquiry, one that does not preclude our agentic, self-determining nature? To be sure, MGTs claim to have avoided the mechanistic/nonagentic determinism they find in modern/conventional psychological science by eschewing the attempt to discover (objective) causal laws, which on their view preclude human agency and which they equate with objective psychological knowledge. I challenge not only that equation but also their claim to have upheld a realist epistemology while abandoning epistemic objectivity and normativity in favor of a "naturalized" epistemology.

Part IV: Truth and Agency

Although I separate matters of being (ontology) and of knowing (epistemology) by placing them in separate sections of this volume (Parts II and III, respectively), it should be obvious that one cannot speak about the nature of being without making some assumptions about the nature of knowing. Conversely, one cannot speak about the nature of knowing without making some assumptions about the nature of being—after all, knowing is itself a form of being (Pols, 2004b, 2005). However, this does not lead to the inexorable epistemological conclusion (of MGTs and radical postmodernists) that knowledge (especially in the human sciences) can never be rightly called objective.

In Part IV (chap. 10), then, I unite ontology and epistemology more expressly and formally, especially by revisiting the MGTs' insistence on the inseparability of our situated being (i.e., their ontology), on the one hand, and our situated knowing (i.e., their epistemology), on the other—all in the name of agency. Put differently, in this section I unite the twin goals that constitute the two-pronged mission of MGTs and that parallel the two questions around which I have organized the entire volume: (a) our capacity for agentic action (an ontological claim) and (b) our capacity to know the truth about the human (psychological) world (an epistemic claim). I especially question whether the ontological and epistemological claims of MGTs allow for an agency that not only is saved from the perceived extremes of modern reductionistic and postmodern nihilistic psychologies but also is "worth wanting" (Dennett, 1984) in the first place. Borrowing Pols's (2004b, 2005) term, I call this form of agency "rational agency," not least because for MGTs agency resides predominately in our interpretive, conceptual, or meaning-making powers.

Here it is well to keep in mind that it is in their views about the nature of the inseparability of being and knowing that MGTs find warrant for a form of psychological knowledge that is itself (for them) both situated and realist, but not objectivist. For example, in arguing on behalf of a realist form of psychological knowledge, MGTs also argue that our situatedness, or the particularity of our social/psychological "being in the world" (i.e., our view from somewhere), precludes our capacity for objective psychological knowledge about that being, or existence. Because on their view objective psychological knowledge consists in (or equates with) indubitable knowledge of timeless, universal, and mechanistically deterministic causal laws that require a "view from nowhere" for their detection, those laws cannot logically coexist with the *locally situated* (or *locally interpretation-based*) agentic psychology that they propound—hence their insistence that agency ultimately necessitates an antiobjectivist epistemology. MGTs, then, seek a realist form of psychological knowledge that cannot be rightly called objective knowledge. In chapter 10, I argue that the concrete localized, contextualized, or situated and thus particularized nature of our "being in the world" (which necessitates a "view from somewhere") does not of necessity or in principle preclude the attainment of objective psychological knowledge—of our own selves as individuals, of particular other selves, or of human beings in general.

I support this claim with two arguments drawn from two philosophers of different generations and somewhat disparate aims. One argument rests on the ontological claim to a fusion of universality and particularity that exists within each and every particular being or entity, including that fusion within each knower and each object of knowing that constitutes the real (Pols, 1963, 1982, 1992, 1998, 2004b, 2005). The other argument rests on the possibility of a "transcultural normative reach," in which warrant for empirical claims can in principle extend well beyond the borders of the particular context in which the claims were first warranted (Siegel, 1997, 1999a, 1999b, 2004). Both arguments appeal to the self-reflexive deployment of our rationality itself, in their defense of the universal features of rationality, including our rational capacity for objective knowing. In the final analysis, I argue that our rational capacity to attain objective knowledge—especially about human social/psychological existence—is essential to the causal agency or efficacy that MGTs hope to save from the mechanistically deterministic causality they find in modern/conventional psychological science.

In chapter 10, then, I make the case that a rational form of agency—one that includes the intentional, causal (including interpretive or meaning-making) power to transcend or overcome the particulars of undesirable circumstances in which we find ourselves—itself depends fully on the objectivist knowing and knowledge that MGTs and radical postmodernists both reject in agency's name. I discuss how both groups have conflated objective knowing with generality or universality (and the denial of particularity or contextuality) on the one hand, and with mechanistic determinism (or reductionism), on the other.

SUMMARY

Throughout this volume I address the same three questions that have rightly prompted the extraordinary efforts of MGTs to forge a new approach to psychology. First, an ontological question: What is the nature of human psychological being or existence (or personhood)? Second, an epistemological question: What kind of knowledge about human psychological existence should any inquiry that attempts to be truth-tracking or realist work to provide? Third, a logical question: What are the consequences of the MGTs' ontological and epistemological commitments for the human agency on whose behalf they labor? Although I separate these three questions into ontological, epistemological, and logical domains, respectively, I argue that they each contain an empirical or experiential component nonetheless—as does the rationality on whose behalf I labor, and on which I myself rely throughout that labor.

2

THE POSTMODERNIST ROOTS OF
THE MIDDLE-GROUND THEORISTS

Those who find some form of postmodernism appealing typically point an accusatory finger at the century-long dominance of a modern scientific approach to psychology by characterizing that approach with various pejoratively intended terms. These include *positivist, scientistic, objectivist, empiricist, rationalist, reductionistic, deterministic, mechanistic, hegemonic, oppressive, dominant, absolutizing,* and *totalizing,* to name just a few (e.g., Fishman, 1999; Freedman & Combs, 1996; S. Friedman, 1993; Gergen, 1994; Kvale, 1992; Mahoney, 2004; Martin & Sugarman, 1999a, 1999b; McNamee & Gergen, 1992; Neimeyer & Mahoney, 1995; Omer & Alon, 1997; Raskin & Bridges, 2002, 2004; Richardson, Fowers, & Guignon, 1999; Rosen & Kuehlwein, 1996; Slife & Williams, 1995; White & Epston, 1990). Indeed, some of these authors find in modern (social) science a source of psychopathology itself. This is no less true of many middle-ground theorists (MGTs) than of bona fide or radical postmodernists. For instance, Richardson, Fowers, and Guignon (1999), who fit my definition of MGTs, do not embrace a radical postmodernist philosophy of psychology. Yet in a section of their (1999) *Re-Envisioning Psychology* entitled "The Modern Scientific Outlook: Problems and Consequences," they speak of postmodernists with approbation, as they too find in the application

27

of modern objectivist epistemologies to human science inquiry a source of some "irrationalities and pathologies of modern life."

> When the method of objectification is taken as the very definition of an epistemically mature stance toward life, trouble ensues. This view rather dogmatically absolutizes a certain detached, dispassionate, spectator view of knowing and relating to the world. . . . Many postmodern and herme-neutic thinkers argue that "the language of science, when applied to the study of human beings, is a relatively impoverished language" (Slife & Williams, 1995, p. 195). A one-sided stress on the objectifying point of view may be an important source of some of the peculiar irrationalities and pathologies of modern life. (pp. 35–36)

Postmodernists have seized on (modern, objectivist) science itself as the culprit, as if *that* were the cause of whatever problems inhere in psychological existence and inquiry. Let us therefore consider some defining features of a generic postmodernist doctrine, to provide an intellectual context for the emergence of the MGTs' less radical approach to psychology.

DEFINING FEATURES OF THE POSTMODERN TURN IN PSYCHOTHERAPY

Because of its many varieties and uses, postmodernism is difficult to capture in one descriptive definition[1] (see Best & Kellner, 1991; Fishman, 1999; Kvale, 1992; Rosenau, 1992). Nevertheless, I previously summarized postmodernists' opposition to modernism by way of three basic commitments (Held, 1995, pp. 10–12): (a) Postmodernists reject general, objective laws and truths, in favor of local, unique, contextualized, relativistic, and subjective "truths"; (b) Postmodernists proclaim an indeterminacy or plurality of meaning in texts/events; and (c) Postmodernists deny the existence (or ontological status) of the self or subject. They instead proclaim the "death of the subject," in which the self/subject is replaced in some cases by infinitely malleable "selves" (Baumgardner & Rappoport, 1996; Gergen, 1991, 1997; Glass, 1993). This position is sometimes called *antisubjectivist*, a term that generates confusion given the antiobjectivist philosophy of postmodernists.[2]

The problem of championing an antiobjectivist (or subjectivist) epistemology while denying the existence of the knowing subject has not gone unnoticed by critics of radical postmodernism (see Held, 1995, pp. 15–20;

---

[1]Fishman (1999, pp. 5–9) differentiates four types of postmodernism—skeptical, critical, ontological, and pragmatic—each of which emphasizes one or more of the following six themes: foundationlessness, fragmentariness, constructivism, critical theory, ontological hermeneutics, and (neo)pragmatism. He says that "within psychology, it is mainly the skeptical and critical visions of postmodernism that have gained prominence," and these visions reject the "hegemony of modernist, positivist psychology" (p. 7).
[2]See chapter 1, note 9.

Martin, Sugarman, & Thompson, 2003, pp. 39–40). Thus the three defining features of postmodernism are attended to critically by the moderates who seek a philosophical middle ground—the MGTs themselves. As we shall see, these moderates put great stock in the existence of historical, sociocultural, and discursive constraints that are said at once to (a) obviate the extreme relativism, antirealism, and indeterminacy of meaning proclaimed by radical postmodernists and (b) make possible subjectivity in the form of real human subjects/selves—that is, the knowing/acting agents or beings whom radical postmodernists (e.g., Gergen, 1991, 1994, 1997) try to eliminate in their "antisubjectivist" dismissal of the "individual psyche" (Martin et al., 2003, pp. 39–40; also see Harré, 1998; Martin & Sugarman, 1999a; Messer, Sass, & Woolfolk, 1988b; Richardson, Fowers, & Guigan, 1999; Woolfolk, 1998).

Although postmodernism's three defining features also help constitute the postmodern turn in psychology, the one feature that unites postmodernism in all its many incarnations is a loyal commitment to the epistemological supposition that we cannot (in either scientific or everyday inquiry) attain knowledge of an objective, or knower-independent, reality. Instead knowers make, construct, or constitute—in the language of their local discursive/interpretive/social contexts—their own biased or subjective "realities." Thus "truth" (with scare quotes) is relative to each subjective knower (or each subjective group of knowers). Moreover, rather than bemoan their "negative philosophical judgment" about knowing (Pols, 1992, 1998), postmodernists celebrate this epistemological state of affairs by reiterating a discourse that proclaims with a unified voice the context dependence or knower dependence, the relativity or subjectivity, of all "truth" claims. Although that voice vigorously denies the claim that science can attain universal truths—it characterizes that claim as nothing less than the oppressive or "totalizing discourse" of modernity and its alleged positivism—the claim to know any objective truth or reality is thoroughly rejected by postmodernists (Held, 1998a).

This utterly universal dismissal of objective truth claims constitutes the antirealist or antiobjectivist[3] epistemology that is a defining feature of all forms of postmodernism, although the way I have characterized that dismissal here is particularly exemplary of the radical social constructionist form of postmodernism that has so influenced social scientific inquiry, including inquiry (as well as therapeutic practice) in psychology (Held, 1998a, 1998b).[4] I have more to say about social constructionism (and its first cousin, constructivism) later in this chapter and again in chapters 3 through 4, in

---

[3]Throughout this chapter I use these terms interchangeably to denote a postmodern/constructionist/constructivist epistemology. At times I select some terms over others, depending on my intended emphasis. See chapter 1 for my equation of an antirealist with an antiobjectivist epistemology, an equation that MGTs reject in pursuing their twin goals.

[4]See Held (1998a) for a discussion of the three most fundamental claims of social constructionism, and Held (1995, pp. 102–105) and chapter 1, this volume, note 4, for distinctions between the doctrines of social constructionism and constructivism.

which I discuss its uses by certain MGTs. In chapter 3, I also clarify my own use of the distinctions between objectivity and subjectivity, realism and antirealism, and objectivism and relativism.

Here note that there are more radical and less radical forms of antirealism, just as there are more radical and less radical forms of realism (see Held, 1995, chap. 1). In the more radical antirealist (or antiobjectivist) view, reality itself is constituted in language—that is, there *exists* no independent or objective reality, apart from the knower's (linguistic) constructions. This of course constitutes an antirealist (or antiobjectivist) ontology, which complements the antirealist/antiobjectivist epistemology of radical postmodernists. As Rosen (1996) put it, "For all practical purposes radical constructivists have banished metaphysical reality from their epistemological worldview: there is no reality that extends beyond the individual's own experience" (p. 6). Osbeck (1993) said something similar: "As described by Shotter, . . . 'A thoroughgoing social constructionist stance . . . seems to suggest that not only our knowledge of the world but the world itself is a social construction'" (p. 344).

In the less radical form of antirealism adopted by many postmodernists, there exists an independent or objective reality, but knowers cannot claim to have any cognitive access to it as it is, in itself. That is because the knower's own theory, language, or social/discursive context—the knower's own "subjectivity"—intervenes or mediates between the knower and that targeted independent reality in a way that alters or distorts as a function of that subjectivity. As Polkinghorne (1992), citing Rorty, expressed the matter, "A common theme of the postmodern epistemology is that linguistic systems stand between reality and experience (Rorty, 1989). Each language system has its own particular way of distorting, filtering, and constructing experience" (pp. 149–150). Slife and Williams (1995) expressly link such mediation (or indirect knowing) with the social construction of our understanding of the world—if not the world itself, which seemingly has an independent existence.

> Gergen (1985) specifically disputes the empiricist assumption that sensory experience dictates the way in which the world is understood. Are not . . . the very words that one might use to describe the world a product of social agreement? If so, the experiences of the empiricist do not directly access the world as it is. These experiences access the world as it is mediated by language, which is itself socially derived. This mediation means that our thoughts and descriptions, including our interpretations of our world, are socially constructed. (p. 80)

To be sure, definitions of postmodernism itself abound, and they typically focus on the antirealist/antiobjectivist and relativistic epistemology (and, sometimes, ontology) that I claim to be postmodernism's most basic defining feature. For example, consider these two substantial definitions, in which we find both ontological and epistemological claims—although many more such statements are available.[5]

First, in *The Case for Pragmatic Psychology*, (neo)pragmatic psychologist (and MGT) Daniel Fishman (1999) gives these definitions of postmodernism, in which there seems to be some form of ontological antirealism as well as an antiobjectivist/antirealist epistemology.

> The changes in the '60s were associated with the emergence of an inter-related family of alternative visions called by such names as "postmodernism," "neopragmatism," "social constructionism," "deconstructionism," "cultural criticism," "hermeneutics," "interpretive theory," and "antifoundationalism." While there are very important differences among these frameworks,[6] they all contrast themselves to modernism, assuming that reality is, to a large extent, "constructed" or "invented" by individuals and groups as a function of particular personal beliefs and historical, cultural, and social contexts. Thus "postmodernism" . . . conceives of the nature of reality as relative, depending upon an observer's point of view. The postmodernist argues against the modernist's claim to achieve fundamental and objective knowledge about the world through the natural science method. (p. xxi)

In this next statement, Fishman (1999) hints at the possible existence of an independent reality, although the scare quotes suggest otherwise.

> A core idea in postmodernism is that we are always interpreting our experienced reality through a pair of conceptual glasses—glasses based on such factors as our present personal goals in this particular situation, our past experiences, our values and attitudes, our body of knowledge, the nature of language, present trends in contemporary culture, and so forth. It is never possible to take the glasses off altogether and view the world as it "really is," with pure objectivity. (p. 5)

Second, constructivist psychologist Robert Neimeyer (1993) gives this definition of constructivist psychotherapy, which is based on the postmodernist doctrine of constructivism itself. Note his nod to ontological as well as epistemological antirealism/antiobjectivism.

> Like the broader postmodern zeitgeist from which it derives, constructivist psychotherapy is founded on a conceptual critique of objectivist epistemology. In particular, it offers an alternative conception of psychotherapy as the quest for a more viable personal knowledge, in a world that lacks

---

[5]See Held (1995, 1998a, 1998b, 2001, 2002b) for additional quotations.
[6]For example, see Richardson et al. (1999) for the ways in which hermeneutics departs from postmodernism/social constructionism, especially in the former's rejection of the moral relativism of the latter. Also see Gantt (1996) and Osbeck (1993).

the fixed referents provided by a directly knowable external reality.[7] (p. 230)

In a later article, Neimeyer (1998) first defines social constructionism in antirealist and antiobjectivist terms, and then goes on to liken constructivism to constructionism. Notice the celebratory spirit in which antirealism and antiobjectivism are embraced; in the next section and throughout this volume, I explain how postmodernists causally link their antirealist/ antiobjectivist philosophies to liberation and agency.

> Social constructionism [SC] endorses a form of postmodernism . . . that turns nearly every aspect of this modern psychological program on its head. Gone is the faith in an objectively knowable universe, and with it the hope that elimination of human bias, adherence to canons of methodology, and reliance on a pure language of observation would yield a "true" human science, mirroring psychological reality without distortion. Gone too is the modern notion of an essentialized self. . . . In their place is a panoply of perspectives cutting across the human sciences and humanities, whose common threads include an acknowledgement (even a celebration) of multiple realities, socially constituted and historically situated, which defy adequate comprehension in objectivist terms. . . . Like SC, constructivism . . . [rejects] "objectivist" psychologies, with their commitment to a realist epistemology, correspondence theory of truth, . . . and mediational view of language. In their place, constructivists endorse a view of knowledge as a personal construction, a coherence-based, neo-pragmatic theory of truth, . . . and a constitutive view of language (Mahoney, 1991; Neimeyer, 1995). (pp. 136, 141)

The "core features of constructivist psychology" are succinctly summarized by Bridges (2002): "Truth is relative; reality is invented and not discovered; meaning is socially or individually constructed; and . . . taking a non-objectivist, non-reductionist stance when working with clients or research participants is beneficial" (p. 309).

HOW ANTIREALIST AND ANTIOBJECTIVIST DOCTRINES "SERVE" AGENCY

Although some postmodernists hold their antirealist/antiobjectivist views for strictly epistemic reasons, others seem to have more practical concerns. For if we make our own psychological truths or realities rather than discover any preexisting psychological truth or reality, we then seem free to construct our lives according to our whims and wishes (Held, 1995, 1998a). Hermeneutic philosopher Charles Guignon (1998) put the matter succinctly.

---

[7]The repudiation of a "directly knowable external reality" does not automatically preclude a realist (or objectivist) epistemology, as the author appears to suppose, because (epistemic) realism does not require that all reality be known directly—that is, without theoretical mediation—in order to be known with objectivity (see Held, 1995, pp. 163–175, 1998a; Pols, 1992).

> Part of the appeal [of constructionist accounts], no doubt, lies in the exhilarating sense of freedom we get from thinking that there are no constraints on the stories we can create in composing our own lives. Now anything is possible, it seems. (p. 566)

Well, maybe not anything. After all, even in his radical brand of postmodernism/social constructionism, Gergen (1985, 1991, 1994, 1997) relies on local discourse communities to "warrant" (with my scare quotes) the knowledge claims that allegedly constitute our social/"psychological"[8] existence. (For critiques of Gergen's view of epistemic "warrant," see Held, 2002b; Martin, Sugarman, & Thompson, 2003, pp. 39–44.) And recall this statement made by (neo)pragmatic psychologist Fishman (1999): "From a postmodern perspective . . . it is not possible to 'discover' 'basic laws of human nature'; and the results of the [modern, positivist] enterprise are substantively irrelevant to the nonlaboratory world—because of the contextual embeddedness of psychological knowledge" (p. 10).

Elsewhere I have discussed in detail the optimistic link between the adoption by postmodernists of antirealist/antiobjectivist philosophies on the one hand and the attainment of liberating, emancipatory, and desirable outcomes in therapy—and in life—on the other (e.g., Held, 1995, 1998a, 2001, 2002a, 2002b). Although M. Brewster Smith (2003) noticed a similar link, he found it fraught with ambivalence, at least in Gergen's writings: "I sense ambivalence between Gergen the tendentious advocate of postmodern liberation—libertinism, it sounds more like—and Gergen the astute social critic. But advocacy has the upper hand" (p. 159). Advocacy indeed. Consider these few exemplary quotations, in which liberation often takes the form of reinventing one's (ever malleable) "self" or "identity." I find little ambivalence in these statements, including Gergen's.

> The doors of therapeutic perception and possibility have been opened wide by the recognition that we are actively constructing our mental realities rather than simply uncovering or coping with an objective "truth." (Hoyt, 1996, p. 1)
>
> Although this may all be frightening without the legitimating guidance of the grand narratives, it is also a liberating possibility. It frees us from the totalizing tyranny of the grand narratives. (Parry & Doan, 1994, p. 25)
>
> People can [in therapy] be enabled to construct things from different viewpoints, thus liberating them from the oppression of limiting narrative beliefs and relieving the resulting pain. . . . [They] may come to transcend the restraints imposed by their erstwhile reliance on a determinate set of meanings. . . . For still others a stance toward meaning itself will evolve; one which betokens that tolerance of uncertainty, that free-

---

[8]I put the word *psychological* in scare quotes to denote Gergen's (1997) "social reconstruction of the mind" or "psyche," in which "the social is given primacy over the individual" (p. 735).

ing of experience which comes from acceptance of unbounded relativity of meaning.[9] (Gergen & Kaye, 1992, p. 183)

[The importation of social constructionist ideas into counselling] involves calling into question the realism entailed in our usual linguistic practices, to the point that even our most "objective" diagnoses of clients are seen as socially constructed discourses that often carry destructive implications. . . . Likewise it undermines the naive hope that we can achieve a position of neutrality . . . and it undermines our taken-for-granted belief in stable, singular, and sustainable identities, instead conjuring an image of selves that subtly or dramatically shift with alternations in the conversational context. . . . An affirmative reading of SC partially compensates for this loss of security by offering fresh images of social life and its possible transformation in psychotherapy. With the demise of an essentialized self, persons are freed (and challenged) to negotiate with others more fluid identities, striving to use the narrative resources of their cultures to script more satisfying lives. (Neimeyer, 1998, pp. 146–147)

One of the positive consequences of psychotherapy's linguistic turn has been the recognition that what serves as truth or normality is not static, but is subject to change and redefinition. It is, then, perfectly possible for a *locally* normative position to be liberating, and for this to challenge prevailing *societal* concepts of normality. . . . The search for paradoxes is enhanced by the end of epistemic certainty, which had, for so long, limited possibilities in the play of ideas. (Stancombe & White, 1998, pp. 590–591)

In addition to the rejection of totalizing explanations . . . postmodern thought also rejects strongly deterministic and reductionistic theories. . . . Individuals are free to choose, adopt and change self-images according to shifting life circumstances and needs. A multiplicity of images is increasingly available to everyone. They are democratic in the sense that individual life circumstances (e.g., race, class, age, etc.) provide less constraint on their adoption than in the past. (Baumgardner & Rappoport, 1996, pp. 126, 128)

I maintain that it is precisely *agency*—indeed, *voluntary* agency—that puts the "construction" into "constructionism." (Kenwood, 1996, p. 534)

All this postmodernist celebration in the name of liberation strikes me as premature. There are questions to be asked—and answered. Do the extreme antirealist/antiobjectivist philosophies of radical postmodernists buy us a social/psychological existence as free of constraint as postmodernists appear to think? Do these philosophies buy us a form of psychological inquiry

---

[9]Gergen seeks more than personal transformation; he seeks social change, as this quotation illustrates: "We can see how constructionist dialogues can stimulate the development of social alternatives to the traditional conception of the self-contained individual. In significant respects, these revisionings of the person are intended as resources for societal change" (Gergen, 1997, p. 742; see also Gergen, 2001a).

or epistemology that can give us knowledge that is warranted (without scare quotes)? And is the radical postmodernist conception of agency one that gives us an agency that is fully agentic—an agency "worth wanting" (Dennett, 1984)?

Enter the MGTs, who say that radical postmodernists have gone too far in clearing out the remnants of modernism from their epistemological and ontological closets. In so doing, they undermine a philosophical foundation for a valid theory of human agency and thus preclude an approach to psychological inquiry/science that can give agency its due—or so MGTs argue. Before we begin to consider their conceptions of agency and the middle-ground approaches to psychology that they offer in agency's name, let us briefly consider the responses of radical postmodernists to the realist charge of contradiction that inheres in postmodern philosophy. Here I include the responses of those postmodernists who find even radical postmodernism to be itself too modern or conventional; these postmodernists therefore propose to radicalize postmodernism even further. It is that proposition that makes the MGTs' attempts at moderation all the more compelling.

RESPONSES OF RADICAL POSTMODERNISTS TO THE REALIST CHARGE OF CONTRADICTION

Radical postmodernists are not unaware of realist/objectivist critiques of their antirealist/antiobjectivist and relativist philosophies (e.g., Erwin, 1997, 1999, 2001; Held, 1995, 1998a, 2002b; Mackay, 1997, 2003; Zuriff, 1998). Indeed, they sometimes respond to those critiques. They especially like to point out that the contradictions, inconsistencies, and incoherence to which realists object when postmodernists make universal, objective truth or reality claims in the context of advancing their antirealist/antiobjectivist and relativist philosophies do not exist, because they do not make any such truth or reality claims in the first place. For instance, in responding to a host of such critiques (by, e.g., Edley, 2001; Hibberd, 2001a, 2001b; Jenkins, 2001; Liebrucks, 2001; Maze, 2001), Gergen (2001a) stated, "I am not trying to 'get it right' about the nature of science, reality, the mind, truth, objectivity, and so on. My chief aims are transformative" (p. 419).

Gergen (2001a) says he prefers to "remain ontologically mute" (p. 425). "Constructionism is ontologically mute. . . . [It] offers no foundation, no ineluctable rationality, no means for establishing its basic superiority to all competing views of knowledge. It is, rather, a form of intelligibility" (Gergen, 1994, pp. 72, 78). Efran and Heffner (1998) said, "Our reality claims do not assume knowledge of a free-standing universe and therefore do not violate constructivist tenets" (p. 96). Raskin (2004) asks, more subtly, "'What if we acted *as if* what is real were dependent on our constructions?' From the 'human involvement' perspective, all of us are invariably committed to particular constructions of how things are" (p. 336). The problem, of course, is how we can remain committed to constructions of how things *are* while remaining antirealists/antiobjectivists. I include in this Gergen's (1997, 2001a) own commitment to his belief that when social constructionist discourse is adopted, liberation or transformation follows (see Held, 2002b).

In the next section of this chapter, I present some of the universal, objective truth claims made by radical postmodernists—despite their insistence that they have not made any such claims. These are claims that even the most radical of the radical postmodernists find problematic, much like postmodernism's realist critics. In later chapters I return to (a) the "ontological mutism" of radical postmodernists (chap. 4), (b) the kind of ontological and epistemological philosophies that can in principle ground a psychological discipline that grants our agentic capacity to transform or transcend (i.e., liberate ourselves from) existing realities (chaps. 6 & 10), and (c) the unnecessary conflation within postmodernism of the active nature of our knowing processes with antirealist/antiobjectivist epistemological doctrines (chaps. 8–9). Here let us turn to the three universal, objective truth claims that I find in postmodernist discourse—universal because they are said to apply to everyone, and objective because their truth status does not depend on postmodernists' (or anyone's) beliefs about their truth status.

Three Universal Truth Claims Made by Radical Postmodernists

The three universal, objective truth claims are intrinsic to the social constructionist and constructivist doctrines advanced by most—if not all—postmodernists in psychology. Following is a capsule summary of, and a brief commentary on, each claim (see Held, 1998a, 2002b, for elaboration).

Claim 1: The Active Nature of Knowing

Our knowledge of the world is actively constructed. In both science and everyday life, we actively construct theories about how the world works, including that aspect of the world that pertains to ourselves. We are not passive knowers.

My Commentary. Recall that all theories are constructions. The fact that we actively work to attain knowledge, which we express by way of theories/propositions that we ourselves construct, does not automatically result in the antirealist/antiobjectivist and relativistic view of reality, truth, and knowledge propounded by postmodernists. Active knowing does not logically preclude the possibility of objective knowledge of the world, including the human world. Thus there is nothing in this claim that establishes a postmodernist philosophy, and its assertion constitutes a universal, objectivist claim (about knowing) that subverts the antirealism/antiobjectivism and relativism of postmodernism.

Claim 2: Our Theories Affect Our Lives

The theories we construct and accept, and even the informal discourses we adopt, can determine the outcomes in life (the reality) that we get. The reality we get as a consequence of the theories or discourses that we adopt can take two forms: (a) linguistic reality, in which case discourse affects discourse, and (b) extralinguistic reality, in which case discourse affects something more than discourse (see Held, 1995, pp. 143–146, for evidence of this in the postmodern therapy literature).

My Commentary. This claim does not necessarily constitute a social constructionist assertion; it depends on how it is interpreted. A conventional realist/objectivist interpretation of Claim 2 is this: How we understand or interpret life affects the options we perceive and the actions we take on those options, and that understanding can in principle (but does not necessarily) give us (some) objective truth about our lives. Moreover, there is nothing antirealist/antiobjectivist or relativistic about this claim itself. A postmodernist interpretation of Claim 2 is this: The theories or discourses we adopt can never in principle give us any objective truth; however, our non-objective, subjective, biased, and relativistic theories and discourses nonetheless determine the life or reality that we ultimately get. Obviously the second part of the postmodernist interpretation of Claim 2 constitutes the universal, objective truth/reality claim that subverts or undermines the antirealist/antiobjectivist and relativistic thrust of the first part—hence the contradiction. Thus in either interpretation of Claim 2 (conventional or postmodernist), there exists a universal, objective causal claim, the kind of truth or reality claim that many—but not all—postmodernists say (in their efforts to be "ontologically mute") they do not make.

Claim 3: The Postmodernist Interpretation of Claim 2 Liberates Us

If we accept the postmodernist interpretation of Claim 2, then we will have more options or possibilities (i.e., more freedom or fewer constraints) in our lives than if we accept the conventional realist/objectivist interpretation of Claim 2.

My Commentary. Claim 3 is illustrated in prior quotations, in which the adoption of a postmodernist/constructionist (or antirealist/antiobjectivist) epistemology is said by postmodernists/constructionists to enhance liberation, freedom, and transcendence. Yet is Claim 3 true? As with Claim 2, only objective empirical observation can give us the answer, because this is an empirical matter. However, because radical postmodernists argue against the possibility of objective empirical observation as a basis for assessing the truth of their claims (e.g., Gergen, 1985), they cannot warrant their universal, objectivist assertions—which, like this one, subvert or undermine their antirealist/antiobjectivist philosophy.

Still, the question of warrant of knowledge claims is one from which postmodernists do not shrink. In taking up a pragmatic standard of warrant, they argue that the reality we prefer should determine the modes of discourse (including the theories) we accept as "true" (with scare quotes). Thus we should decide on the reality we want to attain, and then develop or adopt a mode of discourse (or theory) that helps us attain it. This of course involves making values central to epistemic warrant. I return to the question of warrant in my discussion of the MGTs, who—like radical postmodernists—argue that epistemic warrant must expressly incorporate values, especially when making claims about the human world. Here let us consider the attempt made by the most radical of the radical postmodernists (who take the realist critique seriously) to radicalize postmodernism even further.

Some Proposals for the (Further) Radicalization of Radical Postmodernism

The radical postmodernists who take to heart the realist critique of postmodernists' self-refuting or self-undermining truth/reality claims do more than simply defend themselves by saying they do not make universal, objective claims.[10] Although they do not typically respond directly to my commentary about those claims, they nonetheless attend to the issues by focusing on the ways in which postmodernist doctrines have been deployed in psychotherapy. Of prime importance is this: Rather than resolve the contradictions and inconsistencies by putting the brakes on radical postmodernism's rampant antirealism/antiobjectivism and relativism (the mission of MGTs), these radicals seek even more radicalization in the name of a postmodern, constructionist, or constructivist psychology that follows logically or consistently from postmodern epistemological (if not ontological) tenets. Thus these self-critiquing postmodernists seek to explicate a postmodernist approach to psychology, and especially its applications in psychotherapy, that remains logically consistent with the most radical forms of postmodern antirealism/antiobjectivism and relativism.

In an article entitled "Psychotherapy Without Foundations?" Stancombe and White (1998) accuse postmodern therapists of perpetuating in their theo-

---

[10]Recall the statement by Efran and Heffner (1998): "Our reality claims do not assume knowledge of a free-standing universe and therefore do not violate constructivist tenets" (p. 96). In drawing the distinction between constructivists and objectivists, they also said:

> Objectivists often seem to be speaking on behalf of the universe at large. The constructivist speaks only for himself or herself, with a voice (and vocabulary) that reflects the exigencies of his or her biological structure and the circumstances of the local community. (p. 93)

But if each constructivist's claims escape objectivity because they are true for him or her only (i.e., their warrant depends only on his or her beliefs about their truth), then we may rightly ask why the rest of us should believe them too.

retical systems and practice the expressions of certainty that postmodernism's antifoundationalist critique is supposed to subvert.

> Unable to retreat into logico-empiricism and naive realism because of its own internal critique of these philosophical positions, it [the therapeutic industry] has sought solace in hermeneutics and postfoundationalist epistemology. . . . The end of the search for therapeutic certainties has certain repercussions which have, hitherto, been neglected by theorists and clinicians, whose desire to escape some of the constraints of scientism sits uneasily alongside an unshakeable commitment to therapeutic practices which are essentially normative. . . . [This article] explores some of the contradictions embedded in the new "postfoundational" therapies, arguing that the therapeutic industry may be nearer to crisis than it thinks. (p. 579, abstract)

I shall not attend to Stancombe and White's failure to define foundationalism adequately (except to say it is not synonymous with certain knowledge, despite that implication) and their problematic characterization of the modernist paradigm as requiring certainty and foundations to attain universal, "apodictic truth" (p. 585); these are matters I take up in considering the epistemologies proposed by the MGTs. Here I focus instead on their criticism of postmodern narrative/constructionist therapists, in whom they find problematic endorsements of therapist expertise or authority, hierarchy, prescriptive techniques, and normative outcomes; these elements are said by them to be "ethically problematic once the knowledge claims on which therapeutic authority rests are challenged and undermined" (p. 594). Thus, they say, some have been tempted to maintain that "the remedy . . . is to reaffirm therapeutic certainties (recapture the real). . . . This is not an adequate response, because there are no algorithmic methods of verification for either the theories or the methods of therapy" (p. 594). That unacceptable "postmodernist" response, then, is inconsistent with the antirealist epistemology (and ontology) that constitutes postmodernism's alleged postfoundationalism.

Stancombe and White's solution to this problem is to open a space for what they call "a, yet to be defined, *post*-therapeutics" (p. 594): "Narrative and constructionist approaches are stages along this road, but proponents of these new orientations continue to risk being hoist by their own petard if they insist upon retaining the concept of 'therapy,' with its associated chain of signification" (p. 594). What is post-therapeutics? Here is their answer to that question.

> Approaches which increase the number of voices in the therapeutic conversation, and which recognize the *ordinary* mutuality involved in helping, are stages along the road. . . . Post-therapeutics, then, is about discourse facilitation and reflexivity. . . . Helping is a practical-moral affair, which cannot be approached as if rational technical answers existed. (p. 595)

Accordingly they recast "therapy as generative, co-constructed and dialogic" (p. 596) and give as an example the "Hearing Voices Network, which reclaims 'auditory hallucinations' for those who live with them" (p. 595).

Although Stancombe and White are right to insist on logical consistency, problems abound. Here I comment briefly on just a few.

Stancombe and White's description of post-therapeutics as a practical–moral affair in which "each encounter is a problem 'for the subject who acts'" (p. 595) is not new: There exist a great many "pre-post-therapeutics" attempts to reconcile the idiographic nature of psychotherapy with the nomothetics of general (scientific) psychological knowledge[11] (e.g., Fishman, 1999; Held, 1995, 2001; Miller, 2004; Woolfolk, 1998). And the moral and ethical or value-laden[12] nature of psychotherapy, on whose behalf an allegedly value-free technique has been taken to task, has long been accepted by many (e.g., Frank, 1961; M. Friedman, 1985; Halleck, 1971; London, 1964; Slife, Williams, & Barlow, 2001; Tjeltveit, 1999; Woolfolk, 1998). Regarding epistemology, Stancombe and White do not quite abandon epistemic warrant altogether; that would of course condone the "anything-goes" relativism that even radical postmodernists—such as Rorty (as cited in Stancombe & White, 1998, p. 591)—reject. So they exalt Rorty's call for solidarity or communality by placing "warrant" in the practices/pragmatic consequences of local dialogical community. Indeed, they assert without qualification "the centrality of dialogical communities in the justification of knowledge claims" (p. 593).

As for ontology—what are we to make of the use of scare quotes around the term *auditory hallucinations*? Is this meant to reflect the "ontological mutism" explicitly adopted by Gergen? Although they reject the "realist ontology" of modern psychotherapy as sheer "complacency" (p. 588), in the final analysis we find in Stancombe and White's post-therapeutics a fundamental if not foundational claim, one with all the universalist and absolutistic force that they decry in the claims of others: "It [post-therapeutics] can lead to different ways of doing and being" (p. 595), seemingly because the "normative mission" (p. 594) of psychotherapy—both modern and postmodern—is therein eliminated. Post-therapeutics can help "increase the number of voices in the therapeutic conversation, and . . . recognize the *ordinary* mutuality involved in helping" (p. 595). It can help us see that "what people need is not an analysis of their 'psyches' so much as one of their circumstances" (Smail, as cited in Stancombe & White, 1998, p. 595). After all, if post-therapeutics did not have such practical liberating existential consequences, why would we bother to consider its use in the first place?

---

[11]The vast and diverse eclectic therapy movement constitutes just such an attempt. See Held (1995, chap. 3) for elaboration.
[12]In his *Ethics and Values in Psychotherapy*, Tjeltveit (1999, p. 205) astutely defines ethics to include both moral (obligatory) and nonmoral (aspirational) values.

Yet problems remain. Not least is that in urging us to adopt a post-therapeutics approach to "therapy," Stancombe and White tell us what therapists should or at least should not do (to remain logically consistent and meet the needs of people better); this therefore constitutes a bona fide "normative mission" of their own. Thus it is not obvious that the adoption of a truly postfoundational form of therapy or post-therapeutics eliminates the philosophical contradictions that Stancombe and White find even in radical postmodernist approaches to therapy. That they admit to a "*locally* normative position" in the service of liberation does not solve the problem—"It is, then, perfectly possible for a *locally* normative position to be liberating, and for this to challenge prevailing *societal* concepts of normality)" (p. 590)—because their claims about the virtues of post-therapeutic therapy are not limited to any particular discursive community, and so they are universally applicable. Moreover, what if their "locally normative position" is oppressive for at least some locals?[13]

Most important, their claim that their therapy "can lead to different ways of doing and being" (p. 595) requires at least some form of empirical observation to warrant its assertion, despite Stancombe and White's happy postmodernist pronouncement of the "death-knell of empiricism . . . in therapy" (p. 586; see Held, 1998a). In sum, although they make some version of Claim 2 and some version of Claim 3, Stancombe and White insist that only a post-therapeutics form of therapy—which alone is said to reject the foundationalism still lurking even in postmodernistically informed therapies—can fully liberate us from the oppression of the "hegemonic discourses" (p. 592) that postmodern therapy has not successfully muted, although it allegedly constitutes a step in the right direction: "Narrative and constructionist approaches are stages along this road"—for example, Anderson and Goolishian's (1988, 1992) "not knowing" approach to therapy—but even those postmodernists who question the notion of expertise "risk being hoist by their own petard if they insist upon retaining the concept of 'therapy'" (p. 594).

There are others who seek to radicalize postmodern/narrative therapy, although they do not speak of post-therapeutics per se. Still, they move in that direction as they continue to speak of liberation and empowerment. In his edited volume *Deconstructing Psychotherapy*, psychologist Ian Parker (1999) puts the agenda on the table.

> [The metaphor of deconstruction] invites a connection between the political and the personal which is *more* radical and practical than approaches derived so far from dialectics. . . . But deconstruction also promises us something more liberating, something open enough to respect . . . the contradictions that we live as we either bend to oppression or try to break it. (p. 5)

---

[13]See Hare-Mustin (1994, 2004) for a discussion of this very point in the context of gender inequality.

A chapter in that volume by "discursive therapist" John Kaye (1999) entitled "Toward a Non-Regulative Praxis" squares with the post-therapeutics of Stancombe and White and suggests how oppressive norms may be avoided: "An ongoing critique of its own power-knowledge may help prevent postmodern and post-structuralist deconstructive practice from forging a new hegemony with its own regime of political correctness and certitude" (p. 36).

Chapters by Morss and Nichterlein (1999) and by Riikonen and Vataja (1999) also harken a post-therapeutics vision. The former make the now familiar call for what they term *de-experting*, but it is interesting that they chasten postmodern/narrative therapists for tumbling to the "temptation to emancipate."

> Like the sirens' lure to the familiar yet deadly shallows, the odyssey of emancipation draws its appeal from the good intentions of the therapist. It suggests that emancipation is not only possible (itself a big claim) but that it is achievable if correct techniques are adopted with appropriate sensitivity. (p. 172)

The post-therapeutics vision also reveals itself in a later passage by Morss and Nichterlein, which speaks to the idiographic emphasis (see Held, 1995, chap. 3) typically found in postmodern/narrative therapies: "Knowledge must be painstakingly built up with the client, each block scrutinized, weighed, compared. No pre-cast components may be utilized, and no trusted tools employed: the tools, also, must be fashioned anew, in each new encounter" (p. 174).

Riikonen and Vataja (1999) begin their chapter in Parker's book on this now familiar emancipatory note, in which they seem charmed by the "sirens' lure" of emancipation feared by Morss and Nichterlein: "This chapter is a dual and well-intentioned attempt to create non-knowledge where there was knowledge before. . . . We try . . . to show that there isn't anything which should be called 'psychotherapy'" (p. 175). They seek the liberating idiographics of "happy dialogue" or language, which cannot be found in any expert system of therapy.

> The expression points . . . to the general capacity of certain forms of language and dialogue to undo finalizations and too-perfect constellations of meaning. The happiness of dialogues is their power to refreshen, to bring about joy, to dissolve burdens and oppression. (p. 185)

Happy language, indeed.

Although he speaks of "post-professional" or "anti-professionalised" therapy rather than "post-therapeutics," House (1999, 2003) draws on "Parker's important work on discourse and power" to argue that "therapy's pretensions to being a legitimate professional, clinical practice . . . constitute a self-serving and ethically questionable ideology. The 'scientific' status of therapy as a modernist enterprise is . . . fundamentally undermined by new-paradigm epistemologies" (House, 1999, p. 377, abstract). He goes on to say:

> As soon as we embrace the ideology of professionalisation (. . . a scientific "treatment" mentality . . .), then we quite possibly do a terminal violence to those very intangible, "non-specific" "being" qualities that are in my view what makes at least some therapeutic experiences worth having. (House, 1999, p. 387)

The use of scare quotes to call into question the legitimacy of science, treatment, nonspecifics, and being is noteworthy; they cover much ground, both epistemologically and ontologically, as do the scare quotes around the words *objective*, *reality*, and *truth*, in the quotation that follows. Indeed, in the end House (1999) argues that truth is always a subjective matter, one that cannot be found in general/systematic efforts to attain objectivity.

> It is a fundamental error of the (ironically named) "Enlightenment" project to expect humanly built systems of truth to lead to reliable, "objective" accounts of "reality." Rather, my own particular "truth" is unavoidably "local," based on my own unique experiences of therapy. (p. 389)

I return to the themes of generality, particularity, and objectivity in subsequent chapters, as I discuss MGTs' attempts to retreat from the illogical extremity of such increasingly radicalized views.

A More Ambitious Attempt

In the previous section, we considered the writings of those who work to radicalize the "not knowing," "post-therapeutics," or "postprofessional" approach to therapy (and psychology) now common in the most radical postmodern circles. Although these theorists/therapists decry the negative consequences of yielding to the temptation to rely on predetermined "expert" forms of content and technique in therapeutic practice, they do not solve the problem that persists within postmodern therapies and motivates their efforts: remaining loyal to a radically antirealist/antiobjectivist doctrine—what they sometimes problematically call the end of (epistemological) certainty—while making universal, objective claims about the nature of human psychological existence and, especially, its betterment.[14]

---

[14]See Held (1998a, pp. 208–210) for a discussion of the moral relativism of radical postmodernist doctrines, which can give no basis for accepting any discourse other than one's desires. There the reader is referred to Gantt (1996), Mühlhäusler and Harré (1990), and Osbeck, (1993), who share this concern. Richardson et al. (1999) do as well. Postmodern pragmatic philosopher Richard Rorty, who is often quoted by radical postmodern therapists and psychologists, makes the point clear when he states, "The pragmatist's claim [is] that to know your desires (not your deeply buried 'inmost,' 'true,' desires, but your ordinary everyday desires) is to know the criterion of truth, to understand what it would take for a belief to 'work'" (Rorty, 1991, p. 31).

For the moment I shall leave aside the problem of equating the impossibility of certain empirical knowledge with the impossibility of objective empirical knowledge. Instead I assess a unique effort that is intended to create a philosophical foundation for therapy, one which does not call for therapy's own demise but which is nonetheless consistent with the constructivist insistence on the impossibility of objective knowledge. This effort focuses on the (not quite successful) quest among some psychoanalysts "to propose a central role in both theory and clinical practice for a subjectivity not dependent on any knowable context in external reality" (Moore, 1999, p. 3). In other words, its author explicitly attempts to produce a full metatheory—an internally consistent postmodern metatheory—that does not fall prey to the self-refutation or logical contradiction that obtains when one attempts to say what is objectively true (or what is the case) in the context of a doctrine that denies the possibility of objective knowledge or truth. Robert Holt (2002, pp. 272–273), a prominent psychoanalytic psychologist, warns cogently of the logical contradictions that inhere in such attempts. Yet Holt maintains that these problematic attempts should be examined nonetheless, so that their internal contradictions can be seen as clearly as possible. Let us now consider one such attempt.

Like Stancombe and White, psychoanalytic psychologist Richard Moore (1999) argues that the narrative therapists who claim to have navigated this problem successfully (for Moore these include Donald Spence, Roy Schafer, Robert Storolow, and Irwin Z. Hoffman) have not gone far enough: They too are said by Moore to possess the stubborn internal contradiction, and so there is more work to be done.

> Through a discussion of their explicit and implicit characterization of truth and reality within the psychoanalytic hour, a spotlight is thrown on the contradiction within each of these approaches between their proclaimed subjectivist, and often constructivist, theoretical perspective and an increasingly tenuous clinical base in traditional psychoanalytic reality. . . . The tension between the premises of psychoanalysis and the direction taken by this growing narrative discourse is reflected in the work of each of these writers as a basic logical discontinuity appearing in many of their central concepts. (p. 9)

But whereas others seek a more radicalized "post-therapeutics" (Stancombe & White, 1998) or "post-professional era" (House, 1999, 2003) so they can maintain logical consistency with their "end of certainty" (which they problematically oppose to objectivity), Moore seeks a constructivist metatheory of psychoanalysis that also saves therapy from the radical deconstructive efforts of these others (e.g., Parker, 1999). For this reason his is a more conservative and, at the same time, a more ambitious effort. Recall that other postmodernists—those who have not sought to radicalize postmodern therapy further—have denied the contradiction that Moore seeks to resolve, by claiming to remain "ontologically mute" (Gergen, 1994, 1998, 2001a). In that case they "say" they do not make claims about "a free-standing universe" (Efran & Heffner, 1998, p. 96); they are instead only seeking liberation or transformation (Gergen, 1997, 2001a) or merely "speaking for themselves": "Objectivists often seem to be speaking on behalf of the universe at large. The constructivist speaks only for himself or herself" (Efran & Heffner, 1998, p. 93).

In contrast to the postmodern contradiction deniers (who do not seek more radicalization) and the postmodern contradiction acknowledgers (who do seek more radicalization), Moore asserts his own unique mission: to conceptualize the nature of subjectivity itself in universalist terms, and for no less than bona fide therapeutic purposes. In the final chapter of *The Creation of Reality in Psychoanalysis*, Moore (1999) "attempts to elaborate a more unified metapsychology congruent with the subjectivist perspectives of Spence, Schafer, Stolorow, and Hoffman, but also one significantly less fettered by traditional assumptions about external reality" (p. 9).

Moore rehearses his subjectivist epistemology throughout his book, as he strives to construct an internally consistent narrative/constructivist therapy (among other purposes). However, he repeatedly tells us that he is aware of the burdensome contradiction under which other constructivist therapists have labored.

> We suggest . . . the possibility of constructing a theory of subjectivity based primarily on conscious subjective experience, a theory that understands such experience as a creative process situated in subjective time and grounded in the accumulated subjectivity of the society in which it occurs. (p. 125)

But at the same time, Moore questions "whether, in the absence of any pretense that our experience includes such a thing as an objective world, we can assume an ability to narrate anything about any*thing*" (p. 127). He elaborates, appealing—as do the others—to uncertainty.

> Perhaps it would be useful to conceive of language not as a reflection or sharing of our established knowledge, but rather as a reflection of our never knowing for certain. . . . I refer here not to the gap between people but to . . . the personal one that lies between the experience we can never fully communicate and the world we can never fully know. (p. 127)

Again, there are problems. Not knowing the world fully, or not knowing any aspect of the world with certainty, does not entail epistemic subjectivity (or preclude objectivity). Thus there are replies to postmodernists' preoccupation with the uncertain, limited, and fallibilist nature of our (empirical) knowledge, and with our individualized particularity as knowers, that do not retreat into an antiobjectivist (or thoroughgoing subjectivist) epistemology.

Moreover, there exist philosophical arguments concerning the possibility of objective knowledge of subjective events, states, and entities (including social/psychological entities), which are by nature mind-dependent entities—that is, they could not exist if there were no minds.[15] Indeed, it is possible to conceive of psychological science as including the quest for objective knowledge about the nature of subjective experience (e.g., consider attribution theory in social psychology).[16] I have more to say about the possibility of the objective ontological status of mind-dependent entities in chapters 3 and 5. Here let us consider Moore's attempt to say something generally or universally (if not objectively) true about subjectivity itself, as he tells us just how keenly aware he is of the contradiction that remains within narrative/constructivist psychoanalytic therapies. He is especially determined to avoid the contradiction created by postmodernists' (objective) claims about the advantageous pragmatic consequences of adopting an antiobjectivist epistemology.

> Subjectivity cannot logically be used as a foundation for statements about what is real. Just as it is a contradiction for proponents of physics' uncertainty theory to declare that their view is based on objective observation ("look! *nature* tells us that the world is not determined" . . .),[17] saying that psychoanalysis is *objectively* uncertain involves a similar mistake. It is not reasonable to assert that we cannot know objective reality and also that this not knowing is the most realistic basis for a new psychoanalysis . . . [or] that only by seeing through the lens of the subjective will we understand the *real* human condition. And it seems equally questionable to say that all reality is a construction, but ours actually works better. The best the proponents of any perspective discussed thus far may logically proclaim within the limitations of their perspective is that "it seems to explain things better to me." (pp. 129–130)

As we have seen, some postmodernists try to solve the logical contradiction in the relativistic way that Moore disparages by saying that their

---

[15]See philosopher Charles Siewert's (1998) *The Significance of Consciousness* for a defense of a unique form of first-person warrant for self-knowledge. Nagel (1986) reminds us that "the concept of mind, though tied to subjectivity, is not restricted to what can be understood in terms of our own subjectivity" (p. 21). Yet he goes on to say that "an objective conception of mind acknowledges that the features of our own minds that cannot be objectively grasped are examples of a more general subjectivity, of which other examples lie beyond our subjective grasp as well" (p. 26). Still, he gives subjectivity its place in the world: "Though the subjective features of our own minds are at the center of *our* world, we must try to conceive of them as just one manifestation of the mental in a world that is not given especially to the human point of view" (p. 18).

[16]See social psychologist Daniel Wegner's (2002) *The Illusion of Conscious Will* for research about what causes us to experience our actions as either consciously willed or unwilled.

[17]Contra Moore, this is exactly what physicists are entitled to say (without fear of contradiction), for there is nothing subjective about their "uncertainty theory"! It is based on objective knowledge of some aspects of the physical world, although many postmodernists use it improperly to buttress their antiobjectivist views. See Flanagan (2002, pp. 119–123) for a highly accessible discussion of the distinction between deterministic and indeterministic causation, including how "objective ontological indeterminacy" is employed in quantum physics (p. 120).

proclamations are true for them only; that is, they "speak only for themselves" (e.g., Efran & Heffner, 1998). Yet Moore himself is rightly dissatisfied with that (self) limiting "solution"; he wants to say something universally true that does not undermine the tenets of logical discourse: "Such contradictions in . . . the theorists we have discussed are due to the fact that their work arises in the context of a discipline whose positivist underpinning permeates every aspect of its character" (p. 130). The problem, more precisely, allegedly lies within the conventional/positivistic nature of the data (or facts) with which theorists are said to concern themselves. Spence "never forsakes such data, but largely directs his efforts to regain the secure grip on them which psychoanalysis once believed it had" (p. 130); Schafer "retains his classical facts in narrative clothing"; Stolorow "posits an intersubjective field but typically focuses on individual psychic states and their invariant principles"; and Hoffman "brings his bold recognition of uncertainty largely to the same clinical questions that psychoanalysis has always addressed" (p. 130).

Moore, by contrast, asserts that only by "generating" data about subjectivity itself can constructivist psychoanalysts hope to solve the logical problem.

> A constructivist approach should involve data of its own, data with which it is consonant in terms of logical self-consistency. . . . The data to be discovered . . . concern the role of subjectivity in construction. While these theorists attempt to shift their focus from the objective to the subjective, they have little new and systematic to offer about subjectivity itself. . . . We approach subjectivity differently by making it the center of our concern. . . . We view subjectivity as a process with characteristics that are themselves open to subjective interpretation and all data as primarily data about subjectivity itself. (p. 130)

Here we must ask a question: If there is a way that the "process" of subjectivity actually works—that is, it has characteristics or a way that it *is* (a way that does not depend on beliefs about its nature)—then why is objective knowledge of it precluded? In chapter 5, I explain how the possibility of objective knowledge of mind-dependent entities (e.g., attitudes and emotions) can obtain. Yet in emphasizing the "experience of knowing" and of "not knowing," Moore seems to be speaking about knowledge of consciousness itself; indeed, he later says that the "process of consciousness itself [is] the process whereby we construct" (p. 154). Yet so far there exists no philosophical or scientific consensus about consciousness, although this does not in principle preclude objective knowledge of conscious processes. Still, Moore rejects an objectivist epistemology, as he seeks a "proper" understanding of subjectivity.

> A theoretical perspective on subjectivity on which a constructivist analysis can be based . . . can no longer ground itself on an objective external reality. . . . It . . . must itself be seen as subjective and not as an attempt to

stake out a claim to a closer approximation to any external truth. . . . The perspective offered here does not seek legitimacy by claiming for itself a "higher" objectivity. It simply claims to offer a perspective on the experience of knowing and, even more to the point, not knowing. . . . The idealized experience that replaces truth or virtue in the perspective tentatively offered here is *optimal participation in construction.* (pp. 133–134)

In the final analysis, Moore, like other postmodern therapists, links his antiobjectivist/constructivist philosophy—that we make or construct rather than discover reality—to empowerment, especially if we realize this "fact" (cf. Gergen & Kaye, 1992). Note here as well his implicit nod to the second and third universal truth claims made by radical postmodernists.

Humans control what they contribute to their own consciousness largely by what they do in response to what they have constructed. It is an element of faith within this perspective that for most observers the realization that whatever is observed is also constructed will result in some added degree of empowerment. (p. 154)

Can having faith in the "realization that whatever is observed is also constructed" give us an "added degree of empowerment"? Ironically such "faith" constitutes the "negative philosophical judgment about knowing" that, I argue, undermines agency of any sort. Although the theorists whom we have discussed in this chapter have advanced their antirealism/antiobjectivism and relativism in the context of theories of psychotherapy, their philosophical pronouncements pertain to the discipline of psychology as a whole— including, especially, psychological inquiry. It is therefore time to consider more moderate philosophical views, ones that attempt to mediate between the philosophies of modernism and postmodernism—that is, the intricate arguments of MGTs themselves.

II

THE INTERPRETIVE TURN IN
MODERATION: ONTOLOGY

3

AN INTRODUCTION TO THE MIDDLE-GROUND THEORISTS

In chapter 2, I argued that the radical postmodern/antirealist turn in psychology reflects an optimistic impulse to liberate individuals from the "oppressive" constraints of the universal, objective, mechanistically deterministic causal laws sought by many (but not all) modern/conventional psychologists. As we have seen, for radical postmodernists either (a) there exists no reality independent of our knowing (including interpretive) processes (an ontological matter) or (b) if an independent reality does exist, it is not cognitively accessible to us as it is, independent of our knowing (including interpretive) processes (an epistemological matter). In either case we more or less (respectively) construct or make "reality" in language rather than discover a preexisting independent or objective reality. Thus reality itself cannot be said to constrain our (social/psychological) existence as beings with interpretive powers. For radical postmodernists, then, neither the "laws"[1] (i.e., generalizations) of modern/conventional psychological science (which in principle can be discovered) nor an independent reality (which in principle

---

[1] I put the word *laws* in scare quotes to acknowledge the radical postmodernist rejection of even the idea of objective scientific laws, especially in the human sciences. The legitimacy of seeking causal laws in psychological science is considered in some detail in chapter 9.

warrants those discoveries) can constrain each individual's capacity to rein-vent herself freely in virtue of narrative/interpretive reconstruction. Indeed, these "lawlike" generalizations are seen to compound the problem: They not only subvert the act of narrative self-invention but also, given the postmodernist denial of the possibility of objective truth, commit this sub-versive act with no (objective) epistemological warrant.

In chapter 2, I also illustrated how the radical postmodern emancipatory impulse, in its most extreme incarnations, has led to a program that annihi-lates the notion of psychotherapy itself. This, recall, resulted in the "post-therapeutics" of the most radical postmodern psychotherapists.

In the next four chapters, I explicate the ways in which some psycholo-gists and philosophers have laid claim to what I am calling a "middle-ground" ontology that avoids the alleged excesses of radical postmodern antirealist doctrines on the one hand, and of modern/conventional objectivist (or so-called "positivist") doctrines on the other. Although these theorists some-times speak of transcending the two perceived extremes, as we shall see they more typically speak of integrating, reconciling, or bridging them by locating a more moderate or intermediate ontological position.

In this chapter I introduce the middle-ground theorists (MGTs) by way of quotations that illustrate their use of middle-ground language. In chapters 4 through 7, I explore their four core ontological claims about our psycho-logical existence—that is, their "ontology of personhood." In chapters 8 through 9, I consider the epistemic consequences for psychological inquiry that follow from that ontology. In chapter 10, I discuss the implications of the MGTs' ontology and epistemology for human agency.

Before investigating the ontological claims of the MGTs, I make good on my earlier promise to define with more precision the terminological dis-tinctions that are crucial to a proper understanding of their philosophical (on-tological and epistemological) commitments: *objectivity/subjectivity*, *realism/antirealism*, and *objectivism/relativism*. After all, MGTs put far more effort than do most radical postmodernists into redefining these distinctions. They espe-cially want to challenge—if not obliterate altogether—the objective/subjec-tive distinction, in an effort to eliminate objectivism while maintaining real-ism (in both ontological and epistemic terms). We therefore need more philosophical background, including how these terms have been used conven-tionally, to appreciate the nuanced efforts of the MGTs. This background will also allow me to explain my own use of these terms in more detail than I gave in chapters 1 and 2, to understand and assess the MGTs' uses of them.

THREE KEY DISTINCTIONS: OBJECTIVITY/SUBJECTIVITY, REALISM/ANTIREALISM, AND OBJECTIVISM/RELATIVISM

There is no dearth of discussion about the meanings of the binary oppo-sitions *objectivity/subjectivity*, *realism/antirealism*, and *objectivism/relativism* (and their many variants). Even to oppose these terms in these particular ways invites objection, whether in regard to ontological or epistemological matters. My goal is not to settle the disputes, but rather to settle on some standard usage for my critique of the MGTs. This is necessary because in making their middle-ground cases, MGTs themselves call into question the (standard) meanings of these terms; in so doing they also call into question the legitimacy not only of opposing some of them (i.e., *objectivity* and *subjectivity*) but also of equating others (i.e., *realism* and *objectivism*). In my review of these terms, I discuss epistemological as well as ontological matters, because the two are often intertwined; this state of affairs will become more apparent as we consider their uses in the writings of MGTs themselves.

The Objective/Subjective Distinction

In his famous volume *The Construction of Social Reality*, philosopher John Searle (1995) distinguishes objectivity from subjectivity both epistemically and ontologically.

> Epistemically speaking, "objective" and "subjective" are primarily predicates about judgments. We often speak of judgments as being "subjective" when we mean that their truth or falsity cannot be settled "objectively," because the truth or falsity is not a simple matter of fact but depends on certain attitudes, feelings, and points of view of the makers and hearers of the judgment. . . . In the ontological sense, "objective" and "subjective" are predicates of entities and types of entities, and they ascribe modes of existence. (p. 8)

Searle goes on to say that "we can make epistemically subjective statements about entities that are ontologically objective, and . . . epistemically objective statements about entities that are ontologically subjective" (p. 8). He gives this example of the former: "The statement 'Mt. Everest is more beautiful than Mt. Whitney' is about ontologically objective entities, but makes a subjective judgment about them" (pp. 8–9). And he gives the following example of the latter.

> The statement "I now have a pain in my lower back" reports an epistemologically objective fact in the sense that it is made true by the existence of an actual fact that is not dependent on any stance, attitudes, or opinions of observers. . . . [T]he actual pain, has a subjective mode of existence. (p. 9)

Yet what if one thinks there are no epistemologically objective judgments because there are no "matters of (brute) fact" in the first place? This is held to be the case (a matter of fact?) by both radical postmodernists and MGTs, who try to moderate the former's views while allowing (culturally determined) forms of interpretation to be fundamental to all acts of knowing. However, in eliminating the possibility of epistemically objective judgments (because for MGTs and postmodernists "truth" or "falsity" depends on one's "point of view," to use Searle's words, p. 8), the distinction between (at least epistemic) objectivity and subjectivity loses its meaning. Indeed, MGTs make much of their challenge to this distinction to forge their middle-ground philosophies. I have more to say about the objective/subjective distinction, both ontologically and epistemically, in later chapters; there I consider the logical implications of holding an (anti)objectivist or (anti)realist episte-mology for one's ontology, and the logical implications of holding an (anti)objectivist or (anti)realist ontology for one's epistemology.

Here notice that I tend to use the word *objective* in referring to epistemic matters. However, because we may speak (as does Searle) of an objective (or real) *existence* as well as objective (or realist) *knowledge* about that existence, I sometimes use it ontologically as well. Recall again that MGTs seek a real-ist philosophy (both ontologically and epistemically) that is not objectivist. They therefore do not equate the terms *realist* and *objective*, whereas I have used them interchangeably so far (see chap. 1). My reasons for doing this will become clearer as we proceed in this chapter, and especially in chapters 8 and 9, in which I defend my terminological equation and challenge their terminological distinction. At this point, and for the rest of this volume, I define epistemic objectivity (or epistemic realism) to mean judgments whose truth or falsity does not depend on anyone's beliefs about their truth or fal-sity, including the "attitudes, feelings, and points of view" (p. 8) of which Searle spoke. Philosopher Edward Erwin (1999) offered a definition that covers most of the bases: "An 'objectivist epistemology' is one which holds that propositions are generally true or false independently of any particular para-digm, or school of thought, or language, or indeed of what any human be-lieves" (p. 353; also see Erwin, 1997, p. 74).

The Realist/Antirealist Distinction

The terms *realist/antirealist* and *realism/antirealism* also come with com-plications. Searle (1995) takes to task harshly those who use the term *realism* in an epistemological sense[2] and instead insists that it may properly be used

[2]For example, I have spoken of realist or antirealist epistemologies as those that affirm our ability or inability (respectively) to access realities that exist independently of our knowing processes (see Held, 1995, 1998a, 1998b, 2001, 2002b). I am not alone in this. Philosopher Susan Haack (2002) makes the following statement in "Realisms and Their Rivals":

> "Realism" refers . . . to a whole family of positions; and so contrasts . . . with another whole family of non-realist positions—idealism, nominalism, instrumentalism, relativism, irrealism, etc., etc. . . . The common theme that unites the many and various members of the realist family is that something—the world, truth, universals, numbers, moral values, etc., etc.—is independent of human beings and their beliefs, concepts, cultures, theories, or whatever. What distinguishes the different members of the realist family from each other is exactly what it is that each holds to be independent, in exactly what way, of exactly what about us. . . . Disputes between realists and their non-realist opponents . . . all focus . . . on how much of what we know of the world is properly thought of as the world's contribution and how much as our contribution, on where the line runs between what we discover and what we construct. (pp. 67–69)

only in referring to ontology: "Since the seventeenth century the most common arguments against realism have been epistemic—'all we can ever really know are our own sense data,' . . . —but the thesis under attack, realism, is not . . . an epistemic thesis at all" (p. 154). For Searle, then, realism is a "theory of ontology" (p. 154): "I have defined realism as the view that the world exists independently of our representations of it" (p. 153). Or, more emphatically, "*Realism is the view that there is a way that things are that is logically independent of all human representations. Realism does not say how things are but only that there is a way that they are*" (p. 155). Although philosopher Amie Thomasson (2003), in defiance of Searle, defines conventional forms of "realism" in ontological, epistemological, and semantic terms, her conventional ontological definition squares with his.

> Three elements of a realist philosophical world-view seem to go together:
> The ontological view that there are kinds of things that exist and have
> their nature independently of human beliefs, representations, and prac-
> tices; the epistemological view that acquiring knowledge about such kinds
> is thus a matter of substantive discovery in the face of possibilities of
> gross error and ignorance; and the semantic view that reference to these
> kinds proceeds via a causal relation to an ostended sample, so that the
> extension of the term is determined by the real nature of the kind rather
> than by our associated beliefs and concepts, enabling us to refer to the
> kind despite our possible ignorance and error regarding its nature.
> (p. 580)

We will meet Thomasson again in chapter 5 and thereafter, as she challenges the conventional view of at least ontological realism.

Searle (1995) also denies the possibility of philosopher Hilary Putnam's middle-ground "internal" (ontological) realism, in which "all the reality we can ever really get at, have access to, is the reality that is internal to our system of representations" (p. 174).[3] For example, Searle states, "I do not think there is a coherent position of 'internal realism' that is halfway between external realism, as I have defined it, and out-and-out antirealism, which Putnam also claims to reject" (p. 164).[4] Of course this sort of middle-

---

[3]Pols (1992) refers to this notion of *internal realism* as an "'ontology' of a language" (p. 7). Pols uses scare quotes to indicate that such an ontology is no ontology at all. As he expresses it, "All entities whatsoever are *entities for a language*; each of them is said to belong to the ontology of a certain language and theory. . . . [Philosophers who advance this] are usually called antirealists" (p. 6).
[4]Philosopher Susan Haack (2002), who advocates a middle-ground philosophy that she calls "innocent realism" (p. 85), evidently shares Searle's dismissal of Putnam, if not his reasons for that dismissal.

> Those of more realist inclination . . . are puzzled by what it could mean to say, "relative
> to conceptual scheme C1 there are rocks, but relative to conceptual scheme C2 there
> aren't." . . . Indeed, Putnam himself seems to have felt this realist pull, recently urging
> that . . . we explore what habitable middle ground there may be between metaphysical
> realism and conceptual relativity. Innocent realism occupies just such a habitable
> middle ground between rigid realism and rakish relativism. (p. 85)

About Haack's middle-ground "innocent realism," more in chapter 5.

ground ontology is what MGTs seek: After all, human psychological existence surely depends on human minds, including human minds in the act of knowing—an act that itself is capable of forming theories or representations about that existence (consider, e.g., cognitive psychology). It therefore seems wrong to say that psychological existence cannot properly be called real. Indeed, this is exactly the inclination of MGTs, who rightly want a realist ontology of human kinds—that is, of mind-dependent entities—such as psychological states and processes.

To be sure, then, the waters are deep; and MGTs are not the only ones to notice this. For example, philosopher Susan Haack (2003) defines as real those entities or kinds that are "independent of how anyone in particular believes them to be" (p. 162). This can be true, she says, of social (or human) kinds—including psychological kinds, which are not independent of human beliefs and intentions. Thomasson (2003) too argues on behalf of the realism of human kinds, despite their mind dependence, owing to their possible existence independent of anyone's beliefs about their existence and nature. This latter solution is important, and it departs substantially from what MGTs typically propound in their arguments about the (ontological) realism of human social/psychological (i.e., mind-dependent) entities.

Throughout this volume I will not define ontological realism as narrowly as does Searle. Instead I adopt the view set forth by Haack and Thomasson that what is (ontologically) real can, in principle, include that which depends on human beliefs, representations, and practices. Yet as I explain, it is the exact *nature* of that dependence that determines whether ontological realism can obtain (see note 2, this chapter). Thus for an entity to be considered real ontologically, it must exist independently of beliefs about its existence and nature in some clearly specified way; the entity cannot merely be what anyone believes it to be[5] (Thomasson, 2003). And in keeping with my own (but not the MGTs') equation of realist and objectivist philosophies, I continue to speak of (anti)realist/(anti)objectivist ontologies, just as I speak of (anti)realist/(anti)objectivist epistemologies.

The Objectivist/Relativist Distinction

Opposing the terms *objectivist* and *relativist* is most problematic of all, not least owing to the more typical opposition of the terms *objective* and *subjective*. Nonetheless, I take the objectivist/relativist opposition from philosopher Richard Bernstein's (1983) *Beyond Objectivism and Relativism*, which has had far-reaching influence in postmodernist and MGT circles. Indeed, Bernstein is cited widely by MGTs, who sometimes speak of the capacity for transcendence that the word *beyond* in his book's title invokes even as they

---

[5]Unless, of course, the entity in question consists in a person's or group of persons' beliefs about the nature of some other entity.

claim to have forged middle-ground philosophies. Bernstein begins his distinction by defining objectivism.

> By "objectivism," I mean the basic conviction that there is or must be some permanent, ahistorical matrix or framework to which we can ultimately appeal in determining the nature of rationality, knowledge, truth, reality, goodness, or rightness. An objectivist claims that there is (or must be) such a matrix and that the primary task of the philosopher is to discover what it is. . . . Objectivism is closely related to foundationalism and the search for an Archimedean point. The objectivist maintains that unless we can ground philosophy, knowledge, or language in a rigorous manner we cannot avoid radical skepticism. . . . I am using the term "objectivism" in a way that is far more inclusive than some of its standard uses. "Objectivism" has frequently been used to designate metaphysical realism—the claim that there is a world of objective reality that exists independently of us and that has a determinate nature or essence that we can know. In modern times objectivism has been closely linked with an acceptance of a basic metaphysical or epistemological distinction between the subject and object. (pp. 8–9)

In the first sentence of this definition Bernstein refers to epistemological (e.g., knowledge), ontological (e.g., reality), and ethical (e.g., goodness) matters, although he seems to emphasize epistemology in his mention of foundationalism and skepticism. He also makes reference to the modern (objectivist) distinction between the (knowing) subject and the object (to be known). It is this very distinction that MGTs seek to transcend, reconcile, integrate, bridge, evade, and even obliterate in their middle-ground pursuits.

Linguist George Lakoff (1987) also gives objectivism both epistemic and ontological connotations. More in line with Searle than Bernstein, however, Lakoff emphasizes the ontological proposition that an objective existence does not depend on human cognition, including belief, understanding, perception, or knowledge.

> Objectivism assumes that correctness is independent of the state of people's minds. The Independence Assumption: Existence and fact are independent of belief, knowledge, perception, modes of understanding. . . . Existence cannot depend in any way on human cognition. The world is the way it is, regardless of what people believe or perceive and regardless of any way in which human beings understand the world. (p. 164)

This brings me to Bernstein's (1983) decision to oppose objectivism not to subjectivism, but rather to relativism. It is important to consider this opposition here, because it pertains to the arguments of MGTs, who rely on Bernstein frequently and who reject objectivism outright but accept certain forms of relativism, both ontologically (chap. 5) and epistemologically (chaps. 8–9). Indeed, Haack (2002) makes clear that there are a great many relativist doctrines.

"Relativism" itself refers, not to a single, simple thesis but to a whole family, each holding that something (truth, reality, moral values, and so forth) is relative, in some sense, to something else (language, theory, scientific paradigm, culture, and so on). . . . The most relevant members of the relativist family are those that relativize truth and/or reality to language, theory, paradigm, or conceptual scheme. (p. 82)

Haack (2002) lists what she calls "Varieties of Relativism" (p. 83) and includes "epistemic values," "truth," "metaphysical commitment," "ontology," and "moral values" among the entities that can be considered relative to something else. Thus, like Bernstein, she gives relativism epistemological, ontological, and ethical forms. Yet unlike Bernstein, she opposes relativism to realism rather than to objectivism. However, given her definition of *realism* (see note 2, this chapter), I do not think she would object to my (but not MGTs') equation of realist and objectivist philosophies.

Here is Bernstein's (1983) own definition of relativism, in which—as with his definition of objectivism—we find reference to epistemological (e.g., adjudication or evaluation of competing claims), ontological (e.g., reality), and ethical (e.g., right and good) matters.

The relativist not only denies the positive claims of the objectivist but goes further. In its strongest form, relativism is the basic conviction that when we turn to the examination of . . . rationality, truth, reality, right, the good, or norms[,] we are forced to recognize that . . . all such concepts must be understood as relative to a specific conceptual scheme, theoretical framework, paradigm, form of life, society, or culture. . . . For the relativist, there is no substantive overarching framework or single metalanguage by which we can rationally adjudicate or univocally evaluate competing claims of alternative paradigms. (p. 8)

And about his decision to oppose objectivism to relativism rather than to subjectivism, Bernstein is clear that relativism "must be carefully distinguished from 'subjectivism.'" (p. 11)

A relativist need not be a subjectivist, and a subjectivist need not be a relativist. Husserl is a subjectivist, . . . as he claims that there are a priori structures of transcendental subjectivity that can be apodictically known. . . . However, there is nothing relativistic about Husserl's conception of transcendental phenomenology; it is intended to be the definitive answer to all forms of relativism, skepticism, and historicism. Even if we think of subjectivism[6] . . . to call attention to whatever is "merely" a matter of personal opinion, taste, or bias, . . . a relativist is not necessarily a subjectivist. (p. 11)

---

[6]Recall here again the problem for postmodernists of insisting on a subjectivist epistemology while denying the existence of real selves/subjects. See chapter 1, especially note 9, and chapter 2.

Accordingly for Bernstein (as for Kant),[7] the doctrines of relativism and antiobjectivism (or antirealism) are not necessarily correlated, at least not epistemically speaking.

Most important for my analysis is Bernstein's (1983) appeal to Heidegger to explain his decision to contrast relativism with objectivism, rather than with subjectivism (or even absolutism).[8] He says that Heidegger, having probed "the roots of the various forms of subjectivism that have pervaded modern thought," in the end "questions the whole mode of thinking whereby we take the 'subjective' and the 'objective' as signifying a basic epistemological or metaphysical distinction" (p. 12). MGTs themselves put considerable effort into questioning the legitimacy of the objective/subjective distinction, especially between the knowing "subject" and the "object" to be known, in their quest for a philosophical middle ground between the professed extremes of modernism's objectivist philosophies and postmodernism's subjectivist (and extreme relativist) philosophies. And like Bernstein they often rely on the work of Heidegger—as well as that of Gadamer—to call that distinction into question. In her marvelous little book *Martin Heidegger*, philosopher Marjorie Grene (1957) describes Heidegger's aversion to the Greek philosophy that came after the pre-Socratic thought of Parmenides, for whom

> awareness and its "object" were, not separated by the categorizings of science or religion, but at one. . . . The point is really that *all* our traditional separations, like subject/object, substance/accident, property/relation, and so on . . . are so many veils over Being, so many chasms between ourselves and Being. (pp. 106–107)

Here is how Bernstein (1983) put it.

> Gadamer shows us what is wrong with that way of thinking that dichotomizes the world into "objects" which exist *an sich* and "subjects" that are detached from and stand over against them. We do not comprehend what the things themselves "say" unless we realize that their meaning transcends them and comes into being through the happening or event

---

[7]For example, Kant did not believe in the possibility of objective knowledge, if we consider that to be knowledge of the thing in itself, as it exists independently of the knower. Yet he was also no epistemological relativist. As philosopher Edward Pols (2000a) explained in the following statement,

> Kant . . . is an antirealist about commonsense and scientific knowledge, but he is not a relativist. For Kant, commonsense and scientific knowledge give us appearance rather than reality, but such appearances are not constructed according to the individual or social wishes and whims. Kantian appearances are inevitable appearances, based on a union of sense and understanding that all human beings have in common. (p. 56)

[8]Bernstein (1983) mentions absolutism in the context of his discussion of relativism and subjectivism within Husserl's transcendental phenomenology.

> The most plausible defenses of relativism have nothing to do with subjectivism. So while neither absolutism nor subjectivism is a live option for us now, the choice between a sophisticated form of fallibilistic objectivism and a nonsubjective conception of relativism does seem to be a live—and indeed a momentous—one. (pp. 12–13)

In chapter 8, I challenge postmodernists' and MGTs' tendency to equate objective knowledge with infallible knowledge.

of understanding. And we do not understand ourselves as "subjects" unless we understand how we are always being shaped by effective-history and tradition. We are always *in medias res*: there are no absolute beginnings or endings. (p. 166)

The notion of "coming into being" by way of "understanding" is central to the philosophy of MGTs, some of whom speak of an "emanationist" or "emergent" theory of truth/reality, in which we literally bring what exists into being in the act of knowing or understanding within a discursive community (see chap. 5). Here and throughout this volume, I define the term *relativism* in line with Haack (2002): What is warranted as truth, or what is taken to exist, is relative to, or depends on, "something else" (p. 82). In the case of MGTs, that something else invariably amounts to the point of view of a group or community of knowers, so that truth and reality ultimately depend on the particular discursive practices of (local) cultural/discursive/interpretive contexts or communities.

Last but not least, the term *in medias res* in the quotation of Bernstein does not mean "in the middle ground," certainly not in the way that MGTs define their middle-ground philosophy (of psychology). Yet that term constitutes middle-ground language nonetheless, and so it is to the middle-ground language of MGTs that I now turn, as I begin to lay out their search for a philosophical middle ground.

THE MIDDLE-GROUND LANGUAGE OF MIDDLE-GROUND THEORISTS

In chapter 1, I said that MGTs declare allegiance to at least three theoretical/philosophical traditions—(neo)hermeneutics, (moderate) social constructionism, and (neo)pragmatism. I also said that dividing MGTs in this way is somewhat misleading, because I find more commonalities than differences among them: They all emphasize a determinative role of language or interpretation (within cultural/discursive/interpretive contexts) for social/psychological existence and knowledge about that existence; they all reject objectivist epistemologies and typically adhere to some form of pragmatic, relativistic or value-laden standard of epistemic warrant; and they all share the MGT two-pronged mission of seeking a truth-tracking form of psychological inquiry that does justice to human agency. Despite these commonalities and the absence of clear-cut ideological distinctions among the three constitutive traditions, I nonetheless organize this section along these lines to highlight the exact language used in each. I devote more space to those MGTs who work expressly in the (neo)hermeneutic tradition; there are more self-proclaimed hermeneuticists among the MGTs, and those who work within other "traditions" also make interpretation fundamental to their philosophies of psychology.

The (Neo)Hermeneutic Tradition

The word *beyond* in the title of Bernstein's (1983) book suggests a transcendence of both objectivist and relativist philosophies, rather than laying claim to a philosophical middle ground. However, Bernstein also invokes the metaphor of the middle ground when he challenges the legitimacy of the objective/subjective distinction. As the previous quotation of him suggests, the knowing subject and the object to be known do not exist independently of each other; instead they constitute each other, and in so doing they defy their traditional polarities, their positions as opposed extremes.

Phenomenological and hermeneutic psychiatrist Edwin Hersch (2003), who adopts a relational, Heideggerian ontology of "being in the world" similar to that of hermeneutic MGTs, appeals to Bernstein's book title in formulating what I see as his own "'middle ground' position" (p. 343), in which the language of transcendence (beyond) and integration (blendings) appears.

> To borrow from the title of Richard Bernstein's 1983 book, something "beyond objectivism and relativism" is implied and required. . . . Relatedness is primary. . . . Thus to try to atomistically break down experience into a set of discrete 'objective' and 'subjective' elements would be inappropriate and misguided. (p. 344)

He too speaks of a "'co-constitutional' epistemological position, in which the realities of human experience or *known* reality can be described as 'both given and made'" (p. 60). Thus the allegedly coconstituted "truths of human experience" are "never completely subjective or without any objective truth value" (p. 73). Instead, the "relatively subjective and the relatively objective components offer significant contributions to the interactional truths of human experience that emerge from their blendings" (p. 273).

Cultural and anthropological psychologist Suzanne Kirschner's (1997) review of *Rewriting the Self*—whose author, narrative psychologist Mark Freeman, I include among the MGTs (for reasons that will soon become apparent) is itself entitled "Beyond Positivism and Postmodernism." Although this title invokes transcendence, Kirschner situates Freeman's agentic, hermeneutic, and moderately constructionist psychology between the two untenable extremes of "conventional objectivist psychology" on the one hand and "radical [constructionist] skepticism" on the other—this with the standard MGT eye toward an agentic notion of personhood as well.

> In celebrating this interpretivist [i.e., hermeneutic] vision, Freeman is not only challenging the adequacy of conventional objectivist psychology. . . . He also situates himself in opposition to that family of theoretical movements which includes poststructuralism, deconstructionism, and social constructionism. [These] theorists . . . hold that since we cannot know "objects" (including the self) apart from or prior to the language that articulates them, we should relinquish altogether the quest for any

sort of improved understanding of human beings. . . . He offers an alternative to such radical skepticism. . . . He celebrates hermeneutics as a form of social understanding that acknowledges the centrality and ubiquity of language and interpretation without succumbing to paralyzing doubt and nihilism. Hermeneutics, he asserts, provides a method of understanding self and others that enables us to discriminate between interpretations of greater and lesser adequacy [i.e., "truth value" or "validity"]. It provides, as well, a model of personhood that views selves as capable of agency, innovation, and resistance. (p. 15)

I use Freeman's own words in my discussion of his middle-ground position. Like other MGTs, he holds fast to the two-pronged mission of a truth-tracking form of psychological inquiry that exalts human agency nonetheless.

As I explained in chapter 1, I deliberately use the metaphor of the middle ground only in a loose way; I do not find significant differences among theorists who speak expressly of integrating/reconciling/bridging, moderating/mediating, transcending/overcoming, or avoiding/evading the two philosophical "extremes" in question, and so I use the term *middle ground* to characterize all of them. Indeed, sometimes the same author speaks in many—if not all—of these ways. However, philosopher Thomas Nagel (1986), whom I do not characterize as an MGT despite his nod to integration, speaks in a different way altogether in *The View from Nowhere*. There he suggests that we hold objective and subjective views simultaneously, if not integratively.

Much of what I will have to say will concern the possibilities of integration [of an objective and a subjective standpoint]. . . . But I shall also point out ways in which the two standpoints cannot be satisfactorily integrated, and in these cases I believe the correct course is . . . to hold the opposition clearly in one's mind without suppressing either element. Apart from the chance that this kind of tension will generate something new, it is best to be aware of the ways in which life and thought are split, if that is how things are.[9] (p. 6)

As we shall see, MGTs cannot entertain the objective standpoint: They believe that our necessarily situated existence, our view from somewhere, precludes that. I challenge that claim in chapter 8 and again in chapter 10.

Middle-ground language appears in others whom I do not necessarily place among MGTs "proper"; its appeal is classic (Aristotelian!) and ubiquitous. For example, Driver-Linn (2003) provides some intellectual context in an article entitled "Where Is Psychology Going?" There she too struggles with the possibility of integration, and her conclusions about truth are closer to those of MGTs than of Nagel. Indeed, she spends considerable time ex-

---

[9]See Grene (1957, pp. 106–110), for discussion of Heidegger's view that being/existence (or life) and knowing/awareness are one. See Pols (1998, 2002a, 2004a, 2004b) for a different approach to the argument that knowing is an instance of being, an approach in which the objectivist epistemology that many MGTs denounce in the name of Heidegger is defended nonetheless.

plaining Kuhn's "Middling Position on Truth"[10] (p. 270), a position that, she says, "may hold an implicit appeal to psychologists because it bridges these divisions, falling between a natural/rationalist stance and a social/relativistic stance" (p. 276). It is worth quoting her as she explains the differences between the natural and the human sciences on the basis of "science wars" between "objectivists, rationalists, reductionists, positivists, and empiricists" on the natural science side and "humanists, relativists, postmodernists, and social constructionists" on the social science side. What falls in the middle sounds not unlike the position of MGTs.

> [The natural science] side maintains that scientific laws and truths can be gleaned through rigorous methods that winnow away the subjective from the objective. . . . On the other side . . . [are] humanists, relativists, postmodernists, and social constructionists. This camp maintains that . . . the objective cannot be winnowed away from the subjective. . . . Psychologists . . . either pick a side (against their colleagues) or maintain half a belief in empirical results as sacrosanct and half a belief that science, like many products psychological, is a construction. . . . [Kuhn's] naturalism represents a particularly hopeful approach for psychologists to take when . . . caught between a natural science/rationalist worldview and a social science/relativist worldview. This position suggests that maps, or models, or theories, or results can be empirically based, while acknowledging the subjectivity inherent in psychological inquiry. Results can fit the world in ways that are discernibly good or better than those of the past, without trying to make the shaky claim that psychological science is progressing toward perfect correspondence with a verifiable and objective reality. (pp. 270–271)

The last two sentences in this passage could have been written by any number of MGT authors; I refer especially to the rejection of objectivity, and its (problematic) equation with infallibility ("perfect correspondence"). Driver-Linn (2003) surely squares with Kirschner's (1997) view of Freeman (1993), who is said by her to allow us to "discriminate between interpretations of greater and lesser adequacy," while challenging "conventional objectivist psychology" (p. 15). In the end Driver-Linn questions the long-term goals of psychological inquiry, because she sees contradictions in them. She maintains that if psychologists seek multiple levels of analysis, then they must generate synthesis or meta-analysis to integrate the more "molecular" methods of natural science with the more "molar" analysis of social science (p. 276).[11] (Some MGTs, especially Martin & Sugarman, 1999b, indeed provide a "levels of reality" approach.) But in that case, she asks, why are "his-

---

[10]See Green (2004), who challenges Driver-Linn's interpretation of Kuhn.
[11]I am not sure just what Driver-Linn means by *molecular* methods and *molar* analysis. It seems to me that both within natural science and within social science there can be some methods or analyses that are more "molecular" than others (and thus some that are more "molar").

tory of psychology and philosophy of science relatively undervalued and breadth so routinely sacrificed in favor of specialization?" (p. 276). (This question may provide one reason for the scant attention given to the MGTs' historically and philosophically informed integrative efforts.) And if psychologists "favor a Kuhn-like, naturalistic, middling stance on truth in science," if they "believe that there is truth without claiming that results are not historically, culturally, and psychologically limited," then why is there "such a strong norm for using language of justification . . . instead of an explicit acknowledgment that such products . . . are not truth, but instead represent works in progress?" (p. 276).

I see no contradiction in using the "language of justification" (or truth) and acknowledging that the findings of science are "works in progress." Notice, however, that Driver-Linn reveals her hand: She, like MGTs, wants truth-tracking psychological inquiry, but without either objectivity or *too much* relativism. She too seems in search of a middle-ground position between objectivism and relativism, especially when attending to matters of truth in psychological inquiry. Indeed, MGTs' reformulations of truth and (ontological) realism (chap. 5) play no minor role in their revisionist program for psychological inquiry (chap. 9).

Some MGTs not only invoke a middle-ground philosophy metaphorically in their attempts to integrate/reconcile/bridge, moderate/mediate, transcend/overcome, or avoid/evade the problems they find in both modernist and postmodernist approaches to psychological science but also use middle-ground language quite literally. In the rest of this chapter, I provide examples of their express use of middle-ground language as they explicate an agentic psychology that is truth tracking.

Let us begin with the words of psychologists Jack Martin and Jeff Sugarman, who appeal to middle-ground alternatives more explicitly and frequently than do other MGTs. For example, in an article entitled "Between the Modern and Postmodern," Martin and Sugarman (2000a) use the language of both mediation and transcendence to make their nuanced ontological and epistemological arguments, although mediation dominates. The word *between* appears not only in the title but also in two of three opposition-defying subheadings: "Between Modern Foundationalism and Postmodern Radical Arbitrariness" (p. 402); "Between Modern Essentialism and Postmodern Antisubjectivism" (p. 403); and "Beyond Modern Certainty and Postmodern Anarchistic Relativism" (p. 404). Martin and Sugarman's (2000a) search for philosophical middle ground is unequivocal in this quotation, although the "unsustainable myths" they find in modernity—especially their presumption of foundationalism and certainty—are, as we shall see, harder to find in recent times than they suggest: "Unless it is possible to articulate convincingly some alternative middle ground to the unsustainable myths of modernity on the one hand and some of the more excessively radical medicine of postmodernism on the other, psychology and education are in deep difficulty" (p. 400).

In *The Psychology of Human Possibility and Constraint*, Martin and Sugarman (1999a) make a fuller case for their "neorealist hermeneutics." There, in addition to their typical use of middle-ground language, they deploy the language of avoidance/evasion—for example, in the section entitled "Avoiding Scientism and Relativism" (p. 46). They also use the language of transcending/overcoming—for example, in a chapter entitled "The Challenge: Overcoming the Problems of Dualism Without Sacrificing the Psychological" (p. 1). However, they return to middle-ground language in proposing their "neorealist hermeneutics" (p. 52): "A middle course is charted between the extremes of an overly constraining static, ahistorical, 'outside' standard on the one bank, and an overly enabling, strongly relativistic, nihilistic, 'anything goes' absence of standard on the other" (p. 59).

And in *Psychology and the Question of Agency*, Martin, Sugarman, and Thompson (2003) strive for a compatibilist middle-ground philosophy in which they tackle directly the problem of how humans can have freedom/ agency in the context of a deterministic psychological science.

> By offering a critique of Gergen's [radical] social constructionism in psychology, we hope to succeed in creating an opening between the extremes of traditional scientistic psychology, on the one hand, and what we regard as too radical postmodern reactions to psychological scientism, on the other hand. It is in this clearing that we subsequently will envision a genuinely agentic psychology. (p. 40)

In chapter 3, entitled "Between Hard Determinism and Radical Freedom" (p. 45), the authors say that they seek a "theory of agency understood as self-determination—one that might succeed in positioning a compatibilist-like middle position between hard determinism and the kind of mysterious freedom apparently sponsored by radical libertarians" (p. 49). They literally call this a "middle-ground position" (p. 57) and later refer to it as a "kind of middle-ground agency" (p. 73). Moreover, in the edited volume *Between Chance and Choice* (Atmanspacher & Bishop, 2002), Martin and Sugarman (2002) again articulate a middle-ground agency by way of a soft determinism, one that avoids the extremes of both libertarianism and hard/reductionistic determinism.

Others qualify for MGT status in virtue of their middle-ground language. In *Re-envisioning Psychology*, Richardson, Fowers, and Guignon (1999)—like Martin and Sugarman—make their case for a hermeneutic psychology of human agency that "steers a path" (both ontological and epistemological) between modern objectivism and radical postmodern constructionism. (They also use the language of transcendence/overcoming in the second section, entitled "Beyond Scientism and Constructionism," p. 139.)

The authors credit that steerage to philosopher Charles Taylor, who (not unlike Bernstein) rejects the conventional opposition of objectivity and subjectivity. Here are Richardson et al.'s (1999) own words on this, in the context of their discussion of the nature of emotion.

> The linguistic constitution of our experience undermines one of the most fundamental assumptions of the objectivist outlook, the assumption that an object exists and has determinate features, "independent of any descriptions or interpretations offered of it by any subjects" (Taylor, 1989, p. 34) and that science can give us a correct representation of that object. Given this account of feelings as "always already" interpreted, Taylor steers a path between constructionism, which paves the way to the pop psychological idea that "thinking makes it so," and scientific objectivism, which treats feelings as just "there." (p. 220)

In that same volume, Richardson, Fowers, and Guignon (1999) use the language of transcendence/overcoming—and liberation itself—to describe the hermeneutic philosophy they propound in the name of agency.

> Hermeneutic philosophers generally want to call in question the distinction between "subjective" and "objective" that has dominated our thinking since the rise of modern science. . . . Taylor wants to liberate us from both the objectified view of reality and the subjectified view of values we get from modern science. (p. 215)

And Fowers (1998), in seeking to allay the "Cartesian [A]nxiety . . . fanned by much postmodern rhetoric," says he is "seeking a middle path . . . in which we can justifiably claim that some interpretations are better than others, even though there are no final warrants for such distinctions." Moreover, in an article entitled "Beyond Scientism and Postmodernism?" Richardson (1998) described his hermeneutic realism as one that went "beyond scientism and constructionism," in virtue of its "notion of a practical life-world or a realm of lived experience as our basic reality" (p. 42). All in all, Richardson et al. (1999), Guignon (1991), and Martin and Sugarman (1999b) defend a "hermeneutic realism," in which the deep relation between being and knowing is said to obliterate the conventional distinction between humans as knowing subjects and as objects to be known; for these and other MGTs, humans therefore end up (actually) being what they interpret themselves to be. This proclamation, of course, sounds suspiciously like the radical postmodernism/ constructionism that MGTs reject, and I return to it in subsequent chapters.

In *The Cure of Souls: Science, Values and Psychotherapy*, psychologist Robert Woolfolk (1998) also advocates a hermeneutic position, one that "has [recently] become widespread in the social sciences and the humanities" (p. 65). He says that Gadamer's hermeneutics, in particular, occupies a middle ground or "intermediate" position (both ontologically and epistemologically) between objectivism and constructionism. Note in the following quotation a form of the claim about the relation between being/existence and knowing;

this constitutes one way to express the dependence of being on knowing or interpretation to which MGTs typically appeal to eliminate the possibility of objective (but not realist) knowledge or truth.

> An objectivist might argue that sexism and racism were present in past eras but were unobservable without present-day conceptual apparatus. A social constructionist might argue that sexism and racism (and all other social categories) are present . . . only after the categories are socially constructed and adopted as interpretive tools. Gadamer's hermeneutic position is intermediate. It does not hold that social explanation involves the arbitrary imposition of socially constructed concepts. An external social reality that interpreters can access does exist, but that reality emerges only through interpretation and is delimited by the variety of constraints to which interpretation is subject. (p. 74)

Although I have much more to say about the deep relation between being (ontology) and knowing (epistemology), including the implications of that relation for objective knowing and knowledge, my conclusions depart considerably from those of MGTs. I especially attend (in chap. 5) to the (hermeneutic notion of an) "emanationist" or "emergent" theory of reality/ truth to which Woolfolk only alludes. This notion also appears in the words of phenomenological and hermeneutic psychiatrist Edwin Hersch (2003), who speaks of widespread "claiming the middle ground" in the "objectivism-subjectivism debate" (p. 341)—a debate he works to resolve by way of his "co-constitutional epistemology," in which the "interactional truths of human experience . . . emerge from . . . [the] blendings [of the relatively subjective and relatively objective components]" (p. 273).

Most of the psychologists quoted in this section have cited the work of hermeneutic philosopher Charles Guignon to support their middle-ground philosophical arguments about psychological inquiry and agency. This makes sense, because Guignon (1998) himself supports the two-pronged mission of the MGTs—that is, a moderation of modern scientific (objectivist) psychology and postmodern constructionism, in the name of human agency and truth. In fact, it is Guignon's description of an "emanationist" or "emergent" theory of truth that we will consider in due course. Here he speaks of psychotherapy as an "illustrative example of human science inquiry" (p. 558, abstract).

> Naturalist approaches assume explanation involves describing underlying causes operating beneath the surface phenomena of thought and action. . . . Difficulties this view encounters in doing justice to human agency have given rise to constructionist conceptions of psychotherapy . . . [in which] action is structured by narratives or stories understood as free creations that swing free of any facts and do not involve discovering any truth about a person's life or history. . . . This approach involves a number of excesses and shortcomings and [the author] argues for a more moderate narrativist viewpoint that draws on . . . ontological hermeneutics. (p. 558, abstract)

Guignon (1998), like Bernstein and other hermeneuticists, also calls into question the "subject-object distinction [that] is presupposed by both naturalism or constructionism" (p. 567). Although elsewhere he speaks of moderation, here is his language of transcendence/overcoming.

> Whereas constructionists invite us to celebrate the fact that the meanings we create swing free of any ties to reality, naturalists encourage us to expunge all meaning vocabulary from our theories, so that we can be sure we are getting in touch with reality as it is in itself. . . . The hermeneutic tradition has tried to overcome both naturalism and constructionism by working out a different ontological account of human existence and its relation to the world. (p. 567)

Others in search of a middle-ground philosophy of psychology also seek a hermeneutic "solution." In *Rewriting the Self*, narrative psychologist Mark Freeman (1993) finds in "hermeneutic inquiry" (p. 5) the road to both psychological truth and human agency that Kirschner (1997) attributed to him, and that I claim to be the dual mission of MGTs. If understood properly, he tells us, the "task" of hermeneutics is to acknowledge the "primacy of word [especially in our interpretive/linguistic or knowing/understanding powers] *without losing world* [reality] *in the process*." It is worth attending to this, because he makes the point clearly. Note especially his desire for mediation, which for him is compatible with the attainment of valid or true (although, as with other MGTs, not objective) knowledge.

> On the one hand, there is the attempt to wave the banner of interpretation, to show its unsurpassability in making sense of the world, to show that there does not and cannot exist an unprejudiced, neutral, wholly objective way of doing so. On the other hand, however, there is also the attempt to maintain that the very interpretive prejudices we have, far from obviating the possibility of knowing and understanding, are exactly the prerequisites for our making any sense of things at all. "Word" does indeed achieve a certain primacy from this perspective. . . . The task . . . is to maintain and embrace the primacy of word *without losing world in the process* . . . and to show that this process [of interpretation], rather than being antithetical to . . . generating valid knowledge, is in fact perfectly compatible with it. (p. 16)

Freeman (1993) then explains how his compatibilist hermeneutic "mediation" (between word and world, subjective and objective) does not fall prey to charges of being unscientific, relativistic, and skeptical.

> Hermeneutics ought not to be considered the unscientific, relativistic, skepticism-ridden fantasy land it is sometimes assumed to be. . . . [Some] will reject this attempt at mediation. Mainstream psychologists . . . may continue to find the perspective . . . too "subjective" and imprecise. Others, perhaps, may find the perspective too "objective." . . . There will also be those who just don't like the mediating philosophical positions of the

sort being advanced here. But mediating philosophical positions . . . are only a problem for those who are given to extremes. . . . But if one has any interest at all in positing both the unsurpassability of interpretation and the possibility still of generating what we colloquially call "knowledge," then there is little choice but to inhabit this region. (pp. 16–17)

In this final quotation, Freeman (1993) uses the language of transcendence ("moved beyond") in refusing to view language as a prison from which we cannot escape. This last point certainly moderates the radically constructionist antirealism of Gergen (2001a), who asked, "How should we answer questions about what is 'independent of language' save through language? . . . It is to pound on the walls of the house of language in hopes that we may find our way outside" (pp. 425, 429). Here, by contrast, are Freeman's own words of mediation and transcendence.

To confer primacy upon language need not result in breaking the covenant between word and world; it only breaks the spell . . . which supposes language to be a mere mirror of the world. . . . We have indeed moved beyond this conception. But this is hardly ample reason to leap to the conclusion that words cannot disclose or reveal. . . . [This falls] prey to a fallacy as well as to a particularly crude form of either-or thinking: either language is a mirror or it is a reality unto itself, autistically enclosed, a veritable prison, in which there exist no doors leading out. (p. 223)

Freeman appears to make good sense, but questions remain nonetheless. Most important, just how is this "either–or thinking" to be successfully mediated? By what means can we have truth (without scare quotes), when the particularities of our interpretive/linguistic contexts are said by MGTs to play no minor role in what we warrant as truth (about the human world) *within* those contexts? Although Freeman and other MGTs confront those thorny questions with all due seriousness, they (not entirely unlike radical postmodernists) seem to settle for (local) "truth" (with scare quotes) rather than insist on truth (without scare quotes). In chapter 8, I put forth a theory of (direct) knowing (of reality) that does not preclude a linguistic/conceptual component.

Here let us consider one more hermeneutic psychologist. Unlike those we have considered so far, he characterizes his own position not as more moderate but as more radical than the polarities he—like the others—rejects. In "Humanism, Hermeneutics, and the Concept of the Human Subject," Louis Sass (1988) speaks of doing without various binary oppositions. This sounds like the language of avoiding/evading, although Sass himself describes his position in the language of transcending/overcoming, one that conveys a revolutionary or radical spirit. However, despite his belief that the hermeneutic view is more radical than the objectivism and relativism it is said to transcend, he advances a position that sounds not unlike the ones put forth by those who speak expressly and with approbation of middle-ground philosophies of psychology.

> The hermeneutic alternative to objectivism and relativism . . . does feel at times like something less than a revelation. . . . However, we would have to say that the ontological hermeneutic position is far more radical than the polarized positions it attempts to overcome. In rejecting these extremes, the hermeneutic position is attempting to do without certain dimensions or binary oppositions in which philosophy and psychology have for centuries been rooted . . . e.g., inner versus outer, self versus world, subjective versus objective, . . . and freedom versus determinism. (p. 261)

The attempt to forge a middle-ground philosophy of psychology is not limited to the hermeneuticists whom I have quoted. Like these hermeneuticists, there are social constructionists in search of middle-ground territory, in virtue of their criticism of the radically antirealist version of social constructionism advocated by social constructionist movement leader Gergen (e.g., 1985, 1988, 1991, 1994, 2001a, 2001b) and their concomitant endorsement of more moderate forms of social constructionism (e.g., Edley, 2001; Harré, 1984, 1998, 2002; Liebrucks, 2001). Again, these moderate constructionists are hard to distinguish ideologically from MGTs who inhabit the hermeneutic camp, because the latter also reject Gergen's strong (antirealist) constructionism and embrace the more moderate notion that humans indeed (socially) construct aspects of reality, which reality admits of a realist ontology (and epistemology) nonetheless (e.g., Hersch, 2003; Martin & Sugarman, 1999a, 2000a; Richardson, Fowers, & Guigan, 1999; Woolfolk, 1998). Thus these moderate constructionists, much like the hermeneuticists we have considered, distance themselves from radically antirealist and relativist philosophies as they attempt to work out middle-ground ontologies and epistemologies.

I also include among MGTs some theorists who call or consider themselves (neo)pragmatists (e.g., Fishman, 1999; Miller, 2004).[12] As with the more moderate social constructionists, they too share core philosophical allegiances with the hermeneuticists we have considered. Indeed, all three middle-ground-seeking "constituencies" have much in common: (a) They emphasize the role of language/interpretation in being and knowing; (b) Accordingly they make being and knowing relative to or dependent on local discursive/interpretive contexts or communities; and (c) They deploy pragmatic theories of epistemic warrant, in which the consequences of our knowledge claims determine their truth status. Not least, they hold the dual

---

[12]Miller (2004) calls his approach to the case study method that he, like Fishman, propounds "narrative psychotherapy case study" (p. 211). Still, he makes common cause with Fishman's (1999, 2001) "'pragmatic case study' approach" (p. 210), not least when he speaks with approbation of philosophers (e.g., Wittgenstein, Dilthey, Husserl, and Heidegger) who, "in what they liked to call the *human* sciences . . . encouraged us to pay attention to . . . the pragmatic tasks of everyday living" (p. 205). Accordingly, I consider him to have some pragmatic leanings as well. See chapter 1, note 10.

mission of a truth-tracking form of psychological inquiry that does justice to human agency. In the next two sections, I give exemplary quotations of the two remaining "traditions" from which MGTs hail—social constructionism and (neo)pragmatism, respectively.

The Social Constructionist Tradition

The deep commonality between hermeneutic MGTs and social constructionist MGTs is exemplified in hermeneutically inclined psychologists Martin, Sugarman, and Thompson's (2003) approving words about Rom Harré's "discursive psychology," which they take to be a form of social constructionism. Indeed, they say that it constitutes an attempt to moderate—in the name of agency—radical or "overly deterministic versions of social constructionism," in which agency or self-determination is given short shrift (pp. 70, 72). Martin et al. (2003) find in Harré's view of agency a basis for their own "middle-ground agency," and in so doing they illustrate the joining of hermeneutic and social constructionist forces in their middle-ground pursuits.

> Against what they regard as overly determinist versions of social constructionism, Harré and Gillett (1994) champion the role of the person in adopting sociocultural meanings, norms, conventions, and practices. They explicitly counsel against merely replacing physical forces and causes with social and discursive practices that also negate the active agent in favor of extrapersonal explanations. . . . The conceptualization of agency evident in these accounts . . . may be employed to support the kind of middle-ground agency hinted at [in certain compatibilist arguments]. (pp. 72, 73)

Consistent with Martin, Sugarman, and Thompson's description, Harré (2002) stakes out middle-ground territory (at least ontologically) between postmodernism and critical realism in his moderating (re)formulation of social constructionism. Here he aims for the ontological realism that Gergen (e.g., 1985, 1994, 1997, 1998, 2001a) and other radical constructionists/constructivists deny. Thus for Harré (2002) the discursive domain is considered real, and not everything in life is of our own making.

> Postmodernism and critical realism, with its emphasis on the intractable reality and causal efficacy of social structures . . . , are at opposite poles, the former requiring that all be malleable and the latter that nothing be. Social constructionism, while denying the efficacy of social structures, affirms the reality of the discursive domain without falling into the fallacy of supposing that because many aspects of our lives are our own constructions, all must be. (p. 611, abstract)

Harré (2002) distances himself from the extreme relativism that Gergen celebrates in promoting his "unbounded relativity of meaning" (Gergen &

Kaye, 1992, p. 183) and in insisting that "constructionism is itself 'ontologically mute'" (Gergen, 1998, p. 417; see also Gergen, 1994, p. 72; chap. 4, this volume). Of particular interest is Harré's (ontological) acceptance of the essential or universal attributes (of persons) that even Martin and Sugarman—among other MGTs, including moderate constructionists—sometimes reject, as well as his call for epistemological moderation of radical postmodernism.

> While sharing some insights with postmodernism, there are important ways in which the social constructionist viewpoint is very different. . . . It is no part of the social constructionist approach to deny that there are any universal aspects of human life, nor that . . . there are some essential attributes of persons and processes. Nor is it any part of the social constructionist approach to deny that there are better and worse representations of the social world and of human psychology. In short, social constructionism, while at a very great remove from positivistic mainstream psychology, is not radically relativistic. (pp. 611–612)

In his review of Harré's (1998) *The Singular Self*, Burkitt (2001) also mentions the realist moderation that he finds in "discursive constructionism," not least because Harré rejects the nonreal status given to the self or identity by radical postmodernists/constructionists (e.g., Gergen, 1991; Glass, 1993; see chap. 2, this volume, including notes 8–9).

> Although Harré was among the initial pioneers in social psychology who took the "linguistic turn" and began to develop what he still refers to as a "discursive psychology," he never abandoned a realist philosophy of inquiry for a full-blown discursive constructionism. . . . A unique feature of Harré's constructionism is that he has never adopted a postmodern position on the self. That is, while Harré would agree with postmodernists that the self is multiple and fragmented, he nevertheless wants to argue for a sense of singularity at the heart of the person. (Burkitt, 2001, p. 446)

To use Harré's (1998) own words to describe what he himself calls his "realist theme": "Social constructionism [is not] at odds with at least some versions of scientific realism. There are some conditions that stand outside any discourse whatever that make discourse possible" (pp. 18–19). A bold statement indeed for a constructionist of any sort![13]

In a special issue of the journal *Theory and Psychology* (2001) devoted to "Social Constructionism and Its Critics," constructionist psychologist Alexander Liebrucks (2001) denies the (epistemological) relativism advanced in strong(er) forms of social constructionism, especially in Gergen's strongest form.

---

[13]What makes this statement especially bold is Harré's conventionally realist suggestion that there must exist mind-independent (i.e., nonconstructed) entities for realism to obtain.

Contrary to Gergen's (1985) account . . . no relativist conclusions can be drawn from the arguments and empirical findings of social construction-ist sociology of science. . . . The central theses of the social construction-ists in theoretical psychology are primarily concerned not with episte-mology but with the discipline's construal of its subject matter [i.e., ontology]. (p. 385)

Earlier he said, "[Social constructionists] do not subscribe to a relativist epis-temology. They do not claim that it is impossible to arrive at valid accounts of the psychological properties of persons" (p. 373). Yet as we shall see, Gergen (2001a) finds too much realism and foundationalism even in Liebrucks's modest attempts at moderation.

In that same issue of *Theory and Psychology*, constructionist psycholo-gist Nigel Edley (2001) also seeks a more moderate form of social construc-tionism, one that admits of the ontological realism that Gergen rejects in proclaiming his "ontological mutism." Edley therefore makes ontological common cause both with Liebrucks and (to a lesser extent) Harré when he says, "Most social constructionists do not see language as the only reality" (p. 439) and claims that "it is actually very difficult to find occasions where social constructionists have denied the existence of an extra-discursive realm" (p. 437).[14] For Edley, then, discursively (i.e., socially/linguistically) constructed realities—such as emotional states and other psychological properties of per-sons—are as real as rocks, although his use of scare quotes to adorn the word *real* gives pause for thought: "Discourse can bring into being a whole range of phenomena that are every bit as 'real' as trees and houses" (p. 438). Again, I assess these more moderate forms of constructionism in considerable detail in the chapters to follow. Here let us turn our attention to a (neo)pragmatic form of moderation/mediation.

The (Neo)Pragmatic Tradition

In *The Case for Pragmatic Psychology*, psychologist Daniel Fishman (1999) propounds a pragmatic paradigmatic middle ground between the logical posi-tivism he finds in modern psychology's nomothetic/objectivist form of in-quiry and the social constructionism he locates in postmodern psychology's idiographic/hermeneutic form of inquiry. Unlike the hermeneuticists whom we have considered, Fishman does not seem to think that the "hermeneutic paradigm" itself constitutes a middle ground (between modern and radical

---

[14]Actually it is not all that hard to find dismissal (if not outright denial) of an extradiscursive realm within constructionism. In addition to Gergen's many pronouncements, one prominent example appears in the following statement made by the editor of the *Journal of Constructivist Psychology*:

I am only vaguely interested in the ontological question of whether a real world exists in any meaningful sense beyond our construction of it. . . . I would classify myself as neither realist nor antirealist, but *arealist*, someone for whom the term has little meaning. (Neimeyer, 1995, pp. 341–342)

postmodern psychologies). On his view it is indistinguishable from (radical) social constructionism (at least epistemically), so it constitutes one of the two extremes that must itself be reconciled/integrated or transcended/ overcome (the other is the "positivist paradigm"). However, in his Table 4.1 (pp. 99–100), where the pragmatic paradigm is located between the modern/ positivist and postmodern/hermeneutic paradigms, he also gives his (in-the-middle) "pragmatic paradigm" an "underlying" social constructionist episte-mology. And in the text he calls his pragmatic paradigm "neopragmatic [or just "pragmatic"] postmodernism" (p. 98). It is therefore not clear just what is in the middle of what, and on what dimension or continuum.

I remain equally unclear about this statement: "While the table [4.1] might be interpreted as implying that there are only two categorically distinct epistemological paradigms in quantitative psychology [logical positivism and social constructionism], in practice the positivist and pragmatic paradigms . . . form the endpoints of the continuum" (p. 100).[15] My (mis?)understanding, in any case, is this: Whereas hermeneutic MGTs place themselves philosophi-cally between modern positivism and radical postmodernism/constructionism, Fishman first seems to put his pragmatism between modern positivism and (radical?) postmodernism/constructionism, but then says pragmatism consti-tutes an endpoint on the continuum. Which is it?

To be fair, there are other dimensions that distinguish the three para-digms; the "primary goal of research" (p. 99, Table 4.1) is one of the more prominent ones. Yet here again there is discrepancy between what the herme-neutic MGTs themselves say and what Fishman ascribes to them: The prag-matic paradigm, he says, seeks "solution of context-specific, practical psy-chological problems," whereas the hermeneutic paradigm seeks "qualitative understanding of context-specific psychological events and processes" (p. 99, Table 4.1). But as we shall see, many—if not all—hermeneutic MGTs are searching for practical solutions to (context-dependent) psychological prob-lems too. They also advocate pragmatic forms of epistemic warrant in their empirical work, which includes their asking practical questions about how to make life better (e.g., Martin & Sugarman, 1999a; Richardson et al., 1999; Woolfolk, 1998). Moreover, they do not typically dismiss quantitative re-search out of hand.

By the end of the chapter—it is entitled "The Dialectic: Putting It All Together"—Fishman (1999) says, "We can see that the pragmatic model is a type of hybrid of the other two [the positivist and hermeneutic paradigms]" (p. 101). Perhaps here we should back up and consider his opening remarks

---

[15]Fishman (1999) goes on to make the following statement:
> This continuum includes a large variety of 'mixed' epistemologies that contain varying blends of the elements from the 'pure' types at each end. . . . What I have described as three 'pure' paradigms [positivist, pragmatic, and hermeneutic] are the endpoints of continua. (pp. 100–101)

Still, just what paradigms constitute the endpoints of what continua remains unclear.

about the aims of his pragmatic paradigm, in which he speaks at once of integration/reconciliation/bridging and of transcendence/overcoming.

> The *pragmatic paradigm* in psychology seeks to transcend psychology's dialectical culture wars by developing an integrative alternative. This approach combines the epistemological insights and value awareness of skeptical, critical, and ontological postmodernism—hereafter referred to in group as the *hermeneutic paradigm*—with the methodological and conceptual achievements of the *positivist paradigm*. Thus the natural science methodologies and concepts of positivism are employed, but with a nonpositivist purpose: . . . to achieve the democratically derived program goals of particular, historically and culturally situated social groups, not to uncover purported general laws of human nature. . . . Pragmatism . . . [stakes] out a middle, centrist position between modernistically traditional, conservative positivism . . . and radically liberal, skeptical and critical postmodernism. (p. 8)

In chapter 9, I describe Fishman's (and other MGTs') revisionist goals for psychological inquiry. Because all dismiss the discovery of "general laws of human nature," the commonality among them again becomes apparent.

Fishman (1999) expressly deploys the language of transcendence/overcoming in a chapter entitled "Transcending the Dialectic: The Emergence of Postmodern Pragmatism" (p. 102). There he speaks of "Transcending the Either/Or Question to Practical Action" (p. 113) by appealing, as do his hermeneutic MGT colleagues, to Bernstein: "Bernstein argues strongly for a position outside of the Either/Or of 'absolute' objectivism versus 'anything goes' relativism" (p. 113). Although he considers Bernstein to be an American pragmatist (rather than a hermeneuticist), here he attributes to Bernstein (and other philosophers) goals that square with those of hermeneutic MGTs.

> The recent discovery of American pragmatism is epitomized in the work of . . . Richard Bernstein, Richard Rorty, and Stephen Toulmin. Each in a different way has argued a common theme: the need to go "beyond" the present logical impasse between advocates of objectivism and those of relativism to focus on the practical problems in contemporary life—social, political, and cultural. (p. 109)

By the end of the book, however, Fishman returns to middle-ground language, especially when he calls for a proper balance between generality ("nomothetics") and particularity ("idiographics") in the attainment of a maximally useful or pragmatic form of psychological knowledge. (The hermeneutically inclined MGT Woolfolk, 1998, makes a parallel argument about mediating the tension between nomothetic and idiographic approaches to psychotherapy.) In a section entitled "A 'Middle Way' to Generalization," Fishman (1999) makes the following statement:

> The pragmatist agrees with the positivist about the value of generalizing, but also with the hermeneut about the need to retain context. . . . While

generalizing by logical deduction is not possible, as in the positivist paradigm, the pragmatic paradigm promises a viable way of attaining a reasonable degree of generalization without giving up context. (p. 291)

Like other MGTs, Fishman consistently rejects the attempt (logically) to deduce any general or universal, deterministic causal explanations/laws in psychology.[16] These he equates with modern/conventional (and therefore positivist or objectivist) forms of psychological inquiry. And his ontology is more consistent with that of radical postmodernists, in virtue of its greater emphasis on the "flux and flow," or instability, of social/psychological existence. The epistemological question of the kinds of knowledge a proper form of psychological inquiry should produce is one to which I return in chapter 9, in which I consider the criteria of warrant set forth by MGTs to justify their knowledge claims in the name of realism and agency. As we shall see, a pragmatic standard of warrant is adopted not only by those MGTs who call themselves pragmatists but also by hermeneutic and social constructionist MGTs, in one way or another.

THE SEARCH FOR A MIDDLE-GROUND PHILOSOPHY OF PSYCHOLOGY

Despite their varied philosophical traditions, MGTs hold a common ambition: to integrate/reconcile/bridge, moderate/mediate, transcend/overcome, or avoid/evade the ontological and epistemological extremes of the realism, objectivism, universalism/essentialism, mechanistic determinism, and thus the reductionism they find in modern/conventional forms of psychological inquiry on the one hand, and the antirealism, subjectivism, relativism, indeterminism, and thus the nihilism they find in radical postmodern forms of psychological inquiry on the other. Both these poles are said by them to deprive us of the agentic existence on whose behalf they labor. We should therefore be grateful to them if they shed light on both (a) the nature of human psychological existence, by providing a properly agentic ontology of human psychological kinds; and (b) the attainment of valid knowledge about that agentic existence, by providing a properly truth-tracking or realist (but not objectivist) epistemology for psychological inquiry. Whether they can accomplish this by finding the holy grail of philosophical middle ground both ontologically and epistemologically is the question I take up in what follows.

---

[16]See Held (2006a), for two meanings that Fishman (1999, 2001) gives to the term *inductive generalization.*

4

ONTOLOGICAL POINT 1: AN ONTOLOGY OF "BEING IN THE WORLD," OR, A SITUATED PSYCHOLOGICAL EXISTENCE

THE ONTOLOGICAL MUTISM OF RADICAL POSTMODERNISTS

It may be helpful to begin this initial chapter on the middle-ground theorists' (MGTs') search for a middle-ground ontology by first recalling one extreme that they reject outright: the radical postmodernist denial of any and all ontologies, at least as this has been expressed by some social constructionists (e.g., Gergen, 1994, pp. 68–78; 1998, p. 417) and some constructivists (e.g., Neimeyer, 1995, pp. 341–342).[1] Most prominent is the now famous "ontological mutism" of Kenneth Gergen (1994, 1998, 2001a), a leading proponent of an especially radical or strong version of social constructionism in psychology, according to many who critique or work to moderate his form of constructionism (e.g., Edley, 2001; Gantt, 1996; Harré, 2002; Hibberd, 2001a,

---

[1]See chapter 1, note 4, and note 3 later in this chapter, for the distinction between constructionist and constructivist postmodernists.

2001b; Liebrucks, 2001; Maze, 2001; Nightingale & Cromby, 2002; Osbeck, 1993; Rosen, 1996).

In chapters 2 and 3 I gave evidence of Gergen's desire to remain "ontologically mute." Here I quote extensively from his writings to elaborate his argument. In this first quotation, Gergen (1997) poses rhetorical questions to suggest that an "ontology of the mind" is antithetical to a social constructionist psychology, which must for him remain "minimalist" for "constructionist intelligibility itself" (Gergen, 1998, p. 418). After all, ontologies usually delineate what is real, and antirealism (or at least arealism) prevails in radical constructionism.

> Given a constructionist metatheory [which rejects a "realist metaphysics" and a "correspondence theory of language"], how are we then to view professional investments in psychological research, as well as . . . practices based on ontologies of mental process? If not eradication, what role is the ontology of the mind to play in a constructionist orientation to human action? (Gergen, 1997, p. 724)

And here Gergen's (1998) rejection of (ontological) realism is made explicit, as is his linking of realism to foundationalism.[2]

> Constructionism itself is ontologically mute. . . . To say that "we construct the world together" is more like an invitation to dance than a mapping of the world. . . . The greater the elaboration of constructionist proposals—filling them out with material, social structure, power, thought, emotions, and the like—the more they begin to smack of realist foundationalism. . . . Thus, by "saying too much," one unsays the thesis [of social constructionism]. (pp. 417–418)
>
> How should we answer questions about what is "independent of language" save through language? This is only one reason for my desire to see constructionism remain ontologically mute. (Gergen, 2001a, p. 425)

Constructionist psychologist John Shotter (as cited in Osbeck, 1993, p. 344) also adheres to Gergen's antiontological "dictum": "A thoroughgoing social constructionist stance . . . seems to suggest that not only our knowledge of the world but the world itself is a social construction." However, in "Social Constructionism as Ontology," Nightingale and Cromby (2002) contest this, arguing on behalf of the more moderate version of constructionism: "Constructionism, far from being ontologically mute, must itself be an ontology" (p. 705).

Turning to the doctrine of constructivism,[3] which (at least originally) emphasized the personal or individual as opposed to the social/communal

---

[2]The postmodernist tendency to link realism/objectivism to foundationalism, and therefore to epistemic certitude, is discussed in chapter 8.
[3]See Gergen (1994, pp. 67–69), Held (1995, pp. 102–105), Neimeyer (1998, pp. 140–142), Rosen (1996, p. 15), and Stam (1998) for distinctions between the doctrines of constructionism and constructivism.

construction of "reality," we discover various antirealist ontological proclamations—although Gergen (1994) himself faults constructivists for giving
"ontological status" to any entity whatsoever, as his use of scare quotes makes
clear.

> Constructivist theses are often antagonistic to constructionism. . . . From
> a constructionist perspective neither "mind" nor "world" is granted on-
> tological status, thus removing the very grounding assumptions of
> constructivism. . . . For the constructionist, terms for both world and
> mind are constituents of discursive practices. (p. 68)

But some constructivists may be more consistent with Gergen (at least
ontologically "speaking") than he seems to suppose. As Rosen (1996) said,
"For all practical purposes radical constructivists have banished metaphysical reality from their epistemological worldview" (p. 6). Notice the aversion
to ontology talk altogether in this next statement by leading constructivist
psychologist Robert Neimeyer (1995), which was first presented in chapter 3
of this volume (note 14); it sounds like a version of Gergen's "ontological
mutism."

> I am only vaguely interested in the ontological question of whether a
> real world exists in any meaningful sense beyond our construction of it.
> . . . I would classify myself as neither realist nor antirealist, but *arealist*,
> someone for whom the term [reality] has little meaning. (pp. 341–342)

By contrast, in this next (radically) constructivist quotation, we find the
ontological claim that we make, construct, or constitute reality in our discursive practices: "It is always an observer speaking to another observer (who
might, in fact, be himself or herself) who draws distinctions and thereby brings
entities, living or otherwise, into existence" (Efran & Greene, 1996, p. 102).
It is clear that this is a strong version of the second ontological claim of
postmodernists ("Our theories affect our lives"), which I presented in chapter 2, and which appears in Gergen's own writings (e.g., Gergen, 1985, p.
273). The claim also contradicts Gergen's professed ontological mutism.[4]

To be sure, there is more to be said. Moderate social constructionists
(who therefore qualify as MGTs) have lately argued that social constructionism has been misinterpreted. For example, some say constructionism does
not deny the existence of an extralinguistic reality, including certain human
universals—although not essentials (e.g., Edley, 2001; Liebrucks, 2001), as
many have charged. Some say it allows for the reality of a discursive realm
that constrains thought and action, and it does not deny "universal aspects of
human life" or "essential attributes of persons and processes" (Harré, 2002,
p. 612). Nor does it lead inexorably to the (radically) relativistic epistemology (see Edley, 2001; Harré, 2002; Liebrucks, 2001) that all MGTs (by defi-

---

[4]See Held (1995, 2002b), Katzko (2002), and Maze (2001) for commentary and more quotations.

nition) want to avoid. In short, these more moderate social constructionists distance themselves from the antirealist (or in some cases arealist) ontology and the relativist epistemology of radical postmodernists/constructionists/constructivists, who they suggest have gone too far. In virtue of their search for middle ground or moderation, they qualify as MGTs—both ontologically and epistemologically.

Of interest here is a question raised by critics of the allegedly "mute" ontology of some strong constructionists/constructivists: How can there be real agency—the emancipatory goal of radical constructionists/constructivists as well as MGTs—if there is no commitment to an ontology of the individual agent as a real entity, an entity with all the characteristics deemed necessary for agency? Psychologist Rick Ansoff (1996) expressed the question aptly in the title "How Can There Be Personal Agency Without an Ontology of the Individual?" In his abstract he made the following statement:

> Kenwood (1996) argues that there is room for personal volition and agency in social constructionism. This assertion is examined in light of the social constructionist doctrine of *ontological mutism* enunciated by Gergen, according to which any ontological commitment is refused. . . . [Instead,] a clear commitment to the grounding assumptions of some settled ontology ["of the individual as agent"] is a prerequisite for coherent considerations of agency or even volition, because without such a commitment it is impossible to decide what exists and if it moves. (p. 539, abstract)

I have more to say about the "ontology of the individual as agent" (Ansoff, 1996, p. 540) in my discussion in chapter 10 of Pols's (2004b) "ontology of the rational agent," an ontology in which rationality or "rational awareness" of what exists is made central to agentic human being/existence. Here let us note that Kenwood (1996) herself reveals the postmodernists' supposed link between constructionism and agency or free will (see chap. 2, this volume) when she defends constructionism in the name of agency.

> It is precisely *agency*—indeed, *voluntary* agency—that puts the "construction" into "constructionism." Without the capacity to choose among informed alternatives . . . , people could not meaningfully be said to "construct" anything at all. . . . An intelligible account of volition . . . is more likely to come from social constructionists than from more traditional psychologies. . . . The traditional natural-scientific approach committed psychology to the idea that people's actions were not volitional, but resembled more the behaviour of atoms and molecules. . . . The behaviours of people and atoms alike are subject to the immutable laws of nature that can be uncovered through the application of empirical and experimental methods. (p. 534)

Here, in addition to linking constructionism to agency or free will (an ontological matter), Kenwood finds in constructionism a more proper form of psychological inquiry (an epistemological matter), both in terms of process/method and product: a willing abandonment of the search for the "immutable laws of nature." Recall from chapter 1 the fundamental problem that radical postmodernists and MGTs see in the attempt to discover scientific laws in psychology: How can human agency obtain if there exist mechanistically deterministic causal laws (that for them constitute the objective psychological knowledge they reject)? I therefore find in radical postmodern and MGT circles alike a common tendency to equate mechanistic determinism with objectivism, an equation mediated by a commitment to an agentic psychology (see chap. 1). I have much more to say about this equation in the chapters that follow.

Let us turn now to the MGTs' ideas about what is wrong with the ontology of human psychological existence that they presume informs modern/conventional psychological inquiry. We will then be in a better position to appreciate the four ontological claims they set forth as their middle-ground alternatives.

"MYTHS OF MODERNITY": THE PRESUMPTION OF A UNIVERSALIST AND ESSENTIALIST ONTOLOGY IN CONVENTIONAL PSYCHOLOGICAL INQUIRY

Rather than rehearse the diverse ontologies of modernity, I will let them emerge in the words of various MGTs themselves in the next few chapters. Here I limit myself to this one comment: MGTs and the radical postmodernists from whom they distance themselves have a common view of the ontology that informs modern/conventional (and so allegedly positivist)[5] forms of psychological inquiry. That ontology is typically said to embrace problematically (or mythically) the universalist, acontextualist, fixed, essentialist, objectivist, and reductionist assumptions of the natural sciences. It is also sometimes characterized as foundationalist, although that term is conventionally used to describe epistemological matters.

But that view of a so-called "modernist ontology" is itself fraught with myths. And so we find among radical postmodernists and MGTs some myths about the alleged "myths of modernity," as Martin and Sugarman (2000a, p. 400) put it. The alleged "myths of modernity" consist most fundamentally in this: (a) a mechanistically deterministic ontology, in which universal, context-independent, static/unchanging causal laws that exist objectively (i.e.,

---

[5]The tendency on the part of radical postmodernists and MGTs to equate modern epistemologies with (logical) positivism is problematic, given that logical positivism, in which it was thought that formal (content-free) deductive logic could provide a basis for science, has generally been abandoned in philosophy of science circles (see Haack, 2003, pp. 32–34). Moreover, that doctrine never advanced the objectivist epistemology attributed to it by postmodernists and MGTs.

independently of beliefs about them) govern all human social/psychological existence, thereby obviating agency or self-determination; and (b) an objectivist epistemology, in which humans can attain (objective) knowledge of those universal, objective (social/psychological) laws, which exist independently of human knowing processes that can in principle produce certain or infallible (and therefore foundational and objective) knowledge.

The problem is that these assumptions (myths) about modernist ontological and epistemological "myths" do not accurately reflect the views of many who argue on behalf of realism/objectivism, both ontologically and epistemologically. For example, among many modernist philosophers, objective knowledge is not equated with foundational or certain knowledge. Still, understanding the MGTs' reformulated ontology is necessary to appreciate their dual mission of attaining (a) a valid or truth-tracking form of psychological inquiry/knowledge that nonetheless (b) permits an agentic capacity to avoid the mechanistic determinism they find in conventional/"positivist" psychological inquiry. Understanding this reformulated ontology is also essential to appreciate the MGTs' conviction that the problematic claim to certain and infallible knowledge (which they take to constitute objective knowledge) follows from the conventional ontology of modernism, and that they can avoid this unwarranted epistemological extreme (i.e., certain/infallible and thus supposedly objective knowledge) by advancing a different ontology of social/psychological existence.

In short, the middle-ground ontology they set forth is meant to pave the way for the middle-ground truth-tracking, realist but antiobjectivist epistemology of their preferred form of psychological inquiry. Just how the reformulated ontology is supposed to support an alternative epistemology for psychological inquiry, and whether it indeed accomplishes its intended mission, is a focus of my assessment in the chapters to come. Here I offer some quotations of MGTs, to illustrate in their own words the problems they find in the conventional/modernist (and allegedly positivist) ontology of objectivism, universalism, and essentialism—an ontology that for them is in need of rehabilitation if we are to rehabilitate psychological inquiry properly.

Martin and Sugarman have much to say about this, and so I begin with their most pointed statement: "There is no essential, a priori nature of human psychological, agentic kinds" (Martin, Sugarman, & Thompson, 2003, p. 110). And they take "disciplinary psychology" to task for holding "simultaneously to the idea of psychology as a kind of deterministic, reductive science and to the idea that psychology somehow can contribute to the empowerment of [agentic] human beings" (p. 7). They put the problem most plainly when they say, "The determinism of science . . . seems decidedly at odds with much of our everyday experience of ourselves as agents capable of choice and action" (p. ix). In the quotations that follow, their search for a philosophical middle ground ontologically—and ultimately epistemologically—is made explicit.

Many scholars no longer subscribe ... to two basic ideas. ... that humans have a pregiven, fixed nature that determines their essential being across historical periods and sociocultural contexts ... [and] that humans are capable of attaining a progressively truer understanding of themselves and their world. (Martin & Sugarman, 2000a, p. 397)

Unless it is possible to articulate convincingly some alternative middle ground to the unsustainable myths of modernity on the one hand and some of the more excessive radical medicine of postmodernism on the other, psychology and education are in deep difficulty. ... Is it possible to imagine a scenario for human development and change that makes no "fixed" foundationalist or essentialist assumptions, yet which might be drawn on in a defense of limited forms of realism, subjectivity, and warranted understanding necessary to preserve some rationale for psychological and educational inquiry and practice? ... Our strategy is ... to defend the kind of middle-ground position we seek. (Martin & Sugarman, 2000a, p. 400)

In these next quotations, Martin and Sugarman tell us that the postmodern "solution" has gone too far for their middle-ground sensibilities.

Postmodernists' sensible rejection of the [modern] foundationalist idea that reality is characterized by conceptually independent, ahistorical, unchanging forms or laws that can be apprehended objectively has lead them to conclude that reality is characterized by a chaotic, random flux. ... Postmodernists' well-intended attempts to avoid [modern] psychological essentialism ... [are] thus too radical a solution. (Martin & Sugarman, 2000a, pp. 402–403)

Most of the anti-realism evident in the proclamations of some contemporary, postmodern psychologists (cf. Kvale, 1992) arises from quite legitimate and defensible concerns about essentialism, naturalism, and foundationalist certainty. However, anti-realism is simply not necessary to avoid these excessively restrictive and possibly inappropriate, related doctrines in the conceptualization and conduct of psychological inquiry. (Martin & Sugarman, 1999b, p. 183)

Finally, disciplinary psychology is itself taken to task for failing to embrace the "weighty" (ontological) differences between natural and psychological kinds.

When the full weight of the differences between natural and psychological kinds is acknowledged, it becomes stunningly clear why the scientistic, reductionistic inquiry practices and assumptions of much disciplinary psychology over the past 125 years have resulted in so little in the way of a defensible understanding of psychological kinds. (Martin et al., 2003, p. 125)

Richardson, Fowers, and Guignon (1999), who in *Re-envisioning Psychology* adopt a hermeneutic view not inconsistent with that of Martin and Sugarman, make similar comments about the problems of a modernist approach to psychology. Note their dissatisfaction not only with the conventional quantitative methods of modern psychology but also with the descriptive or qualitative methods that many postmodern psychologists prefer; their dissatisfaction stems from the commitment to objectivity and universality that the authors find in both approaches.

> A significant minority of psychological investigators . . . has felt that some kind of descriptive or phenomenological[6] approach to understanding human action . . . represents a more appropriate and promising path to follow [than "conventional, scientific social science"]. . . . These approaches, too, typically aspire to an impossible objectivity; instead of seeking timelessly true, value-neutral explanations of human behavior [as do conventional psychologists], they seek timelessly true, value-neutral descriptions of meaningful human events. (p. 17)

And here Richardson et al. (1999) reject the universal or context-independent "laws" of modern psychology.

> In his [philosopher Peter Winch's] view, explaining human action means giving an account of why people do the things they do—their motives, reasons, and goals. . . . The acceptability of such an account would depend on its making sense to the social actors themselves. . . . The elucidation of rule-following behavior is seen as different in kind from explaining nature or society via context-independent general laws. (p. 179)

Hermeneutic philosopher Charles Guignon (1998), here discussing "Narrative Explanation in Psychotherapy," sees the modernist view of psychological inquiry as an improper "naturalist model of explanation." Owing to its mechanistically deterministic, law-like generalities, this model encounters ontological difficulties "in doing justice to human agency" (p. 558, abstract), as does (for different reasons) the "radical relativism" (p. 565) of postmodern/constructionist models. Guignon argues for "a more moderate narrative viewpoint that draws on the ideas of ontological hermeneutics," which as we shall see rejects epistemic objectivity in principle (p. 558, abstract).

> First, it [the naturalist model] assumes that there are underlying causal mechanisms operating beneath the surface phenomena, and that explanation is a matter of identifying and describing these mechanisms. Second, these underlying causes generally are seen as reflecting lawlike regularities in nature, and so it is often assumed that explanation involves subsuming particular events under general laws. Finally, this model assumes that explanations can be based entirely on objectively specifiable facts. (p. 559)

---

[6]See chapter 3 of this volume for a quotation of Bernstein's (1983, p. 11) comments about the universalism/antirelativism in Husserl's "transcendental phenomenology."

In these next two quotations, MGTs with social constructionist and pragmatic (rather than expressly hermeneutic) allegiances, respectively, make similar points about the need for ontological—and, following from that, epistemological—overhaul in psychological inquiry. Not least is the now familiar MGT rejection of the universal, context-independent laws that are said to obtain in the natural sciences. First, this from moderate social constructionist Alexander Liebrucks (2001):

> In contrast to the subject matter of the natural sciences, the subject matter of psychology is not a natural kind but an artefact. Consequently, except for a very high level of abstraction, there can be no universal psychological accounts but only accounts of culturally specific psychological phenomena. (p. 385)

From (neo)pragmatist Daniel Fishman (1999), here again this call to a context-dependent middle ground:

> The *pragmatic paradigm* in psychology seeks to transcend psychology's dialectical culture wars by developing an integrative alternative. . . . The natural science methodologies and concepts of positivism are employed, but with a nonpositivist purpose: . . . to achieve the democratically derived program goals of particular, historically and culturally situated social groups, not to uncover purported general laws of human nature. . . . Pragmatism . . . [stakes] out a middle, centrist position between modernistically traditional, conservative positivism on the right, and radically liberal, skeptical and critical postmodernism on the left. (p. 8)

Later Fishman (1999) fleshes out his distinction between the modern positivism he wants to moderate and the postmodern constructionism he embraces fully as pragmatism's "underlying epistemology" (p. 99, Table 4.1). Notice his appeal to the "hermeneutic circle" in advancing the postmodern constructionism that informs his own pragmatic paradigm; it indicates again that the hermeneutic, constructionist, and pragmatic "traditions" of those who hold middle-ground aspirations are not clearly distinguishable—especially when pressed into that service.

> Modern positivism is a worldview based on the assumption that physical and social reality are governed by *general laws* . . . [that] are objectively knowable, and that the *natural science method* is the best means for *discovering* them. . . . Like other biological phenomena, human behavior is *explained* . . . in terms of a collection of impersonal, mechanistic, *machinelike processes*, which are governed by deterministic, general "laws of nature." (p. 94)
>
> Postmodern constructionism is a worldview based on the assumption that reality is not objectively knowable. Rather, reality is *constructed* by individuals and groups as a result of particular beliefs and historical, cultural, and social contexts. The nature of reality is relative, depending on the observer's point of view. The *incompleteness*, limitations, and relativ-

ity in knowledge are illustrated in the concepts of the *hermeneutic circle*, the *web of belief, scientific knowledge as paradigm-driven*, and *language as intrinsic to experienced reality*. (p. 95)

Richard Bernstein (1983), whom Fishman calls an American pragmatist but whom others use to support their hermeneutically inspired psychology (e.g., Richardson et al., 1999), sums up such sentiments succinctly in *Beyond Objectivism and Relativism*—although here he does not necessarily limit his commentary to the human social/psychological world, as do most MGTs.

> Each time that an objectivist has come up with what he or she takes to be a firm foundation, an ontological grounding, a fixed categorical scheme, someone has challenged such claims and has argued that what is supposed to be fixed, eternal, ultimate, necessary, or indubitable is open to doubt and questioning. The relativist accuses the objectivist of mistaking what is at best historically or culturally stable for the eternal and permanent. (p. 9)

Hermeneutic psychologists Messer, Sass, and Woolfolk (1988b) take up Bernstein's challenge to go "beyond objectivism and relativism" in their *Hermeneutics and Psychological Theory*, in which they too reject the universal laws sought in "objectivist social science."

> Unlike objectivist social science, "methodological hermeneutics" does not strive for decontextualized facts, but emphasizes meanings as experienced by individuals whose activities are rooted in given sociohistorical settings. . . . It seeks less to generate universal laws than to understand the specific case in its historical and cultural context. (pp. xiii–xiv)

INTRODUCTION TO A MIDDLE-GROUND ONTOLOGY OF HUMAN PSYCHOLOGICAL EXISTENCE

I have claimed that the recent search for a philosophical middle ground in psychology originated in at least two core commitments: (a) the desire for an agentic psychology and (b) the desire for a truth-tracking form of psychological inquiry. In short, the search for truth and agency is a fundamental motivating force behind the search for a middle-ground philosophy of psychology.

Although MGTs share with postmodernists/constructionists/ constructivists a belief in the possibility of social/psychological transformation or transcendence, or what I will call a capacity for transcendent agency at both individual and societal levels, they do not share the radical postmodernist insistence on ontological mutism. Nor do MGTs share the so-called ontological "irrealism" of those radicals who eschew mutism as they happily engage in ontology talk. That is, MGTs do not share the radical postmodern view that there simply is no one way the world actually *is*, because we literally make or construct our worlds discursively by means of our worldviews. In *Ways of Worldmaking*, philosopher Nelson Goodman famously expresses this radical claim, which philosopher Edward Erwin (2001, p. 8) called the "multiple worlds-constructionist view".[7] Haack (2002) summarized Goodman's claim succinctly.

> Goodman is even more radical, relativizing not just truth but reality, so that his [ontological] position is perhaps best described as "irrealism." There is no one real world, Goodman holds, only many "versions," the descriptions or depictions made by scientists, novelists, artists, etc. Versions of what?—he doesn't say. This radical Goodmanian irrealism has some affinity with radical forms of social constructivism which think of theoretical entities as created by scientists' intellectual activity. (p. 84)

Haack (2002) propounds her own "innocent realism," a realism that occupies a "habitable middle ground between rigid realism and rakish relativism" (p. 85). However, she is no middle-ground theorist in the sense of the MGTs I consider collectively, and so I shall return to her in my critique of the epistemological views of MGTs—especially their rejection of the possibility of objective knowledge about human social/psychological kinds, which Haack defends.

Here I consider MGTs' careful articulations of an ontology of human (psychological) being/existence, one that can ground a carefully articulated ontology of human agency. Yet contrary to what we saw in the words of the radical postmodernists quoted in chapter 2, theirs is an agency that does not permit an unconstrained, endless, free play of self-invention/self-construction and self-reinvention/self-reconstruction (in language or discourse). Thus, theirs is no small undertaking; it is filled with the nuance lacking in radical postmodernist philosophies, and so its nuance deserves the careful consideration I give to it in what follows. The basic questions to which I ultimately address my critique are twofold:

1. Have MGTs in fact integrated/reconciled/bridged, moderated/mediated, transcended/overcome, or avoided/evaded the perceived extremes of modernism and postmodernism, either ontologically, epistemologically, or both?
2. Have MGTs specified an ontology of human psychological existence that (a) helps them attain a form of psychological inquiry/knowing that is valid or truth tracking (the epistemological goal) and that also (b) grants humans the agentic capacity to transform, transcend, or overcome whatever social/psychological conditions they find oppressive, restrictive, or limiting (the ontological goal)? Recall that according to MGTs

---

[7]See Erwin (2001) for extensive critique of Goodman's "multiple worlds-constructionist view."

this agentic capacity is automatically denied in the alleged search within modern/conventional psychology for timeless, universal, and mechanistically deterministic (i.e., objective)[8] causal laws.

Introduction to the Four Ontological Points

I organize my overview of the MGTs' search for a middle-ground ontology around four focal themes or points.

Point 1: Chapter 4

Our psychological existence is constituted by, constrained by, and thus dependent on the historical/cultural/discursive/interpretive/linguistic context of our location—our time and place—in the world. Although all the MGTs whom I consider make this point in one way or another, those who expressly hold hermeneutic (as opposed to constructionist or pragmatist) allegiances refer to this by way of the Heideggerian notion of our (agentic) "being in the world" (Dreyfus, 1991; Grene, 1957; Guignon, 1991, 2002a, 2005). Put differently, the local or situated nature of our (psychological) existence makes our existence "historical all the way down" (Guignon, 2000, 2005); and if this (ontology) is so, then understanding our existence may indeed require "interpretation all the way down" (Dreyfus, as cited in Bohman, Hiley, & Shusterman, 1991, p. 7), as hermeneutic MGTs like to claim. Because for hermeneuticists interpretation or understanding is itself historically constituted, I take these two phrases to be more or less synonymous. However, it remains logically possible for humans to exist historically (all the way down), without requiring that that existence be itself interpretation (all the way down).[9]

Point 2: Chapter 5

Our psychological existence is dependent on the discursive/interpretive context to which we ourselves contribute (i.e., the meanings that are said by MGTs to exist "out there"), and so is ultimately dependent on our own knowing, interpreting, or meaning-making processes. This does not in any way compromise the reality of human psychological existence. Thus the nature of "personhood" in any given context is real: It is not subject to endless reinvention or reconstruction, without constraint. Moreover, the meanings or discourses that constitute the interpretive context in which humans exist and participate as psychological agents are themselves real (e.g., Guignon, 1991, 2005; Harré, 2002; Martin & Sugarman, 1999a, 1999b, 2000a; Richardson et al.,1999). Because these claims depend on MGTs' definitions

---

[8] See chapter 1 for the way in which MGTs link mechanistic determinism with objectivism.
[9] I am indebted to Amie Thomasson (personal communication, February 12, 2005) for this distinction.

of the word *real* and its many variants (see especially Martin & Sugarman, 1999b), I give considerable attention to these definitions.

Point 3: Chapter 6

We have an agentic human capacity that allows us, via the (hermeneutic) process of (self-)(re)interpretation, to transform, overcome, or transcend (to some limited extent) the constraints imposed by our (constitutive) historical/cultural/discursive/interpretive contexts. These constraints are said not only to enable, make possible, or constitute human psychological existence (or the nature of personhood as it manifests itself in particular contexts) but also to enable, make possible, or constitute *knowledge* about that existence, which in turn (reflexively) affects that existence. However, there are no guarantees that such transformation or transcendence will obtain in any particular case.

Point 4: Chapter 7

Owing to the interpretive nature of our agency, the ontology of the human psychological world may best be characterized as nonstatic: It is an ontology of flux and flow, of possibility, malleability, fluidity, and change. And owing to the embeddedness or situatedness of our "being in the world," ours is also an ontology with built-in (contextual) constraints that give rise to a psychological existence with some degree of stability and consistency. Thus we find a tension in "the psychology of possibility and constraint," as Martin and Sugarman (1999a) aptly put it. As we shall see, this tension is crucial for understanding the MGTs' claim to have defended successfully a middle-ground realist philosophy of psychology, in which "not just anything goes" either ontologically or epistemologically. However, because what does "go" is said always to depend on our beliefs about what exists, the MGTs' realism is not equated with objectivism.

These four points constitute a middle-ground ontology of human psychological existence, according to MGTs. It is an ontology that is deliberately situated between (a) the free-floating, emancipatory, invent-your-own "reality" of the muted—if not mute—local "ontologies" expressed by radical postmodernists/constructionists/constructivists, on the one hand; and (b) the stable/static/fixed/immutable, universalist, and mechanistically deterministic (or supposedly objectivist) ontology attributed by MGTs and radical postmodernists to conventional modernists, on the other. This middle-ground ontology makes possible the transformation or transcendence of extant forms of psychological being, but always within the limits of the discursive/interpretive contexts to which we contribute and which in turn constrain what we can contribute.

This middle-ground ontology also has implications for the nature of knowing and its products. Thus the epistemology that follows from this middle-ground ontology is itself said to occupy middle-ground territory. We consider this issue in chapters 8 and 9, but here I flesh out the first of the four onto-logical points—an ontology of "being in the world."

ONTOLOGICAL POINT 1:
AN ONTOLOGY OF BEING IN THE WORLD

In this section I explore the MGTs' claim that our psychological being/existence, or our "personhood" as they often put it, is constituted by, con-strained by, and so continuously dependent on the (local) historical/cultural/discursive/interpretive contexts in which we participate as agents and to which we contribute. Thus our existence is often characterized (especially by MGTs in the hermeneutic camp) by way of the Heideggerian notion of our "being in the world" (Dreyfus, 1991; Grene, 1957; Guignon, 1991, 2002a, 2005). However, it is not clear to what extent the (hermeneutically inclined) MGTs who use Heidegger's language actually are Heideggerians; accordingly I re-main neutral on that question. Although the constructionist and (neo)pragmatic MGTs do not use Heidegger's language per se, they insist on the local or situated nature of social/psychological existence nonetheless. Thus, again, the similarities far outweigh any differences that may exist among the various traditions from which various MGTs originate.

Because the historical/cultural contexts in which we exist are said to be "always already" interpreted, we ourselves are said to be "interpretation" (or, alternatively, "historical") "all the way down"[10] (Dreyfus, as cited in Bohman et al., 1991, p. 7; Guignon, 2000, 2002b, 2005). In *Martin Heidegger* philoso-pher Marjorie Grene (1957) put this most simply: "Human being is being always already in a world: a world into which, beyond its willing, it has been cast" (p. 20). Later she adds this paraphrased translation of Heidegger: "In asking about Being, then, we are seeking to grasp formally and conceptually what 'as human beings we already and always understand'" (p. 76).

To put this a bit differently, humans do not exist (socially and psycho-logically) independently of their beliefs about, or interpretations/understand-ing of, human existence. MGTs are therefore quick to reject what they con-sider the "detached, objective theorizing" of "mainstream scientists," which separates the knowing subject from the object to be known, and in the pro-cess allegedly "distorts and conceals possibilities of understanding that are absolutely crucial in attempts to understand the value-laden aspect of hu-man existence" (Guignon, 2002b, p. 94). Here we catch a glimpse of the antiobjectivist epistemology that follows from the MGTs' ontology of "being in the world."

---

[10]Here I remind the reader that being "historical" (all the way down) does not necessitate being "interpretation" (all the way down).

The Heideggerian notion of "being in the world" is clearly expressed by hermeneutic philosopher (and on my view MGT) Charles Guignon in these two quotations. Of prime importance is the view denied by him and other MGTs who cite Heidegger: that there is a universal or essential human (social/psychological) nature, one which operates independently of culturally or historically constrained beliefs about that human nature.

> Heidegger . . . begins his greatest work, *Being and Time*, with a description of . . . our ways of *being-in-the-world* in its familiar, practical contexts, prior to theorizing and reflection. . . . Hermeneutics . . . [challenges] the belief that humans have an essential nature or innate characteristics that determine what they must be. . . . Humans always find themselves enmeshed in a shared cultural and historical context that provides the possible self-interpretations. . . . And since what we interpret are themselves interpretations that have emerged in the course of our history, we can say . . . that we are "interpretation all the way down." . . . Being human is something we *make* in taking up the possibilities of interpretation and evaluation we find around us. (Guignon, 2000)

At the end of this second quotation, Guignon (2002b) introduces the antiobjectivist idea that there is no "view from nowhere" that can inform the possibilities we take up in defining our existence/being.

> The public language and patterns of action of our community shape the "clearing" . . . in which things show up for us as mattering or counting in determinate ways. This all-pervasive background of shared understanding is the ultimate source of all the possibilities of self-interpretation and self-assessment we take up in forming our identity in the world. . . . As participants in this common world, we are always already committed to goals and concerned about issues that define the life of our community. These commitments and concerns define us; they make us the people we are. Though we may criticize any set of our fundamental beliefs from the standpoint of others that are currently taken as given, there is no vantage point outside our cultural commitments from which we can objectify and criticize all of them at once. (p. 95)

There is much more to consider in these two quotations, and I comment on them extensively in due course. Here I emphasize the sense that there is no aspect of our social/psychological existence that is not constituted, at least in part, by the historical/cultural/discursive/interpretive contexts in which we find ourselves "thrown" but in which we actively participate nonetheless—hence the idea that context both constrains and makes possible or enables our existence as active agents. Thus what may appear to be some essential and/or universal aspect of our social/psychological existence can be no such thing; that existence is always contingent on the particularities of the context that constitutes our being or personhood by way of available interpretations and practices that we "take up." We are therefore said to be historical/cultural/interpretive beings "all the way down."

The link between psychological being or personhood and interpretation within a particular context, including but not limited to self-interpretation, is illustrated most clearly in a telling quotation. The quotation is so important that I return to it repeatedly, not least because the all-important question of just whose interpretations or beliefs anyone's psychological existence depends on has important implications for the objectivist epistemology that MGTs and postmodernists reject (see chap. 3, this volume). That is so because, at least in conventional terms, epistemic objectivity typically requires that what is judged to be true should be warranted independently of what anyone believes to be true. Thus the object to be known should have some sort of independence from the knowing subject,[11] if objective knowledge of it is to be possible (Erwin, 1997, p. 74; 1999, p. 353), although the exact nature of this independence is of utmost importance and the object of considerable philosophical debate (Thomasson, 2003).

Although I return to this matter in chapter 5, here is the all-important quotation.

> Humans just *are* what they interpret themselves as being within their social context. (Richardson, Fowers, & Guignon, 1999, p. 236)

The claim is so important that Martin, Sugarman, and Thompson (2003) gave their own (seemingly independent) version of it.

> Humans simply are what they interpret themselves as being within their historical and sociocultural contexts. (p. 77)

This local or contextualized, antiuniversalist or antiessentialist ontology (of human social/psychological existence) is a philosophy that MGTs share with (radical) postmodernists—although as we saw in chapter 2, the latter do not typically bow as low to the constraints or limits (on being and knowing) of the cultural/discursive context. After all, these contextual constraints (e.g., meanings and practices) are what allow MGTs to lay claim to their middle-ground, not-just-anything-goes ontology in the first place. Here Guignon (1998) expresses the search for just that sort of ontological middle ground (by means of the language of transcendence or overcoming), in a way that subverts the possibility of objectivist strivings.

> The hermeneutic tradition has tried to overcome both naturalism and constructionism by working out a different ontological account of human existence and its relation to the world. . . . For Heidegger, a human being should be thought of not as a subject set over against objective reality but as a unified totality of what he called "being-in-the-world." (p. 567)

---

[11]Of course, when the object of inquiry consists in the nature of the knowing subject's own beliefs or mental states, matters become much more complex. See Siewert (1998) for a sustained argument about a unique type of warrant for first-person knowledge claims.

The alleged prominence of the particularities of cultural/discursive contexts in constituting human psychological being or existence, and the pervasive rejection of the subject(ive)/object(ive) distinction and hence the possibility of an objectivist epistemology, are matters that I investigate—and assess critically—throughout this volume.

Here I offer more exemplary statements in which an ontology of "being in the world" is propounded by MGTs. In this ontology, human psychological existence or personhood is said to be constituted (i.e., both enabled or made possible and limited or constrained) by the historical/cultural/discursive/interpretive context into which we are born and in which we participate actively (or agentically). As the quotations reveal, MGTs seem to think that their ontology eliminates the possibility of any independence between knowing subjects and objects to be known—that is, between selves and the (social/psychological) world. Notice the familiar (we have considered some of these statements in other contexts) middle-ground-like rejection of conventional/modern essentialism, universalism, and objectivism on the one hand, and (radical) postmodern/constructionist relativism and antirealism on the other. Also notice that all but the last three quotations come from hermeneutically inclined MGTs, who rely on Heidegger although speak in ways (e.g., "self," "agency") that he might not.[12] The last three quotations express the similar views of social constructionist MGTs, even though they do not use the language of Heidegger.

> Ontological hermeneutics is well known for its insistence on the embeddedness of the individual in a sociocultural context that profoundly shapes his or her identity. . . . Human beings attain their humanity only through taking up a more or less coherent pattern of interpretations, practices and understandings from their families, communities, and societies. The durable interpretations and social practices in an identifiable and historically constituted group comprise the tradition that largely defines that group and its members (Gadamer, 1975; Heidegger, 1962). (Fowers, 2001b)
>
> Contrary to the conventional wisdom, traditions are not something alien to us, against which we define ourselves. They are always part of who we are and provide the terms through which we define ourselves (Gadamer, 1975). (Fowers, 2001b)
>
> Tradition . . . has a power which is constantly determining what we are in the process of becoming. We are *always already* "thrown" into a tradition. We can see how far Gadamer is from any naïve form of relativism that fails to appreciate how we are always shaped by effective-history (*Wirkungsgeschichte*). It is not just that works of art, texts, and tradition have effects and leave traces. Rather, what we are . . . is always being

---

[12]I am again indebted to Amie Thomasson (personal communication, February, 16, 2005) for this observation.

influenced by tradition, even when we think we are most free of it. Again, it is important to reiterate that a tradition is not something "naturelike," something "given" that stands over against us. It is always "part of us" and works through its effective-history. (Bernstein, 1983, p, 142)

Our being already situated in a shared life world makes up what Heidegger calls our "facticity." As factical beings who are thrown into a world, we are not just active decision makers . . . ; we are also finite beings whose existence is embedded in a world that makes binding demands on us because it makes us the people we are. . . . [But] we are active beings. We find ourselves thrown into a world we neither create nor control, but it is up to each of us to take up the possibilities of self-understanding into which we are thrown, and shape them into lives that are our own. (Guignon, 2002b, pp. 95–96)

For him [Heidegger], being in the world is a unitary phenomenon in which self and world are intertwined in such a way that there is no possible way of separating them. . . . We require the world around us in order to be agents (Guignon, 1991). . . . It is impossible for us to remove ourselves from the world, without ceasing to be human. (Martin & Sugarman, 1999b, p. 184)

The psychological reality of individuals is not only constrained, but is actually constituted in large part, by socioculturally shared beliefs and practices. . . . Unlike physical and biological reality, sociocultural and psychological reality does not exist independently of human perception and activity. However . . . this does not mean that they are not real in the influence that they can exert on human collectives and individuals. (Martin & Sugarman, 1999b, pp. 186–187)

In all such [modern functionalist] approaches, sociocultural meanings, rules, conventions, and practices, which for us play critically important background, contextual, and constitutive roles in the development of human self understanding and agency receive extremely short shrift. (Martin & Sugarman, 2002, p. 420)

The linguistic constitution of our experience undermines one of the most fundamental assumptions of the objectivist outlook, . . . that an object exists and has determinist features "independent of any descriptions or interpretations offered of it by any subjects" (Taylor, 1989, p. 34) and that science can give us a correct representation of that object. Given this account of feelings as "always already" interpreted, Taylor steers a path between constructionism, which paves the way to the pop psychological idea that "thinking makes it so," and scientific objectivism, which treats feelings as just "there." . . . With this conception of humans as beings whose very identity is shaped by self-interpretations and self-evaluations, Taylor fills out Heidegger's claim that humans are self-interpreting beings. . . . Our interpretations *constitute* our being. (Richardson, Fowers, & Guignon, 1999, p. 220)

It is far from clear that human behavior and experience can be characterized [on the naturalistic view] as objects that have a reality independent of and prior to interpretations. (Richardson et al., 1999, p. 278)

To say that our behavior and identity are *constituted* by the interpretations we adopt is to say that these interpretations shape and define the reality of our beliefs, feelings and actions. (Richardson et al., 1999, p. 280)

Achieving a more sophisticated vocabulary . . . helps create a different kind of psychic life and opens up new possibilities of behavior and expression. . . . If these kinds of transformations are possible, then a simple correspondence model is insufficient. (Richardson et al., 1999, p. 281)

[The early work of Heidegger] suggests that the separateness of subject and object is not primary, that such a primary separateness idea is an illusion based on faulty assumptions, and that our primary position in relation to Reality is that of Being-in-the-World. (Hersch, 2003, p. 59)

If there is to be a human science, it must be able to ask questions that do not make false and misleading assumptions about what it means to be human. . . . Individuality arises from and has meaning only within our temporal situatedness, . . . not from our private possession of variable qualities or capacities. Failing to be clear about this is to miss what human being-in-the-world means. (Faulconer & Williams, 1990a, p. 54)

An objectivist might argue that sexism and racism were present in past eras but were unobservable without present-day conceptual apparatus. A social constructionist might argue that sexism and racism (and all other social categories) are present after and only after the categories are socially constructed and adopted as interpretive tools. Gadamer's hermeneutic position is intermediate. It does not hold that social explanation involves the arbitrary imposition of socially constructed concepts. An external social reality that interpreters can access does exist, but that reality emerges only through interpretation and is delimited by the variety of constraints to which interpretation is subject. (Woolfolk, 1998, p. 74)

The social sciences in North America are currently in a state of ferment, with traditional objectivist approaches being questioned. . . . Unlike objectivist social science, "methodological hermeneutics" does not strive for decontextualized facts, but emphasizes meanings as experienced by individuals whose activities are rooted in given sociohistorical settings. The hermeneutic approach insists upon the inseparability of fact and value, detail and context, and observation and theory. (Messer, Sass, & Woolfolk, 1988b, pp. xiii–xiv)

These three final quotations reflect the views of social constructionist MGTs, who also seek a middle-ground ontology of "being in the world" by way of the discursive/interpretive context that allegedly constrains human social/psychological existence. Again, although they do not expressly use the language of Heidegger, their ontology is hard—if not impossible—to distinguish from that of hermeneutically inclined MGTs. That is because, recall, they share with hermeneutic and (neo)pragmatic MGTs the three "core allegiances" mentioned in chapter 3.

Social constructionism points to the many cases in which a type of psychological phenomenon, such as remembering, is at least as much an attribute of a discursive interaction as it is an attribute of an individual mind. . . . It puts considerable stress on the . . . [social and semantic conventions that constrain] human thought and action. Postmodernism and critical realism . . . are at opposite poles, the former requiring that all be malleable and the latter that nothing be. Social constructionism . . . affirms the reality of the discursive domain without falling into the fallacy of supposing that because many aspects of our lives are our own constructions, all must be. (Harré, 2002, p. 611, abstract)

There are properties of persons that exist only in the context of a certain discourse, that is, persons have them only relative to the meaning system of the community to which they belong. . . . An obvious example is furnished by roles. . . . It is the thesis of social constructionists that the same is true for so-called "intentional states" such as emotions, motives, and attitudes. (Liebrucks, 2001, p. 374)

This is not to say that so-called "intentional states" . . . are not real. . . . The point is rather that, since their existence depends on social context, the phenomena that are investigated by psychology are ontologically different from the phenomena studied by the natural sciences. (Liebrucks, 2001, p. 378)

I return to many of these quotations (especially that all-important one) throughout my analysis, as I consider in more particular detail the ontological and epistemological nuance that inheres in them.

A Local "Ontology" of Being in the World?

For MGTs the nature of our "being in the world" (or our context-dependent existence) is nothing short of an ontology of human existence. Because the term *ontology* derives from the Greek word for "being" (Pols, 1992, p. 210; 1998, p. 4), it contains a universal connotation, one that—following from Pols's (1998) discussion of Plato and Aristotle—may be properly called Being (with a capital *B*), to distinguish it from the particular beings (with a lowercase *b*) or entities that give infinitely unique expression to Being. The relation of being to Being suggests that universality inheres in (or pervades) particularity, and this ontological claim appears in my conclusions about the relation between truth or knowing and agency or being—both within and beyond psychological inquiry.

But as we saw in the previous quotations, the antiessentialism and antiuniversalism of MGTs translates into their claim that human psychological existence (or "personhood") is always "constituted," "formed," "molded," "shaped," or "influenced" by the particulars of the discursive/interpretive contexts into which each human being is "thrown." Hence there is a local/particular, or nonuniversal, connotation to the MGTs' use of the word *ontology*, although that local particularity is never quite so particularized as to pertain to just one person. Psychological being or personhood has only as much generality as the sweep of the discursive/ interpretive practices that makes personhood within a discursive/interpretive context possible.

Is it oxymoronic, then, to use the word *ontology* to refer to something that is merely local or regional rather than universal? Well, yes—and no. Yes, if we accept *ontology* in the ancient sense of *prote philosophia* ("first philosophy") put forth by Aristotle, and renamed "metaphysics" by Alexandrian editors who worked perhaps 275 years after his death.[13] And no, if we accept "ontology" only in the more limited, minimalist, or deflationary sense of MGTs, many of whom reject the "traditional metaphysics of transcendental or first principles" (Martin et al., 2003, p. 131). For example, the term *ontology of a language* has been adopted by various (analytic) philosophers to suggest that posited entities are "real for [or relative to] a language"; they are "real" only within a language system (Pols, 1992, pp. 6–8; 1998, p. 79). Pols (1992, pp. 98–99) gives the "internal realism" that Putnam defends and Searle rightly rejects (see chap. 3, this volume, especially notes 3 and 4) this minimalist or deflationary sense of "ontology."[14]

When MGTs reject not only the ontological mutism of radical postmodernists/constructionists but also their antirealism and radical relativism, they ask for nothing less than a fully realist (if not a fully nonrelativist) ontology of personhood. They must, therefore, somehow reconcile the local nature of their ontology with the universality implied by the conventional or nondeflated meaning of the term. An important question to ask is whether for MGTs there are any commonalities among the various forms of "personhood" (or psychological kinds) that emerge in different discursive/ interpretive contexts. Put differently, are there universal features of personhood that exist across such contexts, and if so, at what level of generality or abstraction may they be most properly articulated? After all, if we are self-interpreting beings who are concerned (for example) with what it means to be human, then at that high (enough) level of abstraction, we may speak of a universal or essential human nature that unifies and distinguishes us as

---

[13]The term *ontology* came much later; it belongs to more modern times (Held & Pols, 1985, p. 522, note 1), but contains the Greek root for *being*.

[14]On Quine's view *ontology* refers to nothing more than a catalogue of entities that exist according to a particular theory. This too may be said to use *ontology* in a minimalist or deflationary sense. As Quine (1948) himself put it in a famous essay:

> Viewed from within the phenomenalistic conceptual scheme, the ontologies of physical objects and mathematical objects are myths. The quality of myth, however, is relative; relative, in this case, to the epistemological point of view. This point of view is one among various, corresponding to one among our various interests and purposes. (p. 38)

So when we speak of an ontology, it is a way of speaking of what exists according to a particular theory; it is not a way of asserting what really exists, independent of a theory. Similarly, Quine's criterion of ontological commitment is a criterion for determining what entities a particular theory is committed to the existence of, and not for determining what things really exist (Amie Thomasson, personal communication, February 16, 2005).

human beings—even though the particular content of our self-understandings or interpretations will surely vary in some ways.[15]

In turning now to the second ontological point, we consider whether the MGTs' preference for local ontologies (rather than a universal ontology) of human psychological existence affords them the ontological realism (and the avoidance of an extreme relativism) that they work to defend. In chapters 8 and 9 we consider the epistemological implications of this local, yet allegedly realist, middle-ground ontology.

---

[15]Phenomenological psychologist Frederick Wertz (1999) links universality and particularity by way of "universal horizons of human existence," which include the essential features of meaning itself. In so doing he seeks a "regional ontology" and "indigenous epistemology" for psychology, which in some ways echoes what the MGTs are after. It is worth quoting him on this.

> Brentano . . . provided us with the fundamental essence of all psychic life, the most universal essential feature which distinguishes the psychic from all other phenomena, in *intentionality*. Description of mental life shows that experience is always experience of something. . . . The description of psychological phenomena in their intentionality led Husserl and his followers to recognize the *situated and contextual* character of psychological life (Merleau-Ponty, 1942 & 1945), its being-in-the-world (Heidegger, 1926). Complex unities of *meaning* were shown to manifest such essential characteristics as its corporeality, practical instrumentality, emotionality, spatiality, discourses, sociality, and temporality. . . . These are not inferred laws or hypothetical constructs but the universal horizons of human existence which show themselves in the direct *intuitive* grasp of mental life (Levinas, 1973). Such intuition establishes a regional ontology and an indigenous epistemology for psychology. (p. 144)

5

ONTOLOGICAL POINT 2: A MIDDLE-GROUND REALIST ONTOLOGY?

Humans just *are* what they interpret themselves as being within their social context. (Richardson, Fowers, & Guignon, 1999, p. 236)

Humans simply are what they interpret themselves as being within their historical and sociocultural contexts. (Martin, Sugarman, & Thompson, 2003, p. 77)

In chapter 4, I set forth the first of four core ontological claims of the middle-ground theorists (MGTs). Ontological Point 1, our ontology of "being in the world," established the dependence of human psychological existence (or the nature of personhood) on local historical/cultural/discursive/interpretive contexts. Many of the quotations in that chapter expressed the MGTs' claim to have avoided the ontological mutism, antirealism/irrealism, and extreme relativism of radical postmodernists on the one hand, and the ontological universalism, essentialism, and objectivism of conventional modernists on the other.[1] In seeking an ontological middle ground for psychology, MGTs lay claim to an ontological realism that avoids the extremes that shape radical postmodern and modern/conventional forms of psychological inquiry. It is this more moderate realism that I consider in this chapter.

I divide my discussion of the MGTs' ontological realism into three sections. In the first section, I elaborate a foundational assumption of their on-

---

[1]See chapter 3 of this volume for definitions of *objectivism*, *(anti)realism*, and *relativism*. See chapter 4 of this volume for a discussion of the "ontological mutism" of some radical constructionists. *Essentialism* is the doctrine that entities or kinds have features intrinsic to or necessary for their existence, regardless of their context—hence my equation of universalism with essentialism.

tology of personhood: the (reflexive) relationship between (a) our beliefs about the nature of personhood and (b) the actual nature of personhood itself—that is, the kinds of entities that constitute our existence as psychological beings. The direction of causality is said to be mutual and so works both ways for MGTs: Human psychological existence is dependent on beliefs about psychological existence, and beliefs about psychological existence are dependent on actual human psychological existence. To make this more concrete, recall Richardson, Fowers, and Guignon's (1999) and Martin, Sugarman, and Thompson's (2003) all-important claim quoted at the head of this chapter. If the assertion that we are what we interpret ourselves to be (which is how I will henceforth refer to this claim) is correct, then the object to be known (our personhood or psychological existence) does not and cannot exist independently of ourselves as knowers—independently, that is, of our believing and representing or discursive/interpretive (i.e., knowing or epistemic) practices. In that case knowers actively (agentically!) construct the discourses or interpretations (the "knowledges") about psychological existence that in turn constitute or determine the nature of that existence itself—hence the bidirectional nature of the "causality" that operates between being and knowing.

Of course our knowing practices are themselves part of human psychological existence, part of being a person. Knowing is thus a form of being, and so the waters are deeper than they at first may seem. We must therefore be careful to specify on *whose* beliefs and *which* beliefs psychological existence depends, if we want to assess fairly whether MGTs have indeed succeeded in giving us a realist ontology of psychological existence—in which psychological existence is not merely what anyone believes it to be—rather than simply another form of radical postmodern antirealism and relativism. MGTs sometimes say that they escape postmodern antirealism (and at least extreme relativism) by propounding a definition of realism better suited to the study of human psychological entities than the conventional definitions of realism (see chap. 3, this volume)—definitions in which entities are said to be real only if they exist independently of human beliefs, representations, and practices (Haack, 2003; Searle, 1995; Thomasson, 2003).

Accordingly in the second section of this chapter, I review the revised meanings that some MGTs give to the terms *real, realist,* and *realism,* and contrast these with more conventional meanings. I consider from whose and which beliefs the entity to be known must be independent to qualify for realist (ontological) status. I also explore the nature of the alleged dependence of psychological existence or personhood (in any given context) on knowers' beliefs (within that same context)—for example, whether it is a logical/constitutive or causal form of dependence. This distinction has important implications for the ontological realism (and epistemological realism but not objectivism) that MGTs seek. And it has no less relevance to the human agency on whose behalf MGTs labor.

In the third and final section of this chapter, I turn my attention to the extreme ontological relativism that MGTs suppose themselves to have avoided. The nontrivial question of relativism must be raised whenever it is supposed that what exists depends on beliefs about what exists, within or even beyond any particular discursive/interpretive context (Martin, Sugarman, & Thompson, 2003, p. 77; Richardson, Fowers, & Guignon, 1999, p. 236). I conclude with an assessment of whether an ontology of personhood that is local and relativistic can nonetheless be realist. As the reader surely suspects by now, I have my doubts. But in any case, my goal is to demonstrate that MGTs have not quite avoided/escaped, transcended/overcome, or mediated/moderated the extreme relativism that they in principle reject.

ARE WE JUST WHAT WE BELIEVE OURSELVES TO BE? THE REFLEXIVE RELATIONSHIP BETWEEN PSYCHOLOGICAL BEING AND KNOWING

It will help if we begin with quotations that illustrate and elaborate the all-important claim made by Richardson, Fowers, and Guignon (1999) and Martin, Sugarman, and Thompson (2003)—that we are what we interpret ourselves to be. In reviewing these passages, note that "we" are said to construct the discourses/interpretations (or "knowledges") about "ourselves" within our historical/cultural/discursive/interpretive contexts, which discourses/interpretations in turn reflexively constitute or construct "us" (our psychological being or personhood). Hence we find an appeal to Giddens's use of the concept of the "double hermeneutic [the 'two-way relations between actions and those who study them'] to develop . . . his 'theory of reflexivity'" (Giddens, as cited in Windschuttle, 1996, p. 206). As Richardson et al. (1999) described Giddens's double hermeneutic, "There is a mutually influencing interplay or dialogue between meaning-laden events and the interpretive frameworks of investigators" (pp. 180–181).

Here I call attention to my own deliberate imposition of scare quotes around the words *we, ourselves*, and *us* in the previous paragraph, to ask a question regarding the all-important assertion that we are what we interpret ourselves to be. Just which humans have, in their acts of inquiring (knowing) about personhood, constructed the discourses/interpretations that literally make us what we are now alleged psychologically to be? At the individual or idiographic level, does each person's psychological existence depend on his or her own beliefs about that psychological existence—and nothing more? At the cultural or nomothetic level, does the general nature of personhood within a local discursive/interpretive context depend on the beliefs of those who (collectively) contribute to the discourse/interpretations about personhood in that context—and nothing more? Put differently, are those who inquire about the nature of psychological existence the same persons who make psychological existence what it *is*, in virtue of their discourse about personhood?

Neither Richardson, Fowers, and Guignon's (1999) nor Martin, Sugarman, and Thompson's (2003) extreme version of the all-important claim settles the matter, although they elaborate their views in ways that make their position clearer. So in my assessment of the ontological realism that MGTs consistently defend, I again raise the important question of on whose mind(s) the personhood or psychological existence under investigation depends. Because this question has epistemological as well as ontological implications, I also put the word *knowledges* in the previous paragraph in scare quotes (in addition to using its plural form) to call into question the epistemological realism of the knowledge about personhood that follows from the MGTs' psychological inquiry.

For now note in these quotations an explicit or implicit reference to reality or realism, to actual being or existence. For MGTs there is evidently little doubt about the reality of the psychological existence that humans "bring forth" (or constitute) in their (reflexive) discourses, although just what that reality may consist in is not always delineated clearly or consistently—for example, in some cases it is the nature of personhood, in others the nature of agency, and in still others the nature (or types) of intentional states. Here I begin with two quotations that give context to Richardson et al.'s (1999) and Martin et al.'s (2003) all-important claim. The use of the prefix *self-* in the first quotation pertains to my questions about whose beliefs psychological existence depends on. Notice in both quotations the hint of an antiobjectivist epistemology, by way of the renunciation of epistemic neutrality.

> Our intentions, desires, and beliefs are made possible and given concrete form by the background of self-interpretations and self-assessments circulating in a historical culture. . . . Because humans just *are* what they interpret themselves as being within their social context, according to hermeneutics, it follows that social theory cannot be thought of as a neutral process of recording facts about humans. . . . Interpretations devised by social scientists feed back into the culture and so define and alter the reality they describe. (Richardson et al., 1999, p. 236)
>
> Hermeneutic inquiry depends on our ability to recognize that our "truths" are made possible by a shared background of life into which we are initiated and to which we contribute. . . . Because humans simply are what they interpret themselves as being within their historical and sociocultural contexts, the study of psychological phenomena cannot be conceived as a detached, neutral process of recording objective facts, nor can psychology ignore the agency reflected in human interpretive activity. (Martin et al., 2003, p. 77)

The suggestion in the second quotation that agency is "reflected in interpretive activity" is a theme to which I return in chapter 6.

Here are more quotations that rely on an underlying "double hermeneutic" claim about reflexivity. They too invite us to ask on whose interpretations "our" psychological existence depends; they also vary in just what the
psychological existence brought forth or constituted in discursive/interpretive
practices consists. I therefore put these quotations into two broad categories,
beginning with those that make the most general or abstract ontological claims
(e.g., the world or reality emerges in discourse). I then move on to quotations
in which the aspects of psychological existence that emerge in discourse are
particularized to varying extents (e.g., psychological selves or persons, life
stories, intentional states, behavior, and experiences), as are aspects of the
world that so emerge (e.g., sociocultural traditions, social reality). Some quotations cover the whole ontological range.

First, the quotations that give us the most general or abstract claims:

> The world just *is* what emerges into presence in our discourse, and dis-
> course relies on the disclosedness of the world for its sense. (Guignon,
> 1991, p. 100)

> How is the world affected by our language-based conception of it?
> The nature of reality and its relation to human activity is one of the
> more important problems addressed by hermeneutic thinkers. The sug-
> gestion that the world and our interpretation of it are not separable, much
> less independent, is intriguing. (Slife & Williams, 1995, p. 92, note 11)

> Social science theories do not just describe or explain events that are
> independent of them but help constitute the objects of study. (Richardson
> et al., 1999, p. 305)

And now the quotations in which these abstract claims are made more specific, to a greater or a lesser extent:

> As we try to describe our own or others' behavior and experience, our
> descriptions actively shape those phenomena and help to bring them
> into being. Because our interpretations help make our experience and
> behavior what it is, . . . these interpretations represent an important
> constitutive element of that experience and behavior. (Richardson et
> al., 1999, p. 282)

> Interpretations both grow out of and feed back into the unfolding
> history of our community. . . . The very being of a person's life story is
> preshaped by the background of stories and interpretations that consti-
> tute what Gadamer called the "tradition" of a shared life world. But it
> also shows that our interpretations of our lives . . . feed back into and
> reshape the wider context of tradition in which they appear. (Guignon,
> 1998, p. 573)

> We are beings whose social reality is, in part, constituted by the ways
> in which we interpret and preinterpret this reality. . . . Freudian con-
> cepts, categories, and vocabulary have become constitutive of our
> preinterpreted world. We think, act, and feel differently because of the
> influence of Freud's doctrine. . . . If the vocabulary of psychoanalysis
> were to be abandoned . . . , then we would not only tell different narra-

tives about ourselves, we would become different beings. (Bernstein, 1988, p. 104)

In interpreting the products of human life and relating those interpretations to our concrete historical situation, we open ourselves to the influence of those interpretations. In the fusion of horizons between interpreter and that which is interpreted, there is a codetermination of each. (Woolfolk, 1998, p. 75)

The emergence of psychological phenomena in the life span of a human individual may be seen to originate and evolve within a process of sociocultural embeddedness, which enables and constrains the emergence of a genuinely reflexive psychological self—a self that continues to be enabled and constrained by sociocultural and interpretive practices and means. Further, sociocultural traditions themselves emerge and evolve over a much longer time line in dynamic interaction with the activities of a myriad of individual and collective psychological agents. (Martin & Sugarman, 1999a, pp. 14–15)

[Social constructionists] hold that in psychology . . . there is a reflexive relationship between beliefs about the "objects" of investigation and these "objects" themselves, . . . that psychological discourses can have an effect on persons and their psychological properties. (Liebrucks, 2001, p. 373)

The existence of intentional states is . . . *not* independent of human discourses. This is not to say that so-called "intentional states" like emotions, attitudes, and motives are not real. (Liebrucks, 2001, p. 378)

Social constructionists argue that psychological discourses not only describe the conduct of persons but inevitably also evaluate this conduct, and therefore psychological discourses have a *reflexive impact* on the very phenomena they attempt to represent. (Liebrucks, 2001, p. 385)

Some of the most celebrated pieces of constructionist work have drawn specific attention to the *onto-formative* . . . capacities of language. . . . [Such works] have shown how discourse can bring into being a whole range of phenomena [e.g., sexuality, childhood, community] that are every bit as "real" as trees and houses. (Edley, 2001, p. 438)

Not only the telling of the stories of a life but many of the most characteristic human psychological phenomena are discursive, brought into being through the public and private use of symbols under all sorts of normative constraints. Remembering . . . , deciding . . . , reasoning . . . , persuading . . . generally either are performed wholly discursively or make use of discourse in important ways. (Harré, 1998, p. 35)

Searching for Ontological Realism in an "Emanationist" or "Emergent" Theory of Truth/Reality[2]

The idea that we bring many sorts of psychological entities into existence by way of our discursive/interpretive (knowing) practices presents a prob-

---

[2]Truth and reality are not typically seen as synonymous. For example, Thomasson (2003) regards "truth" as a semantic matter rather than an epistemic or ontological one. By contrast, Slife and Williams (1995) equate "what truth is" with "what the world is like" (p. 181). Because some MGTs

lem for the ontological realism that MGTs defend. For if "what humans are" depends "just" (Richardson et al., 1999, p. 236) or "simply" (Martin et al., 2003, p. 77) on what humans interpret and so believe themselves to be, it is hard to see how psychological entities can have an existence that is sufficiently independent of knowers or interpreters to make them real in any conventional meaning of the term *real* (see chap. 3, this volume). Therefore MGTs who subscribe to these extreme versions of the all-important claim must find ways to bypass this problem. One way some attempt this is by redefining the term *real*; we consider that solution in the next section. The other way (which we consider here) is by reformulating the nature of reality itself, so that the traditional distinction between *being* and *knowing* is blurred. Here is the crux of this solution. For some MGTs the ontological realism of psychological existence, entities, or personhood is accomplished by way of the claim that (social/psychological) life itself is "always already" structured narratively—before any one of us interprets it. That is, life (in the human world) is said to be structured narratively prior to human inquiry (and thus discourse) about it. Put differently, we discover (the truth about a preexisting) psychological existence as we constitute that existence in our local discourses/interpretations—we both discover and make psychological reality simultaneously! This is an odd combination indeed, because realists typically assume that we discover (and then describe in language the nature of) an independently existing (or preexisting) reality, and radical antirealists/ constructionists typically assume that we constitute or construct a nonindependently existing (or nonpreexisting) "reality" in language—which "reality" (or nonreality) we are then sometimes said to know "directly"[3] (see Held, 1995, chap. 6).

By contrast, some MGTs claim that our psychological existence, and the stories we tell about that existence in the act of knowing it, are inextricably fused. However, the exact nature of that fusion, and how it is supposed to work ontologically in the service of realism, remains in need of clarification (although the presumed teleological or agentic nature of human psychological existence plays no minor role). Here I let the quotations speak for themselves, beginning with Guignon (1998), who puts forth this claim most explicitly. Note the foundational role he gives to teleology.

> Life has a narrative structure *before* there is any explicit attempt to put that life into the form of a story. . . . The story-shaped structure of life follows from the basic future directedness of human existence. . . . Nar-

---

merge the notions of "telling" or "narrating" a life (which I consider a matter of truth) with "being" or "living" (which I consider a matter of reality), I take their "emanationist" or "emergent" theory to be a theory of truth/reality. Guignon (2002a) also mentions an "*expressivist ontology*," in which entities have "ways of emerging-into-presence . . . in the clearing that defines our world" (p. 280).

[3]Putting the word *directly* in scare quotes conveys an unconventional meaning of direct knowing that contrasts with the more conventional meaning—unmediated knowledge of an independently existing reality.

rating the events in a person's life must be thought of as a matter of making articulate the often inchoate and tacit stories that *already inform* that life. . . . Storytelling makes explicit what is *already there* in life [all italics added]. (Guignon, 1998, pp. 568–569)

There is no such thing as the reality of a person's life distinct from the various aspects we may uncover in narrating that life. . . . In telling stories in the psychotherapeutic setting, we are realizing and defining a meaning and structure that was *there all along* [italics added]. (Guignon, 1998, p. 573)

In the next two statements, we see a deliberate blurring of the divide between reality and descriptions of reality, between "living" and "telling" or "words" and "world" (as some put it), all in the name of ontological realism.

The disjunction between "living" and "telling" is not nearly so great. . . . Even if we do not live narratives of the same nature and scope as those we tell when we pause to reflect comprehensively on the past, the very act of existing meaningfully in time . . . is only possible in and through the fabric of narrative itself. (Freeman, 1993, p. 21)

Some of the most celebrated pieces of constructionist work . . . have shown how discourse can bring into being a whole range of different phenomena [e.g., sexuality, childhood, communities] that are every bit as "real" as trees and houses. In addition, they have helped us to understand that there is no clear dividing line between words and world or between the material and the symbolic. (Edley, 2001, p. 438)

The idea that reality can "emerge" only by way of interpretation itself surfaces in these next quotations, which bring us closer to the "emanationist" or "emergent" (as I shall call it) theory of truth propounded by some MGTs. In these quotations, but especially in the second one, there seems to be equivocation about whether *what* exists, exists prior to *narrative* about what exists. But the "emergentist" claim stands nonetheless.

Gadamer's hermeneutic position is intermediate [between objectivism and constructionism]. . . . An external social reality that interpreters can access does exist, but that reality emerges only through interpretation and is delimited by the variety of constraints to which interpretation is subject. (Woolfolk, 1998, p. 74)

By means of the narrative, Gadamer (1975, p. 101) says, "what is emerges. In it is produced and brought to light what otherwise is constantly hidden and withdrawn." (Richardson et al., 1999, pp. 258–259)

In various ways these quotations express the MGT claim that aspects of reality "emerge" in discourse/interpretations, narratives, or linguistic constructions (all of which typically contain beliefs about reality). They are therefore also ways of saying that what exists in the social/psychological world depends on human beliefs about what exists in the social/psychological world. We are, then, back at the all-important claim that we are what we interpret ourselves to be. If this statement serves as shorthand for a belief many (if not all) MGTs seem to hold in common, we may then ask whether making what exists (in the human world) dependent on beliefs about what exists allows a route to ontological realism, despite philosophical arguments to the contrary.

In *Against Relativism* philosopher Christopher Norris (1997) examines the Heideggerian claim that "'things' can only emerge against the horizon of intelligibility that constitutes the 'world' of meaningful practices and life-forms" (p. 147). Norris concludes that this claim contains nothing short of an

> implicit anti-realism which attaches to such talk of "things" (or entities) once subject to reinterpretation in the depth-ontological or hermeneutic mode. Thus when Heidegger asks "What is a Thing" . . . his purpose is to question both our everyday ("ontic" or "factical") notions of thinghood and that entire history of philosophico-scientific thought which has always been captive to "metaphysical" ideas of knowledge, truth and representation. (pp. 147–148)

This antirealism is for Norris expressed in the question of how "properties of x can be determined *both* by its intrinsic nature—as revealed through scientific investigation—*and* by its role within some given context of linguistic, cultural or 'world-disclosive' preunderstanding" (p. 147). Norris argues that in the "latter case nothing could count as an object—or as evidence for that object's nature and properties—except in so far as it showed up among the range of currently accepted practices and beliefs" (p. 147).

In short, says Norris (1997), "There could be no escaping the 'hermeneutic circle' which Heidegger and Gadamer . . . have raised to a high point of interpretive principle" (p. 147). If Norris is right about this, it is hard to see how MGTs can successfully defend the ontological realism of social/psychological entities, because they deny the existence of essential or intrinsic properties of those entities. And if there is no escaping the "hermeneutic circle," it is hard to see how MGTs can successfully defend the agentic capacity to transcend, transform, or overcome the discursive/interpretive contexts that are said to constitute human social/psychological existence.

In this chapter I consider the MGTs' defense of the ontological realism of social/psychological entities. I focus especially on how some MGTs argue that an ontology of "being in the world"—in which the distinction between knowing subjects and objects to be known collapses, making possible their antiobjectivism—is perfectly realist, despite the conventional realist requirement that (real) entities have essential or intrinsic properties that are not "constituted in knowing relations" (Hibberd, 2001a, 2001b; Maze, 2001). Here I turn from the MGT view that (social/psychological) reality emerges in our discursive/interpretive (knowing) practices, to the idea that truth also so emerges.

From an Emergent Reality to Emergent/Emanationist Theories of Truth

It would be foolish to overstate the distinction between an emergent view of reality and an emergent theory of truth, because MGTs do not themselves make much of this distinction.[4] For this reason I introduce this view of truth in a chapter on ontology. Accordingly I offer quotations that speak expressly of truth; they provide a basis for the MGTs' views about epistemic objectivity and warrant that we consider in chapters 8 and 9, respectively. I begin again with Guignon, some of whose statements about truth in the first quotation appear in the same passage about reality that I quoted earlier in this chapter; his words may therefore sound familiar.

> On ... an emanationist account, a story does not simply mirror pregiven events as they are independent of the story. Instead, the narrative brings to light and makes explicit a story that previously was inchoate. ... Gadamer's emanationist account suggests ... that, in telling stories ..., we are realizing and defining a meaning structure that was there all along ... [This is an] "emerging-into-presence" of the truth. (Guignon, 1998, pp. 572–573)
>
> Our ability to encounter entities is made possible by a clearing opened by our shared, cultural ways of being-in-the-world. This clearing is called *truth* in the sense of *a-lētheia*, unconcealment. Since there are different clearings at different times and under different circumstances, Heidegger says that things "stand in different truths." (Guignon, 2002a, p. 281)

In the following passages, Freeman (1993) speaks not only of the narrative structure of lived experience or life itself but also of the "poetic figuration of life itself" as lived and as told. Ultimately he seeks a broader conception of truth.

> [Isn't the poet's] truth ... of an entirely different sort from the one social scientists and the like seek? ... Where then do meaning and truth reside? In the texts themselves or in me? The answer is plainly that they reside in *both*; precisely in the dialogic space of interpretation itself. This is so ... for any inquiry—be it "artistic" or "scientific"—that seeks to understand the features of the world. (p. 230)
>
> Can we not say, in fact, that the reality of living in time requires narrative reflection and that narrative reflection, in turn, opens the way toward a more comprehensive and expansive conception of truth itself? (p. 32)

---

[4]Although I cast him as an MGT owing to his moderate form of constructionism, in this quotation about truth and reality Harré (2002) sounds more radically constructionist: He seemingly makes reality and truth nothing more than a matter of discourse.

> There surely are many interpretations of some given sequence of actions, identified and individuated by some commonly agreed criteria. However, one of these interpretations will be dominant in the interpretation of subsequent events, as this or that story-line. This will *be* the social/psychological reality. There is nothing else to which this story might or might not correspond. The social scientist or psychologist who notes down the dominant story-line has the truth of the matter. (p. 622)

As a general rule our ongoing engagement with the world changes and complexifies our own hermeneutical situation, which in turn changes and complexifies the qualities of the things we interpret: a new truth emerges. (p. 142)

In speaking of art, Hersch (2003) also mentions "emergent truth," which complements his "co-constitutional" view "in which the realities of human experience or *known* reality can be described as 'both given and made'" (p. 60; see chap. 3, this volume).

Gadamer would emphasize [that the "meanings generated" in people's encounters with, e.g., the intentions they find in Michelangelo's art] are also significant sources of emergent truths. (p. 113)

In Richardson et al. (1999), we encounter the "emergence of truth" in addition to reality. Note the epistemic thrust behind everyone's alleged recognition of "how things are." I presume that by "everyone," the authors mean everyone within a discursive/interpretive context.

Dramatic narratives articulate and bring to realization the potential coherence already embodied in our life context. Thus, the "transformation into form" is an "emergence of truth," according to Gadamer; through it, the tacit significance of life is "raised up into its truth," and "everyone recognizes that this is how things are." (p. 259)

Taken together, these quotations seem to equate a linguistically structured notion of reality with a linguistically structured notion of truth, both of which are said to emerge (locally) in language or narrative. These conceptions of reality and truth amount to a reduction, if not outright elimination, of any possible independence between "how things are" and (narrated) beliefs or stories about how things are. Let us therefore begin to consider the implications of these ideas about reality and truth for the ontological realism MGTs seek.

How an Emanationist/Emergent Notion of Reality/Truth Is Deflationary

Does the MGTs' insistence that (social/psychological) existence or reality and truth about (social/psychological) existence or reality "emerge" only in accounts of or beliefs about that existence compromise their search for a middle-ground ontology that is realist nonetheless? The answer depends on how MGTs define and use the terms *real*, *realist*, and *realism*. In the next section, I discuss that issue. But first I attend to a potential problem with their emanationist/emergent view of truth/reality—that it could in fact be a "deflated" or "minimalist," and so even a "reductionistic," view. If this problem is real, it would be ironic because MGTs struggle fiercely against the reductionism they find in conventional approaches to psychological inquiry, and the (mechanistically deterministic and so for them objectivist) philosophies that are said to underlie them.

In *The Construction of Social Reality*, philosopher John Searle (1995) mentions common motivations for arguments against realism, which (recall from chap. 3) he defines as "the view that there is a way that things are that is logically independent of all human representations" (p. 155). He settles on one in particular: the attempt to "eliminate the possibility of skepticism by removing the gulf between appearance and reality that makes skepticism possible in the first place" (p. 168). This is just what I find in the words of MGTs who deliberately blur the distinction between "living" and "telling," between "world" and "words." Here Searle refers to the motivations of twentieth-century "verificationists," whose analytic philosophy would produce the "idea that nothing at all exists apart from language and meaning"—just as earlier philosophers "came up with the idea that there is no reality independent of experience and knowledge" (p. 168). However, what he says seems equally applicable to MGTs, whose search for a middle-ground form of (ontological) realism Searle would surely dismiss.

> Since the seventeenth century, the most common argument against realism has been derived from epistemic considerations. . . . If reality consists in nothing but our experiences, if our experiences are somehow constitutive of reality, then the form of skepticism that says we can never get out of our experiences to the reality beyond is answered. (p. 168)

Norris (1997) labels linguistic philosophers' conception of truth "minimalist" (in the sense of being a logico-semantic conception) and couples that conception with the "emergent" conception seen in those who have hermeneutic inclinations, such as "postmodernists, antifoundationalists, neopragmatists"[5]—that is, those who "equate science with a destructive and humanly degrading form of means-end rationality, an instrumental reason wholly devoid of critical or emancipatory values" (p. 137). These are also the values of many MGTs, and there is for Norris an ironic "elective affinity" between (a) "a minimalist (logico-semantic) conception of truth in philosophy of language and science [which, in its logical positivist origins, rejected 'Heidegger's depth-ontological talk']" and (b) "a broadly hermeneutic—Heideggerian—idea of truth as what emerges or stands revealed against the horizon of a meaningful form of life" (p. 137). Norris argues that in both cases (a and b) truth is in some way "reduced" (relativistically) to our local linguistic or interpretive practices, with the further Rortian (neo)pragmatic reductive twist that what is true is merely what is judged "'good in the way of belief'" (Rorty, as cited in Norris, 1997, pp. 136, 138). Truth is, then, not a conventional

---

[5]Although postmodernists, antifoundationalists, and (neo)pragmatists often adopt various antirealisms, a minimalist conception of truth has no necessary (or obvious) tie to any kind of antirealism (Thomasson, personal communication, February 21, 2005).

matter of using "causal-explanatory modes of understanding" (p. 136) that allow correspondence with an objective or independently existing reality; truth is a "*de dicto*" matter of avoiding "any 'metaphysical' commitment to claims about the intrinsic (e.g., causal) properties of this or that real-world object of enquiry" (p. 135). Because MGTs frequently appeal to pragmatic standards of warrant and express an aversion to causal forms of explanation, correspondence theories of truth, essentialism, and objectivist philosophies, Norris's analysis may apply to them as well.

In *The View from Nowhere*, philosopher Thomas Nagel (1986) too makes comments that may apply to MGTs, in virtue of his criticism of the appeal to historical/cultural constraints on human existence to support a local, situated form of "truth." These are constraints to which many MGTs appeal not only for their localized (yet allegedly realist) ontologies of personhood but also for their localized (yet allegedly realist) forms of epistemic warrant. It is noteworthy (and again ironic) that Nagel ultimately equates the historicism that MGTs so value in their commitment to a deeply rich, situated, nonreductionistic ontology of personhood with the reductionism and (extreme) relativism that MGTs reject vehemently.

> It is one thing to recognize the limitations that inevitably come from occupying a particular position in the history of a culture; it is another to convert these into nonlimitations by embracing a historicism which says there is no truth except what is internal to a particular historical standpoint. (pp. 10–11)
>
> To redefine the aim [of truth] so that its achievement is largely guaranteed, through various forms of reductionism, relativism, or historicism, is a form of cognitive wish-fulfillment. Philosophy cannot take refuge in reduced ambitions. It is after eternal and nonlocal truth, even though we know that is not what we are going to get. (p. 10)

Nagel (1986) offers a psychological reason for the appeal of "deflationary" views of truth and reality, an appeal that supplies an interesting counterpoint to Bernstein's (1983, p. 19) famous diagnostic claim that the desire for objective knowledge is a result of an outdated, modernist "Cartesian Anxiety."

> If the theories of historical captivity or grammatical delusion are not true, then why have some philosophers felt themselves cured of their metaphysical problems by these forms of therapy? My counterdiagnosis is that a lot of philosophers are sick of the subject and glad to be rid of its problems. . . . This makes them receptive not only to scientism but to deflationary metaphysical theories like positivism and pragmatism, which offer to raise us above the old battles. (p. 11)

Pols (1958) anticipated the psychological basis for a receptivity to "deflationary metaphysical theories," which is expressed in the title of his essay "To Live at Ease Ever After." Consistent with Pols, Norris (1990)—in his incisive critique of postmodernism—explains how postmodernists "can live quite happily with the absence of . . . [the] delusory props" that enable our erroneous belief that objective knowledge is within our reach (p. 118). About postmodernism Pols (2000b) himself said, "Postmodernism tries to console us by providing the happy ending every comedy must have: our true cognitive task is the pleasant one of creating and recreating our own realities, a task identical with an endless and exuberant *autopoiēsis*, or self-making."

A thoroughgoing or unconstrained self-making (or self-determination) in the name of agency, liberation, or emancipation is not what MGTs want. As we saw in chapter 2, that is the aim of radical postmodernists/constructionists. By contrast, MGTs want a constrained form of self-determination or agency, and it is the existence of constraint that distinguishes them from radical postmodernists, by giving them license to defend the realism that radical postmodernists reject. Their version of realism is what makes them MGTs, and so it is to their claim to realism that we now turn.

DEFINITIONS AND USES OF THE TERM *REAL*

There are in the many writings of MGTs three criteria on which some regularly rely to support their claim to a realist ontology of psychological existence or personhood: (a) The discourses, interpretations, or meanings (what I will call linguistic entities) that constitute our psychological existence are not merely in our heads; they are literally "out there in the world"; (b) Accordingly we cannot simply construct, make, or even select (on the basis of wish or whim) the discourses, interpretations, or meanings that help us attain a preferred form of psychological existence; and (c) Our knowledge claims or interpretations are therefore always fallible, because they must answer to or are constrained by something that exists independently of any *particular* person/knower, something that may (sometimes) be said to exist "objectively"—the discourses, interpretations, or meanings that are "out there in the world."

After giving evidence of these three criteria (which constitute the implicit definitions or uses of the term *real*), I discuss the explicit definitions of the word *real* provided by MGTs. I then turn to more conventional definitions of the word *real* as a basis for comparison. In putting forth these conventional meanings, I ask questions about the nature of the dependence of personhood on discourse—that is, on human beliefs, representations, and practices—alleged by MGTs. Is it a logical or causal form of dependence, a rigid or general form of dependence? On whose beliefs, representations, and practices can the nature of personhood depend—and on whose beliefs, representations, and practices must it not depend—if a realist (if not an objectivist) ontology of personhood is to obtain? Finally, does this realist ontology of MGTs escape the (strong) ontological relativism of radical postmodernists?

The Three Criteria for Use of the Term *Real*: Implicit Definitions

Criterion 1: Discourses, Interpretations, or Meanings Are
"Out There in the World"

According to MGTs, linguistic entities are "out there in the world"; they are not merely in our heads. Thus as MGTs sometimes say, they exist "objectively" in virtue of having some kind of mind independence (Thomasson, 1998). However, consistent with their antiobjectivist philosophy, MGTs also sometimes say that discourses, interpretations, or meanings are not ontologically objective. If existing "out there" (or independently of any *particular* knower's beliefs) does not give linguistic entities an objective existence, then a question arises: Have MGTs merely failed to achieve philosophical consistency, or have they in fact attained a middle-ground ontology? After all, oscillation is not the same as integration/reconciliation/bridging, transcendence/overcoming, mediation/moderation, or avoidance/escape.

In these first quotations, we find the foundational idea that the linguistic entities of cultural/historical/discursive/interpretive contexts (which elsewhere are said to constitute personhood) have some (here unspecified) sort of existence independent of the (individual) persons/knowers allegedly constituted by them. The first quotation comes from a moderate constructionist, the second from hermeneuticists, and the third from a (neo)pragmatist.

> Social constructionism, while denying the efficacy of social structures, affirms the reality of the discursive domain without falling into the fallacy of supposing that because many aspects of our lives are our own constructions, all must be. (Harré, 2002, p. 611, abstract)
>
> Meanings are in the world, not in our heads. (Richardson et al., 1999, p. 236)
>
> The pragmatic psychology view can be characterized as a "moderate" constructionist position that falls in the middle of the realist versus constructionist continuum . . . [and] posits that although it is not possible to apprehend transhistorical and cross-cultural—that is, history-and-culture-free—foundational realities, there are "facts," "theories," and "values" that transcend any individual's idiosyncratic perspective. (Fishman, 2001, p. 279)

In the next few quotations, we find elaboration of the claim that linguistic entities have an existence that is "out there" in the world. We also begin to see signs of struggle about whether this "fact" allows linguistic entities to have an objective existence. The struggle issues from MGTs' pervasive discomfort with objectivist philosophies, even as they embrace realism, and it manifests itself in various ways—for example, in the replacement of the word *objective* with the words *intersubjective* and *real*. I begin again with Guignon.

> It would be wrong to suppose that meanings and values only arise "in here," in our minds. . . . Heidegger calls our attention to the etymology of

the word "existence"—literally, "standing outside"—in order to drive home the point that being human is never a matter of being "in here," encapsulated in a subjective container, but is "always already outside," caught up in the midst of things in a shared world. (Guignon, 2005, p. 85)

Hermeneutic philosophers generally want to call in question the distinction between "subjective" and "objective" that has dominated our thinking since the rise of modern science. . . . There are numerous things that are not tangible or that exist only relative to human interests which nevertheless exist "out there" in a perfectly straightforward sense. . . . Values and meanings are experienced as "out there" in the world rather than as in our minds. . . . If the word *objective* is understood as the opposite of *subjective*, that is, as referring to what exists concretely "out there" in the world, then it seems that we have every reason to say . . . that values are objective. (Richardson et al., 1999, p. 215)

Having just given meanings and values an objective status, though, Richardson et al. (1999) then seem to recoil from both objectivity and subjectivity, preferring instead to speak of meanings and values as real, then later (in the second quotation) as intersubjective.

Taylor wants to liberate us from both the objectified view of reality and the subjectified view of values we get from modern science. . . . He has tried to show that we would not be able to think and live as we do unless we grant that meanings, imports, significances, and values have a real existence. (p. 215)[6]

We are not dealing here with just subjective meanings or interpretations. . . . These kinds of meanings are intersubjective rather than subjective. As Taylor (1985b, p. 36) puts it, "The meanings and norms implicit in these practices [e.g., voting] are not just in the minds of the actors, but are out there in the practices themselves." (p. 283)

In the midst of this, Richardson et al. (1999) renounce the "objectivist outlook" altogether.

The linguistic constitution of our experience undermines one of the most fundamental assumptions of the objectivist outlook, the assumption that an object exists and has determinate features "independent of any descriptions or interpretations offered of it by any subjects" (Taylor, 1989, p. 34) and that science can give us a correct representation of that object. (p. 220)

When they add to this the statement that "it is far from clear that human behavior and experience can be characterized as objects that have a reality independent of and prior to interpretations" (p. 278), they appear to undermine their "emanationist"/"emergent" theory of truth/reality: that we can uncover the truth about or reality of the human (social/psychological) world

---

[6]Martin and Sugarman (1999b, p. 185) quote this passage from Richardson et al. (1999, p. 215).

in our narratives or discourses about that world, precisely because that reality is structured narratively or discursively *prior to* our interpretations of it.

Let me end this section by saying that Richardson et al. (1999, p. 215) are exactly right to "question the distinction between 'subjective' and 'objective'" that has long dominated our (scientific) thinking. Their commitment to a realist ontology of psychological existence that sometimes accepts and sometimes rejects ontological objectivism may well stem from the problematic nature of the objective/subjective distinction in the first place. In any case, they do not go far enough in solving these difficult definitional problems, which is perhaps why they and other MGTs find objectivity problematic—sometimes ontologically, although mostly epistemologically. Contrary to what they seem to think, however, there is a way out of the problem of appreciating how entities that are mind dependent (i.e., they are not independent of human beliefs, representations, and practices), such as discourses, meanings, or interpretations and the forms of personhood (or psychological kinds) to which those entities may contribute, can nonetheless have an objective existence that in turn permits objective inquiry and knowledge about them (Thomasson, 2003, 2007). I discuss this claim later in this chapter and in chapter 8.

Criterion 2: We Cannot Construct Preferred Psychological Realities on the Basis of Wish or Whim—That Is, Without Constraint

Although our psychological existence or personhood depends on (or is constrained by) the discursive/interpretive context to which we ourselves contribute, because any such context exists "out there, in the world" and not "merely in our heads," our psychological existence does not depend entirely on our *own* beliefs about its nature. Any one of us, or perhaps even all of us, could in principle be wrong about its nature. Humans are therefore not merely or just what they believe (or interpret) themselves to be—certainly not individually, although this is still possible collectively; collective beliefs about personhood are said to constitute the discursive/interpretive contexts that exist "out there," and in so doing constitute or constrain the nature of personhood or psychological existence that is possible in any given context.

As a result, none of us can—especially as individuals—(re)invent ourselves (psychologically) out of whole cloth just by constructing a self-constitutive discourse or interpretation about our personhood/psychological existence on the basis of wish or whim, as is the case according to some radical postmodernists (see chap. 2, this volume). Thus there exists some kind (and degree) of independence of (a) the reality or thing to be known, in this case the nature of anyone's (or even—although this is less obvious—perhaps everyone's) personhood or psychological existence (within a discursive/interpretive context), and (b) the discourses or interpretations that constitute the context that allegedly constitutes or constrains personhood/psychological existence (in that context). Moreover, the quasi-independent existence of meanings or interpretations "out there, in the world" from the (individual) persons whom they constitute—and who in turn contribute to them—suggests (again) that our interpretations about ourselves can in principle be fallible. Fallibility is the third MGT criterion for use of the term *real*.

All of this, of course, makes problematic the extreme version of the all-important claim that we "just" (Richardson et al., 1999, p. 236) or "simply" (Martin et al., 2003, p. 77) are what we interpret ourselves to be within our social context. I return to this problem in due course.

In the following quotations, Guignon (1991) takes Richard Rorty's postmodern "playful" pragmatism to task for its invitation to unconstrained self/reality making in language, in which "thinking makes it so."

> [According to Rorty] we do best to think of ourselves as perpetually self-reweaving webs of beliefs and desires who play language games off one another to produce new language games to suit our current purposes. When we see that there is "no way to underwrite or criticize the ongoing, self-modifying know-how of the user of language" in terms of an account of human nature, we will "become increasingly ironic, playful, free and inventive in our choice of self-descriptions." (pp. 89–90)
>
> We most fully realize our potential for freedom when we treat all vocabularies as tools at our disposal and dedicate ourselves to playfully inventing new, idiosyncratic metaphors in composing our own lives as "poems of existence." (p. 92)[7]

Rorty's radical postmodern playful detachment, his seeming dismissal of the constraining influence of the discursive/interpretive context that for MGTs constitutes (the possibilities or terms of) our personhood, selves, or identities, is seen in the radical postmodernism/constructionism that we considered in chapter 2. Recall, for example, these liberating words of Baumgardner and Rappoport (1996): "Individuals are free to choose, adopt and change self-images according to shifting life circumstances and needs" (p. 128). Richardson et al. (1999) similarly and rightly take constructionist psychoanalyst Roy Schafer to task for "treating agency as a free-play of tellings" (p. 259). It is just this sort of free-wheeling, make-your-own (relativistic) reality/existence on the basis of wish[8] and whim from which MGTs recoil, much as they recoil from the alleged objectivism and essentialism of mod-

---

[7]Guignon (1991) criticizes Rorty for buying into the very objective/subjective distinction of the so-called "epistemological model" that Rorty has pronounced dead: "The epistemological model had assumed that we are subjects set over against an independently existing world we want to know" (p. 97). "His [Rorty's] critique of the epistemological tradition therefore must surreptitiously presuppose the initial validity of that very tradition" (p. 94). This presupposition Rorty reveals in taking his "stance of detached objectivity" (p. 95), which Guignon rejects: "The [hermeneutic] awareness that we cannot escape the insider's perspective results from acknowledging . . . our rootedness in a cultural, historical, and linguistic context we can never fully objectify or ground" (pp. 96–97). This, of course, is an expression of the MGTs' ontology of "being in the world."
[8]Gantt (1996) criticizes the hedonism he finds in radical constructionism.

ernism.[9] Indeed, phenomenological and hermeneutic psychiatrist Edwin Hersch (2003, pp. 59–60) uses the term *resistance* when others speak of constraint, to support the ontological realism for which MGTs strive.

The next quotation illustrates this second MGT criterion for establishing the ontological realism of psychological existence or personhood: We cannot wish or will it into existence by interpreting ourselves on the basis of mere whim or desire. It is not without constraint. In this quotation we find a version of the aphorism that "thinking doesn't make it so," which again suggests that our actual personhood has an existence that is in some way independent of how we interpret ourselves to be. Yet if "thinking doesn't make it so," then we are not just or simply what we interpret ourselves to be (even within our social context). Again, contradiction looms. First let us consider the quotation, which—owing to its importance—I give at length. Notice the "reach" for a middle-ground ontology and epistemology.

> There are two inadequate models for describing psychological experience. . . . The first is to see psychological vocabulary as simply describing pre-existing experience—merely as a neutral representation of behavior or an inner reality. This model assumes that behaviors and experiences are independent of our interpretations and that their accuracy is a matter of correspondence with the "real" behavior or inner state. This will not do, because achieving a more sophisticated vocabulary . . . helps create a different kind of psychic life. . . .
>
> The second inadequate mode . . . [is] that thinking makes it so. Recognizing that our interpretations of our experience can transform it may prompt a leap to thinking that we can arbitrarily give our experience any label we choose and thereby change it at will. From this perspective, any talk of the truth, falsity, or erroneousness of interpretations is simply misguided. Yet taking this position overlooks the numerous constraints on the intelligibility and acceptability of interpretations. It discounts the possibility that we can misconstrue ourselves or our situation. We cannot force just any description on our experience—some formulations will seem inauthentic, distortive, or alien. . . . The comforting simplicity of seeking a correspondence between description and reality is insufficient, and the liberating hope of the thinking makes it so viewpoint is misguided. (Richardson et al., 1999, pp. 281–282)

Consistent with their determination to avoid these two extremes, Richardson et al. (1999) earlier said that "[Charles] Taylor steers a path between constructionism, which paves the way to the pop psychological idea that 'thinking makes it so,' and scientific objectivism" (p. 220). However, in that same passage, they said that humans are "beings whose very identity is

---

[9]Siegel (1997) criticizes Rorty's embrace of both unconstrained self-creation and public solidarity, which, "in Rorty's hands [are] not mutually exclusive; one can embrace both public solidarity and private self-creation, even though the two are '"forever incommensurable"'" (p. 215, note 22).

shaped by self-interpretations" (p. 220). They conclude that passage by saying, "Our interpretations *constitute* our being" (p. 220). It is clear that our interpretations must be determined or constrained by something other than ourselves, the truth of our interpretations (about ourselves) must be independent of our beliefs about their truth in some way and to some extent, if we are not *just* what we (individually or even collectively) interpret ourselves to be. Yet in what way and to what extent?

Martin and Sugarman (1999a, 1999b) provide one plausible answer, by situating the psychological (or individual) "level of reality" within the constraining influence of the sociocultural (or collective) level of reality—which itself is constrained by the biological level, which in turn is constrained by the physical level.

> Both physical and biological reality exist outside of human collective or individual perception and constrain (in the sense of limiting possibilities with respect to the development of) sociocultural and psychological realities. (1999b, p. 186)
>
> Within all of the dynamic flux that describes the ongoing mutable interaction between societies and psychological individuals, there exists a kind of non-chaotic, non-arbitrary social and psychological reality that is much more than linguistic. It is not simply a matter of how we decide to think or talk, as some postmodernists appear to claim (cf. Kvale, 1992). (1999b, p. 190)

In subsequent chapters I have more to say about Martin and Sugarman's "levels of reality" ontology and its implications for their views about the realism (and objectivity) of psychological inquiry. Here let me say that we are still not clear about the extent and nature of the independence of our psychological existence (being) from our discourses/interpretations about that existence (knowing). Thus it is still not clear just how psychological existence can be said to be real, either in any conventional sense of the term *real* or even according to Criterion 2.

Finally, compared with these hermeneutically inclined MGTs, one moderate social constructionist seems to want a clearer distinction between the object of knowledge (in this case psychological existence) and knowers' (in this case scientists') beliefs about that existence: "Social constructionists in principle acknowledge that the 'objects' of psychological investigations and their properties exist independently of any beliefs scientists might have about them" (Liebrucks, 2001, pp. 373–374). Here we see raised the all-important question of just whose beliefs, and what kind of beliefs, can affect a psychological existence that still deserves the descriptor *real*. I return to these questions (and this theorist) subsequently.

Criterion 3: There Is a Potential for Fallibility

Implicit in Criterion 2 of realism, that "thinking doesn't make it so," is the possibility that what we believe about psychological existence can be mistaken or wrong owing to constraints on discourses and meanings/ interpretations that exist "out there in the world" and not just "in our heads" (Criterion 1). Put differently, knowledge claims about psychological existence can in principle be wrong. The possibility of fallible knowledge claims is a conventional criterion of realism; it rests on the conventional realist assumption that the entity to be known exists independently of acts of knowing about that entity.

There are two questions to keep in mind. For MGTs does fallibility obtain because psychological existence itself exists independently (enough) of beliefs about that existence so as to permit inquirers to be wrong in principle? Or does fallibility obtain because the discursive/interpretive context that exists "out there" constrains knowledge claims? The latter is problematic, because in that case knowledge claims are fallible only if they violate beliefs or discourses about psychological existence, and not the nature of psychological existence itself. Because MGTs sometimes say that psychological existence is constituted in (or simply consists in) beliefs about that existence, it is hard to see how they can lay claim to the kind of fallibilism that would support a robustly realist ontology. The previous quotation of Richardson et al. (1999) admits of either or even both interpretations; it does not tell us why "some formulations will seem inauthentic, distortive, or alien" (p. 282). I therefore do not find it to be of much help in answering the two questions.

Turning to Liebrucks (2001), the moderate social constructionist whom we considered at the end of the last section, we also find an appeal to the possibility of fallible or erroneous beliefs or interpretations to support the reality of psychological entities. First, let us reconsider Liebrucks's position on the reality of psychological entities despite their dependence on local discourse. Unlike Richardson et al. (1999), he does not make the case that the dependence of personhood on local discourse allows realism owing merely to the "external existence" of that discourse. As we have seen, the issue of just whose beliefs, representations, and practices the object of investigation exists independently of (i.e., that of scientists) is more a matter of consequence for him than for his hermeneutic counterparts.

> The existence of intentional states is . . . *not* independent of human discourses. This is not to say that so-called "intentional states" like emotions, attitudes and motives are not real. . . . The point is rather that, since their existence depends on social context, the phenomena that are investigated by psychology are ontologically different from the phenomena studied by natural sciences. (Liebrucks, 2001, p. 378)

And in this next quotation, we see how Liebrucks (2001)—like Richardson et al. (1999)—uses fallibilism to support his realism. Although Liebrucks does not make this link explicit, it is implicit in what he says—especially if we consider what he says here in the context of the passage that immediately follows.

[Unlike our pain], we can be said to be deceived about our emotions. Therefore we sometimes correct our emotional self-apprehension, we sometimes say that we are unclear about our emotions, and we sometimes even admit that others know our emotions better than we do ourselves. . . . A similar analysis can be given for the concepts "motive" and "attitude." . . . We can mistake our motives and attitudes just as much as we can mistake our emotions. (pp. 376–377)

In this final statement of Liebrucks, which extends a previous quotation, I interpret his claim that social constructionism admits of valid accounts of personhood to mean that it also allows for the possibility of invalid accounts. If I am correct about this, then fallibilism is used to support ontological realism. Note the concern with the correct level of abstraction—that is, the generality versus particularity—of valid accounts. I return to this matter in due course. More important here is the insistence that although "there is a reflexive relationship between beliefs about the 'objects' of investigation and these 'objects' themselves" (p. 373), there is also a form of independence of these objects from those (scientists) who inquire about them—an independence that permits fallibilism and thus the realism that follows from it.

[Social constructionists] do not claim that it is impossible to arrive at valid accounts of the psychological properties of persons. . . . Valid accounts that apply to the psychology of all humankind . . . are possible only on a very high level of abstraction, and . . . more concrete accounts only apply to specific historical epochs and specific cultural spheres. . . . Constructionists acknowledge that the "objects" of psychological investigations . . . exist independently of any beliefs scientists might have about them. How else could they claim that a large amount of psychological research is based on a false conception of its subject matter? When social constructionists say that psychological discourses have an effect on the "objects" of which they speak, this must not be misinterpreted . . . that psychological theories become true just by announcing them. (pp. 373–374)

The final sentence of this quotation invokes Richardson et al.'s (1999) rejection of the claim that "thinking makes it so." However, Liebrucks's reasons for sharing this sentiment may be different: He asserts the independence of objects of inquiry from (scientific) inquirers, whereas Richardson et al. assert the existence of external linguistic/discursive/interpretive constraints on what can rightly be said (to be the case) by anyone in a particular discursive context. Yet they do not say that those constraints issue from a (psychological) reality that exists independently of knowers, and which knowers can in principle have access to that reality. Although Liebrucks would surely agree with them that (scientific) inquirers are themselves psychologically constituted or in some way determined by the discursive contexts that constitute/determine the objects of their psychological investigations, the basis for his perfectly conventional claim to ontological realism—that the entity to be known exists independently (enough) of the knower—is not made sufficiently clear.

Explicit Definitions of the Term *Real*

In the previous quotations, the word *real* is merely used; it is not defined explicitly. We must go further if we are to understand with less inference just what certain MGTs mean by *real* when they refer to psychological entities. Unlike conventional definitions of *real*, MGTs' definitions typically permit a dependence of psychological entities (the objects of knowing) on knowers/inquirers: Their attempt to obliterate the distinction between knowing subjects and objects to be known (the objective/subjective distinction) is one important indication of this. As Richardson et al. (1999) put it,

> It is right to say that the human sciences *constitute* the reality they study.
> . . . This is why the sharp distinction between the knowing subject and
> the object to be known, taken as self-evident in the natural sciences,
> cannot be made in the human sciences. (p. 223)

The problem is that despite the crucial word *sharp*, the all-important claim that humans are what they interpret themselves to be (within their social context) makes possible a complete dependence of psychological existence (the entity to be known) on ourselves as *knowers/interpreters*. Again, a proper understanding of this claim itself rests on just whose and which beliefs/interpretations psychological existence depends on. So too we must know in what way psychological existence depends on beliefs/interpretations, to achieve a proper understanding of this claim. If there is no distinction made between knowing subjects and the objects to be known, then knowers make or constitute (rather than discover) psychological reality (in acts of knowing), in which case the antirealism of radical postmodernism prevails. Yet because MGTs want to avoid this extreme, some of them appeal to an "emanationist" theory of truth/reality (in which reality is both made and discovered simultaneously), and/or the "out there" existence of meanings that constrain (and so permit the fallibility of) psychological claims, to support their ontological realism.

This erosion (if not outright elimination) of the distinction between the knowing subject and object to be known is driven home by the MGTs' (antiobjectivist) view that we not only are constrained by interpretations that exist "out there" in the world but also contribute to those very interpretations. Recall earlier in this chapter the quotations about the "reflexive relationship between beliefs about the 'objects' of investigation and these 'objects' themselves" (Liebrucks, 2001, p. 373). This claim calls into question the actual "out-thereness" (or independence) of the discursive/interpretive context that constrains our mutually influential (social/psychological) being and our knowing about our (social/psychological) being.

As we review MGTs' explicit definitions of the word *real*, then, two questions should be kept in mind: (a) whose minds—which knowers—must objects of psychological inquiry be independent of to warrant the descriptor *real*? (b) relatedly, in what way can those objects of inquiry be dependent on the knower's/inquirer's beliefs, representations, and practices, and yet still be considered to have a real existence? The answers to these questions have bearing on the potential for the fallibilist knowing on which many MGTs and conventional realists rely to support their ontological realism.

We should also keep in mind that MGTs are right to insist that psychological entities, unlike physical/material entities, cannot be independent of all human beliefs, representations, and practices. After all, psychological entities—such as the emotions, motives, and attitudes about which Liebrucks (2001) speaks—depend on the existence of minds that make beliefs, representations, and practices possible in the first place. Let us therefore look more closely at how a few MGTs redefine the term *real*, to accommodate this obvious state of affairs. I begin first with a proposal for "psychological realism" and then consider a proposal for "hermeneutic realism." Both proposals are put forth as more proper forms of realism for human (social/psychological) kinds than are conventional views about realism (see chap. 3, this volume).

Psychological Realism

Slaney (2001) distinguishes "psychological realism" from "classical empirical realism." The latter, she claims, is attached to the "metaphysical commitments" of "metaphysical realism [with its causality], strict objectivism, and materialism" (p. 149), none of which apply to the human world. Hence we need a different way of understanding what is real when we refer to the human (psychological) world, one that does not insist on the independence required by conventional realists (see chap. 3, this volume): "There is some concern that traditional philosophical doctrines of realism may be inadequate for addressing questions having to do with the ontological status of entities which are, by their very nature, contingent on human social systems" (p. 142).

Slaney (2001) then explains how the "classical empirical realism" that she rejects has traditionally worked in psychology: Psychological entities, such as traits, certainly depend on human beings for their existence. However, this does not mean that scientists construct or constitute them out of whole cloth—or what I would in some cases call construct/constitute them in the act of knowing. Therefore, consistent with Liebrucks's claim, they seemingly exist independently of those who conduct scientific investigations about them.

> For the classical empirical realist what makes such entities [electron, gene, warped space, traits] "real" is the fact that they have *objective existence.*
> . . . From this view, what is "real" is that which exists independently of

human conceptual, and, to some extent, perceptual capabilities. . . . Trait theorists do not claim that traits are independent of human *existence*, i.e., that human traits could exist if humans did not. What they do deny, however, is that psychological constructs are *merely constructions*, i.e., convenient labels assigned by the scientist for denoting particular classes of observable phenomena, as opposed to real entities for which the scientific community has particular labels. (pp. 144–145)

MGTs, then, deny that psychological entities are "merely constructions." If they propounded that doctrine, they would be radical postmodernists/ constructionists rather than MGTs in search of a more moderate yet proper ontology for human social/psychological kinds. Evidently the problem for them is any ontology that gives to social/psychological (i.e., human) kinds an objective existential status; again, MGTs tend to want realism, but without objectivism. And so Slaney (2001) provides what she considers a more proper form of realism for psychological entities, "psychological realism." In this we find mention of the local "discursive ontology" of particular sociocultural contexts, which ontology coincides with the ontology of "being in the world" (Ontological Point 1) attributed to Heidegger. Like other MGTs, she does not insist on the independence of the entity to be known (local forms of psychological existence) from (local) beliefs, representations, and practices (i.e., discursive/interpretive contexts). Psychological existence, she rightly says, is human-contingent. However, she does not tell us in just what ways objects of psychological inquiry do and do not depend on ourselves as inquirers, so as to allow the potential for fallibilism that some MGTs use to defend their version of ontological realism.

> Although psychological realists do not deny that there exist entities which are beyond our perceptual capabilities . . ., they dispute the notion that what makes something "real" is that it exists in some objective realm, independent of humans' perception or conceptualization of it. . . . [They assume] a discursive ontology in which psychological reality may be understood in terms of the intentional (rule following) acts of people within particular sociocultural historical contexts. . . . [This] is exemplified in Martin and Sugarman's "levels of reality" approach. . . . The psychological realist considers psychological activity to be as real as objectively existing spatiotemporal entities, but real in a different sense, and, hence, needs to be understood in the context of its human-contingent nature. (pp. 146–147)

Hermeneutic Realism

Here we may ask whether Martin and Sugarman's (1999b) "levels of reality" approach clarifies the nature of the dependence of psychological entities on knowers within a historical/cultural/discursive/interpretive context, in a way that rightly allows those kinds to be called real (but not objective).

In their "levels of reality" approach, Martin and Sugarman (1999b) make a case for what they call "hermeneutic realism," in which we find one of the most explicit and elaborated definitions of realism in the MGT literature.

Martin and Sugarman (1999b), in asking "What is Real?" (p. 178), begin with the definition "familiar to most psychologists": "The doctrine [realism 1] that objects of sense perception have an existence independent of the act of perception" (p. 178). This definition is familiar; it hangs on the conventional view that something is real if it exists independently of human beliefs, representations, and practices (see chap. 3, this volume). Martin and Sugarman (1999b) provide two other definitions of realism—realism defined in "opposition to nominalism" (realism 2), in which "abstractions, generalizations, and especially universals have a real, objective existence" (p. 178), and realism defined by an entity's ability to exert a "causal influence" or "causal force independent of the activity of human inquirers" (realism 3), even if that entity is "misperceived or unperceived" (p. 179). I shall return to realism 3 in discussing the agency that fuels the MGTs' campaign, as well as that of radical postmodernists/antirealists.

Martin and Sugarman (1999b) conclude with a fourth definition of realism: "hermeneutic realism" (realism 4), which does not require that psychological entities exist independently of human beliefs, representations, and practices. Realism 4 "locates psychological phenomena in the historical, cultural world of human existence at both collective and individual levels" (p. 184). Of course if there were no human beings, there would be no (human) psychological entities. Here we are considering a more subtle proposition: If there were no human beings engaged in acts of knowing/rationality—such as producing or constructing discourses/interpretations (including theories), holding beliefs (including theories), and engaging in rule-governed practices—it would be hard to see how there could be personhood in the agentic sense on which MGTs insist. Martin and Sugarman (1999b) therefore ask a good question: "Realism 1 requires existence independent of human perception. Because social institutions and practices and psychological theories and beliefs obviously require human activity and construction, should one conclude that such phenomena are not real?" (p. 180). And in support of their "hermeneutic realism,"[10] they say that even other forms of realism (e.g., realism 1 and realism 3) do not require that "sociocultural or psychological phenomena must be considered to be natural if they are to be thought of as real, or that the obviously contingent character of most such phenomena means that they can not be treated as real" (p. 183).

---

[10]In "Heidegger's Hermeneutic Realism," Dreyfus (1991) compares Heidegger with Rorty, whom Guignon (1991) criticizes, to reveal how Rorty cannot accept even his "minimal hermeneutic realism" (p. 40). Dreyfus also explains how Heidegger is a "plural realist" in holding a "subtle and plausible position beyond metaphysical realism and antirealism" (p. 39). In considering MGTs' interpretations of Heidegger, it is not clear to me that he has indeed transcended the realist/antirealist debate.

Martin and Sugarman (1999a) proclaim the "impermanent, yet none-theless real nature of both sociocultural and psychological phenomena" (p. 52): "Human sociocultural and psychological categories are not arbitrary in that they are definite kinds, even if not natural" (Martin & Sugarman, 1999b, p. 190). In the next quotation, they clarify their view of what makes something real by stating what is not necessary: its ontological fixedness (or essentialism) and its (supposedly foundational) potential to be known with epistemic certainty. Note the equation of causal influence with (real) exist-ence; it goes to the issue of agency. Note also the middle-ground desire to "avoid" the extremes of (post)modernism.

> To say that something exists and/or exerts influence outside of human perception does not mean that the thing posited is fixed essentially, know-able with certainty, or that it is natural and without contingency. . . . Most of the anti-realism evident in the proclamations of some contem-porary, postmodern psychologists (cf. Kvale, 1992) arises from quite le-gitimate and defensible concerns about essentialism, naturalism, and foundationalist certainty. However, anti-realism is simply not necessary to avoid these excessively restrictive and possibly inappropriate, related doctrines in the conceptualization and conduct of psychological inquiry. (Martin & Sugarman, 1999b, p. 183)

There is much to commend in this statement. As I shall argue, human social and psychological entities—which by definition are dependent on human action (in the broadest possible sense)—can indeed be real without being fixed essentially and knowable with certainty. Martin and Sugarman are surely right to insist that a realist ontology of human social/psychological entities does not require mind independence in *all* senses; it need not be defined by the overly restrictive tenets of traditional doctrines of realism (see chap. 3, this volume). Yet the unanswered, all-important question remains: In just what way can human psychological entities depend (as they surely must) on human beings, on human beings who are also knowers about hu-man beings, and yet still merit the label *real*—even according to Martin and Sugarman's less restrictive definition? To put this another way, on whose knowing processes, on whose and which beliefs, must psychological entities *not* depend, so that MGTs can indeed escape the radical postmodernist claim that we make or constitute (social/psychological) "realities" (or nonrealities) in each and every act of knowing—rather than discover some preexisting, or at least (quasi-)independently existing, reality?

To see if Martin and Sugarman (1999b) address this question, let us consider their positive definition of the term *hermeneutic realism*. Notice that the stated elimination of the objective/subjective distinction is made in the service of agency.

> Hermeneutic realism (realism 4) avoids the subjective-objective and mind-dependent/mind-independent turmoil that . . . occurs all too easily

when traditional doctrines of realism are applied to human activities. . . . Heidegger undercuts the idea that we are minds or subjects who somehow happen to be in contact with an external world of material objects. For him, being in the world is a unitary phenomenon in which self and world are intertwined in such a way that there is no possible way of separating them. Heidegger starts afresh with a description of our everyday agency. . . . We require the world around us in order to be agents (Guignon, 1991). (p. 184)

Hersch (2003) reinforces these views in a section entitled "The 'Realist–Non-Dualistic–Co-constitutional–Hermeneutic' Position" (p. 132), which he bases on having "taken a position of *realism* at the ontological level" (p. 273). There "the Relatedness is primary and therefore the *whole* is emphasized as prior to the individual parts" (p. 56).

Whether "hermeneutic realism" in fact avoids the mind-dependent/mind-independent (or subjective/objective) "turmoil," as MGTs claim, is debatable. And even if it does, we are still left with the question of whether the realist (but nonobjectivist) epistemology to which MGTs aspire can in principle follow from their reflexively discursive/interpretive ontology of "being in the world." In chapter 9, I argue that it does not follow, not least because I do not find sufficient answers to the question of just how psychological entities may be said to exist even quasi-independently of acts of knowing in all the various manifestations of those acts. It is, again, especially not clear just how fallibilist knowing (Criterion 3 of realism) can obtain, when what constrains knowledge claims (in a discursive/interpretive context) are meanings (among which I include values) that exist "out there" (Criterion 1 of realism)—meanings/values to which those who participate agentically in that context contribute, both individually and collectively. If the humans doing the (self-)interpreting/knowing are the same humans who constitute the interpretive context that determines their psychological existence, is there then sufficient independence between knowers and entities to be known for fallibilist knowing and hence realism to obtain? Perhaps—although this is still far from obvious, and so the all-important claim that we are what we interpret ourselves to be looms threateningly.

Martin and Sugarman (1999b) here express their version of the reflexive impact of knowing/discursive/interpretive processes and practices on the discursive/interpretive contexts to which humans contribute and which in turn constitute "in large part" the psychological existence of those same humans.

> The psychological reality of individual humans (e.g., memories, intentions, imaginings, experiences . . .) emerges as a consequence of the immersion and participation of biological human individuals in societies and cultures to which such individuals are born and within which they grow and develop. . . . The psychological reality of individuals is not only constrained, but is actually constituted in large part, by socioculturally

shared beliefs and practices. . . . Unlike physical and biological reality, sociocultural and psychological reality does not exist independently of human perception and activity. However . . . this does not mean that they are not real in the influence they can exert on human collectives and individuals. . . . [There is an] interactive and reciprocal pattern of dynamic possibilities across these various levels of reality. . . . *The actions of individual humans may have important consequences for human sociocultural reality* [italics added]. (pp. 186–187)

In this quotation the equation of what is real with causal influence (agency) is noteworthy—as is the claim that humans acting as individual agents can causally affect with "important consequences" the sociocultural realities that constitute them as psychological agents. We are again left with the question of just how psychological reality can exist independently enough of either individual or collective beliefs about psychological reality for realism to obtain.

Like other MGTs, Martin and Sugarman (1999a) claim that a fallibilist, perspectival, and thus neorealist hermeneutic epistemology follows from or is "compatible with" their hermeneutic (ontological) realism (p. 64). Yet unlike Richardson et al. (1999) and Liebrucks (2001), they do not expressly use the possibility of fallibilism (Criterion 3 of realism) to make their case for ontological realism, which they defend by way of their "levels of reality" ontology. Still, their extreme version of the all-important claim leads us to ask in what way humans are not "simply" what they interpret themselves to be (Martin et al., 2003, p. 77). Surely we must be something more than our self-interpretations, if the fallibilist knowing that some MGTs seek is to obtain.

In the next section, I consider in more detail the problem of attaining a realist ontology of psychological entities, which cannot exist independently of human beings (as can entities in the natural sciences). I try to sharpen the distinction between the knowing subject and the object to be known that Richardson et al. (1999, p. 223) claim cannot, in the human sciences, be a sharp distinction. I do so by way of philosophers whose views about these matters have not found their way into the discourse of the MGTs. However, because these philosophers consider the nature of the dependence of human kinds on human knowing processes in ways that transcend what MGTs give us, I find their work to be highly relevant.

Conventional and Unconventional Approaches to the Realism of Human Kinds in Mainstream Philosophy

The Conventional Requirement of Independence

The MGT claim that we are constituted psychologically by our discursive/interpretive contexts has both ontological and epistemological implications. The most fundamental ontological implication is that because humans do not exist (as psychological beings) independently of their "own" beliefs/interpretations about that existence (or at least the beliefs/interpretations circulating in their own discursive/interpretive contexts), psychological entities do not "have their nature independently of human beliefs, representations, and practices"—as philosopher Amie Thomasson (2003, p. 580) puts the standard definition of (ontological) realism (see chap. 3, this volume). She therefore says that ontological realism is thought conventionally to require an "Independence Principle," in which "things of kind K exist independently of the mental, . . . that it is possible that there are things that are of kind K and that there are no mental states whatsoever" (p. 582). This conventional definition of realism precludes mental states from the domain of the ontologically real, a preclusion that creates problems for any form of truth-tracking psychological inquiry—which is exactly what MGTs and Thomasson want to defend.

As we saw in chapter 3, Thomasson (2003) provides a brief but comprehensive synopsis of the conventional view of realism, in which ontology, epistemology, and semantics are brought into play.

> Three elements of a realist philosophical world-view seem to go together: The ontological view that there are kinds of things that exist and have their nature independently of human beliefs, representations, and practices; the epistemological view that acquiring knowledge about such kinds is thus a matter of substantive discovery in the face of possibilities of gross error and ignorance; and the semantic view that reference to these kinds proceeds via a causal relation to an ostended sample, so that the extension of the term is determined by the real nature of the kind rather than by our associated beliefs and concepts. (p. 580)

But Thomasson objects to this ontological view as a universal requirement for all kinds owing to its exclusion of human kinds (e.g., artifacts), which do depend for their existence on beliefs, representations, and practices—on that which is mental.

> A general realist position . . . requires only that . . . there are *some* things and kinds that exist independently of the mental—not that everything is independent. Thus many realists are willing to accept that, along with independent natural kinds and objects, there are also (e.g.) institutional objects and artifacts that neither exist nor have their natures independently of all human beliefs, representations, and practices. . . . As a consequence of the specific ways in which they differ ontologically from the natural objects and kinds of the realist's paradigm . . . we will require a substantively different ontology, epistemology, and semantics if we are to make sense of objects studied by the social and human sciences. (Thomasson, 2003, pp. 580–581)

Although Thomasson here speaks of human kinds in terms of institutional and artifactual kinds, her argument has no less relevance to such psychological kinds as emotions and attitudes. I return to her arguments about the ontological realism of human kinds later in this chapter, and about epistemic realism in inquiry about human kinds in chapter 8.

Philosopher Susan Haack, whom we also first encountered in chapter 3, says something similar to Thomasson. After stating that the "common theme" of the various forms of realism is that "something . . . is independent of human beings and their beliefs, concepts, cultures, theories, or whatever" (2002, p. 67), she gives her own "middle-ground" ontology. This she calls "innocent realism," in which not only physical entities but also the "mental activities" of human beings (which are of course mind dependent) enjoy a perfectly real existence.

> Innocent realism occupies . . . a habitable middle ground between rigid realism and rakish relativism. The world—the one real world—is independent of how we believe it to be; that, as the innocent realist sees it, is what it means to be real. But, of course, human beings intervene in the world in various ways, and they, and their physical and mental activities, are themselves part of the world. (Haack, 2002, p. 85)

So far, so good—but distinctions are in order. To be more precise, I have not yet explicitly distinguished various aspects or functions of the mental domain, and these distinctions play no minor role in the way in which psychological kinds may be (successfully) argued to be real. Although I have until now made these distinctions only implicitly or informally, here now is the explicit, more formal version.

First, we must distinguish between (a) mind (the domain of the mental) in its most general sense—for example, Pols (1998, p. 98) offers a list of mind's (or rationality's) *functions*, in which he includes knowing, making, understanding, thinking, conceiving, perceiving, remembering, anticipating, believing, doubting, attending, intending, affirming, denying, willing, refusing, imagining, valuing, judging, and feeling—and (b) those acts or functions of mind that we think of expressly as knowing acts, acts in which we attain knowledge (or "justified true beliefs") about something. Second, we must distinguish among the many *products* of mind's "formative functions of rationality,"[11] such as artifacts, institutions, and theories, including scientific and commonsense theories about the nature of human psychological existence.

We are now in a position to attend more directly to the distinction between the obvious and necessary dependence of psychological entities on mind for their existence and the more questionable dependence of psychological entities on acts of knowing (in which I include interpreting). This,

---

[11]Pols (1992, 1998) distinguishes between the "rational awareness" and "formative" functions of mind or rationality (Held, 1995, chap. 6). Here consider this to be a distinction between mind's knowing processes and mind's constructing or creating processes, respectively. I elaborate his meanings of these terms in chapters 8 and 10.

after all, is what MGTs claim—especially when they strive to mediate, avoid, or transcend the distinction between the knowing subject and the object to be known, or the subjective/objective distinction.

Here let us return to Thomasson's (2003) critique of the barring of human kinds (including psychological entities/kinds) from the domain of what is real in conventional doctrines of realism, in which entities that depend on human beliefs, representations, and practices would not meet the criteria for a real existence. Recall her view that human kinds cannot pass the test of the "Independence Principle," in virtue of their necessary dependence on the mental. Let us now consider the second principle required for a conventional or "robust realism," the "Natural Boundaries Principle." It is here that we begin to engage the question of the naturalistic status of human kinds: "If a kind K has natural boundaries, then the conditions that determine whether or not something is of kind K are independent of whether or not those conditions are accepted by anyone" (p. 582). Thus, says Thomasson, "The idea that a kind K has natural boundaries may be expressed in ignorance and error principles" (p. 582).

The "Ignorance Principle" states that "for all conditions determining the nature of the kind K, it is possible that these remain unknown to everyone" (p. 583). And the "Error Principle" states that "if a kind K has natural boundaries, since these boundaries are not determined by human beliefs about those boundaries, any beliefs (or principles accepted) regarding the nature of Ks could turn out to be massively wrong" (p. 583). Thus we may ask whether we have "epistemic privilege" about human kinds, because humans determine their "boundaries," or the "conditions for their existence" (Thomasson, personal communication, March 10, 2004). If so, according to conventional doctrines of realism, human kinds are not real.

Alternatively, perhaps social and psychological entities have bona fide natural boundaries—ones not determined by human beliefs about their nature—despite their failure to exist independently of the mental. In that case they could be treated as natural kinds in our inquiry about them, including—but not limited to—psychological inquiry. Because this matter has not been settled in philosophical circles, I do not pursue it here, except to say that some argue that it is possible to make the case that social and psychological entities have natural boundaries (i.e., the ignorance and error principles could apply to them); these scholars argue that we pick out members of such kinds "by ostension," by identifying certain causal or functional roles about the kind, such as those we might find in the case of mental states. For example, pain is said by some (e.g., Putnam, 1967) to be that state mediating between tissue damage and avoidance behavior (Thomasson, 2003, personal communication, March 10, 2004). Yet if human kinds are not natural kinds, as Martin and Sugarman (1999b) say, can they be investigated with the possibility of error and ignorance nonetheless, and therefore be considered ontologically real by that criterion? This is an important question that MGTs do not answer with sufficient clarity to make a determination, even if we take into account the three criteria for realism (including the criterion of fallibilism) put forth by some of them.

I return to Thomasson's arguments momentarily. Here note that Haack (2002) also appeals to the possibility of error to support her "innocent realism."

> Some descriptions describe us, and some describe things in the world that depend on us; and whether such a description is true or is false depends on how we are, or how those things that depend on us are. . . . But whether even such a description is true or is false does not depend on how you or I or anybody *thinks* the world is. . . . The innocent realist is a contrite fallibilist. . . . The tension between independence and accessibility . . . may be altogether superable if our understanding of independence is modest enough and our understanding of accessibility is fallibilist enough. (pp. 87–88)

Is the MGT understanding of dependence modest enough, and of accessibility fallibilist enough, for the ontological realism that Haack defines to obtain?

The Unconventional Allowance of Dependence

Both Thomasson (2003) and Haack (2002) subvert conventional doctrines of realism by allowing human kinds to be real, even though they are dependent on the mental, as long as the dependence is of the sort for which fallibilism can obtain. What kind of dependence would permit such fallibilist inquiry?

To answer that question, I return to the question of natural boundaries raised by Thomasson, who explains how there can be fallibilist inquiry about human kinds or entities—those that exist in virtue of their dependence on human beliefs, representations, and practices, or the mental. Thomasson (2003) begins by saying:

> It is possible for things of kind K to depend necessarily on certain mental states, but not on the acceptance of certain beliefs *about the nature of kind K*, in which case it is in principle possible that a kind have natural boundaries *in spite of its lack of independence* [all italics added]. (p. 584)
>
> Mental state kinds themselves might be plausibly considered examples of such kinds. For mental states certainly do not exist independently of the mental, yet at least according to many, mental state kinds are to be distinguished by the causal or functional roles of the state, regarding which everyone may be in ignorance or error. (p. 584, note 7)

Most important, it is only when things of a kind depend on the mental without also depending on beliefs about the nature or existence of the kind, that the nature or existence of the kind itself may be open to discovery and error. Let us use Thomasson's (2003) example of racism to illustrate.

Some social kinds such as racism . . . do depend on the existence of certain sets of beliefs and intentional behaviors, but may exist without the existence of any beliefs that are themselves *about* racism. . . . Although the Independence Principle clearly fails, these opaque kinds of entities may remain unknown even to those within the relevant society, and thus may require substantive social scientific discovery of their existence as well as nature. (p. 606)

Consider three points. First, although racism certainly depends for its existence on the holding (by some) of certain beliefs and intentional behaviors (i.e., racism depends on mental states, and so it fails the Independence Principle of conventional realism), because racism does not depend on beliefs about racism itself (within or beyond any discursive context), everyone in a particular context can in principle be ignorant of the existence of racism in that same context and/or be massively wrong about the nature of any racism that does exist within that context. As Thomasson says, "No one has to have any beliefs about what it takes for some individual or society to be racist, for there to be racist individuals and societies" (personal communication, December 4, 2001). Thus racism can exist independently of anyone's beliefs about racism as a kind, as long as there exist people who hold certain beliefs (and related behaviors) about the capacities or nature of members of different ethnic groups, even if they never expressed those beliefs to anyone. Even if the word *racism* never occurred to anyone, as long as certain stereotypic beliefs about members of any ethnic group existed, racism would still exist as a social kind and would not depend on any culture's belief in racism's existence, or on any views about its nature. In short, racism could be relevantly similar to a natural kind, with much to be discovered about it along conventional causal natural and social science lines, despite its lack of complete mind independence.

The second point is even more subtle in asking on whose beliefs human kinds can depend and still be real. Even within a community of insiders who "descriptively define" the term *racism* by setting up what counts as racism (i.e., they determine the "boundary conditions" for the use of the term *racism*), racism is perfectly real nonetheless, because it could exist without anyone (inside or outside the community under consideration) ever having invented or used the term—or having stipulated its "boundary conditions." Again, although racism depends for its existence on mental states, and the "boundaries of application" for the use of the term *racism* are in a sense stipulated by language users who either are or are not insiders of the context in which racism is being investigated, racism's existence does not depend on anyone's beliefs or boundary stipulations about racism per se (Thomasson, personal communication, March 10, 2004). In short, contrary to Richardson et al. (1999) and Martin et al. (2003), human beings are not *just* or *simply* what they interpret themselves to be within their social contexts; for example, there could easily be a community of racist people who do not interpret themselves as such.

And so Liebrucks (2001) faces unanswered questions when he claims that "there are properties of persons that exist only in the context of a certain discourse, that is, persons have them only relative to the meaning system of the community to which they belong," in which case they are merely "discursive constructions," including "intentional states such as emotions, motives, and attitudes" (p. 374). This must surely include racism, as an attitude if not an emotion or motive, and it suggests that racism would not exist (in a context) if there were not discourse about racism (in that context).[12] Woolfolk (1998), invoking an "emanationist" theory of reality/truth, seems to suggest a somewhat similar conclusion when he says that "an external reality that interpreters can access does exist, but that reality emerges only through interpretation and is delimited by the variety of constraints to which interpretation is subject" (p. 74).

Here are Thomasson's (2003) words on the possibility of substantive discovery for those who contribute to discourse within the community in which the relevant inquiry takes place.

> Even within a community of insiders involved in sustaining institutional facts or reproducing artifacts, there are many facts to be uncovered by social sciences. . . . [Among] these are issues regarding causal relations involving artifactual and institutional kinds, as are some of the most famous issues in social science, concerning e.g., the Marxist and feminist claims about (perhaps) unintended and unnoticed oppressive consequences of our practices involving money, division of labor, etc. Such causal facts certainly remain opaque and in need of discovery. (p. 606)

It is worth recalling that in some (but not all) ways, MGTs who give explicit definitions of *real* agree with Thomasson; they too defend the realism of human (psychological) kinds, kinds that are mind dependent and so fail the Independence test of more conventional "robust realisms" (e.g., Martin & Sugarman, 1999a, 1999b; Slaney, 2001). Martin and Sugarman (1999b) seem especially appreciative of the independence of artifacts and practices from particular minds.

> Socially constructed artifacts and practices . . . may exist . . . outside of the awareness of particular individuals who encounter, participate in them, and are affected by them . . . even though at a general, collective level, all such practices and actions require human activity for their existence. (p. 181)

But even they shrink from the objectivist epistemological conclusions that Thomasson (1997) draws when she makes a similar observation.

---

[12]See Held (2002b, pp. 660–661) for a discussion of Liebrucks's (2001) relativism.

> [The] dependence on intentionality [of entities in the social and cultural world] in no way makes them phantasms or epistemically subjective entities; instead they remain entities external to each one of us and our particular intentional states, and entities about which we can make objectively true and false claims and acquire genuine knowledge. (p. 133)

In invoking fallibilism (Criterion 3) as a basis for ontological realism, Richardson et al. (1999)—who appeal to the "'out there' in the world" (p. 215) existence of meanings/interpretations—should seem sympathetic to Thomasson's realism. Yet like other MGTs, they too reject the objectivist epistemology that Thomasson equates with realism. I return to these epistemological matters in chapters 8 and 9.

The third point about the realism of human social/psychological entities concerns a foundational assumption about the "conditions" required for the (real) existence of various entities. Thomasson (2007) accomplishes her mission by allowing "the existence conditions for things of different categories [to] vary" (p. 119). So things of a certain kind exist if the existence conditions—the "frame-level criteria" (or boundary conditions that are associated with the use of the term for a kind)—are met. Using her example, "the existence of stories (of the right kind) is not a sufficient condition for the 'real' existence of whales, though it is for that of fictional characters."

> In many cases (where mind-dependent properties are exactly what we should have expected), a certain object's (a fictional character, a work of art) or property's (being married, being a professor) being mind-dependent (or practice-dependent, or discourse-dependent) in no way vitiates its claim to "really" existing. In other cases it might, e.g., if whales were supposed to be real independent animals of a species, and there were only whale stories; or if having cancer turned out to be just a matter of one's doctor signing papers that certify one has cancer, we might legitimately say that there are no whales (whales aren't real animals), or that cancer isn't a real disease. (Thomasson, personal communication, March 10, 2004)

Let us consider Thomasson's distinction between two different sorts of human kinds to clarify how the existence criteria for different entities that depend on the mental can vary. In particular, it is useful to contrast racism (which we have already considered) and marriage (which we have not).

Marriage is, of course, an institutional kind; it can exist only in virtue of our stipulation of its "existence criteria." If humans did not create the institution of marriage, marriage would not exist. By contrast, racism—one hopes for moral reasons—is not an institutional kind, and I have already given Thomasson's (2003) views about how it can exist independently of "boundary or existence criteria" asserted by humans, even though we may *study* it only if (like natural kinds) we first stipulate criteria for its existence. Thus racism, unlike marriage, can exist prior to our stipulations about its existence. Because racism, unlike marriage, can exist independently of our beliefs and stipulations about racism as a kind, we can in principle be ignorant of (or discover) the existence of racism in any given context, whereas we cannot be ignorant of (or discover) the existence of marriage (unless we are extreme outsiders to that context). In this sense racism is more a natural kind than is marriage.

However, once we have stipulated the boundary criteria for marriage—what it takes for something to count as marriage—we can ask many substantive questions about marriage, just as we can ask many substantive questions about racism (once we have stipulated its boundary criteria); and so much remains to discover about both marriage and racism. For example, we can inquire into the effects of marriage on various economic indicators, on the happiness of married (and unmarried) members of a society, and so forth. And once we discover whether racism exists in any society, we can ask many questions about it. For example, how many people in a given society hold racist views? What kinds of people are likely to hold those views? What causal factors affect the tendency to hold (or not hold) those views? And what are the political, social, economic, and legal consequences of holding those views?

In conclusion, the notion of "epistemic privilege" about human kinds need not preclude those kinds from the realm of the real. Thus whatever epistemic privilege we have about human kinds owing to their mind dependence need not preclude the possibility of substantive, objective discovery about any of those kinds (Thomasson, personal communication, March 11, 2004). Still, the nature of the epistemic privilege, the nature of the dependence of human kinds on minds (or beliefs), has all-important implications for the realism of those kinds. These issues have remained largely untouched by the MGTs, who also defend the realism of human kinds.

We will return in chapters 8 and 9 to the implications of Thomasson's ontology of human kinds for psychological inquiry, especially for the possibility of the objective knowledge about those kinds that MGTs reject in principle and Thomasson defends. Just here I return to the question of how MGTs might respond to her ontological claim—that psychological entities, such as racism, are not independent of mental states but are independent of beliefs about racism itself, as a kind. Recall that some MGTs use the possibility of fallible claims to support their ontological realism. Yet their ontology of "being in the world" is said to be constituted discursively and reflexively, by those who participate in the ongoing discourses/interpretations that themselves constitute the social contexts on which the social/psychological existence of those participants depends. The question is this: Can MGTs entertain the existence of social/psychological entities, such as racism, without discourse about those entities? Earlier I used exemplary quotations of Richardson et al. (1999), Martin et al. (2003), Liebrucks (2001), and Woolfolk (1998) to suggest that MGTs might have trouble accepting the existence of human-kind entities such as racism, if there were no discourse about racism.

Although I know of no writings in which MGTs say whether racism per se could exist without discourse/beliefs about racism, two writings shed light on this question. Fowers (1998) and Richardson et al. (1999) use the example of "stonewalling" in contemporary research about marital interactions to question the ontological status/existence of psychological entities that are not interpreted as such. Contrary to Thomasson, we could interpret them as saying that there would be no stonewalling (and by extension no racism) if there were no notions of these entities as distinct kinds/entities, although it is hard to say just where they would come down on this question, and this quotation does not demonstrate that stonewalling does not exist unless it is interpreted as such.

> Does stonewalling exist whether or not it is interpreted as such? It is true that the behaviors identified by Gottman [the failure to provide cues to tell the speaker that the listener is tracking, such as nodding] are publicly observable and identifiable. . . . But does this constellation of behaviors stand up and identify itself . . . ? It does not, of course. Instead it is differentiated by the speaker, the observer, and possibly the listener, as salient in a particular context. (Richardson et al., 1999, p. 288)

Fowers (1998) says that the "importance [of stonewalling] derives, not so much from some independent existence or reality, but from how it figures in . . . marital interaction from the points of view of the speaker and the marital researcher in this particular sociohistorical context." Although Fowers stresses the importance of stonewalling, its "independent existence or reality" (although not directly challenged) seems at least questionable.

By contrast, I concur with Thomasson that stonewalling (like racism, or depression, or altruism) could exist even if the "constellation of behaviors" that constitute it do not "stand up and identify themselves." As long as there exists a co-occurrence of those behaviors that are constitutive of stonewalling in at least some circumstances, as long as the "boundary conditions" that are associated with the use of the term "stonewalling" are met, the stonewalling exists whether anyone realizes or identifies it as such. This, as Thomasson says, is what gives license to think of certain human kinds—including psychological entities—as being open to genuine/fallibilist discovery, in which objective knowledge can obtain, even though they are mind dependent in clearly specified ways. Although we (either as insiders or outsiders of the context under scrutiny) "descriptively define" the boundaries of the *use* of such terms as *racism* or *stonewalling*, we are only putting a label on something that was there prior to that label. We did not bring the racism or stonewalling into existence in virtue of our discourse about racism or stonewalling; they did not "emerge" into being in some "emanationist" sense owing to our discourse about them. In short, they are not mind-independent entities, but they are in a crucial sense discourse-independent entities!

The example of stonewalling we find in Fowers (1998) and Richardson et al. (1999) may share some common features with Nelson Goodman's "irrealism," although it is surely not intended to be as radical in its departure from conventional realism. For example, I cannot imagine MGTs agreeing with this account of Goodman by Haack (2002): "There is no one real world, Goodman holds, only many 'versions,' the descriptions or depictions made by scientists, novelists, artists, etc. Versions of what?—he doesn't say" (p. 84). Erwin (2001) criticizes Goodman's claim that constellations (e.g., the Big Dipper) would not exist if we had not picked out certain stars and identified them as constellations. This argument about (celestial) constellations seems similar to the one about stonewalling (it is a "constellation of behaviors" that does not "stand up and identify itself"). Erwin states, "It is we, Goodman argues, who noticed a certain similarity between a certain constellation of stars and a dipper. We then constructed, rather than discovered, the Big Dipper" (p. 8). Erwin calls this the "multiple worlds-constructionist view": "(a) There are multiple worlds rather than just one, (b) worlds are constructed rather than discovered, and (c) worlds are not independent of mind and language" (pp. 7–8). Although Richardson et al. (1999) and Fowers (1998) distinguish themselves from radical constructionists in virtue of their moderation, as do all MGTs, their discussion of stonewalling seems not entirely at odds with criteria (b) and (c)—if not (a)—of Erwin's description of the "multiple worlds-constructionist view." It would be interesting to hear their views on this matter.

The Blurred Distinction Between Being and Knowing About Being Revisited

These assertions about stonewalling by certain MGTs minimize the distinction between existence and knowledge claims (or beliefs) about that existence—including discourses, interpretations, and narratives about that existence—at least for social/psychological entities. In short, MGTs blur the distinction between being and knowing, although in their commitment to realism, they surely strive to preserve more of a distinction than do radical constructionists. Being very clear and precise about the exact nature of the distinction between the existence of a kind K and beliefs about (the existence and nature of) kind K is, according to Thomasson (2003), just what is necessary for the possibility of substantive, fallibilist, objective discovery/inquiry. And recall that it is on fallibilist inquiry that a realist ontology of social/psychological entities depends,[13] according to Criterion 3 of realism

---

[13]Hibberd (2001a) says that logical independence "is the *sine qua non* of realist philosophy" (p. 309). For Hibberd (2001b), realism requires a nonconstitutive "theory of relations" (p. 343), in which the known is not constituted by the knower or the knower's linguistic framework or forestructure. In that case, she argues, there could be no error (2001a, p. 311), and it is the possibility of error or fallibility that makes real discovery of real entities possible. Maze (2001) also formulates realism in terms of

put forth by these same MGTs. Although these MGTs defend that fallibilism and the ontological realism that they say it supports, they do not tell us how various social/psychological entities (or human kinds) do and do not exist independently of human beliefs, representations, and practices. As Haack (2002) put the matter:

> The key issue in the many and various disputes between realists and their non-realist opponents is how the world, truth, universals, etc., can at once be independent of us, and yet knowable by us. Those disputes all focus . . . on how much of what we know of the world is properly thought of as the world's contribution and how much as our contribution, on where the line runs between what we discover and what we construct. (pp. 67–69)

Richardson et al. (1999) and other MGTs do not indicate where to draw the line between construction and discovery: "Our nature or being as humans is not just something we *find* (as in deterministic theories), nor is it something we just *make* (as in existentialist and constructionist views); instead it is *what we make of what we find*" (p. 212). They, like other MGTs, argue expressly against the "clear distinction" between the knowing subject and the object to be known in psychological inquiry. They seem to blur that very distinction deliberately, so they can claim to have avoided, transcended, or reconciled the thorny objective/subjective distinction. Blurring the distinction between knower and known (or between being and knowing, or between world and words)—for example, in the "emanationist" or "emergent" theory of reality/truth put forth by some MGTs—is what makes them MGTs when compared with (a) radical postmodernists/constructionists, who try to eliminate the distinction altogether, regardless of the object of inquiry, and (b) more (but not completely) conventional realists, such as Thomasson, who want to retain it (albeit in a more precisely nuanced way). However, the MGTs' failure to be precise about just how they have avoided, transcended, or reconciled this distinction presents problems for their ontological realism of human kinds.

The "emanationist" or "emergent" theory of reality/truth expressed by Guignon (1998), Freeman (1993), Woolfolk (1998), and Richardson et al. (1999) claims that we bring into being—in the act of knowing, interpreting, describing, narrating or telling— what already existed. But it is hard to see how we can then be wrong about what we claim to know. And if we cannot be wrong (or fallible in our attempts to know something), then the emanationist account sounds like the radical constructionism that it rejects—

---

fallibilism and a nonconstitutive theory of relations, in which entities have "intrinsic natures" whose existence is not caused by or dependent on "our awareness of them" (p. 395). He rejects the antirealist notion that we have access to nothing more than our mental "representations," because this leads to an "immediate, therefore infallible, fusion" (p. 396) between the knower and the representation, rather than a fallible, direct knowledge of the real/independent thing in itself.

in which case we just make/construct "reality" rather than discover a preexisting reality, no matter how much it claims that, unlike radical constructionism, we both make and discover reality simultaneously. Most of the MGTs' ontological claims are not strictly emanationist; they sound more constructionist, although not radically so. Recall this, from Richardson et al. (1999), in which the words *help* and *element* have critical moderating effects (also see Edley, 2001, p. 438).

> As we try to describe our own or others' behavior and experience, our descriptions actively shape those phenomena and help to bring them into being. Because our interpretations help make our experience and behavior what it is, we can say that these interpretations represent an important constitutive element of that experience and behavior. (p. 282)

If we delete the crucial word "help" from this quotation, then we come close to the extreme version of the all-important claim that we "just" (Richardson et al., 1999, p. 236) are what we interpret ourselves to be in our social context. This may be read as the "perverted direct knowing" of extreme antirealists, although this is exactly what MGTs do not want—that we (each) bring into "existence" or constitute the "entity"/"reality" to be known in each and every act of knowing. In that case no act of knowing can in principle be fallible, because we know our constructions immediately and directly as we constitute them.[14] Hence the radical postmodernist claim that there is no truth, only multiple "truths," each of which is dependent on what a knower (or, depending on the version of postmodernism,[15] group of knowers) has brought into being in the act of knowing. And none of these "truths" can claim hegemony over the others in virtue of its hold on an independent reality, although some are said to be more warranted by way of their fit within the "constraints" of the local discursive/interpretive context (a coherentist standard of epistemic warrant) or by way of their practical consequences (a pragmatic standard of epistemic warrant). I return to the question of warrant in chapter 9.

If the "reality" we make in the act of knowing changes with each act of knowing, it is a matter not only of different cultural groups making different "realities" within their respective discursive contexts but also of the same person making different "realities" as she engages in ongoing acts of knowing. In that less constrained case, it is hard to see how "reality" can stand still long enough for anyone to study it at all, although it certainly lends itself to the free-wheeling, radically postmodernist version of "agency" that MGTs rightly reject. Some of them might say that we are psychologically consti-

---

[14]See Held (1995, 2002b) and Pols (1992, 1998) for discussions of direct and indirect knowing; also see chapter 8 (this volume).
[15]Radical constructivism has traditionally emphasized the knowing or reality-making processes of individual knowers, whereas radical social constructionism emphasizes the knowing or reality-making processes of knowers acting collectively or socially within a discursive/interpretive context.

tuted by or within some previously created sociocultural, discursive context[16] to which we ourselves now contribute, and which to some unspecified extent predetermines what psychological realities we *can* possibly constitute in our (individual and/or collective) acts of knowing. Thus what social/psychological entities can "emerge" or "show up" for us are predetermined (or constrained) by our interpretive contexts, but these entities are real nonetheless (see Dreyfus, 1991).

This is not exactly the "emanationist" account of reality/truth that some MGTs propound, in which we make and discover (social/psychological) reality simultaneously. However, like the emanationist account, it happily accepts some blurring of the distinction between knower and known in matters of inquiry about human (psychological) kinds, insofar as humans make or constitute what exists psychologically in virtue of their acts of knowing what exists psychologically. I return to the epistemic implications of the MGTs' ontology of human kinds in chapters 8 and 9. Here let us turn our attention back to the ontological question of the nature of the dependence of psychological being on discursive/interpretive (knowing) processes about that being.

The Nature of the Dependence of Social/Psychological Entities on Discursive/Interpretive Processes: Logical Versus Causal Dependence

Conventional realists distinguish between logical and causal dependence to assess the ontological realism of various entities. Recall from chapter 3 Searle's (1995) definition of the term *realism*: "*Realism is the view that there is a way that things are that is logically independent of all human representations. Realism does not say how things are but only that there is a way that things are*" (p. 155). Searle clarifies the distinction between logical and causal dependence (and thus realism and antirealism).

> Suppose it should turn out that physical reality is causally dependent on consciousness in such a way that with the last death of the last conscious agent all of physical reality blows up. . . . Would that still be consistent with external realism? It would, because the postulated dependence of matter on consciousness is a causal dependence like any other. When realism claims that reality exists independently of consciousness and of other forms of representation, no causal claim is made or implied. Rather, the claim is that reality is not *logically constituted* by representations, that there is no logical dependence. (p. 156)

The logical dependence of one kind of entity—for example, (psychological) properties of persons such as emotions, motives, and attitudes—on

---

[16]A context which, for Martin and Sugarman (1999a, 1999b) at least, is "nested" within biological and physical "levels of reality," respectively.

another kind of entity—for example, discourses, interpretations, representa-tions, or beliefs about properties of persons—means that the very idea of the first entity presupposes that if the first entity exists, the second exists: In this case the concept "properties of persons" or "psychological entities" presup-poses discourses, interpretations, representations, or beliefs about properties of persons or psychological entities. The very idea of properties of persons makes it clear that these (properties) could not in principle exist if there were no discourses, interpretations, representations, or beliefs about proper-ties of persons.

Causal dependence is a different and in some ways a lesser matter, pre-cisely because it does not involve logical necessity; it may therefore be less constraining. All kinds of things can and do causally affect (psychological) properties of persons, but this does not make any of them logically necessary for these properties to come into existence. For example, attitudes may be causally determined or influenced by one's classmates, but one can be home schooled and still have attitudes. The very idea of attitudes does not depend logically on, contain within it, or presuppose classmates; attitudes (even these very attitudes) do not in principle depend for their existence on the presence of classmates. And even when considering the (causal) laws of nature, the fact that the laws could have turned out otherwise, that there would have been no logical contradiction if they had turned out otherwise, makes causal dependence a less constraining or limiting matter—as Searle (1995, p. 157) suggests in a later passage.[17] About this distinction Thomasson (2003) says,

> The sort of dependence relevant to realism . . . is commonly called "logi-cal" dependence, knowable a priori by analyzing the relevant concepts, not a mere causal or nomological dependence based in laws of nature. . . . The dependencies of institutions and artifacts [human kinds] on col-lective acceptance or individual intentions . . . [are] not causal claims about the creation of these entities, but logical claims, e.g., that the very idea of something being money presupposes collective agreement about what counts as money, and that the very idea of something being an artifact requires that it have been produced by someone with certain intentions. (p. 581, note 2)

How is this distinction relevant to my discussion of the MGTs' ontol-ogy of psychological entities? Other than Woolfolk (1998), I could find no explicit mention of logical versus causal dependence in their writings, but

---

[17]Here are Searle's (1995) exact words.
> Realism does not say that the world had to turn out one way rather than another, but only that there is a way that it did turn out that is independent of our representations of it. . . . On the realist view if it turned out that only conscious states exist, then ships and shoes and sealing wax do not exist. . . . On the antirealist view, such things, if they exist, are necessarily constituted by our representations. . . . [Alternatively], for the realist, it not only *could have* turned out that there are objects other than representations, but in fact it *did* turn out that way. For the antirealist it could not have turned out that there are representation-independent objects. (pp. 156–157)

the distinction is there—if only implicitly. And the explicit use of causal language by MGTs may be no accident, especially given their aversion to a causality-based science of psychology on the grounds that the mechanistic determinism thought to inform such a science subverts the agentic (self-determining, autonomous, purposive, or intentional) functioning they champion (see chap. 1, this volume). Let us begin with this: MGTs claim that psychological entities (or, at the most abstract level, personhood itself) depend on discourses, interpretations, representations, or beliefs about psychological entities (or personhood), within historical/cultural/discursive/interpretive contexts. This, after all, is a version of the all-important claim that we are what we interpret ourselves to be.

But is the claim one of logical or causal dependence? Here a problem emerges. Often it seems that MGTs argue on behalf of the logical dependence of psychological entities or properties of persons on beliefs about those entities—that in principle there could be no such entities if there were no beliefs about those entities in local discursive/interpretive contexts (about this more in due course). Yet sometimes MGTs use what seems like causal language to describe or explain the dependence of psychological entities on discourse/interpretations (including beliefs) about those entities. Is that a mere linguistic slip, or is it intentional?

I do not think this is accidental: Slipping causality into the picture can (but does not necessarily) allow for the kind of agency that MGTs seek. Let me be more precise. If the language of causal dependence is used in a certain way, we can be said to become "self-determining" agents—to use the terminology of Martin and Sugarman (1999a, 1999b) and Martin et al. (2003). Thus the causal dependence of one entity (in this case the nature of our social/psychological existence) on another (our own goals for that existence) may support the profound kind of agency that MGTs are after—the kind in which we as agents can causally affect, and so transcend or transform, our (own) social/psychological existence or circumstances intentionally. If our intentions had no such causal consequences for our social/psychological existence, then we would not have the profound kind of agency that MGTs defend. Although surely less profound, more mundane sorts of agency could still obtain—for example, I could intend to reach for my glass of water and carry out that intention as a self-determining agent, in virtue of the causal powers that inhere in me, without attaining the kind or degree of (self-)transcendence/transformation of which MGTs speak (see chap. 6, this volume).

However, if the language of causal dependence is used in a different way, it could subvert the agency that MGTs work to build into their ontology of human psychological existence. And so whether agency obtains depends in no small part on whose beliefs about psychological existence affect or determine whose psychological existence—that is, on whose intentions do any particular person's psychological properties depend? If my psychological existence depends solely on my own beliefs about that existence, I may have the agency or freedom to be (or make myself) psychologically whatever I choose to believe myself to be, as radical postmodernists would have it (see chap. 2, this volume; I say "may" here because the ultimate source of my "choice" may be beyond "my" control).[18] But such unconstrained freedom could cost MGTs the ontological realism they defend, and so they rightly reject that radical postmodern claim. Alternatively, if my psychological existence depends on the beliefs of others about psychological existence (in general) within my discursive/interpretive context (as MGTs say), I am then less free to become or make myself a different person psychologically than the one I am now. (I may in fact have no freedom whatsoever to be or make myself a different person psychologically, although this does not necessarily follow.)

This second proposition allows my claims about myself to be fallible in principle, and so it upholds the realism that MGTs endorse, but it could come at the expense of the kind of agency they propound. Although MGTs might settle for a lesser form of agency than the capacity for social/psychological (self-)determination—for example, they might settle for the capacity to initiate simple actions such as getting a glass of water—I do not think that is the case, especially given their language of transcendence, transformation, and liberation. Thus a middle ground between no self-determination (e.g., the alleged mechanistic determinism of modern/conventional psychology) and infinite or unconstrained self-determination (e.g., the rampant "anything-goes" freedom of radical postmodern psychology) must be found. I consider the relation between the fallibilism/realism and the agency/self-determination that MGTs simultaneously uphold in chapter 6.

Now we are in a position to revisit some quotations that illustrate how some MGTs oscillate between the logical and causal dependence of psychological entities—or properties of personhood—on (local) discourses, interpretations, representations, and beliefs about those entities/properties. Note that when causal language is used, it sometimes invokes a passive view of persons, ones who are nonagentically determined by discourse that already exists prior to their existence in their local context. Yet at other times that causal language invokes an active view of persons, ones who agentically cause or determine their own (psychological) entities to emerge (sometimes according to an "emanationist" theory of reality/truth). MGTs, then, sometimes oscillate between two different notions of causality—one nonagentically deterministic, the other agentically deterministic.[19] And because the nature

---

[18]Erwin (1997, chap. 1) discusses the source of choice (e.g., conscious vs. unconscious mental states) in assessing autonomy or free will. Martin and Sugarman (2002) and Martin et al. (2003, pp. 98–100) also have interesting arguments about this.

[19]I consider arguments about the causal "laws" of psychological inquiry in chapter 9 and the causality immanent in human agency in chapter 10. The distinction between nonagentic (or mechanistic) causality/determination and agentic (or nonmechanistic) causality/determination is discussed at length in Martin and Sugarman (2002), Martin et al. (2003), and Rychlak (1994, 1997, 2001).

of the dependence of psychological entities on discourse about those entities is not made clear, their case not only for the ontological realism[20] of various psychological entities/kinds but also for (the ontological realism of) agency itself is not clear either.

In his moderate social constructionism, Liebrucks (2001) seems to endorse a logical dependence of properties of persons on the discursive context; these properties could not in principle exist without discourse. These he calls "discursive constructions."

> There are properties of persons that exist only in the context of a certain discourse, that is, persons have them only relative to the meaning system of the community to which they belong [e.g., roles, intentional states such as emotions, motives, and attitudes]. . . . Their existence depends on social context. (pp. 374, 378)

Liebrucks (2001) says that he rejects "causal necessity" in psychology in favor of "normative necessity" and "semantic necessity," the rules and conventions (including meanings) that seem to (logically) constitute psychological entities as just the entities they are understood within a context to be (p. 380). Yet he also seems to make conventional causal claims: Discourse influences, brings about, alters, or reflexively impacts aspects of our human *being*, including our conduct or behavior and our experience (see Held, 1998a, 2002b, for examples of universal ontological/causal claims of radical constructionists). Note that the causal language in these quotations can be interpreted to invoke either an active or a passive view of personhood.

> [Social constructionists] hold that psychological discourses can have an *effect* [italics added] on persons and their psychological properties. (p. 373)
>
> The psychological functioning of persons is *influenced* by discursive practices, that is, the behaviour and experience of people are manifestly *altered* through discourses. [There are] . . . properties of persons that are *brought about* by discourses [all italics added]. (p. 374)
>
> Social constructionists argue that psychological discourses not only describe the conduct of persons but inevitably also evaluate this conduct, and therefore psychological discourses have a *reflexive impact* on the very phenomena they attempt to represent. (p. 385)

Edley (2001) argues that distinguishing ontological from epistemological forms of social constructionism happily "takes away from the apparent radicalism of much of this work" (p. 433, abstract), and he inclines toward a causal dependence of being on discourse. Although it is hard to be sure, he seems to invoke a passive causal view of personhood. However, the last

---

[20]Recall that for Searle (1995), realism is threatened only by logical, not causal, dependence: "Realism is the view that there is a way that things are that is logically independent of all human representations" (p. 155).

sentence also suggests a logical dependence of existence on discourse. (And putting the word *real* in scare quotes calls into question his commitment to realism.)

> Some of the most celebrated pieces of constructionist work have drawn specific attention to the *onto-formative* . . . capacities of language. . . . [These works] have shown how discourse can *bring into being* [italics added] a whole range of different phenomena that are every bit as "real" as trees and houses. . . . There is no clear dividing line between words and the world or between the material and the symbolic. (p. 438)

Turning from moderate social constructionists to hermeneutic MGTs, we find similar claims, with similar oscillations. Much to his credit, Woolfolk (1998) explicitly addresses the distinction between logical and causal dependence.

> The claim here is *not* that self and self-understanding [or interpretation] are one, such that thinking something about the self makes it so. For some descriptions of ourselves to be true, our belief in them is a *necessary* but not sufficient condition. For example, I cannot be a born-again Christian without also . . . believing myself to be a born-again Christian. . . . For the most part, however, the relationship between self and self-understanding is not logical but causal. . . . [For example], examining our emotions, understanding them and their bases more fully, may lead to their alteration. (p. 96)

Richardson et al. (1999) suggest that psychological existence depends causally on discourse, but the word *constitutive* implies a logical dependence. And their causal language is sometimes of the active/agentic sort: We actively make ourselves what we are psychologically, by way of our own descriptions or discourse about our psychological existence. However, others may also be affected psychologically by our descriptions or discourse, in which case these others seem to be more the recipients of our agency than their own. Thus ambiguity abounds, although again the word *help* is important; it suggests, contrary to Richardson et al. (1999, p. 236), that humans are not *just* "what they interpret themselves as being within their social contexts."

> As we try to describe our own or others' behavior and experience, our descriptions *actively shape* those phenomena and help to *bring them into being*. Because our interpretations help make our experience and behavior what it is, we can say that these interpretations represent an important constitutive element of that experience and behavior [all italics added]. (p. 282)
>
> Achieving a more sophisticated vocabulary . . . helps *create* a different kind of psychic life and *opens up* new possibilities of behavior and expression. . . . One of the central premises of talk therapy [is] that verbalizing and reinterpreting one's experience can change it. . . . Attaining a wider emotional vocabulary does not simply allow one to describe one's pre-

existing feelings more accurately—it helps *bring about* a richer sense of one's inner life and *creates* different relationships among one's affect, self-understanding, and behavior [all italics added]. (p. 281)

But in these next quotations, Richardson et al. (1999) reiterate philosopher Charles Taylor's rejection of the causal dependence of psychological existence, experience, or action on discourse/interpretations and instead invoke a logical dependence, by suggesting that psychological experience and action could not in principle exist without a discursive/interpretive context. Still, we find what can be interpreted as more causal language (e.g., the verbs *shape*, *transform*, and *alter*) in the last sentence of each quotation.

Taylor (1985a) clarifies that this connection between self-interpretation and action is not causal in nature: "it is not to say that we change our interpretations and then *as a result* our experience of our predicament alters. Rather, . . . certain modes of experience are not possible without certain self-descriptions" (p. 37). . . . Our descriptions of our actions are not just neutral depictions but part of what constitutes those actions. To say that our behavior and identity are *constituted* by the interpretations we adopt is to say that these interpretations shape and define the reality of our beliefs, feelings, and actions. (p. 280)

In Taylor's words, "To say that language is constitutive of emotion is to say that experiencing an emotion essentially involves seeing that certain descriptions apply" (1985c, p. 71). And seeing what descriptions apply determines the quality of the feelings: "Language articulates our feelings . . . and in this way transforms our sense of the imports involved; and hence transforms the feeling." (p. 220)

Our intentions, desires, and beliefs are made possible and given concrete form by the background of self-interpretations and self-assessments circulating in a historical culture. . . . Interpretations devised by social scientists feed back into the culture and so define and alter the reality they describe. (p. 236)

In this next quotation, Bernstein (1983) suggests a logical dependence of psychological existence on discursive/interpretive contexts; he denies cause–effect sequences. Yet he uses causal language (e.g., the words *determining*, *shaped*, and *influenced*) nonetheless, language that invokes a passive view of persons. In the following quotation, Martin and Sugarman (1999b) stick to logical dependency—the very idea of being "agents" or "human" contains a (hermeneutic) "being in the world." Martin et al. (2003) reiterate this preference, although they do not deny causal relations and in fact rightly distinguish the greater matter of "constitutive" factors from "influencing" factors in psychological phenomena.

Tradition . . . has a power which is constantly determining what we are in the process of becoming. . . . We are always shaped by effective-history (*Wirkungsgeschichte*). It is not just that works of art, texts, and traditions have effects and leave traces. Rather, what we are . . . is always being influenced by tradition. . . . A tradition is not something "naturelike," something "given" that stands over against us. It is always "part of us" and works through its effective-history. (Bernstein, 1983, p. 142)

For him [Heidegger], being in the world is a unitary phenomenon in which self and world are intertwined in such a way that there is no possible way of separating them. . . . We require the world around us in order to be agents. . . . It is impossible for us to remove ourselves from the world, without ceasing to be human. (Martin & Sugarman, 1999b, p. 184)

It is useful to distinguish clearly between the sociocultural constitution of psychological phenomena, like mind and self, and sociocultural influence on such psychological phenomena. . . . Culture is more than influential communications and interactions. It consists in . . . resources that once appropriated and internalized help to constitute psychological persons. (Martin et al., 2003, p. 62)

Disentangling the logical from the causal nature of the dependence of personhood or psychological existence on the discursive/interpretive context has important implications. The logical dependence of psychological entities on discourse, interpretations, or beliefs about those entities can undermine the possibility of psychological inquiry that is fallible—inquiry, that is, in which there can be error in principle: Recall that fallibilism is the third criterion of ontological realism, according to some MGTs. Thus if within a social context, discourse, interpretations, or beliefs about psychological entities constitute those entities logically (the kind of dependence MGTs often seem to prefer), then their lack of independence from knowers' beliefs about their nature is problematic for their realism, because fallibilism cannot then in principle obtain.[21] In that case, what we are psychologically—the nature of our personhood—is indeed just what we interpret it to be. We cannot in principle be other than what we interpret ourselves to be, and so we cannot in principle be wrong about our psychological existence—at least not collectively within a social context.

But as we have seen, MGTs sometimes use causal language to describe the dependence of psychological existence on discourse, interpretations, or beliefs about that existence. Recall that for Searle (1995), realism is threatened only by logical dependence, not causal dependence. "Realism is the view that there is a way that things are that is logically independent of all human representations" (p. 155). Yet even if we are just what we believe ourselves to be only by way of some causal process, can our beliefs about what we are be fallible in principle? And if not, can realism obtain?

Answering that question fully would require a lengthy philosophical exposition. Here I merely consider some possible contenders. Begin by ac-

---

[21]Consider these examples of logical dependence, in which fallibilism cannot obtain. It is not possible logically (or in principle or by definition) for the Pope to be wrong about his edicts; it is not possible logically for an author to be wrong about the attributes she ascribes to her fictional characters. My thanks to Thomasson (1999, personal communication, March 10, 2004) for these examples.

cepting that any causal dependence of psychological existence on discursive beliefs about that existence must be approached in temporal terms, in which case beliefs are indexed to time. We then have two possibilities: (a) we become what we now believe ourselves to be at some later point in time; or (b) we are what we believe ourselves to be in the exact moment we hold a self-referential belief.

To start with (a), let us suppose that at t1 I believe I am a good pop singer (to use the "power of positive thinking"), and holding that belief causes me to become a good pop singer at some later time, t2. It is in that case still logically possible for me to be wrong about my pop-singing abilities at t1, and so at least then I can in principle be fallible about my pop-singing talents. Similarly, at t2, when I have now become a good pop singer in virtue of the causal effects of my positive thoughts at t1, I could start to think that I am a good opera singer, and holding that new belief causes me to become a good opera singer at some later time, t3. Again, it is logically (or in principle) possible for me to be wrong or fallible about my opera-singing abilities at t2. And so on, ad infinitum. To state this more generally, if psychological existence depends causally on beliefs about psychological existence, anyone (or even everyone) can in principle be wrong about the nature of psychological existence, because beliefs about psychological existence can in principle be wrong at any point in time. Thus causal dependence—unlike logical dependence—does not threaten the possibility of the fallibilism on which realism depends.

And even in the less plausible case of (b), in which I instantly am whatever I believe or interpret myself to be in the moment, the possibility of fallibilism still exists. That is because even then there is a way things are that is independent of human beliefs about, or representations of, how those things are (Searle, 1995)—in this case that we are what we believe we are in the moment. And this (causal) "law" would be true whether or not anyone knew about it or understood it correctly. This "law" does not depend on anyone's beliefs about this "law" for its existence. So we could in principle be ignorant of or in error about the "law," but it would govern nonetheless; it does not depend on our beliefs about its existence for its causal powers.

Both (a) and (b) are relevant to the case of racism that we considered earlier in this chapter—that racism, although dependent on mental phenomena in some senses, does not depend on beliefs about racism for its existence and nature. In both cases realism (at least as a general thesis) is saved, because the fallibilism some MGTs use to support their ontological realism is possible. In the case of causal dependence, our (individual and collective) beliefs about our psychological existence are not definitive for that existence; our beliefs just happen to make that existence (causally) what it is. Yet if that is true, it is a feature of the human world that does not depend on human beliefs about it for its existence.

To be sure, this analysis of causal dependence is problematic for MGTs. Despite sometimes using the language of causal dependence, some of them explicitly deny that "thinking makes it so" or that cause–effect sequences obtain (e.g., Richardson et al., 1999). Yet to the extent that they prefer a logical dependence of psychological existence on discourse/beliefs about that existence, the realism they defend is compromised, because the possibility of fallibility hangs in the balance.

There are implications of the distinction between logical and causal dependence not only for the realism of psychological entities but also for agency—for deciding whether humans should be properly seen as active or passive beings, and if the former, in what sense they should be seen as active. Thus these distinctions have implications for the kind of agency—along with the kind of realism—that fuels the MGT campaign. Before moving on to agency, we surely must (while still on the topic of ontological realism) revisit the related problem of relativism. Some MGTs make a point of avoiding at least the extreme relativism of radical postmodernists. Still, have they in fact managed to work out a realist ontology of human psychological existence that is reflexively dependent on the local discursive/interpretive context, without succumbing to a relativism that undermines realism? Can extreme relativism be avoided when what exists is said to depend on what is believed locally to exist? And if not, can realism follow?

CAN THERE BE A (LOCALLY) BELIEF-DEPENDENT ONTOLOGY OF PERSONHOOD THAT IS SUFFICIENTLY NONRELATIVIST TO BE REALIST?

For MGTs psychological entities, properties, or kinds depend for their (real) existence on discourses, interpretations, and thus beliefs about those entities/properties/kinds, beliefs that are held by persons/knowers within particular historical/cultural/discursive/interpretive contexts. Thus MGTs, like radical postmodernists, reject the existence of essential human social/psychological properties. As Martin et al. (2003) state in the following excerpt:

> There is no essential, a priori nature of human psychological, agentic kinds. (p. 110)
>
> Our most basic claim is existential and is congruent with the contingent emergence of psychological kinds, not with any pre-given, essentialist characterization of human psychological individuals. (p. 124)

But if there are no essentials of psychological existence whatsoever, if all psychological properties are contingent on (or emerge only within) local discursive/interpretive contexts, then have MGTs avoided the (strong) relativism (of radical postmodernists) to which they object? Have they gone "beyond objectivism and relativism," to use Bernstein's (1983) famous book title? And if not, then how can they maintain that theirs is a realist ontology of personhood, even by their own criteria of ontological realism—including, especially, the possibility of fallibilist inquiry?

Bernstein (1983) himself claims to have avoided any "naive form of relativism" (p. 142). Martin and Sugarman (1999a) also say that they avoid "strong relativism" and instead support only a "weak relativism," which "holds that our concepts are partly constitutive of the reality about which we offer reasons and evidence" (pp. 48–51). Do such claims put them, and the MGTs who agree with them, in a moderately relativistic position? And if so, is it nonrelativistic enough to buy them the realist ontology that MGTs want to purchase? Can realism and relativism, even a moderate relativism, coexist? Are they compatible?

Recall from chapter 3 that Haack (2002) makes relativism (along with such other forms of "non-realist positions" as idealism, nominalism, and irrealism) a rival to realism.[22]

> "Relativism" itself refers, not to a single, simple thesis but to a whole family, each holding that something (truth, reality, moral values, and so forth) is relative, in some sense, to something else (language, theory, scientific paradigm, culture, and so on). . . . The most relevant members of the relativist family are those that relativize truth and/or reality to language, theory, paradigm or conceptual scheme. (p. 82)

Haack also says that "metaphysical commitment" or "ontology" are seen by some as relative to "language, conceptual scheme, theory, scientific paradigm, version/depiction/description, culture, community, or individual" (p. 83). Because MGTs often make "metaphysical commitments" or "ontology" contingent on local discursive/interpretive contexts, they seem to fit well within Haack's range of relativistic possibilities.

MGTs, who claim to have founded a realist ontology that makes sense for psychological entities, which are necessarily mind dependent in some ways, have not shied away from the use of the word *relative* when describing that ontology—although they certainly deny that theirs is a "radical" relativism (either ontologically or epistemologically). Recall these snippets of previously considered quotations, this time with attention to the word *relative*.

> There are properties of persons that exist only in the context of a certain discourse, that is, persons have them only relative to the meaning system of the community to which they belong. (Liebrucks, 2001, p. 374)
>
> It is useful to focus directly on the implications of Heidegger's hermeneutic realism for human psychology. . . . [N]umerous things [e.g., values and meanings] that are not tangible or that exist only relative to human conception are nevertheless in the world in a straightforward sense. (Martin & Sugarman, 1999b, p. 185)

---

[22]Haack (2002) contrasts relativism with realism, whereas Bernstein (1983) contrasts relativism with objectivism. As we shall see, MGTs do not equate realism with objectivism.

There are numerous things that are not tangible or that exist only relative to human interests which nevertheless exist "out there" in a perfectly straightforward sense. . . . We would not be able to think and live as we do unless we grant that meanings, imports, significances, and values have a real existence. (Richardson et al., 1999, p. 215)

The discursive turn and . . . a generally constructionist orientation in psychology [do] not license a slide into radical relativism. . . . That different discourse genres disclose different aspects of material reality is no ground at all for denying that it is that very material reality . . . that is involved in our adherence to some and abandonment of others. (Harré, 2002, pp. 621–622)

We can see how far Gadamer is from any naive form of relativism that fails to appreciate how we are always shaped by effective-history (*Wirkungsgeschichte*). (Bernstein, 1983, p. 142)

And so relativism simpliciter is not a problem for MGTs' realism. Only extreme or excessive relativism, the kind that allegedly subverts realism, must be avoided—especially the excessive relativism of radical postmodernism/constructionism. Yet can a moderate relativism pass the test of realism? According to Haack (2003), the foundational test of all realisms, including the realism of intentional (human) kinds, is this: "How they are doesn't depend on how you, or I, or anyone in particular believes them to be" (p. 163). And MGTs indeed make much of constraints external to any particular individual (i.e., collectively held beliefs or intentions) on what can possibly exist psychologically—for anyone and everyone—within a historical/cultural/discursive/interpretive context. Moreover, recall that that discursive/interpretive context is said by some to be "nested" within biological and physical "levels of reality" (Martin & Sugarman, 1999b, pp. 186–189) or within "material reality" (Harré, 2002, p. 622). This is said to limit or constrain the kinds of discourses, interpretations, or beliefs that are allowed or possible within a discursive/interpretive context. As Richardson et al. (1999) write,

Some . . . charge Gadamer with a pernicious relativism: the view that whatever anyone *thinks* is true *is* true. . . . [This] overlooks . . . how the tradition provides guidelines and models that constrain our possible claims. (p. 235)

Harré (1998) said that social constructionism is not "at odds with at least some versions of scientific realism," because "there are some conditions [e.g., natural expressions of feeling, perceptual point of view] that stand outside any discourse whatever that make discourse possible" (pp. 18–19).

Still, we are left with the all-important claim that we are what we interpret ourselves to be. And the words *just* and *simply* in the extreme versions of that claim are disconcerting. Is (local) *discursive* constraint on what is, on what therefore can rightly be said about what is, sufficient for the avoidance of extreme ontological relativism? And if so, is (local) discursive constraint sufficient for the attainment of realism, in which entities surely require more constraint on their existence than even a discursive constraint that is not local?

It is not clear that MGTs have made their case for an ontology of personhood that is sufficiently nonrelativistic to support their ontological realism. After all, much hangs on just what they mean by the term *relative*, and this is not always obvious. For example, Liebrucks's (2001, p. 374) assertion that "there are properties of persons that exist only in the context of a certain discourse . . . [or] only relative to the meaning system of the community to which . . . [persons] belong," which seems applicable to most if not all MGTs, sounds close to his own definition of the term *ontological relativism*: "What the world is actually like depends solely on what we believe about it" (p. 386, note 3). The word *solely* is of course crucial, and the MGTs whom I have considered usually reject the claim that properties of persons depend solely on beliefs about personhood that are held by members of a discursive community (e.g., Martin & Sugarman's, 1999a, 1999b, "levels-of-reality" argument). Yet if MGTs agree with Liebrucks that certain properties of persons can (in principle) exist only relative to (or with the benefit of) certain discourses (i.e., they depend logically on discourses about those properties), and if discourses reflect the beliefs of those within any discursive community, then properties of persons (within a community) may exist only relative to— or depend on—the holding of certain beliefs about properties of persons by persons/knowers within the relevant discursive community. Hence my decision to combine the words *beliefs* and *discourses* to form the term *beliefs/discourses*. As Liebrucks (2001) said, "In psychology . . . there is a reflexive relationship between *beliefs* about the 'objects' of investigation and these 'objects' themselves. . . . Psychological *discourses* can have an effect on persons and their psychological properties[23] [all italics added]" (p. 373).

And so it remains to be seen how the fallibilist inquiry (i.e., the realist epistemology) on which many MGTs hang ontological realism's hat can obtain, because we cannot be assured that "facts about the nature of the kind are not determinable by reporting or analyzing anyone's concepts, but are potentially substantive discoveries subject both to possibilities of confirmation and error" (Thomasson, 2003, p. 583).[24] But before we consider

---

[23]Liebrucks (2001) undoes his assertion in the next sentence: "Social constructionists in principle acknowledge that the 'objects' of psychological investigations and their properties exist independently of any beliefs scientists might have about them" (pp. 373–374). Yet why should scientists' beliefs about the objects of their inquiry be exempt from reflexively affecting those objects? This is just the "theory of reflexivity" propounded by Giddens and adopted by some MGTs. I criticize that theory in chapters 7 and 8.

[24]Just as Thomasson (2007) argues that existence criteria may vary for different kinds of entities without sacrificing realism, so too the kinds of things that can be open to substantive discovery and error may vary for different groups of people, without sacrificing realism. She says that we must "talk about what sorts of discoveries are possible between some groups of people and some objects" (personal communication, March 10, 2004). It is worth quoting her at length.

If a realist epistemology . . . for a kind K is accepted universally with regard to *all* groups G, then that presupposes that K has natural boundaries. Nonetheless . . . a realist

epistemology, we must address the question of psychological universals and realism.

Universals in a "Situated Realism"?

Despite their rejection of essential psychological entities or kinds, MGTs do not completely disavow universals in the psychological domain. Instead psychological universals exist only at such a high level of abstraction that they could not give us the kind of psychological knowledge that for MGTs is most worth having: knowledge of the way psychological entities manifest themselves in local historical/cultural/discursive/interpretive contexts. As Liebrucks (2001) put it, "Valid accounts that apply to the psychology of all humankind irrespective of time and culture are possible only on a very high level of abstraction, . . . more concrete accounts only apply to specific historical epochs and specific cultural spheres" (p. 373). Thus what may be said to be universal (or highly general) is of lesser value to most MGTs; and this has implications for the nature of the psychological inquiry that follows from their local/relativistic ontology of personhood. Although several MGTs speak of universality, Harré's middle-ground comments are perhaps the most pointed.

> There is a universal feature of all person concepts, the singular trajectory through space and time of the embodied human being. (Harré, 2002, p. 620)
>
> The social constructionist position entails that there are both universal and local aspects of the human condition and so both universal and local forms of "senses of self." The conditions for developing a language rich enough to construct local diversity are universal! (Harré, 1998, p. 18)
>
> I hope that neither the simplistic universalism of "mainstream" positivist psychology, nor the extreme relativism of some recent distorted expositions of the constructionist point of view, can be sustained. Psychology . . . must . . . seek the universal in the local and the particular, without achieving a false generality by developing concepts of ever higher orders of abstraction, and without elevating the local and the particular to the exclusive status of all that there is. (Harré, 2002, p. 616)

Harré's directive to "seek the universal in the local and the particular" constitutes a compelling theme that will resurface throughout this volume. Here I defend the notion of local reality. As Haack (2003) says, each scien-

---

epistemology may be appropriate for *some* groups G with regard to a certain kind without that kind having natural boundaries. The possibility of members of a group G making substantive discoveries about a certain kind presupposes that it exist and have its nature independently of G members' beliefs and concepts regarding its nature. That, however, does not require that it exist and have its nature independently of *everyone's* beliefs and concepts. . . . So epistemological realism . . . may apply locally (relative to some groups G), but not universally, to kinds that lack natural boundaries. (Thomasson, 2003, pp. 583–584)

tist (or more broadly, each knower) experiences a particular in each and every act of knowing, but if that particular were not an instance of a general, no scientific inquiry (or more broadly, no rational inquiry of any sort) could be conducted. Haack (2003) also says that "a kind is real just in case it is independent of how we believe it to be" (p. 132), although she acknowledges that "unlike natural kinds, social kinds aren't congeries of properties held together by laws of nature but congeries of behaviors held together by people's beliefs and intentions" (p. 165). Haack does not discriminate among the way beliefs and intentions do and do not play a role in determining the existence of different *kinds* of social kinds (e.g., recall Thomasson's, 2003, distinction between racism and institutions like marriage). However, Haack (2003) is at least within shouting distance of Thomasson when she says, "*What* generals are real isn't something we can just read off our language, but something that takes work [substantive, fallibilist discovery] to find out" (p. 132). For her this is no less true in social science than in natural science.

> While some social institutions are universal, many are culturally specific. Everywhere there are differences in status, but only in some cultures are there differences of caste, or Sirs and Lords; everywhere people obtain and distribute food, but only in some cultures are there prices or markets. Real but restricted generalities, rooted in human nature but holding in the context of specific social institutions, allow for the possibility of explanation and even—given appropriate limitations of scope . . . and ordinarily only to a probability—prediction. (p. 165)

It is exactly prediction that is a thorn in the side of the MGTs' commitment to an agentic psychology, in which self-determination obtains.

Psychologist J. R. Maze (2001), who is a harsh critic of social constructionism, makes comments consistent with both Harré and Haack: "Everything cognizable is of a kind, that is, has universality and . . . particularity" (p. 397). Regarding particularity, psychological entities surely take different forms in different contexts, and different aspects of these entities may be of interest to different investigators for a variety of social reasons (Haack, 2003, p. 165; Maze, 2001, p. 407). Even so they can usually be seen as unique instances of general or abstract human qualities. If there were not some universality in most if not all particularities, what Pols (1992, 1998) calls the "U-factor" ("U" for universality), it would be hard to see how there could be the "fusion of horizons"—the incorporation of the other's interpretive "framework of prejudgments" into one's own (Richardson et al., 1999, p. 230)—on which hermeneutic MGTs rely to support the possibility of understanding and ultimately transcendence (i.e., agency).[25]

---

[25]According to Richardson et al. (1999),
> Understanding is achieved through a process of 'fusing horizons,' an attempt at achieving agreement in which the horizon of the present lets the voice of the other be heard as making a truth claim, while the claim of the other transforms the horizon of the present and compels us to rethink our prejudices. (p. 230)

Still, the unique or particular instantiation of a kind in a particular context may be of great interest, in some cases of greater interest than its more broadly conceived instantiation, and its existential particularity need not compromise its conventional reality status. After all, every instantiation of a kind has its own unique features—consider human beings (see Held, 1995, for a discussion of the reality status of unique events). Thus, for example, in social science inquiry we may concern ourselves with caste systems, and not how status in all cultures works, or how status in general works. The proper level of abstraction at which to frame any empirical question rests with the inquirer, and does not automatically deprive any social/psychological kind or entity of inquiry that can be framed in a more general way. Hibberd's (2002) discussion of "situational or contextual realism" is helpful here. Unlike the appeal to context to support an antiobjectivist ontology and epistemology among radical and moderate constructionists alike, Hibberd finds no obstacle to objectivity in contextualized particularity.

> Realism's most distinctive thesis is: whatever there is is an occurrence or situation in space and time. . . . Thus, every situation is contextualized. (p. 686)
>
> Situational realism maintains that all situations have both particularity and generality (are of a certain sort or kind and have objective relations to other situations); that whilst everything that exists is a particular, different things may have exactly the same quality or stand in exactly the same relation. (p. 692, note 2)

Hibberd states the constructionist/realist distinction succinctly.

> The social constructionist and the situational realist agree about the importance of context. The difference . . . is that the former maintains that context renders "internal" what is known . . . (that there is only "truth within traditions"), whereas the latter does not. (p. 687)

As we shall see, MGTs agree with radical postmodernists that there is only truth within (or relative to) traditions, although they sometimes relieve the word *truth* of scare quotes owing to their alleged (ontological and epistemological) realism (but not objectivism).

Just how locally or generally any psychological entity should properly be conceptualized has profound implications for the alleged stability of that (or any) psychological entity across time and space (chap. 7, this volume), and thus for the kind of inquiry about that entity that we can rationally expect to conduct (chaps. 8–9, this volume). I shall make a case for the fusion of generality (the conceptual) and particularity (the experiential) in any act of "rational awareness" (or direct knowing), as Pols (1992, 1998) put it. These include acts of knowing in both everyday and scientific contexts. Recall Nagel's (1986) warning: that because our efforts to understand ourselves is so difficult—"we are in a sense trying to climb out of our own minds, an effort that some would regard as insane and I regard as philosophically fundamental" (p. 11)—we will try to lessen the effort by redefining "the aim so that its achievement is largely guaranteed, through various forms of reductionism, relativism, or historicism." And with no holds barred he added, "Historicist interpretation doesn't make philosophical problems go away. . . . In the name of liberation, these movements have offered us intellectual repression" (pp. 10–11).

Although many MGTs seem to favor some form of "historicist interpretation" to solve the problems they find in modern psychology, I would not tar their *antireductionist* efforts with the brush of "intellectual repression." However, they, like the radical postmodernists they criticize, most certainly labor "in the name of liberation," or what I would prefer to call "agentic transcendence." It is therefore to the matter of agency that I now turn.

6

ONTOLOGICAL POINT 3: AN ONTOLOGY OF SITUATED AGENCY AND TRANSCENDENCE

Whether middle-ground theorists (MGTs) have made their case for the ontological realism of psychological entities or kinds (Ontological Point 2) is, for reasons given in chapter 5, debatable. In any case, deeply intertwined with their (situated) ontology of "being in the world" (Ontological Point 1) is their claim that humans are agentic beings; we play no minor role in determining our own social/psychological existence. Formulating an approach to psychology that is properly agentic constitutes half of the dual theme that fuels the MGT campaign—to attain a truth-tracking form of psychological inquiry that does not deprive us of our agentic capacity to act with intention and purpose. Thus agency is commonly seen by MGTs quite conventionally as the capacity to make choices about how to live one's life—the capacity for reasoned/rational self-determination. Consider these exemplary definitions.

> Broadly speaking, *agency* is the capability of individual human beings to make their own choices and to act on these choices in ways that make a difference in their lives. (Martin & Sugarman, 2002, p. 407)

Agency is the deliberative, reflective activity of a human being in framing, choosing, and executing his or her actions in a way that is not fully determined by factors and conditions other than his or her own understanding and reasoning. (Martin, Sugarman, & Thompson, 2003, p. 82)[1]

The words "not fully" in that second quotation are important, and later Martin, Sugarman, and Thompson (2003) add that their goal is to "argue for . . . a conception of agency as embedded and situated, yet also emergent within historical sociocultural contexts, which in turn are nested in the biological and physical world" (p. 133). However conventional their view of agency may be, they (and other MGTs) put more emphasis on the historical/cultural embeddedness of agency, or what should perhaps be called "situated agency," than do either radical postmodernists/constructionists (who often tout an unconstrained freedom to reinvent ourselves psychologically; see chap. 2, this volume) or conventional modern empiricists (who, according to radical postmodernists and MGTs, reduce our psychological existence to the nonagentic object of mechanistically deterministic causal laws). Even Albert Bandura's influential work on agency is seen by MGTs in this mechanistic way (e.g., Bishop, 2005, p. 157).

In chapter 6, I ask this question: How can we, acting as intentional agents, existentially transcend or overcome the discourses/interpretations that exist "out there" and that allegedly constitute us psychologically, so that we can become new beings socially and psychologically? The capacity to transcend or overcome what now exists socially and psychologically, what now *is*, is central to the MGTs' mission. Although they say we contribute to the historically/culturally grounded discursive context that in turn (reflexively) "constitutes" us, it is not clear how we—acting either as individual or collective agents—can transcend, overcome, or change the constraints that allegedly make each of us what we "already are," and can even hope (or imagine ourselves) to be. After all, these constraints must be constraining enough not only to make us what we are (and are not) within our discursive context but also be constraining enough to make possible the ontological realism that MGTs claim to have defended successfully. These constraints must exist "out there," independently (enough) of what any one of us believes/interprets ourselves—or those constraints themselves—to be, if ontological realism is to obtain.

---

[1]Guignon (2001) uses the term *agency* differently than do Martin and Sugarman.
"Agency" refers not just to "deliberative actions." . . . Instead the term refers to all our *doings*, to whatever we may be said to *do* as opposed to suffer. And so it includes such humdrum, unreflective activities as drinking coffee in the morning, petting the cat, or letting the telephone ring.
Although Guignon suggests these to exemplify a "prior background of unreflective, everyday activities . . . that themselves do not involve any conscious reflection," it is not obvious that these three examples are completely reflection free.

We are now in a position to reformulate our question. How can there emerge new discourses/interpretations—and thus new ways of being (socially/psychologically) that are allegedly constituted by them—when the *possibilities* of interpretation are determined in advance of us by the discursive context into which we are "thrown" and to which we contribute? The constitution (constraint) of social/psychological existence by the local discursive context not only has implications for the ontological realism (Ontological Point 2) of psychological entities but also has implications for the possibility of transcending or overcoming what constitutes us in the first place. It therefore has implications for the agentic existence (Ontological Point 3) that MGTs defend. Our agency in turn has implications for the stability or flux of our psychological existence (Ontological Point 4), which in turn affects the nature of the psychological inquiry (the epistemology) that can follow logically from that agentic ontology.

THE TRIADIC RELATION AMONG CONSTRAINT, REALISM, AND AGENCY

In taking up the problem of agency, I must return to the triadic relationship among constraint, realism, and agency that I began to explore in chapter 5. Here I offer a generic principle, to be fleshed out in due course: The more constraint there is on what persons can and cannot in principle be psychologically[2] and thus what can rightly be said about persons psychologically, the more the ontology of personhood can rightly be called realist, because psychological existence then does not depend logically[3] on anyone's beliefs (or interpretations) about the nature of psychological existence. Psychological being is not merely (the antirealist matter of) what anyone thinks or says psychological being is, because there is a way that that being is. As we saw in chapter 5, although psychological existence is mind dependent in some ways, not all aspects of that existence depend for their existence on beliefs about their existence. Aspects of psychological existence can therefore—in just that way—have an independent existence, one in which there is the possibility of genuine, substantive, fallibilist discovery, so that massive error and gross ignorance are possible (recall Thomasson's, 2003, example of racism in chap. 5).

---

[2]Here I must distinguish between what persons in general can and cannot *be* (psychologically) and what any person can and cannot *become* (psychologically). The latter is a developmental question that is not obviously or directly related to realism about psychological entities and might involve such circumstances of an individual's life as his talents and whether his upbringing nourishes those talents.
[3]Here again the kind of dependence that threatens ontological realism (especially according to Searle, 1995) is the logical dependence MGTs seem to prefer, although they sometimes use causal language (see chap. 5, this volume).

Thus humans are not "just" (Richardson, Fowers, & Guignon, 1999, p. 236) or "simply" (Martin, Sugarman, & Thompson, 2003, p. 77) what they interpret themselves to be within a social context, to reiterate the extreme versions of the all-important claim. Moreover, MGTs do not seem to adhere to that claim consistently, especially in light of the three criteria for realism that Richardson et al. put forth: Thinking it is so does not make it so (Criterion 2), even within the limits of a historical/cultural/discursive/interpretive context, because the constraints on what exists (and thus what can rightly be said about what exists) within that context exist "out there" in the discursive/interpretive context (Criterion 1). This is after all what in large part entitles MGTs to say that fallible inquiry is possible in psychology (Criterion 3).

The road to ontological realism, then, comes at a price: the extent of the agency (or self-determination) in whose name MGTs labor. The dilemma for MGTs is this: On the one hand, the more we exist psychologically independently of our beliefs/discourses about our psychological existence or personhood[4]—that is, the more realist the ontology of psychological existence is—the less "agentic" we may be said to be, if agency is the capacity to generate new beliefs/discourses (about personhood) that in some (unspecified) way reconstitute us as the new persons we have reinterpreted ourselves to be. On the other hand, the less we exist psychologically independently of our beliefs/discourses about our psychological existence or personhood—that is, the less realist the ontology of psychological existence is—the more "agentic" we may be said to be, because our capacity to generate new beliefs/ discourses about our psychological existence or personhood reconstitutes us as the new persons we have reinterpreted ourselves to be.

If we take this second antirealist case to its extreme, then thinking it is so indeed makes it so, because there is no (logical) distinction between what we believe we are and what we in fact are. However, MGTs do not want this extreme; they rightly insist on the existence of constraints on what can validly be said. Yet the question about the nature of those constraints, first asked in chapter 5, reemerges here: Are *discursive* constraints (even ones "nested" in physical and biological "levels of reality") sufficient for ontological realism? And complicating matters is the correct assertion that what one believes oneself to be surely constitutes some part of what one in fact is, even if that belief is erroneous.

In chapter 5 we discussed how MGTs stake their realism on the constraining power of the historical/cultural/discursive/interpretive context

---

[4]Recall from chapter 5 the case, made by Liebrucks (2001) and reinforced by me, that discourses (by definition) reflect beliefs about certain entities. In setting forth Berger and Luckman's "thesis of reflexivity" (from their seminal book *The Social Construction of Reality*), Liebrucks also makes clear that beliefs about psychological entities affect those same psychological entities: "In psychology . . . there is a reflexive relationship between beliefs about the 'objects' of investigation and these 'objects' themselves. . . . Psychological discourses can have an effect on persons" (p. 373).

(which exists "out there," apart from any particular knower) to avoid the wish-it, want-it, think-it/be-it antirealism of radical postmodernism/social constructionism. There thinking it is so allegedly makes it so (because believing is or logically constitutes being), and so fallibilist inquiry cannot obtain. This line of thought reflects the three criteria of realism of some MGTs. First, the meanings (including values) that constitute our psychological existence constrain what can rightly be said about that existence because they exist "out there." Second, thinking does not make it so (at least not logically).[5] Third, fallibilist inquiry follows. To be sure, Criteria 2 and 3 coincide with the conventional definitions of realism given by Searle, Haack, and Thomasson (see chap. 3). By contrast, Criterion 1 poses problems for conventional realism, by blurring the distinction between psychological existence and beliefs/discourses about (or interpretations of) psychological existence; it is just this distinction that makes Criteria 2 and 3 possible (see chap. 5).

MGTs also insist on our ability to transcend or overcome the beliefs/ discourses (or interpretations) that allegedly constitute us psychologically (Criterion 1 of realism), by way of an *agentic interpretive function* that changes our social/psychological existence in some imprecise way. In seeking more precision than they give, I consider at least two possibilities: (a) Do we instantly (and directly) become the new persons we reinterpret ourselves to be (within the constraints of our discursive context) in the agentic moment/act of making new interpretations that reconstitute us psychologically? or (b) do we (indirectly) become the new persons we reinterpret ourselves to be (within the constraints of our discursive context) by first contributing to and thereby altering the interpretive/discursive context that constitutes us psychologically? And in either case, does a logical or causal dependence obtain? That last question has implications not only for agency but also for ontological realism, as we saw in chapter 5.

In sometimes seeming to prefer a constitutive (or logical) rather than a causal dependence of being on interpreting/knowing, some MGTs (e.g., Richardson, Fowers, & Guignon, 1999) appear to reject possibility (b): "This connection between self-interpretation and action is not causal in nature: 'it is not to say that we change our interpretations and then *as a result* our experience . . . alters. Rather . . . certain modes of experience are *not possible* [italics added] without self-descriptions'" (p. 280). However, these same MGTs do not accept possibility (a) either, which seems too radically constructionist/antirealist for them: "Recognizing that our interpretations of our experience can transform it may prompt a leap to thinking that we can arbitrarily give our experience any label we choose and thereby change it at will" (p. 282). Again, their appeal to contextual discursive constraint to support their

---

[5]See chapter 5 for a discussion of the consequences for ontological realism of logical versus causal dependence of psychological existence on discourse about that existence.

realism diminishes the reach of our agency, at least when compared with the "invent your own reality" of radical postmodernism.

To be sure, there are other ways to conceptualize agency. Some of these conflict substantially with MGTs' definitions of agency, in virtue of their appeal both to (a) the individualism that many MGTs reject in their elevation of local community (over individuality) as constitutive of (psychological) personhood and (b) the essentialism that virtually all MGTs reject, in their elevation of local community (over universals of human nature) as constitutive of (psychological) personhood. The MGTs' rejection of individualism on the one hand and essentialism or universalism on the other should not be surprising, given their search for a philosophical middle ground; this they think exists in the contextually constituted nature of personhood. Thus they seem to reject conceptions of agency that include our universal or essential but nonetheless individualistically instantiated capacity for (a) an imaginative function of mind not limited to or constrained by the "horizons" of one's cultural context and for (b) objective knowing, in which there can in principle be knowledge that is independent of the beliefs that help constitute "interpretive frameworks" or "horizons of understanding."

Can MGTs—in their own agentic pursuit of transcendence—avoid the "make our own reality" (either individually or collectively) of radical social constructionist philosophies on the one hand, and the discovery of a preexisting independent reality of modern objectivist philosophies on the other? Does their version of realism succeed in giving us a psychological realism rather than a psychological "realism"? Again, are the constraints on (psychological) existence that the local discursive/interpretive context allegedly supplies substantial and independent enough to support a realist ontology of psychological existence, including the agentic capacity to transcend what exists (see chap. 5)?

In any case, the tension among constraint, realism, and agency remains. If humans are psychologically constituted locally in discursive/interpretive contexts that constrain what can in principle exist psychologically and thus what can be validly said about that existence (because it is in some way real), then how can humans transcend those constraints enough to transform themselves psychologically—how can they self-determine their psychological existence? Put differently, how can they be agentic?

Much to their credit, some MGTs find obstacles to an agentic capacity for self-determination, freedom/autonomy, and ultimately transcendence in their own ontology of "being in the world," in which what anyone can and cannot be within a given context is both constrained and made possible in advance. Some of them rightly question how it is possible to transcend the "hermeneutic circle" they invoke for realist constraint. A very few of them even seem to fear that they may be headed for a form of cultural reductionism (e.g., Jenkins, 2001), a fear analogous to their more ubiquitous concern about other forms of reductionism in psychological inquiry, such as the biological reductionism (e.g., Martin & Sugarman, 2002) that allegedly makes humans nonagentic beings.

This concern is expressed in the following quotations, although some seem more concerned about (a) our ability to be agentic or self-determined persons psychologically, whereas others seem more concerned about (b) our agentic ability to change the traditions that constitute us as agentic or self-determining persons psychologically. Some concern themselves with both (a) and (b). The two concerns correspond, although only imprecisely, to the two possibilities for self-change (one direct, the other indirect) that I pondered earlier in this chapter. Notice the addition of new voices to the discussion.

First, the quotations that pertain to (a), the potential for psychological self-change:

> If culture is so foundational in our way of being, how do we think criti-
> cally, oppose the status quo, and have independent thoughts? How is
> psychological change possible? How do people oppose the mainstream?
> (Cushman, 1995, p. 292)
>
> One's culture might be seen as something like a prosthetic device in
> that agents are only able to live life stories that are possible to imagine
> and undertake in their time and culture. (Howard, 1994, p. 57)
>
> The other limit [other than the human brain] is set by the history of a
> culture. What kinds of cognitive practices and affective reactions are
> implicit in the legitimate practices of a social order? There are limits to
> the sort of being which can be created by Vygotskian appropriation from
> this cultural and anatomical here and now. (Harré, 2002, p. 613)

Now the quotations that pertain either to (b), the capacity to change the traditions that constitute us psychologically, or to both (a) and (b):

> Postmodernists and critical theorists worry that hermeneutics is too cul-
> turally conservative in its emphasis on tradition, social embeddedness,
> and situated truth. . . . Any claims about the metatheoretical status of
> hermeneutics are dependent on showing that critical perspectives can
> arise and be heard within a tradition in such a way that [they] foster
> appropriate and beneficial changes in the tradition. (Fowers, 2001b)
>
> How does one ever manage to become conscious enough of the dis-
> cursive order of one's culture to make transgression and critique pos-
> sible? How . . . does one undergo the transformation from a kind of ob-
> ject, prey to the constrictive forces of society and culture, to a willful
> subject, able both to put into question those narratives assumed to be
> given and to transform in turn the sociocultural surround itself? (Free-
> man, 1993, p. 23)
>
> Social constructionism . . . says relatively little concerning the possi-
> bility of psychologically inspired sociocultural change. And yet, if the
> psychological agency of individual humans could be reduced entirely to
> a hard social determinism, there would be little possibility of explaining

why societies themselves change and evolve over time. (Martin & Sugarman, 1999b, p. 187)

We cannot . . . stand completely outside of all traditions and freely choose what will be preserved and what will be relinquished. This double-edged relationship to tradition Gadamer calls "dialectical." But does simply calling it "dialectical" explain how we can be unable to distance ourselves from tradition and yet have the ability to actively preserve it? (Alcoff, 1996, p. 29)[6]

MGTs must be credited not only for raising these difficult questions but also for working to answer them. Still, I contend that they have not worked out their solutions sufficiently—either for their version of realism or for their version of agency. Before we can consider the success of their solutions, however, let us first consider in more detail their views of agency itself.

AGENCY AS THE CAPACITY FOR TRANSCENDENCE OF CONSTITUTIVE CONTEXTS

Despite giving primacy to culture or tradition and thus rejecting at least any thoroughgoing individualism, MGTs nonetheless claim that individual persons have the potential to reinterpret any local discursive "practice" uniquely. This means we are each potentially free to transcend or overcome the cultural/historical/discursive/interpretive conditions that constitute our thoughts, feelings, and actions—that is, our (allegedly real) psychological existence itself. How is such individualistic agency possible? Is this nod to individualism an oxymoron, given the MGTs' commitment to our local, situated existence within communities? Put differently, are we historical (or interpretation) *all* the way down (see chap. 4, this volume)? If we are, then how is any transcendence possible? After all, "the hermeneutic view makes it clear that we are much more comprehensively embedded in history and culture than the conventional wisdom of modern psychology allows" (Richardson, Fowers, & Guignon, 1999, p. 274).

One way to answer this question is to make the universal or essentialist claim that all humans have the uniquely individual potential to transcend (in uniquely individualistic ways) the limits of the context that only in part makes them what they are. Indeed, it would be hard to conceive of any real agency in completely nonindividualistic or communitarian terms. In chapter 10, I maintain that any rationally based agency has, in its instantiation, both unique particularity and universality built into it (Pols, 1998, 2004b). The question for now is just how MGTs' versions of transcendence (or agency) are supposed to work, given their unqualified ontology of "being in the world"—of being historical, or *local* interpretation, *all* the way down.

---

[6]I am grateful to Jack Martin for bringing Alcoff's work to my attention.

Another solution to the problem of transcendence is to say that the historical/cultural/discursive/interpretive constraints that constitute us are loose or flexible enough for us to stretch them (and so to reconstitute ourselves in the process); this is not necessarily incompatible with the claim that these constraints make us what we are only in part.[7] But in that case these constraints may not be substantial or constraining enough to support the MGTs' version of ontological realism: This of course constitutes the triadic relation among constraint, realism, and agency that we have already considered.

Let us begin with some answers that MGTs give to their own questions about how transcendence of what now exists (i.e., how agency) is possible. Notice the emphasis on the individualistic cognitive (rational/reasoned) processes of knowing/interpreting in many of these answers, which also contain at least implicit definitions of agency. That emphasis links agentic *being* to agentic *knowing*, and hence ontology to epistemology, respectively. Also note that contextual constraints are sometimes said to limit the extent and nature of the transcendence that is possible; this is no doubt said in the service of realism. Finally, although I have divided these answers into several themes, the themes overlap considerably; the initial description of each theme merely gives my intended emphasis. As we saw in the previous set of quotations, within each theme we sometimes find a defense of (a) our ability to be agentic or self-determined persons and at other times (b) our ability to change the traditions that constitute us as (agentic or self-determined) persons, or both.

Theme 1. Each individual's enactment of a practice constitutes a new interpretation of that practice, which transforms it. Because there is freedom to reinterpret each practice "anew," we can transform the practices/contexts that constitute us, and in so doing transform ourselves. The "hermeneutic circle" is therefore not a "vicious circle."

Note especially in the first two quotations a nod to particularity's role in constituting what exists more generally.

> When an individual engages in a practice, he or she does not simply follow a formalized script but interprets the practice anew, . . . in the service of specific purposes. . . . [Thus] there are continual opportunities for innovation and evolution of these social practices. . . . Social norms define the practices and create the context of intelligibility for the action, but the practices and norms would cease to exist were it not for the individuals participating in them. (Richardson et al., 1999, p. 284)
>
> A common fear of . . . dialectical reasoning is that it represents a vicious circle,[8] in which we are entrapped. The hermeneutic circle is not vicious, because the relationship between part and whole are not entirely determinate. The part-whole dialectic is dynamic; it always in-

---

[7] I am grateful to Tim McIntire for suggesting this point.
[8] See Guignon (2002a, p. 278), for further discussion of how the hermeneutic circle is not viciously circular.

cludes the possibility that additional readings of specific examples . . .
will require shifts in the overall interpretation or that a better articulation of the global perspective will lead to alterations and improvements
in the partial readings. (Richardson et al., 1999, p. 303)

The circularity of . . . a hermeneutical understanding is neither vicious nor . . . a defect. It is seen as such only when judged by the mistaken
and unwarranted epistemological demands for empirical verification.
(Bernstein, 1983, p. 134)

On the one hand, we inevitably draw our choices from the culturally
given possibilities available to us. . . . [Thus] we are always tied to our
cultural upbringing. . . . On the other hand, we can reinterpret what we
have inherited to create new prospects for living. . . . Every time we
engage in a cultural practice, we are interpreting it, which makes the
reinterpretation of culture almost continuous. (Fowers, 2001a, pp. 267–
268)

The subject matter of therapeutic conversation is how best to live our
lives in concrete situations where we are already defined by some serious
commitments and identifications but have a measure of freedom to work
out how they might best be interpreted. (Richardson et al., 1999, p. 263)

Psychological individuals, through their imaginings, intentions, and
actions, are capable of influencing the societies that have spawned them
in ways that explain the evolution and change clearly evident in sociocultural history. (Martin & Sugarman, 1999b, p. 187)

That psychological individuals shape societies and cultures is undeni-
able, another ineluctable existential condition. (Martin & Sugarman,
1999a, p. 31)

Theme 2. Reflective or reflexive forms of human agency/consciousness
(including imagination) allow creativity and transcendence (or change) of
the context and thus of experience or existence itself.

Though always rooted in a given practice, theory involves imaginative
reflection on possible modifications of that practice. And though imagination is always constrained by established practice, it is not confined to
slavish, mechanical repetition. Changing circumstances and encounters
with other practices can nourish the imagination; and since no practice
is defined for all possible situations, there is always need for imaginative
projections and creative decisions in pursuing a practice. (Bohman, Hiley,
& Shusterman, 1991, p. 13)

Our theory assumes a shifting emergent ontological status for the psychological, one that develops and changes as the individual gradually
develops and emerges, as reflective forms of human agency come to transcend the basic existential condition of throwness. . . into pre-existing
physical and sociocultural worlds. (Martin & Sugarman, 1999a, p. 38)

[There are] emergent capacities for forms of memory and imagination
that . . . permit a reflexive intentionality capable of entertaining possibilities not available in the sociocultural features of the developmental
context. . . . Through the exercise of human creativity associated with

reflexive consciousness and intentionality, possibilities for new sociocultural practices are made available. (Martin & Sugarman, 1999a, p. 117)

Theme 3. Self-interpretation or self-understanding allows for self-determination (i.e., agentic acts, including experiences), at least to some extent, given the discursive/interpretive (among other) constraints that determine the form and content of self-understanding and self-determination.

In most of the next few quotations, these self-interpretations and understandings—although contextually situated or constrained—are nonetheless conceived in individualistic terms. However, in one quotation (of Richardson et al., 1999), these provide the "background" that is "circulating in a historical culture." This assertion suggests that self-understanding is itself part of the discursive/interpretive context that exists "out there," beyond any particular person's mind, which context determines or constrains the possible self-understanding of any particular person in that context.

> Agency as self-determination equates to a kind of self-understanding that permits a deliberative, reflective activity in selecting, choosing, framing, and executing actions. While there is some limited origination in this, . . . psychological persons can never stand outside of the determining influence of relevant physical, biological, and sociocultural (especially relational and linguistic) factors and conditions. (Martin & Sugarman, 2002, p. 419)
>
> Because human psychological beings are agents who are aware and reflective . . . , their courses of action and ways of being are affected not only by the classifications of societies and cultures, but also by their own conceptions of, and reactions to, such classifications. Thus, an individual's experience . . . is constituted in part by the individual's own understanding [and reasoning][9]. . . . This latter understanding obviously reflects a life of immersion in socioculturally available practices, but also is based on a somewhat inevitably unique set of experiences of any psychological individual within those practices. (Martin & Sugarman, 1999b, p. 190)
>
> Humans must be seen as self-interpreting beings whose defining traits are shaped by the stands they take in being participants in a public life world. . . . Our intentions, desires, and beliefs are made possible and given concrete form by the background of self-interpretations and self-assessments circulating in a historical culture. . . . Humans just *are* what they interpret themselves as being within their social context. (Richardson et al., 1999, p. 236)
>
> We are . . . finite beings whose existence is embedded in a world that makes binding demands on us because it makes us the people we are. . . . We are [also] active beings. We find ourselves thrown into a world we neither create nor control, but it is up to each of us to take up the possibilities of self-understanding into which we are thrown, and shape them

---

[9]The word *reasoning*, which implies rationality, is paired with *understanding* in similar quotations from Martin et al. (2003, pp. 82–83, 112).

into lives that are our own. . . . Human existence involves living in a *tension* between thrownness and projection. (Guignon, 2002b, pp. 95–96)

Theme 4. Self-interpretations and self-understandings (including theories, narratives, and imaginings about the self) constitute the self itself, which is always underdetermined (by contextualized experiences) and thus unpredictable. The unpredictability of individual selves/persons has implications for the nature of (psychological) existence, as well as psychological inquiry.

> Personal theories, including theories of self, arise from but are underdetermined by human experience in sociocultural contexts. . . . Once formed, these theories evolve in unpredictable ways that are not entirely determined by those experiences. (Martin & Sugarman, 1999a, p. 35)
>
> Can I imagine beyond the limits set by the discursive space that presently obtains? Can I leap out of discourse and into the world? . . . It all depends . . . on how much credence we place in the possibility of transcendence. . . . [There are] narratives of human beings who have managed to emancipate themselves, not from history but from the expected course of things. . . . The self would be rewritten again and again. Is it not precisely this plenitude of meaning, as it exists in the dialogic space between the "I" who interprets and the "me" that is the text, that serves in the end to signal the free operation of narrative imagination? (Freeman, 1993, pp. 199, 216, 221)

Theme 5. Agency is rooted in the human capacity for conscious awareness, rationality/reasoning, or understanding of the self and the world in which the self exists (or is constituted)—all of which are necessary for transcendence/freedom.

> [Life] narratives . . . signify our capacity to become conscious of our worlds and to make something of them; they will serve as testimony to our own power to challenge power. . . . I have the power . . . to become conscious enough of my world to shape my destiny. . . . I can, on occasion, move in the direction of becoming conscious of the ways I am determined, [which] suggests that there exists a margin of freedom within which to think, act, and be. (Freeman, 1993, pp. 216–217)
>
> Humans are, at least, partially, aware of many of their choices and actions. . . . Change in sociocultural practices, conventions, and rules that guide human choice and action may . . . reflect human activity that is nondeliberative. . . . [But] our phenomenal experience of ourselves as intentional agents . . . provides sufficient reason to forego a . . . fully random or unconscious determination. . . . Human choice and action, at least in part and sometimes, result from the irreducible understanding and reasoning of human agents. (Martin & Sugarman, 2002, p. 415)

Theme 6. Agency is the capacity to create not only new meanings/interpretations, narratives, and theories (about oneself, others, and the world) but also new categories of knowledge itself. This "transcendence" is sometimes accomplished through contact with other "traditions," and at other times through a universal or essential but locally/situatedly emergent capacity for (new) meaning making that might sometimes be called an imaginative capacity. These two possibilities for transcendence are not mutually exclusive.

> Although we cannot stand outside ourselves by using rational procedures or find an ultimate foundation . . . we do create an understanding of ourselves, of others, and of our world. But this understanding, he [Gadamer] said, is developed within the context of the tradition of the society to which we belong, and while standing in this tradition through interaction with other traditions, we are able to overcome its limitations and create new categories of knowledge organization. (Polkinghorne, 1983, p. 228)

> Because human psychological beings are agents who are aware and reflective . . . , their courses of action and ways of being are affected not only by the classifications of societies and cultures, but also by their own conceptions of, and reactions to, such classifications. . . . The reflections and actions of classified individuals often result in changes in classification. (Martin & Sugarman, 1999b, p. 190)

> Though imagination is always constrained by established practice, it is not confined to slavish, mechanical repetition. Changing circumstances and encounters with other practices can nourish the imagination. (Bohman et al., 1991, p. 13)

> Although . . . culture is "sedimented" in us, we are not influenced by a single, monolithic culture. . . . Each of us lives at an *intersection* of traditions. . . . Our ability to find other traditions or aspects of our indigenous tradition that help us understand what we disapprove of in our normative community frees us to resist the status quo and develop new alternatives. (Cushman, 1995, pp. 292–293)

> Even while we are indeed bequeathed words that were on the scene well before we ourselves were, there nonetheless remained the prospect of . . . transforming their very meaning. . . . The self, despite its inability to be a sovereign origin of meaning, was significantly more than a merely imaginary artifact of words. . . . "I" am often able to do something new with the words bequeathed me, thereby enlarging the scope of my self and my world. (Freeman, 1993, p. 225)

> Because of the reflective self understanding and reason upon which it ["situated, deliberative agency"] rests, such agency also consists in a kind of self-determination that never acts outside of historical and cultural situatedness, but which can aspire beyond, and cannot be reduced to such situatedness alone. . . . [Agency] has an aspect of origination . . . in the capability . . . to selectively take up, modify, and employ available sociocultural practices and conventions. (Martin & Sugarman, 2002, pp. 421–422)

HOW INDIVIDUALS CAN (AGENTICALLY) TRANSCEND THEIR CONSTITUTIVE CONTEXTS: A CLOSER LOOK

There is a common theme in these quotations. On the one hand, cultural/discursive conditions constrain (and so make possible) the nature of social/psychological existence; and it is just these contextual constraints that are said to make the MGTs' ontology of "being in the world" a fully realist ontology. On the other hand, all individual persons have the potential to transcend the constraints that (in no small part) make them what they are, by means of universal agentic rational interpretive powers. Thus, when speaking of an agentic capacity to transcend discursive/interpretive constraints, we must appreciate the tension between the uniqueness of each individual agent and the generality of the constraining context in which that agent is constituted. As Guignon (2002b) aptly puts it, "Human existence involves living in a *tension* between thrownness and projection. . . . It involves both absorption into humdrum worldly affairs and self-formation across a life-span" (pp. 96–97).

The formulation of this tension may be seen as an instance of the hermeneutic circle itself, in which individuals contribute to the context that constitutes or defines them—hence the repeated use of the term *reflexive* by some MGTs. Yet MGTs are nonetheless left with the daunting task of explaining just how individuals can alter the circular process, assuming they cannot break out of the constitutive circle altogether. Such explanation is needed if the capacity to transcend what is—if the capacity to be self-determining or agentic beings—is to be defended successfully. Being MGTs, they hold the aspiration to moderate, not demolish or obliterate. But this of course lessens the reach of agency, the extent of possible transcendence. As some MGTs put it, we can be "mildly innovative" or have "limited origination" in "selecting and choosing, framing and executing actions" (Martin & Sugarman, 2002, p. 419). Alternatively we have "a measure of freedom to work out how they [our commitments and identifications] might best be reinterpreted" (Richardson et al., 1999, p. 263). Also, there is a "margin of freedom within which to think, act, and be" (Freeman, 1993, p. 217).

It is therefore clear that the historical/cultural/discursive/interpretive constraints that MGTs deploy in the name of ontological realism must lessen the possible reach of the agency to which they remain committed. That they celebrate those constraints owing not only to the realism they allegedly ensure but also to their making possible what we can (in principle) become, is of little help in solving the problem, because what we can become is then limited by the same constraints that constitute (and make real) what we now are. The "self-formation" of which Guignon and others speak must stay within interpretive—or humanly made—limits. As psychologist Louis Sass (1988) expressed Guignon's claim, "Thus, even the nature of our self-interpretations or self-understandings are largely determined by the possibilities laid open by a shared 'we-world'" (p. 246). We are, then, back to the question that directs this chapter: how transcendence of the discourse that constitutes us psychologically is possible, especially if we are seen as historical/interpretation "all the way down."

Two Solutions to the Problem of Unique Transcendence of Constitutive Contexts: The Contextual Versus the Individual

Contained within the six thematic sets of quotations are two types of solutions to this problem. On the one hand, there is something universal or essential about the historical/cultural/discursive/interpretive traditions that constitute us: They themselves give us the raw ingredients to transform them and thus (indirectly) transform ourselves. On the other hand, there is a universal or essential feature of mind that allows us to transcend what now exists, regardless of what the context in which we exist does or does not provide. These are not necessarily mutually exclusive, because historical/cultural traditions are not mind-independent entities (see chap. 5); but there is a different emphasis in each formulation nonetheless. Moreover, each formulation appeals to the universalism/essentialism that MGTs eschew, although what is said to be universal or essential differs.

Solution 1: The Multivocal or Pluralistic Nature/Essence of Cultures

One way out of the standoff between uniquely individual agency on the one hand, and general cultural/discursive constraint on the other, is to claim that all cultures are essentially/necessarily "multivocal." Fowers (2001a), responding to Foucault, says just that.

> Cultures are always multivocal and characterized by ongoing debate about what it means to live well. Moreover, we are not simply helpless puppets of an overwhelming regime of power, because the cultural order exists only through our actions. Each individual act is an interpretation of the customs and practices of a form of life and these interpretations can and do lead to new formulations of the cultural order. (p. 272)

And Fowers adds that not only are cultures multivocal but also that our attachments to them are only partial owing to their multivocal nature.

> When we recognize that our attachment to culture is necessarily specific and partial rather than all-encompassing, we can see that differences between members of the same culture are to be expected as part of the multifaceted nature of culture. In fact, cultural traditions always contain a welter of voices that interpret the customs and practices of the group differently, and these alternative views are often in conflict. The ambiguity of culture is also temporal because all cultural traditions are also evolving over time. (pp. 273–274)

Other MGTs support this view of cultures as essentially or universally pluralistic, as we saw in the quotations in Theme 6. For example, according to Martin and Sugarman (1999b), "Because sociocultural reality is pluralistic, both across and within different societies, individual psychological reality may vary considerably from society to society, from individual to individual, and from time to time" (p. 186). Freeman (1993) observes that there is a "plenitude of meaning" in the "dialogic space between the 'I' who interprets and the 'me' that is the text," which "signal[s] the free operation of the narrative imagination" and thus self-(re)construction (p. 221). Cushman (1995) says that "although . . . culture is 'sedimented' in us, we are not influenced by a single, monolithic culture" (p. 293). Rather, we each live "at an *intersection* of traditions" that "sometimes conflict": "Our ability to find other traditions or aspects of our indigenous tradition that help us understand what we disapprove of in our normative community frees us to resist the status quo and develop new alternatives" (p. 293). Howard (1994) says that an agent can "define meaning in her or his life through some subset of the many ontological stories . . . that are offered by one's culture. . . . Since most cultures entertain multiple construals of reality, people are generally not exposed to only one worldview" (p. 57).

Thus no culture is a monolithic whole; each culture allegedly provides more than enough options from which to (freely?) choose, in defining or determining our existence. If this is true, then we might well ask just what it means to speak of a culture or a tradition as some constraining entity/unity, although that nontrivial question is well beyond the scope of this volume.

Despite these answers to the question of how transcendence is possible, questions remain. For example, what determines that of which—to use Cushman's words—we disapprove? What for him moves us to seek out other traditions in the first place? Is that to be found in culture? Howard (1994) says that "each of us has a need to 'see' life in some basic way or ways" (p. 57), a claim that sounds perfectly universal or essentialist. Yet what if the various worldviews circulating in a culture do not suffice? Then what? (And is that even possible?) After all, taking up a "tradition" (or an aspect of a tradition) by choice is not necessarily the same as transcending what now exists, even if each of us interprets/enacts any given practice within a tradition in her "own" unique way. But how unique can any of us be, and how uniquely can each of us take up what already exists, if each of us is historical/interpretation (or culturally constituted) all the way down? That is, to what extent can we hope to transcend our constitutive contexts? What is the length of our agentic reach? If there can only be "mild innovation," is that sufficient for transcendence? It all depends, of course, on just what is meant by transcendence, and this is not spelled out clearly.

Guignon (1991) relies on Heideggerian distinctions to allow agency to depend on culture without precluding the possibility of "authentic" ways to take up what we find: "When we start from a description of our everyday agency before theorizing, we see that our own identity as agents is bound up with concrete situations and a practical life-world that we *find* rather than create" (p. 99). Yet what is this "everyday agency before theorizing" or "our own identity as agents"? Here is how Guignon (2002b) distinguishes those who live the "inauthentic" life, which consists in "fleeing from one's responsibility for owning up to one's life," from those who live an "authentic" life, which is "characterized by resoluteness" (p. 97). The distinction between authentic and inauthentic agency is noteworthy.

> Heidegger [1962] says that resoluteness pulls you back from "the endless multiplicity of possibilities which offer themselves as closest to one" . . . and enables you to be clear-sighted about what is demanded by the current situation in which you find yourself. . . . [It asks you to] identify what are the "basic possibilities" for you, the possibilities genuinely worth pursuing. . . . Authenticity involves "choosing to choose," that is, wholeheartedly taking over the choices you make and making them your own. (pp. 97–98)

In her account of Heidegger, Grene (1957) equates authenticity with transcendence;[10] like Guignon, she suggests that it is in making what exists one's own[11] that authenticity—and therefore transcendence—obtains. Guignon, in his appeal to Heidegger's "endless multiplicity of possibilities," suggests that culture affords us unlimited options from which to choose. Yet again, if that is the case, then what does it mean to speak of culture—constitutive or otherwise? And even if we have made one of these options "our own" by choosing to choose, have we transcended what is?

Richardson et al. (1999) say something similar, although they end with a moderating twist (between determinism and constructionism) that has an "emanationist" (see chap. 5, this volume) ring to it. Note the scare quotes that adorn the terms *essential natures* and *personal identities*; they deprive those terms of their common or conventional meanings. Thus cultural universals seem to preside over any existing "essentials" of individual human

---

[10]Grene (1957) says,

> Conscience is the call of the self to itself, out of forfeiture to authenticity. . . . I am thrown into a world not of my choosing, and . . . precisely this contingent character of my situation *is*, despite myself, the self I have the task of choosing. Thus in conscience the self bids itself transcend the facticity which it yet inalienably is. (p. 33)

[11]See Robinson (1985, chap. 2) for the distinction between what is "one's" and what is "one's own," in the context of a clear discussion of authenticity.

> [The term *authenticity*] makes a distinction between those reasons or beliefs of a person's that have been externally supplied or imposed or are otherwise "determined," and those which are not thus derived. The distinction is between some attribute or psychological disposition being merely "his" in contrast to being "his own.". . . [Thus] a person may be said to act on the basis of reasons, but the reasons themselves are not something over which the actor has total control, nor are they something of his own making. Like other mental entities, reasons too are supplied from the outside—are *learned*—and are not "authentic." Thus, in the sense in which authenticity has already been used, we can say that an actor's reasons are *his* but not *his own*. (pp. 42–44)

beings, however uniquely what is found in culture may be adopted or owned by individuals.

> In drawing on the interpretations circulating in our public world, we compose our own autobiographies, and in the process we constitute our own "essential nature" or "personal identity." . . . Any drives and needs they [humans] have come to have a determinate form only within the framework of interpretations opened by a cultural clearing. . . . Our nature or being as humans is not just something we *find* (as in deterministic theories), nor is it something we just *make* (as in existentialist and constructionist views); instead it is *what we make of what we find*. (pp. 211–212)

Recall Hersch's (2003) similar (although more expressly epistemological) "co-constitutional" argument that "the realities of human experience or *known* reality can be described as 'both given and made'" (p. 60).

Can we make anything we want of what we find? This seems closer to Freeman's (1993) "free operation of the narrative imagination" (p. 221), which is ensured by the "plenitude of meaning" available to us all. Is the agentic transcendence of what exists anything like an artistic or musical composition—there are certain notes (or colors) available, but we can arrange (or mix) them differently, to produce compositions of unlimited novelty? Psychologist Steven Pinker (1997) suggested something like this in explaining "combinatorics."

> The combinatorics of mentalese, and of other representations composed of parts, explain the inexhaustible repertoire of human thought and action. A few elements and a few rules that combine them can generate an unfathomably vast number of different representations, because the number of possible representations grows exponentially with their size. Language is an obvious example. . . . [And] we are unlikely to have a melody shortage anytime soon because music is combinatorial: if each note of a melody can be selected from, say, eight notes on average, there are 64 pairs of notes, 512 motifs of three notes, 4,096 phrases of four notes, and so on, multiplying out to trillions and trillions of musical pieces. (p. 88)

This statement says nothing about how innovative any new composition can in principle be. Yet Martin and Sugarman repeatedly insist that innovation can only be "mild" or "modest" owing to the cultural constraints that make their (middle-ground) realism possible (Martin & Sugarman, 2000a, p. 402; 2002, p. 419; Martin et al., 2003, pp. x, 89). It therefore seems that innovation that is not merely mild or modest, that breaks with tradition in some profound way, is ruled out by their ontology. This strikes me as problematic given the existence of wildly inventive minds—consider Leonardo's notebooks! However, accounting for wild innovation may not be necessary for the MGTs' ontology of agency/self-determination. But is their constrained agency, then, an agency worth wanting?

In "The Internal Critical Resources of Hermeneutics," Fowers (2001b) explains how transcendence of constitutive contexts is possible. He appeals to the existence of universal, "generic sources of change in [positive][12] traditions." These consist in (a) the "multivocal character" of traditions, which he finds "inevitable, because various participants have widely differing roles and viewpoints within the group"; (b) the fact that "traditions are almost always in contact with their own histories and with other ways of life"; (c) the fact that "every tradition confronts difficulties that arise in its institutions and practices and in the participants' lives, . . . [which difficulties] call for critical reflection of what the form of life takes for granted"; and (d) the fact that "traditions . . . must be appropriated, interpreted, fostered, and perpetuated by humans . . . in order to continue. . . . This process . . . [offers] endless variation and potential change in that tradition."

Fowers (2001b) also enumerates "specific sources of changes in traditions," especially in Western traditions, in which the hermeneutics that he and many other MGTs propound "is embedded." These include (a) the "Enlightenment roots" of Northern Atlantic cultures, which originated in "doubt and critique"; (b) "our shared faith in reform"; (c) our "philosophic liberal tradition," in which "reduction of suffering [is] . . . a primary ideal"; (d) the "dialogic perspective . . . at the heart of hermeneutic philosophy"; and (e) the "critique of ideology" found in some Western traditions.

Despite these apparent mechanisms of change, it remains to be seen just how Fowers's (2001b) "generic sources of change in traditions" can work to transcend the tradition itself, to give way to a new tradition, especially in any radical sense. This is especially poignant given his own adherence to the MGT constitutive ontology of "being in the world": "Traditions are not something alien to us, against which we define ourselves. They are always part of who we are and provide *the terms* [italics added] through which we define ourselves" (Fowers, 2001b). The problem is solved if we accept that transcendence is for various MGTs moderate, mild, or limited—it must be limited, if the constitutive constraints (on social/psychological existence) supplied by the historical/cultural/discursive/interpretive context (or tradition) are constraining or substantial enough to support the ontological realism that MGTs defend. Even if one does not accept that solution, one could still argue that what counts as mild or radical change is itself culturally determined. In any case, Martin et al. (2003) express the former as well as any: "Agency, . . . while certainly not radically free, is nevertheless capable of generating possibilities for action that might deviate *somewhat* [italics added]

---

[12]Fowers (2001b) defines a "negative tradition" as "one in which authority is rigidly held, reinterpretations are strictly inhibited, the past is venerated over the present and future, and the core values of the tradition are presented univocally." They "inhibit actively innovation." "Positive traditions," are "living dynamic collectivities" that are "open to change" by being "multivocal" about their "defining features" and their "future."

from possibilities already experienced" (p. x). Yet Martin et al. (2003) themselves make a strong case for such universal or essential (although individually expressed) functions of human mind as "imaginative projection," "critical self-reflection," "oppositional thinking," and "dialogical engagement" (p. x). Let us therefore now consider this second solution to the problem of how there can be transcendence of constitutive contexts.

Solution 2: The Rational or Imaginative Nature/Essence of Human Mind

MGTs who put the sources of change in traditions within the nature/essence of traditions themselves take for granted the deployment of certain human mental capacities. Most frequently mentioned is the universal or essential cognitive/rational capacity for reinterpretation (of practices within the tradition, among other things). Given their commitment to our agentic nature, it would not make sense to see change (or lack thereof) as something that just happens to us—a mechanistic effect of the nature of the traditions that constitute us rather than an effect of our active participation in those traditions. As Fowers (2001b) aptly put it, "Traditions do not continue through the blind force of inertia alone. The tradition needs to be taken up, affirmed, reinterpreted, and cultivated." There must, then, be a way that humans are—that mind is—regardless of the constitutive context, if any amount of (agentic) transcendence or innovation (or adherence to the status quo) is to obtain. Thus, not surprisingly, we find talk of universal or essential features of mind (i.e., agentic features) by those who otherwise reject universalism and essentialism in human (social/psychological) existence. In other words, agency itself is a universal or essential feature of human being, if not (properly speaking) a psychological kind.

This gives rise to a recurrent dilemma: how we can deploy our rationality (or minds) to transcend (or not to transcend) what exists, because what exists in any context (reflexively) constitutes the rationality (or mind) that is itself deployed within that context? Put differently, for MGTs there is no way that rationality or mind is, independent of the context that constitutes rationality or mind. Recall Alcoff's (1996) Gadamerian claim that "we cannot . . . stand completely outside of all traditions and freely choose what will be preserved and what will be relinquished." (p. 29). Let us consider three MGTs who try to resolve this tension, with unusually explicit attention to mind's universal or essential (rational) powers: Liebrucks (2001), who embodies the moderate social constructionist tradition; Martin and Sugarman (1999a, 1999b, 2000a, 2002; Martin et al., 2003), who embody the hermeneutic tradition; and Freeman (1993), who embodies the narrative as well as hermeneutic tradition.

Liebrucks (2001) takes the universals or essentials of mind seriously when he attributes to all persons the capacity for thinking, remembering, and attending (pp. 374, 381). However, he places these at such a high level of abstraction that they can give us no "concrete" knowledge of human psychological existence, which is for him always context dependent (see chap. 9, this volume). To use his own words again, "Valid accounts that apply to the psychology of all humankind irrespective of time and culture are possible only on a very high level of abstraction" (p. 373). Recall his local ontology of personhood.

> There are properties of persons that exist only in the context of a certain discourse, that is, persons have them only relative to the meaning system of the community to which they belong. . . . [e.g.,] roles [and] . . . so-called intentional states, such as emotions, motives, and attitudes. (p. 374)

For Liebrucks psychology should study the rules and practices of specific contexts that give behavior its meaning at the local discursive level: "Psychological explanations make reference to rules and conventions in order to show how a certain event makes sense in the way that it takes place. The psychological concepts just do not fit into the causal model of explanation" (p. 386). That last sentence matters much. In arguing for "normative necessity" and "semantic necessity" over "causal necessity" (p. 380), Liebrucks rejects the causal determinism that is thought to deprive humans of their agentic/self-determining nature. In claiming that humans constitute themselves psychologically in local discourse, he appears to adopt a logical form of dependence of being on discourse, in the name of agency (see chap. 5, this volume). I shall return to the logical versus causal dependence of personhood on the discursive context, to assess their implications for the capacity to transcend what exists, when what exists is said to constitute mind and agency itself.

Much to their credit, Martin and Sugarman (1999a, 1999b, 2000a, 2002) propose an elaborate theory of individual psychological development, in support of a capacity for transcendence or innovation born of universal/essential agentic powers. Although the powers themselves seem at times to be treated as universal/essential, the effects (or contents) of their deployment are always said to be both constrained and made possible by sociocultural context. Thus for Martin and Sugarman our agentic reach at best attains only "mild innovation." But whatever the magnitude of the reach, do they manage to solve the dilemma of transcending the context that constitutes us? Well, yes and no.

First the yes, if we consider that "our developmentally emergent, constantly evolving theories, memories and imaginings" (1999a, p. 38), our "memorial recollection, imaginative projection, and reason" (2002, p. 421), and our "imaginative projection, critical self-reflection, oppositional thinking, and dialogical engagement" (Martin et al., 2003, p. x) allow us to "transcend our biological, experiential, sociocultural origins through creative, innovative constructions that, while constrained by these origins, are not reducible[13] to them" (1999a, p. 38). Moreover, Martin and Sugarman seemingly extend our agentic reach when they say we are determined or constituted by our contexts only in part: "Psychological reality, reflected in individual psychological agency, is *not entirely* [italics added] determined by those same sociocultural conventions [to which we reflexively contribute]" (1999b, p. 187). So we are not completely determined by, nor are we reducible to, the culture that only in part constitutes us.[14]

Now the no, in the form of a question. To what extent are we not determined by culture? Not much, evidently. "Societies require psychological individuals (selves), and psychological individuals (selves) are *mostly constituted* [italics added], but not entirely constrained,[15] by sociocultural means" (Martin & Sugarman, 1999a, p. 32). "The psychological reality of individuals is not only constrained, but is actually constituted *in large part* [italics added], by socioculturally shared beliefs and practices" (1999b, p. 186). Martin and Sugarman's language seems deliberately vague here, and that is surely out of necessity—what empirical observation (or logical argument) can be used to specify the proportion of mind or rationality that must not be constituted by sociocultural beliefs and practices if there are to be agentic/self-determining powers substantial enough to transcend those (constitutive) beliefs and practices? Still, we may ask whether the claim that we are "mostly" or "in large part" constituted by culture gives our universal/essential agentic capacity the (causal) powers it needs to attain transcendence (of the constitutive culture) that is substantial enough to make a difference—that is, actually to transcend.

Martin and Sugarman (1999b) may have solved the problem by giving each individual a unique set of experiences within any cultural/discursive context. In that case, however much mind is constituted in culture, everyone's mental constitution is necessarily unique—a uniqueness that permits decidedly individualistic expression, if not bona fide transcendence.

---

[13]Elsewhere they insert the word *entirely*, to provide qualification. Psychological agency is thus not entirely reducible to "sociocultural reality" (Martin & Sugarman, 1999b, p. 187).

[14]In his review of *Psychology and the Question of Agency*, psychologist Joseph Rychlak (2004) takes Martin et al. (2003) to task for failing to provide a bona fide explanation of agency by way of the construct "emergence."

> It is argued that "human agency cannot be *reduced* to purely biological and/or cultural determinants, yet must be understood as arising *non-mysteriously* within appropriate developmental, historical, and social contexts." . . . The challenge for their theory is to explain how it is possible for an organism to develop agentic capacities which have broken free of earlier sources of influence. . . . But does emergence really explain anything? . . . [Much of this book] has such a quality of merely describing events taking place, as if this resulted in an explanation of such events. . . . Emergence supposedly permits the breaking of new ground, moving into directions that are based on agential choices rather than on social pressures. . . . [Yet] the authors admit that . . . "a detailed development of such emergentist theorizing is admittedly unavailable at this writing." (pp. 766–767)

[15]The difference (or relation) between constitution and constraint is not readily apparent here.

> An individual's experience . . . is not simply a social construction, but is
> constituted in part by the individual's own understanding of . . . [its]
> significance. . . . Understanding obviously reflects a life of immersion in
> socioculturally available practices, but also is based on a somewhat in-
> evitably unique set of experiences of any psychological individual within
> those practices. (p. 190)

But if every person's experience of his or her cultural/discursive context is truly unique, at least two possibilities obtain: (a) culture itself is so "multivocal" (Cushman, 1995, p. 293; Fowers, 2001b) or fluid that its existence as an entity/unity is called into question, in which case it is hard to see how culture can provide enough constraint to support the ontological realism MGTs defend, and/or (b) the universal/essential properties of mind or rationality are such that they cannot be "in large part" or "mostly" constituted in culture (Martin & Sugarman, 1999a, 1999b).

The distinction between mental processes or functions and mental contents or products of those functions is important here. When Martin and Sugarman (1999b) say, "The psychological reality of individuals is not only constrained, but is actually constituted in large part, by socioculturally shared beliefs and practices" (p. 186), is the psychological reality to which they refer the processes/functions/capacities/acts of mind or rationality, such as the "imaginative projection, critical self-reflection, oppositional thinking, and dialogical engagement" that they themselves specify (Martin et al., 2003, p. 10)? Or is the psychological reality to which they refer the content or product of the "formative" functions of mind/rationality,[16] such as the "theories, memories, and imaginings" they also speak of? In their theorizing about individual agency, they seem to make mental process itself context (and therefore content) dependent—although this is again not quite clear.

> We are not born into a world objectified a priori by a natural ability for
> reflexive thought. Consciousness, subjectivity, and our capacities for
> understanding and knowing, emerge not from an innate Cartesian indi-
> vidual mind primed for ratiocination, but from the fundamentally em-
> bodied nature of our existential involvements. Intentionality . . . is en-
> twined with our physical presence in the world and the world itself.
> (Martin & Sugarman, 1999a, p. 18)

As Martin et al. (2003) sum this up repeatedly, theirs is a "theory of situated, emergent, and deliberative agency" (p. 103; see my note 14). The question is this: Does the dependence of universal/essential mental functions or processes (including consciousness/awareness) on local, particular existence/situatedness "in the world" so affect or determine the nature of those

---

[16]See Pols (1992, 1998) and Held (1995, p. 164) for Pols's distinction between the rational awareness and formative functions of mind or rationality. The former pertains to our capacity to know directly that which we do not constitute in the act of knowing; the latter pertains to our capacity to make, create, or produce such temporospatial entities as houses, chairs, and paintings, and such nontemporospatial/linguistic entities as theories, propositions, and narratives.

functions as functions that we can no longer speak of them, and thus of the agency that depends on them, in universal/essential terms? Is there not universal Knowing, but only local knowing? Not Oppositional Thinking, but only local oppositional thinking, and so on? Is that why there can only be mild or modest, rather than wild or immodest, innovation/transcendence?

Martin and Sugarman (1999a) implicitly give rationality a primary role in agency, when they speak of our capacities for "understanding and knowing," and "ratiocination" (p. 18). Elsewhere they speak explicitly of reason itself: "Human choice and action . . . result from the irreducible understanding and reasoning of human agents" (2002, p. 415). Still elsewhere they say that it is in our ability to comprehend the limits of our situatedness that the possibility of transcendence, although still modest, obtains: "The conception of personhood . . . is that of a subjectivity . . . capable of comprehending something of . . . [its] situatedness and its limitations, with the possibility of moving modestly beyond them" (2000b, p. 402). In chapter 10, I elaborate the place of reason/rationality (and of objective knowing or rational awareness) in agency; there I give my own conception of an agency worth having.

As much as they give the universal/essential features of mind or rationality their due, Martin and Sugarman—in insisting that innovation can be only mild or modest (2002, p. 419)—make culture at least as prominent as those features in explaining our agentic powers. Although they insist that mind is not reducible to culture, I nonetheless find in their words nods to cultural reductionism, or at least relativism. For example, in seeking a middle ground between the individualism of "cognitive constructivism" and the contextualism of "social constructionism," they try to integrate the two (1999a, pp. 99–106): although "contemporary Western culture" would not have been the same without the uniquely innovative minds of Da Vinci, Bach, Descartes, and Einstein (Martin et al., 2003, p. 85), "for an individual transformation to be called creative, it must manifest both significance and value" (1999a, p. 110), and these are determined contextually—"creativity requires evaluation according to sociocultural standards" (1999a, p. 112). "If an individual transformation is to be authorized as creative, it must pass from the domain of the private-individual to the private-collective" (1999a, p. 111).

I agree that for a transformation to be called, evaluated as, or authorized as creative, social values are brought to bear. Yet I do not think that a transformation *is* or *is not* creative on the basis of anyone's beliefs about its innovative qualities (although what *counts* as creative may of course vary contextually). Thus the work of Da Vinci, Bach, Descartes, and Einstein would have been innovative/creative, even if no one ever believed it to be such. It is similar to the examples of stonewalling (Fowers, 1998; Richardson et al., 1999) and racism that we considered in chapter 5. As long as certain constellations of behaviors exist, stonewalling and racism exist, even if no one notices or labels them as such. Thus we again arrive at the crucial point in defense of realism. Although certain entities are mind dependent—they could not exist if there were no minds—they are not dependent on beliefs about the existence and nature of those entities (see note 3); hence there can be massive ignorance and gross error, even about their very existence (Thomasson, 2003). These are the very conditions that permit the fallibilist inquiry on which some MGTs rely in defending the ontological realism of human (social/psychological) kinds.

Let us return to Martin and Sugarman's (2000a) suggestion that it is through our capacity to comprehend something of our "situatedness and its limitations" that the "possibility of moving modestly beyond them" obtains (p. 402). In this we at last reach the conclusion that knowledge of the limits of our situatedness can set us free, if only a little. This is important because it suggests that (for them) agentic existence is linked intimately to our capacity to know what surrounds us—what constrains us—to transcend those enabling constraints. Here, then, we find another link between ontology and epistemology in the MGTs' quest for a truth-tracking form of psychological inquiry that preserves human agency. A similar link is made by Freeman (1993), who hinges freedom or transcendence on our ability to become aware of what (necessarily) constrains us.

> [Narratives] signify our capacity to become conscious of our worlds and to make something of them. . . . To speak of the social construction of the self . . . is not to claim that we are prisoners of history, mechanically determined by our conditioning. . . . While what I think and feel and do and say is surely a function of the time and place in which I live, . . . I also have the power—contingent, of course, on the conditions present, whether they are stultifying or liberating[17]—to become conscious enough of my world to shape my destiny. . . . Perhaps, I am relying on a kind of faith when I make this claim; it could very well be . . . that I am nothing but a product or an ideological effect . . . [of] forces I will never know. I just don't happen to believe this is so. . . . That I can, on occasion, move in the direction of becoming conscious of the ways I am determined, suggests that there exists a margin of freedom within which to think, act, and be. (p. 217)
>
> As Bakhtin (1986) has written, "The better a person understands the degree to which he is externally determined, the closer he comes to understanding and exercising his real freedom." (p. 24)

Like Martin and Sugarman, then, Freeman hinges the agentic power to challenge (what now is), to chart our own course (if only with a "margin of freedom"), on mind's (seemingly universal/essential) rational capacity to know the nature of our situatedness, with all its constraining or enabling features—although he, like Fowers (1998), makes this power of mind contingent on the "stultifying or liberating" conditions in which minds exist. This makes the potential for transcendence in oppressive situations less likely; and these

---

[17]This distinction is similar to Fowers's (2001b) distinction between "positive" and "negative" traditions. (See note 12.)

are (ironically) just the situations in which it is most needed (cf. Jenkins, 2001; Rychlak, 1997).

Moreover, nowhere in these quotations of Martin and Sugarman (2000a) and Freeman (1993) do we find the suggestion that our (conscious) awareness or knowledge of what limits or determines us fails to attain the status of (epistemically) realist awareness/knowledge. That is, what we know about these limits is not determined merely by our beliefs about these limits; we seemingly have access to them as they exist, independently of our beliefs about their existence and nature. Yet because these authors (like all MGTs) rightly say we cannot know with certainty, they wrongly conclude we cannot know with objectivity. And so we find another irony in their writings: on the one hand, an implicit faith in our ability to transcend contextual constraints by knowing (something about) what they *are*, but on the other hand, a strong antiobjectivist epistemology that runs throughout the writings of all the MGTs whom I have encountered. We cannot have objective knowledge about the human world, they say, not only because we can never have the certitude they suppose objectivity requires but also because we can never have "the view from nowhere" that they also suppose objectivity requires owing to our situated existence or "being in the world." Freeman anticipates part of the epistemic problem that agency poses.

> We *know* that discourse and all the rest affect us; we can prove it through empirical study. But we can never know, with any certainty, whether freedom exists or whether the self can indeed be seen as an originator of meaning and action, whether it can take what is and do something different with it.[18] (pp. 217–218)

Martin and Sugarman (2002) have somewhat different reasons for saying that there is only "limited origination" in our "deliberative, reflective activity" (p. 419). They appeal to the situated nature of agency (ontology) more than to uncertainty and lack of empirical proof (epistemology). In chapter 10, I make a case for the intimate link between the objectivist epistemology MGTs reject and the agentic ontology they exalt. In making that case, I shall appeal to something more than faith in our rational knowing powers; I shall appeal to demonstrations of those powers in the self-reflexive act of our deployment of them.

THE NATURE OF DEPENDENCE REVISITED: CAUSAL DEPENDENCE, LOGICAL DEPENDENCE, AND AGENCY

Have MGTs made their case for agency/transcendence, either in virtue of the multivocal nature of all traditions or the universal/essential rational

---

[18]Rychlak (1980, 1994, 1997, 2001, 2004), although not an MGT, uses his own extensive empirical evidence to defend free will/agency, in just the way that Freeman denies—that the self is indeed the originator of meaning and (purposive) action. This I consider in chapters 9 and 10.

interpretive functions of human mind, or both? Is the glass half empty or half full? Or is it so full of holes that it holds no water? As we saw in considering the "emanationist" or "emergent" theory of reality/truth (chap. 5), philosopher Christopher Norris (1997) declared the latter. He finds the "hermeneutic circle" to be "viciously circular," because

> nothing could count as an object [or give evidence of its nature/properties] . . . except insofar as it showed up among the range of currently accepted practices and beliefs. . . . There could be no escaping the 'hermeneutic circle' which Heidegger—and Gadamer after him—have raised to a high point of interpretive principle. (p. 147)

Norris (1990) rhetorically asks something akin to what I have asked repeatedly: "Do interpretative conventions go *all* [italics added] the way down, thus rendering 'theory' just a species of rhetorical psychological back-up for beliefs that are always already in place before the theorist gets to work on them?" (p. 107).

Although Norris (1990, 1997) does not cite the MGTs whom I assess,[19] he anticipates and dismisses their arguments about transcendence/innovation and the nature of psychological inquiry. In chapters 8 and 9 we shall encounter MGTs who indeed celebrate psychological theory as a form of practice.[20] They maintain that values are a large and proper part of establishing epistemic warrant; that in fact there is no fact/value distinction in psychological inquiry, nor should there be. In any case, because MGTs equivocate about the nature (i.e., logical vs. causal) of the alleged dependence of psychological existence on historical/cultural/discursive/interpretive contexts (see chap. 5, this volume), their case about agency/transcendence is problematic—as is their case for what psychological inquiry should consist in. Let us therefore reexamine the implications for agency/transcendence of interpreting, first in logical and then in causal terms, MGTs' ontological claims about the dependence of psychological existence on (the prior, although ever-evolving) existence of discourses/interpretations. In chapter 9, I assess how those claims relate to their views about proper forms of psychological inquiry.

Logical Dependence of Psychological Existence on Discourse/Interpretations

In chapter 5, I defined logical dependence or logical necessity as follows: Something (x) cannot, in principle, exist unless something else (y) exists. The very idea of x contains or presupposes the existence of y. When

---

[19]However, he seems to equate the hermeneutic foundation of some MGTs with radical postmodernism in general (Norris, 1997, p. 137), which—if valid—challenges their own claim to have avoided that extreme.

[20]For example, Richardson et al. (1999) entitle their final chapter "Social Theory as Practice."

MGTs say or suggest that personhood, or psychological properties of persons, could not in principle exist if there were no (local) discourses about persons and their psychological properties, they are saying that the very idea of personhood contains or presupposes the existence of (local) discourses (including beliefs) about the nature of personhood. Thus personhood could not in principle exist without discursive/interpretive contexts in which there are discourses or beliefs about the nature of personhood; it cannot be otherwise (Thomasson, 2003). Logical dependence is therefore a matter of logical necessity, and so it is more constraining than causal dependency. In chapter 5, I also gave a series of exemplary quotations, in which MGTs seem to oscillate between two forms of dependency: (a) Within any discursive/interpretive context, psychological properties of persons are logically dependent on discourses about persons; and (b) Within any discursive/interpretive context, psychological properties of persons are merely causally dependent on discourses about persons. This oscillation creates ambiguity about the nature of the agency that MGTs propound, including its reach as well as its ontological realism.

Let us return to the example of stonewalling that we considered in chapter 5. Recall that according to Fowers (1998) and Richardson et al. (1999, p. 288), the "constellation of behaviors" that compose stonewalling does not "stand up and identify itself" unless that constellation is interpreted *as stonewalling*. Richardson et al. (1999) state, "Instead it [stonewalling] is differentiated by the speaker, the observer, and possibly the listener, as salient in a particular context" (p. 288). In both texts the authors suggest that stonewalling does not exist (as stonewalling) unless "it is interpreted *as such*" [italics added] (Fowers, 1998; Richardson et al., 1999, p. 288). Thus the existence of stonewalling is dependent on interpretations that logically constitute certain behaviors as stonewalling; it (and other psychological kinds) is logically dependent on discourse about that kind, and so cannot in principle exist without that discourse. This is precisely the claim Thomasson (2003) opposes about such "opaque" human kinds as racism, which depend on minds but not discourses/beliefs about those kinds for their existence. That stonewalling does not "stand up and identify itself" means it does not have mind-independent boundaries, but that fact does not automatically preclude it from being subject to real/fallibilist inquiry and discovery. It can therefore have the realist ontology that MGTs purport social/psychological kinds to have.

Does this argument pertain to agency as well as to stonewalling and racism? Can there be agency (or self-determination) if agency depends logically on discourse about agency, discourse that exists "out there," apart from any particular agent's mind? If that were so, there might be little hope of agentic or intentional transcendence/innovation, in the sense of the self-determination about which some MGTs speak, because then what I (or anyone) can even hope to be depends logically on what already exists discursively. This could hold even if I (like all members of my "discursive community") am said to contribute reflexively to that discourse in some (unspecified) way. Alternatively, if psychological properties depend logically and literally on *self*-generated discourses about those properties, on *self*-interpretations themselves, then there may be unlimited agency, depending on the extent to which self-interpretations remain unconstrained by the discursive context in which selves are said to interpret themselves—that is, depending on the source or origin of self-interpretations. Martin and Sugarman (2002) logically stake a middle ground between these two extremes by defending only "mild innovation," in which there can be at best "limited origination" (p. 419). They—like other MGTs—seem to appreciate that if self-interpretations are quite unconstrained, then we are back in the radical postmodernist believe-it, think-it/be-it antirealist version of "agency" that MGTs hope to avoid.

Here it might help to introduce some distinctions about logical dependence that could permit greater or lesser choice or agency owing to the way the alleged dependence operates. I refer to the distinction between rigid dependence, or "dependence on a particular individual [or thing]," and generic dependence, or "dependence on something or other of a particular type" (Thomasson, 1999, p. 27). Because Liebrucks (2001) and Richardson et al. (1999) sometimes say that emotion is dependent on the discourse/language that (logically) constitutes it, let us use that example. I begin with two propositions about generic dependence.[21]

Proposition 1

If emotions depend generically on discourse only in the most general way, then there might only need to be discourse sophisticated enough to give those who participate in it the idea of emotion in general. In that case each individual type of emotion need not be picked out or defined within that discourse in order for any particular emotion to exist. So it is in principle (logically) possible for someone to transcend the emotions currently experienced in a discursive context, as long as the dependence of emotion on discourse is generic (enough).

Proposition 2

But if emotions depend generically on much more specific types of discourse, then there might need to be discourse in which that very emotion is picked out or defined for any particular emotion to exist. In that case there could, for example, be no joy unless there was discourse about joy that (logically) constituted joy; there could be no sorrow unless there was discourse about sorrow that (logically) constituted sorrow. If this more specific kind of generic dependence obtains, no new emotions could exist (i.e., be experi-

---

[21]Several discussions with Amie Thomasson during March and April 2003 helped me to formulate these distinctions.

enced and expressed) without the relevant conceptual repertoire of the community first changing. In that case emotional transcendence, at least any thoroughgoing emotional transcendence, would be difficult—if not impossible.

The case of rigid dependence is even more limiting, because then each instance of the relevant emotion depends on an instance of interpreting it as such. So if one did not interpret an emotion to be joy, one would not in that moment be able to experience joy. In that case we must ask if we can in principle be wrong or fallible about the emotions we are experiencing, a question that reopens the issue of the ontological realism of human kinds. Liebrucks (2001), who seems to prefer a logical to a causal dependence of psychological kinds on discourse about those kinds, says we can.

> We can be . . . deceived about our emotions. Therefore we sometimes correct our emotional self-apprehension, we sometimes say that we are unclear about our emotions, and we sometimes even admit that others know our emotions better than we do ourselves. . . . We can mistake our motives and attitudes just as much as we can mistake our emotions. (pp. 376–377)

Although I agree with Liebrucks, I would express the possibility of error in the case of rigid dependence a bit differently. Thus even in rigid dependence (in which each instance of a particular experience depends on an instance of interpreting it as just that experience), there is some room for error: Although "interpreting-as-joy" (to stick with that example) is (logically) necessary for joy to be experienced (and so to exist), this does not say that "interpreting-as-joy" is sufficient for joy to obtain. Presumably, then, the possibility is left open that one could interpret oneself as feeling joy when, for example, one feels some other emotion or even no emotion at all. To be sure, this is a limited kind of fallibility. However, it does seem to follow (logically) that if one has an emotion one must (necessarily) interpret oneself as having just that emotion in the moment one is having it, or one is not (by definition) having that emotion.

Richardson et al. (1999) quote Charles Taylor to imply a generic form of dependence that is more specific (i.e., Proposition 2, although rigid dependence is not ruled out), in that particular types of emotions seem to depend (logically) for their existence (experience or expression) on particular types of descriptions/language.

> "To say that language is constitutive of emotion is to say that experiencing an emotion essentially involves seeing that certain descriptions apply." . . . And seeing what descriptions apply determines the quality of the feelings. . . . Feelings cannot be thought of simply as objects with determinate characteristics independent of any interpretations or meanings. (p. 220)

But what of our (reflexive) input into the discursive/interpretive context? Can we deliberately bring new emotions into existence indirectly by first making the agentic move of contributing to and so altering the discursive context that constitutes us psychologically? This is problematic, because it could make novel emotions causally dependent on our agentic acts, and here Richardson et al. (1999) seem to invoke logical dependence. Elsewhere Richardson et al. (1999) quote Taylor to reinforce their commitment to logical dependence, and their rejection of causal dependence. In doing so they reject the possibility of choice or agency (which they rightly link to causality) in the matter.

> This connection between self-interpretation and action is not causal in nature: "it is not to say that we change our interpretations and then *as a result* our experience of our predicament alters. Rather . . . certain modes of experience are not possible without certain self-descriptions." (p. 280)

Woolfolk, Sass, and Messer (1988), in referring to Taylor and Gadamer, said something similar: "We are constituted by our self-interpretations; but . . . these interpretations are not freely chosen or consciously recognized, since they are so deeply embedded in culture, history, and bodily being" (p. 16).

What about the universal/essential imaginative agentic capacities that Martin and Sugarman entertain as a means to transcendence? I have not noticed in their many writings language that could be fairly interpreted either in terms of logical or causal dependence. However, because imagination is central to what is at stake in the very idea of agency/transcendence, it may be worth considering how the case of imagination could play out logically. Yet it is hard to see how imagination itself would be logically dependent on discourse: What could it possibly mean to say that discourse logically determines, either generically or rigidly, the content of what an individual is able to imagine—that certain imaginative products, or even imaginative activity in general, could not happen without certain forms of discourse?

One sensible answer is that the possibilities within which one can imagine are sketched out in advance by forms of discursive practices in the community. That is, the concept of imagination has built into it (or logically presupposes) the idea that what I imagine must be meaningful, if the (imaginative) act is to count as imagination, and something is meaningful only if it has an accepted meaning in the practices of some community or discursive/interpretive context.[22] This fits with Liebrucks's (2001, p. 380) notions of "semantic necessity" and "normative necessity," as well as with Martin and Sugarman's (1999a, 2002) insistence on possibility and constraint within a context, which complements their settling for "mild" or "modest" innovation. Thus "transcendence" is possible, as long as we limit the imagination

---

[22]I am again grateful to Amie Thomasson for her help in my formulation of this.

that gives rise to it to the possibilities that are laid out for us in advance, or are logically predetermined by local discursive practices. Whether MGTs would find this definition of agency/transcendence acceptable remains to be seen.

Causal Dependence of Psychological Existence on Discourse/Interpretations

Causal dependence, recall, is a lesser matter and so may be seen as less constraining than logical dependence, because it does not involve logical necessity (see chap. 5, this volume).[23] Even if something (e.g., psychological properties of persons) had never come into existence without some other entity (say, discourse about those properties), according to causal dependence, this could in principle have been otherwise (Searle, 1995, p. 156). There is nothing that makes it logically necessary that it turned out the way it did, causally speaking.

Also recall that sometimes MGTs oscillate between language that suggests a logical (constitutive) dependence of psychological existence on discourse about that existence and language that suggests a causal dependence of psychological existence on discourse about that existence. The latter is signaled when MGTs say that discourse/interpretations causally affect, bring about, bring into being, alter, shape, change, create, impact, and influence the psychological properties of persons (see chap. 5 for quotations). In so suggesting causal dependence, MGTs also appear to suggest that it is in principle possible for psychological properties of persons to exist without discourse about those properties. Their position is therefore confusing, because they also say that personhood is constituted logically in discourse (about personhood). The consequence of all this oscillation for their view of agency is that that too seems unclear.

In chapter 5, I also said that when causal language "seeps into" MGTs' discourse, it does so with a purpose: It preserves the agency that MGTs defend, although this preservation depends on the way causal language is used. Causal language sometimes invokes an active and sometimes a passive view of persons; it depends on who or what is the cause of some effect, and who or what is the effect of some cause. Moreover, in the present chapter, I asked if our seemingly universal/essential, agentic interpretive powers allow us deliberately to causally affect our psychological existence indirectly, by first changing our discourse about that existence. First we (causally) change the discursive/interpretive context that constitutes us; then, as a result of this action, we (automatically? instantaneously?) become (logically) "reconstituted." This

---

[23]It should by now be apparent that I am not attempting to work out a causal ontology of human/mental kinds. See Pols (1998) for just such an ontology.

seeming "mix and match" of causal and logical dependence to retain agency is hard to fathom.

Richardson et al. (1999) have been most extensive in rejecting all forms of causal dependence. Yet they sometimes suggest an agentic causal relation between interpretation and existence. They speak of "recognizing that our interpretations of our experience can transform it," although they deny that we can "change it at will" just by giving "our experience any label we choose" (p. 282). Yet they also say that therapists intentionally (or willfully) "focus a good deal of effort on changing this constellation of self-interpretation, behavior, and experience" (p. 280). They use the reasonable example of therapy with victims of sexual assault, in which the therapist aims to reinterpret the victim's sense of powerlessness, to "transform her powerlessness into justified anger about it, thereby moving her from a victim stance to a position of greater strength" (p. 281). If the therapy is successful, "it profoundly changes the survivor's self-understanding, affective experience, behavior, and, indeed, identity as a survivor" (p. 281). Although this suggests a causal dependence of experience and behavior on (in this case therapeutic) interpretation, Richardson et al. (1999) do not say that the broader discursive context must first be changed for personal change to occur. Still, they seem to assume the necessity of at least a contextual basis for such therapeutic intervention in the first place: "We need to . . . reconceptualize therapy as a specialized form of hermeneutic dialogue, one that is shaped . . . by the current cultural conversation and struggle, and, in turn, contributes its own voice and influence to that conversation and struggle" (p. 276).

Despite all due caveats about cultural constraint, these passages about therapy make use of perfectly conventional cause/effect language: (Therapeutic) discourse can causally affect or determine something more than discourse (as well as discourse). If we can indeed choose to change (i.e., self-determine) our psychological existence by changing our discourse/beliefs about our existence, either individually or collectively, do we again achieve agency at the price of realism? Not if we can actually become what we interpret ourselves to be, either individually or collectively. In that case the causal dependence of psychological existence on beliefs/discourse about psychological existence does not threaten the ontological realism of psychological kinds, because there is then a way the (psychological) world is that does not depend on beliefs about the nature of the (psychological) world (Searle, 1995; see chap. 5, this volume). But if we "just" or "simply" are what we interpret ourselves to be (Martin et al., 2003, p. 77; Richardson et al., 1999, p. 236), then the complete logical dependence of psychological existence on beliefs about that existence disallows the fallibilist inquiry that is necessary for ontological realism—that is, we cannot in principle be wrong about the nature of psychological existence. Whether discursive constraint on what exists psychologically is sufficient for realism depends, then, on the logical versus causal nature of the dependence, and that remains unclear owing to linguistic oscillation in MGTs' writings about just that.

In chapter 9, I consider ways in which MGTs' views about causality inform their approaches to psychological inquiry, including its proper products. At this point let us consider the stability of our psychological existence. Although MGTs do not resolve questions about just how our psychological existence depends on local discursive contexts (i.e., the causal vs. logical nature of that dependence) and so do not resolve the tension between (their version of) realism and agency, they seem unified in their reasonable insistence that humans evolve psychologically over time, both individually and collectively. The extent of the stability of their ontology of human psychological existence has implications not only for agency but also for their approach to psychological inquiry. It is to their views about stability, which constitute Ontological Point 4, that we now turn.

7

ONTOLOGICAL POINT 4:
AN ONTOLOGY OF FLUX AND FLOW

There is one more way in which middle-ground theorists (MGTs) attempt to avoid the psychological "ontology" set forth in radical postmodernist inquiry and the psychological ontology set forth in conventional modernist inquiry. On the one hand, they reject the existence of rigidly stable/unchanging psychological entities, kinds, or forms (even within any given discursive/interpretive context); these they attribute to those who work in conventional modernist traditions. Such an ontology cannot obtain owing to our agentic capacity to transcend discursive constraints on our (local) social/psychological existence, by means of our reflexive interpretive powers. Hence we can in principle change ourselves psychologically through acts of (re)interpretation. Knowing about being reflexively affects being.

On the other hand, MGTs also reject an ontology of unmitigated chaotic flux; this they attribute to those who work in radical postmodernist traditions, despite the "ontological mutism" professed by certain prominent members of that tradition (see chap. 4). Such an ontology cannot obtain because the extent of transcendence that we can hope to attain (i.e., our agentic "reach") is always limited by the discursive constraints that are said (alternately) to constitute us logically or affect us causally; it is such constraint, after all, that supports the MGTs' version of ontological realism (see chap. 5). As we saw in chapter 6, the transcendence that we can in principle attain is frequently said to be "mild" or "modest"; it is never so radically transformative that it allows us to become just what we believe or interpret ourselves to be.

And so MGTs once again aim for an ontological middle ground: Although theirs is a psychological ontology of "flux and flow," the psychological entities that "evolve" or "emerge" within historical/cultural/discursive/interpretive contexts are said to be stable enough to be real, and so to allow truth-tracking (or realist) inquiry about them. In short, our psychological existence is somewhat stable, because (a) the contexts in which that existence is embedded are somewhat stable (despite our reflexive contributions to those contexts) and (b) our capacity for agentic transcendence is itself limited by those contexts. Yet this, to be sure, is a psychological stability only within a context, because for MGTs there exist no universal/essential psychological entities. Let us look more closely at these claims.

THE DEFENSE OF STABILITY WITHIN FLUX

A Postmodernist Ontology of Extreme Flux

Not all MGTs have taken a moderate position in regard to the stability of social/psychological entities. In chapter 3, I included Daniel Fishman (1999) among the MGTs in virtue of his extensive effort to "transcend the dialectic" between modern positivist and postmodern constructionist/hermeneutic paradigms by way of his "postmodern pragmatism"; he claims this paradigm to be a "hybrid of the other two" (p. 101). Nonetheless, he (sometimes) propounds what sounds more like a radical postmodernist ontology of extreme flux. In *The Case for Pragmatic Psychology* (1999), he also advocates an antiobjectivist or antirealist epistemology, although in a more recent article Fishman (2001) says he adopts a more moderate epistemology, one that "falls in the middle of the realist versus constructionist continuum" (p. 279). It is hard to say just where he stands ontologically in the 2001 article, because there he says that

> moderate constructionism [which he supports and which he says is based in "pragmatic relativism"] is consistent with pragmatism's de-emphasis on ontological issues of what is real and its alternative focus on morality and the striving toward human betterment and democratic decision-making processes. (p. 280)

This is not quite the ontological mutism of radical constructionists, but it is at least a "muted" form of mutism, and certainly one that departs from the positive ontological pronouncements of other MGTs. In any case, let us consider his views about ontological flux, in which the ontological glass seems more empty than full.

> Philosophical pragmatism is founded upon a social constructionist theory of knowledge. The world that exists independently of our minds is an unlimited complex of change and novelty, order and disorder. . . . We take on different conceptual perspectives, as we might put on different pairs of glasses, with each providing us a different perspective on the world. The pragmatic "truth" of a particular perspective does not lie in its correspondence to "objective reality," since that reality is continuously in flux. Rather, the pragmatic truth of a particular perspective lies in the usefulness of the perspective in helping us to cope and solve particular problems. (Fishman, 1999, p. 130)

In professing an ontology of continuous flux, Fishman makes a perfectly objective claim about how the world/reality is, one that does not seem to require the perspectivally mediating lenses he deems necessary to attain other relativistic "truths." But such a claim in no way compromises the ontological realism that MGTs profess, because the world could in principle be just this way, regardless of our beliefs about its nature. Still, Fishman seems to recognize that such an ontology, to the extent that it is correct, could preclude—or at least make difficult—the scientific knowledge to which he himself aspires, assuming that such knowledge consists in generalities that hold to a greater or lesser extent over time. This includes generalities about what is found to be useful (pragmatically speaking) in certain circumstances, which generalities also constitute the objective claims that Fishman denies (see Held, 2006a, 2006b). Let us leave aside for now the question of how Fishman, given his pragmatic "truth" (with scare quotes), can know the truth (without scare quotes) about just how the world/reality is—that is, without his antiobjectivist[1] mediating lenses—and turn instead to those who take more moderate positions about stability and change.

A Middle-Ground Ontology of Stability Within Flux

Like Fishman, Martin and Sugarman (2000a) attribute the claim that reality itself is merely "chaotic, random flux" to postmodernist/constructionist thought. They offer a middle-ground alternative in the so-called "form–flux debate," but, unlike Fishman's, it is one that seems to renounce any thoroughgoing ontological flux. As in the case of Fishman, epistemological matters appear here too.

> Postmodernists' sensible rejection of the foundationalist idea that reality is characterized by conceptually independent, ahistorical, unchanging

---

[1] Fishman (2006a, 2006b) now argues that his pragmatic model could be considered to reflect an objectivist epistemology by broadening the meaning of the term *objectivity*. However, I do not concur with his argument (Held, 2006a, 2006b).

forms or laws that can be apprehended objectively has lead them to conclude that reality is characterized by a chaotic, random flux, the arbitrary
ordering of which reflects only dominant sociocultural positions and interests. The alternative possibility that reality as flux might not be chaotic but might be possessed of emergent, changing, yet identifiable and
understandable patterns and movements has been ignored in this forced
dialectic. (Martin & Sugarman, 2000a, pp. 402–403)

In his foreword to Martin and Sugarman's (1999a) book, Polkinghorne (1999)
linked an ontology of flux to postmodernism.

> The dark side of the consequences of modernism influenced many phi-
> losophers to reexamine the assumptions about the nature of reality that
> informed modernism. . . . These philosophers—termed
> "postmodernists"—challenged the position that reality consists of per-
> manent, universal forms and laws. Instead they recovered Heraclitus's
> position that the nature of reality is change and that the notion of uni-
> form, unchanging essences and laws is an illusion. . . . In the form-flux
> debate, the postmodernists hold that reality is flux, not form. (p. xi)

Other MGTs agree that although ours is a social/psychological ontology of flux and flow owing to the reflexive impact on our existence of our
interpretive powers, it is not as formless and chaotic as the ontology that
Fishman and radical postmodernists put forth. In chapters 8 and 9 I explain
how this ontology is crucial for the MGTs' approach to psychological inquiry: If (psychological) "reality" is nothing but chaos, then we make or impose whatever order we "find" in the act of "knowing" it; in that case we do
not discover any order that is real in virtue of its existing (in some way)
independently of or prior to our acts of knowing. In making the case that the
ontology of at least the human world is pure chaos, radical postmodernists
relegate (nonchaotic) being/existence to mere *beliefs about* (nonchaotic)
being/existence—in that problematic case, "what anyone *thinks* is true *is* true,"
to reiterate Richardson, Fowers, and Guignon's (1999, p. 235) well-put objection. After all, there is then nothing but chaos to prove anyone's thesis
wrong—other than the thesis of chaos itself! As Thomasson (2003) stated in
discussing epistemological realism:

> If there were no pre-existing characteristics or structure of the world to
> discover, all supposed discovery would be mere imposition [of our con-
> cepts on reality]. A more robust realism is thus often thought to require
> that there be a world that not only exists, but also has a certain structure
> independently of the mental. (p. 582)

MGTs, then, are moved to claim that there is order in chaos, order not
merely or only of our own making/imposing. The order born of constraint is
again the basis for their ontological realism,[2] which in turn grounds their

---

[2]Note here, again, that ontological realism does not necessitate an ordered or structured world; it is
epistemological realism, the possibility of genuine, substantive discovery, that may well depend on
that sort of ontology.

version of epistemological realism. Despite our agentic reflexive capacity to transform interpretively (within limits) our social/psychological existence, that existence must nonetheless have enough stability for truth-tracking, substantive psychological inquiry to obtain. As philosopher Linda Alcoff (1996) said in discussing Gadamer's epistemological/justificatory criterion of coherence for his theory of truth:

> We must assume there is regularity in the world in order to do science; we must assume the world can be made sense of before we attempt to make sense of it . . . that the future will be like the past in order to generate any explanatory and predictive theory. (p. 51)

Historian Keith Windschuttle (1996) criticizes the "theory of reflexivity" contained in the notion of the "double hermeneutic" (the "two-way relations between actions and those who study them," p. 206) set forth by Giddens and accepted by most if not all MGTs. Although Windschuttle's critique is at odds with the MGTs' acceptance of the "double hermeneutic"—MGTs tend to believe it is ubiquitous, whereas Windschuttle limits the conditions of its workings—they both head in the same direction: Like them, he wants to assure us that the human world is not so chaotic as to preclude substantive, truth-tracking inquiry of any sort.

> The "double hermeneutic" thesis, then, commits the . . . fallacy . . . of shifting from a sociological statement to a logical statement. From the premise that there are some examples of reflexive understanding in society, Giddens slides into the claim that reflexivity is therefore a logically necessary component of modern society. . . . Just because an aspect of society is constantly shifting ground does not mean you cannot have knowledge about it. You can have knowledge about its movement. (p. 208)

Although MGTs might not quarrel with the second part of this statement, they would most certainly reject Windschuttle's defense of objective knowledge, which does not reduce to a "total lack of certainty" despite its rejection of absolute certainty (p. 208). As we shall find in chapter 9, they also tolerate forms of epistemological relativism that he rejects. In any event, let us consider a few more statements in which MGTs acknowledge the stability of psychological entities in the context of a (human) ontology of moderate flux and flow.

Like Martin and Sugarman, Harré (2002) finds a tension (or middle ground) between stability and change, in his articulation of a moderate form of social constructionism, one that is not "radically relativist" (p. 612). Because most MGTs find stability (and therefore constraint on what can rightly be said) within the cultural/discursive context, it is interesting that here Harré finds stability in the developmentally driven constructions of individuals and ephemerality in the collective expressions or constructions of the social/cognitive world.[3]

---

[3]Recall that for Harré (2002) "there are both local and universal features of social processes from which higher mental functions are appropriated" (p. 612).

There are major social constructionist contributions to two different interconnected domains of psychology: developmental and cognitive. . . . In the former, the results of construction are fairly long-term and stable attributes of individual persons. In the latter, the results of construction are ephemeral attributes of the flow of jointly created sequences of meaningful actions. (p. 612)

In distinction (if not opposition) to Harré, Richardson, Fowers, and Guignon (1999)—in their discussion of "truth" within the hermeneutic tradition—point to possible but seemingly improbable discoveries and upheavals in the cultural/discursive world owing to their unimaginable or inconceivable status. Again, we should usually anticipate modest innovation in traditions; they tend to be more or less conserved as a result of constraint on our interpretive practices.

> [Gadamer emphasizes] how the tradition provides guidelines and models that constrain our possible claims. . . . Such guidelines and truths may be interpreted in different ways with the appearance of new perspectives and interests, but, barring some currently unimaginable discovery or some inconceivable cultural upheaval, they will not be cast aside. (p. 235)

Martin and Sugarman (1999b) also seem to agree that cultural upheavals are not that easy to come by and so should not be expected as a matter of course.

> [T]he inter-relational, communicative practices and conventions of societies and their members make available coordinating systems of meaning and understanding that cannot be changed overnight—or sometimes, as many would-be reformers have discovered, even over years and lifetimes. (p. 188)

Polkinghorne (1983) too relies on the continuity of human existence to explain new developments that permit flux, but not random or chaotic flux. Yet in contrast to Alcoff, who says that we must assume "the future will be like the past," he sees the future as open ended. Still, he qualifies for middle-ground status by avoiding both the chaos of postmodernism and the purportedly stable universals or essentials of modernism.

> The human realm . . . continues to develop by creating new patterns of integration and then incorporating them as structures which will form still newer patterns. This process . . . is not random; it is built up out of itself, and its own past accomplishments are used as the images out of which further developments emerge. The human realm is in flux, but it never begins over. Its change is continuous with its past, and the past continues as a developmental trend. The realm is not static; it evolves historically. The future, however, is open ended. (p. 263)

Woolfolk, Sass, and Messer (1988) attribute to psychoanalyst and psychologist Donald Spence a preference for a "know-nothing or random view of the world," a view that should be subjected to "hermeneutic methods of interpretation to generate hypotheses," which must then be subjected to "re-lentlessly skeptical criticism" (p. 10). Spence's (1988) own words on this do not make clear whether he qualifies for middle-ground status on the onto-logical question of stability: Here he seems to speak, as does Alcoff, only of what it is best (or necessary) to *assume* ontologically, not of how the world actually *is* (outside of its "sheer richness"). Whereas Alcoff says that we need to assume regularity to do science (an epistemic matter), Spence (1988) as-sumes the opposite.

> If the hermeneutic approach . . . is coupled with a belief in a nonrandom universe, then we have the worst of both worlds. Given the sheer rich-ness of the physical world, it is ridiculously easy to find patterns once we look for them; and if we assume that a pattern is waiting to be discov-ered, the hermeneutic method only adds more grist for the mill. . . . If the hermeneutic approach is coupled with a belief in a random universe, then we are protected against weak pattern matches. . . . If pattern is the exception rather than the rule, then every pattern match must meet some kind of parsimony test. (pp. 70–71)

Despite the pragmatism expressed in the next quotation (i.e., the con-cern with what is useful), Spence (1982, 1988, 1994) nonetheless endorses a far more conventional modernist epistemology or approach to psychological inquiry/science than do many MGTs and (therefore) radical postmodernists, some of whom have taken him to task for just that.[4] Like conventional real-ists, then, he prefers pattern finding to pattern making, which I interpret to mean he prefers *discovery* to *construction*: "There is a world of difference be-tween pattern finding and pattern making, and only the former can qualify as useful" (Spence, 1988, p. 83). Still, that his ontological preference is for "be-lief in a random universe" calls the realism of his epistemology into question, at least according to Thomasson (2003, p. 582).

Martin and Sugarman (1999a, 1999b) provide sharp ontological con-trast to Fishman and even Spence. Indeed, they have gone considerably fur-ther than many MGTs in working out an ontological basis for their theory of the emergent but nonchaotic patterns that constitute our contextualized psy-chological existence (see chap. 6, this volume, note 14). They do this by way of their "levels of reality" ontology, which they claim is needed for a more appropriately realist (i.e., middle-ground) approach to psychological inquiry than either modernist or postmodernist inquiry has offered. Recall that al-though "psychological phenomena" are said by them to be "emergent, evolv-

---

[4]See Held (1995) for a discussion of Spence's attempt to reconcile the hermeneutic/interpretive discipline of psychoanalysis with rigorous science. The title of Spence's 1994 book, *The Rhetorical Voice of Psychoanalysis: Displacement of Evidence by Theory*, indicates his commitment to evidential rigor. In *The Creation of Reality in Psychoanalysis*, radical constructivist/postmodernist psychoanalytic psychologist Richard Moore (1999) takes Spence, among others, to task for failing to attain a "consistent postmodern metapsychology" (on the dust jacket of the book). (See chap. 2 of this volume for elaboration.)

ing, and mutable" (1999a, p. 52), these phenomena are real nonetheless: We must develop "an appreciation of the impermanent, yet nonetheless real nature of both sociocultural and psychological phenomena" (p. 52). It is worth reconsidering their "levels" argument.

> Because of their embeddedness within sociocultural, biological, and physical [levels of] reality . . . psychological actions and experiences are far from chaotic, arbitrary, or fleetingly irrelevant. . . . Human sociocultural and psychological categories are not arbitrary in that they are definite kinds even if not natural.[5] . . . Within all of the dynamic flux that describes the ongoing mutable interaction between societies and psychological individuals, there exists a kind of non-chaotic, non-arbitrary social and psychological reality that is much more than linguistic. It is not simply a matter of how we decide to think or talk, as some postmodernists appear to think. . . . The physical, biological, and sociocultural world simultaneously constrains and enables the emergence and interpretation of human psychological kinds. (Martin & Sugarman, 1999b, pp. 190–191)

Thus Martin and Sugarman (1999b) rightly conclude that if psychological inquiry worthy of that name is to exist, there must be an ontology of psychological kinds/entities that is sufficiently stable—what I would consider an ontology of moderate stability owing to the rejection of the universals/essentials that would grant profound stability.

> That all four levels of reality are in a constant state of dynamic evolution . . . [indicates] the potential inadequacy of any philosophical or psychological system of thought that would assume fixed, foundational, essential, or non-contingent categories of things. . . . And yet, even at these [sociocultural and psychological] levels of reality, things are not so ephemeral as to escape entirely human attempts to inquire into them in ways that might yield useful, even if inevitably temporary and contextualized understandings. (p. 188)

Here we see rejected the search for the timeless, acontextual, and thus noncontingent (i.e., universalist/essentialist) psychological knowledge or truth that, according to MGTs, drives more conventional forms of inquiry. These forms of inquiry are for them in desperate need of moderating reform, owing not least to the contextualized nature of the pragmatic epistemology that Martin and Sugarman (1999b) and Fishman (1999, 2001) express in their epistemic standard of usefulness, which appears in the quotations of them earlier in this chapter. Yet if there are no universals/essentials, how can any

---

[5]Here there seems to be some resonance with Thomasson's (2003) views about the realism of human kinds, despite the lack of natural boundaries in the case of mind-dependent entities. See chapter 5 of this volume for a discussion of the possibility of what amounts to "natural boundaries" of some human (i.e., mind-dependent) kinds, for purposes of inquiry.

claim then be expected to hold up across time within any one culture, let alone across cultures? And if this is the case, is their form of inquiry doomed to the strong relativism to which they object when they reject radical postmodernism?

In fact, Martin and Sugarman (1999a) renounce at least strong relativism—especially in their discussion of psychological inquiry. In so doing they acknowledge the necessity of generals/kinds (cf. Haack, 2003) in any form of inquiry (see chap. 5, this volume). After all, if there were no kinds or types of entities, if each entity were nothing but a now-you-see-it-now-you-don't, utterly unique and ephemeral particularity, we could not generalize (with benefit of our rational, conceptual, or interpretive powers) from the unique particularity of our experiences to at least some proper extent, so as to produce what may be deservedly called *knowledge*. We are back to the ancient problem of the relation of universality (or at least generality) to particularity. (About this, more in chap. 10, this volume.) Here note that Martin and Sugarman (1999a) do not specify the extent of warranted generalization. This is important. In the subsequent quote, are they speaking of generals that are general enough to constitute psychological universals? It is hard to say for sure, but it seems at least logically possible.

> To adopt strongly relativistic approaches to psychological inquiry seems to deny the possibility that there are, on the one hand, undeniable aspects of human experience that spring from the very nature of our existence in the world, and, on the other hand, ways of communicating across the sociocultural, linguistic, interpersonal, and personal conventions and practices that separate us. If taken to its logical extreme, such relativism would seem to deny the possibility of psychology itself, reducing human experience to nothing more than entirely local, individual occurrences and fleeting impressions that resist generalization, understanding, and explanation. (pp. 51–52)

That last sentence is the most compelling plea on behalf of the ontological stability of psychological kinds that I have yet to find in the MGT literature. On my reading Martin and Sugarman seem to insist that if there is to be a discipline of psychology, if there is to be (realist) psychological inquiry, then psychological entities, kinds, or phenomena must hold still or exist long enough to be identified and studied substantively.

THE TENSION BETWEEN AGENCY AND STABILITY

In chapter 6 we considered the potential tension (or inverse relation) between agency and realism, including the constraint on which realism depends. If agency consists in our reinterpretive/imaginative (or rational) capacities to reconstitute ourselves linguistically, which is what MGTs sometimes say, then the ontological realism of social/psychological kinds may be diminished as agency defined in this way increases. For if (logically speaking) "humans just *are* what they interpret themselves as being within their social context" (Richardson, Fowers, & Guignon, 1999, p. 236), or "humans simply are what they interpret themselves as being within their historical and sociocultural contexts" (Martin, Sugarman, & Thompson, 2003, p. 77), then there is no distinction between what we believe we are and what we "just" or "simply" are—between our social/psychological existence and our beliefs about our social/psychological existence.[6] In that case, we cannot in principle make claims about the nature of that existence that turn out to be wrong. Recall that the potential for fallibility is the third criterion of ontological realism given by some MGTs (see chap. 5, this volume).

The second criterion of ontological realism given by some MGTs, that "thinking [doesn't] make it so" (Richardson et al., 1999, p. 282) or that reality "is not simply a matter of how we decide to think or talk" (Martin & Sugarman, 1999b, p. 190), so converges on the definition of the term *realism* I have used—that there is a way things are that is independent of human beliefs about those things—that some MGTs may have unwittingly painted themselves into an antirealist corner in the name of a robust agency. This is so even if the historical/cultural/discursive/interpretive constraints (i.e., the meanings that exist "out there") that limit what we can justifiably say about ourselves are invoked in the name of realism, insofar as we have the agentic powers to reconstitute ourselves by adopting new beliefs about or interpretations of ourselves (see chap. 6, this volume). Again, can discursive constraint be sufficient constraint for realism to obtain (see chap. 5, this volume)?

There is a similar relation between agency and stability. If agency consists in our reinterpretive/imaginative (or rational) capacities to reconstitute ourselves linguistically, then ontological stability may be diminished as agency defined in this way rises. Although the extreme ontology of "chaotic, random flux" attributed to postmodernists (e.g., by Martin & Sugarman, 2000a, pp. 402–403) does not equate with the "ontological mutism" of some radical postmodernists/constructionists (see chap. 4, this volume), the effect is the same: We are free to be whatever we wish to be, without constraint. This is exactly what Charles Guignon (1991) rightly takes Rorty and other postmodernists to task for. This absence of constraint also constitutes one of the two extremes that MGTs seek to avoid (see chap. 5, this volume). The other is the profound ontological stability that is said to ground the search for timeless, unchanging universals in modern/conventional forms of psychological inquiry.

---

[6]See chapter 5 of this volume for extensive consideration of the consequence for ontological realism of making psychological existence logically versus causally dependent on beliefs about psychological existence.

Unlike agency and realism and agency and stability, stability and realism are not necessarily related. Human kinds (among other entities) can be ephemeral and still be real; there is nothing about ontological realism that requires a stable world. Yet if human psychological kinds are infinitely unstable, infinitely ephemeral, owing to our agentic/self-determinative (re)interpretive powers (or even for other reasons), then we may wonder whether they are stable enough to allow for real, substantive inquiry of any sort. After all, even in particle physics—in which existence is ephemeral—entities must exist long enough to be detected.

Thus MGTs must find enough stability in psychological entities to permit the truth-tracking/realist form of psychological inquiry that they want. But they also must give humans enough agency, enough power of self-determination, to avoid the mechanistic form of determinism they find in modern/conventional psychological inquiry, inquiry which for them fails to give agency its proper due. As we saw in chapter 6, they attempt this by arguing on behalf of agentic powers that are limited by their essential situatedness in culture—that is, by our "in the world" agency (Martin & Sugarman, 2002, p. 421), our "situated, emergent agency" (Martin, Sugarman, & Thompson, 2003, p. 159). This agency is always constrained by the discourse that exists "out there" in the interpretive context, rather than in any particular knower's mind.

A Culturally Situated Agency Revisited

Making agency itself culturally situated, which is to make it culturally determined (to some degree), limits the extent of the transcendence (of what now exists) that is possible. By setting limits in advance on how much (but not exactly how much) transcendence or innovation is possible—recall it is said to be "mild" or "modest" (Martin & Sugarman, 2000a, 2002), because agents have only "measures" (Richardson et al., 1999, p. 263) or "margins" (Freeman, 1993, p. 217) of freedom—MGTs ensure some ontological stability, at least enough for realist inquiry to obtain. To be sure, Martin and Sugarman (2002) and others speak of such constraint in the positive terms of what it can enable, allow, or make possible; it is not a "negative" matter of mechanistic or full determination.

> Socioculturally governed meanings change over historical time. Such change could not occur if past sociocultural rules, conventions, and practices were fully determining of meaning. Therefore, past sociocultural rules, conventions, and practices cannot be fully determinate of meaningful human action, but must be at least partially open-ended. . . . [They allow] for the development of personal understanding and possibilities for action that may contribute significantly to sociocultural change. However, allowance is not determination. (p. 414)

Still, for MGTs the cultural/discursive context sets limits on what is possible (in that context) only by making some other things impossible (in that context). Hence transcendence (of that context) is limited—it must be "mild" or "modest" or "measured" or within "margins"—and moderation is once again maintained in the matters of agency, stability, and realism. Martin and Sugarman (2002) make their middle-ground ontology of agency apparent in two ways. They claim that "by bringing agency 'into the world'" (p. 421) they have (a) located a viable compatibilist position that avoids the excesses of both libertarianism and hard determinism and (b) articulated a "proper 'metaphysics'" that avoids the "traditional metaphysics" of modernism without resorting to either the ontological mutism or the ontological chaos of radical postmodernism.

> It is this nesting of the psychological within the historical and sociocultural, which in turn are nested within biological and physical reality, that we regard as a proper "metaphysics" of the human condition. This is not a traditional metaphysics of transcendental or first principles, certainty, and essentials, but a "neo-metaphysics" consisting in historical, situational, and developmental contingencies that are inseparable from, the "acting-in-the-world" of embodied, biologically evolved human beings. (p. 422)

As was the case with MGTs' various views of agency, this quotation again suggests that the capacity to "act in the world" should never be conceived apart from the cultural/discursive context that allegedly constitutes that capacity. That capacity is nothing less than our (agentic) rational/imaginative powers to (re)interpret and thereby transcend what now exists in any context. Whatever the universal/essential nature of those agentic powers may be, for MGTs they are realized only in virtue of our existence in the contexts that constitute them. Thus those agentic powers are, as a matter of principle, limited in the degree of transcendence or innovation they can generate—again, stability (or constraint) at the price of agentic reach.

But maybe there is a way around the tension between stability/constraint and agency that seems so inescapable. Because MGTs often define our agentic powers in terms of (what I interpret to be) a perfectly universal/essential capacity to know the realities of the particular circumstances that allegedly constitute human social/psychological existence (see chap. 6), it seems fair to speak of the *universal* nature of our rational/imaginative capacity on the one hand, and the uniquely *particular* nature of what is known or experienced in deploying that capacity on the other. Put differently, it is not logically necessary to give culture the determinative or privileged position in constituting the rational power itself, as MGTs often (but not always) seem to suggest. By elevating culture above the universal or essential properties of mind/rationality (and thus agency) itself, MGTs—to the extent that culture is sufficiently stable—retain the (discursive) constraint that makes their ontological and epistemological realism possible. However, they then must shortchange agency and the potential for transcendence or innovation that comes with it. For MGTs there is no radically free postmodernist lunch.

To be sure, it is fair to ask if we can rightly speak of the universals of mind/rationality (or of agentic powers) without reference to the particular contents in play. As we shall see in chapter 10, some social psychologists claim that culture figures much in the way rationality works on any particular contents. Contrary to such views, I will argue that the necessity of being "in the world" to know the world (for purposes of transcendence/innovation or otherwise) does not necessitate putting culture first. To appreciate this claim, we must first appreciate the universals of mind as instantiated in individual minds, as they in turn are instantiated in cultural contexts. To do this, we must again appreciate the claim that universality (what Pols, 1998, calls the "U-factor") inheres in all particularity (what Pols, 1998, calls the "P-factor")—that is, that every particularity has universality within it (see chap. 5, this volume).

In chapter 10, I discuss how agents must be situated in all their particularity to both be and know with the particularity that is vital to all existence. However, this does not mean that humans are first and foremost historically/culturally particular beings. Put differently, we are not necessarily historical/cultural all the way down. Nor does human situatedness in particular contexts preclude our ability to know with the generality (i.e., with an epistemic agentic "reach") that the capacity for objective knowing grants. This epistemic preclusion is typically attributed to the fact that no one has a "view from nowhere," a view that is presumed necessary for objective knowledge by MGTs and radical postmodernists alike.

Because the ability to know one's situation (an epistemic matter) is central in some MGTs' conceptions of agency (an ontological matter), and insofar as psychological inquiry (an epistemic matter) is implicated in MGTs' discussions of agency, stability, and realism, let us now turn to epistemological matters to see just how MGTs seek moderation in that regard.

III

THE INTERPRETIVE TURN
IN MODERATION:
EPISTEMOLOGY

8

SITUATED KNOWING: A MIDDLE-GROUND ANTIOBJECTIVIST EPISTEMOLOGY?

So far we have considered four interrelated ontological claims about human psychological existence made by middle-ground theorists (MGTs): (a) the local or situated nature of that existence—that is, an ontology of "being in the world"; (b) the self-reflexive and yet realist nature of that existence; (c) the agentic/self-determining but only mildly or modestly transcendent/innovative nature of that existence; and (d) the evanescent yet quasi-stable nature of that existence. The qualifications in these claims reflect the attempt to articulate an ontological middle ground—one that reconciles, moderates, transcends, or avoids the universalist/essentialist ontology of conventional modernist psychology on the one hand, and the now-you-see-it-now-you-don't chaotic or muted "ontology" of radical postmodernist psychology on the other.

Whether MGTs have in fact successfully defined a *realist* middle-ground ontology that permits a middle-ground epistemology—one that reconciles, moderates, transcends, or avoids the professed epistemological excesses of modernism and radical postmodernism—is questionable at best. These excesses are said to consist in (a) the objectivism of modernist inquiry, which is thought to bring with it certain, foundational, universal, mechanistically deterministic knowledge; and (b) the antiobjectivism of radical postmodernist inquiry, which is thought to bring with it skeptical, antifoundational, radically relativist, antirealist "knowledge." Although MGTs themselves reject objectivist epistemologies, they also—in seeking a realist epistemology—reject the antirealism, radical relativism, and extreme skepticism of radical postmodernists. Have they succeeded in defining a realist epistemology that is not objectivist?

In what follows I focus on MGTs' attempts to navigate between the epistemological objectivism of modernists and the epistemological relativism and antirealism of radical postmodernists. The question of warrant is central to the journey. What, for MGTs, warrants knowledge claims, or warrants them enough so that they do not end up sailing either an objectivist or a relativist/antirealist sea? Can there be a warrant that gets them "beyond objectivism and relativism" (Bernstein, 1983) to a moderate, situated (epistemological) realism? Although MGTs are as diverse a lot epistemically as they are ontologically, they speak in epistemic concert enough for us to begin to answer these questions. In answering these questions, I again include some whose philosophical voices have not been included in the MGT discourse.

CONVENTIONAL VIEWS OF REALIST
OR OBJECTIVIST EPISTEMOLOGIES

Recall from chapter 3 of this volume that Searle (1995) applies the terms *realism* and *antirealism* only to ontological matters; for him it is improper to speak of realist and antirealist epistemologies.[1] Yet many do so, and although there are different versions of epistemological realism,[2] let us begin with an all-purpose, conventional definition: A realist epistemology requires that knowers can, in principle, attain knowledge of reality that is objective in the sense that it does not originate in the knower or knowing subject—reality that is therefore independent of the knower and her knowing processes. Here we see the dichotomy between the knowing subject and the object or reality to be known that MGTs reject.

First, because I invoke objectivity in this definition, I equate realist and objectivist epistemologies. Because MGTs seek a realist epistemology that is not objectivist, my equation should be troublesome to them. Second, my definition can be elaborated to specify that the knower can attain knowledge

---

[1]Martin and Sugarman's (1999b) definition of objectivism incorporates both ontological and epistemological doctrines: "Objectivism (cf. Fay, 1996) 'may be defined as the thesis that reality exists in itself, independently of the mind, and that this reality is knowable as such'" (p. 189).
[2]See Held (1995, chap. 1) for a spectrum of both realist and antirealist epistemological positions.

of a reality that is independent of the knower's theory, language, context, culture, community, conceptual scheme, discourse, interpretive practices, and so forth (Haack, 2002, p. 83). This of course presumes that there exists a reality that is independent of these things. Because for MGTs social/psychological reality (which they rightly say is mind dependent) does not exist independently of most if not all of the mind-dependent items in Haack's list—for example, for them psychological existence is not independent of cultural beliefs, interpretations, or discourses about psychological existence—that existence does not constitute an objective existence. It therefore seems hard if not impossible for MGTs to subscribe to a conventional realist or objectivist epistemology when investigating social/psychological matters, and in fact they do not.

Philosopher Edward Erwin (1999) put forth this definition of an objectivist epistemology.

> An "objectivist epistemology" . . . holds that propositions are generally true or false independently of any particular paradigm, or school of thought, or language, or indeed of what any human believes; and, furthermore, that they can often be warranted independently of what anyone believes.[3] (p. 353)

Although philosopher Susan Haack (2002) wrote of "realisms" rather than "antiobjectivisms," she said that what "unites the many and various members of the realist family is that something—the world, truth, universals, numbers, moral values, etc., etc.—is independent of human beings and their beliefs, concepts, cultures, theories, or whatever" (p. 67). Philosopher Amie Thomasson (2003) too wrote of "realism" rather than "antiobjectivism." She defined the term *epistemological realism* as "the view that facts about the world [including the nature of any kind] are genuinely discoverable through substantive investigation subject to possibilities of confirmation and error, not just imposed by or to be read off of our concepts or beliefs" (p. 582). The similarity in these definitions provides more support for my decision to use the terms *realist epistemology* and *objectivist epistemology* interchangeably—although again, this should be problematic for MGTs, who want to keep the two distinct.

Thomasson (2003) says that one's "version of ontological realism" must be "robust" enough to support epistemological realism (p. 582). In chapters 5 and 7 we saw that Thomasson finds robustness (or structure) in some human (social/psychological) kinds, despite their necessary mind dependence, owing to their structured existence independent of knowers' beliefs about their existence. Thus in the earlier example, racism could exist even if everyone were ignorant of its existence or massively wrong in their beliefs about its nature. By contrast, MGTs say that we do not exist psychologically indepen-

---

[3]Erwin (1997) gave this alternate definition of an objectivist epistemology: "a set of epistemic standards the truth of which is independent of what any human believes" (p. 74).

dently of our discourses about our psychological existence—independently, that is, of our "concepts or beliefs" about our psychological existence. Recall that for some, humans are what they interpret themselves to be (to para- phrase Richardson, Fowers, & Guignon, 1999, p. 236, and Martin, Sugarman, & Thompson, 2003, p. 77). Thus humans do not have an objective (psycho- logical) existence. We may now ask if the MGT version of ontological "real- ism" is robust enough to support the epistemological realism they want. Put differently, can there be a realist epistemology that is not an objectivist epis- temology? To answer that question, let us turn to the antiobjectivist episte- mologies of MGTs, especially to their three arguments about why objective knowledge of human kinds is impossible.

THE ANTIOBJECTIVIST STANCE

MGTs do not see their adoption of an antiobjectivist epistemology as a weakness or failing; to the contrary, it is celebrated as consistent with their antiobjectivist ontology and as proper for psychological inquiry. As we dis- cussed in chapter 5, for MGTs being and believing—or being and knowing about our being—are inseparable: "Human beings not only come to know through the hermeneutic process, but are formed and constituted by it" (Woolfolk, Sass, & Messer, 1988, p. 17). The "believing/knowing (about being) *constitutes* being" equation brings with it problems that must be sur- mounted for any form of realism to obtain. That MGTs themselves realize this can be gleaned from their use of fallibilist inquiry to support their own version of ontological realism. Yet it would be inconsistent for them to reject an objectivist ontology on the one hand, and then (on the other hand) to insist on an objectivist epistemology, in which claims about psychological existence can indeed be "warranted independently of what anyone believes" (Erwin, 1999, p. 353).

In addition to being inconsistent with an antiobjectivist ontology, an objectivist epistemology is also considered by MGTs to be a liability for in- quiry into the human world. It constitutes a detached stance that is not only impossible but also allegedly robs the subject matter (our social/psychologi- cal existence) of its richness, significance, and moral import—of its "real" nature. Many MGTs therefore claim to hold a realist but not an objectivist epistemology. In short, they see their antiobjectivism as a correct and desir- able consequence of (a) the necessary fusion of "facts" about our psychologi- cal existence with (local) values (i.e., they reject the attempt to maintain the fact/value distinction they find in conventional modernist inquiry) and (b) the necessary fusion of our empirical "observations" with interpretive/ conceptual apparatus (i.e., they reject the attempt to maintain the conceptual/ empirical or theory/observation distinction they find in conventional mod- ernist inquiry). Messer, Sass, and Woolfolk (1988b) put this succinctly: "The hermeneutic approach insists upon the inseparability of fact and value, detail and context, and observation and theory" (p. xiv).

MGTs see their rejection of so-called "brute facts/data"[4] and/or "brute observations" (i.e., aconceptual or interpretation-free facts/data and observations) as a humanistically inspired epistemic virtue, not a scientistically or positivistically inspired epistemic vice. Although this view may distance them from the conventional modernist approach to psychological science that they find lacking, does it also give them the desired distance from the radical postmodernist/constructionist approach to psychological "science"? We can see evidence of the antiobjectivist stance of MGTs in quotations that link objectivist epistemologies with controversy and problems—including social, emotional/psychological, and, not least, epistemological "pathology."[5] Messer, Sass, and Woolfolk (1988b) gave an early heads-up on the controversy that would only heighten in the 15 years to come: "The social sciences in North America are currently in a state of ferment, with traditional objectivist approaches being questioned in a variety of ways" (p. xiii). Indeed, a decade later Richardson, Fowers, and Guignon (1999) made explicit the "pathology" that accompanies an objectivist epistemology.

> When the method of objectification is taken as the very definition of an epistemically mature stance toward life, trouble ensues. This view rather dogmatically absolutizes a certain detached, dispassionate, spectator view of knowing and relating to the world. . . . In many situations they will only hamper us or have harmful consequences. Many postmodern and hermeneutic thinkers [e.g., Slife & Williams, 1995, p. 195] argue that "the language of science, when applied to the study of human beings, is a relatively impoverished language." . . . The objectifying point of view may be an important source of some of the peculiar irrationalities and pathologies of modern life. (pp. 35–36)

In making his seminal antiobjectivist case years earlier, Bernstein (1983) linked the need for objective knowledge (to avoid rampant relativism) with

---

[4]Meichenbaum (1988), in discussing Charles Taylor's (1971) article entitled "Interpretation and the Sciences of Man," says Taylor uses the term "brute data" to "refer to the acts of people (behaviors) . . . which supposedly are 'beyond interpretation.' These are the observational building blocks for the empiricist" (pp. 121–122). Taylor (1971) himself defines "brute data" as "data whose validity cannot be questioned by offering another interpretation or reading, data whose credibility cannot be founded or undermined by further reasoning" (p. 8). In note 4 (p. 8) Taylor distinguishes his "brute data" from the "brute facts" of others. Searle (1995) distinguishes between brute facts and institutional facts.

> Brute facts [e.g., that the sun is ninety-three million miles from the earth] exist independently of any human institutions; institutional facts [e.g., that Clinton is president] can exist only within human institutions. Brute facts require the institution of language in order that we can *state* the facts, but the brute facts *themselves* exist quite independently of language or of any other institution. (p. 27).

Searle (1995, p. 229, note 1) attributes his notion of "brute fact" to Anscombe's (1957–1958) "On Brute Facts" (*Analysis* 18, no. 3). The "brute facts" and "brute observations" of which I speak are not necessarily the same kind of entity.

[5]See Koch (1985) for discussion of "the pathology of knowledge," or what Koch also called *epistemopathy*, owing especially to "method-fetishism" as opposed to "meaningful thinking" (pp. 76–82).

pathology: "We need to *exorcize* the Cartesian Anxiety and liberate ourselves from its seductive appeal" (p. 19). The problem here is that the "Cartesian Anxiety" Bernstein diagnoses in those who seek objective knowledge is surely a psychological rather than an epistemic condition, as philosopher Harvey Siegel (2004) astutely pointed out.[6]

Although Slife and Williams (1995) do not link epistemic objectivity to pathology, they make common cause with Richardson, Fowers, and Guignon (1999), who cite them with approbation. As Slife and Williams (1995) put it, "To study human action from an 'objective' perspective is to study it as an abstraction from the lived world" (p. 89). Slife and Williams (1995) later say that scientists not only cannot have objectivity but also that they do not need it, because it affords no "special warrant."

> The very definitions and framing of a research question are shot through with traditions, history, expectations, values, and other subjective factors. It seems unlikely that at any stage the research process is objective. ... [However] it is questionable whether this kind of objectivity is necessary for the work of science to continue. Science ... can be (and is being) done without this sort of objectivity. ... It is only when we expect science to be capable of making truth claims that objectivity seems to be so important. (p. 194)

In criticizing objectivists' alleged determination to obtain certitude through their (futile) search for an "Archimedean point upon which we can ground our knowledge" (p. 16), Bernstein (1983) himself strives for a moderation to get "beyond objectivism and relativism." But he, like more recent MGTs, fails to appreciate that many who defend an objectivist epistemology do not do so by way of an Archimedean point (or any sort of foundationalism)—or with the hope of certitude. Recall that an objectivist epistemology is typically defined as one in which a proposition's truth is warranted independently of beliefs about the truth of the proposition (Erwin, 1999; Haack, 2003; Thomasson, 2003). Indeed, Erwin (1997) expressly disputes the alleged link between an objectivist epistemology and foundationalism, which he defines as a theory in which "our non-basic beliefs are ultimately justified by so-called 'basic beliefs,'" which "are either self-justifying or are in no need of justification" (p. 69). He says that "one of the main reasons given for the turn to a postmodernist epistemology is that all foundationalist theories are said to have failed," but even if "all current solutions to the problem [that motivated foundationalism] are wrong[,] it does not follow that there is no objective supporting evidence for any belief

---

[6]According to Siegel (2004), to reason that "'she is (Cartesianly) anxious, therefore her objectivism is misguided'—is straightforwardly to commit the freshman-level fallacy of psychologizing, i.e., of evaluating the epistemic status of a belief in terms of the psychological state or motivation of the believer." Thus "a person's anxiety concerning relativism ... has no tendency to undermine either her arguments against it or her arguments for a non-relativist alternative" (p. 776).

at all, or . . . that we cannot articulate general objective epistemic principles" (p. 69).[7]

Although here he speaks of therapy and not psychological inquiry in general, Woolfolk (2001)—like Richardson et al. (1999)—rejects the "dragon of objectivism" in the human world.

> Slaying the dragon of objectivism . . . is simply one step that leads to a more holistic, complex, humanistic, interpretive view of all the health care professions. . . . Health itself is understood not as a thing definable apart from culture and human interests, as, for example, mass or velocity might be. (p. 297)

Freeman (1993), like Woolfolk, slays the dragon of objectivity in the name of understanding others.

> In claiming that our understanding of others is . . . contingent upon our understanding of the worlds they inhabit, the myth of observational neutrality and objectivity—traditionally defined—is exploded: the faceless observer, sans history, sans prejudice . . . could understand absolutely nothing. (p. 201)

And so the stage is set for the MGTs' rejection of objectivist epistemologies in favor of their moderate, nonobjectivist, but nonetheless (allegedly) realist epistemology. Let us turn to their three negative descriptive arguments about why objective knowing and knowledge are not only undesirable but also actually impossible, before we consider their prescribed epistemology in chapter 9.

THREE ARGUMENTS AGAINST OBJECTIVE KNOWING AND KNOWLEDGE: THE NEGATIVE ARGUMENT

MGTs put forth three arguments against the possibility of objective knowing and knowledge, arguments that lead them to the inexorable conclusion that objectivist epistemologies are indefensible, at least in social/psychological inquiry. First, there is no subject/object dichotomy; therefore, there can be no objective knowledge. Second, there is no (value-free) view from nowhere; therefore, there can be no objective knowledge. Third, there is an ontology of flux and flow in the human world; therefore, there can be no objective knowledge. For each argument I set forth the ontological claim

---

[7]Erwin (1997, pp. 69–70) mentions Haack's "foundherentist" alternative to foundationalism (and coherentism), and he refers to Haack's (1993b, pp. 182–194) incisive rebuttal of Rorty's antiobjectivist epistemology, a rebuttal that does not depend on foundationalism. Moreover, Siegel (1997) says, "It is quite fashionable, in these postmodern days, to trash or dismiss foundationalism; . . . however, many criticisms of it are . . . aimed at doctrines quite different from foundationalism properly so called" (p. 114). For Siegel a "modest foundationalism . . . [as developed by] Goldman [1988] offers important arguments for foundationalism, while insisting that foundational beliefs need not be certain or infallible" (p. 203).

on which the argument is based, describe the epistemological conclusion that is said to follow logically from the ontological claim, and critique both. In some cases I outline and then critique corollaries to the primary antiobjectivist argument. Although the claim that we are situated knowers—that there exists no "view from nowhere"—inheres in all three arguments, I shall emphasize that idea most explicitly in the second argument, in which "facts" are said to be necessarily (and therefore properly) infused with local/situated values and interests.

Antiobjectivist Argument 1: There Is No Subject/Object Dichotomy; Therefore, There Can Be No Objective Knowledge

The Ontological Claim

We have already considered the ontological claim at length in chapter 5. Accordingly here I will review it concisely, before turning to its presumed epistemological implications.

In the human world at least, there is no (allegedly Cartesian) distinction between the object to be known (in this case our psychological existence) and ourselves as knowing subjects. In the parlance of MGTs, there is no "subject/object dichotomy," a dichotomy deemed necessary for objective knowledge.

> Gadamer is critical of the traditional/(Cartesian) conception of knowing as the confrontation of a knowing and controlling subject with an external object. . . . [He rejects] this subject-object dichotomy with its premise of detached, objectified knowledge. (Woolfolk, Sass, & Messer, 1988, p. 16)
>
> Hermeneutic philosophers generally want to call in question the distinction between "subjective" and "objective" that has dominated our thinking since the rise of modern science. (Richardson et al., 1999, p. 215)
>
> To have a subjective world is to imply that there is an objective world, and the hermeneuticist specifically denies that the world can be divided neatly into these two realms. (Slife & Williams, 1995, p. 89)

In light of such statements, perhaps Antiobjectivist Argument 1 would be better expressed as saying that because there is no subject/object dichotomy, the very idea of "objective knowledge" is meaningless—or at least ill defined.

I agree that the subject(ive)/object(ive) distinction needs to be reconsidered, especially in the pursuit of knowledge about human/psychological entities, which are necessarily mind dependent: If there were no minds, there would be no psychological (i.e., mental) entities to study. However, I do not agree that the distinction should be eliminated altogether; there are ways to rework the distinction that leave objective psychological knowledge intact. Yet for MGTs the entity to be known (the nature of our psychological existence) does not exist independently of our beliefs about that existence—independently, that is, of the local discourse (or the conceptual/interpretive/linguistic apparatus) about our psychological existence that we as knowers bring to the knowing process when we try to understand human psychological existence. In so doing we reflexively (re)constitute that existence. Again, our being and our knowing about our being are not distinct: "The supposed objectivity of reality is not its independence from interpretation and bias. So-called objective views of the universe are themselves a *type* of bias, a type of interpretation" (Slife & Williams, 1995, p. 88).

In my critique of the MGTs' rejection of the subject/object dichotomy, and therefore their rejection of the very idea (and hence possibility) of "objective (psychological) knowledge," I confront in more detail the reasons they give for these rejections; I also argue that striving for epistemic objectivity (i.e., for the reduction of bias) is indeed a value-laden endeavor, or a moral matter. However, that in no way compromises the desirability of just that striving or the possibility of so striving with success.

The Epistemological Conclusion

What is said by MGTs to follow epistemologically from these ontological claims is this: We are so psychologically constituted (or caused) by our local historical/cultural discourses/interpretations about our psychological existence that there can be no "brute facts" (or data) about our psychological existence—no aconceptual or interpretation-free knowledge about our interpretation-laden/nonbrute psychological existence. That existence is said, especially by hermeneutically inclined MGTs, to be historically/culturally discursive/interpretive (i.e., linguistic) all the way down: "Understanding psychological phenomena requires interpretation of the meanings of these phenomena within historical, sociocultural, and linguistic context. . . . To understand someone . . . is to penetrate the relevant interpretive contexts within which such emotion and action occur" (Martin & Sugarman, 1999b, pp. 189–190).

Because MGTs believe that brute (i.e., aconceptual or interpretation-free) facts (or data) are necessary for objective knowledge to obtain, knowledge about the human (social/psychological) world cannot be rightly called objective. If the necessary brute facts or data can be attained at all (and this is indeed a big if—for example, Richardson et al., 1999, p. 299, say that "brute data" about human behavior are "inherently impossible"), they can be gained only if the object to be known exists independently of knowing subjects—that is, if the object is a brute or interpretation-free object, such as a rock. And for MGTs beliefs and conceptions about human psychological existence make us what we are: We *are* what we interpret ourselves to be in our social context (to paraphrase Richardson, Fowers, & Guignon, 1999, p. 236, and Martin, Sugarman, & Thompson, 2003, p. 77, once again). This means that objective knowledge about human psychological existence can never be ours for the asking—or so they think.

Here I offer evidence of the MGTs' insistence that objectivist epistemologies are beyond the reach of those who conduct psychological inquiry because the alleged inseparability of the object to be known and the knowing subject precludes the attainment of the brute facts deemed necessary for objective psychological knowledge. Again, if there can be no subject/object distinction in psychological inquiry, and if objective knowledge depends logically on that very distinction, then there can be no objective knowledge.

> Heidegger's conception of human existence as an event seems to collapse the distinction between subjective and objective. In place of the traditional picture of subjects confronting a world of brute, meaningless objects, we get a picture of life as an unfolding "happening" that is enmeshed in a meaningful lifeworld and woven into a shared history. (Guignon, 2005, p. 87)

Miller (2004) outlined the "received or mainstream view of science" (pp. 125–142), in which he proclaimed the supposed orthodoxies of science to be problematic for a practical psychological science. Miller equates naturalism/materialism with objectivity, which he pits against the "nonnatural/ideational/subjective world of mind and consciousness" (p. 128). Like most MGTs, he says that both worlds are real nonetheless. Although Fishman (1999) is less decidedly realist, he strikes a similar note in saying that "a hallmark of the natural sciences is the study of [brute/interpretation-free] phenomena that can be objectively, directly, and reliably observed" (p. 23).

Richardson et al. (1999) explain, in ways that invoke Giddens's "theory of reflexivity" (see chaps. 5 & 7, this volume), why the human sciences cannot yield the objective knowledge of the natural sciences.

> Because there is no clear way to draw a distinction between the "facts" of the matter and the way they are interpreted . . . Gadamer can say that there is no "object in itself" to be studied by historiography. "This is precisely what distinguishes the human sciences from the natural sciences." . . . The human sciences *constitute* the reality they study in a way the natural sciences do not. This is why the sharp distinction between the knowing subject and the object to be known . . . cannot be made in the human sciences. (p. 223)
>
> [The naturalistic approach] fails, because every observation is an interpretation—there are no brute data that can help us break out of the circle. (p. 303)

Richardson et al. (1999) deny the possibility of brute facts in the human sciences. Here we find a familiar objection to reification (see Slife & Williams, 1995, p. 88) and a nod to an ontology of change, instability, or contingency: "There has been an overwhelming tendency in mainstream social science toward reification, toward mistaking historically conditioned social and political patterns for an unchangeable brute reality which is simply 'out there' to be confronted" (Bernstein, as cited in Richardson et al., 1999, p. 289). Bernstein (1983) also said, "According to Gadamer, 'historical objectivism,' which treats the 'object' as if it were ontologically independent of the 'subject,' 'conceals the involvement of the historical consciousness itself in effective-history'" (p. 142).

In this next quotation, Martin and Sugarman (2000b) speak expressly of "'self' understanding," which contains complexities that do not plague third-person understanding of psychological phenomena (see Freeman, 1993). Yet there are similarities, to be sure, so the same conclusion is reached nonetheless: There is no subject/object dichotomy and therefore objective knowledge cannot obtain.

> "Self" understanding is not a matter of hurdling a Cartesian barrier to confront an unsituated subject standing apart from its own being. . . . Self and other psychological kinds cannot be conceived apart from interpretations and descriptions given to them within historical, sociocultural traditions of living.

A Critique of the "No Subject/Object Dichotomy, Therefore No Objective Knowledge" Argument

For MGTs, because humans do not exist (psychologically) independently of their minds, humans do not exist (psychologically) independently of their beliefs/discourses about (or interpretations/understandings of) their psychological existence/minds. Ours is thus not a brute or interpretation-free existence, like that of rocks. Hence humans cannot know with objectivity the nature of mind: neither their own minds, nor the minds of particular others, nor mind in general—certainly not with the objectivity with which humans can know rocks, which do exist independently of minds owing to their brute or interpretation-free status. Here the distinction between self-knowledge (i.e., knowledge about one's own mind) and psychological knowledge (i.e., knowledge about mind in general) is relevant, because it invokes that important question of on *whose* mind(s) psychological entities depend (see chap. 5), and how that dependence affects our ability to conduct substantive psychological inquiry.

The nature of self-knowledge brings with it special epistemic problems that are beyond the scope of my analysis,[8] which concerns itself with knowledge about psychological existence as it manifests itself generally, if not universally. I make the distinction between "generally" and "universally," because MGTs reject a universalist/essentialist account of mind owing to their

---

[8]See Charles Siewert's (1998) *The Significance of Consciousness* and Timothy Wilson's (2002) *Strangers to Ourselves*, for opposing views about our access to first-person knowledge and, in the case of Siewert, distinctive forms of warrant for first-person knowledge.

belief that we exist "in the world"; our psychological existence therefore depends on the local cultural/discursive/interpretive contexts that exist "out there" (beyond any particular mind) and in which psychological existence is locally constituted. In chapter 5 we discussed how some MGTs use the possibility of (epistemic) fallibilism to support the (ontological) realism of human psychological kinds. Now the realism of human kinds becomes necessary to support the possibility of fallibilism, which is deemed necessary for the realist, although not objectivist, epistemology MGTs defend.

Yet if truly fallibilist inquiry obtains, then so can objective knowledge, at least according to the definitions of objectivist or realist epistemologies we have considered so far. It seems odd that MGTs would embrace fallibilism to support their ontological realism, but then reject the objective knowledge that truly fallibilist inquiry makes possible. The mystery is solved when we see that many (if not all) MGTs equate objective knowing with certitude or indubitability—the very source of all that "Cartesian Anxiety" Bernstein (1983) finds in objectivists, even though objectivists embrace fallibilism (about this, more later). Two quotations document the MGTs' equation of epistemic objectivity with certitude. In the first quotation, Martin and Sugarman (1999b) express discomfort about equating the realism they propound with the objectivism they reject.

> An understanding of realism as objectivism commits . . . [one] to both the ontological and epistemological doctrines of objectivism. . . . By claiming that something is real, one also is claiming that one can have certain knowledge of it, in the sense that one's knowledge of the thing in question corresponds to the thing-in-itself. . . . [This] is a mistake with respect to psychological phenomena. (p. 189)

Richardson et al. (1999) also link objective data to certitude or indubitability, in calling on us to "accept that there is no ultimate appeal to surefire methods or indubitably objective data or to any final truth of the matter" (p. 303).

I shall have more to say about the problematic equation of objective knowing and knowledge with certain or infallible knowing and knowledge, as well as the crucial question of whether the realism that MGTs desire can be defended in the face of their antiobjectivist epistemologies. Here let us return to Thomasson (1998), who accepts the possibility of objective knowledge of social and psychological entities or kinds, which are mind dependent in *some* senses (see chap. 5, this volume). This she achieves by reworking our understanding of objective and subjective judgments, a reworking at least implicitly recommended especially by hermeneutically inclined MGTs, who also rightly "call into question the distinction between 'subjective' and 'objective' that has dominated our thinking since the rise of modern science" (Richardson et al., 1999, p. 215).

Historically there have been two dominant ways of defining "subjective" judgments, the first as those judgments dependent (in some way) on mental states, the second as judgments about mental states. . . . Both of these methods . . . take us far afield from the original intuitive understanding of the subjective and objective. More importantly, both make it a mere matter of definition that certain kinds of judgments (ethical, psychological, social scientific) must be subjective, when these ought to be issues for substantive philosophical debate. (Thomasson, 1998, abstract)

Thomasson makes good on her promise to offer a "new way of understanding subjective and objective judgments that is able to avoid these problems [of deeming subjective any judgment that depends on mental states or is about mental states] while preserving the intuitive distinction between the subjective and objective" (abstract). In place of the "dependence-based" and "aboutness" definitions of "subjective," she offers a "type-subjective" definition.[9] What makes a judgment subjective is not whether its truth condition depends on anyone's mental states or is about anyone's mental states, but whether there

are no properties of the kind described by the property term (so that no judgment involving facts of that kind can be made true, *and* the source of the mistake lies in false projection from inner [mental] states [onto the external world]). (Thomasson, 1998)

For example, if there exist no aesthetic properties that make the claim "That building is beautiful" either true or false, then it is a type-subjective judgment, a false projection of one's subjective perception on the world. Yet if there exist such aesthetic properties, the judgment is type objective (Thomasson, 1998). Because mental states exist, objective judgments can in principle be made about them, including the knower's own mental states, provided there is cognitive access to them. To use her example, if instead of saying "That building is beautiful" our aesthetic judge had said, "I believe the building is beautiful," the statement could be objective even if there were no aesthetic properties in the world, because it could be made true (or false)[10] by the existence of his beliefs.

Still, as we saw in chapter 5, Thomasson relies on the existence "external to each one of us" of social and psychological kinds—which necessarily depend on intentionality/mind for their existence—to support the possibility of objective knowledge about those kinds. In this next quotation,

---

[9]See Thomasson (1998) for her distinction between "type-subjective" and "token-subjective" judgments.
[10]The mere fact of a judgment being wrong does not consign it to subjective status. As Thomasson (1998) points out, "Judgments, e.g., about phlogiston are indeed mistakes and lack any truthmaker in the world, yet they are not generally accused of being subjective statements (but merely wrong)."

Thomasson (1997) might appear to sound like MGTs who use the "out there" in the world existence of meanings or practices to support their own ontological realism (e.g., Martin & Sugarman, 1999b, p. 181; Richardson et al., 1999), were it not for her embrace of and their rejection of the possibility of objective knowledge about human kinds.

> It is not the case that . . . every object about which we can acquire genuine knowledge . . . is an object postulated by the physical sciences and completely describable in physicalistic terms. In fact the great majority of entities in the social and cultural world . . . from governments to monuments, songs to theories, artifacts to fictional characters, are those which depend on . . . intentionality. Their dependence on intentionality in no way makes them phantasms or epistemically subjective entities; instead they remain external to each one of us and our particular intentional states, and entities about which we can make objectively true or false claims and acquire genuine knowledge. (p. 133)

MGTs not only differ from Thomasson in their rejection of the possibility of objective knowledge about human kinds but also in their heavy reliance on discursive or linguistic constraint (the meanings that allegedly constitute us psychologically) to support their ontological realism. This linguistic constraint is used not only to support their ontological realism; it also extends to the related matter of what we are justified in claiming or saying about our existence. It therefore extends to some form of epistemic realism. Given the MGTs' emphasis on language to support their realisms, the divide between Thomasson and MGTs should not be underestimated: Recall that for Thomasson racism (and other human social/psychological kinds) can exist even if there exists no concept or conception of it as a kind, as long as there exist people who hold certain beliefs about the members of different ethnic groups. Thus if there exists a certain constellation of behaviors and mental states, racism exists, whether anyone identifies that constellation *as* racism or not. Put differently, although we "descriptively define" the boundaries for the *use* of such terms as *racism* (or *stonewalling*), we are merely putting a label on something that existed prior to the label. We did not bring the racism (or stonewalling) into existence in virtue of our discourse about racism (or stonewalling). Those entities did not "emerge" into being in some "emanationist" sense owing to our discourse about them. In short, although they are mind-dependent entities, they are also in a crucial sense discourse-independent entities (see chap. 5).

By contrast, Fowers (1998) and Richardson et al. (1999) seem to suggest that stonewalling, for example, cannot exist unless it is interpreted as such—although their exact position on this is not quite clear (see chap. 5, this volume). Moreover, Guignon (1998), Freeman (1993), Richardson et al. (1999), and Woolfolk (1998), among others, speak expressly of an "emanationist" or "emergent" theory of reality/truth, in which we bring into being what was already there all along, in the act of knowing/interpreting or narrating/telling (see chap. 5, this volume). Recall again Woolfolk's (1998) examples of sexism and racism to illustrate this: "An external reality that interpreters can access does exist, but that reality emerges only through interpretation and is delimited by the variety of constraints to which interpretation is subject" (p. 74). Presumably on his view there would, for example, be no racism, sexism, and stonewalling without our interpretive awareness of them as racism, sexism, and stonewalling.

Here we are again confronted with the role of language in the existence of human psychological kinds, but this time with its epistemological consequences—its preclusion of objective psychological knowledge. Let us examine that epistemic implication more closely.

Corollary to Antiobjectivist Argument 1: Linguistically Constitutive ("Direct") Versus Linguistically Mediated ("Indirect") Knowing of Psychological Entities Precludes Objective Knowledge

Because meanings and interpretations are linguistic entities, it may seem unnecessary to emphasize the role played by our use of language in the antiobjectivist epistemological arguments of MGTs. Yet that linguistic role cannot be emphasized enough owing to a convergence between MGTs and the radical postmodernists/constructionists whom they oppose epistemically. In short, it is not clear for either group whether language—especially local discursive/interpretive practices—(a) constitutes the psychological realities or entities to be known in the knowing process (what I referred to as "perverted direct knowing" in chap. 5 and what I will henceforth call "direct" knowing, with intended scare quotes) or (b) mediates between preexisting psychological realities or entities and the knower's attempt to access them (what I and others refer to as indirect or mediated knowing; see Held, 1995, pp. 7–9, 174–189 and Pols, 1992, 1998).

In either case a nonobjectivist epistemology is said to obtain, because in either case we can have no brute facts/data—no aconceptual or interpretation-free facts/data, which are said by MGTs (and radical postmodernists) to be necessary for objective knowledge. Because many MGTs equate objective knowledge with certitude (e.g., Bernstein, 1983, p. 19; Fishman, 1999, p. 113; Martin & Sugarman, 1999b, p. 189; Richardson et al., 1999, p. 303), and because interpretations are always open to revision (e.g., Richardson et al., 1999, p. 298, rightly say, "There is always room for reinterpretation"), the interpretation-laden (or nonbrute) facts/data that for MGTs constitute knowledge about the human world cannot constitute objective knowledge. Put differently, once language enters the epistemic picture, whether constitutively or mediationally, all objectivist bets are off!

Here I speak not of some MGTs' oscillation between the logical and causal dependence of psychological existence on discourse, although the epistemic matter now under consideration is not unrelated to that ontological matter, because causation is again (sometimes) invoked in "direct" knowing. That the knower supposedly constitutes the psychological reality to be known in the act of knowing again reflects the "emanationist" or "emergent" theory of reality/truth that we considered in chapter 5, in which the distinction between being and knowing or telling about being is deliberately blurred by MGTs. The radical constructionist version of this "perverted" form of direct or unmediated knowing implies that there can be no error in the act of knowing, because we constitute/make (or bring into being) in language the "reality" we then know "directly," exactly as it has been so constituted by us (Held, 2002b). On this account there is thus no distinction between the knowing subject and the object to be known. Polkinghorne (1983) put this most boldly: "Reality is views; it is not a thing which lies behind views and causes them" (p. 251).

By contrast, when MGTs say that we constitute in language the reality that was there all along, they distance themselves from this radically constructivist claim, so they make the fallibilist knowing that they endorse seem possible. However, it is not clear just how that fallibilism works. Especially apt is Maze's (2001) critique of antirealists' "immediate, therefore infallible, fusion" (p. 396) between the act of knowing and the representation that is "known," which alleged "knowledge" negates realism itself, because there could then be no error/fallibility in knowing[11] (see chap. 5, this volume, note 13; Held, 2002b, p. 667).

This form of the constitutive/emanationist/emergent view of reality/truth (we bring into being and so can know "directly" what was there all along) seems to pervade the thinking of quite a few MGTs and is distinctive to them (see chap. 5, this volume). However, I am not convinced that it makes sense or gives them their moderate realism, either ontologically or epistemically. In any case, they sometimes seem to endorse a linguistic, mediated (or indirect) form of knowing, which appears regularly in radical postmodernist/constructionist literature as well (see Held, 1995, for quotations).

In contrast to their constitutive/emanationist "direct" form of knowing, MGTs—when propounding an indirect or mediated form of knowing—seem to endorse a constructionist/antirealist doctrine: that our linguistic forestructures, conceptual schemes, or interpretive contexts always mediate between the knower and the entity to be known, and moreover in so doing alter or color in experience whatever the real, true, or "independent" nature of the entity to be known consists in (Held, 1995, p. 7). However, because

---

[11]Maze (2001) insists that only direct/unmediated knowing in which the entity to be known exists independently of the knowing process can be fallible. By contrast, I maintain (Held, 1995, 2002b) that indirect or theoretically mediated knowing can also be fallible, although indirect knowing (of entities that, although independent of the knowing process, are not directly accessible, such as the physics of the very large or very small) always depends ultimately on direct knowing (see Pols, 1992, 1998).

MGTs claim that psychological entities do not have a nature independent of human knowing (i.e., interpretive/conceptual/linguistic) practices (hence my use of scare quotes around the word *independent*), it is hard to see how this idea of mediation serves their epistemological realism. In short, neither their constitutive/emanationist form of "direct" knowing nor *their* version of indirect knowing supports the epistemic realism MGTs defend.

By contrast, MGTs who claim that we linguistically constitute or bring into being in the act of knowing a reality that was *already there* seem to be drawing some type of distinction between being and knowing, or between the object to be known and the knowing subject. Still, it remains unclear just what the nature of that distinction is and so how fallibilist knowing can obtain. In any case, let us here review statements of a few MGTs, who in addition to endorsing a constitutive view of knowing also seem to endorse a mediational or indirect view of knowing. The use of theory or language in the knowing process (including their expression in "background" cultural assumptions/beliefs/discourses) precludes the aconceptual or interpretation-free "brute data" that these (and all) MGTs, like the radical postmodernists/constructionists they find too extreme, deem necessary for objective knowledge. Note that in the second quotation there seems to be some slippage from the mediational or indirect view of knowing to the constitutive or "direct" view of knowing.

> Schafer (1980c, p. 49) correctly observes that human reality "is always mediated by narration." (Richardson et al., 1999, p. 259)
>
> We do not directly perceive "facts" about how things are. Instead, our encounters with things are always mediated by interests, feelings, and background assumptions. . . . If there are no absolutes outside us that determine the correct way of interpreting things . . . we alone are the source of the interpretations entities have in our world. In this sense, reality is *made*, not *found*[12]—it is a matter of invention rather than discovery. (Richardson et al., 1999, p. 118)
>
> The inescapability of interpretation is a severe blow to the traditional concept of scientific objectivity in psychology. (Richardson et al., 1999, p. 290)
>
> Individual humans gradually . . . construct progressively more elaborate theories of their contexts and themselves. Understanding resident in such theories . . . shifts the nature of such engagement from one of unmediated, direct perception and prereflection to one of mediated, reflective consciousness. (Martin & Sugarman, 1999a, pp. 21–22)
>
> Are not reports of one's experiences grounded in language conventions . . . ? If so, the experiences of the empiricist do not directly access the world as it is . . . [but rather] as it is mediated by language, which is

---

[12]Recall Richardson et al.'s (1999) somewhat different claim that "our nature or being as humans is not just something we *find* (as in deterministic theories), nor is it something we just *make* (as in existentialist and constructionist views); instead it is *what we make of what we find*" (p. 212).

itself socially derived. This mediation means that our thoughts and descriptions, including our interpretations of our world, are socially constructed. (Slife & Williams, 1995, p. 80)

The point in discussing whether, in pursuing knowledge about human psychological existence, linguistic constitution ("direct" knowing) or linguistic mediation (indirect knowing) is said to obtain, is this: Because theory/language[13] is involved in *any* way in the knowing process (as well as in our existence), brute facts/data cannot be attained, so the possibility of objective knowledge—which is said to depend on them—is seemingly precluded.

A Critique of the "Use of Language in Knowing, Therefore No Objective Knowledge" Corollary to Antiobjectivist Argument 1

For MGTs as well as radical postmodernists/constructionists, the use of language in the knowing process precludes objective knowing (at least about human kinds), owing to the local, situated nature of language use. On the MGTs' view, different discursive/interpretive contexts constitute or cause different experiences or understandings of social/psychological existence. These experiences or understandings may therefore be said to be relative to the context in which they occur.

Here we catch a glimpse of the epistemological relativism that pervades the MGTs' theory of knowing and knowledge, which—despite their claims to ontological and epistemological realism—complements their ontological relativism (see chap. 5, this volume). In short, each discursive/interpretive context so colors, conditions, or biases the knowing process in its own particular way that no knower can ever claim to know the thing in itself[14] as it exists objectively or independently of the knower's situated (and therefore presumably biased) discourse or language use. Thus there can be no "brute" (interpretation-free/aconceptual) facts (see note 4), and so objective knowledge cannot obtain. As Woolfolk, Sass, and Messer (1988) stated, "Since what is known is always known by a knower situated within history and society, interpretation is always conditioned and influenced by the tradition and horizon of understanding within which one operates" (p. 17).

Add to this the MGTs' ontological claim that our social/psychological existence is itself constituted or caused/conditioned by the local discursive/

---

[13]Theory and language are often conflated by antirealists; hence my use of a slash to convey that conflation (see note 15).

[14]My use of the Kantian term "thing in itself" is deliberate. Recall from chapter 3 (note 7) Pols's (2000a) claim that although Kant was an antirealist (he thought "commonsense and scientific knowledge gives us appearance rather that reality"), such appearances are not relative to local discursive contexts. They are, rather, "inevitable appearances, based on a union of sense and understanding that all human beings have in common." But Kant "took the paradoxical step of calling this world of appearance objective" because for him objectivity was subjective in origin; it emerged from the universal properties of mind (p. 56). Also see Held (1995, p. 257, note 2).

interpretive context in which we reflexively participate, and it becomes clear that not only are there no brute facts about that existence but also no brute *existence*—that is, we are interpretation/historical "all the way down." The two of course go together: If humans do not exist psychologically independently of their beliefs about their psychological existence, then how can they know (and so make factual statements about) that existence as it is, independent of their beliefs, interpretations, and concepts about that existence? And if they cannot know that existence as it is, independent of their beliefs about that existence, then there can be no objective knowledge of that existence, at least not according to conventional definitions of an objectivist (or realist) epistemology.

Here we again confront the "blurred distinction between being and knowing about being" (see chap. 5, this volume) that leads MGTs straight to their antiobjectivist epistemology. This blurring is otherwise known in MGT circles as the "double hermeneutic" that allegedly pervades psychological (and all social science) inquiry—"the two-way relations between actions and those who study them" (Windschuttle, 1996, p. 206). This incorporates Giddens's "theory of reflexivity," in which humans are said to be "always already" interpreted entities when they (re)turn to (re)interpret themselves and each other time and again (see chaps. 5 & 7, this volume). In short, the "emanationist" or "emergent" theory of reality/truth, in which we allegedly constitute or bring into being in our discourses/narratives (about our social/ psychological existence) what was there "all along," itself "emerges" in the words of some MGTs.

> The inescapability of interpretation is a severe blow to the traditional concept of scientific objectivity in psychology and other social sciences, for . . . no matter how carefully we specify and measure the phenomena of interest, these descriptions are dependent on a background of meanings that are not being measured, and the descriptions help bring the phenomena into being. (Richardson et al., 1999, p. 290)

Again, I must ask this question: If social/psychological existence and the act of knowing about that existence are not distinct enough to permit even the possibility of objective knowledge about that existence, then how can they be distinct enough to allow for the fallibilist inquiry some MGTs use to defend their version of realism? Yet despite deploying just that defense, Richardson et al. (1999) remain resolute in their determination to preclude the possibility of objectivist inquiry in the social sciences. In addition to their emanationist theory of truth/reality, they approvingly cite Slife and Williams (1995) to proclaim that all methods of inquiry, in presupposing "a number of things about what the world is really like," are so infused with theory (that which is conceptual/linguistic or interpretation-laden) that "methods are hardly in a position to serve as an independent test of our theories or beliefs" (Richardson et al., 1999, p. 178). Here I take "independent" to mean "objective," and so the point remains: When language enters the epistemic door—whether in the form of formal theoretical or everyday conceptualization[15]—objective knowledge flies out the window.

To be sure, there are ways around the presumed "obstacles" to objective knowing that are supposedly caused by a conceptual/linguistic component in all acts of knowing that may be properly called *rational* acts of knowing. However, these other possibilities do not seem to occur to MGTs, who—in their search for an alternative epistemology—oscillate between (a) rejecting the possibility of the interpretation-free/aconceptual "brute facts" presumed necessary for objective knowledge and the epistemic certainty that they erroneously equate with it; and (b) reformulating "objective" (or what they prefer to call realist) knowledge in more middle-ground, interpretation-laden/conceptual and fallibilist terms. That there exist arguments that support conventional views of epistemic objectivity that require neither (a) eliminating from the knowing process a conceptual component nor (b) retaining in the knowing process certainty/infallibility seems to elude them. Indeed, facts (about the nature of a kind, including human kinds) need not be interpretation-free/aconceptual "brute" facts to be objective facts, in perfectly conventional terms. Nor must they preclude indirect or mediated (i.e., theoretical) knowing in the process of attaining them. But to be objective facts, they do need to be warranted "independently of . . . what anyone believes" (Erwin, 1999, p. 353).

In his incisive critique of Richard Rorty, Guignon (1991) said that Rorty "buys into and reflects the very epistemological model that Rorty intends to reject" (p. 94). On Guignon's view, Rorty promotes pragmatic solidarity ("what a group happens to find commendable in the way of belief," p. 94) over epistemic truth. Yet, says Guignon, Rorty nonetheless suggests "the stance of detached objectivity and ironic playfulness" (p. 95) that not only contradicts his antiepistemic stance but also fails to make sense of his own deep (moral) commitments: "Rorty's pragmatism looks plausible only because it buys into the key assumptions of the epistemological tradition and because it surreptitiously presupposes commitments that its own position makes unintelligible" (p. 96). Just as Guignon suggests that Rorty depends on the very object/subject dichotomy (of the epistemological tradition) he rejects, so I argue that MGTs rely on the very epistemic objectivity they reject to make their (objective) case for their antiobjectivist epistemology.

---

[15]Pols (1992) aptly described the conflation of theory and language.
> Many academic philosophers today . . . seem to think of the holding of a theory as a kind of language use. Curiously, they also tend to think of language use as a kind of theory holding. In short, they blend what, on the face of it, are separate notions or concepts, "language" and "theory." . . . They make all knowledge a function of language-cum-theory, so much so that for them there is no way to get outside language-cum-theory to know *anything* directly. (p. 5)

Continued Critique of the Corollary To Antiobjectivist Claim 1: Finding a Place for the Conceptual in Direct (Objective) Knowing and the Theoretical in Indirect (Objective) Knowing

Let us continue our critique by first reviewing the antiobjectivist claims of MGTs. Because we bring background concepts, theories, discourses, paradigms, beliefs, interpretations, meanings, and ideas (i.e., linguistic entities) to our attempts to know human (social/psychological) kinds, we cannot have access to interpretation-free/aconceptual (or brute) facts about our psychological existence (which itself is said to be constituted in interpretation). Therefore we cannot have objective knowledge about our nonbrute/interpretation-laden existence—or so the argument goes.

Another way to express this argument is in terms of direct and indirect knowing. Because all acts of knowing (including observational experiences) are infused with a conceptual element, we supposedly cannot have the direct access we are said to need for objective knowledge to obtain. Moreover, to the extent that our conceptual apparatus gives us indirect or mediated knowledge (as opposed to constituting or bringing forth psychological entities in the act of knowing—what I have called "perverted direct knowing"), we still cannot have access to brute facts, because cognitive mediation brings interpretation (or interpretive bias) into the act of knowing. That act therefore cannot give us the "brute" thing in itself (assuming there are brute things, at least in the physical world), as it exists independently of our background/situated beliefs, interpretations, discourses, theories and so forth. So for antiobjectivists there exists no direct knowing, and indirect or mediated knowing cannot even in principle supply the interpretation-free/aconceptual (or brute) facts presumed necessary for objective knowledge. Add to this the problematic assertion that objective knowing necessitates certitude or indubitability, and the case is closed. How can we be certain about anything in the empirical world, if knowing about the world always requires us to make use of our interpretive/conceptual processes and products, which themselves always remain open to revision?

But what if we took a more positive and flexible (but still fallibilist) view of knowing in general, including knowing about human kinds, in the name of conventional objectivism? What if language were viewed not as an inherent impediment to knowing, but as a potential aid to the direct knowing ultimately needed for objective knowledge? And what if theory, which is expressed in language but is not synonymous with language (see note 15), were seen as having the potential to provide objective—albeit indirect or mediated—access to a reality to which we can have no direct access, such as the physics of the very large or very small or causality in general? And what if, as we find in conventional definitions of objectivist/realist epistemologies (e.g., Erwin, 1999; Haack, 2002; T. Smith, 2004; Thomasson, 2003), objective knowledge did not necessitate certitude, but rather allowed for the fallibilist knowing MGTs themselves endorse? All this is what philosopher Edward Pols maintains in *Radical Realism* (1992) and again in *Mind Regained* (1998).

Pols unites the generality/universality of the conceptual realm and the (unique) particularity of the experiential realm in his concept "rational awareness," which we first encountered in chapter 5. *Rational awareness* is Pols's term for the direct (unmediated) knowing on which all knowing (even theoretically mediated knowing) ultimately depends; it is the basis for the objective knowledge that we can in principle attain. Thus contrary to the usual antirealist/antiobjectivist assumption that language must, by its very nature, preclude access to the thing in itself, for Pols language makes direct knowing—*rational* awareness—possible. It is important to note again that for him language and theory are not interchangeable (see note 15): Language is a component of direct (unmediated) rational knowing of entities to which we can have direct access, such as trees and x-ray machines (which are nonlinguistic entities) and poems and theories (which are linguistic entities); theory is necessary for indirect (mediated) rational knowing of entities to which we cannot have direct access, such as the causes of racism and stonewalling (which are social/psychological entities) and cancer and black holes (which are physical entities). However, neither the use of language (in direct knowing) nor of theory (in indirect or mediated knowing) necessarily precludes objective knowledge of the thing in itself, the thing as it exists independently of our knowing processes—or, if the thing is a social/psychological entity (e.g., attitudes), at least independently enough to permit substantive fallibilist inquiry (cf. Thomasson, 2003). That is the point of Pols's "radical realism," for the presumed preclusion of objective knowledge is the negative (antiobjectivist) judgment about knowing that prevails in radical postmodernist and MGT circles alike.

Rational awareness, to be sure, is an active knowing process, and in that sense it is agentic. Pols claims that knowers bring *universal* cognitive/conceptual (i.e., rational) functions to their active engagement with whatever *particular* reality they are at any moment experiencing (i.e., aware of). The knowing process is thus one of active, directed attention, in which the knower engages the real and attains it in a sense that can only be called active knowing. Rational awareness, then, incorporates two components unified in any one act of knowing. The first component, the *awareness or experiential (or empirical) pole* of knowing, consists in the particulars of whatever here-and-now one is experiencing (e.g., that the cat is on the mat). The second component, the *rational pole* of knowing, consists in one's conceptual understanding of that here-and-now experience—understanding that entails all the generality that the conceptual bestows on any particular act of knowing.

It is of prime importance that the two poles are inextricably fused in any act of direct knowing.

The term "awareness" is not meant to call attention to a mode of experience that functions at a subrational level, nor is the term "rational" meant to call attention to some purely conceptual or propositional way of functioning. Rational awareness is *reason experiencing* rather than reason responding to experience. (Pols, 1992, p. 155)[16]

This is important: Rather than our conceptual/linguistic activity (a) constituting or bringing forth "directly" the "reality" to be known (the perverted direct knowing of some radical postmodernists/constructionists) or (b) altering in experience the real nature of some independent reality in virtue of an indirect or mediational process that distorts in experience the nature of the reality to be known, language—the conceptual—helps govern and stabilize our direct experience of the particular real. As Pols (1992) put it, "The fusion of the rational and the experiential poles in direct knowing means that the awareness [or experiential component] supports and justifies the articulation, while the articulation [or rational component] focuses, intensifies, and stabilizes the awareness" (p. 156).

Even the possibility of this fusion is a bitter pill for MGTs and radical postmodernists to swallow. For them local linguistic/discursive contexts so constitute, determine, or affect our local/relativistic existence, and so color or bias our local/relativistic knowledge about that existence, that it is inconceivable that the linguistic/conceptual component of direct knowing, and the theoretical component of indirect or mediated knowing, could help us understand ourselves and the world around us in objective (or unbiased or nonrelativistic) terms. Yet that is exactly Pols's (1992, 1998) claim, in part because he finds universality in all particularity (what he calls the "U-factor" for universality and the "P-factor" for particularity; see chaps. 5 & 7, this volume), including the particularity each of us embodies in his unique existence (e.g., just *this* person, just *his* joy, just *her* smile). It is the U-factor that gives us rational/cognitive access to the particularities (P-factor) that we encounter/experience in the first place. That Pols insists on the fusion of the P-factor and the U-factor indicates the egalitarian importance he gives to particularity as well as universality.

Because rational awareness is reason experiencing, not reason responding to experience, Pols can speak of mind's (rational) functions[17] as universal functions. Even some MGTs seem so inclined when they invoke universal cognitive processes in particular acts of (for example) imagining, remembering, thinking, and attending—including attending reflexively to oneself (see Freeman, 1993; Harré, 2002; Liebrucks, 2001; Martin & Sugarman, 1999a, 1999b). It is just such universal cognitive acts that make possible an agentic ability to transcend some aspects of what we now are, as we reach for a differ-

[16]For more detail about what Pols calls the rational-experiential engagement characteristic of direct knowing, see Pols (1992, pp. 33–35, 130, 138–144, 176–179).
[17]Pols (1998, p. 98) gives a quasi-comprehensive list of mind's functions, which includes knowing, among many others. For this list see chapter 10 of this volume, note 13.

ent, presumably better way of being. Put differently, the context that is said to constitute us psychologically cannot make us *all* that we are; we cannot be historical/interpretation *all* the way down, if each of us—in virtue of being human—has a (mindful) capacity to become something other than what we have until this moment been constituted to be within our discursive context (cf. Jenkins, 2001; Rychlak, 1997; see chap. 6, this volume).

Returning now to the MGTs' antiobjectivist epistemology, we find that despite their rejection of other dichotomies (e.g., the subject/object dichotomy), they seem to accept a dichotomy between facts about (a) brute entities, such as trees, rocks, and other physical kinds, which are not constituted by discourses/interpretations or linguistic practices, and (b) nonbrute entities, such as attitudes, emotions, and other mental kinds, which are said to be constituted by (local) discourses/interpretations or linguistic practices. For example, Miller (2004) and Richardson et al. (1999) seem to accept the possibility of objective knowledge of physical (aconceptual/interpretation-free or brute) entities, but not of social/psychological (conceptual/interpretation-laden or nonbrute) entities.

Searle (1995) similarly distinguishes brute facts (which do not depend on human intentionality) from institutional facts (which do depend on human intentionality). Moreover, he insists that whereas brute facts "require the institution of language" to state them, they themselves (or at least the reality to which those facts refer) "exist quite independently of language or any other institutions" (p. 27; see note 4, this chapter).

But if, as many MGTs seem to believe, the necessary infusion of *all* observation (or knowing/awareness) with a conceptual, interpretive, or linguistic component in principle precludes objective knowledge, then it becomes questionable whether we could have objective knowledge even of brute entities. It would therefore help to know with more precision the implications for objective knowledge that MGTs find in (a) the distinction between brute (or physical) and nonbrute (or mental/intentional) entities and (b) the role of a conceptual, interpretive, or linguistic component in knowing any kind of entity. Can a brute entity, which is thought to be subject only to a so-called "single hermeneutic" in the act of knowing it, be known with objectivity (unlike a nonbrute entity, owing to its alleged "double hermeneutic" status)? Again, if interpretation is involved (either singly or doubly) in knowing any kind of entity, and if interpretation is the source of fallibility (because interpretations must always remain open to revision), and if—as MGTs (erroneously) claim—objective knowledge is by definition indubitable knowledge, then how can there be objective knowledge about any kind of entity?

Here it might help to return to our philosophers who do not accept an antiobjectivist conclusion based on the reasonable premise of a linguistic/conceptual or theoretical component in observation/knowing. Recall that

Pols uses the fusion of the conceptual/rational "pole" of direct knowing with the experiential/empirical "pole" of direct knowing in the service of his objectivist epistemology (which he prefers to call realist). By contrast, MGTs use the (locally situated) linguistic and/or theoretical nature of observation (their version of the conceptual/empirical fusion) in the service of their antiobjectivist epistemology (which they also call realist).

Pols is not the only philosopher who finds a place for the conceptual in objective knowing. In *Defending Science—Within Reason*, Haack (2003) does not use the term *rational-experiential engagement* or speak of *reason experiencing*. Pols's articulation of rational awareness goes deeper metaphysically than anything Haack offers. However, in her use of the term *experience-and-reasoning* (p. 125), she supports the "intimate" "interdependence" (if not Pols's "fusion") of reason/rationality on the one hand, and experience/observation on the other, as necessary for objective knowledge or truth nonetheless. This she makes especially clear in her crossword puzzle analogy,[18] in which prior entries are analogous to background reasons/beliefs, and clues to each entry are analogous to empirical observations/evidence. But this intimate interdependence does not preclude objective truth, because even the world of human kinds (or "we, and the world") is, according to Haack, "a certain way" (p. 124): "There are objective truths, and the sciences sometimes succeed in discovering some of them; but truth is not transparent,[19] and progress is not guaranteed" (p. 124).

> The method of everyday empirical inquiry, and the method of science . . . , is the method of experience and reasoning; or, since the two work so intimately together, perhaps "the method of experience-and-reasoning." . . . It is sometimes assumed that to acknowledge the inter-dependence of perception and background belief, of observation and theory, is eo ipso to deny that experience can be a real evidential constraint. But this is a mistake. Is perception dependent on background beliefs, observation on theory? Yes. . . . Is there a privileged category of infallible observation statements, or of observable things? No, and no again. And yet the evidence of the senses ultimately anchors our theories in the world, and it is a real constraint. (p. 125)

In defending objective knowledge or truth in science and in everyday life, Haack (2003) seemingly dismisses any sharp distinction between raw (aconceptual/interpretation-free) data, experiences, and observations on the one hand, and conceptualized/interpretational judgments on the other. In this next quotation, she accepts fallibilist inquiry in attaining epistemic ob-

---

[18]Also see Haack's (1998c) "Puzzling Out Science," in *Manifesto of a Passionate Moderate*.
[19]That Haack finds truth not to be transparent in the human world is reminiscent of our discussion in chapter 5 of Thomasson's claim that questions about some human kinds (e.g., the nature and existence of racism) can remain "opaque" (open to gross ignorance and massive error) even within any given context.

jectivity. Although she links fallibilism to interpretation (that which is conceptual), she does not allow local interpretive/discursive contexts to preclude objectivity in principle, as do MGTs.

> In every perceptual event . . . there is something received, something resistant to one's will and independent of one's expectations. In every judgment . . . there is something in some degree interpretive, and hence fallible. There is no sharply distinguishable category of statements the meaning of which is exhausted by experience. . . . The meaning of any statement depends on the links between its words and others as well as on the links with the world learned directly by ostension. . . . To deny that there is a sharply distinguishable category of interpretation-free observation statements is not to say that "it's a glass of water" or "it's gone green" or "lo, a raven" are really theoretical statements after all. (p. 128)

Let us return to the conclusions reached by MGTs that stand in distinction to those of philosophers such as Pols and Haack, who accept the possibility of objective knowledge given an intimate interdependence—or even a fusion—of the conceptual and observational realms in acts of knowing. Recall that MGTs take this fusion necessarily to imply an antiobjectivist epistemology (at least regarding knowledge of human kinds). Pols and Haack, by contrast, use it to support their objectivist epistemologies (including knowledge of human kinds). Who is right? Only substantive philosophical debate can settle the matter, but I side with Pols and Haack: I do not think that MGTs have made their case that all knowledge of the human world is so colored or biased (or, as they like to put it, prejudiced) by local discursive/interpretive practices that no objective knowledge of that world can obtain—that the infusion of observation with a conceptual/linguistic (or what Pols considers a rational) component necessarily defeats epistemic objectivity.

One way to argue that the MGTs' antiobjectivist conclusion does not follow from their premise that all observation is infused with (locally based) concepts, interpretations, or language (so that all observation is necessarily colored or biased in a way particular to the relevant context) is to appeal to Pols's argument: that the conceptual component of direct knowing brings with it the universality or generality on which rationality (and the objective knowledge to which rational awareness can give rise) depends. Therefore the local situatedness of the knower—especially as it pertains to the knower's linguistic/conceptual background—does not necessarily color or bias (or corrupt) the knower's access to the real, as it exists independently of the knower's cognitive activity. Instead that linguistic/conceptual background makes (objective) access to the real (both direct and mediated or indirect) possible in the first place owing to the universality that inheres in *its* particularity. A different way to express this argument is to appeal to the universal (context-transcendent) features of mind/rationality (including mind's knowing, observational, or attentional processes), as do some MGTs (see chap. 6).

Another, perhaps less metaphysically daunting, way to challenge the MGTs' antiobjectivist conclusion is closer to Haack's (2003) claim that the intimate interdependence between reasoning and experience or between theory and observation does not necessarily preclude objective knowledge—because even the world of human kinds is, according to Haack, "a certain way" (p. 124). That certain way does not depend for its existence on beliefs about its existence and nature. Hence there can in principle be objective knowledge about that world.

Indeed, if these philosophers are correct, it would seem that objective knowledge is possible even for some mind-dependent (nonbrute) entities. Here recall from chapter 5 Thomasson's arguments about human kinds, especially her example of racism. Racism is a mind-dependent entity; if there were no minds there would be no racism. Moreover, we certainly use language to stipulate the boundary or existence conditions/criteria for the use of the term *racism*, and racist acts themselves often involve the use of language within discursive/interpretive/linguistic communities. Nonetheless, it does not follow that racism is merely a matter of what anyone (or everyone) in a certain discursive/interpretive/linguistic community (or even outside that community) says or believes racism is. That is because racism could exist even if the word *racism* never occurred to anyone and no one ever stipulated the boundary conditions of its existence; it can exist prior to anyone's stipulating how the term is to be used even if one possessed the relevant concept.

That we must stipulate racism's boundary conditions to *study* racism, then, does not itself mean that we cause racism to come into *existence*. That is because racism can exist without beliefs about racism as a kind. It is mind independent in just that respect. Thus in principle we can make perfectly objective observations about the existence of racism in any given context, about the factors that increase or decrease its presence, and so on. These sorts of questions about racism (and other social/psychological kinds) are open to substantive, fallible discovery, as are certain questions about such brute entities as rocks, whose boundary conditions we must also stipulate to study them. In short, we can be grossly ignorant of any existing racism or massively wrong about its nature, within or beyond any given context (see chap. 5).

By now it should be evident that holding an objectivist epistemology does not deny or diminish the importance of the unique particulars that humans encounter across different cultural/discursive contexts, or even within any one context. Most profound in this regard is Pols's explication of rational awareness, which is highly respectful of the cultural diversity that MGTs exalt in their rejection of universals/essentials in the human world. After all, Pols's rational awareness grants direct access to unique (and thus diverse) particulars—this is just what the "awareness" component of the term *rational awareness* is meant to emphasize. Moreover, direct access to particularity can rightly be called objective knowledge of particularity—hence his use of the term *P-factor* to call attention to the importance of particularity in the act of knowing something (particular) that is not constituted by the knower in the act of knowing. The universals of rationality (including the rationality enjoyed in everyday and scientific inquiry) do not trump or eliminate the particularities of culture; they make possible culture or cultural particularity—including cultural evolution, transcendence, or change—by allowing us to know (objectively) what we might wish to preserve or overcome.

In this final quotation of Pols (1992), we see how overcoming or transcending what exists "here and now" (which is just what MGTs themselves emphasize in their descriptions of agency; see chap. 6, this volume) can obtain only with the help of the universality/generality of the rational pole. His term *openness to particularity* is also reminiscent of hermeneutically inclined MGTs, who deploy a Gadamerian "fusion of horizons" as a means to (agentic or intentional) transcendence of constitutive cultural contexts (see chap. 6, this volume). But for Pols the openness to particularity is also openness to reality itself, as it exists independently of acts of knowing any particular reality. In this way he makes no truck with the antiobjectivist epistemological conclusions of MGTs.

> The rational pole is a universal, symbol-generating transcendence of the here and now, but its functioning depends on the presence of the experiential pole—and the latter is unfailingly present, even in our most formal intellectual exercises. . . . The fusion of the two poles must be taken seriously: although the rational pole plays the governing and active role in our cognitive access to the real, it does so only under the constraint of the experiential pole. The experiential pole, on the other hand, is our sense-based receptivity to the real by way of the particularity of the here and now, but only under the governance of the rational pole; so the receptivity is not merely an openness to particularity but rather an openness to reality by way of particularity. (p. 156)

What better starting point for any account of agency than "openness to reality by way of particularity"? I return to this account in chapter 10. Here let us assess another argument used by MGTs to support their antiobjectivist epistemology.

Antiobjectivist Argument 2: There Is No Value-Free "View From Nowhere," No "God's-Eye View"; Therefore, There Can Be No Objective Knowledge

The Ontological Claim

Recall that for MGTs human social/psychological existence is one of "being in the world"; it is an existence that is constituted (or caused) by the particulars of the historical/cultural/interpretive/discursive contexts into which humans are "thrown." This means that we are situated beings and so can enjoy what is called "situated personhood" (see chap. 4). All the particulars of local contexts (including the linguistic/conceptual and theoretical particulars on which we focused in Antiobjectivist Argument 1) can help make us what we are. That is why some MGTs maintain that we are historical/interpretive beings all the way down. Thus, on their view, facts about human kinds—which are not aconceptual/interpretation-free (or brute) kinds—cannot in principle be objective or brute facts.

In addition to giving prime attention to the particularities of the linguistic/conceptual aspect of our local or situated existence as that affects both our being and our knowing about that being, MGTs emphasize the local values that help to make us what we are. Therefore, it is to values that we now turn. It is not immediately obvious that values are linguistic entities, although surely they are conceptual in some sense, and so I will join MGTs and treat them as conceptual/interpretation-laden, or nonbrute, entities. After all, they help constitute (or contribute to) the discourse/interpretations of discursive/interpretive contexts, and MGTs themselves (e.g., Richardson et al., 1999, p. 202) often speak of "meanings and values" as if they were inextricably fused—which in some ways seems right.

However, it does seem obvious that we need values to exist socially and psychologically—not least because, as MGTs rightly point out, our social/ psychological existence is necessarily a moral (or immoral) existence. It cannot be an amoral existence, because what we say and do—the choices we make, the goals we set, and the routes we take to attain those goals—often have consequences (judged right or wrong) for how we (and others) live our lives (Cushman, 1995; Fowers, 2003, 2005; Fowers & Richardson, 1996; Freeman, 1993; Guignon, 1991; Harré, 1984; Howard, 1986; Martin & Sugarman, 1999b; Martin et al., 2003; Miller, 2004; Polkinghorne, 1983; Richardson et al., 1999; Robinson, 2002a, 2002b; Slife & Williams, 1995; Tjeltveit, 1999, 2003; Woolfolk, 1998). In short, values are a fundamental and necessary component of our (psychological) personhood.

It is beyond the scope of this book to argue whether values should be viewed in morally realist or relativist terms,[20] although the question of whether MGTs have articulated a local—and by my lights relativist—ontology of being in the world that is nonetheless realist is surely relevant to this question (see chap. 5). Rather, my concern is with the epistemological implications of the locally value-laden nature of our psychological existence. Does an existence fraught with values pave the way for the realist but antiobjectivist epistemology to which the MGTs aspire?

---

[20]See Pols's (1982) *The Acts of Our Being* and Robinson's (2002b) *Praise and Blame*, for defenses of moral realism. See Tjeltveit's (1999) *Ethics and Values in Psychotherapy* for the distinction between moral (i.e., prescriptive) and nonmoral (i.e., aspirational but not prescriptive) goods, both of which are subsumed by ethical values.

The Epistemological Conclusion

What follows epistemically from the value-laden nature of our exist-ence in the world is this: Because our psychological existence is fraught with values (owing to our local "being in the world"), so too are our knowing practices—or so MGTs argue. Thus our local historical/cultural situatedness so constitutes or conditions our wants, desires, interests, and aspirations (i.e., our values), and this value-laden constitution or conditioning in turn so con-stitutes or conditions (affects, prejudices, or "infects") our knowing processes, that we cannot be said (even in principle) to have non-value-laden knowl-edge about our social/psychological existence. Moreover, just as any concep-tual/interpretive or linguistic element in the act of knowing is thought by MGTs to deprive us of the brute facts that are presumed necessary for the certitude that they equate erroneously with objective knowledge (see Antiobjectivist Argument 1), so too the alleged pervasion of the knowing process with values is thought to preclude certain/objective knowledge. In short, for MGTs there can be no distinction between facts (or "facts") and values (at least in the human world); for them there exists no fact/value distinction—a "fact" that precludes the possibility of objective knowledge, in which facts and values are indeed distinguished.

The "fact" that values are said to contribute not only to the content of interpretive/discursive contexts but also to the interpretive/discursive (i.e., knowing) processes that exist within those contexts necessitates a blurring of the distinction between values and discourses/interpretations, including knowledge claims or beliefs. Indeed, all claims may then be fairly said to embody the values that inhere in the local contexts from which those claims originate; values are in that case a necessary or inherent/essential feature of discourses, interpretations, knowledge claims, and/or beliefs. Put differently, insofar as values may be said to embody meanings (and meanings values), they too are not interpretation-free/aconceptual or nonlinguistic (i.e., brute) entities. Therefore (a) the "no conceptual/observational distinction" (or the "no theoretical/observational distinction") and (b) the "no fact/value dis-tinction" contain common assumptions, and they both contribute to an antiobjectivist epistemological conclusion.

Consider these statements of MGTs, many of whose antiobjectivist sen-timents were quoted earlier. Notice that the role of values in producing facts/knowledge is considered desirable; the attempt to eliminate them is said to make conventional psychological inquiry detached, sterile, and ultimately useless—if not altogether impossible.

> The effort [in naturalistic psychological science] to maintain a sharp dis-tinction between fact and value has been entirely unsuccessful, resulting in an ostensibly objective scientific endeavor that in fact perpetuates a disguised ideology. (Richardson et al., 1999, p. 277)

Psychological inquiry is better characterized as the morally motivated activity of concerned citizens who want to improve the life of their community and nation, rather than as the austere work of disengaged, neutral observers. (Richardson et al., 1999, p. 304)

Most contemporary psychology researchers write as if they believe themselves to be accumulating neutral, objective facts in a value free, transhistorical, epistemological arena. . . . Such an approach ignores the extent to which such facts are inextricably interwoven with theory, with the researcher's biases, with the choice of language used to describe the terms employed, and with sociocultural and historical influences. (Woolfolk et al., 1988, p. 24)

The discipline of psychology has . . . [attempted] to separate presumably objective facts about behavior and presumably subjective considerations about morality and values. . . . The attempt to create a value-neutral science and practice, valiant as it has been, has failed us in many ways. (Fowers, 2005, p. 6)

It seems unlikely that we would ever achieve . . . objective grounds from which to observe anything, including experimental results. . . . The very definitions and framing of a research question are shot through with traditions, history, expectations, values, and other subjective factors. It seems unlikely that at any stage the research process is objective. (Slife & Williams, 1995, pp. 193–194)

Most important in considering these arguments is the epistemological question of what warrants or justifies claims to psychological knowledge. MGTs make two points about the relation between epistemic warrant and values: (a) We cannot avoid the imposition of values in bestowing warrant or justification on knowledge claims in psychology, but (b) this is a good thing, because our psychological knowledge claims affect us reflexively, and so the good and bad consequences of those claims *should* play a strong role in epistemic warrant. Put differently, our situated existence (our "view from somewhere") predeterministically "colors" not only our value-laden existence but also the value-laden way in which we warrant knowledge claims about the nature of that existence, so that they cannot be rightly called objective claims. Again, these two descriptive claims (about being and knowing about being) are often expressed by MGTs as a rejection of the fact/value dichotomy.

But MGTs go further, for they not only *describe* our ontological and epistemic natures and practices but also *prescribe* them. Inquiry about human psychological existence *should* appeal to our wants, desires, interests, and aspirations (our values) to establish warranted claims; modern/conventional psychological inquiry has (mistakenly and failingly) tried to eliminate contextualized values from its epistemology. That is, even the doomed attempt to attain objective (non-value-laden) knowledge is seen as wrong headed, given (a) the (conceptual/nonbrute and value-laden) nature of human social/psychological existence and (b) the nature of inquiry about that existence, which is said always to affect that existence reflexively (see chaps. 5 & 7). Following are two quotations that we have seen before and that reinforce the MGTs' point.

> Social constructionists argue that psychological discourses not only describe the conduct of persons but inevitably also evaluate this conduct, and therefore psychological discourses have a reflexive impact on the very phenomena they attempt to represent. . . . Thus . . . there can certainly be no value-free psychology. (Liebrucks, 2001, p. 385)

> Because humans just *are* what they interpret themselves as being within their social contexts, . . . it follows that social theory cannot be thought of as a neutral process of recording facts about humans. Insofar as interpretations devised by social scientists feed back into the culture and so define and alter the reality they describe, . . . the practice of interpreting humans has wide-ranging ethical and political implications. Far from being a neutral, value-free form of inquiry, the human sciences always operate with culturally mediated value assumptions and always influence the cultural context they address. Hermeneutics therefore calls for . . . moral and political awareness that is . . . overlooked in both mainstream scientistic and constructionist approaches to studying human phenomena. (Richardson et al., 1999, p. 236)

There is much in the second passage on which to comment. First, note that the opening sentence—which I have quoted repeatedly in the chapters on ontology—is now recast in epistemic terms. Second, note that the praiseworthy hermeneutic approach avoids both (modern) "scientistic" and (postmodern) constructionist forms of social/psychological inquiry. Third, note how mediated or indirect knowing is supposed to challenge the conventional attempt to "record [brute] facts." And fourth (and most important), note the implicit suggestion that values should be part of the criteria we use to establish epistemic warrant: Because the (social/psychological) theories that we accept as true reflexively affect our contextualized existence, we are morally obligated to consider their moral and political impact as a legitimate part of our deliberations about their truth status. This last point is important, and juxtaposing it with this statement made by Gergen (1985)—in his call for the radical social constructionism that MGTs reject—reveals just how close some MGTs come to taking a position that they say explicitly is too extreme for their attempts at moderation.

> Unlike the moral relativism of the empirical tradition, constructionism reasserts the relevance of moral criteria for scientific practice. To the extent that psychological theory (and related practices) enter into the life of the culture, sustaining certain patterns of conduct and destroying others, such work must be evaluated in terms of good and ill. The practitioner can no longer justify any socially reprehensible conclusion on the grounds of being a "victim of the facts"; he or she must confront the pragmatic implications of such conclusions within society more generally. (p. 273)

Richardson et al. (1999) are not quite clear about just how mediation operates in human science inquiry. I presume this: Just as the role of theory in indirect or mediated knowing is sometimes used by MGTs and radical postmodernists to deny any possible access to an independent or objective reality (assuming one exists), Richardson et al. assume unavoidable "culturally mediated value assumptions" (in the previous passage) to be the mediating obstacle to objective inquiry/knowledge. Richardson et al. (1999) go further in suggesting that values (or at least interests) always stand between, or mediate, our knowing efforts and the entity to be known; those knowing efforts must therefore always be of the indirect sort. This alleged state of affairs automatically precludes for them the attainment of (objective or, in this case, non-value-laden) facts. Instead all we can have are (value-laden) "facts"—although again, this is not seen as problematic. I presume these value-laden "facts" are nonobjective, in virtue of a postmodernist-like use of scare quotes around the word *facts*: "We do not directly perceive 'facts' about how things are.[21] Instead, our encounters with things are always mediated by interests, feelings, and background assumptions we bring with us to the encounter" (p. 118).

In that last statement, no room is left for the possibility that, even in regard to human kinds, (a) a conceptual component (e.g., "background assumptions" or prior entries in Haack's crossword puzzle analogy) can make possible direct knowing/rational awareness and (b) the interpretive realm of theory can make possible indirect or mediated knowing that is objective nonetheless. Thus both (a) and (b) can in principle aid those of us who seek objective knowledge about the human world (and beyond). Again, in the name of moderation, we find in MGTs what amounts to a negative philosophical judgment about knowing—however much that judgment is celebrated as a more proper, human-friendly, morally engaged form of psychological science.

Here are some quotations in which epistemic warrant (or deciding what should count as a fact) is said always to be (and on this view *should* always be) laden with the values or interests embedded in the relevant discursive/interpretive context. This constitutes the antiobjectivist pragmatic standard of warrant seen in the writings of radical constructionists and MGTS. In some of these quotations of MGTs, the perspectival nature of knowing (from a "vantage point" or "standpoint")—the idea that there is no "view from nowhere"—is emphasized. In others, values are emphasized. In some, both are made prominent and are sometimes linked.

---

[21]I am not sure just what Richardson et al. (1999) mean when they say "we do not directly perceive 'facts' about how things are" (p. 118). In the next sentence they mention the mediation of "our encounters with things," which things I take to be the objects of our presumably mediated knowing. If "'facts' about how things are" are also things themselves, then we can rightly ask whether we can know facts directly.

In the next quotation of Richardson et al. (1999), note that the uncertain nature of knowledge about humans results from our "interpretive perspectives and interests." Recall that for them and other MGTs, objective knowledge is problematically equated with certain or indubitable knowledge.

> The truths we discover about humans generally must be treated as defeasible not simply because new data may show up but because different interpretive perspectives and interests can compel us to rethink and revise the discoveries we make. (p. 235)

In the first two of the next three quotations, Richardson et al. (1999) emphasize values, whereas in the third they emphasize the perspectival nature of observation and interpretation (which are equated) in the name of a properly value-laden science.

> Serious doubts have been voiced for decades . . . about whether the ideals of . . . true value neutrality ever have or could be achieved in accounts of human activities in their real-life social and historical setting. . . . David Hoy (1986, p. 124) observes that "theory choice in the social sciences is . . . more relativistic than in the natural sciences, since the principles used to select social theories would be guided by a variety of values." (p. 178)
>
> Knowledge claims are adjudicated within a social order that incorporates and strives to fulfill a more or less explicit set of values, in contrast to the distortions incurred in the attempt to maintain factitious distinctions between facts and values and between objective and subjective domains. (p. 154)
>
> A "view from nowhere" is simply inaccessible, . . . all observation is interpretation. . . . Every interpretation has some standpoint, a perspective from which it is made, even when the interpreting is done in the name of a would-be value free science. (p. 304)

In the statement that follows, Polkinghorne (1983) links his antiobjectivist pragmatic epistemology to a view from somewhere, in which values play some part.

> We cannot approach objects in a value-free, undistorted context as proposed by the methods of an "objective" science. Instead we want to know what is useful. . . . [Gadamer] does not believe that methods will ever carry us beyond our culturally shaped context to some ultimately free standpoint from which we can see the things-in-themselves. (p. 225)

Values are emphasized in the first of these two quotations of Bernstein (1983), whereas the "view from somewhere" is emphasized in the second, in which pragmatism prevails.

> In a lecture . . . entitled "Objectivity, Value Judgment, and Theory Choice" . . . [Kuhn] emphasizes that criteria of choice "function not as rules, which determine choice, but as values, which influence it." (pp. 54–55)

Gadamer is appealing to a concept of truth that (pragmatically speaking) amounts to what can be argumentatively validated by the community of interpreters. . . . This does not mean that there is some transcendental or ahistorical perspective from which we can evaluate competing claims to truth. We judge and evaluate such claims by the standards and practices that have been hammered out in the course of history. (p. 154)

Here Martin and Sugarman (1999a) link their antiobjectivist epistemology to the lack of an "outside vantage point" (or "view from nowhere").

There is no outside vantage point, complete with its own set of unimpeachably objective standards, from which to make judgments concerning the relative merits of different interpretations. (p. 57)

And in these final quotations, Woolfolk (1998) says that understanding is a conceptual matter that is situatedly value laden, so the conceptual component of knowing that we considered in Antiobjectivist Argument 1 is here linked to the value-laden component of knowing. This reflects the tendency of MGTs to speak of "meanings and values" as a fused entity. The second quotation goes further than the first: Understanding is not just orchestrated in a field of value-laden concepts but is constituted by values.

Our understanding of ourselves and of other people is orchestrated within a field of practical, value-laden concepts. (p. 75)
Our picture of the empirical world is constituted by values. (p. 54)

A Critique of the "No (Value-Free) View From Nowhere, Therefore No Objective Knowledge" Argument

For MGTs local values contribute not only to human social/psychological existence (i.e., ontology) but also to knowledge claims about that existence (i.e., epistemology). On their view, values always do—and moreover should—affect the knowing process and the "knowledge" that arises from that process, a "fact" that obliterates any distinction between facts and values as merely the wishful, Cartesian-infused anxious thinking of conventional inquirers. But as we have seen, MGTs believe the elimination of the fact/value distinction to be a proper state of affairs that should be celebrated rather than lamented, for it allegedly makes intelligibility (within a discursive/interpretive context) possible in the first place. The elimination of the fact/value distinction, then, paves the way for psychological knowledge that is more properly engaged, more practical or useful, than the "detached, dispassionate objectivity" (Guignon, 2002a, p. 274) sought in physical science inquiry. And so MGTs proclaim their approach to psychological inquiry to consist in a more human or user-friendly epistemology/science, one more morally infused and hence more realistic—although not more realist in any objectivist sense, given their rejection of objective knowledge.

I am not the only one to see confusion in this, although those who "unite" (albeit unofficially) against the celebration of the fact/value fusion (and the antiobjectivist epistemology that follows from it) tend to speak of knowing simpliciter, rather than knowing about human social/psychological entities in particular (even though they hardly preclude the latter). The fact that we bring local or situated values (e.g., wants, desires, interests, and aspirations) and meanings (e.g., concepts and interpretations), including background assumptions/beliefs, to acts of knowing (about our psychological existence) does not automatically obliterate any possible distinction between facts and values in the act of knowing, and so does not obliterate the possibility of objective knowledge. That is because we do not need to rely on or use (local) values to warrant knowledge claims about human psychological existence, including the pragmatic claims to which many MGTs attend.[22]

Those who make this objectivist assertion take objectivity to be "an essentially moral disposition" (Robinson, 1997). Theirs is an engaged, passionate commitment to seek the objective truth of the matter under scrutiny to the very best of their ability, and to accept not only the fallible nature of all acts of knowing but also their epistemic limits. The objectivist commitment also requires the acceptance only of warranted findings, no matter how much inquirers may at times wish the content of such findings were not the case. In making the objectivist commitment to truth that in no way depends on what anyone believes (or wants) the truth of the matter to be, objectivist inquirers work to put aside their own interests (other than their interest in objectivity) as much as possible, rather than celebrate their allegedly unavoidable inclusion as a necessary and valuable part of engaged inquiry.

> The objectivity that many take to be the defining mark of science, and which postmodernism takes to be a chimera is, in fact, an essentially moral disposition whose validity must be granted as a precondition for both science and critiques of it.[23] (Robinson, 1997)

For Robinson the "culture of science" is not a value-neutral enterprise; nor does it pretend to be, as its critics (including MGTs) allege. Rather, that culture values the striving for indifference otherwise known as objectivity. This moral epistemic value means that other moral nonepistemic values (e.g., the social outcomes we think ought to obtain) cannot be used to warrant knowledge claims.

Haack (2003) too speaks of certain moral commitments as bona fide epistemic values, including especially the commitment to honesty in inquiry—a commitment surely shared by MGTs (e.g., Slife & Williams, 1995, p. 194) in their proper commitment to fallibilist inquiry. Moreover, philosophers

---

[22]Haack (1998a, 1998b) challenges Rorty's and others' claim that pragmatism (especially that of Peirce) rests on an antirealist epistemology. See Held (1998a) for discussion of the antirealist use of pragmatism in psychology and psychotherapy.

[23]In due course we shall see how philosopher Harvey Siegel (1997) argues that in challenging rationality, postmodernist challengers presuppose the very rationality they challenge.

Alven Neiman and Harvey Siegel (1993), in describing the epistemology of Israel Scheffler, offer a more objectivist-friendly "middle-road in epistemology" (p. 59) than that typically offered even by MGTs.

> Certain interests, motives, and even desires are not only *not* antithetical to objectivity but are, in fact, presupposed by it. . . . Scheffler has begun to elaborate a conception of rationality as objective yet emotional and interested. . . . Scheffler's conception of . . . objectivity [involves] . . . public testing and criticism in accordance with impartial criteria, which leaves room for emotion, commitment and interest. . . . [He insists] that rationality cannot be divorced either from emotion or from morality. (pp. 76, 79)

Siegel (1999c) also quotes philosopher Stephen Toulmin on this.

> "To be objective does not require us to be *uninterested*, . . . devoid of interests and feelings; it requires us only to acknowledge those interests and feelings, to discount any resulting biases and prejudices, and to do our best to act in a *disinterested* way." (p. 918)

Of course the *existence* of impartial (or unbiased) criteria for warranting knowledge claims is the bone of contention. MGTs deny both their existence and their desirability; on their view we cannot have any such criteria—at least in the human sciences—owing to our situatedly value-laden knowing about our situatedly value-laden existence. But that seemingly universal epistemic condition is for them a good thing. Consider again Slife and Williams (1995), and note especially the antirealist use of scare quotes on the word *actually*.

> Objectivity calls for . . . some grounds from which to observe that are independent of, or shielded from, all subjective influences. . . . Because subjective influences—values, emotions—are essential to the very identity of the scientist as a person, and because our history, culture, and so forth are often held implicitly . . . , it seems unlikely that we would ever achieve this kind of objective grounds from which to observe anything. . . . [But] it is questionable whether this kind of objectivity is necessary for the work of science to continue. . . . All that is required is that scientists be open to alternative explanations, be honest, and reserve judgment about what is "actually" going on. (pp. 193–194)

To sum up the MGT position so far, what we are (psychologically) and how we know about what we are (psychologically) are always tied inextricably to our local historical/cultural/discursive/interpretive contexts (which include values), and so to each other. This allegedly precludes the possibility of objective knowledge about psychological existence. Put differently, psychological being and knowing about psychological being are both relative to discursive/interpretive contexts (see chap. 5); and if they are relativistic, they cannot then be objectivist.

Here we might well recall from chapter 3 the words about (strong) relativism of Richard Bernstein (1983), whose aim was to go "beyond objectivism and relativism."

> In its strongest form, relativism is the basic conviction that when we . . . [examine the] concept of rationality, truth, reality, right, the good, or norms—we are forced to recognize that . . . all such concepts must be understood as relative to a specific conceptual scheme, theoretical framework, paradigm, form of life, society, or culture. . . . There is no substantive overarching framework or single metalanguage by which we can rationally adjudicate or univocally evaluate competing claims of alternative paradigms. (p. 8)

Although some MGTs (e.g., Martin & Sugarman) claim that theirs is not a strong relativism owing to the discursive constraints that radical postmodernists tend to deny, their *perspectival* warrant is indeed a form of epistemological relativism. The point is that we must once again engage the matter of relativism, this time in epistemological rather than ontological terms.

Haack (2003) rejects any form of relativism (weak or strong) by arguing that epistemic warrant may begin in the realm of the "personal" and then proceed to the realm of the "social," but must ultimately end up in the realm of the "impersonal" if it is real or legitimate warrant (pp. 60–77). Although *judgments* of evidential criteria (in all forms of inquiry, both scientific and everyday) are always perspectival or situated, filled with "background beliefs" (p. 76) of all sorts, and hence may even be said to be value laden, evidential criteria *themselves* are not; they are therefore objective. This important epistemic distinction gets lost despite MGTs' laudable commitment to nuanced formulations.

> What has been taken for paradigm-relativity of evidential quality [or value] is a kind of epistemological illusion; . . . whether evidence is relevant, whether this is a good explanation of that, how strong or weak this evidence really is, how well or poorly warranted this claim actual is, is an objective matter. . . . Since evidential quality is not transparent, . . . a scientist may be reasonable in giving a claim a degree of credence which is disproportionate to the real, objective quality of his evidence, if that real quality is inaccessible to him. Reasonableness, *so understood* [italics added], is perspectival. (Haack, 2003, p. 77)

Here Haack seems to be suggesting something fundamental to current explications of objectivity made by those who support its possibility in straightforward ways—that objective knowledge (knowledge of how something in the world is, independent of the knower's beliefs about how it is) is never certain or infallible. Objective knowledge is instead always uncertain (or at least comes only with degrees of certainty), fallible, and thus open to revision, not least because "evidential quality [though itself objective] is not transparent." "The innocent realist is a contrite fallibilist," says Haack (2002, p. 88). She also inclines toward a view articulated by many conventional objectivists: That knowers are always (locally) situated, and so must make epistemic judgments from the vantage point of their (local) situatedness, does not preclude the possibility of objective epistemic criteria and thus objective knowledge. This is because all rational or reasonable knowers *with the same background information* could in principle reach consensus about the epistemic value of the available evidence. So although warrant starts out personal and social (i.e., perspectival), it can end up impersonal (i.e., nonperspectival)—although there are no guarantees.

In the views that favor epistemic objectivity, objectivity and rationality are put forth as deeply intertwined. It is not surprising, then, that the proponents of these views can allow for the universality of rationality/objectivity (what Pols, 1992, 1998, calls the "U-factor") without failing to acknowledge the crucial role played by local particularity, circumstance, or situatedness (what Pols, 1992, 1998, calls the "P-factor") in the act of knowing or experiencing an independent reality. Philosopher Nicholas Rescher is one such proponent.

Continued Critique of the "No (Value-Free) View From Nowhere, Therefore No Objective Knowledge" Argument: Rescher on the "Circumstantial Universality of Reason"

In *Objectivity: The Obligations of Impersonal Reason*, philosopher Nicholas Rescher (1997) argues on behalf of the "circumstantial universality of reason" (p. 8). He propounds the universals of objectivity and rationality (which he equates) without ignoring the particular circumstances in which knowers exist as knowers. He begins by factoring out of the equation the personal and communal "allegiances" (which we may consider to be values in a broad sense) that are key elements in the MGTs' antiobjectivist epistemology.

> An objective judgment is one that abstracts from personal idiosyncrasies or group parochialisms. It is a judgment made without the influence of individual or communal preferences and predilections, a judgment in line with generic standards of rationality that can plausibly be seen as abstracting from the personal or communal inclinations or allegiances. (p. 7)

This sounds like the "detached" abstracted knowledge to which many MGTs vehemently object in their call for local/situated, value-laden knowledge of the human (social/psychological) world; for them it strips knowledge of that world of its all-important circumstantial, moral qualities. The notion of universal features of mind (including universal rationality)[24] is at best given

---

[24]In chapter 10, I consider the empirical data that allegedly support the existence of different forms of reason/rationality in Eastern versus Western cultures.

ambivalent endorsement by most MGTs (see chap. 6), whose ontology of "being in the world" is the foundational point of both their middle-ground ontology and the middle-ground epistemology believed to follow from it.

Then Rescher does something unexpected: He puts the personal/communal factor back into the equation. However, I doubt this is done in a way that would be acceptable to MGTs, because Rescher defends a universal feature of rationality (as objectivity) nonetheless.

> The distinction is not that between a personal vision of things and an impersonal vision of them, but between those aspects of personal views that are (or should be) compelling for rational people in general and those which are shaped by the particular biases, preferences, and loyalties of particular individuals or groups. To strive for objectivity is to seek to put things in such a way that not just kindred spirits but virtually *anyone* can see the sense of it. It is not so much a matter of being impersonal as impartial—of putting aside one's idiosyncratic predilections and parochial preferences in forming one's beliefs, evaluations, and choices. (p. 8)

To be sure, it is hard to imagine MGTs tumbling to this: For them local historical/cultural/discursive/interpretive contexts give us the biases or "prejudices," the beliefs and values, that (a) make us what we are and (b) make our local/situated form of understanding or knowing possible in the first place. To give up such "allegiances" (as Rescher calls them) is to relinquish our (belief/value) commitments, and thus our ways of being and knowing; this would be tantamount to giving up (on) ourselves. For many MGTs we can transcend our beliefs/values or biases/"prejudices" by way of a Gadamerian "fusion of horizons," in which we strive to remain open to the "horizons" of others (see chap. 6, this volume). Still, recall that we cannot put aside our context-based commitments altogether; they help constitute us significantly. Quoting William James, Rescher says, "'There is no point of view absolutely public and universal'" (James, as cited in Rescher, 1997, p. 8). Rescher himself continues with a prescriptive thrust.

> We must judge from the vantage point of a position in space, time, and cultural context. But it is not the absoluteness of an unrealizable point of view from nowhere or from everywhere-at-once or from God's vantage point that is at issue with objectivity. Objectivity is a matter of how we *should*—and how otherwise reasonable people *would*—proceed if they were in our shoes in the relevant regards. (p. 8)

Rescher resonates with Haack's (2003) insistence that epistemic criteria (or reasons for warrant) are themselves objective, although they are not necessarily transparent. Thus Rescher's use of the words *in principle* is important.

> Reason is (circumstantially) universal, and it is objectivity's coordination with rationality that links it to universality. That which . . . is the sensible thing for us to do in the circumstances is thereby the reasonable

thing for ANYBODY—any rational individual—to do *in those circum-stances.* . . . Reason is agent-indifferent. . . . An intelligent, detached observer, apprised of the facts of the case, must be in a position to say: "While I myself do not believe or value these things, I can see that it is appropriate that sensible people placed in the agent's circumstances should do so." (pp. 8–9)

If something makes good rational sense, it must be possible *in principle* [italics added] for anyone and everyone to see that this is so. The matter of good reasons is not something subjective or idiosyncratic; it is objec-tive and lies in the public domain. (p. 10)

As he continues, Rescher makes clear just how he brings particularity into the equation, in a way that sounds decidedly Aristotelian![25]

Rational resolutions, while indeed universal, are only *contextually and circumstantially* universal in a way that makes room for the variation of times, places, and the thousands of details encountered with each indi-vidual and situation. This circumstantiality of reason makes for an un-avoidable aspect of person-relativity. . . . What is rational for someone to do or to think *hinges on the particular details of how this individual is circum-stanced*—and the prevailing circumstances of course differ from person to person and group to group. (pp. 10–11)

Would MGTs accept this? As good as the very last part may sound to their relativistic ears, I have my doubts. If we are historical/interpretation *all* the way down, can there be a rationality pervasive enough to meet even the *circumstantial* universality of rationality/reason on which Rescher hinges his view of objectivity? If our existence and knowing about our existence are profoundly constituted in or caused by culture, can we even hope to imagine ourselves in each other's shoes well enough to converge on a universally accepted rational choice in any given situation? Put differently, if MGTs are right, would not rationality/reason itself be constituted locally or relativisti-cally to a large extent (see chap. 6)? If so, then even if two "rational" people from two very different discursive/interpretive contexts were apprised of all the relevant circumstances or background information of a third rational agent, they might still disagree about what that third agent should think or do.

Here we should let MGTs weigh in. For example, consider Guignon (2002a), who at first seems similar to Rescher but then parts company with him.

Most cases of apparent conflict [about interpretation] can be resolved once one grasps the contexts to which claims of correctness are relativized.

---

[25]Blaine Fowers (2005) exquisitely summarizes Aristotle's attention to particularity, especially in ethical matters; I am grateful to him for our many discussions about this. See Robinson's (1989) *Aristotle's Psychology,* for elaboration of this point and many others.

> . . . [But the] "fore-meanings," or "prejudices," that make up our cultur-
> ally and historically conditioned pre-understanding . . . determine what
> can count for us as data or facts, [therefore] we have no access to an
> uninterpreted given that could ground our interpretations. But neither
> can we turn to an overarching standard of reason that could adjudicate
> among conflicting interpretations, for, as Gadamer says, "the idea of an
> absolute reason is not a possibility for historical humanity." (p. 282)

And in this next quotation, Polkinghorne (1983) seems even less inclined
than Guignon toward anything resembling Rescher's position.

> The loci of truth claims, according to Ogilvy, are various communities of
> like-minded interpreters.[26] We cannot escape our contexts, and so the
> limits of knowledge are contained in these communities. . . . The idea of
> what is reasonable varies from community to community. (p. 250)

To summarize: Rescher's appeal to the circumstantial universality of
rationality/reason as a condition for objectivity would probably fail to sway
those who see psychological existence as so constituted in or determined by
culture/context that—all "fusions of horizons" notwithstanding—the universality of rationality/objectivity on whose behalf Rescher argues could not
obtain, even under the circumstantial conditions he specifies. But if that is
the case, it again becomes hard to see how transcendence or overcoming of
circumstance is possible, including even the "mild or modest innovation" to
which some MGTs appeal (e.g., Martin & Sugarman, 1999a, 1999b). Those
who make agency in this circumstance-transcending sense possible (e.g.,
Jenkins, 2001; Rychlak, 2001) seem to appeal more to the universal features
of mind/rationality (if not also to objectivity) than do MGTs. Let us now
consider the critique of antiobjectivist epistemologies made by philosopher
Harvey Siegel, who defends transcendence in epistemic terms by deploying
the universals of rationality/reason.

Continued Critique of the "No (Value-Free) View From Nowhere, Therefore No Objective Knowledge" Argument: Siegel on Neutral Epistemic Standards

Siegel might state the position against which he argues more precisely:
No view from nowhere means no neutral epistemic standards or impartial
epistemic criteria, and therefore no objective knowledge. Siegel (1999c) also
finds merit in Rescher, although in his review of Rescher's (1997) book, he
criticizes his tendency to equate objectivity with rationality and to make
rationality primary, to have objectivity "follow in rationality's wake" (Rescher,
1997, p. 18). Instead Siegel (1999c) offers this alternative formulation of the
deep relation between objectivity and rationality.

---

[26]In *Self-Knowledge and the Self*, philosopher David Jopling (2000) discusses the problem with using
like-minded interpreters as the basis for warrant of self-knowledge.

Rationality and objectivity are not equivalent, nor is the former primary, and the latter secondary. Rather, they are importantly intertwined. . . . (i) For a belief/judgment to be rational, it must be based upon evidence that is objectively assessed; in this respect objectivity is necessary for rationality. (ii) For a belief/judgment to be objective (-ly held), it must be based upon appropriate evaluation of the strength of relevant reasons/ evidence and must implicitly presuppose or claim that impartial assessment favors it; in this respect rationality is necessary for objectivity. (p. 919)

In so intertwining objectivity and rationality, Siegel makes possible the epistemic transcendence of our local situatedness that he needs to refute epistemic relativism—including (a) the pan-relativism of those who claim that because we have no "God's eye view," we cannot make objective judgments about anything and (b) the more limited relativism of those (e.g., MGTs) who emphasize our inability to make objective judgments about human social/psychological existence. He refutes the relativist claim that because the neutral epistemic criteria that relativists insist on for objectivity is not possible (owing to situated knowing), relativism (or antiobjectivism) follows. This Siegel (2004) does first by demonstrating the "self-refuting" or "self-referentially incoherent" (p. 747) feature of relativist claims—that it is universally true that there is no universal truth—and then by challenging two related assumptions made by relativists: Owing to our situatedness, which brings with it local "conceptual schemes or frameworks" and local "forms of life" (p. 750), (a) there can be "no *neutral* standards in accordance with which knowledge-claims can be adjudicated" (p. 750); and (b) there is no "possibility of transcending one's (relative) perspective" (p. 750). Hence epistemic relativism obtains.

Here I consider the "no neutral standards" argument for relativism, because it pertains to the argument against the existence of impartial criteria made by MGTs when they maintain that, owing to our situated existence, (local) values always do (and always should) play a role in warranting knowledge claims about human social/psychological existence, and that therefore at least no human science can rightly be said to yield objective knowledge.

Siegel (2004) flatly rejects the relativist contention that "disputes can be resolved only relative to our respective standards (and not 'absolutely')" because there "are no 'meta-' or higher-order standards available to which we can appeal which will fairly or non-question-beggingly resolve our dispute" (p. 750). He argues that relativists make an unnecessary assumption that, when considered critically and rejected, makes possible the objective judgments they deny. The unnecessary assumption is that to refute relativism, we need a standard that is "neutral *generally*, i.e., neutral with respect to all possible disputes" (p. 751). Siegel says we can grant that there is no such universal standard neutrality and still allow that there are "standards which . . . are neutral in the weaker sense that they do not unfairly prejudice any particular, live (at a time) dispute" (p. 751).

Siegel (2004) uses the example of the famous dispute between Galileo and the Church regarding the existence of moons orbiting Jupiter. Galileo appealed to telescopic observation to warrant his claim that there were such moons; the Church appealed to naked-eye observation, Scripture, and Aristotle to warrant its claim that there were not. Still, Siegel says, both sides "recognized *logic* (or, more broadly, '*reason*') as a standard to which either disputant may fairly appeal" (p. 751); they both "agreed that, were Galileo able adequately to explain the workings of his newly invented telescope . . . , that explanation would undermine his opponents' rejection of the proposed Galilean standard of telescopic observation" (p. 751). Thus they both acknowledged "*adequate explanation* as a relevant meta-standard for evaluating first-order standards" (p. 751)—in this case, Scripture versus telescopic observation. In short, universal neutrality—"neutrality with respect to *every* possible dispute or *all* conceivable conceptual schemes"—is not needed. Instead we need only "neutrality with respect to the issue at hand" (p. 752).

> Such neutrality . . . does not require that standards cannot discriminate among better or worse competing views, but rather simply that such discrimination must be fair to competing views, i.e., cannot be prejudicial toward or irrelevantly biased against one or another of them. There is no reason to think that *this* weaker sort of neutrality cannot, in principle, be had. (p. 752)

To be sure, the controversy in which Galileo found himself bitterly embroiled concerned astronomical matters and not the nature of human social/psychological existence. It is the human sciences, after all, that are the object of MGTs' plans for epistemological overhaul. Still, MGTs themselves—indeed all who have taken the "interpretive turn" (see Hiley, Bohman, & Shusterman, 1991)—typically accept that some interpretations are better than others, even when judging claims made within the human sciences. That is because MGTs seek to avoid a rampant relativism; if they did not, they would not be MGTs. So they too must think there are criteria that are fair/impartial or objective enough to judge the relative merits or truth of discrepant claims, at least *within* discursive/interpretive contexts.[27]

Siegel (2004) acknowledges that "the two meta-standards noted, logic (or 'reason') and explanatory adequacy, are not neutral with respect to all possible disputes"—that is, they "might fail to be neutral with respect to disputes concerning the character and force of logic, and . . . the character of explanation and its possible tie to truth" (p. 751). These are just the kind of

---

[27]A *conventional* realist (as opposed to someone who adopts the unconventional epistemic "realism" of MGTs) might prefer to speak of knowledge about what is the case *regardless of* the discursive context. I am grateful to Amie Thomasson (personal communication, January 17, 2002) for this insight (see Held, 2002b).

disputes that interest MGTs, in their quest to articulate epistemic warrant within cultural contexts. These disputes lead us to questions about descriptive or naturalized versus prescriptive or normative epistemologies, questions that pertain to epistemic relativism (see chap. 9, this volume). Still, as Siegel (2004) himself says, in order for someone to challenge the impartiality/objectivity of evidential standards or criteria to resolve a dispute, "the challenger must presuppose some (other) standard, one which is neutral with respect to the challenge at hand. Otherwise, there would be no reason to regard the originally proposed standard as problematic" (p. 752). As Siegel compellingly concludes,

> Thus successfully challenging the appeal to . . . [an unfair or biased] standard appears to require acceptance of a general (meta-) standard of neutrality, or fairness. Consequently, the relativist cannot challenge all such appeals to standards as unacceptably non-neutral except by presupposing that particular (meta-) standard herself. (p. 753)

In short, the objectivity that is denied is necessarily presumed by the relativistic challenger. (Robinson, 1997, said something similar: "[Objectivity's] validity must be granted as a precondition for both science and critiques of it.") Moreover, in discussing the self-justificatory nature of rationality, Siegel (1997, pp. 81–87) argues (along similar lines) that if someone challenges the value of rationality, the challenger presupposes the very rationality he or she calls into question (see chap. 10, this volume).

If MGTs believe that cultural discourses or interpretations—including the diverse values held within different discursive/interpretive contexts—constitute or determine rationality/reason itself, then they may well say that there can in principle be no way to warrant objectively one culture's claims over those of another, because each has its own equally "valid" logic, rationality, or reason. But in that case they endorse the rampant relativism they say they hope to avoid in their spirit of moderation. Can MGTs hold to their celebration of value-laden warrant or epistemic criteria, the obliteration of the fact/value distinction, while also rejecting rampant relativism—or, as Martin and Sugarman (1999b, p. 191) eloquently put it, "anarchistic relativism"? Can they lay claim to an epistemology that is at once realist *and* antiobjectivist? Again, we must examine their epistemic standards regarding claims about human kinds to answer these questions.

Antiobjectivist Argument 3: There Is an Ontology of Flux and Flow in the Human World; Therefore, There Can Be No Objective Knowledge

The Ontological Claim

According to MGTs, our psychological existence is reflexive in nature. Therefore our ever-evolving interpretations about our psychological existence determine reflexively the nature of that existence. Put differently, the distinction between being and knowing about being is blurred (see chap. 5), so our psychological existence is not and cannot be one comprised of fixed, stable, or unchanging kinds/entities whose continuity can be counted on for purposes of inquiry (see chap. 7). Recall that all-important quotation:

> Humans just *are* what they interpret themselves as being within their social context. . . . Interpretations devised by social scientists feed back into the culture and so define and alter the reality they describe. (Richardson et al., 1999, p. 236)

Or alternatively,

> Humans simply are what they interpret themselves as being within their historical and sociocultural contexts. (Martin et al., 2003, p. 77)

Now add this one, and the claim is complete.

> If our self-understanding makes us who we are, then the truth about us may be too malleable and multifaceted to be amenable to a single, overarching, consensual scientific account, now or at any time in the future. (Richardson et al., 1999, p. 299)

Of course this is a bit of a red herring, because objectivists do not necessarily insist on a single unified truth: There can be many objective accounts of the same phenomenon, as long as they are logically compatible with each other (e.g., Erwin, 1997; Haack, 2003).

Having proclaimed the unstable nature of our reflexive psychological existence, MGTs also proclaim that there nonetheless is enough stability in that existence for psychological inquiry to obtain. The truths yielded by psychological inquiry are not for them timeless truths, but humans evidently hold still long enough psychologically to allow the realities of that existence to be captured (see chap. 7).

> Even at these [sociocultural and psychological] levels of reality, things are not so ephemeral as to escape entirely human attempts to inquire into them. . . . Because of their embeddedness within sociocultural, biological, and physical reality . . . psychological actions and experiences are far from chaotic, arbitrary, or fleetingly irrelevant. (Martin & Sugarman, 1999b, pp. 188, 190)

The question is this: Why should an ontology of flux and flow preclude objectivist inquiry? This quotation of Bernstein suggests an answer to that question, by linking the brute facts or reality deemed necessary for objective knowledge to stability. Thus it is not merely that there exists no aconceptual/interpretation-free (or brute) reality in the human world to be known objectively; there exists no *unchanging* or *stable* brute reality in the human world to be known objectively: "'There has been an overwhelming tendency in mainstream social science toward . . . mistaking historically conditioned social and political patterns for an unchanging brute reality which is simply 'out there' to be confronted'" (Bernstein, as cited in Richardson et al., 1999, p. 289). Still, the reasoning behind the antiobjectivist argument regarding ontological instability is not so transparent. This next quotation makes that reasoning more apparent, by linking the certitude deemed necessary for objective knowledge to stability. Note the appeal to the "no view from nowhere" problem, as well: "Because the sociohistorical context constantly changes, as well as does our vantage point within it, there can never be final or absolutely certain interpretation" (Woolfolk et al., 1988, p. 17). Nonetheless, the claim that an ontology of flux and flow necessarily precludes objective knowledge is not evident.

The Epistemological Conclusion

One way to think about the "ontology of flux and flow, therefore no objective knowledge" argument is to appreciate that behind it lies the MGTs' commitment to the blurred distinction between the knowing subject and the object to be known (see chap. 5). If our beliefs about (or interpretations of) our psychological existence continually change, and in so doing always alter or reconstitute that existence, then that existence is not only in constant flux but also fails to be an aconceptual/interpretation-free, or brute, existence. According to MGTs, then, our psychological being cannot be *known* as it exists independently of our beliefs about (or interpretations of) it, because our psychological being does not *exist* independently of our beliefs about (or interpretations of) it. In short, on the MGTs' view, that being or existence cannot be known with objectivity.

Here it would help to revisit what MGTs mean by "objective knowledge." We have already considered their insistence on investigation of (a) an aconceptual/interpretation-free (brute) reality and (b) a value-free reality, if objective knowledge is to obtain. Another striking commonality is that objective knowledge is often said to consist in indubitable knowledge of timeless, universal, and mechanistically deterministic causal laws about the unchanging or stable essences of the (brute) entities under investigation. However, according to MGTs, humans are agentic beings whose unending reinterpretations of their own psychological existence reconstitute or reshape the nature of that existence. Therefore mechanistic laws cannot capture the nature of human psychological existence for two reasons: (a) human psychological existence is agentic or self-determined and thus is not mechanistically determined and (b) because humans reconstitute themselves psychologically, humans cannot possess the enduring, essential, and universal psychological qualities deemed necessary for the mechanistically deterministic causal laws that can in principle be discovered (with certainty or indubitability) in the natural sciences, in which objects of inquiry do exist independently of inquirers' beliefs about them and so are presumed to remain stable—or at least more stable than human kinds.[28] If objective knowledge consists solely in universal mechanistic laws that govern the allegedly unchanging or stable essences of brute (nonagentic/mind-independent) entities, and these laws can be known with certainty or indubitability, then there can be no objective psychological knowledge. Thus the problem that fuels the MGTs' two-pronged mission resurfaces: how to conceive of a form of psychological inquiry that is epistemically truth tracking or realist but not objectivist, because the latter would preclude the agency they seek to preserve.

Later in this chapter, I revisit the argument that objective knowledge—contrary to what MGTs claim—is not limited to timeless, universal, and mechanistically deterministic causal laws about unchanging brute entities that can in principle be known with certainty or indubitability. To the contrary, according to the objectivists whom I review, empirically derived knowledge of any sort is always fallible. Here let us review quotations in which the natural sciences are said by MGTs to yield the objective knowledge (especially the universal deterministic causal laws) that cannot obtain in the human sciences owing to the agentic "objects" of inquiry in the latter.[29] Notice especially that the mind-dependent, interpretive, or conceptual (i.e., nonbrute) and situated or value-laden nature of psychological existence factors into the link between a changing ontology of flux and flow and the preclusion of objective knowledge.

Martin and Sugarman (1999b) link objective "apprehension" to "conceptually independent," "unchanging forms or laws." They end with middle-ground language.

> Postmodern psychologists . . . are right to reject the foundationalist idea that psychological and sociocultural reality is characterized by conceptually independent, ahistorical, unchanging forms or laws that can be apprehended objectively. However, . . . to conclude that psychological and sociocultural reality is nothing more than a chaotic, random flux, the arbitrary ordering of which reflects only dominant positions and interests, goes too far. . . . There is room for warranted interpretive navigation between the Scylla of essentialism and the Charybdis of ephemeralism. (p. 191)

In the next quotation, agentic control is an obstacle to discovering "causal connections" in psychology. That plus the value-laden/situated, in-

---

[28]Needless to say, physical or brute entities may change over time (consider the weather, or climate change!), although this does not in principle preclude the attainment of objective knowledge about them.

[29]The claim that causal laws cannot obtain in the human sciences ultimately rests on the distinction between the reasons that agentically propel the actions of human agents and the causes that mechanistically propel the actions of physical entities. See Erwin (1997) and Grünbaum (1988) for arguments about how reasons can be seen to act as causes in a straightforward or commonsense way. See Pols (1998, 2002a) for metaphysical explication of this commonsense view.

terpretive, and thus uncertain nature of psychological existence seemingly preclude objective psychological knowledge. In the second quotation, causal explanatory laws are precluded by agency, which is seen as teleological.

> The ontological status of psychological phenomena prevents their penetration by known means of establishing causal connections in physical sciences. . . . The methods and epistemic strategies of physical science do not apply in the same way to psychological phenomena because such phenomena are morally constituted, agentically controlled, contextual, and uncertain. . . . Relevant empirical evidence in psychology . . . inevitably will be less generalizable, less definitive, and more interpretative. . . . [Much psychological inquiry] can be stripped of its unsupportable vestiges of objectivism. (Martin & Sugarman, 1999a, pp. 45, 47–48, 56)
>
> Charles Taylor . . . declared that human actions cannot be explained by causal laws of the deductive-nomological form . . . and proposed that human actions require a teleological form of explanation. (Polkinghorne, 1983, p. 170)

Causal laws or principles are problematic for psychology in these next few quotations, in which objective knowledge is equated with abstract, unchanging/timeless, and universal causal laws about decontextualized, value-free, aconceptual/interpretation-free (brute) entities.

> The pragmatic "truth" of a particular perspective does not lie in its correspondence to "objective reality," since that reality is continuously in flux. . . . Pragmatism focuses on case studies that address particular practical problems in local and time-specific contexts rather than on the abstract, universal, quantitative knowledge of timeless principles and laws. (Fishman, 1999, pp. 130–131)
>
> The goal of the natural sciences is to *explain* events by subsuming them under general laws, [which requires treating] the world as a collection of decontextualized objects that may appear in various causal interactions. Such an objectifying stance toward things presupposes a capacity for *abstraction* in which all meanings and values are removed from what is experienced so that the things we study are encountered as inherently meaningless spatiotemporal objects subsumable under covering laws. (Richardson et al., 1999, p. 202)
>
> [Naturalistic psychology] relies on an unnecessary and ultimately implausible division of the world into objective facts ordered by causal laws that are what they are independent of our interpretations, and subjective experiences. (Richardson et al., 1999, p. 277)
>
> Unlike natural scientific explanations, which make reference to causes in order to elucidate why a certain object has the properties it has . . . , psychological explanation makes reference to rules and conventions in order to show how a certain event makes sense in the way that it takes place. The psychological concepts just do not fit into the causal model of explanation. (Liebrucks, 2001, pp. 385–386)

A Critique of the "Ontology of Flux and Flow, Therefore No Objective Knowledge" Argument

The most obvious response to this argument is one that MGTs have anticipated: There must be enough stability in the psychological world to allow us to attain some truth about it. If the ontology of flux and flow means that psychological existence is too unstable for knowledge that consists in causal/explanatory psychological laws, then that existence is also too unstable for knowledge that does not consist in causal/explanatory psychological laws, such as the "reasons" or "understanding" (as opposed to "causes" or "explanation," respectively) to which many antiobjectivists appeal (see note 29).

Recall the earlier quotations, in which various MGTs state that human social/psychological kinds do not morph so quickly as to elude inquiry altogether; for them there can in principle be warranted "realist" claims about our psychological existence. Even if MGTs are correct that psychological knowledge cannot consist in timeless, universal, and mechanistically deterministic causal laws owing to the locally situated, reflexively agentic nature of human psychological existence, it does not follow that there can be no objective knowledge about that existence altogether—unless objective knowledge is redefined to include only indubitable claims about the mechanistic causal forces that allegedly govern the unchanging essences of interpretation-free or brute/physical entities.

In short, that we may change psychologically over time—even in response to new ways of understanding our psychological existence—does not in itself lead to the inexorable conclusion that we cannot have objective psychological knowledge about our psychological existence—in the conventional meaning of the term *objective* (that the truth of a proposition does not depend on beliefs about the truth of that proposition).[30] This requires that what we are psychologically is not merely a matter of what we believe we are; that what we are psychologically permits enough of a distinction between knower and known to allow for the fallibilist inquiry that MGTs themselves endorse in defense of their ontological and epistemological realism (see chap. 5).

Underlying the MGTs' argument that our agentic capacity for ongoing reinterpretation of ourselves means the ontology of human psychological existence is one of ongoing change, in which no objective knowledge about our psychological existence can obtain, is the notion of the "double hermeneutic" attributed to Giddens. According to historian Keith Windschuttle's

---

[30]Unless, of course, the proposition is about whether certain persons hold that proposition to be true, in which case their belief about the proposition is the proposition under consideration. So, it is in principle possible to know objectively whether I or anyone thinks it is possible for objective knowledge to obtain (see Thomasson, 2003).

(1996) account of the Gadamerian hermeneutics adopted by many MGTs, because "the interpreter always brings his own meanings, prejudices and pre-conceptions to the task," he cannot "understand the meanings of others . . . in any objective sense,[31] but only through the web of his own meanings and culture" (p. 205).

> Social science, he [Giddens] says, is not insulated from its subject matter in the way that natural science is. For example, no matter what evidence a physicist finds or what theory he supports, his published work does not have any affect on the laws of physics. However, Giddens argues, the publications of social scientists often have a considerable impact on what happens in human affairs. . . . Even those sociological activities that ap-pear to be "objective," such as the compilation of statistics on the distri-bution of population, birth and death rates, marriage and the family, all "regularly enter our lives and help redefine them." (Windschuttle, 1996, p. 206)

This sounds like MGT talk—recall Bernstein's (1988) claim that "we are beings whose social reality is, in part, constituted by the ways in which we interpret and preinterpret this reality" (p. 104). Our lives would not be "lived differently because phlogiston theory has been rejected, but if the vocabulary of psychoanalysis were to be abandoned . . . then we would not only tell different narratives about ourselves, we would become different beings" (p. 104). It is therefore not surprising that some MGTs themselves refer to Giddens. Recall this claim made by Richardson et al. (1999), in which the allegedly value-laden (and so non-neutral or nonobjective) nature of social science inquiry is reinforced or supported by Giddens's "theory of reflexivity."

> Insofar as interpretations devised by social scientists feed back into the culture and so define and alter the reality they describe, . . . the practice of interpreting humans has wide-ranging ethical and political implica-tions. Far from being a neutral, value-free form of inquiry, the human sciences always operate with culturally mediated value assumptions and always influence the cultural context they address. (p. 236)

Richardson et al. (1999) link Giddens's theory of reflexivity to their antiobjectivist epistemology more explicitly in their own discussion of Giddens. Here they take to task the descriptive or qualitative forms of re-search in which postmodernists have sought refuge from the objectifying re-ductionism they find in quantitative methods.

---

[31]See my critiques of the "Corollary to Antiobjectivist Argument 1," in which antiobjectivist argument about the use of language/interpretation (or concepts/meanings) in knowing is said by MGTs (and others) to preclude objective knowledge.

Giddens (1976) argues that social inquiry is characterized by a "double hermeneutic." . . . However, [even] descriptivist views of social inquiry do not take the full measure of this interplay or double hermeneutic. . . . Phenomenological and descriptivist writers either state or imply that we should try to give a thoroughly objective characterization of the lived experience or patterns of meaningful human action that are being scrutinized. . . . That would be neither possible nor desirable. We bring our cultural concerns and commitments to the work of understanding such that "our" accounts of "their" reality will always be creative, somewhat value-laden interpretations. (pp. 180–181)

And so we see yet again that objectivity not only is impossible (even in qualitative terms) but also is undesirable—hence the MGTs' celebration of antiobjectivist epistemologies in the name of more proper, value-laden interpretive commitments, which are said to make the human sciences more realistic (i.e., more deserving of the descriptor "human"). Not so fast, says Windschuttle (1996), who challenges Giddens's claim that the reflexivity of the double hermeneutic produces knowledge that "itself contributes to the 'unstable or mutable character' of the social world" and so cannot grant us truth in any conventional sense (pp. 206–207). Windschuttle (1996) alerts us to a "subtle and unacknowledged shift in . . . [Giddens's] account of reflexivity and the double hermeneutic."

> In his early writings about this process . . . , reflexivity was something that "could" happen, not something that "must" happen. . . . However, by the 1990s, Giddens was confident he had grasped one of the inherent features of contemporary society . . . that the modern world is "thoroughly constituted" by "wholesale reflexivity" . . . that reflexivity is a *necessary* component of contemporary society and . . . *must* change the world to which it refers. (p. 207)

Windschuttle (1996) rejects the thesis of wholesale reflexivity. He writes that "people are so bombarded with contradictory opinions from academic 'experts' in the media that most take them all with a grain of salt" (p. 208). Yet MGTs take Giddens's reflexivity thesis even further, by saying it is not just the findings of human science but our own everyday lay interpretations that constitute or cause and continually alter what we are psychologically.

To be sure, the extent to which the reflexivity thesis obtains is an empirical question. Yet according to MGTs, we cannot get an objective answer even to that question—not least because we may change psychologically in the process of trying to answer that question, in which case we may render the findings obsolete before they are expressed. As we saw in chapter 7, Windschuttle (1996) finds a fallacy in Giddens's thesis—"shifting from a sociological statement to a logical statement" (p. 208): "From the premise that there are some examples of reflexive understanding in society, Giddens slides into the claim that reflexivity is therefore . . . logically necessary"

(p. 208). Moreover, he defends conventional or objective historical knowledge in the face of claims to the contrary made by philosophers of sociology.

> Even in those cases where we recognize reflexivity is at work . . . they do not provide grounds for a total lack of certainty.[32] Just because an aspect of society is constantly shifting around does not mean you cannot have knowledge about . . . its movement. . . . There is nothing in Giddens's hermeneutics or theory of reflexivity that undermines history's claims to provide knowledge. (p. 208)

MGTs might agree with Windschuttle, because they too defend epistemic realism. But given their antiobjectivist epistemology, I am not sure that what they mean by knowledge and truth is what Windschuttle has in mind. After all, in criticizing Foucault and Giddens (whose views are supported by some MGTs), Windschuttle (1996) defends objectivist notions of truth and knowledge and rejects relativism altogether (pp. 137, 209–211). Consider this statement about Foucault, whose views as put forth by Windschuttle (1996) are consistent with what pervades the antiobjectivist epistemic pronouncements of MGTs.

> The discipline of history, Foucault claims, cannot aspire to produce objective knowledge. Rather, it should aim at purging us of the pretence that historians are detached, objective observers of the past. This can only be accomplished by the "affirmation of knowledge as perspective." . . . In other words, objectivity is impossible, so historians should be deliberately biased in their interpretations. (p. 137)

Substitute the word *psychology* for *history* and that statement could have been written by any number of MGTs.

In this last statement, Windschuttle harshly challenges attempts to change the conventional meanings of epistemological terms.

> By trying to eliminate the truth content of words such as "know," "fact," "proof," and "discover," they [academics influenced by Giddens and Foucault] are all involved in an arrogant but tawdry attempt to change the meaning of the language for no better reason than to shore up their own misconceived and otherwise self-contradictory theories. (p. 211)

To be fair, we must remember that MGTs seek moderation in these matters; they are certainly not arrogant, and I would hardly call their valiant efforts "tawdry." Nor are they as extreme as the relativists/antirealists whom Windschuttle takes to task—or are they? To answer that question, in chap-

---

[32]Here I take Windschuttle's use of the words "total lack of certainty" to mean that he accepts the conventional objectivist view that certainty comes in degrees, and thus reflects the extent of warrant/justification (or evidence in support) of a knowledge claim or proposition. This is a different view of certainty than what inheres in some MGTs' attempts to refute the possibility of epistemic objectivity by rejecting the possibility of certain (psychological) knowledge. On their view the word "certain" is equated with indubitable or infallible (knowledge), at least at times.

ter 9 we consider their positive views about psychological inquiry, which for them can be realist without being objectivist. Here let us review what I will now call the "straw man" of conventional epistemic objectivity that the MGTs have constructed and to which they address their critiques. We will also review the reformulated version of objectivity offered by some.

THE STRAW MAN OF OBJECTIVITY REDUX

In this chapter I have attempted to refute the grounds on which MGTs reject an objectivist epistemology for psychological inquiry, by challenging their three core antiobjectivist arguments: First, there is no subject/object dichotomy, no independence of the knowing subject from the (psychological) object or reality to be known. Therefore there can be no aconceptual/interpretation-free or brute (psychological) facts/data, a fact that is thought to preclude objective (psychological) knowledge. Second, there is no value-free "view from nowhere." Therefore the local values that allegedly constitute human social/psychological existence also so infuse all (locally situated) knowing (about that existence) that there can be no fact/value distinction. Thus there are no value-free (psychological) facts/data, a fact that is thought to preclude objective (psychological) knowledge. Third, there is no stable psychological existence but rather an ontology of flux and flow, owing to human agentic interpretive capacities, which reflexively impact psychological existence. Therefore there can be no timeless, universal, and mechanistically deterministic causal laws that govern the unchanging or stable essences of (brute) psychological entities, a fact that is thought to preclude objective (psychological) knowledge.

Note that the first and third arguments contain true premises (knowing has an interpretive component and the psychological world changes, respectively) but a false conclusion, whereas the second contains a false premise (nonepistemic values necessarily infuse the knowing process) as well as a false conclusion. Add to this the belief that if (a) language/interpretation, (b) values of any sort (including epistemic values), and (c) change/flux enter the epistemic picture, then there cannot be the certainty or indubitability deemed necessary for objective knowledge, and the possibility of objective psychological knowledge vanishes.

In my critique of these three arguments, I cited philosophers whose own objectivist epistemologies embrace the fallibilist, conceptual, and situated nature of all inquiry, including inquiry into entities that are mind dependent in some ways and subject to change (for that reason). Although they do not insist on the discovery of universal mechanistically deterministic causal laws, they do insist on the inclusion of proper epistemic values in the service of objective knowing and knowledge. But the familiar voices of those philosophers do not reach the ears of MGTs. This leads me to see the MGTs' understanding of epistemic objectivity as a straw man: Theirs is an extreme view that, although not without historical precedent, is hardly the only objectivist game in town. It is ironic that those who seek moderation would not incorporate the arguments of objectivists who take moderate positions about objectivity. Although Hersch (2003, pp. 341–344) is an MGT who says that objectivists, subjectivists, and relativists all build straw men of their opponents as they each "claim the middle ground," he too does not cite the philosophers to whom I refer.[33]

To their credit, MGTs sometimes offer nuanced reformulations of the extreme view of objectivity that they take to be pervasive, reformulations that are thought by them to fit their mediational or moderating aspirations for psychological inquiry. Martin and Sugarman (1999a), Fishman (2006a, 2006b), and Bernstein (1983) are particularly prominent in this regard. First, although Martin and Sugarman (1999a) subscribe to a "fallibilist objectivity" that many objectivists would and do accept, conventional objectivists would not accept a fallibilist objectivity qualified by the word *perspectival* (which here does not seem to be the "circumstantial universality of reason/rationality" propounded by Rescher, 1997, in the name of objectivity, but rather invokes relativism): "What strikes interpreters as sense or nonsense depends on the traditions in which they are embedded, and these traditions, while always contingent, are accessible in a way that can warrant a kind of *perspectival, fallibilist objectivity* [italics added]" (p. 120).

Fishman (2006a, 2006b), in a recent exchange with me (Held, 2006a, 2006b), now states that he embraces an "objectivist" epistemology as I define it, as long as we broaden "the concept of objectivity to include . . . coherence and pragmatic criteria of truth" (2006b, abstract), in which case truth is internal (or relative) to a knowledge system, which for Fishman consists in "the internal assumptions and logic of a particular paradigm, culture, or language" (2006b, p. 4). Thus, like Martin and Sugarman, Fishman (2006b) subscribes to a "perspectival objectivity." Moreover, Fishman (2006b) acknowledges this both by calling attention to his use of quotation marks to distinguish his postmodernist form of "objectivity" from "my" conventional one, and by again, as before (Fishman, 1999, 2001), endorsing Rorty's "model of 'pragmatic relativism.'"

Martin and Sugarman (1999a) also speak of "linguistic objectivity," but this offers nothing new, because many objectivists include a linguistic component in the pursuit of knowledge. Thomasson (2003, 2007), for example, argues that we must stipulate the "boundary criteria" of the kinds we want to study, whether they are physical or mental, to determine if there exist entities in the world that fulfill those criteria (which sounds close to what Martin and Sugarman say here). However, that does not mean we linguistically con-

---

[33]Recall that Hersch (2003) offers his own "co-constitutional or interactional view of knowledge" (p. 343) as the best (intermediate) resolution of the extreme positions taken by all the others.

stitute the entities themselves, or that they are objective only in some linguistic sense (see chap. 5, this volume). Moreover, perspectivism (or relativism) reappears at the very start of this quotation.

> Within a particular sociocultural tradition, our descriptions and interpretations of human actions and social practices are *linguistically objective* [italics added] because their accuracy, appropriateness, or correctness can be adjudicated according to whether the phenomena concerned have the properties attributed to them by our descriptions and interpretations. (p. 54)

And as for Martin and Sugarman's (1999a) rejection of "singular, objective truths" in this next quotation, recall again that conventional objectivists do not insist on single descriptions of any entity, as long as the multiple descriptions are not incompatible (cf. Erwin, 1997; Haack, 2003). Although Martin and Sugarman's "perspectivism" would be problematic for objectivists, the endorsement here of "fair-mindedness" and "accountability" across traditions of understanding would no doubt appeal nonetheless.

> The kind of perspectivism advanced by Gadamer . . . entails a critical recognition that no psychological inquiry possibly can yield singular, objective truths that correspond directly to a fixed sociocultural/psychological reality. Instead, the only kind of objectivity that is possible is one of critical intersubjectivity that might be achieved through fair-minded criticism and accountability both within and across traditions of understanding and inquiry. (p. 60)

Richard Bernstein (1983) also makes common cause with Martin and Sugarman when he speaks of a "sophisticated form of fallibilistic objectivism" (pp. 12–13; see chap. 3, this volume, note 8). Of special interest in some of these last few quotations is the conception of objectivist inquiry as fallibilist and fair minded, conceptions reminiscent of such defenders of conventional epistemic objectivity as philosophers Siegel, Rescher, Haack, Thomasson, T. Smith, and Erwin. Still, the relativistic or perspectival "objectivity" (or forms of warrant/justification) that some MGTs propound in their reformulated versions of "objectivity" would not be tolerated by conventional objectivists.

CONCLUDING COMMENT

MGTs oscillate between two opposing positions regarding objective knowledge. These opposing positions each reflect an emphasis on one prong of their two-pronged mission—the attainment of (a) a truth-tracking or realist form of psychological inquiry that (b) preserves human agency. The first position is their inclination to reject the possibility of objective psychological knowledge altogether. This impulse reflects their desire to banish from psychological inquiry the search for the mechanistically deterministic causal laws of the natural sciences. Such laws, which are equated by MGTs with objective knowledge, are seen both as dehumanizing (when applied to human agentic or self-determining beings) and as known with certainty or indubitability. Thus the outright rejection of epistemic objectivity is done primarily in the name of human agency (although it also supposedly makes way for the epistemic fallibility that supports their commitment to the ontological realism of psychological kinds). Given the problems that inhere in the objective/subjective distinction, I can appreciate the MGTs' inclination to reconcile, mediate, transcend, or avoid it. However, I do not agree that the quest for objective psychological knowledge must limit itself to discovering universal mechanistic causal laws, even without the indubitability that MGTs wrongly equate with objective knowledge.

The second position consists in MGTs' occasional attempts to reinstate the epistemic objectivity that they have rejected, albeit in reformulated terms. But why do this after going to such great effort to reject an objectivist epistemology in the first place? One possible reason is that they may appreciate that the objective/subjective distinction, although surely in need of rehabilitation, has virtue nonetheless. For example, Richardson et al. (1999), who are as adamant as any in rejecting an objectivist epistemology in psychological inquiry, still find uses for it in the value-laden form of psychological knowledge that they propound: "If the word *objective* is understood as the opposite of *subjective*, that is, as referring to what exists concretely 'out there' in the world, then it seems we have every reason to say . . . that values are objective" (p. 215). The virtue that may inspire such objectivist pronouncements consists in what Robinson (1997) called "the morals of objectivity," the relentless striving to get at the truth (the reality) of the matter under scrutiny, although we know full well that the effort could be fraught with error every step of the way. Such conventional objectivist acceptance of fallibility may explain why some MGTs reformulate their understanding of objectivity as "fallibilist objectivity." I contend that this supposed reformulation is offered in the service of the epistemic realism that MGTs seek as one of their twin goals.

But in striving for objectivity (or even "objectivity"), MGTs subvert their hoped-for obliteration of the fact/value distinction in the service of a more morally informed, value-laden, human science. Thus we see a circular process, or oscillatory movement, in rejecting the subject(ive)/object(ive) distinction altogether (in the name of agency) and reinstating it in reformulated terms (in the name of epistemic realism).

MGTs are consistent on at least this point: Although they reject an objectivist epistemology in the excessive form in which they understand it, they want to adhere to a realist epistemology nonetheless. That dual stance seems odd if not contradictory, given that epistemic objectivism and epistemic realism are usually seen as compatible if not interchangeable. Again, those who speak of objectivist or realist epistemologies typically agree that bona fide truth or knowledge is not merely a function of (or relative to) what anyone believes to be the case, including the beliefs that constitute the conceptual schemes, paradigms, and language systems of knowers. This is so even in the case of knowledge claims about mind-dependent entities, such as mental states and processes—that is, knowledge claims about the social/psychological world.

To appreciate MGTs' attempts to maintain a realist epistemology that is not objectivist, we must first understand how they use the term *realism* in their epistemic arguments. That means we must look more closely at just what for them should properly warrant knowledge or truth claims about human psychological existence. Only then can we assess whether the word *realist* may be fairly applied to their own psychological claims.

9

SITUATED WARRANT: A MIDDLE-GROUND REALIST EPISTEMOLOGY?

Middle-ground theorists (MGTs) insist that psychological knowledge is not and cannot be objective knowledge. On their view objective knowledge (or an objectivist epistemology) consists in indubitably known, timeless, universal, and mechanistically deterministic causal laws about the unchanging essences of brute or mind-independent entities. Yet many conventional objectivists adopt a more moderate view of objective knowledge: that the truth of a proposition (causal or otherwise) can in principle be warranted independently of beliefs about its truth or of the conceptual/linguistic/discursive context of knowers. Claims about an entity can thus in principle be warranted independently of anyone's beliefs about the nature of the entity. Moreover, fallibility always obtains: There is no indubitability in empirical matters.

MGTs also insist that psychological knowledge is realist knowledge nonetheless; for them "thinking doesn't make it so," and therefore fallibility can obtain (see chap. 5, this volume). In realist knowledge (or a realist epistemology), "facts about the world are genuinely discoverable through substantive investigation subject to possibilities of confirmation and error, not just imposed by or to be read off of our concepts and beliefs" (Thomasson,

2003, p. 582). Thus realist claims can be justified independently of anyone's beliefs about the entity in question or the conceptual/linguistic/discursive context of knowers, and they are always fallible. Given these conventional definitions, we can equate realist and objectivist epistemologies (or forms of inquiry/knowledge)—in sharp contrast to the epistemology of MGTs, who try to defend a realist epistemology that is not objectivist, at least not in any conventional sense.

This proclamation—that psychological inquiry can be realist but not objectivist—constitutes the basis of the MGTs' claim to a middle-ground epistemology, one that attempts to integrate/reconcile/bridge, moderate/ mediate, transcend/overcome, or avoid/escape both the objectivism of modern science and the relativism/antirealism of radical postmodern "science." It is to this proclamation that they appeal in the name of their dual mission: the attainment of a truth-tracking or realist form of psychological inquiry that preserves human agency.

To evaluate their claim to have found an epistemic middle ground, we must first examine MGTs' arguments about what *should* warrant or justify claims about human psychological existence. After all, if such claims are not properly warranted or justified, they cannot in principle give us the truth— the reality—of human psychological existence, which truth/reality is just what MGTs seek in calling their epistemology "realist." But whether they call their epistemic realism a "neorealist hermeneutic" epistemology (e.g., Guignon, 1991, 2002a; Martin & Sugarman, 1999a, 1999b; Richardson, Fowers, & Guignon, 1999; Woolfolk, 1998), a "(neo)pragmatic" epistemology (e.g., Fishman, 1999, 2001), or a moderate "social constructionist" epistemology (e.g., Edley, 2001; Harré, 1998, 2002; Liebrucks, 2001), all insist that there exists realist epistemic warrant for claims about psychological existence, in which (in conventional terms) warrant is not merely a matter of what anyone thinks to be the case. Moreover, MGTs do not accept the radical postmodern view that we are in a "post-epistemological" era, in which knowledge and truth are reduced to "knowledge" and "truth," because our desires constitute the only possible standard of warrant. I refer here to Rorty's (1991) famous statement: "The pragmatist's claim [is] that to know your desires . . . is to know the criterion of truth, to understand what it would take for a belief to 'work'" (p. 31).

Do MGTs manage to attain truth and not "truth," knowledge and not "knowledge"? Do they manage to resist the "deflationary" view of truth/ reality against which Nagel (1986) warned (see chap. 5, this volume)? Recall Gergen's (1985, p. 273) strong constructionist argument—that warrant should be a function of the "good or ill" that (reflexively) follows from our knowledge or truth claims; that is, there are and should be "moral criteria for scientific practice" (see chap. 8, this volume). Like Rorty, Gergen adopts pragmatic criteria of warrant—but then so too do many MGTs, despite their desire to distance themselves from Gergen's radical constructionism and

Rorty's radical postmodernism. After all, MGTs often ask us to maintain "moral and political awareness" when we study human phenomena, which study cannot deploy "neutral, value-free forms of inquiry"—not least because for them the "human sciences . . . always [reflexively] influence the cultural context they address" (Richardson, Fowers, & Guignon, 1999, p. 236). As Bohman, Hiley, and Shusterman (1991) put it, "If there is nothing that is not an interpretation against which to judge, choices among competing interpretations . . . raise important moral and political issues about the relationship between interpreters and the subjects of their interpretations" (p. 8).

Are the epistemologies of radical constructionists/postmodernists and MGTs different enough to allow MGTs to claim access to truth/reality in ways that Gergen and Rorty cannot? Does the MGTs' value-laden form of inquiry avoid the strong relativism implied in Rorty's and Gergen's pragmatic standards of warrant? If so, does it avoid epistemic relativism altogether? And if it does not, can their weaker form of relativism be sufficiently "truth tracking" to be rightly called a realist epistemology? To answer these questions, let us consider MGTs' views about what can and should warrant knowledge claims in psychology.

STANDARDS OF WARRANT

In this section I set forth four forms of warrant espoused by MGTs. All four appeal to some form of situated or perspectival warrant, in which local or situated meanings and values are said to play a legitimate justificatory role. Yet they have different emphases that can be distinguished on that basis.

Criterion 1: Perspectival Warrant and Fallibilist Inquiry/Knowing

Martin and Sugarman are among the most explicit proponents of perspectival, fallibilist warrant, or what can alternatively be called "warrant within a tradition." Accordingly I quote them almost exclusively, because I do not find evidence that other MGTs—who say similar things—reject their statements. For example, Hersch (2003) speaks expressly of a "perspectival realist" epistemology (p. 60).

In this quotation notice first the (discursively) contextualized nature of warrant (which conventional objectivists/realists reject) and then the uncertain nature of knowing or understanding (which conventional objectivists/realists accept).

> The reality of psychological phenomena within other levels of reality allows psychologists to warrant claims concerning their interpretative

findings by tapping into, and participating within, systems of meaning and practice extant in relevant historical, sociocultural contexts. However, the same reality ensures that our understanding of psychological phenomena never can be absolute, certain, or complete. (Martin & Sugarman, 1999b, p. 191)

These next two quotations emphasize empirical demonstrations and criteria for warrant (which conventional objectivists/realists accept). However, because those are made relative to (discursive/interpretive) context, they are "stripped of objectivism"—that is, the kind of objectivism conventional objectivists often accept. Martin and Sugarman also tout a more fallibilist epistemology than what they think exists in conventional forms of psychological inquiry, although it is not obvious why they consider their epistemology to be more fallibilist.

> The evaluation of competing theories, and the means and criteria of any such evaluation, must be considered not only in relation to relevant demonstrations themselves, but also in relation to the traditions of understanding and knowing in which both demonstrations and theories are embedded. (Martin & Sugarman, 1999a, p. 53)
>
> Much extant inquiry in social science and psychology . . . can be stripped of its unsupportable vestiges of objectivism and positivism, and seen as a valuable source of necessarily socioculturally and temporally constrained demonstrations. . . . This more fallibilist construal of social and psychological inquiry assumes that its focal phenomena . . . cannot be construed in manners unsupported by relevant sociocultural traditions, including those that define the inquiry practices of psychologists and social scientists. (Martin & Sugarman, 1999a, pp. 55–56)

Next we see "the no view from nowhere, therefore no objective knowledge" argument. Fallibilist knowledge and relativist standards of warrant are linked together and invoked in the antiobjectivist campaign, although in middle-ground terms.

> There is no outside vantage point, complete with its own set of unimpeachably objective standards, from which to make judgments concerning the relative merits of different interpretations. . . . The possibility of illegitimate interpretations exists (i.e., interpretations not appropriately constrained by any identifiable tradition). (Martin & Sugarman, 1999a, p. 57)
>
> Epistemological claims concerning psychological phenomena can only be adjudicated in relation to relevant sociocultural traditions. . . . A middle course is charted between the extremes of an overly constraining static, ahistorical, "outside" standard on the one bank, and an overly enabling, strongly relativistic, nihilistic, "anything goes" absence of standard on the other. (Martin & Sugarman, 1999a, p. 59)

In these last two quotations, a middle-ground appeal to "fusion" (of horizons/traditions) or integration/reconciliation is again made in the service of a fallibilist, perspectival (here linked to a critically intersubjectivist), but nonetheless "neorealist" epistemology.

> Once objectivism and positivism are abandoned in favor of a fallibilist, perspectivist epistemology, some powerful, coherent notion of "critical intersubjectivity" is required to enable the necessarily imperfect (but all that is available) possibility of Gadamer's fusion of horizons. (Martin & Sugarman, 1999a, p. 60)
>
> We endorse a fusion of hermeneutic and neorealist epistemologies . . . [that] is capable of warranting a progressive perspectivist program of psychological inquiry. (Martin & Sugarman, 1999a, p. 41)

Guignon (2002a) perhaps best summed up the sentiment seen in the previously mentioned quotations: "Truth is always relativized to a context of interests and aims. . . . Standards . . . are relative to the framework of interpretation in play, and therefore cannot give us a higher court of appeal" (p. 282). In short, the necessary "view from somewhere" allegedly precludes a nonrelativist or objectivist epistemology (see chap. 3, this volume).

Criterion 2: Practical Reason Within a Context

In these next quotations, we see an appeal to reason or rationality (or judgment) for epistemic warrant. However, that reason or rationality itself is said to be relative to context, or "perspectival." Therefore there can be no universal reason/rationality, such as that maintained in Rescher's "circumstantial universality of reason" and in Siegel's argument that the universals of rationality are presupposed by those who challenge them (see chap. 8)—this despite the (tentative) appeal made by some MGTs (especially Martin and Sugarman) to a universal reason/rationality in their attempt to explain how agentic transcendence of (or innovation within) the constitutive context is possible (see chap. 6).

> The [epistemic] criteria we present here cannot be fully formalized. . . . They require a certain degree of discernment and judgment that cannot be encompassed in an explicit list of rules or procedures. . . . What counts as good judgment in these matters is worked out over time in a community of inquirers. (Richardson, Fowers, & Guignon, 1999, p. 302)
>
> What we draw upon in reflection on our own historically-effected understanding and our efforts to extend it, is the necessarily perspectival, but nonarbitrary, warranted reason that flows from our historical and sociocultural situatedness. (Martin & Sugarman, 1999a, p. 120)

Bernstein (1983), here appealing to the "practical rationality of theory-choice" (p. 52), gives his appeal to reason/rationality a pragmatic (as well as a relativist or perspectival) twist.

> The challenge . . . is to give the best possible reasons and arguments that are appropriate to our hermeneutical situation in order to validate claims

to truth. . . . Gadamer is appealing to a concept of truth that (pragmatically speaking) amounts to what can be argumentatively validated by the community of interpreters who open themselves to what tradition "says to us." This does not mean that there is some transcendental or ahistorical perspective from which we can evaluate competing claims to truth. (pp. 153, 154)

Guignon (1991), like Bernstein, adopts a hermeneutically informed notion of "practical reason" to warrant knowledge claims perspectivally—that is, with a "view from somewhere."

Hermeneutic thinkers show how this project of working out a post-Epistemological epistemology might go. These include attempts to clarify the role of practical reason . . . in justifying knowledge claims, reflections on rationality as the ability to adopt multiple partially disengaged perspectives rather than a totally disengaged stance of pure "objectivity." (p. 100)

Again, because there is no "view from nowhere," for these scholars there can be no nonrelativist or objectivist epistemology. In due course we consider whether a relativist/nonobjectivist epistemology can rightly be called "realist."

Criterion 3: Weak Relativism

In chapter 5, I argued that despite their claim to ontological realism and their ostensible rejection of ontological relativism, MGTs are nonetheless committed to a relativist ontology of human psychological existence. Can they manage to support a relativist ontology while (on some occasions) rejecting a relativist epistemology? In principle, this might seem possible. For example, Liebrucks (2001) says that "properties of persons" exist "only relative to the meaning system of the community to which they belong" (p. 374), but he also says social constructionists "do not subscribe to a relativist epistemology" (p. 373). By contrast, some MGTs admit to a weak form of epistemic relativism. For example, Hersch (2003) defends "*realism at the ontological level*" (p. 269) but describes his epistemology as "relatively relativistic" (p. 169). Is a weak, qualified form of epistemic relativism compatible with the realist epistemology that MGTs typically proclaim?

We begin with Martin and Sugarman (1999a), who distinguish strong versus weak relativism in terms of *truth* as opposed to what it is *reasonable* to believe, respectively. In so doing they once again appeal to rationality in their notion of epistemic warrant, although it is a relativistic rather than a universal notion of reason/rationality that they propound.

Strong relativism . . . holds that *what is true* is relative to a conceptual scheme, and that what is true in one such scheme . . . will be false for another. Weak relativism . . . [holds that] what it is *reasonable to believe* is relative to a conceptual scheme, and what it is reasonable to believe in one conceptual scheme may not be reasonable to believe in another [all italics added]. (p. 48)

Perspectivism does not eschew reasons and evidence as essential warrants for understanding, nor is it committed to finding that all conceptual schemes are equally valuable. (p. 50)

Freeman (1993), by contrast, says that truth itself is relative, so he would appear to fit Martin and Sugarman's definition of strong relativism. However, he denies that his is a strong relativism owing to the existence of linguistic/discursive/interpretive constraints on what can rightly be said. Those constraints consist in the relation of the old interpretation to the new, and the tradition or language in which truth emerges. In short, he seemingly appeals to something like the emergent or emanationist theory of "truth/reality" that we first considered in chapter 5, a theory I there called "deflationary." At the least, the nature of what we interpret is here said to change as a result of our interpretive activity; there is a reflexive relationship between being and knowing about being.

The idea of truth must be clearly relativized on some level; we cannot compare the thing-for-them to the thing-for-us; we live in two different worlds, two different hermeneutical situations. . . . Doesn't this relativization of the idea of truth entail in the end a complete and total relativism, where every reading is as sound as every other? Not at all. For . . . our ongoing engagement with the world changes and complexifies our own hermeneutical situation, which in turn changes and complexifies the qualities of the things we interpret: a new truth emerges. (pp. 142–143)

Woolfolk (1998), who like Freeman proclaims an emanationist or emergent theory of truth/reality (see chap. 5, this volume), rejects the epistemological relativism he finds in social constructionism and constructivism (p. 135). Yet he gives signs of adopting a form of epistemic relativism nonetheless: Although he relieves the word *truth* of its postmodernist scare quotes, he also qualifies the definition of truth so as to relativize it to context, horizon, framework, or perspective. In short, this is only truth within a tradition—that is, perspectival truth that emerges in a "view from somewhere."

Understanding the actions of human beings involves uncovering truth, but truth that is constrained by a sociocultural horizon, truth that can be identified only from a particular vantage point. (p. 136)

A presumption seems to be at work in these statements: that a conceptual component of knowing (which is seen by MGTs as perspectival) necessarily precludes objective knowledge/truth.

Criterion 4: Pragmatic/Value-Laden Warrant

Pragmatic and relativistic notions of warrant cannot be separated in MGT circles, for the obvious reason that values—which are said to be relative to traditions—are themselves the basis for the MGTs' pragmatic form of epistemic warrant. What one tradition values or desires in consequences that follow from warranting a belief as a justified true belief may therefore differ from what another tradition values or desires (cf. Rorty, 1991, pp. 30–31). For example, in Tradition A liberation is valued, so in that tradition claims that have liberating consequences are warranted; whereas in Tradition B oppression is valued, so in that tradition claims that have oppressive consequences are warranted.[1] Still, that pragmatic consequences are used to justify truth or knowledge claims does not in itself necessitate a relativistic epistemology, weak or strong: If there is universal agreement about just what constitutes desirable or good consequences/outcomes (of holding certain beliefs), then the pragmatic standard of warrant is only antirealist (or antiobjectivist);[2] it is not also relativistic.[3] But for MGTs, who make much of cultural differences when speaking of meanings and values, this is a moot point: The practical reason to which MGTs appeal for epistemic warrant is reason *in a context*; it is not the (circumstantially) universal reason/rationality of Rescher or Siegel (see chap. 8, this volume). As Martin and Sugarman (1999a) put it in defending weak relativism, "The use of traditions as pragmatic nondogmatic warrants . . . counters the kind of strong relativism and nihilism many associate with the subjectivism of modern life" (pp. 118–119).

In the final chapter of *Re-envisioning Psychology*, Richardson, Fowers, and Guignon (1999, pp. 298–302) give seven epistemic criteria for "evaluating interpretations" in psychology. Some of these criteria are not inconsistent with those sometimes found in objectivist epistemologies (e.g., whether a new theory can make "sense of observations that did not fit within previously available accounts," p. 301).[4] Yet some are. However, it is the beneficially transformative potential of theory within a context (p. 306) that is of most interest to them, and this makes their standards of warrant seem pragmatic in the Rortian sense. They call their epistemic criteria "nonfoundational

---

[1]Although Gergen (1985, 2001a) equates objectivism with authoritarianism and constructivism with liberation, Maze (2001) turns Gergen's equation on its ear: It is authoritarianism that denies (access to) objective truth, implies Maze (p. 412). Oppression should therefore follow consequentially from Gergen's antiobjectivism, rather than from Maze's own fallibilist epistemic realism/objectivism!

[2]To know the consequences of holding a belief requires a realist/objectivist epistemology about *that* question. Yet then the belief itself reflects an antirealist or antiobjectivist epistemology, in which true belief is held only to the standard of what knowers want to believe is true, rather than what is true according to nonpragmatic epistemic or evidential criteria.

[3]See chapter 3, this volume, note 7, for Pols's (2000a) discussion of Kant's antirealism but not relativism. See Haack (1998b), who argues against the Rortian view that pragmatists (especially C. S. Peirce) are necessarily antirealists.

[4]Regarding the latter criterion, see Erwin (1997), who propounds an objectivist epistemology but warns of the use of "inference to the best explanation" to warrant theory choice (pp. 76–77).

suggestions" (p. 299). They again call on the lack of distinction between (a) the knowing subject and the object to be known, and between (b) facts and values to argue their pragmatic standard of warrant for psychological inquiry. Let us consider a few exemplary quotations, some of which we have encountered in the context of other arguments. Note in the second quotation the realization that objectivity is itself an epistemic value.

> David Hoy (1986, p. 124) observes that "theory choice in the social sciences is . . . more relativistic than in the natural sciences, since the principles used to select social theories would be guided by a variety of values." (p. 178)
>
> Knowledge claims are adjudicated within a social order that incorporates . . . a more or less explicit set of values, in contrast to the distortions incurred in the attempt to maintain factitious distinctions between facts and values and between objective and subjective domains. Of course, we will continue to adhere to openness and objectivity as paramount values of inquiry. (p. 154)
>
> Because any data . . . are partly constituted by the investigator and those she studies, there are no simple "facts of the matter" that can arbitrate between the higher-order interpretations of different theories. . . . If our self-understanding helps make us who we are, then the truth about us may be too malleable and multifaceted to be amenable to a single, overarching, consensual scientific account. (p. 299)

Although the search for an "overarching scientific account" is rejected by Richardson et al. (1999), in this next quotation they state their overarching pragmatic epistemic criterion of beneficial social/psychological transformation nonetheless. This criterion, they say, is aided by "the interpretive perspective" that they propound.

> Our theory and research are certainly not neutral; by challenging, altering, reinforcing, or enriching our self-understandings and actions, they are in fact potentially transformative. . . . The naturalistic approach is unable to answer the question of whether a given theory is the *best transformative account* [italics added], because the possibility that theory can transform practice is seen as an extrascientific question. (p. 306)

In his essay "Pragmatism or Hermeneutics? Epistemology after Foundationalism," Guignon (1991) pits his "hardy hermeneutic realism" (p. 99) against the radically playful, ironic, freewheeling postmodern pragmatism of Rorty (see chap. 5, this volume). Yet he, like other hermeneutically inclined MGTs, defines epistemic warrant in pragmatic terms nonetheless. For example, in "Narrative Explanation in Psychotherapy," Guignon (1998) again suggests a pragmatic (transformative) criterion for judging the truth of narratives about our lives, as he does in the quotation from his (2002a) essay "Truth in Interpretation" that follows. Guignon (1998) concludes on an optimistic note about our ability to detect truth in our stories, although he does not tell us just how he knows this assertion to be true.

> Deciding which story is the best or truest will depend on such factors as the ... quality of the future it implies. ... Generally this does not present any major problems in practice. As beings whose very being is shaped by stories, we are remarkably good at spotting the truth in the stories we tell. (Guignon, 1998, p. 575)
>
> The best interpretations ... reveal that the possibilities they disclose are just that, *possibilities*, and that other possibilities of interpretation are therefore possible. (Guignon, 2002a, p. 284)

In contrast to Guignon, Fishman (1999, 2001)—who appealed to a pervasive ontology of flux and flow to argue against an objectivist epistemology (see chaps. 7–8, this volume)—embraces Rorty's "epistemology" unambivalently. He (1999) deliberately fuses what he considers the postmodern (neo)pragmatism of Rorty with the perspectival relativism of hermeneutics to propound Rorty's "pragmatic relativism" (pp. 119, 131). In so doing he adopts an antirealism more radical than that of other MGTs, both ontologically and epistemically. Indeed, he does not characterize his epistemology as "realist," as do other MGTs. He explicitly calls his Rortian version of pragmatism (which he rightly contrasts with the pragmatism of James, Dewey, and Peirce, p. 296) postmodernist, because it is "founded on a social constructionist theory of knowledge" (p. 130). This is interesting, given that Fishman also seeks a middle ground by integrating/reconciling hermeneutic and positivist paradigms in the service of his "(neo)pragmatic psychology." However, because he seeks a middle ground by way of integration/ reconciliation and transcendence, and because warrant for him is context-dependent/perspectival/relativist and pragmatic, we may count him as a bona fide MGT. After all, he himself (2001) describes his own version of social constructionism as "moderate."

> The pragmatic psychology view can be characterized as a "moderate" constructionist position that also falls in the middle of the realist versus constructionist continuum. The moderate constructionist posits that although it is not possible to apprehend transhistorical and cross-cultural ... foundational realities, there are "facts," "theories," and "values" that transcend any individual's idiosyncratic perspective because they have developed functional authority within society. (p. 279)

Given Fishman's use of scare quotes in this quotation, he sounds as "realist" as any of the versions of "realism" propounded by other MGTs (see chap. 5, this volume). Here let us consider a few more quotations in which Fishman (1999), unlike other MGTs, appeals epistemically to a Rortian "pragmatic relativism," in which truth is indistinguishable from values or desires. Note also Fishman's appeal (especially in the second and third quotations) to a naturalized rather than a normative epistemology, and his implicit rejection (especially in the first quotation) of Rescher's (1997) "circumstantial universality of reason" (see chap. 8, this volume). In the fourth quotation, the "ontology of flux and flow, therefore no objective knowledge" argument resurfaces.

> Which glasses [language, paradigm, web of belief] we should use in [viewing the world] depends not upon which pair purports to best correspond to the "real" external world, but rather which is best pragmatically. . . . If two different groups have different interests in a certain situation, each might justifiably be led to choose different glasses with which to view the situation. (p. 118)
>
> Rorty argues that "anything goes" relativism does not necessarily follow from perspectivism [or pragmatic relativism]. . . . "There is nothing to be said about either truth or rationality apart from description of the familiar procedures of justification which a given society—*ours*—uses in one or another area of inquiry. . . . Each of us will commend as true beliefs those which he or she finds good to believe" [Rorty, 1989a, pp. 37–38]. (p. 119)
>
> Rorty's concept of "pragmatic relativism," which . . . [denies] transhistorical and cross-cultural "foundational" standards, points to the already established and agreed-upon procedures and standards our society now has for determining truth and morality in particular contexts. (p. 131)
>
> The pragmatic "truth" of a particular perspective does not lie in its correspondence to "objective reality," since that reality is continuously in flux. Rather, [pragmatic truth] . . . lies in the usefulness of the perspective in helping us to cope. (p. 130)

CRITIQUE OF A PERSPECTIVAL/RELATIVIST, PRAGMATIC FORM OF WARRANT

In this section I offer my critique of MGTs' standards of warrant—that is, their epistemology. In particular, I ask whether their fallibilist, perspectival, (weakly) relativist, and pragmatic form of warrant can—even in principle—constitute the realist (or truth-tracking) epistemology to which they lay claim. This set of questions may be addressed independently of the agency that MGTs seek to preserve within (or owing to) their (hoped-for antiobjectivist) version of epistemic realism.

Can a Weak Relativist Epistemology Be a Realist Epistemology?

This question functions as the counterpart to the one posed in chapter 5—namely, can a (locally) belief-dependent and, in that sense, relativist ontology of human psychological existence or personhood constitute a realist ontology? In this chapter we have seen how some MGTs, especially Martin and Sugarman (1999a), defend a weak form of epistemic relativism in the service of the perspectival warrant that many (but not all) MGTs support. For example, recall (chap. 5, this volume) that Liebrucks (2001) appeared to defend a relativist ontology of personhood: "There are properties of persons that exist only in the context of a certain discourse, that is, persons have them only relative to the meaning system of the community to which they belong" (p. 374). Yet Liebrucks then propounded what he considered to be a perfectly realist and nonrelativist epistemology or science of psychology, one that could in principle provide objective psychological knowledge (in which a claim's truth does not depend on beliefs about its truth or the conceptual schemes of knowers). However, Liebrucks seems to invoke knowledge (of what is the case) within any (discursive) context rather than—as bona fide objectivists might insist—regardless of the (discursive) context (see chap. 8, this volume, note 27). Thus Liebrucks's caveat might appear to call into question the objective, or nonrelativist, epistemic status of his psychological knowledge.

In the first quotation, notice Liebrucks's claim that valid psychological accounts "apply to" (or are about) particular times and cultures; this is a claim that objectivists could in principle accept. That is, he does not suggest the relativist or perspectival (antiobjectivist) view that truth depends on the perspective of the knowers, so that knowers in different cultural/discursive contexts could in principle make different *valid* judgments about the same (psychological) claim; this is a claim that objectivists would surely reject. In the second quotation, he disavows the view that the relativism of social constructionists qualifies their epistemology, but leaves open the possibility that it is (as I argue) relevant to their ontology.

> [Social constructionists] do not subscribe to a relativist epistemology. They do not claim that it is impossible to arrive at valid accounts of the psychological properties of persons. They only claim that valid accounts that apply to the psychology of all humankind irrespective of time and culture are possible only on a very high level of abstraction, and that more concrete accounts only apply to specific historical epochs and specific cultural spheres. (p. 373)
>
> Contrary to Gergen's (1985) account . . . no relativist conclusions can be drawn from the arguments and empirical findings of social constructionist sociology of science. . . . The central theses of the social constructionists in theoretical psychology are primarily concerned not with epistemology but with the discipline's construal of its subject matter. (p. 385)

Here it may be instructive to compare Martin and Sugarman's (1999a) weak epistemic relativism with Liebrucks's relativist ontology but (self-proclaimed) nonrelativist epistemology: There are differences despite the moderate position that each claims to hold. Recall that Martin and Sugarman (1999a) said that strong relativism consists in "committing oneself to the view that reality and truth are relative to differing conceptual schemes" (pp. 48–49). Their mention of reality itself gives strong relativism an ontological element, and because Martin and Sugarman reject strong relativism outright, we may assume that here they reject the ontological relativism Liebrucks seems to accept. Weak relativism, by contrast, consists for Martin and Sugarman in the view that what we take as "reasonable to believe is relative to a conceptual scheme" (p. 48). Thus weak relativism, or the perspectivism Martin and Sugarman propound, is strictly epistemological: It concerns reasonable (or justified) belief.[5] Indeed, for them epistemic warrant is a matter of what claims may be rightly thought justified/warranted in or for a discursive context—that is, *for* knowers in a context (rather than what, in objectivist terms, may be rightly thought justified *about* phenomena observed in a context, but regardless of the conceptual schemes or contexts of the knowers).[6] The former fits standard definitions of epistemological relativism, which is often opposed to objectivism (see chap. 3, this volume).

The problem is that I do not see how Martin and Sugarman's purportedly weakly relativist epistemology can also be considered a realist epistemology, in which (in more conventional terms) what is reasonable to believe, or what is epistemically justified/warranted, is independent of conceptual schemes, theories, discourses, cultures, and (most important) what anyone believes or desires to be true. These forms of independence, after all, form the backbone of more conventional definitions of realist or objectivist epistemologies, which I equate and MGTs do not, and which allow the fallibilist knowing that both "objectivist realists" and MGTs (who try to make themselves "antiobjectivist realists") propound (see chaps. 5 & 8).

That Martin and Sugarman and other MGTs appeal to constraints that operate *within* a discursive context to justify or warrant what can be rightly said *in that context* does not make theirs a realist epistemology—certainly not in any thoroughgoing meaning of the term *realist* (in which justification or warrant operates independently of the conceptual schemes and beliefs of knowers). Their epistemology may indeed provide more constraint (on what can be "rightly" said) by way of the epistemic criteria accepted within any given discursive community than does the "epistemology" of radical postmodernists/constructionists. However, that (discursive) constraint may not be sufficient to make the MGTs' less radically relativist epistemology realist, even in the more lenient terms of Thomasson (2003), Erwin (1997), and Haack (2002), who make the convincing case that many human kinds,

---

[5]Siegel (2004) challenged the strong/weak distinction in saying, "Constructing a conception of relative truth such that . . . '*p* is true for members of Culture C'" is stronger than the conception that "'Members of Culture C believe that *p*.'" But constructing the stronger conception has nonetheless "proved to be quite difficult, and is arguably beyond the conceptual resources available to relativists" (p. 749).

[6]The failure to make this "prepositional" distinction—what is true *for* them versus what is true *about* them—may account for much of the epistemological confusion expressed by postmodernists. See Held (2006a, 2006b) for elaboration.

or mind-dependent entities, (a) are real ontologically and so (b) can be known with fallibility and objectivity (see chaps. 5 & 8, this volume).

Apropos of this, Richardson, Fowers, and Guignon (1999) say that critics are wrong to "charge Gadamer with a pernicious relativism: the view that whatever anyone *thinks* is true is true," because this criticism overlooks "Gadamer's emphasis on how the tradition provides guidelines and models that constrain our possible claims" (p. 235). Although Richardson et al. here and elsewhere say there are tradition-determined limits on what can be rightly claimed within a tradition, they merely avoid the wanton, anything-goes relativism of radical postmodernists. They do not keep their own epistemology free of relativism per se—even if, as Martin and Sugarman (1999a) claim, theirs is a weaker relativism. Again, in adopting this allegedly weaker epistemic relativism, MGTs do not make the case that their epistemology affords realist knowledge—that is, knowledge that can be justified independently of the conceptual scheme of (including the beliefs held within) the discursive/interpretive tradition in which knowledge claims are "justified" relativistically. By making truth relative to discursive/interpretive contexts, MGTs cannot claim to attain knowledge of how things are, independent of the beliefs (about how things are) that are held by those who participate in those contexts—hence their self-proclaimed antiobjectivist epistemology. But this precludes a realist as well as an objectivist epistemology, if objectivity is not given a straw-man definition (see chap. 8, this volume).

And yet Richardson et al. (1999) themselves say (as do other MGTs) that their epistemic goal is to know how something actually is. They seemingly seek truth simpliciter, although they invoke the straw man of an infallible objectivism in the process (see chap. 8, this volume): "Although finding the truth is still a matter of revealing the way things really are, the truths we discover about humans generally must be treated as defeasible" (p. 235). So too with the truths we discover about the natural/physical world, I would add! Here I appeal to Siegel's (1997) notion of "absolutistic fallibilism" (p. 119), in which "absolutistic" carries a meaning quite different from the one MGTs and radical postmodernists give it when qualifying the objectivism they dread. Siegel (1997) says that

> a fallibilist but absolutist conception of truth [is] absolutist in that the truth of a proposition, sentence, belief or claim is independent of the warrant or justification it enjoys on the basis of the relevant evidence, and fallibilist in that our judgments concerning truth are always open to challenge and revision. (p. 6)

Siegel supports "a view of justification as a fallible indicator of truth" and a "rejection of epistemological relativism" (p. 6).

Moreover, the use of "critical intersubjectivity" to allow for agentic transcendence of belief (and warrant for belief) beyond any given context— "the necessarily imperfect (but all that is available) possibility of Gadamer's fusion of horizons" (Martin & Sugarman, 1999a, p. 60)—does not make the MGTs' epistemology realist: that we may agree to substitute new relativistic or (local) discourse/tradition-dependent beliefs and criteria of warrant for old ones does not make the new ones more objectively true—or even more adequate. Although MGTs often accept the greater epistemic adequacy of "fused horizons," even these cannot purchase objective knowledge owing to our alleged inability to escape "from the sociocultural traditions in which societies and psychological individuals are embedded" (Martin & Sugarman, 1999a, p. 57)—this, even though their weak relativist perspectivism is not "committed to finding that all conceptual schemes are equally valuable" (p. 50).

What, then, makes one conceptual scheme more valuable than another? The answer remains unclear. Martin and Sugarman (1999a) tell us that "the ultimate aim . . . is to forge a more adequate conceptualization, understanding, and explanation of humans . . . than might be forthcoming if psychological inquiry is more conceptually restricted" (p. 50). By "conceptually restricted," I take them to mean the restrictions imposed by nonperspectival, allegedly nonfallibilist, and brute-entity focused epistemologies, such as the ones they think they find in the straw man they build of objectivity (see chap. 8, this volume). In any case, recall that in their "weak relativism" Martin and Sugarman do not define "what it is reasonable to believe" in terms of the "circumstantial universality of reason" proposed by Rescher (1997), in which all rational persons put in a given circumstance could in principle agree about what is the case, or how things should be judged.

Rescher's sense of reason/rationality could not obtain for MGTs, because they seem to allow no unflinchingly universal reason/rationality on which to base universal epistemic standards. Thus reason or rationality itself must be relative to conceptual schemes or discursive/interpretive contexts (see chap. 6, this volume). Recall Richardson et al.'s (1999) proclamation: "What counts as good judgment in . . . [evaluating competing interpretations] is worked out over time in a community of inquirers" (p. 302). Also recall this from Guignon (2002a): "Standards . . . are relative to the frameworks of interpretation in play, and therefore cannot give us a higher court of appeal" (p. 282). Moreover, Fishman (1999), who adopts Rorty's "pragmatic relativism," quotes Rorty as saying that "rationality is what history and society make it" (p. 118). Bernstein (1983) says that "discursive truth" is, "pragmatically speaking," "what can be argumentatively validated by the community of interpreters who open themselves to what tradition 'says to us'" (pp. 153–154). In short, the "practical reason" of MGTs, unlike reason simpliciter, is by definition context-dependent; it cannot be otherwise (see Criterion 2).

Given their context-dependent view of reason/rationality, hermeneutically inclined MGTs (e.g., Martin & Sugarman, 1999a, p. 60) may be right to insist that a fusion of interpretive "horizons" (or beliefs and standards of warrant) is all "that is possible" in adjudicating knowledge claims. But is it? That we must use "discernment and judgment" (Richardson et al., 1999, p. 302), or reason/rationality, to warrant knowledge claims constitutes no sound argument against the possibility of bona fide objective knowledge (see chap. 8, this volume). Yet reason/rationality seems to Richardson et al. (1999) to hinder the possibility of objective knowledge: The use of "discernment and judgment" is "directly at odds with the kind of naturalistic approach in which formalization" (or "an explicit list of rules or procedures") is "the keystone of objectivity." They say that because "interpretations are central to all human activities, including scientific observations, then . . . the aspiration to complete formalization is unattainable" (p. 302).

Here again the MGTs' straw man of objectivity makes an appearance—this time by insisting that objective knowledge consists not only in indubitably known, timeless, universal, and mechanistically deterministic causal laws about the unchanging essences of brute or physical entities but also requires the "formalization" that seemingly precludes the use of discernment and judgment (i.e., reason). If by "formalization" Richardson et al. (1999) mean the hoped-for content-free formal logic of a long-abandoned logical positivism,[7] then they are erecting another straw man to deny the possibility of objective knowledge. As Haack (2003, pp. 60–68) has cogently argued, objective knowledge does not require leaving our rational, conceptual, or interpretive powers at the door of inquiry; it requires that we bring them inside, as we work to make sense of our empirical observations in light of reasons or background beliefs/knowledge (which is not necessarily "perspectival knowledge").[8] Pols (1992, 1998) similarly argues not on behalf of a "fusion of horizons," but rather a fusion of a rational/general/conceptual "pole" and an experiential/particular/awareness "pole" in any act of direct knowing (or "rational awareness")—an act on which all epistemic objectivity (with all its indirect or theoretically mediated knowing) ultimately depends (see chap. 8, this volume). In short, philosophers such as Pols, Haack, Siegel, and Rescher appeal to universal features of mind/rationality/reason to which we can turn in making objective knowledge claims about the empirical world, claims that are not merely perspectival and are never infallible (see chap. 8, this volume). For them rationality is neither constituted in nor compromised by the local situatedness of knowers.

Finally, there is the obvious problem of the self-refuting or self-undermining nature of relativism, a problem not limited to strong relativism: From what neutral standpoint do MGTs make their universalist, nonrelativist, or nonperspectival claim about the nonuniversal, relativist, or perspectival nature of *all* knowledge claims (see chap. 8, this volume)? Siegel (1997, 1999a,

---

[7]Haack (2003) speaks of the failed attempt within logical positivism to construct "rules for deriving observation statements" (p. 32).
[8]See Haack's (2003) crossword puzzle analogy, in which clues function as experiential or empirical evidence and prior entries function as reasons or background knowledge (p. 58).

1999b, 2004) has much to say about the potential of claims made from necessarily particular situations, viewpoints, or perspectives to extend well beyond those situations, so that claims are not "true" only for certain knowers.

Can a Pragmatic, Value-Laden Epistemology Be a Realist Epistemology?

To the extent that pragmatic standards of warrant are relative to the values of a tradition or historical/cultural/discursive/interpretive context, they contain all the obstacles to epistemic realism that inhere in relativism, weak or strong. Yet the "values" problem is complex, for the desire to obtain objective knowledge is itself a value (e.g., Haack, 2003; Robinson, 1997). In the final analysis, good science works. Still, many scientific realists do not hold a theory's ability to predict empirical outcomes successfully to be the sole criterion of its truth; for example, rival explanations of the outcome must be ruled out as well (Erwin, 1997; Siegel & Erwin, 1989). Moreover, recall Erwin's (1997) argument that the best available theory or explanation (what he calls an "inference to the best explanation") should not be accepted as true simply because it is either the only theory available or the best of all available theories; a theory must have sufficient evidence to warrant its acceptance.

The way in which many MGTs speak about pragmatic warrant highlights two problems. First, some MGTs—following Gadamer—regularly proclaim that the values and "prejudices" of a tradition are necessary for the achievement of understanding within that tradition. Thus the needs, interests, and goals of the members of the tradition do and moreover should warrant knowledge claims, because that form of "warrant" humanizes the human sciences—including psychological science. Recall from Richardson et al. (1999) that "knowledge claims are adjudicated within a social order that incorporates . . . values, in contrast to the distortions incurred in the attempt to maintain factitious distinctions between facts and values and between objective and subjective domains" (p. 154). Yet on the other hand, when speaking explicitly of warrant, these MGTs sometimes revert to the conventional realist/objectivist epistemic norm (or value) of trying to eliminate bias as much as possible. Note these two sentences from Richardson et al. (1999).

> We will continue to adhere to openness and objectivity as paramount values of inquiry—by trying to characterize states of affairs in a manner as free of personal bias as possible. (p. 154)
> Objectivity remains important in the sense that we do our level best to avoid unnecessary bias, personal agendas, and premature foreclosure of our interpretive options. (p. 299)

Other than their implication of the existence of "necessary bias," these statements could have been written by conventional realists, who seek objective knowledge. I therefore wonder if MGTs, despite all their objections to epistemic objectivity, in fact want their psychological inquiry to have the potential to yield objective knowledge in a conventional sense: that the truth of (or warrant for) a claim does not depend on beliefs about the truth of that claim or on the conceptual, linguistic, or discursive context of knowers.

The second problem to emerge from the MGTs' pragmatic, value-laden warrant consists in their tenacious insistence on celebrating the demise of the fact/value distinction, as was illustrated in the first quotation of Richardson et al. (1999) in the previous paragraph and in chapter 8 of this volume. This celebration stems from many MGTs' insistence on the all-important "trans-formative aspect of psychological theory" (Richardson et al., 1999, p. 306), which is not unrelated to their view of agency or transcendence. In short, moral and political values—the reality that we prefer—*should* be the basis for warrant, because the theories we accept "feed back into the culture and so define and alter the reality they describe" (Richardson et al., 1999, p. 236; see chap. 5, this volume). Because, according to MGTs and radical postmodernists alike, there exists no "neutral, value-free form of inquiry" in the human sciences, a condition said to preclude objective knowledge (see chap. 8, this volume), we should justify claims according to local political and moral values—including the value of transcendence. We should there-fore warrant as "true" those theories or interpretations that help us (as a practical consequence of their adoption) to transcend what now exists in ways that we value or desire; and these values or desires usually contain at their core liberating goals (see chaps. 2 & 6, this volume).

But how can such a pragmatic, value-laden form of warrant constitute a realist epistemology? How is what MGTs propose different from Rorty's (1991, pp. 30–31) radically postmodern/antirealist equation of knowledge of our "ordinary everyday desires" with the "criterion of truth"? How is their episte-mology different from Gergen's (1985, p. 273) radically constructionist/ antirealist insistence on "moral criteria for scientific practice," in which we are urged to evaluate theory "in terms of good and ill" effects of its adoption within "society more generally" (see chap. 8, this volume)? After all, Rorty and Gergen sometimes speak about the values and desires of (or constrained by) the community; they sometimes invoke solidarity or community and not the rampant or wanton individualism that some MGTs abhor (e.g., Richardson et al., 1999). Thus the difference between MGTs' pragmatic, value-laden warrant and radical postmodernists'/constructionists' pragmatic, value-laden warrant cannot consist merely in the cultural constraints on warrant to which MGTs say they, but not radicals like Rorty or Gergen, adhere. I say this even taking into account Guignon's (1991) compelling argument that Rorty tumbles to the very epistemic stance of "detached objectivity" that he pro-fesses to reject (see chaps. 5 & 8, this volume).

Gergen's strong social constructionism has been widely criticized. One source of criticism is that it provides no "external standard by which cultural practices are to be evaluated" (Osbeck, 1993, p. 347)—that it allows no "prior moral order" (Mühlhäuser & Harré, as cited in Osbeck, 1993, p. 346)—which leaves it open to the very moral relativism that Gergen (1985, p. 273) imputes to those who follow in the "empiricist tradition." This problem is ably demonstrated in Gantt's (1996) account of the social constructionist perpetuation of the hedonism he finds in the pragmatic and utilitarian philosophy that grounds much social constructionist theory. Recall again Rorty's (1991, pp. 30–31) equation of "ordinary everyday desires" with the "criterion of truth" to get a sense of the regrettable link between pragmatism and hedonism.

But immorality, and even amorality, is just what MGTs wish to avoid. How can they manage to achieve that, while holding to pragmatic/utilitarian standards of warrant? Richardson et al. (1999) criticize the radical postmodernist version of pragmatism, by finding contradiction within it.

> We are being asked [by postmodern theorists] to endorse postmodern relativism as the most humane and authentic viewpoint. . . . They are embroiled in the contradiction of treating all moral values as purely relative or subjective in order to promote certain moral values, such as human solidarity, which they do not appear to view as purely relative or optional. (p. 193)

This well-wrought argument is clear and convincing, and Richardson et al. (1999) should be commended for it. Nonetheless, I suggest that an antiobjectivist epistemology, and not the individualism that they implicate in this next quotation, is the real root of the moral problem.

> [The postmodernist confronts] us with such a wide-open cafeteria of options that it would . . . undermine the possibility of meaningful choice . . . because it tends to deny that there are any good grounds for choosing one option over another. . . . It reverts to . . . a radical choosing of values in a highly individualistic manner. (p. 195)

Richardson et al. (1999) lay claim to what they think is a better alternative (to either modernism or postmodernism)—"contemporary hermeneutics." Here we are said to be what our historical/cultural/discursive/interpretive contexts help to make us—we are historical (or interpretation) "all the way down"—and so our existence, including moral choice, is constrained: Our self-interpretations cannot consist in just anything, so we cannot be (or choose to be) just anything. This constraint makes us capable of real moral commitment, commitment to something greater than our individual wishes and whims (see chap. 4, this volume). No anything-goes (ontological) relativism (and the hedonism that goes with it) for these MGTs (see chap. 5, this volume).

But maybe not. After all, what is to prevent any given culture from adopting values that reflect a thoroughgoing hedonism—if not outright evil—or from going off its moral track? Many say that these are the values of our own culture (e.g., Cushman, 1995). If we cannot escape cultural constraint in both our existence (ontology) and our claims to knowledge of that existence (epistemology), or if we can so escape that it is only a "mild innovation" or "modest transcendence" to which we can aspire (e.g., Martin & Sugarman, 1999a, 1999b; Martin, Sugarman, & Thompson, 2003, pp. x, 115), then we may be just as likely to make things (mildly) worse, instead of (mildly) better. What is to prevent us from using bad values for the pragmatic, value-laden form of warrant that many MGTs happily endorse? Why should liberating rather than oppressive values serve as pragmatic criteria for the MGTs' preferred form of epistemic warrant (see note 1)?

There is an alternative, if we do not accept a pragmatic, value-laden standard of warrant in the first place. But that means accepting the very distinction between facts and values (on the basis of the existence of objective evidence) that MGTs and radical postmodernists alike find problematic, if not impossible. Richardson et al. (1999) offer many statements in their final chapter, entitled "Social Theory as Practice," to justify their rejection of the fact/value distinction in favor of a pragmatic, value-laden epistemology. Here is one example (see chap. 8, this volume, for more quotations).

> Psychological research . . . appears to be a fundamentally moral enterprise designed to improve human welfare, an enterprise that will inevitably tend to promote some ideals over others. . . . Portraying science in culturally relative terms . . . makes the relevance and importance of social inquiry clearer and more compelling. The price of this social relevance is that we accept our accountability for the values and aims that guide our research. (p. 172)

To be sure, if there is no possible or even clear-enough distinction to be made between facts and contextual values—that is, if there are no facts (which require objective evidence), but only "facts"—then perhaps there is some logic to the use of social utility, practical consequences, or values as the criterion for the acceptance of any particular theory, discourse, or interpretation. To put this another way, it is easier to appeal to the value of utility (or the utility of values) as the criterion for theory acceptance if one has denied the possibility of objective evidence in the first place. Yet if one does that, one also denies the possibility of ascertaining real or true utility—that is, assessing utility objectively. So the whole argument becomes thoroughly self-defeating (see Held, 1998a).

Haack (1993a) unwinds the illogic of this in her critique of an argument made by some feminist scholars: that (a) the "underdetermination of theories by data" (p. 34) and/or (b) the "value-ladenness" of all science (p. 34) may be used to advance a so-called "feminist epistemology,"[9] which would obtain "if the aspiration *to legitimate the idea that feminist values should determine what theories are accepted* could be achieved" (p. 34). Haack demon-

---

[9]Richardson et al. (1999) rightly share Haack's concern that by "undermining the grounding of all forms of knowledge, one also undermines the emancipatory ideas of the women's movement and feminist social critique" (p. 197).

strates that neither premise (a) nor (b) logically entails the conclusion that "we may legitimately choose to believe whatever theory suits our political purposes" (p. 35). This is a conclusion that MGTs also seemingly reject by means of the cultural constraints to which they appeal for epistemic warrant and theory choice. Yet unlike them, Haack adheres to an objectivist epistemology nonetheless. In this next quotation, Haack (1998a) challenges the antiobjectivism of feminist epistemologies, but her comments are applicable to all antiobjectivist epistemologies—including those of MGTs.

> If the [antiobjectivist] conclusion were true, it would also undermine the possibility of a science informed by feminist values, in which evidential slack was taken up by reference to women's interests. For if there were no genuine inquiry, no objective evidence, we could not know what theories are such that their being accepted would conduce to women's interests, nor what women's interests are. (p. 118)

Haack is of course saying that if we decide to use even collective (rather than individual) needs, desires, goals, and interests—our (collective) values—to warrant our beliefs about our existence, then we must first know what those needs, desires, goals, and interests (values) are; that is, we must know them with objectivity. In this way even a pragmatic standard of warrant may be said to have an objectivist epistemology within its workings, if not in its actual findings of truth.[10]

Even so I contend that we must think twice before accepting any discourse, theory, or interpretation on the basis of a pragmatic/utilitarian or political agenda rather than striving to get at the objective, value-free facts/truth of the matter. This is the case however well intended that agenda might be, because even well-intended agendas can backfire. For example, Hare-Mustin and Marecek (1990) explain how the use of feminist values to warrant knowledge claims about gender differences have actually intensified some forms of discrimination, despite the emancipatory ideals of their advocates (see Held, 1998a). If there is truth in the claim that the type of discourse we accept has real-world consequences for our social/psychological existence—and MGTs are right to insist that it does—then it is all the more important that we try to get at the objective facts of our social/psychological existence as best we can. That endeavor is not easy, but that is no reason to proclaim the necessity of value-laden "facts," and then celebrate that "negative philosophical judgment about knowing" (and the "deflationary" epistemology that follows from that argument) as a good thing, a legitimate form of "truth" or "realism" for the human sciences.

---

[10]See chapter 8, this volume, note 22, for Haack's (1998b) critique of Rorty's problematic conflation of pragmatism with an antirealist epistemology.

Can a Naturalized (vs. Normative) Epistemology
Be a Realist Epistemology?

In *Real Knowing* philosopher Linda Alcoff (1996) adopts a hermeneutic ontology of "being in the world" in which there is "no absolute separation between human beings and the world . . . [as we are] always already in the world, . . . encumbered with myriad beliefs and commitments, and constitutively linked . . . to that about which we are seeking to know" (pp. 12–13). This of course sounds just like the ontology of MGTs (see chap. 4, this volume). Like them, Alcoff argues on behalf of "real knowing" or "realistic knowing" (as opposed to a more conventionally realist epistemology)[11] to insist that justification should be a matter of how people actually justify beliefs within discursive/interpretive contexts; justification does not and should not consist in the imposition or prescription of normative epistemic criteria, which are derived from "traditional, armchair a priori epistemological theorizing" (Siegel, 1996, p. 5). Alcoff (1996) also propounds an emergent notion of truth, one not entirely unlike that expressed by various MGTs (see chap. 5, this volume). In this quotation she advocates coherentism over foundationalism, as she does a descriptive or naturalized epistemology over (traditional) prescriptive or normative epistemologies.

> For coherentism, knowledge is ultimately a product of phenomena that are immanent to human belief systems and practices . . . , whereas for foundationalism, if a belief is to count as knowledge it must ultimately be able to establish some link to . . . something that is entirely extrinsic to human existence. . . . [For coherentism] justification is an immanent feature of beliefs in that it refers to their interrelationships, and if truth is defined as what coheres, truth is also emergent from immanent relationships rather than from relationships with an external or transcendental realm. . . . No absolute separation should exist between the way in which we actually justify our beliefs and the way in which we *should* justify them: all prescriptive proposals must be grounded firmly in current, actual practices since these alone can circumscribe the possible. . . . There is a normative relevance to having realistic accounts of the production of knowledge. (pp. 12–13)

Alcoff says we *should* justify beliefs as we *do* justify beliefs (within our interpretive contexts). This, according to philosopher Harvey Siegel (1996), constitutes the "naturalistic fallacy"—deriving an "ought" from an "is," or arguing "from facts concerning the formation, sustaining, and alteration of belief to conclusions concerning what ought to be believed" (p. 6). The naturalistic fallacy is but one of the problems that Siegel finds in so-called "natu-

---

[11]The dust jacket of *Real Knowing* states, "'Real' knowing always involves a political dimension. . . . But this does not mean we need to give up realism or the possibility of truth." In this Alcoff sounds much like other MGTs.

ralized" epistemologies, in which epistemology is "reconceived as an empirical discipline and pursued in accordance with the techniques of natural science" (p. 4).

Siegel (1996) contrasts naturalized or descriptive epistemologies with the "traditional, normative nonnaturalism" of prescriptive epistemologies (p. 8).

> Epistemology traditionally has been conceived as a *normative* discipline. . . . Ideally, it informs us of . . . the nature of warrant and justification themselves. . . . According to the naturalized epistemologist, traditional epistemological questions concerning the nature of evidence, warrant, and justification can be solved (if at all) only by "going natural," i.e., by scientifically studying the natural processes by which beliefs and theories are acquired, maintained, and altered in the light of experience. On this view, epistemology relinquishes its traditional autonomy from, and instead takes its place as part of, empirical psychology or cognitive science. (p. 4)

Siegel distinguishes nonnormative naturalized epistemologies from normative naturalized epistemologies and finds problems in both camps. He defines *normative naturalism* as "versions of naturalism that endeavor to acknowledge and account for epistemic normativity," and he says that these "face different but equally powerful difficulties" (p. 14, note 4) when compared with *nonnormative naturalism*, in which we just "give up [traditional] epistemology's pretensions to extrascientific normativity . . . [and replace this with] empirical psychology" (p. 5). Alcoff (1996) may fit within some version of the "normative naturalized" camp in virtue of her claim that there is "normative relevance to having realistic accounts of the production of knowledge" (p. 13). Still, she may be guilty of committing some version of the naturalistic fallacy—"deriving an ought from an is"—in saying that any form of epistemic warrant that should obtain must be derived from forms of warrant that do obtain. However, it is not obvious that she is right to claim that "all prescriptive proposals must be grounded firmly in current, actual practices since these alone can circumscribe the possible" (p. 13). For example, it seems perfectly possible for members of a discursive/interpretive context to adopt an epistemic practice that surpasses those on which they had previously relied. This, after all, would constitute one way (an epistemic way) in which the transcendence that MGTs seek could obtain.

Here we might ask questions that parallel one raised by Siegel (1996): "Can epistemology be naturalized in a way that preserves . . . normativity?" (p. 4). The parallel questions are (a) whether MGTs advocate some form of naturalized epistemology and (b) if so, whether theirs is a form of "normative naturalism," such that they in effect prescribe the epistemic practices they find to be operative in the many discursive/interpretive contexts in the world. Beginning with question (b), we see that the pragmatic, value-laden standard of warrant preferred by many MGTs, although fraught with problems for epistemic realism (at least as understood in the sense we have considered),[12] does seem to have a normative thrust: After all, they prescriptively tell us repeatedly that what we should accept as true belief is that which we (empirically) find gives us the consequences we seek, desire, or value, as a function of adopting a belief as true. They try to persuade everyone—on what appear to be a priori moral grounds—to adopt a pragmatic, value-laden standard of warrant, rather than the more traditional, normative standards of warrant to which many now adhere in modern/conventional forms of psychological inquiry, in which, for example, facts should be distinguished from (nonepistemic) values. Evidently MGTs (in distinction to Alcoff) think it is possible to "transcend" (traditional normative) epistemic practices that, on empirical investigation, are found to exist—if only as aspirations.

Responding to question (a) is more difficult, because the MGTs' ontological and epistemological relativism (however weak it may be) seems relevant to and so complicates the answer. First, on the MGTs' view, the particular consequences that we hope to generate (as a result of adopting certain beliefs or theories) are context dependent; they are expected to vary as a function of the tradition in which knowledge claims are made, so they are relative to contexts/traditions. When we consider the perspectival or relativist notions of warrant, truth, and knowledge endorsed by MGTs, we find that they seem to converge on a "naturalized"[13] epistemic view in at least this sense: The value-laden or moral criteria used within a discursive/interpretive context to justify knowledge claims presumably constitute an empirical question, one for social scientists to discover. Moreover, these empirically detectable (or natural), context-dependent criteria should be used to warrant knowledge claims (within that context), unless they are morally objectionable (because they then warrant claims that produce unacceptable consequences), or unless they are of the traditional, normative nonnaturalistic sort; those who adopt traditional normative epistemic criteria take seriously the objective psychological evidence (in which facts are distinguished from values) that for MGTs cannot be found, because for them it does not exist. In any case, for MGTs an "ought" is seemingly derived from an "is," so their "naturalistic" epistemology has a decidedly prescriptive or normative thrust at the highest level of abstraction—that is, pragmatic, value-laden epistemic criteria (of various sorts) can, do, and so (assuming they are morally acceptable) should always prevail.

---

[12]That definition of *epistemic realism* can be summarized succinctly: A claim that is accepted as true can in principle be warranted independently of (a) beliefs (and desires) about its truth and of (b) the conceptual schemes of knowers (see chap. 8).

[13]I use scare quotes around the word *naturalized* here and henceforth to distinguish whatever naturalized element MGTs include in their epistemology from the naturalism of other epistemologists, such as Quine, who do not necessitate a relativistic thrust. See Siegel (1996, p. 6) for a discussion of Quine's epistemic naturalism.

These two quotations from Fishman (1999), one of and the other about Rorty, support a "naturalized" or descriptive (as opposed to a normative or prescriptive) epistemology and are quite consistent with what other MGTs have said about epistemic justification—even though some MGTs (e.g., Guignon, 1991) have been rightly critical of Rorty's ("anti-epistemic") stance of "ironic playful detachment" (see chaps. 5 & 8, this volume).

> "There is nothing to be said about either truth or rationality apart from description of the familiar procedures of justification which a given society—*ours*—uses in . . . inquiry." (Rorty, as cited in Fishman, 1999, p. 119)
>
> Rorty's concept of "pragmatic relativism" . . . points to the already established and agreed-upon procedures and standards our society now has for determining truth and morality in particular contexts. (Fishman, 1999, p. 131)

To be sure, problems lurk in justifying any type of naturalized or descriptive epistemology. Most notable is the problem of how to justify the claim that beliefs *should* always be justified by the criteria (e.g., moral values) that (we find) *do* justify beliefs in any particular context. By what universal/nonrelativistic standards of reason, rationality, or warrant can the insistence on the virtues of adhering to a context-dependent, "naturalized" form of justification itself be justified (see Siegel, 1996, p. 7)? Because MGTs tend to eschew universal/essential properties of mind/rationality, this question is especially problematic for them (see chaps. 6 & 8, this volume). Do MGTs have the extracontextual view (from nowhere) that they deem necessary for making universal proclamations, including proclaiming their universal epistemic criteria (see, e.g., Richardson et al., 1999, pp. 298–302)? Put differently, on what universal epistemic (as well as moral) norms do they rely to justify their view that epistemic warrant should always be a matter of which locally pragmatic, value-laden factors are used by us (or, if put in more naturalized terms, cause[14] us) to accept social/psychological beliefs as true beliefs within any discursive context?

Moreover, it is not clear how—given their own relativistic, pragmatic, value-laden epistemic criteria—MGTs can claim to know just what pragmatic, value-laden criteria are actually used in any particular discursive context to justify knowledge claims made within that context. After all, they reject even the possibility of the objective knowledge deemed possible in conventional forms of psychological inquiry, in which hypotheses are judged (with all due acknowledgement of fallibility!) to be true or false independently of anyone's beliefs (or desires) about their truth or falsity, based on available empirical evidence.

---

[14]See Siegel (1996, p. 9) for a discussion of how naturalized approaches to justification (or the "evidence relation") are causal—unlike traditional normative approaches, which are epistemic in the nonempirical or a priori sense of providing "probative support for beliefs and theories."

Although Siegel's distinctions may be applied to MGTs' epistemic arguments, it is not clear just how they might respond to his distinctions, because they do not typically use the language of normative versus naturalized epistemology. To be sure, we find in their writings the (normative) prescription of one or more of the following universal "epistemic" norms for the acceptance of interpretations or beliefs: the reliance on the coherence of "facts"; the opening up of new lines of inquiry; the importance of empirical evidence or demonstrations in discerning "facts" or truth; and the pragmatic consequences of warranting and accepting certain beliefs or theories (e.g., Alcoff, 1996; Fishman, 1999; Howard, 1986; Martin & Sugarman, 1999a; Polkinghorne, 1983, 1988; Richardson et al., 1999). Consider this statement about the problem of justifying interpretations within a hermeneutic framework, which itself sounds perfectly normative and nonrelativist.

> The practical tasks of interpretation are better served by a good transcendental theory, one that supplies a proper understanding of the normative epistemology of interpretation. . . . Shared, weak holistic constraints provide a possible basis for the possibility of the public validity of interpretation, much as Kant saw that the very constraints on our knowing apparatus could make objective knowledge[15] possible. (Bohman, 1991, pp. 152–153)

What is not clear is how the promotion of universal (or "transcendental") epistemic norms squares with the relativistic or perspectival standards of warrant that MGTs promote. No problem necessarily appears, as long as each discursive/interpretive context has (at a lower level of abstraction or generality) its own particular version of coherence, empirical demonstrations, pragmatic goals/criteria, and so on—all of which particularized versions (i.e., those subsumed under more abstract or general normative principles) could be judged as equally legitimate, at least in principle. Yet on what universal normative or nonperspectival basis are they so judged? According to Martin and Sugarman (1999a), "Perspectivism does not eschew reasons and evidence as essential warrants for understanding, nor is it committed to finding that all conceptual schemes are equally valuable" (p. 50). "Valuable" does not necessarily equate with "valid," but we may nonetheless ask certain questions. For example, what if the members of a particular discursive/interpretive context, who both exist and "know" about their existence by way of particular conceptual schemes, do not believe that reasons or empirical demonstrations matter in ascertaining truth? Or what if they accept as empirical demonstrations what most others would not? Does "anything go" in the way of standards of warrant, as long as epistemic constraints of some sort or other are merely shown (objectively?) to exist within a context?

---

[15]See chapter 8, this volume, note 14, for a discussion of Kant's view that all objectivity is subjective in origin (Pols, 2000a, p. 56).

Martin and Sugarman (and other MGTs) suggest not, but they also seem to agree that standards of warrant exist within and are relative to traditions, and that this empirical state of affairs allows for a realist epistemology in virtue of the existence of those local constraints. Indeed, it is to just such local/relativistic (discursive) constraints that MGTs appeal when distinguishing *their* "realist" epistemology (see chap. 5) from the (allegedly constraint-free) antirealist epistemology of radical postmodernists/constructionists on the one hand, and from the objectivist (and supposedly foundationalist) epistemology of conventional modernists on the other (see chaps. 2–3). Yet to what universal norms can MGTs appeal to decide whether, for example, the particular pragmatic criteria used in a particular discursive context are adequate for warranting truth—or even perspectival "truth"?

In short, we are left with at least two questions: Would MGTs agree that their pragmatic, value-laden epistemology constitutes some form of naturalized epistemology? And if so, on what philosophical basis could they argue that their naturalized epistemology constitutes a realist epistemology, in which truth does not depend on beliefs (or desires) about what is true (see chap. 5)? Let us turn now to a normative/prescriptive question: According to MGTs, what kinds of empirical questions should and should not be asked in psychological inquiry?

"PROPER" QUESTIONS FOR PSYCHOLOGICAL INQUIRY

We are now in a position to consider MGTs' arguments about the kinds of questions that psychological inquiry itself should properly ask, especially a psychological inquiry in which realist (or truth-tracking) knowledge is sought and human agency is to be preserved. These constitute the twin goals of the MGTs, some of whom accept modern/conventional forms of psychological inquiry (in which causal claims are empirically tested), as long as we do not interpret the findings as the infallibly known, timeless, universal, and mechanistically deterministic causal laws that are thought (by MGTs) to constitute objective knowledge. Other MGTs, by contrast, say that we should dispense with investigating causal claims altogether and establish instead a different form of psychological knowing and knowledge. Most agree about the value of qualitative forms of inquiry, in which variables are not quantified (see, e.g., Slife & Williams, 1995, pp. 199–200; Wertz, 1999). Rather than pursuing that argument here, let us review several proposals—most of which assess the question of causal knowledge—to see if these proposals help MGTs attain their twin goals, or two-pronged mission.

The Elimination of Causal Laws

The causal laws that are said by MGTs to constitute the foundational object of conventional scientific inquiry are problematic in two ways. First, these "laws" are seen as fixed and universal. And because the ontology of psychological existence is alleged to be context-dependent, reflexive, and thus unstable (see chap. 7, this volume), there can be no universal, immutable causal "laws," such as those sometimes sought in the natural sciences (see Rozin, 2001, for a discussion of how natural science relies heavily on purely descriptive work). Second, because causal laws are seen as mechanistically (or nonagentically) deterministic, they are not compatible with the agentic or self-determined view of human psychological nature that MGTs propound. This compatibilist problem is more intractable, and I do not pretend to solve it here.[16]

The problem, of course, is that any form of psychological inquiry that is truth tracking or realist—be it quantitative or qualitative, descriptive or causal—is, as I have maintained, also (by definition) objectivist. In objectivist inquiry, claims can be warranted independently of beliefs about the truth of those claims—of beliefs about what the reality under consideration is (unless the subject of investigation consists in beliefs themselves, in which case objective knowledge can still obtain). This is why a realist or objectivist epistemology (which MGTs do not equate) can be fallibilist in the first place: The answers to our empirical questions are not merely "read off" an analysis of anyone's beliefs, ideas, theories, or concepts about the reality under consideration, even when the questions are about human thought/conceptual (and other cognitive and attitudinal) processes (see Erwin, 1997, 1999; Haack, 2002, 2003; Thomasson, 2003).

To be sure, MGTs give various answers to the question of just what psychological knowledge should consist in, because they say we must abandon the search for universal causal psychological laws (which they equate with the objectivist knowledge that they reject). To define knowledge that is proper for the human sciences, with their uniquely reflexive ontology of "being in the world," most MGTs rely on the distinction between (a) personal/ "subjective" meanings or reasons for the actions of situated agentic beings and (b) impersonal/"objective" mechanistically deterministic causal explanations (or laws) about brute/physical entities. Consider these statements made by MGTs: The first two reflect a hermeneutic view, the third a social constructionist view, and the fourth a narrative/quasi-pragmatic view.

> The goal of the natural sciences is to *explain* events by subsuming them under general laws, . . . to treat the world as a collection of decontextualized objects. . . . [In] such an objectifying stance . . . all meanings and values are removed from what is experienced so that the things we study are encountered as inherently meaningless spatiotempo-

---

[16]Martin et al. (2003) and Martin and Sugarman (2002) propose a compatibilist solution to the problem of a deterministic psychological science about agentic/self-determined beings, by appealing to a soft determinism in which agency is said not to be undetermined but underdetermined. I review some of their solutions in this chapter.

ral objects. . . . The objectified world view requires that we remove ourselves from the picture. (Richardson et al., 1999, p. 202)

Human actions are not caused by antecedent events; people, he [Richard Taylor] said, are agents of their own actions. And Charles Taylor . . . declared that human actions cannot be explained by causal laws of the deductive-nomological form . . . that human actions require a teleological form of explanation. (Polkinghorne, 1983, p. 170)

The adoption of the traditional natural-scientific approach committed psychology to the idea that people's actions were not volitional, but resembled more the behavior of atoms and molecules. This was part of the view that the behaviours of people and atoms alike are subject to the immutable laws of nature that can be uncovered. (Kenwood, 1996, p. 534)

Reasons, rather than causes, point us to the importance of the *concept of understanding* in psychology and that understanding the meaning of behavior is not the same intellectual task as explaining the causes of the behavior, if explaining is taken to mean prediction and control. (Miller, 2004, p. 133)

Here let us consider more specific alternative recommendations for a psychological inquiry that is not expected to produce knowledge that consists in causal laws. We will then consider the recommendations of those MGTs who support the search for causal explanations, as long as their contextualized and fallibilist nature is appreciated—even though that caveat reveals the straw man of objectivity erected by MGTs.

Meaning Rules and Conventions That Make Behavior Sensical Within a Context

Recall from chapter 5 that in his moderate social constructionism, Liebrucks (2001) proclaimed a relativistic ontology of personhood: "There are properties of persons that exist . . . only relative to the meaning system of the community to which they belong" (p. 374). In contrasting the human sciences with the natural sciences, Liebrucks (2001) makes a foundational distinction: Because the existence of intentional states such as emotions, attitudes, and motives "depends on social context, the phenomena that are investigated by psychology are ontologically different from the phenomena studied by the natural sciences" (p. 378). Owing to this ontological difference, we must ask different kinds of questions— noncausal questions—about these human/psychological kinds than we would ask about natural/physical kinds. Presumably, therefore, we need a different "explanatory scheme."

Unlike the natural scientific explanations, which make reference to causes . . . , psychological explanations make reference to rules and conventions in order to show how a certain event makes sense. . . . The psychological concepts just do not fit into the causal model of explanation. (pp. 385–386)

In place of the causal model or "causal necessity," Liebrucks (2001) recommends "normative" and "semantic" necessity (see chap. 5, this volume).

> Rules are not causal laws. . . . Rules are standards of correctness . . .
> [which] do not have the force of *causal necessity*, but only of *normative*
> *necessity*. . . . Unlike causal laws, rules can be violated, and the attempt to
> conform to a rule can fail. . . . [Conventions] also do not determine the
> conduct of persons mechanically, but they have *semantic necessity*. . . . To
> be understood . . . one has to employ the expressive means that are as-
> signed the meaning one would like to express. Yet here again the possi-
> bility of refusal and failure exists (Harré, 1989). (p. 380)

And so a proper psychological science should ascertain not causal laws,
but rather the (meaningful) rules and conventions that make sense of human
behavior in its discursive/interpretive context. It is not surprising that we
find similar language in the moderate social constructionism of Harré (2002),
who writes that "social and semantic conventions replace laws" (p. 614).
Moreover, there is nothing necessarily relativistic about this form of inquiry.
Note the moderating language that closes this quotation of Harré (2002).

> The most important step in the move to a social constructionist point of
> view is to drop the Humean causal metaphysics of the positivist school
> in favour of normative explanations. . . . Intentionality (meaning) and
> normativity (conformity) to rules and conventions, not cause and effect,
> need to be adopted as the framing concepts of psychological studies. . . .
> The positive claims of social constructionism fall short of the radical
> relativism of postmodernism. (Harré, 2002, pp. 614–615)

The problem (first described in chaps. 5–6 of this volume) is that like
other MGTs, Liebrucks (2001) does not specify whether the dependence of
psychological properties on the rules and conventions of local discourses is
logical or causal. Liebrucks (2001) distinguishes so-called (a) "discursive constructions" from (b) "material constructions," in which "properties of persons" either are not (in the case of "a") or are (in the case of "b") identifiable
independently of the discourses that bring them into being (p. 374). However, he does not tell us whether each type is merely causally dependent on
discourse or is fully logically dependent—in which case the properties of persons could not in principle exist without discourse. Recall that the logical/
causal distinction has implications for the agentic properties of humans (see
chap. 6, this volume); it also has implications for what questions a psychological science may be said to ask legitimately. For if "properties of persons"
are causally dependent on discourse, we may ask how specific forms of discourse cause the emergence of specific psychological kinds. However, despite eschewing a psychological science of causal explanations, recall that
Liebrucks and other MGTs indeed use perfectly causal language to explain
the emergence into being and evolution of psychological kinds (see chap. 5,
this volume).

In short, Liebrucks (2001)—like other MGTs and radical postmodernists/constructionists—propounds nothing less than a conventional causal claim, one so very general or universal that it qualifies as an ontological claim: Discourse determines, causes, or affects human social/psychological existence, including conduct/behavior, mental states/traits, and experience itself (see Held, 1998a). We saw many quotations indicative of this in chapters 5 and 6. Recall, for example, Richardson et al.'s (1999) claim that "descriptions actively shape those phenomena [behavior and experience] and help bring them into being" (p. 282).

The discourses we accept as true are said to have *extradiscursive* causal consequences (for the way we live our lives) that are judged acceptable or unacceptable. Indeed, this judgment gives discourse its moral currency, and it is just such currency that leads MGTs (and radical postmodernists such as Gergen and Rorty) to argue that (nonepistemic)[17] values should play a primary role in warranting discourse (or theories/beliefs).[18] Although such value-laden "warrant" compromises the realism (and hence objectivity) of MGTs' knowledge claims (see chap. 8), it in no way vitiates the causal nature of those claims—which is what some MGTs seek in the name of situated agency. Agentically speaking, we may indeed have some degree of choice (or causal efficacy) over (a) which theories or beliefs to accept as true, on the basis of (b) the forms of warrant that we decide to adopt. But that interpretive latitude does not itself make theories or beliefs true, not least because it does not automatically make the preferred form of epistemic warrant valid.

To put all this a bit differently, if truth is whatever is judged (locally) to be "good in the way of belief," then we have indeed embraced such descriptive or naturalized (and relativistic) forms of "epistemic" warrant as those propounded by Rorty and Gergen, whose radical postmodernism/antirealism most (but not all) MGTs[19] reject. Recall that truth, in more conventionally realist terms than those seemingly preferred by MGTs, is what obtains independently of what anyone believes or desires to obtain (Erwin, 1997, 1999; Haack, 2002, 2003; Thomasson, 2003). Moreover, in making truth a pragmatic, value-laden matter (in which the beliefs we accept as true are those that we find empirically to produce valued or desired consequences), MGTs who do so not only compromise the epistemic realism they seek but also invoke the very causal relations (between the beliefs we accept as true and

---

[17]See chapter 8 for a discussion of how striving for objectivity itself depends on holding an epistemic value, and in this sense constitutes a moral matter—what one ought to do.

[18]Even Liebrucks (2001), who finds Gergen's "identification of social constructionism with a relativist epistemology" (p. 364) unfortunate, nonetheless appeals to (a) "local investigative practices" (abstract), (b) "different conceptual schemes" (p. 371), and (c) the "thesis of reflexivity" (p. 365), according to which "there can certainly be no value-free psychology" (p. 385). Although he does not speak expressly of any "pragmatic, value-laden warrant," it seems possible that that is what he implicitly accepts.

[19]In due course I again quote Fishman (1999), who seems to approve of Rorty's postmodern antirealist epistemology in ways other MGTs do not.

how we then live our lives) that they sometimes say cannot in principle obtain in social/psychological (i.e., human science) inquiry.

Here let us briefly reconsider questions about objectivity and relativity, this time as they pertain to some MGTs' proposed inquiry into the (meaning) rules and conventions (within a discursive context) that, they claim *independently of their own discursive contexts*, always play a role in the existence of psychological properties/kinds (within a discursive context), as well as in the intelligibility of psychological properties/kinds (within a discursive context). If we were to take some MGTs' advice and adopt that research agenda, we would be in a position to ask questions to which we could obtain objective answers (despite the typical MGT insistence that objective knowledge is in principle impossible in human science inquiry). That is because the answers would not themselves necessarily depend on the inquirers' own discursive contexts/perspectives (or beliefs about the answers).

Thus perfectly realist, nonrelativist (i.e., objective) knowledge about the proposed (universal and seemingly causal) relation between discourse and the emergence/existence of mental properties and behaviors may be sought (even as that relation may exist uniquely in the content of a particular discursive context). So, too, we can seek an objective answer to Liebrucks's (2001, pp. 385–386) question about how "a certain event makes sense in the way that it takes place" by referring to the "rules and conventions" that exist within a discursive context, because that answer similarly does not necessarily depend on the discursive context (including the beliefs) of the inquirer (as Liebrucks himself seems to suggest in saying that social constructionists "do not subscribe to a relativist epistemology," p. 373). In short, if any form of realist or truth-tracking psychological inquiry about different discursive contexts is to obtain, there must be a way that discursive rules and conventions themselves operate in relation to psychological properties and their intelligibility, a way not "determined" (relativistically) by the various discursive rules and conventions of the contexts in which different inquirers function. Put differently, what is true *about* any particular context is in principle true *for* all knowers, regardless of their contexts.

We may now ask if Harré and Liebrucks are right in asserting that the conventions and rules that allegedly make psychological properties what they are (or are understood to be) within any given context constitute the only knowledge to which we can legitimately aspire in conducting psychological inquiry. Recall from chapter 5 Thomasson's (2003) insistence on the possibility of substantive inquiry about human kinds, kinds that are mind dependent in specified ways but that admit of full causal inquiry nonetheless. To reuse her example of racism, reconsider this: Although racism depends for its existence on the holding (by some) of certain beliefs or intentions (i.e., racism depends on mental states that may be considered discursive or interpretive in some sense), racism itself does not depend on beliefs about racism itself (within or beyond any discursive context). Therefore everyone in a particular context can in principle be ignorant of the existence of racism in that context and/or massively wrong about the nature of any racism that does exist (and so may be known to exist) within that context. Hence it is not, as Liebrucks (2001) might say, merely a matter of discovering the (discursive) rules that make certain "emotions, motives, and attitudes" (p. 374) and overt behaviors racist in any given context (or even universally), because beliefs or ideas about racism itself, *as a kind*, are not needed within a given context for racism to exist within that context. We can therefore study the causes of racism, just as Thomasson (2003) says we can study such "causal relations" as, for example, the "(perhaps) unintended and unnoticed oppressive consequences of our practices involving money, division of labor, etc. Such causal facts certainly remain opaque and in need of discovery" (pp. 606–607).

In chapters 5 and 8, I suggest some perfectly conventional causal questions that could be asked about racism, including the political, social, economic, and legal (to name a few) consequences of holding racist attitudes. I am not here endorsing a pragmatic epistemology, in which consequences such as these should be used to warrant the truth of a theory or belief about the nature of racism, or other human social/psychological kinds. I am only suggesting that such consequences can themselves be assessed objectively, by appealing to evidence judged adequate according to traditional, normative epistemic criteria, in which (nonepistemic) values are not themselves sources of warrant.

"Regularities" in Human Thought and Action in Context

Not all MGTs dismiss the value of conventional forms of psychological inquiry, in which "causal" questions are asked. For example, Richardson et al. (1999), Martin and Sugarman (1999b), and Martin et al. (2003) find merit in just that—as long as there is no objectivist or neutral "pursuit of universal, context-free laws of human behavior" (Richardson et al., 1999, p. 164). Thus it seems that conventional explanatory research is acceptable if its products are interpreted within the limits of what human agency/self-determination is said to allow. As Richardson et al. (1999) put it, "Identifying regularities in beliefs or behavior can be quite illuminating to the extent that these regularities are understood in a broader interpretive perspective" (p. 278). Therefore correlational data should not be taken as a basis for the discovery of lawful (nonagentic or mechanistic) determinants/causes of human thought and action.

> Correlations should not be thought of as approximations or stepping stones to strict empirical theory and universally applicable laws of human activity. Rather, these correlations indicate regularities or systematic interrelationships in the personal or social existence of particular

historical communities, which evolve and ramify in varied and unpredictable ways. (p. 179)

Hermeneutics is offered as the framework that can subsume both interpretive and empirical forms of inquiry about the human world. For example, Fowers (2001b) said, "Hermeneutics has significant promise as a metatheory for psychology, one that can accommodate the best of both standard empirical theory and many of the critics of the dominant approach to the discipline." Or as Richardson et al. (1999) put it in their discussion of marital research:

> Marital behavior, like most important human activity, is clearly rule governed. In a hermeneutic perspective, however, we need not see these rules as either universal or as describing causal processes that bypass human agency and creativity. . . . We should understand them as reflecting norms and conventions that embody a societal vision of the good and decent life. (p. 171)

Here again we see the rules and conventions of such moderate social constructionists as Liebrucks and Harré. Thus, like them, Richardson et al. (1999) reject any psychological science (beyond "neuropsychology or basic sensory psychology," p. 278) that mimics natural science by relying on a "division of the world into objective facts ordered by causal laws that are . . . independent of our interpretations, and subjective experiences that are either epiphenomena of this 'objective reality' or the results of objectively specifiable causal processes" (p. 277).

The problem is not unlike that discussed in the section on the proposed "elimination of causal laws." For when Richardson et al. (1999) say that the way we conduct empirical research on marriage (with all our background assumptions and values) affects the way married lives get lived, they seemingly make an objective (as well as a universal) claim about the causal consequences for our lives of the findings of social science research. The claim is objective because it is put forth independently of the discursive/interpretive context and beliefs of its propounders; its truth or falsity is independent of Richardson et al.'s own background/context-dependent beliefs and their own beliefs about its truth. In short, there is nothing relativistic *epistemically* about the claim; it is said to hold true *for* all knowers, even if it is not true *about* all marriages! The claim expresses the "reflexivity thesis" of Giddens, to which Richardson et al. (1999) appeal (see chap. 8, this volume): "Unless marital researchers participate in developing or reclaiming some deeper language of marital relationships, we will continue to perpetuate the current self-defeating and brittle character of marital relationships" (pp. 171–172).

However true the reflexivity thesis may be in this case, it does not itself necessitate that values should give warrant to any particular claim, thereby obliterating the fact/value distinction and epistemic objectivity or realism. As I explained in chapter 8, that we should be as disinterested as possible in our role as psychological scientists does not mean we can or should be uninterested. Nor does the reflexivity thesis eliminate its own causal nature, or the causal nature of many of the claims made by MGTs (see chaps. 5–6).

Finally, Richardson et al. (1999) list as one of their epistemic criteria the ability of an interpretation to "capture the meaning of the behavior to the actor," who is always self-interpreting and acting teleologically or purposefully within a context that makes the action intelligible (p. 300). This expresses their commitment to an agentic psychology: "If an observer disregards these constitutive elements in favor of a causal, mechanistic account, the observer is . . . ruling out the very features of the action that make it what it is for the actor and for others" (p. 301).

It is not clear to me whether this is about capturing (a) what the actor means/intends to do or (b) what the actor believes he means/intends to do—after all, it is in principle possible for any of us to be "self-deceived" about our own purposes (e.g., I may think I am trying to help my boss when I am in reality trying to subvert her). In either case, the point is that to ask about the meanings/intentions of an actor's behavior from the actor's own point of view is a straightforward psychological question that requires objective evidence—that is, evidence that does not merely consist in or depend on anyone's beliefs about the correct answer, including the actor in question. Similarly, even when asking what one believes one's own meanings/intentions are, there is a way that one's beliefs about one's intentions are, independent of one's own beliefs about one's intentions. Thus there is an independent or objective state of affairs about beliefs that does not depend about one's beliefs on anyone's beliefs about what the relevant beliefs are (for elaboration see D. W. Smith, 2005; Thomasson, 2005). Moreover, there is nothing in this objectivist account that necessitates the "causal, mechanistic account" that Richardson et al. hope to avoid.

Still, to ask how the actor's meanings and intentions relate to his behavior or action is a straightforward causal question about how mental states affect behavior or action. There is nothing in that question itself to suggest a nonagentic (or mechanistic) form of causation/determination. Indeed, if mental states (thoughts, purposes, intentions) did not stand in some form of causal/determinative relation to behavior or action, then an agentic psychology—in which self-determination is prominent—would be defeated at the outset. It is only when mental states are deprived of any *telic* force that a nonagentic or mechanistic causal account obtains.[20]

---

[20]In *The Illusion of Conscious Will*, social psychologist Daniel Wegner (2002) gives an intricate account of the conditions under which voluntary behavior or action is experienced as unwilled, and involuntary behavior or action is experienced as willed. Although Wegner argues that conscious thoughts can be seen as causally connected to action, they are (he says) not necessarily the *actual/empirical* cause of any given action (see p. 68, Figure 3.1). His account of the actual causes of action and of the experience of consciously willing and causing action seems to me to fit a mechanistic model of behavioral causation.

Categories of Psychological Kinds: Pragmatism Without Causality?

In calling for a (neo)pragmatic paradigm for psychology, Daniel Fishman (1999) rejects the hypothetical deductive model of conventional science, in which general laws are sought, for reasons both like and unlike those given by other MGTs.

> Modern positivism is a worldview based on the assumption that physical and social reality are governed by *general laws* that can be stated in *propositional* and *quantitative terms*, that these laws are objectively knowable, and that the *natural science method* is the best means for *discovering* them. (p. 94)

Recall from chapter 7 that Fishman (1999) sees his "pragmatic model" as a hybrid of positivism on the one hand and hermeneutics on the other. To produce his hybrid, he claims to take what is best from the data-based nomothetic (generalized) ideal of modern positivist psychology and from the contextually or interpretively nuanced idiographic (individualized) ideal of hermeneutic psychology (cf. Woolfolk, 1998). Fishman says that his pragmatism shares with hermeneutics a social constructionist (or antiobjectivist) epistemology, an idiographic emphasis, and a preference for conducting research in natural settings. With positivism, he says, his pragmatism shares empiricism or observation as the primary source of knowledge and an "emphasis on behavior as determined and predictable" (p. 99, Table 4.1). Given Fishman's opposition to the possibility and value of discovering general causal laws in psychological inquiry, it is noteworthy that he nonetheless sees behavior as determined and predictable. One question to ask, then, is how—given his ontology in which "reality is continuously in flux" (p. 130)—behavior can be determined (or deterministic) enough to grant its predictability (cf. Martin & Sugarman, 1999a, 2002).

In rejecting a science of universal decontextualized causal laws in his case study method, Fishman (1999) makes way for an ever-expanding database of clinical cases. Therapists can then match target cases to the cases in the database for guidance in selecting interventions that fit the particularities they inevitably encounter in their search for solutions that work with unique individuals. Fishman (1999) seeks "guiding conceptions" (p. 236) or "practical guidelines" (p. 230) whose standard of warrant is limited to pragmatic utility within a particular context. In so doing he evidently accepts that operating only at the level of unique particularity prohibits the construction of a new discipline of psychology, because any discipline necessitates generality (or general categories of entities) at some level of abstraction. Here he describes his "'Middle Way' to Generalization."

> The pragmatist agrees with the positivist about the value of generalizing, but also with the hermeneut about the need to retain context. . . . A rising number of cases in the database increases the probability that there

are specific cases that as a group generalize to any particular target case. While generalizing by logical deduction is not possible, as in the positivist paradigm, the pragmatic paradigm promises a viable way of attaining a reasonable degree of generalization without giving up context. (p. 291)

Does Fishman (1999) achieve his positivist-hermeneutic (nomothetic-idiographic) hybrid? He recognizes the need for inductively derived "generals" to establish any scientific discipline, even as he eschews "generalizing by logical deduction"[21] and general causal laws. Yet given his extreme ontology of flux and flow, how can he also maintain that our psychological existence holds still long enough to enable the generals of existence on which all (scientific and everyday) inquiry ultimately depends (see chap. 5, this volume)? Other MGTs also propound the unstable nature of psychological existence (owing especially to the reflexive impact of our interpretations on that existence), but they adhere to a more moderate ontology of "stability within flux" than does Fishman (see chap. 7, this volume). He seems somewhat less interested in advancing an agentic psychology than do other MGTs: Behavior is "determined and predictable," he says (p. 99, Table 4.1). He therefore seems more concerned with the tension between generality and particularity than with the destabilizing effects of our agentic interpretive activity on our psychological existence (see chap. 6, this volume). Moreover, although Fishman supposes that he avoids the general causal laws of "positivism" in his pragmatism, does he succeed?

Although Fishman may have managed to avoid the causal laws of "positivism," he does not avoid causality altogether (and indeed claims he did not intend to; see Fishman, 2006a, 2006b). Instead, he moves causality from one place, in which it is made explicit (the general, supposedly deductively derived laws he rejects), to another place, in which causality is implicit (the categories of cases whose use, he claims, will cause beneficial outcomes). In creating his system of flexible categories of clinical cases (his "database")—a system that, he says, becomes more differentiated over time as more cases are added—Fishman holds an implicit assumption: that any clinical case can ultimately be matched to a proper category of cases in the database, a category whose recommended interventions can then be tailored to the specifics of the clinical case in question. "These databases provide a vehicle for matching the contexts of particular past cases to the contexts of cases for which planning is needed" (p. 133).

> The whole cumulating case database would be used to develop expectations for how this type of patient should progress. . . . As the case database developed, there would be more . . . cases of a particular type with "superior" or "inferior" outcomes, allowing for cross-case analyses of fac-

---

[21]See Held (2006a) for a discussion of Fishman's use of the term *induction* to refer sometimes to the way we arrive at generalizations themselves and sometimes to the way we extend existing generalizations to new cases, as well as ambiguity in his use of the term *deductive generalization*.

tors and themes to provide guidelines for improving the overall practice of therapy with that type of patient. As more . . . "superior" outcome cases emerge, newly differentiated categories of type of patient might emerge. (p. 226)

This passage requires comment. Conventional science (what Fishman calls "positivism") relies on flexible categories or generals whose names and contents continually evolve, as the categories or generals themselves become more refined and particularized (see Haack, 2003, chap. 5). Fishman's (1999) (neo)pragmatic paradigm can therefore be put in the causal language of modern/conventional (clinical) psychological, rule-driven science: If a client has a type of problem, then see what worked for others in similar circumstances (i.e., use the closest category) and thoughtfully tailor those interventions to the unique particularities of the case under consideration to obtain beneficial outcomes. The implicit assumption is that the application of *this* kind of psychological science will cause better outcomes; that is why clinicians are justified in holding "expectations for how this type of patient should progress" (p. 226) in the first place. But is this kind of psychological science all that different? After all, that certain kinds of interventions produce better effects than others for certain kinds of cases is nothing other than the "specificity question" proposed 40 years ago.[22] And that Fishman (1999) supports the notion of the "thinking clinician" who is "flexible" and "reflective" (p. 210) in tailoring generals to the particulars of cases (over the robotic user of nomothetic or standardized therapy manuals) lessens the objectivity and causality that inhere in his claims no more than the use of conceptual/linguistic entities lessens our direct access to knower-independent realities (see chap. 8, this volume).

In short, Fishman (1999) makes much of subverting the search for general causal "laws" in conventional objectivist psychological science and embracing a constructionist/pragmatic epistemology (which he now, in Fishman, 2001, considers moderate) in the service of a more idiographic form of practice. In response to my interpretation of his philosophy (Held 2006a, 2006b), he now (Fishman, in 2006a, 2006b) states that his pragmatic model contains "causal mechanisms," although he gives them no objective/independent ontological status: In the context of denying the possibility of "ontologically true objective knowledge," Fishman (2006a) reduces causality to a "conceptual tool" within a perspective. Hence he can speak of "causality" (with scare quotes), but not an ontologically objective or real causality (without scare quotes).

Miller (2004) shares Fishman's aversion to the causal laws of objectivist science and his preference for a case study method, if not Fishman's pragmatism (see this volume, chap. 1, note 10, & chap. 3, note 12). Like

---

[22]As Paul (1967) put it, "*What* treatment, by *whom*, is most effective for *this* individual with *that* specific problem, and under *which* set of circumstances?" (p. 111).

Richardson et al. (1999, p. 278), Miller (2004) asserts that physiological psychology, sensation and perception, and learning "lend themselves to causal analysis," whereas "developmental, social, personality, and abnormal clinical psychology are biographical and [so] do not" (p. 141). More like Richardson et al. (1999) than Fishman (1999), Miller (2004) appeals to "moral agency" to bolster his case against "causal analysis" (with its presumed mechanistic determinism) in some areas of psychology: "The moral point of view asserts that human beings are agents who actively pursue their various interests, goals, and purposes, not entirely passive objects that are manipulated and controlled by natural or external forces" (p. 78). Miller (2006a) also states that "goal directed reasons for acting have so many properties that differentiate them from material and efficient causal explanations [in the physical sciences] that . . . using the same term [causality] for both is confusing" (p. 9).

Yet Miller (2004) rightly accepts that developmental, social, personality, and clinical psychology require generalization (and rules) if a psychotherapeutic *discipline* (i.e., clinical *knowledge*) is to obtain. He therefore advocates "heuristics (rules of thumb)" (p. 130) or "laws" (p. 210) that are backed by what seem to be causal assumptions about what interventions will bring about desirable effects under different circumstances, however implicit that "causal analysis" may be.

> Without the knowledge of clinical patterns and processes that are relatively constant across individuals there would be little clinical knowledge. . . . The most powerful clinical generalizations are rules of what therapists should or should not do for clients . . . to better their own lives. (p. 193)

Still, like Fishman, Miller (2004) actively repudiates the laws of science, which he deems nonconducive to the particularities of therapy. Yet his prescriptive generalizations, rules, or principles seem to offer contextualized, lawlike generalities (if not universal laws) nonetheless, although he gives them a moral emphasis.

> The moral dimension is much more in the foreground than in scientific laws. . . . Science can ignore the uniqueness of the person . . . because its goal is not the description, understanding, or betterment of the individual but the advancement of an explanatory set of principles (scientific knowledge). (p. 193)

In presumed contrast to conventional clinical science, Fishman and Miller say that they work inductively, starting with particular cases from which they build general rules of practice. Yet they do not mention that induction is characteristic of most conventional science, in which general laws (or at least regularities) originate in an inductive process (Haack, 2003; Rozin, 2001). Fishman (2001) reasserts his commitment to the general knowledge that I value but differs from me on the basis of the inductive/deductive distinction.

Held [1995] and I are arguing for the pursuit in applied psychology of knowledge that is generalizable across persons and situations. While Held follows a more traditional, deductive approach in this pursuit, I am advocating a more descriptive and inductive approach, starting with the systematic description of many individual cases, and then inductively deriving generalizations as they emerge from cross-case analysis. (p. 280)

Although Fishman and Miller may eschew any "explanatory set of principles" (or causal explanations) that lie behind the lawlike regularities, general principles, or descriptive generalizations that they discover empirically (see Fishman, 2006a, 2006b, for disagreement with this interpretation), the causal nature of the regularities, principles, or descriptions obtains in this generic sense: The use of interventions derived from prior cases that best fit the case at hand will (probably) cause improvement in the client's condition/life, or so they claim. That improvement is itself defined relative to the client's and therapist's life contexts and goals makes therapy a relativistic value-laden or ethical matter, which Miller (2004, p. 71)—in quoting Tjeltveit (1999, p. 231)—equates with moral matters (although, as I stated in chap. 8, note 20, Tjeltveit distinguishes moral from nonmoral goods). Still, even this profoundly value-laden[23] and relativistic dimension of therapy does not in any way diminish the objective/nonrelativistic and causal nature of the generic claim: The truth of the generic (causal) claim does not itself depend on Miller's or Fishman's (or anyone's) own discursive/interpretive (including value-laden/moral) contexts; nor does it depend on their (or anyone's) beliefs about its truth (see Held, 2006a, 2006b). I conclude that no middle-ground epistemological hybrid of "positivism" and "hermeneutics" (or objectivism and constructionism, or modernism and postmodernism) has been achieved by Fishman.

A True Hybrid of Causal Explanation and Noncausal Understanding?

Unlike Liebrucks, Harré, and Miller, Martin and Sugarman (1999a, 1999b) do not dismiss a causal deterministic science of psychology out of hand, although they certainly approach it critically. Let us consider their arguments both for and against the generation and warranting of causal laws, in the context of their own compatibilism, which they characterize as "agency and soft determinism" (Martin & Sugarman, 2002).

In this first quotation, Martin and Sugarman (1999a) do not deny the causal determination of human psychological existence, but instead question our epistemic resources for warranting causal claims about that existence. This is an important distinction; it conveys a more moderate or nu-

---

[23]Miller (2004) says, "Psychological knowledge does contain general principles, but they resemble more moral than scientific principles" (p. 130). However, to the extent that they make causal claims, they remain empirical principles nonetheless (see Held, 2006a, 2006b). Also see Miller (2006a, 2006b), for rebuttals to my critique of his philosophy.

anced position than that taken by those MGTs who reject causal explanation outright on the grounds that it subverts a truly agentic psychology, in
which determinism of any sort cannot be tolerated and so "noncausal" understanding must be the only legitimate form of psychological knowledge
(see chaps. 5–6, this volume).

> Psychological phenomena may be causally determined, but . . . such causal
> relations cannot be warranted in the manner in which causal claims are
> established in physical science. . . . The ontological status of psychologi-
> cal phenomena prevents their penetration by known means of establish-
> ing causal connections in physical science. (p. 45)

Martin and Sugarman (1999a) intensify their stance against conventional deterministic/causal accounts of human psychological existence owing to (a) their failure to account for our agentic and context-dependent/
value-laden existence on the one (ontological) hand, and (b) their alleged
certainty on the other (epistemological) hand. Here they sound more like
Liebrucks, Harré, Fishman, and Miller than in the previous quotation.

> The belief that the methods of physical science . . . inevitably will pro-
> duce . . . highly deterministic, causal understandings and explanations of
> . . . human actions and experiences is scientistic, not scientific. . . . The
> methods and epistemic strategies of physical science do not apply in the
> same way to psychological phenomena because such phenomena are
> morally constituted, agentically controlled, contextual and uncertain.
> (pp. 46–47)

But Martin and Sugarman (1999a) then moderate that intensity, as
they propound the value and validity of conventional psychological knowledge nonetheless. In this next quotation they sound more like Richardson et
al. (1999), who also accept the findings of conventional psychological inquiry but only if they are interpreted within context-dependent limits and
with proper agentic/interpretive circumspection.

> Much existing research in psychology . . . may have a certain amount of
> epistemic value, even if it has not, and will not, yield the kinds of lawful
> causal understandings that are the hallmark of success in physical sci-
> ence. . . . Empirical evidence in psychology . . . will be less generalizable,
> less definitive, and more highly interpretative. (pp. 47–48)

In what should this warranted psychological knowledge consist? Socially embedded rules and conventions? Meanings and intentions of actors
in context? Localized regularities in human thought and action? Categories
of psychological kinds pressed into pragmatic service? Martin and Sugarman
(2002) do not deny the "epistemic value" of conventional mechanistically
deterministic forms of psychological science, but neither do they rule out the
epistemic value of attending to meanings, rules, and conventions: "Sociocultural meanings, rules, conventions, and practices, which for us play critically

important background, contextual, and constitutive roles in the development of human self understanding and agency receive extremely short shrift" (p. 420).

Ultimately Martin and Sugarman maintain that accounting for human agency itself constitutes no small portion of legitimate psychological inquiry. They do not stop at studying the local rules and conventions that make action and experience intelligible within a discursive context, as Liebrucks (2001) advocates. Instead Martin and Sugarman (2002) seem to want a bona fide causal account of "human choice and action" (p. 415)—of agency/self-determination itself—that is as complete an account as agency will permit. Thus they seek a *compatibilist* solution to the problem of attaining a truth-tracking/realist form of psychological inquiry—that is, one that denies neither mechanistic/nonagentic forms of causal determination nor agentic forms of causal (self-)determination. Notice the universality, nonrelativity, and objectivity that inhere in Martin and Sugarman's (2002) claim about the "irreducible understanding and reasoning of human agents"; this claim is not limited to those who live within any particular kind of sociocultural context, or to anyone's point of view, or to anyone's beliefs about its truth.

> Human choice and action, at least in part and sometimes, result from the irreducible understanding and reasoning of human agents. The underdetermination of human agency by . . . other conditions and factors does not mean that human agency is undetermined, only that it figures in its own determination. Such self-determination means that human agency is not reducible to physical, biological, sociocultural, and/ or random/unconscious processes. (p. 415)

Not only do Martin and Sugarman commit to the universal existence of agency (see chap. 6, this volume) but they also want to subject agency to a form of scientific inquiry that is properly deterministic, given the nature of that entity. Thus there must be a way that agency itself is—an essence or nature of agency that transcends its local expressions and is in some way independent of our beliefs about its essence/nature—if the realist inquiry about agency to which they aspire is to succeed (see chap. 5, this volume). Let us try to grasp Martin and Sugarman's (2002) admirable struggle to reconcile at least two oppositions: first, reconciliation of (a) a deterministic science of agency/psychology (or of an agentic psychology), including all the generality that inheres in science, with (b) the local, situated, embodied expressions of agency, including all the particularity of those expressions; and second, reconciliation of (a) agency's aforementioned underdetermination with (b) a deterministic science of agency/psychology.

> The kind of compatibilist theorizing we have attempted herein eventually may contribute to an understanding of psychology as a rigorous, but nonreductive study of the experiences and actions of human agents in historical, sociocultural, and developmental context. . . . There is much

of importance to learn about the physical, neurophysiological, and biological requirements, operations, and conditions that permit human agency, just as there is much still unanswered concerning the sociocultural constitution of agency. (p. 422)

The possibility of a deterministic science of psychology still exists, so long as the self-determination of individual agents can be accessed through methods of scientific inquiry. However, the practical difficulties of achieving veridical access to such self-determination should not be underestimated. . . . Our underdetermination thesis with respect to human agency, if true, while not denying the possibility of a deterministic psychological science, may imply the practical impossibility of such a science. For, even if human agency is not undetermined, so long as self-determination is admitted, it may prove to be indeterminate in the sense of being outside the reach of the methods of psychological science. (p. 423)

Martin and Sugarman (2002) seemingly want to account for or explain agency in terms that are amenable to conventional realist inquiry. In particular, they appear to make agency the dependent variable in their proposed form of psychological inquiry. Yet it also sometimes seems as though they want to account for human experience, choice, and action—that is, our psychological existence—by appealing to our (essential!) agentic nature as the cause of experience, choice, and action, in which case an agentic force or power functions as an independent variable (also see Martin et al., 2003). MGTs who eschew a causal form of psychological inquiry/analysis altogether would perhaps see such ambiguity as a consequence of Martin and Sugarman's (2002) refusal to relinquish determinism of any sort, although the former may fail to distinguish the mechanistic/nonagentic from the agentic forms of causality/determinism that we considered in chapters 5 and 6. In any case, Martin and Sugarman's (2002) equation of agency with "irreducible understanding and reasoning" (p. 415) puts them near the view of agency propounded by philosopher Edward Pols (1998), who—in criticizing what he called "the received scientific doctrine of causality"—rejected the view that agency is "something to be explained, not something that is in itself explanatory" (p. 81). Pols (2004b, 2005) stated his position positively in saying, "The act itself, not an earlier one of which it is an effect, not a set of conditions including earlier ones, is itself an irreducible factor in explanation."

Causal Laws of a Different Kind?

Martin and Sugarman (2002) suggest that agency/self-determination may be studied scientifically—or at least allow for a conventionally deterministic psychological science—if it is determinate (or determined) enough. Again we must ask if there is a way that agency (or agentic functioning) is, independent of beliefs about its nature, so that realist/fallibilist inquiry about it can obtain. If so, then perhaps it can be accessed through conventional scientific methods, without reducing it to a nonagentic object of mechanistically deterministic inquiry. In that seemingly paradoxical or incompatible case, the problem may not lie in the methods of conventional (psychological) science as much as in the way those methods are *interpreted*. This is the position of psychologist Joseph Rychlak, whose extensive investigation of "dialectical reasoning" or "transpredication" in his Logical Learning Theory (LLT)[24] some MGTs cite to support their claims to a truth-tracking/realist form of psychological inquiry in which agency (including the possibility of agentic transcendence) is preserved.

> As Rychlak (1988, 1997) might say, as agents, we are capable of framing "transpredications" (alternative possibilities) that draw upon but purposefully transform what we have experienced and learned as participants in sociocultural and linguistic practices and forms of understanding. (Martin & Sugarman, 2002, p. 419)
>
> Rychlak . . . has demonstrated through both philosophical argument and experimental demonstrations that human learning and information-processing studies can be viewed as establishing the role of freedom in human action. . . . Before the stimulus "conditions" one's response, one makes a choice, conscious or unconscious, to accept or reject it. It is not that experimental data are unimportant in considering the sources of human action. Rather it is the interpretation of that data in a deterministic, mechanistic manner that distorts one's view of human agency. (Miller, 2004, p. 80)
>
> A defining feature of dialectical thought is the human capacity to imagine alternatives, even in the presence of a clearly defined stimulus situation. There is always more than one way to view a situation, which "demands that the human being affirm some . . . meaning at the outset for the sake of which behavior might then take place" (Rychlak, 1988, p. 295). . . . Individuals contribute to their lives by how they choose to frame events within the contexts in which they find themselves. (Jenkins, 2001, p. 353)
>
> Some theorists point to the existence of metaphysical givens and do so in defense of human agency. Rychlak (1994) offers a conceptualization of mind, suggesting that although the mind is innate, and logically a priori to human experience, it has the capacity to transcend the given and generate genuine alternatives to thought and behavior. (Slife & Williams, 1995, p. 165, note 13)

---

[24]Here are Rychlak's (1997) own words on LLT.
   [Predication is] the logical process of affirming, denying or qualifying precedently broader patterns of meaning in sequacious extension to narrower or targeted patterns of meaning. The target is the point, aim, or end (telos) of the meaning extension. . . . Predication and intentionality are identical notions. To behave intentionally is to behave for the sake of certain *affirmations* of meaning (rather than others), targeting them to some end (telos). This is how thought is directed or psychically determined. . . . LLT holds that people are intentional organisms. They intend with purpose. . . . [Transpredication means] that in a state of consciousness the content-meaning framed as a predication is not limited to the target. There is some sense of implied meanings outside of—or in opposition to—the predicated meaning. (pp. 41, 45, 53)

Rychlak has shown that even though one must necessarily be determined by one's goals and purposes (final causation), one may nevertheless have the free will ability to formulate those goals and purposes. Rychlak . . . refer[s] to this ability as the *dialectic*, the ability to think oppositionally. . . . With a dialectic capacity, final causation becomes a type of self determination and thus a variation on free will. (Slife & Williams, 1995, p. 217)

About transcendence Rychlak (1980) himself said the following:

Transcendence refers to a human being's capacity to take a vis-à-vis stance toward the contents of his or her own thought contents, to rise above the course of such mentation . . . and to realize that other possibilities than the ones then under meaningful extension can be entertained. (p. 1150)

On his view "only a transcending intelligence would be capable of such insight"[25] (p. 1150).

Although Rychlak indeed shares with MGTs the dual mission of advancing psychological inquiry that is both truth tracking and mindful of human agency, I would not put him in the same boat with them. First, unlike MGTs, he does not emphasize the role of culture in determining our psychological existence; indeed, he speaks unabashedly in universal (rather than culturally circumscribed) terms about mind, rationality, and agency (for which he has been taken to task harshly).[26] Thus his is not a psychology whose truth or validity stops at the door of any cultural domicile: "Even a prisoner in solitary confinement has the same free will he or she enjoyed before internment" (Rychlak, 1997, p. 162). Nor does he find in conventional psychological science the mechanistic determinism/causality that most other MGTs reject or question, in their own determination to articulate an agentic psychology.

Rychlak (1997) faults outmoded behavioral paradigms based on a limited, efficient, Newtonian view of causation, rather than the form of causality that inheres in conventional psychological science: "Just because a mecha-

---

[25]Rychlak (1980) fleshes out the insight by saying, "I would therefore modify the Cartesian proof of self-existence and self-identity from 'I think, therefore I am' to 'I think and (dialectically) could be thinking otherwise, therefore *I* exist'" (p. 1150).
[26]For example, psychologist Edwin Gantt (2004) said the following:

The key to understanding the problematic nature of Rychlak's [2003] conception of agency . . . is to appreciate the way in which he defines agency as the ability to think or do otherwise, "all circumstances remaining the same." Such a qualification seems to reduce agency to a matter of arbitrary desire or random whimsy, in that the particular real-world circumstances that provide the occasion for a particular choice play no substantive role in guiding or shaping the choice. Were they to do so, then those circumstances would become the determining grounds of one's choice, and thus one's choice would no longer be truly free. (p. 613)

First, it is not obvious that Rychlak's conception of agency reduces to arbitrary desire or whimsy. This sounds more like the postmodern position of Rorty, whom Guignon (1991) ably criticized on those grounds. Second, that the circumstances provide "determining grounds" for choice does not automatically make the choice any less agentic or free, as Rychlak himself explains.

nistically oriented therapist has introduced them [behavioristic therapeutic techniques] does not mean that the explanation for why they work need rest on mechanism (i.e., efficient causation)" (Rychlak, 2000, p. 1129). He also finds no problem in the independent variable (IV)–dependent variable (DV) design used in conventional psychological science: "It [this method] tests through the logic of its design whatever theory is put to it: The IV–DV sequence does not dictate how it is to be understood or interpreted as a testing manipulation" (Rychlak, 2004, p. 768). Thus Rychlak has spent much of his career deploying the methods of conventional psychological science to give evidence of our universal capacity for oppositional or dialectical reasoning, which forms the basis for agency (or free choice) in any situation. He defines the term *agency* as "the capacity that an organism has to behave or believe in conformance with, in contradiction of, in addition to, or without regard for what is perceived to be environmental or biological determinants" (Rychlak, 1997, p. 294).

In short, Rychlak finds no necessary incompatibility in (a) adopting Aristotle's final or telic causality and (b) using the methods of conventional psychological science, which for him give empirical evidence of the human telos that MGTs defend. Rychlak (2000) asks, "Should we turn our backs on traditional science?" (p. 1130). He answers with a resolute no.

> Nothing is wrong with the scientific method. The problem is with the theories used, the confounding of method with theory. . . . Human beings are, and can be empirically proven (i.e., paradigmatically understood) to be, teleological organisms. . . . It is just plain silly to view them as being moved by meaningless impulsions of the billiard-ball (efficiently caused) variety. . . . Students are blaming the scientific method . . . as if it were the messenger of mechanism rather than the disinterested testing vehicle of the paradigmatic theoretical assumptions advanced by the dominant language community in psychology. . . . So why not shift paradigms and frame people as human beings rather than as no-fault robots from the outset? (Rychlak, 2000, p. 1131)

In advocating (a) the methods of conventional psychological science and (b) the universally agentic (vs. the culturally relativistic) features of mind (which universals can be accessed by such science), Rychlak stands in opposition to those MGTs who (a) find in the scientific method itself an inherent mechanistic determinism and (b) eschew the existence of psychological universals/essences. For those MGTs this inherent methodological determinism itself rests on an unacceptable, antiagentic/mechanistic ontology (of causality), so conventional causal forms of inquiry must be abandoned in favor of other, noncausal forms of inquiry, which are said to rest on a psychological ontology that gives agency its proper due—although always within the confines of some discursive/interpretive context. For example, such "proper" inquiry might consist in discovering the local meaning rules and conventions that allegedly constitute context-dependent psychological kinds—kinds that can exist only relative to a discursive/interpretive context (as Liebrucks, 2001, among others, argues).

But Rychlak (2004) finds little virtue in the "alternatives" to conventional psychological science offered by its many critics, including Martin and Sugarman. He writes in his (2004) review of Martin, Sugarman, and Thompson's (2003) book, "The alternatives suggested often boil down to a reliance on untested plausibility, verbal suasion, and fanciful promise. I have watched the development of such approaches in psychology for over 40 years, and am still waiting for the predicted renaissance" (p. 767). And he again says there is nothing in the methods of traditional science that necessitate a reductionistic and mechanistic view of human nature: "Rather than rejecting traditional science, we [should] clarify our thinking about just how we can use it in more humanistic ways" (p. 767).

Having considered Rychlak's nonrelativistic views about (a) the universally agentic nature of human psychological existence and (b) our ability to study or access that existence by way of conventional scientific methods, we may now ask where he stands on the question of the epistemic relativism that I find in the MGTs' (problematic) appeal to perspectival warrant. Rychlak appears to see truth as relative to a conceptual scheme or intellectual paradigm, although he does not equate these with the local discourses/interpretations (or "constitutive" cultural contexts) on which MGTs depend so deeply for their version of epistemic warrant. Yet we see at least some form of epistemic relativism in his equation of "empirically proven" with "paradigmatically understood" in a previous quotation. Indeed, Rychlak (2000) speaks approvingly of Kuhn's suggestion, in *The Structure of Scientific Revolutions*, that scientific evidence is a product of "decisions to retain or reject a paradigmatic assumption [that] take place in the common sense of a community of scientists" (p. 1130). Rychlak (2000) continues, "These communities develop their own language of description, so that they might look at the same empirical data yet describe them differently on the basis of how they conformed to the plausibility of their respective paradigms" (p. 1130).[27]

Rychlak (2000) also seems to agree with a relativistic-sounding physics supposition that he quotes from Prigogine and Stengers: "'The reality studied by physics is also a mental construct; it is not merely given'" (p. 1129). Rychlak (2000) himself says the following:

> The theoretical predication of subject matter affirmed by a scientist from the very outset is a crucial ingredient of the findings eventually observed in the empirical research. . . . Modern scientists are acknowledging their

---

[27]See Haack's (2003, pp. 43–44) and Erwin's (1997, pp. 70–71) critical responses to Kuhn's relativism, including his disclaimer in the revised edition of *The Structure of Scientific Revolutions* regarding the nature and extent of his relativism.

theoretical hypotheses as framed by an . . . "I" or "self" whose point of view must be taken into consideration to fully understand a scientific investigation. (p. 1129)

Rychlak[28] would probably find problematic the notion of objective knowledge or truth as independent of conceptual schemes or paradigms. If I am right in my interpretation, his views about objectivist and relativist epistemologies may be more consistent with the epistemologies propounded by most (if not all) MGTs than is his argument about the full-fledged compatibility of the methods of conventional psychological science and the investigation of the agentic nature of human psychological existence.

In any case, given what appears to be his adoption of some form of epistemic perspectivism, it is hard to see how Rychlak can lay claim to empirical/scientific evidence of the *universal* features of human mind, such as rationality or agency. Moreover, although MGTs typically share his interest in putting telic or final causality into psychological science, many shy away from using conventional psychological scientific methods to prove the existence and nature of agency/self-determination—this owing to the mechanistic determinism that they, unlike Rychlak, automatically find in those methods. Martin and Sugarman perhaps come closest to Rychlak: Recall from chapter 6 their appeal to the universals of rationality and imagination to explain the possibility of transcendence, which they (unlike Rychlak) qualify as "mild" or "moderate" innovation. However, like Rychlak, they do not reject the methods of conventional psychological science out of hand; they ask only if agency is determined enough to assess its (causal) determinants and consequences scientifically/empirically. What is not clear is whether for Martin and Sugarman (2002) agency should be seen as an "independent" or "dependent" variable. That is, does our agentic nature explain human experience, choice, and action, or is it itself the object of explanation?

By contrast, Rychlak is more consistent in treating what he claims is our universal/essential dialectical rational capacity—our agentic nature itself—as an irreducible causal entity or force that explains the acts for which it accounts (e.g., in his research on logical learning theory). In this way, but

---

[28]Rychlak (1998a) said this about his own epistemology.

> I have always considered myself an objective idealist. A "modest, limited" idealism need not be antirealism, but merely hold that knowledge predicates experience rather than traces or maps it directly. All that is required in the accumulation of knowledge is that any theoretical claims be framed understandably (i.e., objectively), and then tested empirically. . . . Held [1995] begs the question of whether reality can be understood through direct awareness without a framing predication lending it meaning from the outset. The problem with most postmodernists is that they are extremely subjective idealists, to the point of becoming nihilists. (p. 603)

First, Rychlak's equation of "objective" with "understandable" is not the common meaning given to "objectivity" by those who hold objectivist epistemologies (see chap. 8, this volume). Second, Rychlak fails to notice that "direct awareness," or "rational awareness," as Pols (1992, 1998) calls it, requires a fusion of the conceptual domain with the experiential domain in any act of direct knowing/ rational awareness (see Held, 1995, chap. 6; see also chap. 8, this volume). Thus this question has not been begged, at least not by me!

certainly not in others, he makes common cause with Pols, whose view of agency we considered earlier. Recall that in contesting the so-called "received scientific doctrine of causality," Pols (1998) lamented the elimination of agency as a causal explanation in its own right—or what he also called an "irreducible factor in explanation" (Pols, 2004b, 2005).

Here let us accept Rychlak's (2000) contention that people freely choose to see things in a positive or negative way. Such "affective assessment" (p. 1129) constitutes agentic or real choice (it is not itself mechanistically determined by something else), and it is just that agentic choice that then determines other acts—for example, how well and quickly anyone will learn and recall items on a list (Rychlak, 1997, p. 286). Rychlak's findings are interesting, but questions arise. First, could people choose to see or frame things in a different way? Rychlak (2000, p. 1129) suggests that they can. Yet he (1997) also says affective assessments are not usually "transpredications," but rather "unipredications" (p. 286)—that is, "psychic unconsciousness" (p. 308), in which there is "no cognizance . . . taken of a realm of possible meaning outside of the course that thought is taking at the moment" (1997, p. 307). Second, does this (scientifically discovered) causal (lawlike) link between (a) affective choice, predication, or assessment and (b) extent of learning or recall constitute an agentic causal/deterministic process or a nonagentic/mechanistic one (Semro, 2003)? For example, once someone knows that this causal link exists, can she then intentionally subvert it by making affective assessment irrelevant to the learning process?

I am not clear about this second question, although the answer has implications for the stability of scientific psychological knowledge, and thus for the "lawlikeness" (if not lawfulness) of its findings. Although many MGTs claim a Giddens-inspired "reflexive impact" of knowing (or knowledge) on psychological existence/being (see chaps. 5, 7, & 8), they also say that we cannot *intentionally* use the fruits of psychological inquiry reflexively to change our psychological existence. That is just what gives mind an existence independent enough of beliefs about mind to be the object of realist/fallibilist inquiry in the first place. Whatever Rychlak's response to this question may be, he is more committed than are MGTs to a way that mind/rationality *is*, a way that mind/rationality works, regardless of beliefs or discourses *about* mind/rationality. Because mind/rationality is a certain way, it may be determined enough (to use Martin and Sugarman's terminology) to study empirically just how mind/rationality makes human choice and action possible.

Causal "Laws" Reconsidered

The controversy about causality in psychological inquiry—both the causal force of the psychological agent and the causal force of whatever is thought to constrain agents—expresses the compatibilist problem of adhering to mechanistically deterministic causal laws in a science that purports to uphold the agentically deterministic causal powers of its human subjects. The struggle to overcome this dilemma is seen most profoundly in the nuanced arguments set forth by Rychlak (1997, 2000) and Martin and Sugarman (2002; Martin et al., 2003). And it also inheres in the work of those MGTs (e.g., Fishman, 1999, 2001; Miller, 2004; Richardson et al., 1999) who do not limit the legitimate content of psychological inquiry to the meaning rules and conventions that are said to constitute intelligible behavior.

Philosopher Edward Erwin (1997) finds one source of the dilemma in the fact that attempts to discover a causal relation between two or more variables are automatically cast as a search for the universal laws of natural science. Yet this, he writes, need not be the case: One "metaphysical objection" to a "science of psychotherapy" is that "there are no psychotherapeutic laws awaiting discovery." However, "for a science of psychotherapy to exist . . . there need not be such laws" (pp. 77–78). Erwin continues with the following:

> It is enough that there be clinically significant true generalizations stating causal relationships between certain causally relevant factors and certain effects. . . . Such generalizations need not be of the form "All B-type events are caused by A-type events." Instead, they may be of the sort "Under certain initial conditions, C, A-type events generally make an important causal difference to the occurrence of B-type events." (p. 78)

Erwin (1997) also says that if the causal relationships that are discovered today turn out to be inapplicable later, "this need not be because the original generalizations were false, but because the initial conditions no longer hold. . . . A science of psychotherapy does not need such [timeless] generalizations" (p. 78).

Erwin (1997) states his own compatibilist solution to the "dilemma of determinism" (p. 13): "Can the twin goals of achieving client autonomy and transforming the field [of psychotherapy] into a [deterministic] science be jointly met?" (p. 2). His answer is yes, as long as we understand that this is not a full-blown "metaphysical autonomy," which "presupposes the freedom needed for moral responsibility," but only an "inner autonomy," which "comes in degrees" and consists in "certain capacities and skills, such as the capacity to reflect on one's preferences, desires, and wishes, and the capacity to change [or eliminate] them in the light of higher-order preferences or values" (pp. 17–18). He adds, "Increasing inner autonomy . . . includes increasing the capacity for self-control" (p. 18). Thus he makes self-determination (i.e., agency), or at least autonomy, dependent on—if not identical with— rationality itself.[29]

---

[29]In making autonomy dependent on, if not identical with, some form of rationality, Erwin (1997, chap. 1) offers a view of autonomy that is to some extent consistent with Pols's notion of agency as "rational agency."

How might MGTs respond to Erwin's views about psychological science? Again, some do not dismiss conventional psychological science out of hand, although even they ask for a different way to interpret the findings of that science—that is, they want to interpret those findings in what they take to be an antiobjectivist way, by not equating them with indubitable knowledge of timeless, universal, and mechanistically deterministic causal laws about the unchanging essences of brute entities. Nor do they believe that psychological claims can be warranted independently of discursive/interpretive contexts or conceptual schemes. That too would defy their antiobjectivist epistemologies.

Recall from chapter 8 that equating objective knowledge with timeless, universal truths (about the mechanistically deterministic laws of unchanging brute essences) that can be known with certainty constitutes the straw man of objectivity erected by many MGTs. By contrast, the possibility of warranting claims independently of knowers' discursive/interpretive contexts, so that truth or knowledge need not be perspectival truth or knowledge (in which case what is true *about* some aspect of the human world can be true only *for* the members of a certain discursive/interpretive context but not for all others), is indeed a feature of bona fide objective knowledge. Because MGTs reject objective psychological knowledge outright, and because objective knowledge (in non-straw-man terms) is realist knowledge, we are left to wonder just how the MGTs' antiobjectivist epistemology can be considered realist in any way at all—including the moderate way that they claim to have defended successfully.

THE CALL FOR METHODOLOGICAL PLURALISM

Some MGTs have made much of psychology's need for methodological pluralism if an agentic psychology is to obtain (e.g., Slife & Williams, 1995, p. 200). They especially proclaim the virtues of qualitative research, which is thought to be more consistent with an agentic ontology than are quantitative methods. According to Slife and Williams (1995), "Many human science methods are grouped under the rubric *qualitative methods*. . . . Researchers avoid measurement and quantification, allowing subjects to describe their own behaviors and experiences in the language native to their experience" (p. 199). Miller (2004) asks, "What makes psychologists think that dreams, fantasies, goals, and intentions are the sorts of things that can be systematically measured to begin with?" He states, "An articulate minority" argues that "this is an area for only qualitative and narrative analysis (e.g., Hoshmand, 1992; Howard, 1991; Polkinghorne, 1998)" (p. 137). Given the consensus even among these qualitatively oriented psychologists that if there is to be a *discipline* of psychology, generalities of some sort must obtain (e.g., Fishman, 1999; Miller, 2004), it is not immediately obvious that the use of statistics is inherently dehumanizing or antiagentic. If the use of statistics is ruled out in advance, the methodology of psychological science becomes less—not more—pluralistic.

Another way to inject methodological pluralism into psychology is to view different methods of inquiry themselves as different cultural/discursive/interpretive contexts. Polkinghorne (1983), for example, makes this case for methodological pluralism.

> Each of the various systems of inquiry is a context or "community" and represents an epistemological position. In this sense, an epistemological pluralism is proposed. . . . One's point of view is transformed . . . when alternatives are admitted. Out of the syncretic interaction of various positions, a fuller understanding arises. (p. 251)

The epistemic relativism that seems to pervade the first part of this quotation seems to recede in the last part, although it does not vanish completely. Here I suggest another, less relativist, more realist/objectivist way to argue on behalf of methodological pluralism. This consists in a case made by philosopher Susan Haack (2003), who says that "there is less to the 'scientific method' than meets the eye" (p. 94) and who sees science as "the long arm of common sense" (p. 93) rather than as a unique method of inquiry.

> Scientific inquiry is continuous with everyday empirical inquiry—only more so. Is there a mode of inference or procedure of inquiry used by all and only scientists? No. There are only . . . modes of inference and procedures of inquiry used by all inquirers, and . . . special mathematical, statistical, or inferential techniques, and special instruments, models, etc. local to this or that area of science. . . . "There is no reason to think that [science] is in possession of a special method of inquiry unavailable to historians or detectives or the rest of us" [Haack, 1993b, p. 137]. (pp. 94–95)

Although psychologist George Howard's (1986) defense of an expressly human science may not square with what Haack has in mind, he at least shares with her one point about methodological pluralism in all sciences: "In general, each science must develop a set of techniques, methods, procedures, and theories which are *appropriate for understanding the characteristics of the subject-matter in that discipline*" (p. 26). In addressing the social sciences, Haack (2003) said that they indeed have a different subject matter than that of the physical sciences. Yet she also said, "The underlying patterns of hypothesizing, reasoning, and testing are the same for all empirical investigation, but the special techniques overlaid on them will differ from field to field" (p. 168).

Still, MGTs would surely object to Haack's presumption of even the potential for objective forms of epistemic warrant. But they might nonetheless tumble to Haack's (2003) assertion that "if any discipline is properly so-called ["the physics of the social sciences"], it is psychology, the discipline to which it falls to investigate the basic contours of human motivation" (p. 169). On the other hand, many MGTs might not appreciate Haack's conclusion owing to their desire to use political or pragmatic consequences as the correct criteria for epistemic warrant—a desire that stems from their celebration of a morally infused (or value-laden) approach to psychological science: "Physics envy . . . is not the only pitfall of intentional social science. There is an equal and opposite danger: transmuting what could and should be inquiry into social phenomena into socio-politico advocacy" (Haack, 2003, p. 169).

EPISTEMIC FAITH AND HOPE

In this chapter I have described how MGTs have worked to uphold an agentic psychology by trying to define a realist yet antiobjectivist epistemology—one that avoids the radical relativism of strong postmodernism /constructionism on the one hand, and the objectivism of modern/ conventional (psychological) science on the other. I have also argued that despite their many nuanced, interesting, and diverse efforts, they have not propounded a form of epistemic warrant that constitutes a bona fide realist epistemology.

Why do MGTs hold so tenaciously to their antiobjectivist epistemology in the first place? Two answers seem likely: (a) they are convinced of the objective truth of their antiobjectivist epistemology, a position that would make their argument self-refuting, self-undermining, or incoherent (see Siegel, 1997, 2004), and/or (b) they are convinced that an antiobjectivist epistemology is the only route to an agentic psychology, one in which transcendence or innovation is possible. We have already considered (a) at length in chapter 8; (b) is the subject matter of chapter 10. The important point is that it is exactly in our capacity to have objective knowledge about (some aspects) of the world, including the world of human social/psychological existence, that the possibility of transcending (problematic) aspects of that world lies.

In this quotation Martin and Sugarman (1999a), who wrestle admirably with the question of whether agency can be studied scientifically, exemplify the link between the search for a proper epistemology of psychology on the one hand and a capacity for agentic transcendence (especially *epistemic* transcendence) on the other.

> [This workable epistemology] avoids both the scientism involved in applying objectivist, positivist, physical scientific methodologies and epistemologies to psychological phenomena without regard to the agentic, contextualized nature of such phenomena, and the strong relativism that seems too often to accompany the necessary endorsement of a perspectivism and fallibilism in psychology and social science. . . . Our neorealist hermeneutics embraces . . . the possibility of transcending the current forms of these practices [of inquiry] and the knowledge claims

and warrants they contain. Such transcendence is made possible by virtue of our agentic intentionality and capacity for critical reflexivity (both subjective and intersubjective), when these are targeted at a deeper understanding of our own nature. (pp. 64–65)

The words "a deeper understanding of our own nature" are important. In using them Martin and Sugarman (1999a) express their hopeful belief that knowledge of human nature is indeed within our reach, however "necessarily imperfect knowledge of it" must be (p. 65). Moreover, Martin and Sugarman link the possibility of transcendence to our capacity to know the nature of human social/psychological existence at a deeper level. I could not agree more. Knowledge is power, but not in Foucault's necessarily oppressive, antiobjectivist sense. The possibility of knowledge of what is the case—objective knowledge—is a prerequisite for the power to transcend what now exists, which is how MGTs define and defend agency (see chap. 6, this volume).

Martin and Sugarman are not alone in expressing their belief in our ability to know the nature of human psychological existence in real, commonsensically objective terms—that is, without qualifying that belief in perspectival, relativistic, or pragmatic/value-laden terms. Although most MGTs support some form of perspectival, (weakly) relativist, and/or pragmatic standard of epistemic warrant, and although they eschew objective knowledge as both impossible and undesirable (because its supposed absolutes and mechanistic determinism are thought to diminish human agency), they convey faith in our ability to know the (objective) realities of human social/psychological existence, as well as the "conditions of constraint and possibility" that warrant that necessarily fallibilist knowledge (Martin & Sugarman, 1999a, p. 65). To be sure, they oscillate even in the expression of that faith, but it is expressed nonetheless. Their own use of the word *faith* is important; it is the most powerful expression of nothing less than a positive philosophical judgment about knowing, and it provides a strong counterpoint to the "Cartesian Anxiety" about which Bernstein (1983) writes and to which MGTS sometimes turn to support their antiobjectivist "negative philosophical judgments about knowing" (Pols, 1992)—however much they may celebrate those judgments in the name of agency.

Mark Freeman (1993), writing about self-knowledge, conveys his (epistemic) faith in our knowing powers and links them to agency in words we considered earlier.

> [Life narratives] signify our capacity to become conscious of our worlds and to make something of them; they will serve as testimony to our own power to challenge power . . . [and] as vehicles of revelation, uncovering those rules and regulations of the social world . . . that often take us unawares. . . . While what I think and feel and do and say is surely a function of the time and place in which I live, . . . I also have the power

... to become conscious enough of my world to shape my destiny. . . .
Perhaps, I am relying on a kind of faith when I make this claim; it could
very well be, I suppose, that I have no power at all. . . . I just don't happen
to believe this is so. . . . That I can, on occasion, move in the direction of
becoming conscious of the way I am determined suggests that there exists a margin of freedom within which to think, act, and be. (pp. 216–
217)

Charles Guignon (1998) expresses his belief in our ability to "spot" the
truth in the stories we tell about our lives: "As beings whose very being is
shaped by stories, we are remarkably good at spotting the truth in the stories
we tell" (p. 575). Guignon (2002a) extends his faith in our epistemic powers
to a pervasive capacity for "clear-sightedness" about our actions in general:
"Nothing general can be said about interpretation aside from descriptions of
what usually goes on. But our actual practices show that we have no real need
for anything more than clear-sightedness about what we in fact do" (p. 284).

Richardson et al. (1999) appear to speak of truth in conventional objectivist terms in the first two quotations. However, in the third quotation
they seem to equivocate owing to a Giddens-like "reflexivity thesis," although
even there they express epistemic faith in our ability to "gain some degree of
accurate knowledge."

> Finding the truth is still a matter of revealing the way things really are.
> (p. 235)
>   It is still necessary that our interpretations, hypotheses, and theories
> be consistent with our clearest apprehension of the facts. (p. 299)
>   We face something of a paradox. On the one hand, our attempts to
> formulate descriptions must strive to be faithful to something. On the
> other hand, . . . these accounts are not entirely distinct from the behav-
> ior or experience in question. It is clearly possible to gain some degree of
> accurate knowledge about human behavior and this possibility suggests
> that a correspondence between our knowledge and social reality is at-
> tainable. Yet the achievement of lucidity about our own or others' be-
> havior often redefines that behavior or experience. (p. 282)

Frederick Wertz (1999), who propounds a phenomenological approach
to psychological inquiry, deploys a version of the word *faith* in his own
epistemic account. His call for an "indigenous epistemology for psychology"
is not unlike the phenomenological (and hermeneutic) approach of Edwin
Hersch (2003), in which we find the "concept of *field-specific or discipline-
specific epistemology*" (p. 115).

> [The] fundamental characteristics of psychological subject matter are
> revealed reflectively and expressed descriptively using ordinary language.
> . . . These are not inferred laws or hypothetical constructs but the univer-
> sal horizons of human existence which show themselves in the direct
> *intuitive* grasp of mental life (Levinas, 1973). Such intuition establishes a

regional ontology and an indigenous epistemology for psychology. . . . The gold standard is . . . the rich description of the lifeworld events which faithfully exhibits the lived experiences and conduct of individual persons. (Wertz, 1999, p. 144)

These authors speak with somewhat different theoretical interests, yet all express their faith in our ability to know the realities of human psychological existence. Indeed, it is this "positive philosophical judgment about knowing" that constitutes the foundation for a *universal* human agentic capacity to transcend *particular* existential (and in some cases epistemological) realities/situations. Although their faith can be warranted in virtue of a reflective or reflexive process, it is not the reflective/reflexive process that MGTs usually invoke (i.e., the "double hermeneutic" or "reflexivity theory" of Giddens; see chap. 8, this volume) in their efforts to deny our ability to know the nature of human social/psychological existence with objectivity. It is to this form of warrant that we now turn.

IV

TRUTH AND AGENCY

10

RATIONAL AGENCY

I have organized this volume around the twin goals of the middle-ground theorists (MGTs): to attain a truth-tracking form of psychological inquiry and yet maintain an agentic view of human nature. Their quest has led them to conclude that objective knowledge of human psychological existence is not only impossible to obtain but also an undesirable goal to hold in the first place. Recall that they equate objective knowledge with indubitable knowledge of timeless, universal, and mechanistically deterministic causal laws that allegedly govern the unchanging essences of brute or nonagentic entities—entities that are not constituted by discourses/interpretations or linguistic/conceptual practices and so are said to be mind-independent entities. On their view, it is the futile search for these "laws" that defines modern/conventional psychological science, which they therefore judge to be inappropriate for the study of human agents (see chap. 8, this volume).

Owing to their equation of objective knowledge with knowledge of mechanistically deterministic causal laws, MGTs argue that to have a psychological science that upholds our agentic capacities—especially our interpretive/meaning-making or nonmechanistic bases for self-determination—we must forgo objective knowledge. If there are universal mechanistically deterministic causal laws that govern our psychological existence, how can we be agentic beings capable of self-determination and transcendence by way of nonmechanistic interpretive acts? And if we lack agency in *that* sense, how can we dare to hope for any transcendence of (the particulars of) our current social/psychological circumstances? That capacity for transcendence of our particularity is, after all, what MGTs want from agency; it constitutes an agency "worth wanting" (cf. Dennett, 1984).[1]

Here we should also recall our earlier discussion of radical constructionist/postmodernist psychologist Kenneth Gergen (1997, 1998), who—unlike his more moderate colleagues—prefers to remain "ontologically mute" (see chaps. 2 & 4, this volume). He nonetheless makes common cause with those more moderate colleagues when he invokes his radical constructionism in the name of agency, liberation, and transcendence: "There is simply no place within the metaphysics of the mainstream tradition [of empiricist psychology] for an unmoved mover, that is, a personal capacity to step outside the fundamental flow of cause and effect" (Gergen, 2001a, p. 428). Although (like Gergen) MGTs reject both the possibility and desirability of objective psychological knowledge, they (unlike Gergen) lay claim to the potentially realist nature of that knowledge nonetheless.

I have argued that the MGTs' realist epistemology is at best "realist" owing to the perspectival or relativist and pragmatic epistemic criteria that they propound (see chap 9, this volume). According to those epistemic criteria, any belief accepted as true (a) can be "true" only relative to (beliefs or interpretations held within) a cultural/discursive context and (b) should be warranted pragmatically by the context-dependent outcomes that follow from holding a belief as "true." Therefore, a proposition (call it Proposition X) that is "true" *for* those who inhabit Context A may not be "true" *for* those who inhabit Context B, even though Proposition X is *about* the same entity in both cases (see Held, 2006a). In short, the MGTs' "realist" epistemology is not only antiobjectivist but also not fully realist in this sense of epistemic realism/objectivism: that the truth of a proposition is independent of beliefs about its truth or conceptual schemes within discursive contexts.

Although MGTs appeal to local/perspectival discursive or interpretive and pragmatic constraints to support their ontological and epistemic "realisms," those constraints also necessarily limit the "reach" of the agency that they wish to propound (see chaps. 6–7, this volume). Therefore, for example, Martin and Sugarman (1999a, 1999b; Martin, Sugarman, & Thompson, 2003) are left to speak logically of the possibility only of "limited transcendence" or "mild innovation" owing to those "realism-granting" cultural discursive or interpretive and pragmatic constraints. My claim that the shortchanged version of "realism" that MGTs propound also shortchanges agency brings to-

---

[1] I refer here to the title of philosopher Daniel Dennett's (1984) book *Elbow Room: The Varieties of Free Will Worth Wanting*. Dennett does not appear to find in mechanistic psychological laws any threat to a free will worth wanting.

gether the two themes of the MGTs' mission, and of this volume as well: truth and agency.

Let me put all this a bit differently. I have argued that the perspectival, (weakly) relativistic, or antiobjectivist epistemology of MGTs not only fails to avoid fully the radical postmodernist/antirealist epistemologies that they reject but also deprives them of the thoroughgoing agentic psychology that they seek. My reason for saying this is based on a foundational claim: It is precisely in a universal capacity to attain objective knowledge in general, and to attain objective knowledge of human social/psychological existence in particular, that *"rational* agency" (Pols, 2005) resides. Therefore the ability to attain objective knowledge is necessary not only for (a) truth-tracking or realist inquiry (which is itself an expression of rational agency) but also for (b) an agency that grants the possibility of transcending our current circumstances, at least on the basis of reasoned or rational considerations.

Taken together (a) and (b) of course constitute the twin goals that drive the MGTs' turn to middle-ground philosophies. Yet I maintain that there is no middle-ground philosophy that grants rational agency, because no middle-ground philosophy—at least none propounded by MGTS—grants the objectivist/realist epistemology (i.e., knowledge) necessary for an agency that promotes the capacity to (self-)determine a different way to be psychologically and socially, *on rational grounds.* In their rationality-based definitions of agency, MGTs make our capacity to reason (to make sense of our circumstances in ways that are intelligible) and our capacity to know the realities of our circumstances central to their views of agency and agency's capacity for transcendence (see chap. 6, this volume).

That MGTs unite reason and knowing in their various definitions of agency may be explained by reasons that transcend their own reasons for doing so. Recall from chapter 8 our discussion of the deep relation between rationality and epistemic objectivity advanced by philosophers Nicholas Rescher and Harvey Siegel. Whereas Rescher (1997) either equates objectivity with rationality or says that objectivity "follows in rationality's wake" (p. 18), Siegel (1999c) says that rationality and objectivity are "intertwined" (p. 919) in a way that makes each a requirement for the other. Neiman and Siegel (1993) further observe, "Objectivity requires fair assessment on the basis of relevant reasons, evidence, and tests; rationality requires that such assessment be objective, i.e., fair, impartial, and independent" (p. 61). Pols (1992, 1998) unites rationality and epistemic objectivity in a different way, by calling our capacity for objective knowing *"rational* awareness."

However negatively MGTs might respond to the assertion that rationality and objective knowing are inseparable, I nonetheless contend that their search for a philosophical middle ground reflects a pervasive refusal to give mind the complete ontological/causal status it deserves. Thus despite their many valiant efforts to retain epistemic realism in the face of their antiobjectivist epistemology, MGTs not only hold a "negative philosophical judgment about knowing" but also in consequence have a lessened if not altogether negative philosophical judgment about the ontological powers (or causal force) of mind/rationality (or rational *agency*) itself. This power includes the capacity for rational awareness (or objective knowledge) of a reality that mind/rationality does not constitute in any act of knowing. This reality may therefore be properly called an independent reality, even in those cases in which the aspect of reality under investigation depends on mind in certain ways, including such mind-dependent entities as institutions and attitudes (see chaps. 5 & 8, this volume). That MGTs sometimes appeal, although in different words, to the function of mind (or mode of rational agency) that Pols (1992, 1998) calls "rational awareness"—for example, when they express their faith or belief in the existence of just that knowing power—gives us reasonable cause for hope (see chap. 9, this volume). Thus despite their antiobjectivism, some MGTs might nonetheless appreciate the deep relation between rational awareness (or objective knowing) and a rational agency (or causal power) that can help us transcend the objectively known particularities of our current circumstances.

In this final chapter, then, I focus on objective knowing as it pertains to rational agency. I argue that the act of knowing something (in the human world) that is not merely a matter of what the knower wishes or believes to be the case (i.e., objective knowing) is integral to agency (in the sense propounded by MGTs) in a way that makes objective knowing and agency inseparable. I continue to rely on the work of Siegel and Pols, each of whom finds an inherent relation between epistemic objectivity and rationality, although they express that relation in very different ways and for different purposes. Despite their profound differences, both make a case for the self-justifying nature of rationality (Siegel) or rational awareness (Pols), a justification that each claims is not viciously circular. However, the forms of justification differ: Siegel (1997) relies on rational argument to answer the question "Why be rational?" (p. 73), whereas Pols adds to his use of rational argument a self-reflexive (experiential) demonstration to justify the existence of rational awareness/objective knowing—which is a fundamental mode or expression of the rational agency he defends. Still, both claim that our universal capacity for rationality (with all the capacity for objective knowing that inheres therein) is necessary for transcendence in some sense (i.e., ontological and/or epistemic) of the particularities of our local, situated circumstances. Thus Siegel and Pols defend a form of transcendence without resorting to the antiobjectivist epistemology on which MGTs depend for *their* agentic psychology.

To put their commonality in different terms, neither Siegel nor Pols accepts the MGT claim that we are historical (or interpretation) all the way down. Nor do they accept the MGTs' belief that we need a view from nowhere (or fixed foundations) to know what is objectively true, both within and beyond the borders of our own particular circumstances. In other words, neither Siegel nor Pols accepts that warrant is merely a local, relativistic, perspectival, or pragmatic/value-laden matter. Instead warrant is a thoroughgoing epistemic matter, in the conventional normative sense of what *should* give warrant universally for any particular claim, rather than in the empirical or naturalized sense of what *does* give (perspectival or relativistic) warrant within any particular discursive context (Siegel, 1996; see chap. 9, this volume). Already we here begin to see that to appreciate transcendence in rational terms, we must appreciate the relation between particularity and universality in both ontological (Pols) and epistemic (Pols and Siegel) terms.

It is important, then, that Siegel and Pols—much like Rescher (see chap. 8, this volume)—do not find in universality and particularity an odd couple; rather, they are seen as deeply intertwined, compatible twins (as are rationality and objectivity). However, this common ground is defined differently by each, and for different purposes. Pols (1963, 1982, 1998, 2004b, 2005) makes more metaphysical commitments than does Siegel (1997, 1999a, 1999b, 2004), owing not least to his linkage of "rational awareness" (or knowing) with "rational agency" (or being). He claims that causality (a conventionally metaphysical notion) inheres in the act of objective knowing (rational awareness)[2]—which is a universal causal power deployed by any particular, embodied mind. Yet this universal causal power is "owned" by every one of us nonetheless: It is embodied within each of us, and thus we can deploy it reflexively—that is, with heightened intention (Pols, 1998, 2004b)—so that we may each demonstrate its existence to ourselves experientially.

In the final analysis, we may say that our capacity for objective knowing serves rather than subverts the cause of an agentic psychology, one grounded in a view of human nature that is rational and telic. Here I make two assertions. First, there exist no good reasons to assume that objective knowledge of human psychological kinds must consist in indubitable knowledge of timeless, universal, and mechanistically deterministic causal laws that govern the unchanging essences of brute or nonagentic entities; indeed, this constitutes the "straw man of objectivity" against which I have already argued (see chaps. 8–9). Second, there are good reasons to consider objective knowing to be a fundamental feature of a rationally agentic psychological existence. Accordingly I conclude this volume by arguing that rational agency, which I consider to be an agency "worth wanting," necessitates the power of objective knowing (not least about the human world). It is this very power of

---

[2]Although Pols equates rational awareness with direct knowing, the two terms refer to objective knowing. Hence I sometimes use the combined term *rational awareness/direct knowing* and sometimes *rational awareness/objective knowing*, depending on my intended emphasis. See chapter 8 for considerable discussion of how he and others give indirect or theoretically mediated knowing the same potential for epistemic objectivity, although Pols insists that indirect knowing ultimately depends on direct knowing/rational awareness.

mind that, ironically, MGTs deny—especially when they explicitly proclaim their negative philosophical judgment about knowing in the service of their agentic psychology.

RATIONAL TRANSCENDENCE: PARTICULARITY AND UNIVERSALITY

In chapter 6, I explored the problems that MGTs encounter when they defend agency—including agency's power to transcend the particulars of local social/psychological circumstances—while simultaneously denying mind's or rationality's power to know those circumstances with objectivity (i.e., as they are, independent of beliefs about how they are). In chapter 8 we reviewed three of their arguments against the possibility of objective knowledge of social/psychological kinds, but the one of greatest concern here is the objective fact of our local or particular situatedness, our "being in the world." This objective fact paradoxically forms the basis of the MGTs' "Antiobjectivist Argument 2": The particulars of our local situation, especially of the values that inhere in any historical/cultural/discursive/interpretive context, are said by MGTs to constrain (or determine) both (a) what we can *be* (see chaps. 4–6) and (b) what we can *know* (or rightly claim) about that being, within that context (see chaps. 8–9).

Those particulars are therefore said to constrain the generality—the (epistemic) "reach"—of what can be said with warrant (or rightly said) about human social/psychological existence. In consequence, one cannot make warranted claims about human social/psychological existence in general; that would stray well beyond the bounds of the cultural/discursive/interpretive context's practices (including the standards of warrant) in which the maker of those claims participates, however nonoppressive those practices may be. For MGTs this would constitute the wrongful imposition of "knowledge" attained within, or relative to, any local context (with all its particular, perspectival/value-laden standards of warrant) on those who inhabit other contexts (with all their particular, perspectival/value-laden standards of warrant). This would not constitute the "fusion of horizons" that hermeneutically inclined MGTs seek, but rather a bona fide imposition.

MGTs therefore typically reject epistemic objectivity, in which empirical claims about human social/psychological existence can in principle hold true *for* everyone *as knowers*, even though an objectivist epistemology does not necessitate that such claims hold true *about* everyone *as subjects of knowledge*. For example, that members of Context A argue all the time can—according to the objectivist epistemology that MGTs reject—in principle hold true for everyone who is able to entertain that claim rationally enough, regardless of their discursive/interpretive context, because it can in principle enjoy universal warrant, even though that claim may not hold true about members of Contexts B through Z.[3] In rejecting the objectivist notion that a claim can be warranted as true for all knowers, regardless of their particular discursive/interpretive contexts, MGTs hold in opposition the notions of universality and particularity—even though they work to reconcile or transcend other oppositions.

Here I present the work of Siegel and Pols, each of whom challenges the opposition of universality and particularity presumed by MGTs and radical postmodernists. Although they differ in how they appreciate the deep relation between universality and particularity, both nonetheless extend the "epistemic reach" of knowledge claims beyond the particular contexts in which those claims were warranted, in virtue of their appeal to the universals of human reason/rationality that MGTs seem at times to reject (see chaps. 6 & 8). These are the very universals of reason/rationality that make objective (or nonrelativistic/nonperspectival) knowing and knowledge possible in the first place, because they make possible the establishment of epistemic norms— or standards of warrant—that transcend the particularities of local discursive/interpretive contexts. In so extending our epistemic "reach," Siegel and Pols extend the human capacity for transcendence beyond the "reach" of what MGTs now seem to accept, especially when they speak of "mild" or "modest" transcendence or innovation.

It is important to notice that here the term *transcendence* contains two meanings, one epistemological and one ontological. The epistemological meaning we have already considered in this chapter and in chapter 9: the capacity to make claims that can in principle hold true for (although not necessarily about) those who inhabit vastly different contexts than the one in which the claims were first made and warranted. The ontological meaning we have considered in previous chapters, especially in chapter 6: the capacity to exceed what now exists—that is, to be a different way or live a different kind of life. The two meanings are of course related. To exist or live in a different way on rational terms, it must surely help to know with objectivity the realities of our own circumstances, as well as the realities that transcend our own circumstances. To be capable of knowing both kinds of realities objectively—as they are, independent of beliefs about how they are—not only enhances our capacity to take rational, "deliberative, reflective [action] . . . in framing, choosing, and executing [our actions]," which is how Martin, Sugarman, and Thompson (2003, p. 82) define "agency." Having such knowledge also makes us different beings. I elaborate that last point in due course.

---

[3]Thus there can indeed be cultural, social, or psychological differences among different groups of humans, which differences can in principle be known objectively—that is, independently of (local) beliefs about those differences.

Transcultural Normative Reach: Siegel on Epistemological Transcendence

Harvey Siegel has devoted much of his prolific career to explicating the nature of (and deep relation between) rationality and epistemic objectivity. In so doing he has made a case for what he calls "transcultural normative reach." Let us begin by considering his arguments about transcendence and relativism, especially his arguments about how we can epistemically transcend the particulars of our local situations to attain objective knowledge. Recall that although all objective truths are true *for* everyone, and so are universal truths in that sense, not all objective truths are true *about* everyone (or everything). However, Siegel also makes possible the existence of some truths that are universal in the sense that they are not only true for everyone but also (in the human world) about everyone: These are truths that pertain to the workings of rationality/reason itself, especially its deployment for purposes of judging the adequacy of claims and arguments.

In chapter 8, I presented Siegel's (2004) rejection of the MGTs' second antiobjectivist argument: that because there is no value-free view from nowhere, there can be no objective knowledge, and so relativism obtains. He refuted this argument by insisting that there can in principle be neutral epistemic standards with regard to specific disputes, despite our situated perspectives. Here I extend that argument to his views about epistemic transcendence or "reach." "Is it possible to 'transcend' one's perspective?" Siegel (2004, p. 754) asks, and he reminds us that

> it is widely acknowledged in contemporary discussion that one can never completely escape one's perspective, framework, or conceptual scheme and achieve a "God's eye view" or "a view from nowhere" (Nagel, 1986); that all cognitive activity is inevitably conducted from some ongoing perspective or point of view. (p. 754)

But Siegel (2004) dismisses this caveat; that there exists no "perspectiveless perspective" does not necessarily inhibit our ability to transcend our "frameworks and perspectives" (p. 754). Siegel continues, "We must distinguish between transcending or escaping any given perspective from transcending *all* such perspectives. Once this distinction is drawn, the 'no transcendence, therefore relativism' argument collapses" (p. 754).

Would MGTs disagree? After all, some MGTs themselves make the case for (limited) transcendence of cultural/discursive perspectives or views by way of the pluralistic or multivocal nature of culture and/or the rational/ imaginative capacities of humans (see chap. 6, this volume). Yet Siegel's (2004) call to reject relativism would be problematic for them, given their antiobjectivist commitment to perspectival and pragmatic/value-laden (and therefore relativistic) forms of warrant (see chap. 9, this volume). In any case, he gives many examples—from developmental psychology to advances in mathematical and scientific theories to consciousness raising about women and minorities—to illustrate the ability of humans to go well beyond previously held beliefs, all without having a "view from nowhere." Because the "cognizers" can themselves give good reasons for the superiority of their new beliefs/perspectives—can, that is, subject them to "critical scrutiny"—"the argument for relativism" is, according to Siegel, defeated (p. 755). Still, MGTs allow ideas to evolve within a discursive/interpretive context, without giving up their perspectival knowledge—that is, their relativist epistemology. We therefore need more to defeat the epistemic relativism that MGTs defend, however weak that form of relativism may be.

Siegel (2004) gives us more, especially in arguing that the capacity for critical scrutiny is itself not relativized (see chap. 8, this volume). This argument should prove problematic for those MGTs who rely on intracultural pluralism or multivocalism rather than on the universals of rationality/reason, to support our capacity for transcendence of the views held within our own discursive/interpretive contexts. He rightly raises the question of just what "frameworks," "conceptual schemes," or "perspectives" consist in, to refute the "framework relativist" who says that "our judgments and our ability to know is bound by them [frameworks] in a way which precludes transcendence" (p. 756). He defines these terms in general or at least generous ways (e.g., the difference between Galilean and Aristotelian views of the universe discussed in chap. 8, this volume) and concludes that the framework relativist fails even then (p. 756).[4] Yet because MGTs would surely accept the commonsense examples of transcendence given by Siegel (e.g., the possibility of consciousness raising about women and minorities), they might not qualify as "framework relativists" in his sense—despite their acceptance of at least a weakly relativistic epistemology, in which we are said always to view the world and ourselves through locally ground, value-colored "lenses" (see chap. 8, this volume).

It is when we turn to Siegel's arguments about "argument quality" and "transcultural normative reach," in his analysis of multiculturalism, that MGTs might well part company with Siegel. For it is here that he makes a case for "criteria of argument quality" or "principles of argument evaluation" that can be universal. At the least they allow arguments advanced by those working *within* a particular historical/cultural context to be valid *across* historical/cultural contexts, so they make possible arguments that are valid universally. Recall this from Rescher (1997): "That we work from within a historio-

---

[4]Siegel (2004) goes on to say,

> Attempts to resuscitate the ["no transcendence, therefore relativism"] argument minimally require a more careful explication of these terms [frameworks, conceptual schemes, or perspectives] than . . . defenders of "framework" relativism have typically given them. (p. 756)

cultural context does not limit the validity of what we say to such a context. ... That we make our assertions within time does not prevent us from asserting timeless truths" (p. 61). I cannot imagine that all MGTs would object to this statement.

Argument Quality and Transcultural Normative Reach

In an article entitled "Argument Quality and Cultural Difference," Siegel (1999b) says that the "multiculturalist argument against impersonal [i.e., abstract, transcultural] conceptions of argument quality fails ... because it itself presupposes just the kind of impersonal[5] account of argument quality it seeks to reject" (p. 183, abstract). Siegel calls this presupposition "transcultural normative reach" (p. 183) and his argument on its behalf contains elements of his argument against the antiobjectivist "no neutral standards, therefore relativism" claim (see chap. 8, this volume). Because we have been considering arguments about the nature and extent of transcendence in rational terms (i.e., rational agency), which includes arguments about both being (ontology) and knowing about being (epistemology), let us see how his argument applies to the epistemic question of argument quality itself.

Siegel (1999b) rejects the opposition of universality and particularity that he finds among some who advance the multiculturalist argument against impersonal, abstract, transcultural conceptions of argument quality. Even though some MGTs astutely criticize aspects of multiculturalism (e.g., Fowers & Richardson, 1996),[6] their historical, cultural, perspectival/relativistic conceptions of epistemic warrant support the "incompatibility" of universality and particularity that Siegel refutes.

> Let us grant that all principles of argument evaluation and criteria of argument quality are local and particular in the sense that they are inevitably articulated and endorsed in particular historical/cultural circumstances. ... Does it follow that they are therefore not universal? ... Acknowledging [this] ... does not preclude us from proclaiming their universality: that is, their legitimate applicability to arguments, considered independently of their location. ... All proclamations of universal principle emanate from particular locales. It does not follow from this, though, that such values have no legitimacy or force beyond the bounds from within which they are proclaimed or embraced. The problematic move is to regard "particularity" and "universality" as contraries, such that a principle or criterion's being one precludes it from being the other. (Siegel, 1999b, p. 193)

---

[5]See chapter 8 of this volume for Haack's (2002, 2003) argument that warrant proceeds from personal to social to impersonal forms.

[6]Fowers and Richardson (1996) discuss the "absolutistic claims" that "many postmodern, social constructionist, and multicultural theorists" inevitably make when formulating "extreme relativistic viewpoints" (p. 617).

In saying that our local, particular situatedness does not in principle preclude our setting forth principles that can legitimately transcend that situatedness, Siegel gives rationality/reason the epistemic force or "reach" that MGTs deny it. Put differently, Siegel (1999b) here rejects the MGTs' insistence that we are historical all the way down—a claim that necessarily limits the scope (as well as the objectivist backing) of the epistemic transcendence that Siegel defends. Recall from chapter 8 Siegel's antirelativistic defense of the generality, scope, or reach of rationality/reason, and objectivity's role in that defense. Also recall from chapter 9 his defense of a normative (vs. naturalized) epistemology.

None of this should appeal to MGTs, most if not all of whom would no doubt find in Siegel's epistemic arguments the decontextualized, disengaged, impersonal abstractions that they deplore when advancing their antiobjectivist/relativist forms of psychological inquiry. They might therefore be tempted to dismiss the logic of his argument (about universality and particularity) and then go on, in a more pragmatic spirit, to decry its "absolutist"[7] (or oppressive) implications. However, when we turn to Siegel's arguments against culturally relative conceptions of argument quality to defend his claims about "transcultural normative reach," we might well find that MGTs who support even weak versions of relativistic warrant are themselves vulnerable to Siegel's logic.

We have already considered Siegel's (1999b) first argument against culturally relative conceptions of argument quality in his critique of the "no neutral criteria, therefore relativism" claim. That claim, he says, contains the (hidden) presupposition of what relativists/antiobjectivists wish to refute on rational grounds.

> Any such argument must presuppose "transcultural normative reach" . . . [because it] will proceed from premises to a conclusion which is said by its proponents to follow from those premises. That it does so, if it does, will not be dependent on the cultural characteristics or commitments of those either advancing or contemplating the argument. The argument is taken by its proponents to provide good reasons for embracing its conclusion, reasons which should be found compelling by any person who fair-mindedly considers it. . . . Such transcultural normative reach must be accepted by any advocate of a culturally relative conception of argument quality who thinks that her advocacy is not only nonarbitrary, but *rational*—warranted by the reasons offered in its support. . . . The rational advocacy of commitment to the culturally relative view of argument quality presupposes the transcultural character of the normative standing of arguments (and reasons) as such. (p. 194)

---

[7]See chapter 9 of this volume for Siegel's (1997) notion of "absolutistic fallibilism" (p. 119) and his explication of a "fallibilist but absolutist conception of truth" (p. 6).

Siegel (1999b) adds to this a second challenge—that denying the possibility of transcultural normative reach (or principles of argument evaluation) prevents its critic from advancing any argument about epistemic criteria whatsoever, because the critic then has no basis for accepting or rejecting any such argument. Thus it is a self-undermining argument, as are the arguments against an objectivist epistemology and in favor of a relativist epistemology made by MGTs and others (see chap. 8, this volume).

> By denying the possibility of overarching, transcultural principles of argument evaluation and criteria of argument quality, the advocate of a culturally relative view of argument quality denies herself the ability to criticize particular, culture-bound argument-related principles and criteria; and, in doing so, likewise denies herself the ability to criticize alternatives to her favored culturally relative view itself. . . . She must . . . therefore reject the culturally relative view of argument quality. (p. 196)

MGTs are surely vulnerable to this line of argument, insofar as they want to advance the (objective) truth of their own arguments against an objectivist epistemology and in favor of a relativist epistemology, on rational grounds. Thus they too must depend on the "overarching, transcultural principles of argument evaluation" that they seem to reject in making "knowledge" (of human kinds) relative to local cultural discursive/interpretive practices. Here I would add that that dependence itself depends on the universals of rationality/reason that their epistemic relativism precludes. This makes their argument self-undermining, and what undermines itself cannot (logically or rationally) be used to advance anything else. Let me put this important point more precisely: Because the antiobjectivist epistemology MGTs advocate in the service of human agency (including the capacity for transcendence of current circumstances) is self-undermining, it also undermines any form of psychological inquiry, including one based on an agentic view of human nature. Thus it cannot be used in the service of agency itself.

Siegel, then, helps us see the universality that inheres in rationality/reason, at least in the form of "overarching, transcultural principles of argument evaluation" (1999b, p. 196) or what he elsewhere calls the "universality of argumentative force" (1999a, p. 406). That universality pierces the heart of arguments on behalf of situated (i.e., nonuniversalist) epistemologies, including those advanced by MGTs. After all, one need not be a positivist in the sense of advocating the formal or content-free deductive rules[8] sought (unsuccessfully) by logical positivists/empiricists to agree that reason—as well as observation—is integral to objective knowing and knowledge. In posing his argument with a fair-minded or open-minded opponent,

---

[8]Siegel (1999a) argues against the separation of formal logic and content: "The universality of argumentative force . . . involves . . . not just 'formal principles of logical relation' but 'the assertive content of thought' as well" (p. 406).

Siegel (1999b) asks for the open-mindedness that many MGTs themselves propound when speaking of transcendence in terms of a Gadamerian "fusion of horizons" or a dialogical stance. However, unlike them, Siegel does not contend that we are limited by an "open-mindedness" or "fairness" (i.e., a form of rationality/reason) itself limited by its historical/cultural constraints or constitution—after all, transcending particularity to attain universality in the knowing process (on objective terms) is not only possible but also has been actualized in many different domains (see Siegel, 2004, p. 755). For Siegel this constitutes bona fide transcendence, and not absolutistic dogma.

Siegel, of course, has the universal features of rationality (with its attendant objectivity) at his disposal to make his case for the possibility of universal, objective knowledge arrived at by those who necessarily inhabit particular contexts (see chap. 8). That case consists in his argument for epistemic transcendence on the basis of transcultural normative reach. But then so too do MGTs have the universal features of rationality (with its attendant capacity for objectivity) at their disposal in making their case against the possibility of objective knowledge of both (a) universals about human social/psychological existence and (b) aspects of human social/psychological existence that may apply only to those who inhabit certain contexts (e.g., cultural differences; see note 3). MGTs have this rational capacity, agency, or power, however much they may deny their own use of rationality's universal features to make their negative case.

Argument Quality and Transcultural Normative Reach Continued: Multiculturalism

Despite touting only perspectival/relativistic forms of epistemic warrant (see chap. 9, this volume), some MGTs seem to acknowledge—or at least openly deploy—universal features of rationality in ways that call to mind Siegel's arguments. For instance, Fowers and Richardson (1996), in an article entitled "Why Is Multiculturalism Good?," rightly call for the "recognition that multiculturalism is self-undermining . . . because it untenably combines an overarching relativism with specific universal ethical principles" (p. 615). How, they ask, can we accept the equality of all cultural practices—including those that reject tolerance and respect—while adhering to universal moral standards regarding tolerance and respect? "For how could one defend the principles of cultural equality, tolerance, and respect within a relativistic viewpoint?" (p. 616).

Although Fowers and Richardson (1996) speak here of moral values and not epistemic values per se, given their (and other MGTs') claim that there can be no fact/value distinction in the human sciences (see chap. 8, this volume), their argument can be extended to epistemic principles, in which rationality typically plays some role. It is therefore noteworthy that they appear to advance a universal conception of rationality, although only implicitly, in saying, "The price of seeing all cultures as equal is nothing less than the loss of the rational defense and promotion of any way of life" (p. 616). Note that "rational defense" is not here qualified or relativized by the words "our type of." Thus they seem to take for granted that there exists the rational defense that we all have at our disposal and that we all presuppose when we promote the virtues of any way of life—including our own. In this they sound like Siegel, who says that cultural relativists presuppose the very transcultural or universal rationality that they deny when making their case for cultural relativism.

But perhaps I make too much of all this. For rather than explicitly propounding a universal rationality/reason or "transcultural normative reach," Fowers and Richardson (1996) express their familiar desire to get "beyond objectivism and relativism." They do not expressly acknowledge that they themselves rely on their own universal powers of rationality to defend their hermeneutic solution to the problem of cultural relativism in particular, and human science inquiry in general. Thus Fowers and Richardson (1996) seem to pitch their rational defense not just to the converted, but also to fair- or open-minded (i.e., rational) opponents.

> Fostering openness to cultural truth claims offers a promising alternative to untenably objectivist and enervatingly relativist views of culture. The hermeneutic claim that it is appropriate to speak . . . of the validity or "truth" of cultural or moral values presupposes that some norms and practices, in particular contexts, are better or more decent than others. . . . We do feel that it is possible to move beyond objectivism and relativism (Bernstein, 1983) in human science inquiry. (p. 617)

Much to their credit, Fowers and Richardson (1996) recoil from the extreme relativism of radical postmodernists, especially that of Gergen and Rorty. Thus their hermeneutic solution is said to moderate the epistemic objectivism of modern/conventional psychological science and the radical relativism of strong postmodernism.

> Many postmodern, social constructionist, and multicultural theorists respond to these dilemmas by insisting that all standards of rationality and value are ultimately arbitrary conventions of a particular society (Gergen, 1994; Rorty, 1987), or mere "truth effects" or the effects of power (Foucault, 1984). But it seems impossible to formulate such extreme relativistic viewpoints without making absolutistic claims that rival the pretensions of the scientism or objectivism they wish to displace. (p. 617)

Do Fowers and Richardson (1996) notice that they too seem to presuppose (and thus rely on) an impersonal, transcultural or universal (conception of) rationality (or argument quality), with all its objectivist epistemic potential, when making their case for contextualized, situated knowing and being—a case in which perspectival/relativist (i.e., nonobjectivist) forms of warrant obtain (see chap. 9, this volume)? Although they say that "it is possible that this [moral] relativism may be ultimately irrefutable" (p. 617), here

they also seem to hope for the possibility of universal/transcultural normative reach, at least with regard to moral truth.

> The hermeneutic perspective regards the moral visions inherent in cul-
> tural traditions as legitimate claims to truth that have validity not only
> for those living in the tradition, but potentially for all of us. Genuinely
> and openly engaging in this exploration of what is of value does not
> involve rejecting the idea of standards or ideals in a relativistic manner.
> (pp. 618–619)

The problem is that the hermeneutic "fusion of horizons" propounded
by Fowers and Richardson does not operate between or beyond objectivism
and relativism in any obvious way. As they indicate elsewhere, it contains all
the perspectival pragmatic/value-laden forms of epistemic warrant that such
forms of relativism invoke. For example, Richardson, Fowers, and Guignon
(1999) quoted philosopher David Hoy (1986, p. 124) in saying that "'theory
choice in the social sciences is . . . more relativistic than in the natural sciences, since the principles used to select social theories would be guided by a
variety of values'" (p. 178). They also said that "knowledge claims are adjudicated within a social order that incorporates and strives to fulfill a more or
less explicit set of values" (p. 154; see chap. 9, this volume, for more quotations). That they repeatedly pronounce all beliefs to be fallible or defeasible
does not make a particular belief any less objectively true, because fallibility
is a feature of objectivity (see chap. 8, this volume). However, Fowers and
Richardson's (1996) belief in our ability to arrive at "moral visions" that
"have validity . . . potentially for all of us" (p. 618), by "hazard[ing]" our
"deepest beliefs in the flux of conversation" (p. 619), suggests a belief in, or
at least the possible presupposition of, a universal rational capacity or function (see chaps. 8–9, this volume)—something that invokes Siegel's notion
of "transcultural normative reach."

We thus return to Siegel (1999b), who anticipates that some may accuse him of imposing his own particular form of "reason" to make his case for
the universality of reason or transcultural normative reach. I refer here to a
section entitled "Argumentation, Rhetoric, and Power," in which he considers "skepticism toward the very idea of argumentative or epistemic
normativity."

> The claim that a given argument is a good one, in that its premises pro-
> vide justification for its conclusion, is (it may be said) not really a claim
> about normative status at all, since there is "in the world" no such thing.
> Such claims, rather, are simply rhetorical devices, which serve to mask
> the exercise of power. . . . That certain principles and criteria of argu-
> ment quality are seen as legitimate is itself no more than a reflection of
> the power enjoyed by those able to establish them as such. (p. 196)

Siegel (1999b) makes three points in response to this anticipated charge.
First, he points out that "this skepticism concerning the very idea of argu-

ment quality . . . plagues culture-relative as well as transcultural views of argument quality, since according to it the former as well as the latter are mere rhetorical exercises of power" (p. 197). Thus (and second), why should we embrace this view of argument quality? "The rational defense of the view requires that some rhetorical efforts are more probatively forceful, and some exercises of rhetorical power more legitimate, than others—and so, that argument quality is not *merely* a matter of rhetoric and power" (p. 197)? Third, if the "advocate" of the rhetorical view denies "any sense of 'rational superiority' other than the rhetorical/power one . . . , [she may] be flatly uninterested in establishing the rational superiority of her view" (p. 197).

The problem with such disinterest, says Siegel, is that although it "embodies an admirable consistency" it comes with a cost: "This 'advocate' seems clearly enough not to be engaging the issue [of argument quality]" (pp. 197–198). Here I would add that any such "advocate" who embraced the (culturally dependent or local) pragmatic/value-laden criteria of warrant advanced by many MGTs (see chap. 9, this volume), could say that argument quality is rationally assessed on the basis of those (relativistic) criteria. However, her very advocacy of those relativistic criteria—although different than Siegel's normative (nonrelativistic) criteria—would require some (nonrelativistic) notion and use of rationality nonetheless. We have seen a similar argument in the writings of radical postmodernists/constructionists who say that they do not claim their views to be any more true or rational than those of others—except in virtue of their (true and rational) pragmatic consequences: "I am not trying to 'get it right' about the nature of science, reality, the mind, truth, objectivity, and so on. My chief aims are transformative" (Gergen, 2001a, p. 419).

To be sure, Siegel (1999b, pp. 194, 196) would reject such pragmatic epistemic criteria on the grounds that they do not rely on rationality in his normatively intended sense, in which the force of an argument should depend on how well its conclusions follow logically from its premises. Siegel (1999a, 1999b) defends the universality that inheres in his normative (nonnaturalized) epistemic criteria, in explaining how such universality is presupposed by anyone who tries to persuade an opponent of the correctness of his views, which persuasive force or "reach" is not "dependent on the cultural characteristics or commitments of those either advancing or contemplating the argument" (1999b, p. 194; see also Siegel, 1996, and chap. 9, this volume). Some, however, would disagree on the empirical (or naturalized) epistemic grounds that different cultures have different tacit epistemologies, which give rise to different basic cognitive processes. For these critics, then, the type of argument one uses to persuade an open- or fair-minded opponent must take that opponent's culture—especially its accepted form of argument—into consideration. This is in fact an implication of the argument espoused by Nisbett, Peng, Choi, and Norenzayan (2001).

Nisbett, Peng, Choi, and Norenzayan (2001) find radically different forms of what they call "sociocognitive systems" (p. 294) in their comparison of Eastern and Western approaches to perception and cognition. They therefore speak of "situated cognition" (p. 306) in ways that sound not unlike the "situated knowing" of MGTs: "Thought always occurs in a pragmatic problem setting, including the cultural assumptions that are brought to the task" (p. 306). They say that although "the assumption of universality of cognitive processes lies deep in the psychological tradition" (p. 305), "tacit or even explicit normative standards for thought will differ across cultures" (p. 306). At the most abstract level, they characterize the cognitive processes of East Asians to be holistic and those of Westerners to be more analytic. To be more precise, there is a "tradition in Eastern philosophy that is opposed at its roots to the formal logic tradition [of the West], namely the dialectical approach. . . . It involves transcending, accepting, or even insisting on the contradiction among premises" (p. 301). Westerners, by contrast, are committed "to avoiding the appearance of contradiction" by way of such laws as the law of "identity," of "noncontradiction," and of the "excluded middle . . . [in which] any statement is either true or false" (p. 301). They predict that evidence of such differences in traditions will be found upon contemporary empirical investigation.

> One of the strongest implications of the notion that Westerners adhere to a logical analysis of problems is that, when presented with apparently contradictory propositions, they should be inclined to reject one in favor of the other. Easterners, on the other hand, committed to the principle of the Middle Way, might be inclined to embrace both propositions, finding them each to have merit. (Nisbett et al., 2001, p. 302)

Nisbett, Peng, Choi, and Norenzayan's (2001) findings are vast and impressive, and the authors put them forth with all due objectivity. They conclude that "psychologists who choose not to do cross-cultural psychology may have chosen to be ethnographers instead" (p. 307). Yet questions remain. Not least is this: Which form of rationality do they themselves use to persuade the reader of the correctness of *their* views about the existence of culture-dependent forms of rationality, and would they use different forms of argument to persuade East Asians of these differences than they would use to persuade Westerners of these differences? They do not say. Instead, they give us a generic or culture-free conclusion: "We hope to have persuaded the reader that the cognitive processes triggered by a given situation may not be so universal as generally supposed" (p. 307).

I do not question the obvious (objectivist) claim that different cognitive approaches to problems exist, even within cultures. Yet despite their own conclusion, Nisbett et al. (who themselves come from and work in different cultural contexts) nonetheless collaborated to obtain their findings of cultural difference, and evidently hope to persuade others of the legitimacy of their findings—independently of the cultural contexts of those others. This suggests that they at least implicitly presuppose—and thus rely on—the universals of human rationality that enable them (as scientists) and the rest of us (as consumers of their science) to appreciate cultural differences, in a spirit of open-mindedness called for by Siegel and by those MGTs who hope for (epistemic) transcendence by way of a "fusion of horizons" or dialogical encounter with the "other."

In *Rationality Redeemed?* Siegel (1997) says that he has "been arguing only that the particular *can* be universal as well; the two are not mutually exclusive. A stronger thesis, that universality is *required* for the justification of particular claims, is one that I endorse" (p. 216, note 31). He criticizes Alisdair MacIntyre, to whom Richardson et al. (1999) appeal, for failing to notice that his claim that "there are no general timeless standards" is "*itself* a 'general timeless,' i.e. acontextual/ahistorical, standard of the sort he claims to eschew. The same can be said of his acontextual/ahistorical *defense* of that standard" (Siegel, 1997, pp. 216–217, note 31).

The Inherently Transcendent Fusion of Universality and Particularity: Pols on Ontological and Epistemic Transcendence

Given his commitment to the universality of rationality, Edward Pols would probably have agreed with Siegel's epistemic arguments about transcultural normative reach. However, Siegel's logical/rational defense of the compatibility of universality and particularity in judging argument quality (and even the necessity of universality for the justification of particular claims) might also have left Pols unsatisfied, owing to the deep metaphysical commitments that he makes in expressing his views about the inherent existential (or ontological) fusion of universality and particularity in all aspects of being. In setting forth his metaphysics, Pols therefore insists on a universality both in being and in knowing (itself an instance of being) that MGTs might reject, owing to their claims about our situated or nonuniversal (social/psychological) ontology of "being in the world" and about our situated or nonuniversal and nonobjective/relativistic "knowledge" of that local being or existence.

In chapter 8 we considered Pols's (1992) expression of the fusion (in any act of rational awareness/direct knowing; see note 2, this chapter) of the "rational pole's" "universal, symbol-generating transcendence of the here and now" with the "experiential pole's" "sense-based receptivity" to reality by way of the "particularity of the here and now" (p. 156). Recall this statement: "Rational awareness is *reason experiencing* rather than reason responding to experience" (p. 155). Here I elaborate Pols's (1998) ontological extension of this fusion to the entity to be known, as well as to the knower herself,[9] by way of the so-called U-factor (for unity/universality) and P-factor (for particularity).

> The U-factor . . . can be understood as a universal source of order of which the laws of nature as formulated in any era of history give us a partial expression. . . . That formal order . . . [is] the source of the order we try to express in morality, art, and science. We appeal to it whenever we refuse to accept as thoroughly definitive any particular inherited code of conduct. . . . Any truly creative artist appeals to it in the same way. When Mozart is composing, he is not confined to what is particular to himself, nor does he work only under the formal strictures of an inherited style and tradition. So also with science. Max Planck . . . did not work exclusively on the basis of his own temperament and tradition, nor was he confined within the theoretic framework of the science he had in mind. (pp. 123–124)

Pols's arguments about being and knowing are not of the usual sort: He does not expect us to accept them on the basis of rational/logical argument alone, but rather directs our attention to our own knowing process in the act of rational awareness/direct knowing itself, to test them experientially. We shall consider this "reflexive" form of justification in the next section. Here we must attend directly to Pols's description of the tension that he finds between the U-factor and the P-factor, which are inextricably fused in any entity that is known directly (e.g., a tree, bird, person, house, equation, theory, painting, or poem). Thus human kinds—indeed, human beings themselves and the products of the "formative function of their rationality"[10] (e.g., houses, equations, theories, paintings, and poems)—are included in his ontology.

In this next quotation, Pols (1998) deliberately uses causal language (mind quite literally "reaches out," although not in Siegel's sense of "transcultural normative reach") to describe an agent's rational awareness (or objective knowing; see note 2) of an independent reality; it is the *causal* feature of the knowing process that gives agents one aspect of their (rational) agency, including their capacity for transcendence. In a sense, then, we transcend our own particularity as we causally "take in" what is independent of our knowing faculties.

> The *rational* pole of rational awareness reaches out at first to a concept or universal ("tree," "person," "triangle," for example) whose ontological

---

[9]Who, in the case of self-knowledge, is of course also the entity to be known.
[10]See Pols (1992) and Held (1995, chap. 6) for the distinction between what Pols calls the "rational awareness" (or direct knowing) and "formative" (or constructive) functions of mind/rationality, a distinction whose conflation he and I find at the root of much postmodernist/antiobjectivist epistemological confusion. In short, the formative function makes entities—both temporospatial (nonlinguistic) entities, such as houses and paintings, and nontemporospatial (linguistic) entities, such as theories and propositions—that can then themselves be known directly by way of rational awareness. Theories may give us indirect (objective) knowledge of a reality that we cannot know directly, such as the physics of the very large or very small.

status remains a continuing puzzle, and it uses this universal to classify or categorize the particular thing. Sometimes [e.g., as in Plato's forms or Aristotle's essences] the knower imputes to the universals a causal role in the particular. . . . Our modern epistemological tradition, troubled by a lack of confidence in the mind's powers, tends to think of universals as originating in mind and used by mind to project an *apparent* entity—in effect producing a unity and stability where there is in fact only a multiplicity of particular stimuli. (p. 118)

That last sentence gives one explanation—a negative philosophical judgment about knowing—for the unstable "ontology of flux and flow" to which some MGTs appeal to deny universals/essences (in the human world) and on that basis to reject the ontological stability needed for objective psychological knowledge (see chap. 8, this volume). Yet Pols (1998) insists that "the unity of the [thing] known is intrinsic rather than imposed, and that absolute universality is intrinsic to its unity" (p. 118).[11]

Most important, Pols maintains that we find rather than impose universality in whatever particularity we encounter when we access any reality directly by means of our powers of rational awareness. We nonetheless deploy (general) categories or concepts (see chap. 8, this volume) formed by other rational powers (i.e., the formative function of rationality; see note 10, this chapter) to articulate the nature of the particular reality that we can in principle know—get hold of—with objectivity, as we actively/agentically "reach out" to take it in. That we can "do violence" (Pols, 1998, p. 119) to that particular reality in the process of characterizing the generality that inheres in our (own particular) experience of it does not mean we must do violence to it. Still, the possibility of such violence suggests a fallibilism that Pols (1998) nonetheless shares both with other epistemic objectivists and with MGTs (who are antiobjectivists): "Like common sense in general, direct knowing can be in error; but closer attention to the matter at hand [at least in commonsense settings] is usually enough to rectify its mistakes" (p. 101).

Recall, for example, this statement made by Guignon (2002a), in which he expresses a variation on Pols's last assertion. In so doing he too reveals a faith in our knowing powers, although his faith serves a relativistic notion of truth that is logically problematic, as well as inconsistent with Pols's antirelativistic epistemology: "Since truth is always relativized to a context of interests and aims, most cases of apparent conflict can be resolved once one grasps the contexts to which claims of correctness are relativized" (p. 282). Presumably neither Guignon's (and our) grasp of the "contexts to which claims of correctness are relativized" nor the universal/nonrelativistic truth that "truth is always relativized to a context," is itself relativized—hence the logical problem of which Siegel spoke.

---

[11]For elaboration see Pols (1998, pp. 118–119).

Pols (1998) has much to say about the particularity of the experiential pole of rational awareness, which particularity he does not shortchange in the least.

> It is indeed a multiplicity of particulars we are experientially engaged with, and the simultaneous confrontation of the U-factor only means that when we are rationally aware of a particular we are also aware that it shares in a unity that all particulars share in. (p. 119)

In *Radical Realism* Pols (1992) expressed this a bit differently, but the same message is given. Note that our concepts and categories are themselves derived from experience with the real and hence are fallible. Yet it is the participation of all particular beings or entities in an "ontic universality"— in reality itself—that makes possible our derivation of concepts that can and often do make contact with and express the real by virtue of the "formative powers of our rationality" (see note 10). These rational powers are themselves "participants" in the universals of which Pols speaks.

> Any directly known particular is thus attained not just as something that may be brought under the universality of concepts and categories but as something that participates in an ontic universality that makes possible the derivative universality of concepts and categories. (p. 212)

Although others who work to justify our capacity for objective knowledge do not do so on the basis of Pols's grand-scale metaphysics, they nonetheless make observations consistent with his. For example, the previous quotation calls to mind the words of Maze (2001; see chap. 5, this volume): "Everything cognizable is of a kind, that is, has universality, and . . . also has particularity" (p. 397). Recall also Haack's (2003) contention that inquiry requires that particulars be instances of generals (see chap. 5, this volume). Even Liebrucks (2001), himself an MGT, allows for universals of personhood at the highest level of abstraction, although these universals are too abstract for the contextualized or local concrete meaning rules and conventions that should constitute the content of a "proper form" of psychological inquiry (see chaps. 5 & 9, this volume).

According to Pols (1998), our rational agentic capacity for transcendence is dependent on the participation of each particular entity in universality. Here he offers a glimpse of his conception of transcendence in the epistemic sense of cognitive access to the universality or Being (with a capital B) that is the Reality (with a capital R) that transcends the particulars we experience/know rationally. It is just that universality or Being that, he claims, inheres (ontologically) in all particularities (or beings) in virtue of the U-factor.

> Characterization of the U-factor is always flawed: break it up, for whatever good reason—and the imperatives of science, theology, morals, or art are very good reasons—and we have lost it. Lost it, however, only if

we do not acknowledge that one consequence of finitude is that we tend to make things [via the formative function of rationality] out of the presence of that which we have not made and which is not exhaustively available to us. We have not made the U-factor, and it is not exhaustively available to us. That does not mean that Being in the sense of transcendence is not accessible to our reason: it is as cognitively accessible as my cat on the mat or your book before your eyes. But it is accessible as *transcending* each of the particulars that participate in it. (p. 119)

"Being in the sense of transcendence is . . . accessible to our reason," says Pols (1998). This is so because, recall, "any directly known particular . . . participates in an ontic universality that makes possible the derivative universality of our concepts and categories" (Pols, 1992, p. 212). Would Siegel (1997) agree? He does not, to my knowledge, draw a distinction (and then claim a deep metaphysical relation) between Being and being, as does Pols. Nor does he speak of universality and transcendence in (Pols's) expressly metaphysical terms. Yet he does speak of access to "universals" in epistemic terms when he defends the "universality of argumentative force" (Siegel, 1999a, p. 406), which itself depends on the possibility of a normative epistemology that is in no way relativistic. It is just that epistemic normativity that allows claims to transcend the time or place (i.e., the circumstances) in which they were first articulated and warranted—that is, to have "transcultural normative reach." Recall his (1997) endorsement of this "stronger thesis": "that universality is *required* for the justification of particular claims, is. . . [a thesis] that I endorse" (p. 216, note 31). Siegel, then, propounds the necessity of a universal *rationality* for epistemic purposes—that is, to justify claims of any sort. These are the "general timeless acontextual/ahistorical standards" of rationality/reason in action for which he takes MacIntyre to task for denying—even as MacIntyre, according to Siegel (1997), deploys them in the act of denying them to justify his particular claims. This is certainly an epistemological argument, and so it relies on (the universals of) logical force, good reasons, or rationality itself.

Although Pols would surely agree, he does not limit his discussion of transcendence to epistemic matters of justification. He also provides an ontological basis for nonrelativistic epistemologies, such as the one Siegel propounds, in which "transcultural normative reach" or epistemic transcendence is made possible in the first place. That is, Pols concerns himself with our being, in all its (ontological) particularity, but with the insistence that we are always "participating actively" in Being (with a capital B) that transcends our particularity (i.e., universality or the U-factor). We achieve such ontological transcendence by way of our "participant powers" (or "rational agency"), among which our agentic capacity for rational awareness/objective knowing is prominent. (Recall that for him knowing about being is itself an instance of being.) Pols (1992) recognizes that his metaphysical commitments will be seen as going too far by those who recoil from "metaphysical speculation": "To some readers this will seem hopelessly speculative" (p. 213).

I submit that Pols's metaphysical "speculation" is no more speculative than that of MGTs, who reject Gergen's (failed) attempts to remain "ontologically mute" (see chap. 4) and who in the name of realism limit our ontological and epistemological potential or agency to the constraints of the historical/cultural/discursive/interpretive contexts that allegedly make us what we are "all the way down" (see chaps. 4–6). Siegel and Pols, by contrast, give us all the potential for ontological (Pols) and epistemological (Pols and Siegel) transcendence of circumstantial particularity that one could want in seeking an agentic view of human nature on which to ground the discipline of psychology. Although they do this in different ways, neither Siegel nor Pols resorts to the antiobjectivist epistemology of MGTs.

To be more precise, Pols (1998) supports his objectivist epistemology ontologically by maintaining that although knowers can rationally access even a human reality that is independent of—or "distinct from"—their knowing processes, they can do so owing to "a profound affinity between knower and known by way of the U-factor intrinsic to each" (pp. 119–120). Pols's appeal to the U-factor to justify our capacity to "cognitively assimilate" (p. 119) or know an independently existing reality is "metaphysically speculative" in ways that exceed my own cognitive comfort, grasp, or intuitions. Nonetheless I am reminded of others who say something similar, although certainly in less far-reaching (metaphysical) terms. For example, recall Haack's (2002, p. 88) attempt to resolve the tension between independence (of the entity to be known) and accessibility (of that entity by the knower) by way of a "modest enough" understanding of independence and a "fallibilist enough" understanding of accessibility (see chap. 5, this volume).

Pols's metaphysics, by contrast, can hardly be characterized as middle ground or modest: After all, he uses the term *radical realism* to describe his epistemology, and that term surely applies as well to the metaphysics (e.g., the U-factor) that supports it. He continually emphasizes without qualification the independence of the knower and the known; it is just that independence that grants us the ability to know the other with all due objectivity. Yet the knower and the known's simultaneous participation in and/or expression of the U-factor gives them an "affinity" that makes possible our rational awareness or objective knowledge of that independent reality (including the reality of human psychological existence) as it exists, independently of our knowing processes and beliefs about its nature.

To put Pols's point somewhat differently, whatever the particulars of our cultural situatedness may be (among other forms of particularity), they are not as limiting as MGTs suppose, because they have within them all the universality needed for our ability to transcend their constraining influence. We always "participate" (to use Pols's term) in that universality—indeed, we cannot not participate in it—in virtue of our existence itself. Pols (1998) includes in his categorization of the many aspects of that existence our (mental) acts of rational awareness (or objective knowing; see note 2) of particulars, which acts always grant some nonexhaustive access to the universality in which those particulars participate.

If Pols is right about the relation of universality and particularity, the implications are profound. Most relevant to our current discussion is that we then require a "view from somewhere"—that is, a particular or situated view—to gain access to generality by way of particularity. This runs contrary to the prevailing wisdom of many, including MGTS, who think that we need a "view from nowhere" or "God's-eye view" to know (especially entities in the human world) with objectivity (see chap. 8, this volume). That Pols (1998) takes particularity as seriously as possible is indicated in his expression "P-factor" and in his use of the term *rational respect* (p. 117) to characterize the demand made on us by the particular entities we work to know, in all their distinct and independent existence.

And yet, Pols says, we always in a sense do transcend even our own particularity in the everyday process of being and knowing, owing to the universality that inheres in any instance of particularity. Moreover, we always have the potential to transcend what now exists in remarkable ways (rather than in the merely limited or modest ways on which some MGTs insist), although that potential may not always be fulfilled for a multitude of reasons (e.g., contentment with the status quo, or overwhelming demoralization). In any case, according to Pols, we must heighten the reflexivity inherent in every act of rational awareness of some particular entity to see that this is so—that is, to justify his claims about rational awareness itself. In considering rationality with attention to its reflexive features, we should be in a better position to assess whether Siegel's and Pols's arguments about our ability to reach beyond or transcend the particulars of our local circumstances (on objectivist terms) can be justified—by the self-justificatory or reflexive nature of rationality itself.

REFLEXIVITY REVISITED

Recall from chapter 5 the "reflexive ontology" or "theory of reflexivity" put forth by MGTs (e.g., Martin et al., 2003; Richardson et al., 1999) to deny the possibility of objective psychological knowledge, because that theory precludes the independence of the knower and the known deemed necessary for epistemic objectivity (see also chaps. 7–8, this volume). Given many MGTs' reliance on the Giddens-like reflexive relationship between being and knowing (about being) to champion their antiobjectivist epistemology (i.e., we are what we interpret ourselves to be), it is noteworthy that Siegel and Pols also rely on reflexivity to serve their objectivist epistemologies. Yet the latter deploy reflexivity in different ways and for different purposes, not only from each other but also from MGTs, whose antiobjectivist epistemology both Siegel and Pols reject. Given the deep relation between rationality and objective knowing on which both Siegel and Pols insist, it is not surprising that they would want to justify (the use of) rationality (Siegel) and the objective knowing powers that help constitute our rational agency (Pols). Can any of this be done by appealing reflexively to reason or rationality itself?

Although Siegel and Pols rely on rationality reflexively in different ways to defend their claims about rationality, they both deploy rationality's powers to justify the powers or force of rationality and claim to avoid any vicious circularity in so doing. Siegel's defense consists in a self-reflexive use of reason to justify the use of reason: He makes a rational case for being rational (which for him is intertwined with epistemic objectivity; see chap. 8, this volume). Pols, by contrast, asks us to take a reflexive turn literally—that is, to turn our attention inward—so that we may attend directly to rational awareness/direct knowing itself in action. He aims to help us observe directly and personally our universal capacity to know the real objectively, as it is, so that we can each see for ourselves that his is not an objectivist's illusion or expression of mere "Cartesian Anxiety." Although he says that taking this reflexive turn will heighten for us (and so make directly accessible to us) the "belief component" inherent in any act of rational awareness, he does not want us to believe this merely on the basis of (a) his (or anyone's) rational arguments, (b) how things merely "seem" to us in first-person terms (cf. Dennett, 1991; Wegner, 2002) without benefit of (direct) observation, or (c) faith/belief itself—hence his reflexive exercise. Their taken-for-granted (universal) capacity for just this kind of reflexivity/self-awareness in the act of knowing may explain how some MGTs manage to maintain faith in their own ability to know with all due objectivity both (a) the historical/cultural/discursive/interpretive circumstances in which humans exist and (b) the implications of those circumstances for psychological existence (see chap. 9, this volume), despite their commitment to an antiobjectivist epistemology.

Siegel's "Self-Reflexive" Defense of Rationality

Siegel (1997) defends rationality against a pervasive charge made by its many critics: that there is a vicious circularity, an "unremovable circularity in offering reasons for being rational" (p. 74), such "that attempts to justify rationality must be question begging or circular" (p. 75). Hence the critics conclude, "The impossibility of providing a noncircular justification of rationality shows that the demand for such a justification is an illegitimate demand; that it is a mistake to suppose that rationality needs to be justified" (p. 75). There is, according to the critics, "'something paradoxical in the very attempt to produce a reasoned defence of reason itself'" (O'Hear, as cited in Siegel, 1997, p. 75).

Siegel (1997) claims that reasoned defense of reason is not only possible but also necessary. The demand for such a defense is thus legitimate. Accordingly he responds to the "fundamental reflexive difficulty" that the critics of rational justification of rationality find in that endeavor, by showing that they are wrong in concluding that "what it [rationality] urges generally, it cannot satisfy itself" (p. 77). Siegel says, "The demand for reasons which warrant a commitment to rationality is as legitimate a demand as is the demand for reasons which warrant any other claim, position or commitment" (p. 77). He argues that there is a "self-reflexive strategy" that can justify rationality without producing reasons that "must be viciously circular or question-begging" (p. 77).

Siegel (1997) rejects Popper's "solution" to the problem that we "irrationally embrace rationalism" (p. 79) by simply accepting an irrational reason for being rational—faith in reason: "Critical rationalism . . . recognizes the fact that the fundamental rationalist attitude results from an . . . act of faith—from faith in reason" (Popper, as cited in Siegel, 1997, p. 78). This is interesting given the faith in our ability to know (at least local) aspects of human social/psychological existence (as they are), faith that is sometimes expressed explicitly by MGTs (see chap. 9, this volume). To be sure, MGTs' faith in knowing the conditions of our social/psychological existence objectively is not necessarily the same as faith in the universals of reason/rationality itself, although Siegel indeed links rationality and objectivity by asserting their interdependence (see chap. 8, this volume). Recall, moreover, that in Pols's description of *rational* awareness, we see that rationality/reason (in the form of a conceptual factor) is intrinsic to objective knowing (see chap. 8, this volume).

Here notice that Siegel (1997), like Pols, does not settle for faith in these matters. He demands reason—more precisely, the justification *of* reason *by* reason—to defend not a limited (e.g., "critical") form of rationalism, but a "comprehensive rationalism" (p. 79). The logical problems that critics find in this defense disappear, says Siegel, if we are willing to accept "a certain kind of argument strategy—a *self-reflexive* strategy—that promises to supply the wanted justification without the attendant logical difficulties" (p. 80). He finds just this kind of strategy in a variety of circumstances in which "charges of inconsistency, circularity, and question-begging seem to threaten" (p. 80), beginning with evolutionary theory.

> Evolutionary theory can explain . . . the evolution of creatures capable of reformulating evolutionary theory itself. It can [also self-reflexively] explain (at least in principle) its own evolution, . . . from its earliest formulations to a theory very much more complex. . . . The theory contributes to its own explanation . . . without being inconsistent or engaging in viciously circular or question-begging reasoning. (p. 80)

Siegel goes on to say that "philosophical theories often need to be, and are, self-reflexive in this way" (p. 80), and he uses theories of epistemic justification to illustrate his point.

> Theorists of various epistemological persuasions—foundationalists, coherentists, pragmatists, naturalists, etc.—regularly offer accounts of epistemic justification which they hope . . . will turn out themselves to be justified in their own terms. Such accounts self-reflexively apply to themselves. But they are not necessarily logically defective for doing so. . . . Foundationalists hope to show that foundationalism follows appropriately from appropriate foundational beliefs; coherentists hope to show that coherentism most adequately coheres with other relevant beliefs; naturalists hope to show that naturalism is the theory of justification most justified by naturalist epistemological inquiry. (pp. 80–81)

To these examples I would add pragmatists, who hope to show that pragmatism—the preferred epistemology of many (if not all) MGTs (see chap. 9)—is itself justified by the pragmatic consequences of advocating that form of epistemic warrant.

Siegel's (1997) answer to the skeptic's question "Why be rational?" deploys a form of the argument that we have already seen in his response to relativists who challenge the "transcultural normative reach" of justified claims and in his response to those who advance the "no neutral criteria, therefore relativism" argument (see chap. 8, this volume). The form of argument Siegel deploys is one in which the critic presupposes what he sets out to refute.

> [In asking "Why be rational?"] the sceptic is playing the rationalist's game. Indeed she is presupposing rationalism, in that she is asking for reasons which justify a position in order to determine whether or not the position is actually justified or is worthy of embrace. . . . In presupposing it [rationalism], she is inadvertently determining the outcome of her inquiry: rationality, and the commitment to it, cannot help but turn out to be themselves rationally justified. (p. 82)

In short, Siegel (1997) argues that the skeptic cannot genuinely or seriously ask the question without undermining her own position—that is, without

> committing herself to take seriously putative reasons for being rational. Consequently, she is acknowledging the potential epistemic force of reasons which purport to answer her question. . . . That reasons are legitimate and forceful just is the position of the rationalist. (p. 82)

Siegel put the matter most succinctly in saying, "Asking for a justification of rationality is asking for a *rational* justification of it" (p. 85).

To be sure, MGTs do not challenge the necessity of rationality/reason in advancing human agency on rational grounds (see chap. 6, this volume), so they might be inclined to think that asking for rational justification of rationality is beside the point. They also might agree with Siegel's (1997) defense of "the potential epistemic force [or strength] of reasons" (p. 85). In so defending reason, Siegel gives reason a force, strength, or power that amounts to nothing less than a causal power to which the term *agency* could be properly applied.[12] Yet because that rational power is not only universal but is also deeply intertwined with our capacity for epistemic objectivity (see chap. 8, this volume), which in turn allows epistemic transcendence in the form of "transcultural normative reach," MGTs would probably say no thanks. So too they cannot be expected to appreciate Pols's views about rationality/ reason. Despite defending our rationally agentic capacities against the forces of mechanistic determinism that MGTs themselves combat as one of their twin goals, Pols also defends our capacity for objective knowing or rational awareness—one of the many universal modes of rational agency or mind.[13]

Pols's Self-Reflexive Demonstration/Defense of Rational Awareness

Whereas Siegel makes a reasoned case on behalf of reason, Pols makes a case for rational awareness by asking us to deploy our capacity for rational awareness in a special way: He asks us to turn inward to see for ourselves that among rational agency's many powers is the power to attain knowledge of a reality that is independent of the knowing process—that is, an objective reality.[14] In *Mind Regained* Pols (1998) says, "The reflexive turn is devoted to justifying and extending the claims made for direct knowing/rational aware-ness (see note 2, this chapter),[15] for this function is central to our reflexive discrimination of the other functions [of mind/rationality] on the list" (p. 115; see note 13, this chapter). Displaying some resonance with Siegel's ra-tional defense of rationality, he says, "We cannot find a fulcrum outside di-rect knowing to establish those claims" (p. 115). "If the function of direct knowing/rational awareness is real, it is a self-justifying function" (p. 116). Elsewhere Pols says (2004a) that "there is nothing viciously circular about

---

[12]Regarding the "reasons" versus "causes" debate within the human sciences, Erwin (1997, pp. 74–75, 134) discusses reasons as causes of mental states and actions in a commonsense understanding of cause as "causally relevant." Grünbaum (1988) rebuts the hermeneutic argument that reasons cannot function as causes within psychoanalytic theory. Pols (1998, pp. 135–136), by contrast, gives a more metaphysical account of "How Reasons Can Be Causally Effective."

[13]In his list of "mind's functions," Pols (1998) states that "mind knows, makes (that is, forms, produces, creates), understands, thinks, conceives, perceives, remembers, anticipates, believes, doubts, attends, intends, affirms, denies, wills, refuses, imagines, values, judges, and feels" (p. 98). Although he does not include consciousness in this list, he does say, "Consciousness, or awareness, qualifies all of the functions I have listed, and at least some of them—knowing, doubting, attending, and feeling, for instance—may fairly be described as modes of consciousness or modes of awareness" (p. 98).

[14]Pols (1998) equates objectivity with "reality, actuality or being" (p. 116), and he gives a common definition of *objective*: "We call a conclusion objective [if] we mean that it expresses what is in fact the case—what is real in the sense that it is independent of the mind of the person who draws the conclusion" (p. 108).

[15]Pols (1998) provides two more names for direct knowing: "rational consciousness and rational subjectivity" (p. 110), and he is careful not to equate subjectivity with "self-enclosure" (p. 116).

this enterprise of justification, for direct knowing is by nature reflexive." Put differently, Pols here claims we can attend directly to (or become rationally aware of) our rational awareness/direct knowing itself, to justify the existence and nature of rational awareness.

Pols (1998) then appeals uniquely to the satisfaction that he says we each necessarily experience when we attain cognitive access to the real and on which we can rely for justificatory purposes (rather than relying on a nonexistent "fulcrum outside direct knowing").

> I turn instead to something intrinsic to the function [of rational awareness], namely, the satisfaction that takes place within the knower when rational awareness completes or actualizes itself in something whose being is independent of the knower. As a satisfaction, it must take place in the knower, but . . . it is wholly taken up with the thing known (person, tree, bird, word, proposition . . .), so much so that . . . [it is] a satisfaction in acknowledging the known as what it is. . . . The factor of rationality, however, means that the satisfaction is impersonal and universal, both as to its "interior" quality and as to its neutral receptivity to that which is other than awareness/subjectivity/consciousness. (pp. 116–117)

Pols (1998) makes common cause with Siegel in at least this sense—that self-reflexive forms of justification are not limited to those who advance objectivist epistemologies: "The authority of direct knowing/rational awareness is by no means at odds with the justificatory procedures that are common in philosophy and science, not to speak of other fields" (p. 116).

What is this reflexive turn that justifies the existence of rational awareness? In the preface to *Radical Realism*, Pols (1992) refers to the epiphany about knowing that he attained in making his own reflexive turn, and there—parting company with Siegel—he hints at the exercise in which he will later ask his readers to participate.

> My eye rested on only a worn bedstead and a chest of drawers. What I enjoyed was a rational awareness (as I now call it) of ordinary things, but a rational awareness suddenly qualified and heightened by a surge in the intensity of the reflexive feature that is always native to it. And what that surge brought me was the assurance that we, the knowers, do not endow the known thing with the structure that comes through to us in our knowing it. (pp. ix–x)

Pols (1992) dates the epiphany to his senior year at Harvard, and in *The Recognition of Reason* (1963), he calls this exercise "radically originative reflection": "In this act we do not merely exercise a familiar function. Risking the charge of hubris, we describe the act as an ontological expansion of reason"[16] (p. 53). The act is radical, he says, "because it is concerned with reason's

---

[16]The term "ontological expansion of reason" carries with it the connotation of transcendence, at least transcendence of any particular object/instance of rational awareness.

whole footing in experience—concerned not with some particular act of knowing . . . but with the whole framework of knowing" (p. 57). The act is originative, he says, "because it produces an awareness and understanding that was not there before" (p. 57): Once the reflexive turn is taken, we intensify what was there all along but not *noticed*.[17] Then (1963) as now (1992, 1998, 2004b), Pols calls on each of us to take our own reflexive turn by attending to knowing itself—not outside of the particular thing being known, but in the act of knowing/experiencing that particular entity. When we do this, he says, we heighten in experience and so find that there is a belief *intrinsic* to every act of rational awareness/direct knowing. Yet this belief (component of knowing) is not itself usually noticed or known outside of the exercise of "radically originative reflection." The belief consists in our satisfaction that we are indeed attaining what is real.

Before considering skeptical challenges to Pols's claim, let us first consider a simple example of everyday knowing to make his argument more concrete. When I direct my gaze outward to a glass of water on my table, I am aware that there is a glass of water that is clear, cylindrical, and half empty (I am a pessimist). But when I take the reflexive turn and look inward, by attending directly to my awareness of the glass of water, I will notice something else, something I did not notice before I took the turn—hence the originative part of radically originative reflection. I will notice that I also hold a belief, or a sense of satisfaction (we can also call it faith or trust), that I am indeed taking in what is independent of me, and that my mind is doing this in a causal/active sense: I am "reaching out" to the entity and "bringing it into" myself, to use Pols's (1998, pp. 117–118) agentic/causal language[18]— hence mind's fundamental agentic/causal power of rational awareness. I will also notice the universality in the particularity of just this glass, says Pols: that is, I am rationally aware of it and so can see its universal/categorical/conceptual nature, as well as its particularity in being just *this* glass of water (Pols, personal communication, April 2004). That this also applies to interpersonal relationships is made clear in a passage from *Mind Regained* (1998): "In that kind of primary rational awareness in which two persons meet, know,

---

[17]It is interesting to compare Pols's (1963) claim that in taking the reflexive turn we merely intensify what was there all along but did not notice with more recent attempts to defend "inner awareness" without appeal to a "higher-order" function that operates in addition to consciousness. As D. W. Smith (2005) put it in his own notion of "reflexive inner awareness," "Consciousness can include an awareness of itself without a higher-order activity that rides along with the basic act of consciousness" (p. 93, abstract). Thus in both Pols's and more recent accounts, there is something intrinsic or integral to consciousness that grants first-person knowledge about mental states or acts, although the nature of the arguments differs. Thomasson (2005) seeks "distance from all inner-observation accounts" and advocates a "contemporary 'cognitive transformation view'. . . about the source of self-knowledge" (p. 115, abstract). Also see Siewert (1998) and D. W. Smith and Thomasson (2005).
[18]When Pols (1998, p. 118) speaks of mind "reaching out" to "take in" the entity being known, he does not limit the causal act to the particular entity itself, but speaks to generality as well.

and acknowledge each other, the mutual satisfaction resonates with reflexive intensity"[19] (p. 118).

If Pols is right about this, it could explain some MGTs' explicit expression of faith in our power to know our social/psychological circumstances correctly (i.e., objectively) enough to transcend them on rational grounds—that is, with benefit of active deliberation and choice about the realities before us (see chap. 9, this volume). But more to the point, we take the intrinsic belief component in rational awareness for granted unless we make the reflexive turn, in which case it is heightened. We therefore may well fail in everyday "cognitive occasions" to appreciate its presence (Pols, 1992, p. 211). That failure of appreciation could explain, at least in part, how we have ended up with the antiobjectivist epistemologies[20] of MGTs and radical postmodernists. Yet faith in our knowing powers slips explicitly into at least some MGTs' discourse nonetheless, perhaps because the belief component of rational awareness is really (objectively!) there, and even they notice it on occasion.

Pols (1992) maintains that this belief component is present even when we find we are in error in (or in doubt about) some particular instance of knowing. This, he says, in no way undermines the existence of the belief component of rational awareness, because it enjoys a universality that transcends particularity.

> Acknowledging yourself to be subject to error, you may nevertheless recognize that the universal factor in the function [of rational awareness] transcends each instance it is integral with, and so possesses a general authority that is not touched by its failure in a particular instance. Knowing yourself mistaken about just *what* is before you in some particular instance, you nevertheless know the misidentified thing is other than yourself and so independent of your cognitive act. Confident that your failure can only be defined within the framework of a general competence, you find that you are in a position to try again. (Pols, 1998, p. 116)

It is hard to miss the expression of agency that pervades this passage, especially when Pols speaks expressly of transcendence of particularity even in any particular failed act of rational awareness/direct knowing. Despite Pols's (1998) assertion that "we cannot find a fulcrum outside direct knowing to establish those claims" (p. 115), the skeptic will no doubt press for what—outside of introspection—justifies belief in the existence of a "belief compo-

---

[19]Here we may have an objectivist version of the hermeneutically inclined MGTs' "fusion of horizons." In *Self-Knowledge and the Self*, philosopher David Jopling (2000) argues that self-knowledge can be gained only through "dialogic encounter" with an other who is not like minded. That is, it is only in virtue of the other's "otherness" that legitimate self-knowledge can be gained. Unlike the hermeneutically inclined MGTs whom we have considered, Jopling questions the value of participating in like-minded communities as a source of true human understanding, especially self-understanding.
[20]See note 10.

nent" of rational awareness (now heightened by the self-reflexive turn and so accessible to us). Moreover, even if there were such external (to each knower) or third-person evidence, would it be sufficient to justify our capacity for rational awareness, and hence epistemic objectivity, itself? After all, the warrant or justification for self-knowledge of any sort is called into question on a regular basis in these anti-introspective[21] days, in which self-reflexive turns allegedly cannot in principle yield any truths about the workings of mind in general or of our own individual minds in particular.

Consider three recent books in which the possibility of self-knowledge is challenged on empirical grounds. In *Strangers to Ourselves*, social psychologist Timothy Wilson (2002) argues that introspection does not—indeed cannot—give us the truth about ourselves, and so we must look outward to others for valid "self" knowledge, which amounts to third-person knowledge about oneself rather than bona fide first-person knowledge.[22] In *Stumbling on Happiness*, social psychologist Daniel Gilbert (2006) finds that our ability to know/predict what will make us happy is consistently fraught with error. In *The Illusion of Conscious Will*, social psychologist Daniel Wegner (2002) argues that we cannot trust our subjective/first-person experience or sense of conscious will (also called "phenomenal will") as an accurate guide to the objective/actual causes of our action: Empirical investigations demonstrate that there are many cases in which "conscious will is present but verifiably voluntary action is not present, and there are also cases in which verifiably voluntary action occurs without benefit of the feeling of conscious will" (Wegner, 2004, p. 682).[23] Thus the experience of conscious will is not a reliable guide to what causes action, which Wegner (2002) ultimately attributes to unconscious processes, both psychological and biological. This line of argument is supported by Daniel Dennett's (1991, 2005) philosophical case against the possibility of attaining knowledge about the nature of consciousness/mind based on "first-person approaches to consciousness."

Let us therefore consider the skeptic's challenge more carefully by posing two questions: First, has Pols shown that a belief component inherent to rational awareness exists? And second, if it does exist, is it sufficient to justify his claim about our capacity for rational awareness or objective knowing (see note 2)? The answer to the first question depends on whether one thinks

---

[21]Rychlak (1997) is one notable exception: Self-reflexivity is "the introspective capacity for mentation to turn back on itself by transcending the process taking place, and thereby realizing that it 'is' involved in the pro forma framing of experience" (p. 304).

[22]See *The Significance of Consciousness*, in which philosopher Charles Siewert (1998) argues on behalf of a distinctive form of warrant for the justification of first-person knowledge claims—that is, for the existence of bona fide self-knowledge. Also see note 17.

[23]As Wegner (2004) put it in his answers to "Frequently Asked Questions About Conscious Will":
Conscious will is based on interpreting one's thought as causing one's action. The experience of will comes and goes in accord with principles governing that *interpretive mechanism* and not in accord with a causal link between thought and action. The experience of conscious will thus is not direct evidence of a causal relation between thought and action. (p. 679)

introspection (or self-reflection) can give evidence of the workings of mind (see note 17). Pols (2002a) says that "rational awareness [of an independent reality] . . . cannot be demonstrated independently of its own reflexive exercise. This is a bootstrap operation. No theory, brought to the bar of a supposed independent empirical test[,] can help us" (pp. 11–12). Does Pols's "reflexive exercise" give evidence that a "belief component" of rational awareness exists? After all, Pols offers the exercise for justification purposes; he describes what we will find to call our attention to what he claims we can see for ourselves if we direct our rational awareness to our own knowing process itself. I invite readers to perform the exercise to decide for themselves.

Regarding the second question—the issue of whether the "belief component" of rational awareness warrants the claim that we can (in principle) know with objectivity—we find even more complexity. For I have consistently defined objective knowledge about an entity or event (call it X) as knowledge that is independent of beliefs about the existence and nature of that entity or event (see chaps. 1, 3, 5, and 8–9, this volume). The objective truth about X is independent of anyone's beliefs about X (unless the truth in question is the truth about someone's belief). Although Pols asks us to use a belief (i.e., the belief component of rational awareness) to justify his claim about our capacity for objective knowing, he is not asking us to believe in that belief component on the basis of mere belief/faith alone: His reflexive demonstration is meant to give us empirical evidence of the existence of the belief component. Whether any experience we may have of said "belief component"—even if it is the universal experience he claims it to be—justifies his claims about knowing is another question. Pols (2002b) himself indicates that he appreciates the complexity in this.

> Belief . . . is intrinsic to direct knowing. Belief of that kind does not call for a justification distinct from itself: the point is rather that any rational justification of belief must include reflexive instances of direct knowing, and so will also include the belief-component that is always part of direct knowing. Deep waters again! (p. 96)

To be sure, objective knowledge (or an objectivist/realist epistemology), even regarding social/psychological kinds, does not depend on the fate of Pols's philosophy. Two arguments should not be dismissed, in any case. First, an antiobjectivist epistemology is self-undermining, and what undermines itself cannot be used rationally to advance anything else—including the agency MGTs defend in part by adopting an antiobjectivist epistemology (see chap. 8, this volume). Second, if we dismiss out of hand the possibility of rational awareness, if we cannot trust our ability to access cognitively an independent reality (including the reality of human kinds), we are then left with the "negative philosophical judgment about knowing" (Pols, 1992, 1998) that is endemic to radical postmodern thought, in which agency/liberation/transcendence is sought by way of an antiobjectivist/antirealist epistemology (see chap. 2, this volume). Is an agency that denies us objective knowledge of human social/psychological circumstances an agency "worth wanting"?

Ironically even scholars who say that introspection gets us nowhere, as they seek without apology what many take to be the mechanistic/nonagentic forms of causation/determinism in psychology that MGTs reject (e.g., Dennett, 1991; Gilbert, 2006; Wegner, 2002; Wilson, 2002), evidently trust their own ability to know something about how mind is, independent of beliefs about its nature, when they take their findings to constitute objective psychological knowledge. As we saw in chapter 9, the mechanistically deterministic causal laws that they seem to seek are not the only kind of objective psychological knowledge. However, these scholars, in virtue of their belief in the potential objectivity of our knowing powers, at least give humans a rational capacity—a form of rational agency—denied by MGTs, who say we cannot know just how the human world is and then celebrate that antiobjectivist proclamation in the name of an agentic psychology.

AGENCY, RATIONALITY, AND OBJECTIVITY

Throughout this volume I have returned repeatedly to the two-pronged mission of the MGTs—the explication of an antiobjectivist yet truth-tracking epistemology for psychological inquiry that is consistent with an ontology of human agency, or self-determination.

The exact form of the psychological inquiry (and the knowledge it can yield) varies among MGTs. For example, there is disagreement about the use of causal explanations in a human science that for some should seek Dilthian interpretive "understanding" rather than causal "explanation" (see chap. 9 and chap. 10, note 12). Recall that some MGTs (e.g., Liebrucks, Harré) reject attempts to answer the causal/explanatory questions of conventional science, and instead propose that psychologists discern the meaning rules and conventions that make acts intelligible within their local discursive/interpretive contexts. Some (e.g., Fishman, Miller) say that psychologists should work inductively to develop categories of context-dependent psychological kinds (e.g., a database of cases) for pragmatic purposes, without resorting to the testing of general or nomothetic (i.e., causal/lawlike) theoretical claims. Others (e.g., Martin and Sugarman; Richardson et al.), by contrast, find various methods of conventional science suited to the purposes of psychological inquiry, but only if we reject the belief that through their use we can establish objective, mechanistically deterministic causal laws that operate on (or in) mind, independently of cultural context.

Members of the last group also say that we should warrant psychological claims by way of the local pragmatic/value-laden epistemologies of the cultural contexts in which psychological claims are made and to which they pertain. Some (e.g., Howard, Polkinghorne, Woolfolk) maintain that we need more humanistic, interpretive/qualitative forms of inquiry to supplement (although not necessarily supplant) the limitations of conventional scientific methods. Martin and Sugarman (1999a) summed up the matter succinctly when they said, "The methods and epistemic strategies of physical science do not apply in the same way to psychological phenomena because such phenomena are morally constituted, agentically controlled, contextual, and uncertain" (p. 46).

Whatever their differences about a proper form of psychological inquiry and the type of knowledge we should gain from that inquiry, one similarity pervades the various proposals of MGTs: the necessarily antiobjectivist epistemic status of the findings of any form of psychological inquiry. For most (if not all) MGTs, an objectivist epistemology is synonymous with the methods of natural science—by which methods natural scientists are problematically said to discover indubitably known, timeless, universal, and mechanistically deterministic causal laws that govern the unchanging essences of brute entities. This view constitutes the straw man of objectivity erected by MGTs (see chap. 8, this volume); and it is used to argue that the methods of natural science cannot apply to human kinds owing to the core ontological feature of humans, which is put forth by MGTs with complete certitude in all its timeless universality: the agentically reflexive capacity for (re)interpreting ourselves and each other, which itself underwrites a contextually constrained capacity for transcendence (of any supposed "laws" or forms of discourse). Yet if there is no way that we are that is independent of our beliefs about what we are—if we just or simply are what we interpret ourselves to be in our social contexts, to recall the all-important quotation of prominent MGTs (see chap. 5, this volume)—then the "interpretive turn," like the "linguistic turn" that preceded and coexists with it (see Bohman, Hiley, & Shusterman, 1991), is an antirealist turn. We are therefore left with the possibility that the interpretive turn taken by MGTs in the name of agency is not only epistemically antiobjectivist but also ontologically antirealist. This makes it hard to distinguish them from the radical postmodernists whose philosophy they find too extreme.

Moreover, in denying the possibility of objective knowledge of human psychological existence, MGTs are throwing out the agentic baby with the mechanistically deterministic bathwater. Given current definitions of an objectivist epistemology—that the truth of a claim does not depend on beliefs about its truth (unless the claim is about someone's beliefs)—there is no reason to equate objective knowledge with indubitable knowledge of timeless, universal, and mechanistically deterministic causal laws. However, objective knowledge is necessary for agency itself—including the agentic capacity to transcend current circumstances as they exist, with benefit of deliberation and choice about the objective realities of those circumstances. This is the very agency defined in the rational terms of many MGTs.

Rational Transcendence Revisited

In chapter 6 we considered the various definitions of agency put forth by MGTs. Although these definitions vary, they also typically point to a universal capacity to interpret our social/psychological situations in novel terms, and so to act on those interpretations in novel ways. For MGTs, then, a capacity for meaning making is necessary for the culmination of agency's powers in action itself—especially action that transcends whatever was given in the context that constitutes meaning (and thus, allegedly, being) in the first place. That the meaning making MGTs endorse in agency's name consists in rational meaning making is clear; many of them speak explicitly of making sense of our social/psychological circumstances in ways that are intelligible within (if not beyond) the contexts that constitute those circumstances. That the knowledge of the realities of those circumstances is realist knowledge is at least implicit in the epistemic realism that MGTs explicitly want to endorse. Thus reason and (realist) knowing are unified in the MGTs' view of agency, and in the capacity for transcendence that inheres in their view of agency.

MGTs are not alone in uniting reason and knowing in their views of agency and transcendence. For example, although I do not consider Rychlak to be an MGT (see chap. 9, this volume), some prominent MGTs nonetheless rely on his important work, in which he speaks expressly about transcendence in terms of our rational capacities: "*Transcendence* refers to a human being's capacity to take a vis-à-vis stance toward the contents of his or her own thought contents, to rise above the course of such mentation . . . , and to realize . . . other possibilities" (1980, p. 1150). Later Rychlak (1997) added this to his definition: "Because human cognition involves . . . the taking of a position within oppositional possibilities, there is always this capacity to extend meanings away from the 'given' to a realm of awareness that is 'not given'" (p. 307).

Tying transcendence to reason's powers more explicitly, Rychlak (1994) also said, "Through . . . oppositional (dialectical, etc.) reasoning people can reflexively examine their views and thereby transcend what they know to frame alternatives . . . [and to] take on as goals" (p. 70). Implicit in this is that humans have enough (rational) awareness of their circumstances to form predications—or take stands—about them in the first place, predicating contents and stands that themselves may be judged reasonable or rational (in virtue of making sense). Thus for Rychlak (as well as MGTs), human rationality/reason is central to our capacity to act agentically both within the confines of any particular context and (in Rychlak's case at least) to transcend context in ways not predetermined by context.

Still, we must not forget that there exists no agreement about just how to construe agency itself (see Davies, 2005). For example, few have responded to Pols's (1998, 2002b, 2004a, 2004b, 2005) deliberate qualification of the term *agency* in putting forth his ontology of "rational agency" and the "rational agent" who enacts it. (One notable exception is Rychlak, 1998b, who responded with approbation.) However, I again find at least an implicit nod to a rational/conceptual component in the views of agency propounded by many MGTs, especially when they make central to agency an interpretive or meaning-making process that is intelligible (see chap. 6, this volume). Of course Rychlak's (1994, 1997) construal of agency as rooted in a universal capacity to reason oppositionally certainly makes rationality/reason (as a process) central to his own conception of agency,[24] which he once defined as a "capacity to influence a course of action" (1994, p. 63) and equated with "freedom of the will"[25] (1997, p. 297).

Rychlak, Pols, and most MGTs converge on at least this point: that the agentic ability to act in and on the world (with the possibility of transcending current circumstances) involves a rational capacity in some sense. Whether we consider that rational capacity to consist in the conceptual component of rational awareness and agency (Pols), dialectical or oppositional reasoning (Rychlak), or deliberative reflection and choice (Martin and Sugarman), these disparate conceptualizations of rationality share a commitment to mind's rational powers. The questions that must be confronted now are these: However our rationality is defined and linked to agency, what does our rationally agentic capacity require most fundamentally to be maximally efficacious? And what does it not require?

Beginning with the second question, I suggest that absence of constraint is not needed. For agentic powers to exist, they must be a certain way, and that way of being necessitates the constraint that MGTs appreciate in their efforts to advance their version of realism (see chap. 5, this volume). Rychlak indicates his appreciation of this in claiming that the cognitive processes that serve agency are determined enough to be studied scientifically—in his own case by way of his Logical Learning Theory (see chap. 9, this volume). Martin and Sugarman indicate that they appreciate this when they speak of the psychology of "possibility and constraint," although they also say that if agency is too "underdetermined," then it may not be determined enough to study scientifically. Pols, whose ontology of the "rational agent" is as

---

[24]In his review of Pols's *Mind Regained*, Rychlak (1998b) says that what is purposive is rational: "Rational action is essentially what we mean by mind. . . . Mind thus has the (higher) power to order events purposively or rationally" (p. 451). Rychlak (1994) also said, "The very core of a free-will notion is that the organism can behave in conformance with, in opposition to, or without regard for . . . rational grounding" (p. 66). If I interpret him correctly, here he may mean that the *content* produced by agentic acts of "transpredication" may not itself be judged reasonable, but rationality itself, as a (logical) *process*, is intrinsic to the ability to so act nonetheless.

[25]Rychlak (1997) goes on to say about "freedom of the will": "The person has *free will* who is capable of affirming the ground or assumption for the sake of which she or he will be determined" (p. 297). Earlier he (1994) said that "the 'free' . . . refers to the generation of alternatives by way of opposite implications in all the meanings that we human beings affirm, and the 'will' . . . is the resultant determinism that always follows once a position has been affirmed and enacted" (p. 70). In sum, "Determinism does not itself contradict freedom" (p. 70). See Howard (1994) and Slife (1994) for relevant comments.

nonmechanistic, nondeterministic, and antireductionistic as an ontology of human mind can be, permits predictability in human matters—although in taking particularity seriously, he must limit the extent of that predictability. In this quotation Pols's (2004b) language comes close to Martin and Sugarman's language of "possibility and constraint."

> Agents seem to be at the mercy of a received self-identity that defines the possibility of action. From this self-identity there appears to be no escape: it affords certain opportunities for action and also sets certain limits upon it. . . . Whatever freedom the rational agent possesses, it is never free from the lot of being just that self-identical particular which at a given time and place is capable of certain acts and not of others. . . . Great things in music in his maturity were legitimately, though not de-terministically, predictable from the childhood career of Mozart, and analogous if more modest predictions can be made about others by some-one familiar with the developmental patterns of children. (2004b)

Making matters more complex, Pols (2004b) reminds us of this about self-identity, and in so doing he invokes our capacity for (self-)transcen-dence—within limits or constraints: "Whatever self-identity we attributed to that agent would have to be consistent with its capacity to alter it in fundamental respects.[26] Self-identity . . . is not so much a given feature of an agent as a task for it." Freeman (1993) in *Rewriting the Self*, no less than Martin and Sugarman (1999a)[27] in *The Psychology of Human Possibility and Constraint*, would no doubt agree.

"A person capable of rational action must decide [a great many things]," states Pols (2004b). Such a person must make decisions that ultimately cul-minate in the decision to remain the same or change, to transcend or not to transcend. Returning now to my first question (What does our rational agentic capacity require most fundamentally to be maximally efficacious?), I main-tain that the capacity to know our circumstances objectively, as they are, independent of beliefs about how they are, is the answer. An objectivist epis-temology—not in the straw-man sense that MGTs and others put forth, but in the fallibilist sense that many contemporary philosophers endorse (see chap. 8, this volume)—is our best and most justifiable ally in our rational pursuits. If we want to transcend what is, we should at least in principle have the capacity to know (a) what it is that we want to transcend, as it exists (in all its particularity and universality), and (b) whether and to what extent we have indeed transcended it. To deny us that epistemic capacity is to deny a

---

[26]Pols (2004b) also said this about self-transcendence:
> With respect to self-identity . . . , it [rational consciousness] . . . sets up an inner discourse between different aspects of the self. . . . It drives a wedge into the kind of unity that we take for granted . . . , opening a great space within which then play all the possibilities of both self-integration and self-dissolution. The inner diversity of rational consciousness makes possible the discontinuities in our history that are necessary preludes to any change in self-identity.

[27]Also see Martin and Sugarman's (2000b) "Is the Self a Kind of Understanding?"

great deal in agency's name. After all, what can it possibly mean to say that we have or have not "transcended" what we cannot know to be the case—that is, with nonrelativistic/objectivist warrant?

But that epistemic capacity is just what MGTs deny us, even as they claim to have articulated an epistemic realism that precludes objective knowledge about the human world. And so they cannot hold a belief in our rational (agentic) capacities to transcend our current circumstances without first overcoming or transcending a profound obstacle of their own making: their refusal to grant mind a universal capacity to know the (objective or independent) realities of the human world, including the realities of human social/psychological existence. Because the antiobjectivist epistemology that they propound undermines itself, it cannot be used rationally to advance anything else, including agency's capacity to transcend. Yet another problem looms, and it is not merely logical; it is fully epistemological. For in making what we can know about the human world relative to the discursive communities we inhabit, MGTs allow us to see ourselves and each other only through the contextually ground lenses that necessarily color what lies beyond them. However enabling (of intelligibility) such lenses may be, these lenses also constrict or limit what we can in principle see/know, so they also necessarily reduce what is potentially available to mind/rationality without local/relativistic coloration: reality itself.

Although the capacity for rational awareness on which Pols insists affords no guarantee of rational transcendence of what exists in any particular case, it at least offers the "negative" assurance that we are not in principle reduced to innovation or transcendence that is only "mild" or "modest" (Martin & Sugarman, 1999a, 1999b), owing to the constricting lenses of discursive contexts. Whatever its fate, Pols's philosophy does not reduce the knowing powers of mind on which rational transcendence depends. Let us conclude, then, with the problem of reductionism, against which MGTs have struggled valiantly in the name of agency.

Reductionism Redux

Behind the two-pronged mission of the MGTs—to attain a truth-tracking form of psychological inquiry that gives human agency its due—lies a strong antireductionistic impulse. For this, and for their efforts to differentiate themselves from radical postmodernists, MGTs of all stripes are to be applauded. Still, although they are well aware of the dangers that biological forms of reductionism pose to agency's place in psychological inquiry, they do not seem as concerned about the dangers of cultural forms of reductionism. Yet they are more vulnerable to the latter, owing to the historical/cultural/discursive/interpretive contexts that they themselves emphasize over the universalities of mind (including rationality) in their own ontology and epistemology. In propounding their theory of agency/transcendence, Martin and Sugarman (1999a, 1999b, 2000a, 2002) go further than most in taking seriously the threat of cultural reductionism, but ultimately they too make social/psychological existence and epistemic warrant relative to culture (see chaps. 6 & 9, this volume). And so even they cannot explain innovation and transcendence that is more than "mild" or "modest."

MGTs are right to continue their efforts to provide an ontology of psychological existence that can lay the groundwork for the questions they ask in their desire for realist psychological inquiry. However, their antiobjectivist epistemology remains the most daunting obstacle to their own aspiration to tell us how mind *is*, such that it can allow for agency on the rational grounds on which they put agency.

To say this another way, rationally agentic action ultimately depends for its existence on the agent's ability to inquire about the world in everyday, commonsense ways. Rationally agentic inquiry (which is one form of agentic action) ultimately depends on our ability to access a reality that is not merely the product of (or synonymous with) our own or others' knowing processes, rationality, or mind—that is, our own or others' beliefs/interpretations about the nature of that reality. If we want to transcend current forms of human existence in the hope of a better tomorrow, we must be able to know the realities of that existence in nonrelativist/objectivist terms—that is, as they are, independent of our (contextually determined) wishes, desires, values, beliefs, and interpretations. If we cannot in principle attain *that* objective knowledge, then we cannot act rationally—with deliberate goals in mind—in the most trivial ways (e.g., getting a glass of water), let alone in ways that promote great social transcendence/innovation (e.g., eliminating racism). This is so no matter how much an antiobjectivist epistemology is celebrated in the name of agency. Thus psychology's *antiobjectivist* interpretive turn deprives both MGTs and their more radical postmodernist colleagues of the liberation/transcendence they relentlessly seek, and in this sense the former's reach even for moderation fails.

Recall that those who advance a reductionistic psychology—those who, for example, say that the subjective experience of agency or will (or even of self-knowledge in general) is merely epiphenomenal, an illusion, or a denial of reality—do not deny their own ability to know that alleged reality with all due fallibility and objectivity. These scientists and the philosophers who ground and/or depend on their findings may perhaps contribute to the wrongful equation that MGTs make between objective knowing and knowledge on the one hand, and mechanistically deterministic (or nonagentic) causal laws on the other (see chaps. 8–9). In any case, MGTs surely deploy their own powers of rational awareness/objective knowing (and the objective knowledge those powers afford) to (a) propound *nonrelativistically* the universal existence of human agency/will and (b) conduct the realist psychological inquiry about human psychological existence that their agency affords. That they deploy those rational agentic powers while simultaneously denying agency a capacity for objective knowing and knowledge does not seem to bother them. But this denial should bother them to the extent that rational agency is at stake.

It seems only fitting to end with the words of some MGTs themselves. I especially appreciate this excellent antireductionist pronouncement from Martin and Sugarman (2002), here speaking about psychological interventions or practice: "In psychology, we should not reductively make human beings small as a means of doing large things to them" (p. 423). I am inclined to modify that good thought in accord with the theme of this volume: In psychology, we should not reductively give human beings only small knowing "powers" as a means of giving them "agency." By this I mean that we should not settle for relativistic psychological knowing and knowledge; we should not deprive ourselves of the capacity for objective psychological knowing and knowledge in the name of agency. About this there can be no middle ground.

REFERENCES

Alcoff, L. M. (1996). *Real knowing: New versions of the coherence theory.* Ithaca, NY: Cornell University Press.

Anderson, H., & Goolishian, H. A. (1988). Human systems as linguistic systems: Preliminary and evolving ideas about the implications for clinical theory. *Family Process, 27,* 371–393.

Anderson, H., & Goolishian, H. A. (1992). The client is the expert: A not-knowing approach to therapy. In S. McNamee & K. J. Gergen (Eds.), *Therapy as social construction* (pp. 25–39). London: Sage.

Anscombe, G. E. M. (1957–1958). On brute facts. *Analysis, 18,* 69–72.

Ansoff, R. (1996). How can there be personal agency without an ontology of the individual? *Theory & Psychology, 6,* 539–544.

Atmanspacher, H., & Bishop, R. (Eds.). (2002). *Between chance and choice: Interdisciplinary perspectives on determinism.* Thorverton, England: Imprint Academic.

Baumgardner, S. R., & Rappoport, L. (1996). Culture and self in postmodern perspective. *The Humanistic Psychologist, 24,* 116–139.

Bernstein, R. J. (1983). *Beyond objectivism and relativism: Science, hermeneutics, and praxis.* Philadelphia: University of Pennsylvania Press.

Bernstein, R. J. (1988). Interpretation and its discontents: The choreography of critique. In S. B. Messer, L. A. Sass, & R. L. Woolfolk (Eds.), *Hermeneutics and psychological theory: Interpretive perspectives on personality, psychotherapy, and psychopathology* (pp. 87–108). New Brunswick, NJ: Rutgers University Press.

Best, S., & Kellner, D. (1991). *Postmodern theory: Critical interrogations.* New York: Guilford Press.

Bishop, R. C. (2005). Cognitive psychology: Hidden assumptions. In B. D. Slife, J. S. Reber, & F. C. Richardson (Eds.), *Critical thinking about psychology: Hidden assumptions and plausible alternatives* (pp. 151–170). Washington, DC: American Psychological Association.

Bohman, J. F. (1991). Holism without skepticism: Contextualism and the limits of interpretation. In D. R. Hiley, J. F. Bohman, & R. Shusterman (Eds.), *The interpretive turn: Philosophy, science, culture* (pp. 129–154). Ithaca, NY: Cornell University Press.

Bohman, J. F., Hiley, D. R., & Shusterman, R. (1991). Introduction: The interpretive turn. In D. R. Hiley, J. F. Bohman, & R. Shusterman (Eds.), *The interpretive turn: Philosophy, science, culture* (pp. 1–14). Ithaca, NY: Cornell University Press.

Bridges, S. K. (2002). Now what? The personal and professional in constructivist thought. In J. D. Raskin & S. K. Bridges (Eds.), *Studies in meaning: Exploring constructivist psychology* (pp. 307–319). New York: Pace University Press.

Burkitt, I. (2001). Multiple and singular selves. [Review of the book *The singular self: An introduction to the psychology of personhood*]. *Theory & Psychology, 11,* 445–447.

Cheney, L. V. (1995). *Telling the truth: Why our culture and our country have stopped making sense—and what we can do about it*. New York: Simon & Schuster.

Crews, F. (2001). *Postmodern pooh*. New York: North Point Press.

Cushman, P. (1995). *Constructing the self, constructing America: A cultural history of psychotherapy*. Reading, MA: Addison-Wesley.

Davies, P. S. (2005, March). *What kind of agent are we? A naturalistic framework for the study of human agency*. Paper presented at the Second Mind and World Working Group Conference [Theme: Distributed Cognition and the Will: Individual Volition in Social Context]. Birmingham, AL.

Dennett, D. (1984). *Elbow room: The varieties of free will worth wanting*. Cambridge, MA: MIT Press.

Dennett, D. (1991). *Consciousness explained*. New York: Little, Brown.

Dennett, D. (2005, April). *Philosophers, zombies, and feelings: The illusions of "first-person" approaches to consciousness*. Harvard Review of Philosophy Lecture, Department of Philosophy, Harvard University. Cambridge, MA.

Dreyfus, H. L. (1991). Heidegger's hermeneutic realism. In D. R. Hiley, J. F. Bohman, & R. Shusterman (Eds.), *The interpretive turn: Philosophy, science, culture* (pp. 25–41). Ithaca, NY: Cornell University Press.

Driver-Linn, E. (2003). Where is psychology going? Structural fault lines revealed by psychologists' use of Kuhn. *American Psychologist, 58,* 269–278.

D'Souza, D. (1991). *Illiberal education: The politics of race and sex on campus*. New York: Free Press.

Edley, N. (2001). Unravelling social constructionism. *Theory & Psychology, 11,* 433–441.

Efran, J. S., & Greene, M. A. (1996). Psychotherapeutic theory and practice: Contributions from Maturana's structure determinism. In H. Rosen & K. T. Kuehlwein (Eds.), *Constructing realities: Meaning-making perspectives for psychotherapists* (pp. 71–113). San Francisco: Jossey-Bass.

Efran, J. S., & Heffner, K. P. (1998). Is constructivist psychotherapy epistemologically flawed? *Journal of Constructivist Psychology, 11,* 89–103.

Ellis, J. M. (1989). *Against deconstruction*. Princeton, NJ: Princeton University Press.

Erwin, E. (1997). *Philosophy and psychotherapy: Razing the troubles of the brain*. London: Sage.

Erwin, E. (1999). Constructivist epistemologies and therapies. *British Journal of Guidance and Counselling, 27,* 353–365.

Erwin, E. (2001). The rejection of natural science approaches to psychotherapy: Language and the world. *Journal of Clinical Psychology, 57,* 7–18.

Farber, D. A., & Sherry, S. (1997). *Beyond all reason: The radical assault on truth in American law*. New York: Oxford University Press.

Faulconer, J. E., & Williams, R. N. (1990a). Reconsidering psychology. In J. E. Faulconer & R. N. Williams (Eds.), *Reconsidering psychology: Perspectives from continental philosophy* (pp. 9–60). Pittsburgh, PA: Duquesne University Press.

Faulconer, J. E., & Williams, R. N. (Eds.). (1990b). *Reconsidering psychology: Perspectives from continental philosophy.* Pittsburgh, PA: Duquesne University Press.

Fishman, D. B. (1999). *The case for pragmatic psychology.* New York: New York University Press.

Fishman, D. B. (2001). From single case to database: A new method for enhancing psychotherapy, forensic, and other psychological practice. *Applied and Preventive Psychology, 10,* 275–304.

Fishman, D. B. (2006a). Finding objectivity and causality in pragmatism. *Pragmatic Case Studies in Psychotherapy, 2,* Article 3. Retrieved February 14, 2007, from http://pcsp.libraries.rutgers.edu/include/getdoc.php?id=509&article= 84&mode=pdf

Fishman, D. B. (2006b). Round 4A: Not a knock-out punch, but rather a call for pluralism. *Pragmatic Case Studies in Psychotherapy, 2,* Article 6. Retrieved February 14, 2007, from http://pcsp.libraries.rutgers.edu/include/getdoc.php?id= 527&article=90&mode=pdf

Flanagan, O. (2002). *The problem of the soul: Two visions of mind and how to reconcile them.* New York: Basic Books.

Flew, A. (1984). *A dictionary of philosophy* (Rev. 2nd ed.). New York: St. Martin's Griffin.

Fowers, B. J. (1998, August). *Self-constitutive understanding and psychological inquiry.* Paper presented at the annual meeting of the American Psychological Association, San Francisco, CA.

Fowers, B. J. (2001a). Culture, identity, and loyalty: New pathways for a culturally aware psychotherapy. In B. D. Slife, R. N. Williams, & S. H. Barlow (Eds.), *Critical issues in psychotherapy: Translating new ideas into practice* (pp. 263–280). Thousand Oaks, CA: Sage.

Fowers, B. J. (2001b, August). *The internal critical resources of hermeneutics.* Paper presented at the annual meeting of the American Psychological Association, San Francisco, CA.

Fowers, B. J. (2003). Reason and human finitude: In praise of practical wisdom. *American Behavioral Scientist, 47,* 415–426.

Fowers, B. J. (2005). *Virtue and psychology: Pursuing excellence in ordinary practices.* Washington, DC: American Psychological Association.

Fowers, B. J., & Richardson, F. C. (1996). Why is multiculturalism good? *American Psychologist, 51,* 609–621.

Frank, J. D. (1961). *Persuasion and healing: A comparative study of psychotherapy.* Baltimore: Johns Hopkins University Press.

Freedman, J., & Combs, G. (1996). *Narrative therapy: The social construction of preferred realities.* New York: Norton.

Freeman, M. (1993). *Rewriting the self: History, memory, narrative.* London: Routledge.

Friedman, M. (1985). *The healing dialogue in psychotherapy.* New York: Jason Aronson.

Friedman, S. (Ed.). (1993). *The new language of change: Constructive collaboration in psychotherapy.* New York: Guilford Press.

Gantt, E. (1996). Social constructionism and the ethics of hedonism. *Journal of Theoretical and Philosophical Psychology, 16*, 123–140.

Gantt, E. (2004). A flawed image of human agency in a postmodern world. [Review of the book *The human image in postmodern America*]. *Contemporary Psychology, 49*, 612–614.

Gergen, K. J. (1985). The social constructionist movement in modern psychology. *American Psychologist, 40*, 266–275.

Gergen, K. J. (1988). If persons are texts. In S. B. Messer, L. A. Sass, & R. L. Woolfolk (Eds.), *Hermeneutics and psychological theory: Interpretive perspectives on personality, psychotherapy, and psychopathology* (pp. 28–51). New Brunswick, NJ: Rutgers University Press.

Gergen, K. J. (1991). *The saturated self: Dilemmas of identity in contemporary life.* New York: Basic Books.

Gergen, K. J. (1994). *Realities and relationships: Soundings in social construction.* Cambridge, MA: Harvard University Press.

Gergen, K. J. (1997). The place of the psyche in a constructed world. *Theory & Psychology, 7*, 723–746.

Gergen, K. J. (1998). The place of material in a constructed world. *Family Process, 37*, 415–419.

Gergen, K. J. (2001a). Construction in contention: Toward consequential resolutions. *Theory & Psychology, 11*, 419–432.

Gergen, K. J. (2001b). Psychological science in a postmodern context. *American Psychologist, 56*, 803–813.

Gergen, K. J., & Kaye, J. (1992). Beyond narrative in the negotiation of therapeutic meaning. In S. McNamee & K. J. Gergen (Eds.), *Therapy as social construction* (pp. 166–185). London: Sage.

Gilbert, D. T. (2006). *Stumbling on happiness.* New York: Knopf.

Glass, J. M. (1993). *Shattered selves: Multiple personality in a postmodern world.* Ithaca, NY: Cornell University Press.

Green, C. (2004). Where is Kuhn going? A comment on Driver-Linn (2003). *American Psychologist, 59*, 271–272.

Grene, M. (1957). *Martin Heidegger.* London: Bowes & Bowes.

Gross, P., Levitt, N., & Lewis, M. W. (Eds.). (1996). *The flight from science and reason.* Baltimore: Johns Hopkins University Press.

Grünbaum, A. (1988). Are hidden motives in psychoanalysis reasons but not causes of human conduct? In S. B. Messer, L. A. Sass, & R. L. Woolfolk (Eds.), *Hermeneutics and psychological theory: Interpretive perspectives on personality, psychotherapy, and psychopathology* (pp. 149–167). New Brunswick, NJ: Rutgers University Press.

Guignon, C. (1991). Pragmatism or hermeneutics? Epistemology after foundationalism. In D. R. Hiley, J. F. Bohman, & R. Shusterman (Eds.), *The interpretive turn: Philosophy, science, culture* (pp. 81–101). Ithaca, NY: Cornell University Press.

Guignon, C. (1998). Narrative explanation in psychotherapy. *American Behavioral Scientist, 41*, 558–577.

Guignon, C. (2000, August). *Hermeneutics, authenticity, and the aims of psychotherapy.* Invited paper presented at the annual meeting of the American Psychological Association, Washington, DC.

Guignon, C. (2001, August). *Meaning and possibilities: Heidegger's picture of human agency.* Paper presented at the annual meeting of the American Psychological Association, San Francisco, CA.

Guignon, C. (2002a). Truth in interpretation: A hermeneutic approach. In M. Krausz (Ed.), *Is there a single right interpretation?* (pp. 264–284). University Park: Pennsylvania State University Press.

Guignon, C. (2002b). Hermeneutics, authenticity, and the aims of psychology. *Journal of Theoretical and Philosophical Psychology, 22*, 83–102.

Guignon, C. (2005). Heidegger's anti-dualism: Beyond mind and matter. In R. Polt (Ed.), *Heidegger's being and time: Critical essays* (pp. 75–88). Lanham, MD: Rowman & Littlefield.

Haack, S. (1993a). Epistemological reflections of an old feminist. *Reason Papers, 18*, 31–43.

Haack, S. (1993b). *Evidence and inquiry: Towards reconstruction in epistemology.* Oxford, England: Blackwell.

Haack, S. (1998a). Science as social?—Yes and no. In S. Haack, *Manifesto of a passionate moderate: Unfashionable essays* (pp. 104–122). Chicago: University of Chicago Press.

Haack, S. (1998b). "We pragmatists. . . .": Peirce and Rorty in conversation. In S. Haack, *Manifesto of a passionate moderate: Unfashionable essays* (pp. 31–47). Chicago: University of Chicago Press.

Haack, S. (1998c). Puzzling out science. In S. Haack, *Manifesto of a passionate moderate: Unfashionable essays* (pp. 90–103). Chicago: University of Chicago Press.

Haack, S. (2002). Realisms and their rivals: Recovering our innocence. *Facta Philosophica, 4*, 67–88.

Haack, S. (2003). *Defending science—within reason: Between scientism and cynicism.* Amherst, NY: Prometheus Books.

Halleck, S. L. (1971). *The politics of therapy.* New York: Science House.

Hare-Mustin, R. T. (1994). Discourses in the mirrored room: A postmodern analysis of therapy. *Family Process, 33*, 19–35.

Hare-Mustin, R. T. (2004). Can we demystify theory? Examining masculinity discourses and feminist postmodern theory. *Journal of Theoretical and Philosophical Psychology, 24*, 14–29.

Hare-Mustin, R. T., & Marecek, J. (1990). Gender and the meaning of difference: Postmodernism and psychology. In R. T. Hare-Mustin & J. Marecek (Eds.), *Making a difference: Psychology and the construction of gender* (pp. 22–64). New Haven, CT: Yale University Press.

Harré, R. (1984). *Personal being: A theory for individual psychology.* Cambridge, MA: Harvard University Press.

Harré, R. (1998). *The singular self: An introduction to the psychology of personhood.* London: Sage.

Harré, R. (2002). Public sources of the personal mind: Social constructionism in context. *Theory & Psychology, 12,* 611–623.

Harré, R., & Stearns, P. (Eds.). (1995). *Discursive psychology in practice.* London: Sage.

Held, B. S. (1995). *Back to reality: A critique of postmodern theory in psychotherapy.* New York: Norton.

Held, B. S. (1998a). The many truths of postmodernist discourse. *Journal of Theoretical and Philosophical Psychology, 18,* 193–217.

Held, B. S. (1998b). The antisystematic impact of postmodern philosophy. *Clinical Psychology: Science and Practice, 5,* 264–273.

Held, B. S. (2001). The postmodern turn: What it means for psychotherapy—and what it doesn't. In B. D. Slife, R. N. Williams, & S. H. Barlow (Eds.), *Critical issues in psychotherapy: Translating new ideas into practice* (pp. 241–256). Thousand Oaks, CA: Sage.

Held, B. S. (2002a). The tyranny of the positive attitude in America: Observation and speculation. *Journal of Clinical Psychology, 58,* 965–992.

Held, B. S. (2002b). What follows? Mind dependence, fallibility, and transcendence according to (strong) constructionism's realist and quasi-realist critics. *Theory & Psychology, 12,* 651–669.

Held, B. S. (2006a, October 16). Round 1: Does case study knowledge need a new epistemology? *Pragmatic Case Studies in Psychotherapy, 2,* Article 2. Retrieved February 14, 2007, from http://pcsp.libraries.rutgers.edu/include/getdoc.php?id=496&article=87&mode=pdf

Held, B. S. (2006b, October 16). Round 3: Regarding objectivity and causality—A rejoinder to Fishman and Miller. *Pragmatic Case Studies in Psychotherapy, 2,* Article 5. Retrieved February 14, 2007, from http://pcsp.libraries.rutgers.edu/include/getdoc.php?id=521&article=88&mode=pdf

Held, B. S., & Pols, E. (1985). Rejoinder: On contradiction. *Family Process, 24,* 521–524.

Henriques, G. (2003). The tree of knowledge system and the theoretical unification of psychology. *Review of General Psychology, 7,* 150–182.

Hersch, E. L. (2003). *From philosophy to psychotherapy: A phenomenological model for psychology, psychiatry, and psychoanalysis.* Toronto: University of Toronto Press.

Hibberd, F. J. (2001a). Gergen's social constructionism, logical positivism and the continuity of error: 1. Conventionalism. *Theory & Psychology, 11,* 297–321.

Hibberd, F. J. (2001b). Gergen's social constructionism, logical positivism and the continuity of error: 2. Meaning-as-use. *Theory & Psychology, 11,* 323–346.

Hibberd, F. J. (2002). Reply to Gergen. *Theory & Psychology, 12,* 685–694.

Hiley, D. R., Bohman, J. F., & Shusterman, R. (Eds.). (1991). *The interpretive turn: Philosophy, science, culture.* Ithaca, NY: Cornell University Press.

Himmelfarb, G. (1994). *On looking into the abyss: Untimely thoughts on culture and society.* New York: Knopf.

Holt, R. R. (2002). Postmodernism: Its origins and its threat to psychoanalysis. *International Forum of Psychoanalysis, 11,* 264–274.

House, R. (1999). "Limits to therapy and counselling": Deconstructing a professional ideology. *British Journal of Guidance and Counselling, 27,* 377–392.

House, R. (2003). *Therapy beyond modernity: Deconstructing and transcending profession-centred therapy.* London: Karnac Books.

Howard, G. S. (1986). *Dare we develop a human science?* Notre Dame, IN: Academic Publications.

Howard, G. S. (1994). Some varieties of free will worth practicing. *Journal of Theoretical and Philosophical Psychology, 14,* 50–61.

Hoyt, M. F. (1996). Introduction: Some stories are better than others. In M. F. Hoyt (Ed.), *Constructive therapies* (Vol. 2, pp. 1–32). New York: Guilford Press.

Jenkins, A. H. (2001). Individuality in cultural context: The case for psychological agency. *Theory & Psychology, 11,* 347–362.

Jopling, D. A. (2000). *Self-knowledge and the self.* New York: Routledge.

Katzko, M. W. (2002). The construction of "social constructionism": A case study in the rhetoric of debate. *Theory & Psychology, 12,* 671–683.

Kaye, J. (1999). Toward a non-regulative praxis. In I. Parker (Ed.), *Deconstructing psychotherapy* (pp. 19–38). London: Sage.

Kenwood, C. (1996). Does volition need social constructionism? *Theory & Psychology, 6,* 533–538.

Kimball, R. (1990). *Tenured radicals: How politics has corrupted our higher education.* New York: Harper & Row.

Kirschner, S. R. (1997). Beyond positivism and postmodernism. [Review of the book *Rewriting the self: History, memory, narrative*]. *Psychoculture, 1,* 15–16.

Koch, S. (1985). The nature and limits of psychological knowledge: Lessons of a century qua "science." In S. Koch & D. E. Leary (Eds.), *A century of psychology as science* (pp. 75–97). New York: McGraw-Hill.

Koertge, N. (1998). *A house built on sand: Exposing postmodernist myths about science.* New York: Oxford University Press.

Kvale, S. (1992). (Ed.). *Psychology and postmodernism.* London: Sage.

Lakoff, G. (1987). *Women, fire, and dangerous things: What categories reveal about the mind.* Chicago: University of Chicago Press.

Lehman, D. (1991). *Signs of the times: Deconstruction and the fall of Paul de Man.* New York: Poseidon Press.

Liebrucks, A. (2001). The concept of social construction. *Theory & Psychology, 11,* 363–391.

London, P. (1964). *The modes and morals of psychotherapy*. New York: Holt, Rinehart and Winston.

Mackay, N. (1997). Constructivism and the logic of explanation. *Journal of Constructivist Psychology, 10,* 339–361.

Mackay, N. (2003). Psychotherapy and the idea of meaning. *Theory & Psychology, 13,* 359–386.

Mahoney, M. J. (2004). What is constructivism and why is it growing? [Review of the book *Studies in meaning: Exploring constructivist psychology*]. *Contemporary Psychology, 49,* 360–363.

Martin, J., & Sugarman, J. (1999a). *The psychology of human possibility and constraint.* Albany: State University of New York Press.

Martin, J., & Sugarman, J. (1999b). Psychology's reality debate: A "levels of reality" approach. *Journal of Theoretical and Philosophical Psychology, 19,* 177–194.

Martin, J., & Sugarman, J. (2000a). Between the modern and the postmodern: The possibility of self and progressive understanding in psychology. *American Psychologist, 55,* 397–406.

Martin, J., & Sugarman, J. (2000b, August). *Is the self a kind of understanding?* Paper presented at the annual convention of the American Psychological Association, Washington, DC.

Martin, J., & Sugarman, J. (2002). Agency and soft determinism in psychology. In H. Atmanspacher & R. Bishop (Eds.), *Between chance and choice: Interdisciplinary perspectives on determinism* (pp. 407–424). Thorverton, England: Imprint Academic.

Martin, J., Sugarman, J., & Thompson, J. (2003). *Psychology and the question of agency.* Albany: State University of New York Press.

Maze, J. R. (2001). Social constructionism, deconstructionism and some requirements of discourse. *Theory & Psychology, 11,* 393–417.

McNamee, S., & Gergen, K. J. (Eds.). (1992). *Therapy as social construction*. London: Sage.

Meichenbaum, D. (1988). What happens when the "brute data" of psychological inquiry are meanings: Nurturing a dialogue between hermeneutics and empiricism. In S. B. Messer, L. A. Sass, & R. L. Woolfolk (Eds.), *Hermeneutics and psychological theory: Interpretive perspectives on personality, psychotherapy, and psychopathology* (pp. 116–130). New Brunswick, NJ: Rutgers University Press.

Messer, S. B., Sass, L. A., & Woolfolk, R. L. (Eds.). (1988a). *Hermeneutics and psychological theory: Interpretive perspectives on personality, psychotherapy, and psychopathology.* New Brunswick, NJ: Rutgers University Press.

Messer, S. B, Sass, L. A., & Woolfolk, R. L. (1988b). Preface. In S. B. Messer, L. A. Sass, & R. L. Woolfolk (Eds.), *Hermeneutics and psychological theory: Interpretive perspectives on personality, psychotherapy, and psychopathology* (pp. xiii–xvi). New Brunswick, NJ: Rutgers University Press.

Miller, R. B. (2004). *Facing human suffering: Psychology and psychotherapy as moral engagement.* Washington, DC: American Psychological Association.

Miller, R. B. (2006a, October 16). Round 2B: Facing human suffering—A response to Held. *Pragmatic Case Studies in Psychotherapy*, *2*, Article 4. Retrieved February 14, 2007, from http://pcsp.libraries.rutgers.edu/include/getdoc.php?id=515&article=85&mode=pdf

Miller, R. B. (2006b, October 16). Round 4B: How real is clinical wisdom? A further reply to Held. *Pragmatic Case Studies in Psychotherapy*, *2*, Article 4. Retrieved February 14, 2007, from http://pcsp.libraries.rutgers.edu/include/getdoc.php?id=538&article=86&mode=pdf

Moore, R. (1999). *The creation of reality in psychoanalysis: A view of the contributions of Donald Spence, Roy Schafer, Robert Stolorow, Irwin Z. Hoffman, and beyond.* Hillsdale, NJ: The Analytic Press.

Morss, J., & Nichterlein, M. (1999). The therapist as client as expert: Externalizing narrative therapy. In I. Parker (Ed.), *Deconstructing psychotherapy* (pp. 164–174). London: Sage.

Mühlhäusler, P., & Harré, R. (1990). *Pronouns and people: The linguistic construction of social and personal identity.* Oxford, England: Blackwell.

Nagel, T. (1986). *The view from nowhere.* New York: Oxford University Press.

Neiman, A., & Siegel, H. (1993). Objectivity and rationality in epistemology and education: Scheffler's middle road. *Syntheses*, *94*, 55–83.

Neimeyer, R. A. (1993). An appraisal of constructivist psychotherapies. *Journal of Consulting and Clinical Psychology*, *61*, 221–234.

Neimeyer, R. A. (1995). Limits and lessons of constructivism: Some critical reflections. *Journal of Constructivist Psychology*, *8*, 339–361.

Neimeyer, R. A. (1998). Social constructionism in the counselling context. *Counselling Psychology Quarterly*, *11*, 135–149.

Neimeyer, R. A., & Mahoney, M. J. (Eds.). (1995). *Constructivism in psychotherapy.* Washington, DC: American Psychological Association.

Nightingale, D. J., & Cromby, J. (2002). Social constructionism as ontology: Exposition and example. *Theory & Psychology*, *12*, 701–713.

Nisbett, R. E., Peng, K., Choi, I., & Norenzayan, A. (2001). Culture and systems of thought: Holistic versus analytic cognition. *Psychological Review*, *108*, 291–310.

Norris, C. (1990). *What's wrong with postmodernism: Critical theory and the ends of philosophy.* Baltimore: Johns Hopkins University Press.

Norris, C. (1997). *Against relativism: Philosophy of science, deconstruction and critical theory.* Oxford, England: Blackwell.

Omer, H., & Alon, N. (1997). *Constructing therapeutic narratives.* Northvale, NJ: Jason Aronson.

Osbeck, L. M. (1993). Social constructionism and the pragmatic standard. *Theory & Psychology*, *3*, 337–349.

Parker, I. (1999). Deconstruction and psychotherapy. In I. Parker (Ed.), *Deconstructing psychotherapy* (pp. 1–18). London: Sage.

Parry, A., & Doan, R. E. (1994). *Story re-visions: Narrative therapy in the postmodern world*. New York: Guilford Press.

Patai, D., & Corral, W. H. (Eds.). (2005). *Theory's empire: An anthology of dissent*. New York: Columbia University Press.

Paul, G. L. (1967). Strategy of outcome research in psychotherapy. *Journal of Consulting Psychology, 31*, 109–118.

Pinker, S. (1997). *How the mind works*. New York: Norton.

Polkinghorne, D. (1983). *Methodology for the human sciences: Systems of inquiry*. Albany: State University of New York Press.

Polkinghorne, D. (1988). *Narrative knowing and the human sciences*. Albany: State University of New York Press.

Polkinghorne, D. E. (1992). Postmodern epistemology of practice. In S. Kvale (Ed.), *Psychology and postmodernism* (pp. 146–165). London: Sage.

Polkinghorne, D. (1999). Foreword. In J. Martin & J. Sugarman, *The psychology of human possibility and constraint* (pp. vii–xiv). Albany: State University of New York Press.

Pols, E. (1958). To live at ease ever after. *Sewanee Review, 66*, 229–251.

Pols, E. (1963). *The recognition of reason*. Carbondale: Southern Illinois University Press.

Pols, E. (1982). *The acts of our being: A reflection on agency and responsibility*. Amherst: University of Massachusetts Press.

Pols, E. (1992). *Radical realism: Direct knowing in science and philosophy*. Ithaca, NY: Cornell University Press.

Pols, E. (1998). *Mind regained*. Ithaca, NY: Cornell University Press.

Pols, E. (2000a). Appearances and realities. [Review of the book *The social construction of what?*]. *First Things, 103*, 56–58.

Pols, E. (2000b). *Analyzing social construction*. Unpublished manuscript.

Pols, E. (2002a). Rational action and the complexity of causality. *Journal of Theoretical and Philosophical Psychology, 22*, 1–18.

Pols, E. (2002b). The psychologist as rational agent. *Bulletin fra Forum for Antropologisk Psykologi, 11*, 92–96.

Pols, E. (2004a). *Radical realism*. Retrieved April 27, 2004, from http://www.radicalrealism.com

Pols, E. (2004b). *The ontology of the rational agent*. Unpublished manuscript.

Pols, E. (2005). The rational agent as a primary being: Continuity and change. In E. Pols, *On rational agency*. Retrieved May 10, 2005, from http://www.rationalagency.com

Putnam, H. (1967). Psychological predicates. In W. H. Capitan and D. D. Merrill (Eds.), *Art, mind, and religion* (pp. 37–48). Pittsburgh, PA: University of Pittsburgh Press.

Quine, W. V. (1948). On what there is. *Review of Metaphysics, 2*, 21–38.

Raskin, J. D. (2004). The permeability of personal construct psychology. In J. D. Raskin & S. K. Bridges (Eds.), *Studies in meaning 2: Bridging the personal and social in constructivist psychology* (pp. 327–346). New York: Pace University Press.

Raskin, J. D., & Bridges, S. K. (Eds.). (2002). *Studies in meaning: Exploring constructivist psychology*. New York: Pace University Press.

Raskin, J. D., & Bridges, S. K. (Eds.). (2004). *Studies in meaning 2: Bridging the personal and social in constructivist psychology*. New York: Pace University Press.

Rescher, N. (1997). *Objectivity: The obligations of impersonal reason*. Notre Dame, IN: University of Notre Dame Press.

Richardson, F. C. (1998). Beyond scientism and postmodernism? *Journal of Theoretical and Philosophical Psychology, 18*, 33–45.

Richardson, F. C., Fowers, B. J., & Guignon, C. B. (1999). *Re-envisioning psychology: Moral dimensions of theory and practice*. San Francisco: Jossey-Bass.

Riikonen, E., & Vataja, S. (1999). Can (and should) we know how, where and when psychotherapy takes place? In I. Parker (Ed.), *Deconstructing psychotherapy* (pp. 175–187). London: Sage.

Robinson, D. N. (1985). *Philosophy of psychology*. New York: Columbia University Press.

Robinson, D. N. (1989). *Aristotle's psychology*. New York: Columbia University Press.

Robinson, D. N. (1997, August). *The morals of objectivity*. Paper presented at the annual meeting of the American Psychological Association, Chicago, IL.

Robinson, D. N. (2002a). Inventing the subject: The renewal of "psychological" psychology. *Bulletin fra Forum for Antropologisk Psykologi, 11*, 6–26.

Robinson, D. N. (2002b). *Praise and blame: Moral realism and its applications*. Princeton, NJ: Princeton University Press.

Rorty, R. (1991). *Essays on Heidegger and others: Philosophical papers* (Vol. 2). Cambridge, England: Cambridge University Press.

Rosen, H. (1996). Meaning-making narratives: Foundations for constructivist and social constructionist psychotherapies. In H. Rosen & K. T. Kuehlwein (Eds.), *Constructing realities: Meaning-making perspectives for psychotherapists* (pp. 3–51). San Francisco: Jossey-Bass.

Rosen, H., & Kuehlwein, K. T. (Eds.). (1996). *Constructing realities: Meaning-making perspectives for psychotherapists*. San Francisco: Jossey-Bass.

Rosenau, P. M. (1992). *Post-modernism and the social sciences: Insights, inroads, and intrusions*. Princeton, NJ: Princeton University Press.

Rozin, P. (2001). Social psychology and science: Some lessons from Solomon Asch. *Personality and Social Psychology Review, 5*, 2–14.

Rychlak, J. F. (1980). More on the meaning of transcendence. *American Psychologist, 35*, 1149–1150.

Rychlak, J. F. (1994). Is free will a process or a content: Both? Neither? Are we free to affirm a position on this question? *Journal of Theoretical and Philosophical Psychology, 14*, 62–72.

Rychlak, J. F. (1997). *In defense of human consciousness*. Washington, DC: American Psychological Association.

Rychlak, J. F. (1998a). Individuality and commonality in the reality of psychotherapy. [Review of the book *Back to reality: A critique of postmodern theory in psychotherapy*]. *Contemporary Psychology, 43*, 603.

Rychlak, J. F. (1998b). [Review of the book *Mind regained*]. *Journal of Mind and Behavior, 19*, 451–454.

Rychlak, J. F. (2000). A psychotherapist's lessons from the philosophy of science. *American Psychologist, 55*, 1126–1132.

Rychlak, J. F. (2001). Psychotherapy as practical teleology: Viewing the person as agent. In B. D. Slife, R. N. Williams, & S. H. Barlow (Eds.), *Critical issues in psychotherapy: Translating new ideas into practice* (pp. 195–204). Thousand Oaks, CA: Sage.

Rychlak, J. F. (2004). Turning reductive science around to make way for the emergence of human agency. [Review of the book *Psychology and the question of agency*]. *Contemporary Psychology, 49*, 766–769.

Sass, L. A. (1988). Humanism, hermeneutics, and the concept of the human subject. In S. B. Messer, L. A. Sass, & R. L. Woolfolk (Eds.), *Hermeneutics and psychological theory: Interpretive perspectives on personality, psychotherapy, and psychopathology* (pp. 222–271). New Brunswick, NJ: Rutgers University Press.

Searle, J. R. (1995). *The construction of social reality*. New York: Free Press.

Semro, K. (2003). *Can a scientific psychology incorporate human agency?* Unpublished senior honors thesis, Bowdoin College, Brunswick, Maine.

Siegel, H. (1996). Naturalism and the abandonment of normativity. In W. O'Donohue & R. F. Kitchener (Eds.), *The philosophy of psychology* (pp. 4–18). London: Sage.

Siegel, H. (1997). *Rationality redeemed? Further dialogues on an educational ideal*. New York: Routledge.

Siegel, H. (1999a). Multiculturalism and the possibility of transcultural educational and philosophical ideals. *Philosophy, 74*, 387–409.

Siegel, H. (1999b). Argument quality and cultural difference. *Argumentation, 13*, 183–201.

Siegel, H. (1999c). [Review of the book *Objectivity: The obligations of impersonal reason*]. *Ethics, 109*, 917–919.

Siegel, H. (2004). Relativism. In I. Niiniluoto, M. Sintonen, & J. Wolenski (Eds.), *Handbook of epistemology* (pp. 747–780). Dordrecht, The Netherlands: Kluwer Academic Publishers.

Siegel, H., & Erwin, E. (1989). Is confirmation differential? *British Journal for Philosophy of Science, 40*, 105–119.

Siewert, C. P. (1998). *The significance of consciousness*. Princeton, NJ: Princeton University Press.

Slaney, K. L. (2001). On empirical realism and the defining of theoretical terms. *Journal of Theoretical and Philosophical Psychology, 21*, 132–152.

Slife, B. D. (1994). The possibility of possibility. *Journal of Theoretical and Philosophical Psychology, 14*, 96–101.

Slife, B. D., & Hopkins, R. O. (2005). Alternative assumptions for neuroscience: Formulating a true monism. In B. D. Slife, J. S. Reber, & F. C. Richardson (Eds.), *Critical thinking about psychology: Hidden assumptions and plausible alternatives* (pp. 121–147). Washington, DC: American Psychological Association.

Slife, B. D., Reber, J. S., & Richardson, F. C. (Eds.). (2005). *Critical thinking about psychology: Hidden assumptions and plausible alternatives.* Washington, DC: American Psychological Association.

Slife, B. D., & Williams, R. N. (1995). *What's behind the research? Discovering hidden assumptions in the behavioral sciences.* Thousand Oaks, CA: Sage.

Slife, B. D., Williams, R. N., & Barlow, S. H. (Eds.). (2001). *Critical issues in psychotherapy: Translating new ideas into practice.* Thousand Oaks, CA: Sage.

Smith, D. W. (2005). Consciousness with reflexive content. In D. W. Smith & A. L. Thomasson (Eds.), *Phenomenology and philosophy of mind* (pp. 93–114). Oxford, England: Oxford University Press.

Smith, D. W., & Thomasson, A. L. (Eds.). (2005). *Phenomenology and philosophy of mind.* Oxford, England: Oxford University Press.

Smith, M. B. (2003). Selfhood at risk: Postmodern perils and the perils of postmodernism. In M. B. Smith, *For a significant social psychology: The collected writings of M. Brewster Smith* (pp. 167). New York: New York University Press.

Smith, T. (2004). "Social" objectivity and the objectivity of value. In P. Machamer & G. Wolters (Eds.), *Science, values, and objectivity* (pp. 143–171). Pittsburgh, PA: University of Pittsburgh Press.

Spence, D. P. (1982). *Narrative truth and historical truth: Meaning and interpretation in psychoanalysis.* New York: Norton.

Spence, D. P. (1988). Tough and tender-minded hermeneutics. In S. B. Messer, L. A. Sass, & R. L. Woolfolk (Eds.), *Hermeneutics and psychological theory: Interpretive perspectives on personality, psychotherapy, and psychopathology* (pp. 62–84). New Brunswick, NJ: Rutgers University Press.

Spence, D. P. (1994). *The rhetorical voice of psychoanalysis: Displacement of evidence by theory.* Cambridge, MA: Harvard University Press.

Stam, H. J. (1998). Personal-construct theory and social constructionism: Difference and dialogue. *Journal of Constructivist Psychology, 11,* 187–203.

Stancombe, J., & White, S. (1998). Psychotherapy without foundations? Hermeneutics, discourse, and the end of certainty. *Theory & Psychology, 8,* 579–599.

Sternberg, R. J. (Ed.). (2005). *Unity in psychology: Possibility or pipedream?* Washington, DC: American Psychological Association.

Taylor, C. (1971). Interpretation and the sciences of man. *Review of Metaphysics, 25,* 3–51.

Thomasson, A. L. (1997). The ontology of the social world in Searle, Husserl and beyond. *Phenomenological Inquiry, 21,* 109–136.

Thomasson, A. L. (1998, October). *The subjective/objective distinction.* Paper presented at the annual meeting of the Alabama Philosophical Association, Orange Beach, AL.

Thomasson, A. L. (1999). *Fiction and metaphysics*. Cambridge, England: Cambridge University Press.

Thomasson, A. L. (2003). Realism and human kinds. *Philosophy and Phenomenological Research, 67*, 580–609.

Thomasson, A. L. (2005). First-person knowledge in phenomenology. In D. W. Smith & A. L. Thomasson (Eds.), *Phenomenology and philosophy of mind* (pp. 115–139). Oxford, England: Oxford University Press.

Thomasson, A. L. (2007). *Ordinary objects*. New York: Oxford University Press.

Tjeltveit, A. C. (1999). *Ethics and values in psychotherapy*. London: Routledge.

Tjeltveit, A. C. (2003). Implicit virtues, divergent goods, multiple communities: Explicitly addressing virtues in the behavioral sciences. *American Behavioral Scientist, 47*, 395–414.

Wegner, D. M. (2002). *The illusion of conscious will*. Cambridge, MA: Bradford Books/MIT Press.

Wegner, D. M. (2004). Précis of the illusion of conscious will. *Behavioral and Brain Sciences, 27*, 649–692.

Wertz, F. J. (1999). Multiple methods in psychology: Epistemological grounding and the possibility of unity. *Journal of Theoretical and Philosophical Psychology, 19*, 131–166.

White, M., & Epston, D. (1990). *Narrative means to therapeutic ends*. New York: Norton.

Wilson, T. D. (2002). *Strangers to ourselves: Discovering the adaptive unconscious*. Cambridge, MA: Belknap Press/Harvard University Press.

Windschuttle, K. (1996). *The killing of history: How literary critics and social theorists are murdering our past*. New York: Free Press.

Woolfolk, R. L. (1998). *The cure of souls: Science, values, and psychotherapy*. San Francisco: Jossey-Bass.

Woolfolk, R. L. (2001). "Objectivity" in diagnosis and treatment: A philosophical analysis. In B. D. Slife, R. N. Williams, & S. H. Barlow (Eds.), *Critical issues in psychotherapy: Translating new ideas into practice* (pp. 287–298). Thousand Oaks, CA: Sage.

Woolfolk, R. L., Sass, L. A., & Messer, S. B. (1988). Introduction to hermeneutics. In S. B. Messer, L. A. Sass, & R. L. Woolfolk (Eds.), *Hermeneutics and psychological theory: Interpretive perspectives on personality, psychotherapy, and psychopathology* (pp. 2–26). New Brunswick, NJ: Rutgers University Press.

Zuriff, G. (1998). Against metaphysical social constructionism in psychology. *Behavior and Philosophy, 26*, 5–28.

AUTHOR INDEX

Grünbaum, A., 254n29, 350n12

Guignon, C. B., 6, 27, 32, 65, 66, 67, 68, 83, 84, 88, 90, 91, 92, 94, 99, 100, 101, 102, 103, 105, 105n, 106, 108, 116, 116n, 124n, 126, 138, 158n, 160, 161, 164, 165n8, 168, 170, 172, 173, 194, 196, 200, 210, 211, 212, 215, 216, 220, 226, 235, 241, 247, 266, 267, 269, 270, 272, 273, 274, 278, 282, 289, 309n, 319, 337, 342

Haack, S., 54n, 55n4, 56, 57, 58, 60, 81n, 87, 100, 129, 131, 137, 138, 150, 150n, 151, 153, 154, 199, 209, 212, 213n, 227, 231, 231n18, 233, 242, 242n22, 244, 245, 246, 252, 272n3, 277, 280, 280nn7–8, 281, 284, 284– 285, 285, 285n, 292, 295, 302, 303, 311n, 316, 332n5, 343, 345

Halleck, S. L., 40

Hare-Mustin, R. T., 41n, 285

Harré, R., 6, 12, 29, 43n, 70, 71, 72, 77, 79, 88, 96, 104, 108n, 113, 151, 153, 163, 195, 195n, 229, 235, 266, 294

Heffner, K. P., 35, 38n, 45, 47

Heidegger, 93, 98n, 173

Held, B. S., 4, 4n, 5, 7, 7n, 11n9, 18, 18n, 19, 28, 29, 29n4, 30, 31n5, 32, 32n, 33, 36, 37, 40, 40n11, 41, 42, 43n, 54n, 76n, 79n, 97n13, 105, 129n, 133n, 139n, 144, 155, 179n, 193, 193n, 197n, 208n2, 221, 222, 222n, 223, 224n14, 242n22, 250n, 261, 284, 285, 295, 301n, 302, 304, 304n, 312n, 324, 341n10

Henriques, G., 5

Hersch, E. L., 6, 12, 61, 67, 70, 95, 109, 117, 174, 261, 261n, 267, 270, 319

Hibberd, F. J., 35, 77, 107, 137, 155

Hiley, D. R., 6, 88, 166, 250, 267, 357

Himmelfarb, G., 9

Holt, R. R., 44

Hopkins, R. O., 7n

Hoshmand, 315

House, R., 42, 43, 44

Howard, G. S., 6, 163, 172, 235, 290, 315, 316, 359n25

Hoy, D., 240, 273, 337

Hoyt, M. F., 33

Jenkins, A. H., 35, 162, 182, 230, 248, 308

Jopling, D. A., 248n, 353n

Katzko, M. W., 79n

Kaye, J., 42, 72

Kellner, D., 28

Kenwood, C., 34, 80, 293

Kimball, R., 9

Kirschner, S. R., 61, 63

Koch, S., 211n5

Koertge, N., 9

Kuehlwein, K. T., 4, 27

Kvale, S., 27, 28, 83, 118, 125

Lakoff, G., 57

Lehman, D., 9

Levin, N., 8

Levinas, 98n, 319n

Lewis, M. W., 8

Liebrucks, A., 12, 35, 70, 72, 78, 79, 85, 96, 104, 118, 119, 121, 122, 127, 133, 135, 144, 150, 152, 152n23, 153, 160n, 176, 177, 185, 186, 187, 229, 238, 255, 266, 270, 276, 293, 294, 295, 295n18, 296, 297, 306, 343

London, P., 40

Mackay, N., 35

Mahoney, M. J., 4, 27, 32

Marecek, J., 285

Martin, J., 6, 12, 27, 29, 33, 63, 64, 65, 66, 70, 71, 74, 81, 82, 83, 88, 89, 92, 94, 97, 99, 100, 101, 102, 104, 105, 114n, 116, 118, 123, 124, 125, 126, 127, 130, 132, 133, 135, 140n, 142, 143nn18–19, 146, 147, 149, 150, 151, 152, 157, 158, 160, 163, 164, 168166, 167, 167n, 169, 170, 172, 174, 175, 176, 178, 178n, 179, 180, 181, 182, 185, 187, 189, 193, 194, 196, 197, 198, 199, 200, 201, 202, 208n1, 210, 215, 217, 218, 220, 221, 223, 229, 235, 241, 248, 251, 252, 254, 255, 261, 262, 266, 268, 269, 270, 272, 275–276, 276, 278, 279, 284, 290, 292n, 297, 300, 304, 305, 306, 307, 311, 312, 314, 317, 318, 324, 329, 346, 357, 360, 360n27, 361, 361–362, 363

Maze, J. R., 35, 78, 79n, 107, 137, 154, 222, 222n, 272n1, 343

McNamee, S., 27

Meichenbaum, D., 211n4

Merleau-Ponty, 98n

Messer, S. B., 6, 29, 86, 95, 187, 196, 210, 211, 214

Miller, R. B., 7n, 12, 12n, 40, 70, 70n, 216, 230, 235, 293, 302, 303, 304, 304n, 308, 314, 315

Moore, R., 45, 197n

Morss, J., 42

Mühlhäusler, P., 43n,

Nagel, T., 46n15, 62, 111, 155, 330

Neiman, A., 243, 325

Neimeyer, R. A., 4, 4n, 13, 27, 31, 32, 34, 73n, 78n3, 79

Nichterlein, M., 42

Nightingale, D. J., 78

Nisbett, R. E., 338, 339

Norenzayan, A., 338

Norris, C., 8, 9, 107, 110, 183, 183n19

Omer, H., 27

Osbeck, L. M., 30, 31n6, 43n, 78, 282

Parker, I., 41, 44

Parry, A., 33

Patai, D., 8, 9

Paul, G. L., 302n

Peng, K., 338

Pinker, S., 174

Polkinghorne, D. E., 6, 30, 169, 194, 222, 235, 240, 248, 255, 290, 293, 315, 316

Pols, E., 16, 23, 24, 29, 32n, 55n3, 59n7, 62n, 80, 96, 97, 97n13, 111, 112, 129, 129n, 139, 154, 155, 164, 179n, 188n, 196, 203, 221, 222n, 224n14, 226n, 228, 229, 229n17, 234, 235n, 245, 254n29, 272n3, 280, 290n, 307, 312n, 313, 318, 325, 326, 327, 340, 341, 341n10, 342, 342n, 343, 344, 345, 345–346, 346, 350, 350nn12–15, 351, 352, 352n17–18, 353, 355, 358, 360, 360n26

Putnam, H., 130

Quine, W. V., 97n14

Rappoport, L., 28, 34, 116

Raskin, J. D., 27, 35

Reber, J. S., 6

Rescher, N., 245, 246, 248, 261, 275, 279, 325, 331

Richardson, F. C., 6, 7n, 12, 27, 29, 43n, 65, 66, 70, 74, 83, 84, 86, 88, 92, 94, 95, 99, 100, 101, 102, 103, 105, 106, 109, 114, 115, 116, 117, 119, 120, 121, 127, 132, 134, 135, 136, 137, 138, 139, 145, 146, 149, 151, 154, 154n, 160, 161, 164, 165, 166, 167, 170, 173, 180, 183n20, 184, 185, 186, 187, 189, 194, 196, 200, 201, 210, 211, 212, 213, 214, 215, 216, 217, 218, 220, 221, 223, 223n, 225, 230, 235, 236, 237, 238, 239, 239n, 240, 252, 253, 255, 257, 263, 266, 267, 269, 272, 273, 278, 279, 280, 281, 282, 283, 284, 284n, 289, 290, 293, 295, 297, 298, 299, 303, 305, 314, 319, 332, 332n6, 335, 336, 337, 340, 346

Riikonen, E., 42

Robinson, D. N., 173n11, 235, 242, 251, 263, 281

Rorty, R., 30, 43n, 266, 272, 275, 282, 283, 336

Rosen, H., 4, 27, 30, 78, 78n3, 79

Rosenau, P. M., 3n3, 5, 28

Rozin, P., 292, 303

Rychlak, J. F., 16, 143n19, 178n15, 182, 182n, 230, 248, 308, 308n, 309, 309n, 310, 311, 312n, 313, 314, 354n21, 358, 359, 359nn24–25

Sass, L. A., 6, 29, 69, 86, 95, 170, 187, 196, 210, 214

Schafer, 223

Searle, J. R., 53, 54, 55, 100, 110, 140, 141, 141n, 144n, 147, 148, 159n, 188, 189, 208, 211n4, 230

Semro, E., 313

Sherry, S., 9

Shusterman, R., 6, 88, 166, 250, 267, 357

Siegel, H., 24, 117n, 212, 212n, 213n, 242n23, 243, 248, 249, 250, 251, 277n5, 278, 280, 281, 286, 287, 288n13, 289, 289n, 325, 326, 327, 330, 331, 331n, 332, 333, 333n, 334, 334n, 334–335, 335, 337, 338, 340, 344, 347, 348, 349, 350

Siewert, C. P., 46n15, 92n, 217n, 352n17, 354n22

Slaney, K. L., 122, 123, 133

SUBJECT INDEX

and faith in knowing, 320
and hermeneutic circle, 107
Agentic functioning, and MGTs on science of psychology, 142
Agentic human nature, and MGTs, 12
Agentic interpretive function, 161
Agentic notion of self-determination, 3n2
Agentic ontology
as MGT goal, 76
and radical postmodernism, 11
Agentic psychology
and antiobjectivist epistemology of MGTs, 317
and causal laws, 292
and meaning of behavior, 299
and methodological pluralism, 315
objectivism against, x
Alcoff, Linda, 164, 176, 195, 196, 197, 286, 287, 288
American Psychological Association, Division 24 (Society for Theoretical and Philosophical Psychology) of, ix
Analytic philosophy, Searle on, 110
Ansoff, Rick, 80
Antiobjectivism, x
and agency, 32–35
of MGTs, 208
Siegel against, 332, 333
Antiobjectivist epistemology, 3–4, 29n3, 283
and agency, 9, 355–356
and causality, 9
and fact/value fusion, 242
in feminism (Haack on), 285
of MGTs, 182, 225, 226, 227, 228, 230, 232–233, 260, 278, 317, 362
agentic psychology undermined by, 325, 334, 361, 362
and conventional psychology, 315
as interpretive commitments, 258, 259
and methods of natural science, 357
and realist epistemology, 324
and reflexivity, 346–347, 353
and values, 235, 236
and moral problem, 283
of postmodernism, 29, 29n3, 228
and constructivist psychotherapy, 31–32
radical, 38, 353
pragmatic consequences of, 46
in renunciation of epistemic neutrality (Richardson et al. and Martin et al.), 102

as self-undermining, 355, 361
Antiobjectivist ontology, and MGTs, 210
Antiobjectivist pragmatic standard of warrant, 239
Antiobjectivist stance, 210–213
arguments for, 213–214
ontology of flux and flow, 251–260
no subject/object dichotomy, 214–234
no value-free "view from nowhere," 234–251, 268, 330
and straw man of objectivity, 260–262
Antirealism
and agency, 32–35
contention over meaning of, 15
Martin and Sugarman on, 125
MGTs' rejection of, 97, 266
more and less radical forms of, 30
and Norris on Heidegger, 107
and perverted direct knowing, 139
in postmodern psychology, 11
and radical constructionism (Gergen), 78
of radical postmodernists, 8
Searle on, 208
Antirealist epistemology, 3–4, 29n3
and agency, 9
and causality, 9
and objective psychological knowledge, 39, 43–48
of postmodernism, 29, 29n3
and constructivist psychotherapy, 31–32
radical, 38
Antisubjectivism, 28
Arealism, 13, 73n, 79
Argument quality, and transcultural normative reach, 332–335
and multiculturalism, 335–340
Aristotle
and causality, 310, 342
and "golden mean," 18
and ontology, 96, 97
Authenticity, 173, 173n11
Autonomy
agency as, 16
client, 314
inner, 11n8
metaphysical, 11n8
Awareness, rational, 228–229, 325, 340, 341–342 347
and cultural diversity, 233

and direct knowing, 327n
fusion of universality and particularity in, 155, 228, 343, 346
and objective knowing, 327n, 348
Pols's epiphany about, 351
Pols's self-reflexive defense of, 350–356
and Rychlak, 312n

Back to Reality (Held), *ix*, 7, 18
Bandura, Albert, 158
Being
    and Heidegger on separations, 59
    and knowing, 23, 67, 100, 105, 137–140, 210
        agentic, 18, 165
        and antiobjectivist epistemology, 225
        and change through reinterpretation, 191
        and MGTs, 223
        Pols on, 341
        and reflexivity, 251–252
    Pols on, 96, 343–344
    situated, 23
    universal meaning of, 96
Being in the world, 20, 22, 24, 61, 88, 89, 90–98, 126, 146, 147, 162
    and Alcoff, 286
    and local discursive ontology, 123
    and MGTs, 162, 170, 246, 292, 340
        constitutive ontology, 175
        realist epistemology, 126
        realist ontology, 107
        on social/psychological existence, 234
    ontology of, 90–98, 135, 157, 170, 175, 207
    and situatedness, 328
Belief, Pols on, 355
Beliefs/discourses, 152
Bernstein, Richard, 6, 86
    and agency, 166
    on being in the world, 94
    and "Cartesian Anxiety," 11, 111, 211–212, 218, 318
    on Gadamer, 151
    on historical objectivism, 217
    on instability, 252–253
    on interpretation, 257
    on objective knowledge or objectivity, 211–212, 212, 261
        fallibilistic, 262

and objectivist/relativist opposition, 56–57, 58–60, 61, 66, 75, 149–150
    and practical rationality, 269–270
    on relativism, 58, 244
        vs. subjectivism, 58
    on tradition, 146–147
    on truth, 279
    and values, 240
    and "view from somewhere," 240, 241
    and warrant, 208
Between Chance and Choice (Atmanspacher & Bishop), 65
"Between the Modern and Postmodern" (Martin & Sugarman), 64–65
Beyond Objectivism and Relativism (Bernstein), 6, 56, 86
"Beyond Scientism and Postmodernism" (Richardson), 66
Bohman, J. F., 6, 10, 166, 250, 267
Brentano, Franz, 98n
Brute facts or data, 211n4, 217, 224
    access to impossible (MGTs), 227
    and certitude, 236
    and knowing process, 223
    MGTs on absence of, 215–216
    and nonobjectivist epistemology, 221
    and stability, 252

"Cartesian Anxiety," 11, 111, 212, 212n6, 218, 318, 347
Case for Pragmatic Psychology, The (Fishman), 6, 31, 73–76, 192
Case studies, in Fishman's pragmatism, 255, 300–301, 301–302
Causal analysis, 7n
Causal dependence
    vs. logical dependence, 140–149
    of psychological existence on discourse/interpretation, 188–190
Causal determination, Martin and Sugarman on, 304–305
Causal determinism, 177. *See also* Determinism
Causal explanation
    in hybrid with noncausal understanding, 304–307
    and MGTs, 356
Causality
    and affective assessment (Rychlak), 313
    and agency, 299, 299n
    and compatibilism, 313–315
    and epistemologies, 9

in Fishman's (neo)pragmatic model, 302
nonagentically vs. agentically deterministic, 143
pragmatism without, 300–304
Causal laws
vs. agency (MGTs), 16–17
and conventional scientific methods, 307–313
elimination of, 291–293, 298
vs. generalization, 314
and MGTs, 23, 24, 76, 262–263
and modern/conventional psychology, 11
and natural vs. human sciences, 255
and radical postmodernism, 11
Certainty
interpretive/conceptual processes preclude, 227
and objective knowledge, 182, 218, 227, 230, 236, 240
Choi, I., on situated cognition, 338–340
Choice, and constructionism, 80
Circumstantial universality of reason, 245–248, 269, 275, 279
Co-constitutional epistemology, 67, 109, 174
Coherentism, 286
Combinatorics, 174
Compatibilism, 11n, 292, 292n, 304, 313–314
and Erwin, 314
of Martin and Sugarman, 202, 306–307
and middle-ground agency, 71
as middle position (Martin, Sugarman, & Thompson), 65
Conflation of active knowing with antirealist epistemology (postmodernism), 36
Conflation of epistemic objectivity with mechanistic ontology, 17
Consciousness
and existential involvements (Martin & Sugarman), 179
Moore on, 47
and Pols on mind, 350n13
self-awareness in (Smith), 352n17
Constraint(s)
and agency, 359
in contemporary hermeneutics, 283
of cultural/discursive context (MGTs vs. radical postmodernists), 92
local situation as, 328 (see also Local context)
local discursive/interpretive context, 139

and ontological realism, 158-159
order born of, 194, 201
in relation with realism and agency, 159–164, 165
Construction(s)
vs. discovery, 138, 197
discursive vs. material, 294
Constructionism
and agency, 80–81
and consequences over rationality, 338
and constructivism, 78n3, 79
on discourse and reality, 106
discursive, 12, 72, 133, 144
moderate, 13, 70, 192
on moral criteria for scientific practice, 238
multiple worlds-constructionist view, 87, 137, 262
and objects of psychological investigation, 120
as ontologically mute, 35
and ontology (Nightingale & Cromby), 78
and postmodernism, 41
and pragmatic paradigm, 85
and warrant, 266
Construction of Social Reality, The (Searle), 53, 110
Constructivism, 4, 29, 32, 78–79
and constructionism, 78n3, 79
radical, 30, 139n15
truth claims of, 36
Constructivist psychotherapy, 31–32
and subjective-objective relation, 47
Contemporary hermeneutics, 283
Context-dependent psychological kinds, and MGTs, 356
Context(s)
agency as capacity for transcending (constitutive), 158, 164–182
and innovation (sociocultural), 177–178
limits on, 201–203
and rationality or mind, 176
behavior sensical within (social), 293–297
beliefs and values out of (historical/cultural/interpretive), 246
discourses/interpretations constructed in, 101
emerging of social/psychological entities in (interpretive), 140

Gadamer on (cultural), 240
intentional states dependent on (social), 119
interpretation within (social/historical), 92
intervention-improvement relative to, 304
practical reason relative to, 269–270, 279
reality obscured by, 361
reason in (MGTs on warrants), 272
regularities of thought and action in, 297–299
Rescher on, 331–332
truth as dependent on, 324
and warrant, 315
See also Local context
Contextualized experiences, and self, 168
Contextualized values, and modern/conventional psychology, 237
Contextually constrained capacity for transcendence, 357
Contextual realism, 155
Contradiction, in Western vs. Eastern thought, 339
Conventional modern psychology. *See* Modern/conventional psychology
Conventions
    making behavior sensical within context, 293–297
    in warranted psychological knowledge, 305–306
Correlational data, 297
Correspondence theories of truth, 111
Creation of Reality in Psychoanalysis, The (Moore), 45
Creativity, Martin and Sugarman on, 180
Critical intersubjectivity, 262, 269, 278–279
Critical realism, 96
    vs. postmodernism (Harré), 71
Critical scrutiny, 331
Critical theorists, on hermeneutics, 163
Critical Thinking About Psychology (Slife, Reber, & Richardson), 6
Crossword puzzle analogy, of Haack, 231, 239
Cultural/discursive context, 201–203
Culturally grounded discursive context, and MGTs on agency, 158
Culturally situated agency, 201–203
Cultural reductionism, 162, 180, 362
Culture(s), 147

determination by (Martin & Sugarman), 178–179
and independent thinking, 163
multivocal or pluralistic nature/essence of, 171–176
as pluralistic, 169, 172
Richardson et al. on, 102
Rychlak vs. MGTs on, 309
and universals of rationality, 234
unlimited options in, 173
See also Multiculturalism
Cure of Souls: Science, Values, and Psychotherapy, The (Woolfolk), 66–67

Dare We Develop a Human Science? (Howard), 6
Data. *See* Brute facts or data
Deconstructing Psychotherapy (Parker), 41
Deconstruction
    Moore's metatheory against, 44
    Parker on, 41
De-experting, 42
Defending Science—Within Reason (Haack), 231
Definitions, of "real," 112
    explicit, 121–127
    implicit, 112, 113–121
Dependence
    causal
        vs. logical dependence, 140–149
        of psychological existence on discourse/interpretations, 188–190
    on context, 324
    generic vs. rigid, 185–186
    of human kinds
        and fallibilism, 131
        Haack on, 131
        on mental states vs. on beliefs about mental states, 131–132, 135, 137
    logical
        vs. causal dependence, 140–149
        and fallibilism, 147, 147n21
        of psychological existence on discourse/interpretations, 183–188
    logical vs. causal, 140–149, 294
    and MGTs, 159n3
    of psychological entities
        on mind vs. on acts of knowing, 129
        of psychological entities on human beings, 122
Determinism
    causal, 177

dilemma of, 314
nonagentic (mechanistic/nonagentic),
    3n2
soft, 65, 304
Dewey, John, pragmatism of, 274
Dialectical reasoning or thought, 165, 308,
    309
    in Eastern philosophy, 339
Direct knowing, 155, 227, 341n10, 342, 347,
    350–351, 352, 353
    perverted, 139, 221, 222, 227, 229
    rational awareness as, 228, 327n (see also
        Rational awareness)
Discourses, 152
    extradiscursive causal consequences of,
        295
    as "out there in the world," 113–115
Discourses/interpretations
    and agency, 158–159
    causal dependence of psychological ex-
        istence on, 188–190
    logical dependence of psychological
        existence on, 183–188
Discovery, vs. construction, 138, 197
Discursive constraints, and ontological real-
    ism, 160, 191–192
Discursive constructionism, 12, 72, 133, 144
Discursive Psychology in Practice (Harré &
    Stearns), 6
Discursive psychology, 71
Distinctions, 20, 52–53
    brute vs. institutional facts, 230
    brute vs. nonbrute entities, 230
    conceptual/empirical or theory/observa-
        tion, 210
    evidential criteria vs. judgments of evi-
        dential criteria, 244
    fact/value, 183, 210, 236, 241, 260, 263,
        273, 281, 282, 284, 335
        and pragmatic vs. epistemic war-
            rants, 288
    between knowing subjects and objects
        to be known, 66, 138, 253
    between logical and causal dependence,
        149, 294
    objective/subjective, 20, 52, 53–54, 281
        (see also Objective/subjective dis-
            tinction)
    objectivist/relativist, 56–60
    between personal/subjective and imper-
        sonal/objective meanings or reasons,
        292

prepositional (true for vs. true about),
    277n6, 330
realist/antirealist, 20, 54–56
warrants as epistemic vs. empirical, 327
warrants as epistemic vs. pragmatic, 288
Double hermeneutic, 101, 103, 195, 225,
    230, 256–257, 258
Dramatic narratives, 109
Driver-Linn, E., 62–64

Eastern philosophy, sociocognitive system of,
    339
Edley, Nigel, 12, 73, 144, 266
Emanationist theory of truth/reality, 60, 67,
    114, 121, 138–139, 222, 225
    and interpretation (Woolfolk), 133
    ontological realism in, 104–112
Emancipation, in post-therapeutic vision, 42.
    See also Liberation
"Emancipatory" psychology, 19
Emergence, Rychlak on, 178n14
Emergent theory of truth/reality, 60, 67, 114,
    138, 222, 225
    and Alcoff, 286
    ontological realism in, 104–112
Emotion, and dependence, 185–187
Empirical knowledge
    as certain vs. as objective, 44
    as fallible, 254, 265
Empiricism, death-knell of, 41
Empowerment
    and constructivist philosophy (Moore),
        48
    Martin and Sugarman on, 82
End of certainty, 34, 43, 44
Epistemic faith and hope, 317–320
Epistemic objectivity. *See* Objectivist epis-
    temology
Epistemic privilege, about human kinds, 130,
    135
Epistemic "reach," 328, 329, 330
Epistemic warrant. *See* Warrant
Epistemological model, 116n7
Epistemological question, fundamental, 5.
    See also Questions
Epistemological realism. *See* Realist episte-
    mology
Epistemological relativism. *See* Relativist
    epistemology
Epistemology(ies)
    feminist, 284–285
    field-specific or discipline-specific, 319

and agency, 166, 181
and being in the world, 94
and cultures as multivocal, 171
on Gadamer, 278
on good judgment, 269
on hermeneutics, 298
on influence of human sciences, 267
on interpretation, 220
    evaluating of, 272
as MGT, 27, 65
on modernist approach, 83–84
on multiculturalism, 332, 335–337
and neorealist hermeneutic, 266
on objectivist epistemology, 211
on personhood and interpretation, 92,
    99, 100, 101, 102, 160, 210
on postmodernism, 194
and radical constructionists,137
on stonewalling, 136, 184
on theory choice in social sciences, 337
on traditions, 175, 176
    negative, 175n
and truth, 196
Frame-level criteria, 134
Framework relativist, 331
Freedom, human
    agency as, 16
    and causal laws, 11
    and interpretive turn, 6
    See also Agency; Free will
Freeman, Mark, 6, 13
    on agency, 163, 182
        and self-identity, 360
    on emanationist or emergent theory of
        reality/truth, 138, 220
    and hermeneutics, 13, 68–69
    on knowledge and power, 318–319
    as MGT, 12, 61–62
    on narrative imagination, 174
    on narratives, 168
    and objectivity, 213
    and rationality/tradition, 176
    on self, 169
    on transcendence, 168, 181, 201
    on truth, 108–109, 271
Free will. 359
    Rychlak on, 309, 359n24
    See also Agency; Freedom, human
Freudian doctrine, 103
From Philosophy to Psychotherapy (Hersch), 6
Fusion of horizons, 154, 154n, 234, 246, 278–
    279, 328, 335, 337, 340

Fusion of universality and particularity, 24,
    154, 203, 327, 340–346

Gadamer, 59, 66, 95, 103
    on absolute reason, 248
    on culturally shaped context, 240,
        241
    and emergent truths, 108, 109
    and fusion of horizons, 234, 246, 278–
        279, 335
    and hermeneutic circle, 183
    hermeneutic position of, 106
    on historical objectivism, 217
    on historiography, 216
    on object-subject distinction, 214
    perspectivism of, 262
    and relativism, 151, 278
    and self-interpretations, 187
    and tradition, 93, 164, 196, 278, 281
        and understanding, 169
    on truth, 195, 270
Gadamerian hermeneutics, 256–257
    and Freeman, 13
Galileo, and neutral epistemic standards
    (Siegel), 250, 331
Generalization, vs. causal laws, 314
Generic dependence, 185–186
Gergen, Kenneth
    on language, 69
    on moral criteria for scientific practice
        282
    and objectivity, 37
    and ontological mutism, 35, 72, 78, 79,
        80, 324, 345
    relativism of, 71–72, 72–73, 276, 336
    on selves, 28
    social constructionism of, 4, 36, 70, 77–
        78, 282–283 (*see also* Social con-
        structionism)
    vs. empiricist assumptions, 30
    radical social constructionism of, 238
    transformative aim of, 35
    on warrants, 33, 266, 295
Giddens, Anthony, 101, 216, 225, 256–259,
    298, 313, 319, 346
Gilbert, Daniel, 354
Goodman, Nelson, 87, 137
Grene, Marjorie, 59, 90, 173
Guignon, Charles, 6, 83–84
    and agency, 168, 172–173
    and being in the world, 90, 94
    on cultural conditioning, 247–248

on emanationist or emergent theory of reality/truth, 138, 220
on evaluating interpretations, 272
and fallibilism, 342
on Gadamer, 278
on good judgment, 269
on hardy hermeneutic realism, 273
on Heidegger, 113–114, 216
on influence of human sciences, 267
as MGT, 27, 65, 67–68
on narrative, 105–106, 108
and neorealist hermeneutics, 266
on objectivist epistemology, 211
on objectivity in physical sciences, 241
on personhood and interpretation, 92, 99, 100, 101, 102, 103, 160, 210
and postmodernism, 194
on practical reason, 270
on Rorty, 116, 116n7, 200, 226, 273, 282, 289, 309
and self-formation, 170
on spotting truth in stories, 319
on standards, 269, 279
on tension between thrownness and projection, 170
on theory choice in social sciences, 337
and truth, 196
on "view from nowhere," 91

Haack, Susan, 87
crossword puzzle analogy of, 231, 239
on epistemic criteria, 246
on feminist epistemology, 284–285
antiobjectivism in, 285
and foundherentist alternative to foundationalism, 213n
on Goodman, 137
on human kinds, 277–278
on interdependence of reason and experience, 231
and mind-dependent items, 209
on moral commitments as epistemic values, 242
on objective knowledge, 231, 233, 280
and objectivist epistemology, 212
and objectivity, 262
on particulars and universals, 153–154, 343
on realism, 56, 138, 151, 209, 345
"innocent realism" of, 55n, 87, 129, 131, 245
on relativism, 244

vs. realism, 54n, 58, 150
on science and common sense, 316–317
"Happy dialogue," 42
Harré, Rom, 6
and agency, 163
and causal explanation, 356
on conventions and rules, 296
and levels of reality, 151
as MGT, 12
and psychology vs. natural science, 298
and realism, 72n
and relativism, 151
and social constructionism, 71–72, 73, 95–96, 113, 266, 282
as radically constructionist, 108n
on social and semantic conventions, 294
on stability and change, 195
and truth, 196
and universality, 153
Hearing Voices Network, 40
Heidegger, Martin, 59
and being in the world, 90, 91, 93–95, 126, 147
on "existence," 113–114
and hermeneutic circle, 183
and hermeneutic realism, 150
on humans as self-interpreting, 94
as plural realist, 124n
on resoluteness, 173
and subjective-objective distinction, 216
and thinghood, 107
and truth, 110
Heraclitus, 194
Hermeneutic circle, 85, 85–86, 107, 162, 165, 170, 183
Hermeneutic dialogue, theory as (Richardson et al.), 189
Hermeneutic MGTs, 145, 154
Hermeneutic ontology, 286
Hermeneutic paradigm, Fishman on, 74–75
Hermeneutic philosophy, 66
and subjective-objective distinction, 214
Hermeneutic psychology of human agency, 65
Hermeneutic realism, 123–127, 150
Hermeneutics, 12, 74, 102, 163
and being in the world, 88, 91
contemporary, 283
double, 101, 103, 195, 225, 230, 256–257, 258

"*In medias res*," 60
Inner autonomy, 11n8
Innocent realism, Haack on, 55n, 87, 129, 131, 245
Innovation, 174, 196
Institutional kind, marriage as example of, 134
Intention(s)
    and agency, 142
    objectivist but not mechanistic account of, 299
Intentionality, 98n, 220, 294, 294
    and existential involvements (Martin & Sugarman), 179
    Thomasson on, 134
Intentional states, 104
    as discursive constructions, 133
    social constructionists on, 96
    and social context (Liebrucks), 119
"Internal Critical Resources of Hermeneutics, The" (Fowers), 175
Internal realism, 55, 55n, 97
Interpretation(s), 10, 93
    choices among, 267
    dependence of psychological entities on, 129
    and external reality (Woolfolk), 133
    and fallibilism, 230, 232
    Freeman on, 68–69
    and hermeneutics, 62, 88
    of Gadamer, 95
    historicist, 156
    latitude in, 295
    and MGTs, 13, 70
    normative epistemology of, 290
    as "out there in the world," 113–115, 115–116
    and tradition (Martin & Sugarman), 268
    and postmodernist inquiry, 11
    Taylor on, 146
Interpretation and personhood, relation of, 92, 99, 100, 117, 160, 200, 210
    and antirealism, 357
    and being-knowing relationship, 101–112
    and beliefs about personhood, 189
    and brute facts, 215
    and collective beliefs, 115
    within contexts, 142
    and discourse of others, 145
    and fallibilism, 127

and Heidegger, 94
and logical vs. causal dependence, 147
and reflexivity, 252
vs. social kinds (racism example), 132–133
and social theory values, 238
as transforming (Richardson et al.), 189
Interpretative conventions, depth of, 183
Interpretive agentic powers, 16
Interpretive function, agentic, 161
Interpretive turn, 6–7, 10, 250, 357
    vs. liberation and transcendence, 362
    vs. linguistic turn, 6n
    and MGTs, 6–7, 13
    and MGTs on postmodernists, 8
Interpretive Turn, The (Hiley, Bohman, & Shusterman), 6
Intersubjectivity
    critical, 262, 269, 278–279
    as substitute for objectivity, 113
Intuitive grasp, of universals, 319–320
Irrealism, 86–87, 137

James, William
    on points of view, 246
    pragmatism of, 274
Jopling, David, 353n19

Kant, Immanuel, 59, 59n7, 224n14, 290
Kaye, John, 42
Kenwood, C., 80–81, 293
Kirschner, Suzanne, 61
Knowing
    active nature of, 36, 228 (*see also* Rational awareness)
    and being, 23, 67, 100, 105, 137–140, 210
    agentic, 165
    and antiobjectivist epistemology, 225
    and change through reinterpretation, 191
    and MGTs, 223
    Pols on, 341
    and reflexivity, 251–252
    direct (Pols), 155, 342, 347, 350–351, 352, 353
    direct and indirect, 227, 341n10
    perspectival nature of, 239 (*see also* "View from nowhere")

perverted direct, 139, 221, 222, 227, 229
Knowing acts, 129
Knowledge
    and generalization, 199
    and human psychological existence, 89
    as power to transcend, 318
    See also Objective knowledge; *at* Warrant(s)
Knowledge claims
    and further radicalization of postmodernism, 39
    justification or warrant of, 23, 38, 40
Kuhn, Thomas, 62–63, 240, 311

Lakoff, George, 57
Language and linguistic entities
    and brute facts (Searle), 230
    as combinatorial, 174
    in construction of reality (postmodernists), 51
    and emotion, 186
    and human psychological kinds, 221
    and MGTs, 70
    middle-ground, 60, 64
        and (neo)hermeneutic tradition, 61–70
        and (neo)pragmatic tradition, 73–76
        and social constructionism, 70, 71–73
    and objective knowledge, 226, 227
    and objectivism, 113, 221–222, 223–224
    objectivity of, 113, 261–262
    onto-formative capacities of, 104
    ontology of, 97
    in rational awareness (Pols), 229
    and reality (antirealist view), 30
    relation of to world (Freeman vs. Gergen), 69
    and Rorty's pragmatism, 116
    of science (as impoverished), 28, 211
    and theory, 224n13, 226n
Levels of reality
    and discursive/interpretive context, 151, 152
    Martin and Sugarman on, 118, 123–124, 127, 151, 197–198
Levinas, 319
Liberation
    and antiobjectivist/antirealist epistemology, 355–356
    vs. antiobjectivist interpretive turn, 362

from constructivist approach, 45
    as goal, 282
    and postmodernists, 32, 33–34
    and post-therapeutics, 40–41
    and pragmatic criteria, 272n1, 284
    as social constructionist goal, 36
    See also Emancipation
Liebrucks, Alexander
    and causal explanation, 356
    and dependence, 186
    on discursive constructions, 133
    on emotion, 185
    on fallibility, 119–120
    on local rules and conventions, 306
    as MGT, 12
    on mind, 176–177
    on properties of persons, 270
    on psychological explanation, 255
    on psychological properties and rules or conventions, 294–295
    on psychology, 85
        vs. natural sciences, 293, 298
    and racism, 297
    and realism, 122
    and relativism, 72–73, 152
        and universals, 153
    and relativist ontology of personhood, 153, 276, 293
    on rules and conventions, 296
    on semantic and normative necessity, 187
    on social constructionism, 96, 118, 144, 266
    on universals of personhood, 343
Linguistic philosophers, Norris on, 110
Linguistic turn, ix, 357
    of Harré, 72
    vs. interpretive turn, 6n
    of postmodern psychology, 12
    and "truth or normality," 34
Local context(s)
    as constraint, 328
    cultural/discursive contexts (psychological existence dependent on), 218
    discourse as, 119
        and psychological existence, 215
    discursive/interpretive contexts
        beliefs about psychological entities in, 142
        and meaning rules or conventions, 356
        social/psychological existence conditioned by, 224–225

and warrant for "truths," 139
and MGTs, 246, 247
    and objective knowledge, 232
historical/cultural discourses/interpretations as
    brute facts precluded by, 215
    values included in, 243
meaning rules and conventions (and psychological kinds), 310–311
normative position as, 34
ontologies as
    discursive (and being in the world), 123
    and MGTs, 96–98
    of personhood, 177
reality of, 153
values (*see also* Values)
    and MGTs, 235
    vs. objectivity, 260
See also Context(s)
Local dialogical community
    and MGTs, 70
    in post-therapeutics, 40, 41
Logical dependence
    vs. causal dependence, 140–149
    and fallibilism, 147, 147n21
    of psychological existence on discourse/interpretation, 183–188
Logical Learning Theory (LLT), 308, 308n, 359
Logical positivism, 81n, 280

MacIntyre, Alisdair, 340, 344
Marriage, as example of institutional kind, 134–136, 154
Martin, Jack, 6, 12, 64–65, 82–83
    on agency, 157, 158, 163–164, 166–167, 168, 169, 175–176, 180, 202, 307
        and comprehension of situation, 181
        definition of, 329
        and self-identity, 360
    and being in the world, 147, 194
    and belief in ability to know human nature, 318
    and biological reductionism, 162–163
    and causal deterministic science of psychology, 304
    causal/noncausal account by, 304–307
    and causal questions, 297
    and compatibilism dilemma, 314
    on conceptualization, 279
    on constraint, 359

and cultural reductionism, 361–362
on cultural upheavals, 196
and cultures as pluralistic, 172
on discursive psychology, 71
and double hermeneutics, 101
on epistemic standard of usefulness, 198
on epistemology and transcendence, 317–318
on equating realism with objectivism, 218
on essential human nature, 149
on flux and stability, 193
on forms of psychological inquiry, 357
and fusion of horizons, 279–280
and hermeneutic realism, 66
on human kinds, 130
and individual psychological development, 177–179
and interpretation, 215
and language of causal dependence, 142
and levels of reality, 118, 123–124, 127, 151, 197–198
on logical dependency, 146
on mediation, 223
on myths of modernity, 81–82
and neorealist hermeneutics, 266
on objectivism, 208n1
and objectivity, 254, 255, 261, 262
and ontological realism, 220
on personhood and interpretation, 92, 99, 100, 102, 116, 160, 210, 252
and perspectival, fallibilist warrant, 267
on postmodernists, 200
on psychological inquiry, 356
and psychology of possibility and constraint, 89
and rationality/tradition, 176
on realism, 200, 277
    hermeneutic, 123–127
on reductionism, 363
and relativism, 150, 180, 199, 244, 251, 270–271, 275–276, 276–277, 278, 317
Rychlak on, 311
and self-understanding, 217
and situated agency, 201
and soft determinism, 65
and stability, 198, 199, 252
on tradition as pragmatic warrant, 272
    and innovation, 174, 185, 187
and transcendence, 170, 187, 201, 324
    as innovation, 174, 185, 187

and universal reason/rationality, 269
on "view from nowhere," 241
and warranted generalization, 199
on warranted reason, 269
on warrants, 290, 291
Martin Heidegger (Grene), 59, 90
Maze, J. R., 154, 222, 222n, 343
Meaning(s)
  constructivist view of, 32
  Freeman on, 108
  indeterminacy of (postmodernists), 28
  objectivist but not mechanistic account of, 299
  as "out there in the world," 113–115, 115–116, 121
  Taylor on, 114
  unbounded relativity of (Gergen), 71
  in warranted psychological knowledge, 305–306
Meaning making, rational, 358
Meaning rules and conventions, 293–297, 356
Mechanistically deterministic causal laws
  and agency, 81, 356
  vs. human psychological existence, 253
  and objective knowledge, 323, 327
Mechanistically deterministic ontology
  epistemic objectivity conflated with, 17
  in "myth of modernity," 81–82
Mechanistic determinism
  and MGTs on psychology, 142
  and objectivism, 81
Mechanistic/nonagentic or mechanistic determinism, 3n2
Mechanistic view of human nature, traditional science not linked to (Rychlak), 311
Mediation
  Freeman on, 68, 69
  Martin and Sugarman in, 64
Mental states, 131
Messer, S. B., 6, 86, 196, 210–211, 211
Metaphysical autonomy, 11n8
Metaphysics, proper (Martin & Sugarman), 202
Methodological hermeneutics, 86, 95
Methodological pluralism, 315–317
Methodology for the Human Sciences (Polkinghorne), 6
MGTs. *See* Middle ground theorists
Middle ground, Flew on, 3
Middle-ground epistemology, 207, 266

Middle-ground language, 60, 64
  and (neo)hermeneutic tradition, 61–70
  and (neo)pragmatic tradition, 73–76
  and social constructionism, 70, 71–73
Middle-ground ontology, 52, 55–56, 77, 82–83, 86–90, 192, 207, 243
  of being in the world, 90–98
  as ontological realism, 99
  realist, 207
  of stability within flux, 193–199
Middle-ground realism, 89
Middle-ground realist ontology, 99, 157
  and question of which beliefs, 100, 118
  and relation of personhood to beliefs, 100–112
Middle-ground theorists (MGTs), 4–8, 52, 62, 323–326
  and agency, 8–9, 12, 13–14, 16, 87, 89, 157, 162, 174, 182–183, 199–200
  and antiobjectivist epistemology, 361, 362
  and beliefs about psychological existence, 142–143
  vs. causality, 16
  and meaning making, 358
  and objective knowledge, 253, 357, 362–363
  rational agency, 24, 24–25, 325, 326, 356, 358–359
  and rationality, 358, 359
  and universality of rationality, 234
  aims of (two-pronged mission), 8–10, 12–14, 16, 19–20, 62, 67, 86, 254, 266, 323, 325
  antireductionist impulse in, 76, 361
  and common ambition, 76
  and objective knowledge, 262
  and reformulated ontology, 82
  and varieties of psychological inquiry, 356
  antiobjectivist epistemology of, 182, 225, 226, 227, 228, 230, 232–233, 260, 278, 317, 362
  agentic psychology undermined by, 325, 334, 361, 362
  and conventional psychology, 315
  as interpretive commitments, 258, 259
  and methods of natural science, 357
  and realist epistemology, 324

and reflexivity, 346–347, 353
and values, 235, 236
antiobjectivist ontology of, 210
and antirealism, 266
and being in the world, 162, 170, 246, 292, 340
  constitutive ontology of, 175
  realist epistemology, 126
  realist ontology, 107
  on social/psychological existence, 234
and belief-dependent ontology of personhood, 140–149
  and relativism, 149–152
and causal language, 188
and causal laws or explanations, 23, 24, 76
and coming into being by way of understanding, 60
and definition of "real," 109
and dependence, 159n3
  logical vs. causal, 184, 188, 189–190
and dichotomy between knowing subject and known object, 208
and distinctions, 20, 52–53
  evidential criteria vs. judgments of evidential criteria, 244
  fact/value, 183, 210, 236, 241, 260, 263, 281, 282, 284, 335
  humans as knowing subjects vs. objects to be known, 66, 253
  objective-subjective, 52, 53–54, 59, 260, 263
  objectivist/relativist, 56–60
  personal/subjective meanings or reasons and impersonal/objective explanations or laws, 292
  realist/antirealist, 54–56
diversity among, 12–13, 356
and faith in reason and knowing, 318–320, 348, 353
on fallible inquiry, 160
and fusion of rational and experiential, 229
hermeneutic, 145, 154 (see also at Hermeneutic)
and inseparability of being and knowing, 24
and interpretive turn, 6–7, 13
lack of critical response to, 5
on limits to liberation, 19
and link between agency and knowing, 9

and local context, 246, 247 (see also Context; Local context)
and local ontologies, 96–98
and methodological pluralism, 315–317
and moderate social constructionists, 79–80
and modern/conventional psychology, 12, 191, 356
and modernist ontology, 81–86
on modern objectivist epistemologies, 27
and objective knowledge, 220, 253, 262–263, 265, 323, 324
and objective psychological inquiry, 18
and objective standpoint, 62
and objectivism of, 207–208, 266
and objectivist epistemology, 9, 210, 263, 328
and objectivity
as certitude, 218
  reformulations of, 261
ontological commitments of, 20
ontological realism of, 99, 218
  and agency, 200
and ontological relativism, 101
and opposition of universality and particularity, 329
on order in chaos, 194
and personhood, 184
and Pols, 340
and postmodernism, 7–8, 9, 10, 12, 29
  and agency, 35
  radical, 12, 38, 112, 191
  and tradition, 155
and pragmatic criteria of truth, 295–296
  over cultural constraints, 285
problematic assumptions made by, 14
and proper questions for psychological inquiry, 291–315
and psychological entities, 223
and psychological knowledge, 265
on psychological stability and evolution, 190
and rationality/reason, 349–350
"real" as defined and used by, 112
  and being vs. knowing about being, 137–140
  and explicit definition, 121–127
  and implicit definition, 112, 113–21
  and logical vs. causal dependence, 140–149
  and realism of human kinds, 127–137

and realism, 8, 13–14, 160–161, 222, 324–325
  criteria for, 113–121, 161
  and culture as constraint, 202–203
realism and objectivism distinguished by, 9, 15, 17, 18, 89, 150n, 218
and realist epistemology, 9, 15, 76, 263, 265, 278, 324
  mediation in, 222–223
  vs. objectivist, 208, 210
and reflexivity, 251, 346
and relativism, 100, 224, 249, 250, 251, 266, 267, 280, 330
  on psychological existence, 149–152
relativist ontology of, 270
and sciences, 85
and Siegel, 333
and situated knowing, 22, 23
and stability, 201, 252, 256
and transcendence, 330, 346
  contextually constrained capacity for, 357
and transcultural normative reach, 334
and universals, 153, 192, 342
and values, 235–236, 237–238, 239, 241
and warrants, 208, 243, 266–267, 318
  (*see also at* Warrants)
Middle Way, of Eastern thought, 339
Miller, R. B., 12, 216, 293, 302–303, 315, 356
Mind
  functions of (Pols), 129, 129n, 179n, 341n10, 350n13
  MGTs' view of, 325–326
  rational or imaginative nature/essence of, 176–182
  See also Psychological entities; Rationality/reason
Mind-dependent entities
  and beliefs or knowledge claims, 180–181, 264
  natural boundaries lacking for, 198n
  and objective existence, 115
  objective knowledge of, 46, 46n15, 47, 233
  ontological realism of, 56
  and question of whose mind or beliefs, 92, 102, 217
  and social/psychological reality, 209
  See also Psychological existence
Mind Regained (Pols), 228, 350, 352
Modern/conventional psychology, 10–11

and contextualized values, 237
facts vs. values in, 288
and Fishman's paradigm, 302
and Fishman on universal laws or explanations, 76
and mechanistically deterministic causality, 4, 8, 323
MGTs on, 12, 191, 356
and ontology, 81–86
reductionist doctrines of, 4, 5
Modernism, 194
Modernist philosophies of psychology, 4
Moore, Richard, 44–45, 46–47, 48
Morals of objectivity, 263
Moral viewpoint, vs. causal analysis (Miller), 303, 304
Morss, J., 42
Multiculturalism, 335–340
Multiple worlds-constructionist view, 87, 137, 262
Music, as combinatorial, 174
Mutism, ontological. *See* Ontological mutism
"Myths of modernity," 81–82, 83

Nagel, Thomas, 46, 62, 111, 155–156, 330
Narrative approaches, and postmodernism, 41
"Narrative Explanation in Psychotherapy" (Guignon), 84, 273
Narrative framework, 12n
Narrative imagination, 172, 174
"Narrative psychotherapy case study," 70n
Narrative (s)
  dramatic, 109
  Freeman on, 181
Narrative structure, of life, 105–106
Narrative therapists, 44
Natural Boundaries Principles (Thomasson), 130, 131, 132
Naturalistic fallacy, 286, 287
Naturalistic model, 7n
  Guignon on, 84
Naturalized epistemology, as realist, 286–2091
Necessity
  causal vs. normative and semantic, 144, 294
  semantic vs. normative, 187
Negative philosophical judgment
  about knowing (Pols), 29, 342, 355–356
Neiman, Alven, 243, 325

Neimeyer, Robert, 13, 31–32, 34, 73n, 79

(Neo)hermeneutics, 12, 60, 61–70

Neo-metaphysics (Martin & Sugarman), 202

(Neo)pragmatic epistemology, 266

(Neo)pragmatism, 12, 13, 60, 70, 73–76

Neorealist hermeneutics, 65, 266, 317

Neutral epistemic standards, Siegel on, 248–251

Neutral value-free form of inquiry, 282

Nichterlein, M., 42

Nihilism, in postmodern psychology, 4, 5

Nisbett, R. E., on situated cognition, 338–340

Nominalism, realism defined in opposition to, 124

Nomothetics, and Fishman, 75

Nonnormative naturalism, Siegel on, 287

Norenzayan, A., on situated cognition, 338–340

Normality, local vs. societal, 34

Normative epistemologies, vs. naturalized, 287, 290

Normative naturalism, Siegel on, 287

Normativity, Harré on, 294

Normativity (argumentative or epistemic), skepticism toward, and Siegel's response, 337–338

Norris, Christopher, 107, 110, 111–112, 183

"Not knowing" approach to therapy, 41

Objective idealism, of Rychlak, 312n

Objective knowing

    and agency, 326, 327–328

    and rational awareness, 348 (*see also* Rational awareness)

Objective knowledge, 254, 281–282

    and agency (MGTs), 323, 325, 357, 362–363

        and MGTs' self-contradiction, 362–363

    as absent in psychology, 254

    Bernstein on, 211–212

    and brute facts/data, 224

    as certitude or indubitability, 218, 227, 230, 236, 240

    as fallible, 244–245

    and foundational or certain knowledge, 82

    about human kinds, 220

    about human world, 215

    and language, 226

    and mechanistically deterministic causal laws (MGTs), 323, 327, 357

    and MGTs, 220, 253, 262–263, 265, 323, 324

    moderate view of, 265

    and Pols's belief component, 355

    as power to transcend, 318

    and psychological existence, 256

    and Rychlak, 312

    and stability, 252, 253

    straw man of, 353, 260–262

    as timeless/universal, 251–260

    and transcendence, 362

    and true for vs. true about, 330

    and values, 234–251

    and "view from nowhere," 203

    Windschuttle's defense of, 195

Objective psychological inquiry, 18

Objective standpoint, and MGTs, 62

Objective/subjective distinction, 20, 52, 53–54, 281

    challenge to, 61

    and dependence of psychological entities on acts of knowing, 130

    as factitious (Hoy), 273

    hermeneutic philosophers on, 114

        hermeneutic realism,125–126

    MGTs against, 22, 214, 263, 260

    and objective knowledge, 214–221

Objectivism, *ix*, 292

    Bernstein on, 57

        and relativist criticism, 86

    contention over meaning of, 15

    Martin and Sugarman on, 208n1

    and mechanistic determinism, 81

    MGTs' rejection of, 13–14, 15, 111, 207–208, 266

    of modern/conventional psychologists, 8–9

    moving beyond (Fowers & Richardson), 336–337

    and realism, 9, 14, 15, 17, 18, 89, 150n, 218

    and self-determination, 16

    on social categories, 95

Objectivism-subjectivism debate

    and co-constitutional epistemology, 67

Objectivist epistemology, 15, 209

    and agency, 9, 360

    and agentic psychological ontology, 17

    and causality, 9

    consequences of adopting, 14–15

and foundationalism, 212
and local context, 224–225
mechanistic ontology conflated with, 17
MGTs' turn away from, 9, 210, 263, 328
in "myth of modernity," 82
in modern/conventional psychology, 4
and particulars, 233
and Pols, 345
and pragmatic standard of warrant, 285
and realist epistemology, 208, 209, 210, 277, 266

Objectivist ontology, 15
Objectivist/relativist distinction, 20, 56–60
Objectivity
certainty equated with, 182
fallibilist, 263, 337
impossibility of in history (Foucault), 259
and interpretation or mediation, 226
and Kant, 224n14
linguistic, 261–262
and MGTs, 218, 261
in modern and postmodern psychologies (Richardson, Fowers, & Guignon), 84
as moral disposition, 242, 263
perspectival, 261
and rationality (Siegel), 248–251
Rescher on, 245, 246, 248
Richardson et al. on, 281
Slife and Williams on, 243
straw man of, 22, 260–262, 279, 280, 315, 327, 357

"Objectivity, Value Judgment, and Theory Choice" (Kuhn), 240
Ontic universality, Pols on, 343
Onto-formative capacities of language, 104
Ontological commitments, of MGTs, 20
Ontological expansion of reason, Pols on, 351–352
Ontological hermeneutics, 84, 93
Ontological middle ground. See Middle-ground ontology
Ontological mutism
and agency, 80
of constructionism, 72, 73, 78
Gergen on, 35, 71–72, 78, 79, 80, 324, 345
and MGTs vs. radical postmodernists, 86, 191
MGTs' rejection of, 97
"muted" form of, 192

and Neimeyer, 79
of postmodernists, 35, 36, 37, 40, 44–45, 77–81
of social constructivism, 77–78
Ontological question, fundamental, 5. See also Questions
Ontological realism, 15, 55, 56
and agency, 160, 170
and constraints, 158–159
and emanationist or emergent theory of truth/reality, 104–112
and epistemological realism, 209, 210
and fallibilism (Richardson et al.), 134
Gergen's rejection of, 78
and historical/cultural/discursive/interpretive context, 175
and Independence Principle (Thomasson), 128
and logical dependence of psychological existence, 189
and MGTs, 99, 162, 193, 200, 207, 218
and relativism, 150
of psychological entities and agencies, 144
of psychological entities or kinds, 157
and stability, 201
and structured world, 194n
Ontological relativism, 101, 152
Ontology
of being in the world, 90–98, 135, 157, 170, 175, 207 (see also Being in the world)
derivation of term, 96, 97n13
expressivist, 105n
of flux and flow, 22, 76, 89, 192–193, 194, 251–260, 301
and agentic interpretive capacities, 260
MGTs' appeal to, 342
and postmodernism, 194
and predictability (Martin & Sugarman), 300
hermeneutic, 286
of the individual as agent, 80
of a language, 97
levels-of-realism (Martin & Sugarman), 118
local connotation for, 97
middle-ground, 52, 55–56, 82–83, 86–90, 192, 207, 243
as ontological realism, 99
realist, 207

antiobjectivism of, 32, 228
breadth of, 5
and critical realism, 96
defining features of, 28–32
and descriptive or qualitative forms of
    research, 257
disenchantment with, 4
in "form-flux debate," 193–194
and Heraclitus, 194
on hermeneutics, 163
MGTS on, 7–8, 9, 10, 12, 29
    and agency, 35
    and tradition 155
on modern scientific approach, 27, 28
Pols on, 112
and "prepositional" distinction, 277n6
on reality, 83
as social constructionism (Harré), 71
and subjectivity without subject, 11n9,
    15, 28–29
truth claims of, 36–38, 79
types of, 28n
Postmodernism, radical, 7, 8, 10, 19–20, 51–
    52
and agency, 34–35
antiobjectivist epistemology of, 353
on being as beliefs, 194
and consequences over rationality,
    338
critique of, 9
further radicalization of, 38–43
and rejection of fusion of rational and
    experiential, 229
vs. MGTs, 12, 38, 112, 191
and modernist ontology, 81
on multiple "truths," 139
and objective judgments, 53
on objective psychological inquiry, 18
ontological mutism of, 35, 36, 44–45,
    77–81, 191
and opposition of universality and par-
    ticularity, 329
subjectivist-objectivist contradiction in,
    43–48
universal truth claims of, 35–38, 48
Postmodernist ontology, of extreme flux,
    192–193
Postmodern pragmatism, 192
Postmodern relativism, and moral values, 283
Post-therapeutics, 39–42, 43, 44, 52
Practical reason, as context-dependent, 269–
    270, 279

Pragmatic Case Studies in Psychotherapy
    (online journal), 13n
Pragmatic epistemology, 198
Pragmatic paradigm, 85
    Fishman on, 74, 75
Pragmatic relativism, 274, 274–275, 279, 289
Pragmatic solidarity, Rorty promotes, 226
Pragmatic standard of warrant, 285
Pragmatic truth, 193, 266, 285, 295
    and "objective reality," 255, 275
    pragmatic relativism, 274, 275
Pragmatic value-laden epistemology
    as realist, 281–285
Pragmatic/value-laden warrant, 272–275,
    338
    MGTs' espousal of, 288
Pragmatism, 12, 13, 12n
    case studies for, 255, 300–301, 301–302
    without causality, 300–304
    and epistemic warrants (MGT theo-
        rists), 70
    and Fishman, 13, 113
    justification of, 349
    philosophical, 193
    postmodern, 192, 274
    and Rorty, 43n, 116
    See also (Neo)pragmatism
"Pragmatism or Hermeneutics? Epistemology
    after Foundationalism" (Guignon),
    273
Prediction, and generalities, 154
Professionalization, and therapeutic experi-
    ences, 43
Psychoanalysis, vocabulary of, 103–104
Psychological entities
    and "classical empirical realism"
        (Slaney), 122
    as discourse-dependent, 149
    linguistically constituted vs. linguisti-
        cally mediated knowing of, 221–234
    MGTs on, 123, 223
    As nonbrute, 215
Psychological entities or kinds, ontological
    realism of, 157
Psychological existence
    causal dependence of on discourse/in-
        terpretation, 188–190
    as dependent on local cultural/discur-
        sive/interpretive contexts, 218
    and discourse/beliefs, 145–149
    and fallibilism, 118–121, 126, 134, 137–
        138, 147–149

and realism, 137–138n
logical dependence of on discourse/interpretation, 183–188
and MGTs, 6, 9
as nonbrute existence, 215
and objective knowledge, 254–255, 256
as partly independent, 159
and question of whose beliefs, 100, 118
as reflexive, 251–252
stability of, 190, 192
See also Mind-dependent entities; Ontology; Personhood
Psychological existence or agency, nature of, 18
Psychological existence and interpretation. *See* Interpretation and personhood, relation of
Psychological explanation, 256
Liebrucks on, 255
Psychological inquiry
and MGTs, 6, 9
proper questions for, 291
on causal laws, 291–293, 298, 307–315
on hybrid of causal explanation and noncausal understanding, 304–307
on meaning rules and conventions, 293–297
on pragmatism without causality, 300–304
on regularities in thought and action in context, 297–299, 304
and values, 237–241
See also at Epistemology
Psychological kinds, stability of, 199
Psychological knowledge or truth, nature of, 18
Psychological ontology, 191–192
Psychological realism, 122–123
Psychological reality
and realism, 127
and socioculturally shared beliefs and practices, 126–127
Psychological scientism, 65
Psychologizing, Siegel on, 212n
Psychology
discursive, 71
"emancipatory," 19
fragmentation of, 5
fundamental questions of, 5 (*see also* Questions)

indigenous epistemology for, 319–320
innovative philosophy of, 5
modern/conventional, 10–11, 12, 191, (*see also* Modern/conventional psychology)
postmodern, 11
subject matter of, 85
Psychology of Human Possibility and Constraint, The (Martin & Sugarman), 6, 65, 360
Psychology and the Question of Agency (Martin, Sugarman, & Thompson), 6, 65
Psychotherapy(ies)
constructive, 31–32
postmodernistically informed, 41–43
and post-therapeutics, 39–42, 43, 44, 52
value-laden nature of, 40
See also Therapy
"Psychotherapy Without Foundations" (Stancombe & White), 38–39
Putnam, Hilary, 55, 97

Questions
on consequences of MGTs' commitments for agency, 25
fundamental, 12
on possibility of objective psychological knowledge, 5, 14, 16, 23
on relationship of objective psychological knowledge to human agency, 5, 14, 16, 23
on human psychological being, 25
on knowledge of human psychological existence, 25
from MGT message, 8
for psychological inquiry, 291
on causal laws, 291–293, 298, 307–315
on hybrid of causal explanation and noncausal understanding, 304–307
on meaning rules and conventions, 293–297
on pragmatism without causality, 300–304
on regularities in thought and action in context, 297–299, 304
Quine, Willard Van Orman, 97n14

Racism, 233, 297
marriage contrasted with, 134–136, 154

as opaque, 184
and rational awareness, 228
Thomasson's example of, 131–133, 148, 180, 209, 220, 233, 296–297
Radical constructivism vs. social constructionism, 139n15
Radical postmodernism. *See* Postmodernism, radical
Radical realism (Pols), 228, 345
Radical Realism (Pols), 228, 343
Rational agency, 24, 24–25, 325, 326, 356, 358–359
Rational awareness, 228–229, 325, 340, 341–342, 347
   and cultural diversity, 233
   and direct knowing, 228, 327n
   fusion of universality and particularity in, 155, 228, 343, 346
   and objective knowing, 327n, 348
   Pols's epiphany about, 351
   Pols's self-reflexive defense of, 350–356
   and Rychlak, 312n
Rational/imaginative capacities, universal nature of, 202
Rationality/reason
   in agency, 358, 359
     Erwin on, 314
     Freeman on, 181–182
     Martin and Sugarman on, 180
     Rychlak on, 359n24
     Siegel on, 350
   circularity charged against justification of, 347
   circumstantial universality of (Rescher), 245–248, 269, 275, 279
   and context, 176, 279–280
   empirical or experiential component of, 25
   formative functions of, 129
   and multiculturalism (Fowers & Richardson), 335–336
   as objective yet emotional (Scheffler), 243
   perspectival, 269
   as purposive (Rychlak) 359n24
   as relative, 279
   and Siegel, 347
     and objectivity, 248–251
     and self-reflexive defense of rationality, 347–350
   universals of, 176–177, 203, 232, 234, 245–248, 269

See also Argument quality
Rationality Redeemed? (Siegel), 340
Rationally agentic existence, and objective knowledge, 17
Rational nature of human mind, 176–182
Rational transcendence, 328–329, 358–361
   and Pols on fusion of universality and particularity, 340–346
   and transcultural normative reach, 330–332
   and argument quality, 332–340
"Real"
   definitions and uses of, 112
     and being vs. knowing about being, 137–140
     and explicit definition, 121–127
     and implicit definition, 112, 113–121
     and logical vs. causal dependence, 140–149
     and realism of human kinds, 127–137
   redefining of, 105
   as substitute for "objective," 113
Realism, 54–55, 128, 277
   and agency, 189, 190
   and beliefs about mind-dependent entities, 180–181
   and causal vs. logical dependence, 140, 147
   contention over meaning of, 15
   criteria for, 113–121, 161, 200
   critical, 96
     vs. postmodernism (Harré), 71
   epistemological, 194–195
     and structured world, 194n
   fallibility as criterion of, 119
   Haack on (innocent realism), 54n, 55n, 56, 58, 87, 129, 131, 151, 245, 345
   hermeneutic, 66, 123–127, 150
   of human kinds, 127–137, 198n5, 218
     and epistemic privilege, 135
   internal (ontological), 55, 55n, 97
   on mediation, 223
   and MGTs, 8, 13–14, 100, 160–161, 222, 324–325
     criteria for, 113–121, 161
     and culture as constraint, 202–203
   and objectivism, 9, 14, 15, 17, 18, 89, 150n, 218
   ontological, 56, 99, 200 (*see also* Ontological realism)

plural (Heidegger), 124n
psychological, 122–123
radical (Pols), 228, 345
in relation with constraint and agency,
    159–164, 165
and relativism, 54n2, 150, 151
scientific, 72
Searle on, 54–55, 208
situational or contextual, 155
and stability, 201
and structure, 194
Realist/antirealist distinction, 20, 54–56
Realist epistemology, 15, 152, 194–195, 208–
    209, 265–266
    and agency, 9
    and causality, 9
    and local/relativistic (discursive) con-
        straints (and MGTs), 291
    and MGTs, 9, 15, 76, 263, 265, 278,
        324
        mediation in, 222–223
        vs objectivist, 208, 210
    in modern/conventional psychology, 4
    naturalized epistemology as, 286–291
    and objectivist epistemologies, 208, 209,
        210, 266, 277
    pragmatic value-laden epistemology as,
        281–285
    and structured world, 194n
    weak relativist epistemology as, 275–
        281
Realist/objectivist epistemology, and know-
    ing consequences of belief, 272n2
Realist ontology. See Ontological realism
Reality(ies)
    and act of knowing, 139
    emanationist or emergent theory of, 60,
        67, 104–112, 114
    emanationist theory of, 121, 133, 138–
        139, 222, 225
    emergent theory of, 138, 222, 225
    local, 153
    multiple construals of, 172
    objectivity of, 215
    as obscured by context, 361
    Pols on, 343
    and postmodern constructionism, 85
    postmodernism on, 29, 30, 31, 32, 83
        and constructivist psychotherapy,
            31–32
    psychological, 94
    in radical postmodernist view, 51–52

and realist or objectivist epistemology,
    32n
reductionists' awareness of, 362
social, 103
and truth, 104n
as views (Polkinghorne), 222
Reality claims, and postmodernists, 35–36,
    38n
Real Knowing (Alcoff), 286
Reason. See Rationality/reason
Reber, J. S., 6
Recognition of Reason, The (Pols), 351
Reconsidering Psychology (Faulconer & Will-
    iams), 6
Reductionism, 361–363
    cultural, 162, 180, 362
    MGTs' struggle against, 109–110
        and Nagel on historicism, 111
    in modern/conventional psychology, 4,
        5
    traditional science not linked to
        (Rychlak), 311
Reductionist ontology, of modern/conven-
    tional psychology, 8–9
Re-envisioning Psychology (Richardson,
    Fowers, & Guignon), 6, 27–28, 65,
    83–84, 272
Reflection, radically originative (Pols), 352
"Reflexive," and MGTs, 170
Reflexive impact, 313
Reflexivity, 251–252, 346–347
    and being-knowing relation, 101–112,
        191, 215, 271
        and beliefs about objects of investi-
            gation, 100, 104, 120, 121, 152
    and constraints, 89
    and discursive context, 158, 184–185,
        187
    and double hermeneutics (Giddens),
        103, 195, 258–259
    Martin and Sugarman on, 126–127, 179
    and MGTs
        antiobjectivist view of, 121
        and ontology of being in the world,
            126, 135
        and realism, 149
        and stability vs. flux, 192, 194,
            195
    Pol's self-reflexive defense of rational
        awareness, 350–356
    and post-therapeutics, 39
    and rational awareness, 353

and Siegel's "self-reflexive" defense of rationality, 347–350

social constructionists on, 104, 144

theory or thesis of, 101, 152n23, 195, 225, 257, 259, 298–299, 319, 346

and transcendence, 166

Regional ontology, 98n

Regularities in human thought and action in context, 297–299

Fishman and Miller on, 304

Reification, 216–217

Relatedness, vs. objective/subjective distinction, 61

Relations, theory of, 137–138n

Relativism, 60

Bernstein on, 58, 244

and contextualization vs. universals (Fishman; Martin & Sugarman), 198–199

epistemic, 23

and Rychlak, 311

epistemological, 224, 244

Haack on, 57–58, 60

and Martin and Sugarman, 150, 180, 199, 244, 251, 270–271, 275–276, 276–277, 278, 317

and MGTs, 100, 224, 249, 250, 251, 266, 267, 280, 330

on psychological existence, 149–152

moving beyond (Fowers & Richardson), 336–337

in multiculturalism, 335

vs. objective psychological truth, 48

ontological, 101, 152

pragmatic, 274, 274–275, 279, 289

and radical postmodernism, 31, 38

and realism, 54n2, 150, 151

rejection of, 40

and Rescher on universality and particularity, 247

Siegel on, 249, 251, 280–281, 330–331

strong, 150, 270–271

strong vs. weak forms of (Martin & Sugarman), 276–277

strong-weak distinction for (Siegel), 277n5

and transcultural normative reach (Siegel), 333

of value-laden warrants, 272

weak, 150, 270–271

Relativist epistemology, 224

of social constructionists, 276

weak, 275–281

Relativist ontology

and MGTs, 270

of personhood, 276

Rescher, Nicholas, 245–248, 261, 262, 269

and circumstantial universality of reason, 275, 279

on contexts, 331–332

and rationality, 280

universal reason/rationality of, 272

Research

methodological pluralism in, 315–317

and pragmatic vs. hermeneutic paradigm, 74

Rewriting the Self (Freeman), 6, 61, 68, 360

Richardson, F. C., 6, 12, 114–115

and agency, 116, 165, 166, 167

and being in the world, 94–95

on "brute facts," 215

on causal analysis, 302–303

on causal laws, 255

and causal questions, 297

and compatibilism dilemma, 314

on contemporary hermeneutics, 283

and conventional psychological inquiry, 305

and dependence, 187

causal, 189

on descriptions, 295

on discourse and psychological existence, 145, 146

on emanationist or emergent theory of reality/truth, 138, 139, 220

on emotion, 185

on explanations in natural science, 293

and fallibilism, 119, 134

on formalization, 280

on Gadamer, 278

on good judgment, 269, 279

on hermeneutic philosophers, 214

and hermeneutic realism, 66

on human sciences, 216

on influence of human sciences, 267

on interpretation, 220, 257–258, 299

evaluation of, 272

on knowledge claims, 281

and MacIntyre, 340

on marital behavior, 298

on meanings, 113

as MGT, 27, 65

on modernist approach, 83–84

on multiculturalism, 332, 335–337

on natural vs. human sciences, 121
and neorealist hermeneutic, 266
on objective knowledge, 280
on objectivist epistemology, 211, 263
and objectivist inquiry in social sciences, 225
on objectivity, 281
    as certainty, 218
and ontological realism, 220
and "overarching scientific account," rejection of, 273
on personhood and interpretation, 92, 99, 100, 101, 102, 103, 116, 117–118, 160, 210, 252 (*see also* Interpretation and personhood, relation of)
on postmodernism, 194
on pragmatism, 283, 284
on psychological inquiry, 356
and psychology vs. natural science 298
vs. radical constructionists, 137
on realism, 120, 151, 200
on stonewalling, 184
on theory choice in social sciences, 337
on transcendence, 173, 201
and truth, 196, 278, 319
and values, 282
    in social theory, 238, 239, 240
Rigid dependence, 185, 186
Riikonen, E., 42
Rorty, Richard
    on agency, 309n
    on desire and truth, 266
    on differences between traditions, 272
    and "epistemological model," 116n7
    and Fishman, 274
    Guignon on, 116n7, 200, 226, 273, 282, 289, 309
    and Heidegger, 124n
    on justification, 289
    and linguistic systems, 30
    and naturalized epistemology, 289
    on objectivity, 282
    and ontological mutism, 200
    on pragmatic relativism, 275
    on pragmatism, 43n14, 75, 116
        and truth, 110
    on rationality, 279
    and relativism, 40, 336
    Siegel on, 117n
    on truth, 266, 282, 283
    on warrants, 295

Rules
    making behavior sensical within context, 293–297
    in warranted psychological knowledge, 305–306
Rychlak, Joseph, 16, 308–313, 314, 354n21, 358, 359

Sass, Louis, 6, 69, 86, 95, 170, 187, 196, 210–211
Schafer, Roy, 44, 45, 47, 116
Scheffler, Israel, 243
Science
    vs. agency (Martin & Sugarman), 82
    categories of, 302
    as common sense (Haack), 316
    cultural relevance of, 284
    culture of, 242
    human, 95, 121, 216, 237–241
    language of (as impoverished), 28, 211
    and MGTs, 85
    Miller's repudiation of, 303
    paradigmatic assumptions in (Kuhn), 311
    and Pols on universality, 341
    and postmodernists, 28
Science wars (Driver-Linn), 63
Scientific approach, and volition, 80
Scientific method, Rychlak on, 310, 311
Scientific realism, 72
Scientism
    Martin's and Sugarman's avoidance of, 317
    psychological, 65
Searle, John, 53, 54–55,
    on brute vs. institutional facts, 230
    and Lakoff, 57
    and logical vs. causal dependence, 141, 147
    on realism and antirealism, 110, 140, 141n, 144n, 208
    and "internal realism," 97
Self
    singularity in (Harré), 72
    social construction of, 181
Self-deception, 299
Self-determination
    and action, 187
    and agency, 16, 142, 306, 323
    agentic notion of, 3n2
    and causal laws, 11
    desire to preserve, 3

and MGTs, 9
and objectivism of modern/conventional psychologists, 8–9, 16
and postmodern movement, 4, 11
See also Agency
Self-formation, 170
Self-identity, and agency (Pols), 360
Self-interpretation, 168
and action (Taylor), 146
and agency, 167
constraints on, 283
and psychological properties, 185
therapists' efforts to change, 189
See also Interpretation
Self-knowledge, 217
challenging of, 354
first-person warrant for, 46n15
through encounter with "otherness" (Jopling), 353n19
Self-reflexivity, 21, 22, 24, 182, 207, 348, 354, 354n21
Self or subject
postmodernists' denial of, 28
MGTs' attempt to reinstate, 29
and social constructivism, 32, 34
theories of, 168
and words (Freeman), 169
Self-transcendence, Pols on, 360n26
Self-understanding, 168
and agency, 167
and truth about ourselves, 252
Shotter, John, 30, 78
Shusterman, R., 5, 166, 250, 267
Siegel, Harvey, 248–251, 330–335, 337–338
on Cartesian Anxiety, 212
on cultural relativists, 336
on epistemology of Israel Scheffler, 243
on fallibilism, 278
on naturalized epistemology, 286–287, 290
and objectivity, 262
vs. opposition of universality and particularity, 329, 340
and Pols, 344
on rationality, 280
defense of, 347–350
and objectivity, 249, 325, 326
as universal, 344
and reflexivity, 346–347
on relativism, 277n5, 280–281, 330–331, 342
and transcendence, 345

and transcultural normative reach, 24, 330–335, 337
on universality and particularity, 327
on universals of rationality, 269, 272
Singular Self, The (Harré), 6, 72
Situated agency, 158, 179–180, 182, 201–203
and particularity, 203
Situated being, 23
Situated cognition, 339–340
Situated epistemologies, vs. universality of argumentative force, 334
Situated form of knowing, 22, 23
Situated personhood, 235
Situational or contextual realism, 155
Skepticism
toward argumentative or epistemic normativity (Siegel's response against), 337–338
radical, 61–62
about rationality (Siegel's response to), 349
Slaney, K. L., 122–123
Slife, B. D., 6, 30, 103, 212, 243, 315
Smith, M. Brewster, 33
Social constructionism, 4, 12, 29, 30, 32, 70, 71–73, 95–96, 104
conduct evaluated by, 238
in counseling, 34
and discursive practices, 144
and Gadamerian hermeneutics (Freeman), 13
of Gergen, 77
moderate, 60, 79–80, 118, 144–145, 274
and realist epistemology, 266
and stability vs. change, 195–196
and moral relativism, 282–283
and normative explanations (Harré), 294
and personhood, 120
and "pragmatic paradigm," 74
and pragmatic standard, 76
radical, 162
vs. radical constructivism, 139n15
and relativist epistemology, 270, 276
and scientific realism (Harré), 151
on social categories, 95
on sociocultural change, 163–164
truth claims of, 36–38, 79
and universals, 153
"Social Constructionism as Ontology" (Nightingale & Cromby), 78

Social construction of self, 181
Social constructivism
    and Goodman, 87
    and reality of discursive domain, 113
Social kinds, 154
Social norms, and agency, 165
Social and psychological entities and reality, 130, 209
    and fallibilism, 137–138
    and interpretive contexts, 140
    See also Human kinds
Social and psychological kinds, Thomasson on, 219
Social reality, 103
Social sciences, 103
    Haack on, 316
    human affairs affected by, 25
    and philosophies of being and knowing, 3
    theory choice in, 273, 337
Social theory, and values, 238
Sociocognitive systems, 339–340
Sociocultural beliefs and practices, and psychological reality, 126–127
Sociocultural contexts
    and innovation (Martin & Sugarman), 177–178
    and personal theories, 168
Sociocultural reality, as pluralistic, 172
Specificity question, 302
Spence, Donald, 44, 45, 47, 196–197
Stability
    and agency, 199–201
    within flux, 193–199, 252–253
        and Fishman, 301
        and universals, 198–199, 200
    and MGTs, 201, 252, 256
    of psychological existence, 190
    and realism, 201
Stancombe, 34, 38–39, 40, 41
Statistics, use of, 315–316
Stearns, P., 6
Stonewalling, 136–137, 180, 184, 220
    and rational awareness, 228
Storolow, Robert, 44, 45, 47
Strangers to Ourselves (Wilson), 354
Straw man
    of objectivity, 22, 253, 260–262, 279, 280, 315, 327, 357
    opponents pictured as (extremes contrasted with middle ground), 261
Structure of Scientific Revolutions, The (Kuhn), 311

Stumbling on Happiness (Gilbert), 354
Subjective judgments, two ways of defining, 219
Subjective/objective distinction. *See* Objective/subjective distinction
Subjectivism
    contention over meaning of, 15
    vs. relativism (Bernstein), 58
Subjectivity, 11n9
    as barrier to knowledge, 30
    and existential involvements (Martin & Sugarman), 179
    and objective knowledge, 44–48
    personhood as (Martin & Sugarman), 180
    in postmodern psychology, 11
Sugarman, Jeff, 6, 12, 64–65, 82–83
    on agency, 157, 158, 163–164, 166–167, 168, 169, 180, 202, 307
        and comprehension of situation, 181
        definition of, 329
        and self-identity, 360
    and being in the world, 147, 194
    and belief in ability to know human nature, 318
    and biological reductionism, 162–163
    and causal deterministic science of psychology, 304
    causal/noncausal account by, 304–307
    and causal questions, 297
    and compatibilism dilemma, 314
    on conceptualization, 279
    on constraint, 359
    and cultural reductionism, 361–362
    on cultural upheavals, 196
    and cultures as pluralistic, 172
    on discursive psychology, 71
    and double hermeneutics, 101
    on epistemic standard of usefulness, 198
    on epistemology and transcendence, 317–318
    on equating realism with objectivism, 218
    on flux and stability, 193
    on forms of psychological inquiry, 357
    and fusion of horizons, 279–280
    on human kinds, 130
    and individual psychological development, 177–179
    and interpretation, 215
    and language of causal dependence, 142
    and levels of reality, 118, 123–124, 127, 151, 197–198

on logical dependency, 146
on mediation, 223
on myths of modernity, 81–82
and neorealist hermeneutics, 266
on objectivism, 208n1
and objectivity, 254, 255, 261, 262
and ontological realism, 220
on personhood and interpretation, 92, 99, 100, 102, 160, 210
and perspectival, fallibilist warrant, 267
on postmodernists, 200
on psychological inquiry, 356
and psychology of possibility and constraint, 89
and rationality/tradition, 176
on realism, 200, 277
    hermeneutic, 66, 123–127
on reductionism, 363
and relativism, 150, 180, 199, 244, 251, 270–271, 275–276, 276–277, 278, 317
Rychlak on, 311
and self-understanding, 217
and situated agency, 201
and soft determinism, 65
and stability, 198, 199, 252
on tradition as pragmatic warrant, 272
and transcendence, 170, 187, 201, 324
    as innovation, 174, 185, 187
on "view from nowhere," 241
and warranted generalization, 199
on warranted reason, 269
on warrants, 290, 291

Talk therapy, 145–146
Taylor, Charles, 66, 94, 117, 146, 186–187, 211n4, 255, 293
Theory(ies)
    and language, 224n13, 226n
    and life outcomes, 37
    and objective knowledge, 227
    of self, 168
    social (and values), 238
    as transformative account, 273
Theory & Psychology (journal), 72, 73
Theory (thesis) of reflexivity, 101, 152n23, 195, 225, 257, 259, 298–299, 319, 346
Theory of relations, 137–138n
Therapy
    case-study database for, 300–301
    individualization of, 18n

and objectivism (Woolfolk), 213
and regularities in psychological phenomena (Miller), 304
self-interpretation in, 189
talk, 145–146
Thomasson, Amie
    on being and knowing, 137, 138
    on boundary criteria, 132, 134, 135, 136, 233, 261
    on epistemological realism, 194
    on fallibilist inquiry, 228
    on human kinds, 115, 233, 277–278, 296–297
    on intentionality, 133–134
    and knower-known distinction, 138
    on logical vs. causal dependence, 141
    and objective knowledge, 218–219
    on objectivist epistemology, 212
    and objectivity, 113, 133–134, 262
    and ontology of human kinds, 135, 136
    on "realism," 209
    realism of, 134
    on realist epistemology, 265–266
    and realist ontology, 21, 55, 56
        and human kinds, 128–129, 130
    on social kinds, 154
        racism as example of, 131–132, 296–297 (see also Racism)
    on subjective and objective judgments, 219–220
Thompson, J., 6, 101, 102, 158, 201
    on agency, 329
    on discursive psychology, 71
    on personhood and interpretation, 92, 99, 100, 160, 210
    Rychlak on, 311
"To Live at Ease Ever After" (Pols), 111
"Totalizing discourse," 29
Toulmin, Stephen, 75, 243
"Toward a Non-Regulative Praxis" (Kaye), 42
Tradition(s), 93, 146–147
    affirmation of needed (Gadamer), 176
    and consequences of knowledge claims, 288
    and Gadamer, 93, 164, 196, 278, 281
        on understanding, 169
    intersection of, 169
    negative, 175n
    sources of change in (Fowers), 175
    and transcendence, 172
    and truth, 155, 271

and values, 272
warrant within (Martin & Sugarman), 267–268
Transcendence
and agency, 86, 181, 324 (*see also* Agency)
and antiobjectivist/antirealist epistemology, 355–356
vs. antiobjectivist interpretive turn, 362
and cultural/discursive context, 202
and culturally situated agency, 201
and dependence, 185–186
epistemological and ontological, 329
and imagination, 187–188
justification of, 282
as limited, 170, 187–188, 192, 201, 324
as innovation, 174, 185, 187
and MGTs, 4, 330, 335
contextually constrained capacity for, 357
through neorealist hermeneutics, 317–318
and objective knowing or knowledge, 317, 326, 360–361
and ontological expansion of reason, 351n
of particular perspectives, 330, 331, 332, 335
Pols on, 341, 343–345, 346
on rational awareness, 353
rational, 328–329, 358–361
and Pols on fusion of universality and particularity, 340–346
and transcultural normative reach, 330–340
and Rescher, 248
Rychlak on, 309, 358
of situated existence, 21, 22
Transcendence of constitutive contexts
agency as capacity for, 164–171
and multivocal or pluralistic nature/ essence of cultures, 171–176
and rational or imaginative nature of human mind, 176–182
Transcending/overcoming
language of, 65, 66, 68, 69, 75
Transcultural normative reach, 24, 330–332, 337, 344
and argument quality, 332–335
and multiculturalism, 335
Transformative account, theory as, 273

Transformative aspect of psychological theory, 282
Truth
and agency, 324–325
as context-dependent, 324
correspondence theories of, 111
criteria of, 281
definition of, 16
emanationist or emergent theory of, 60, 67, 104–112, 114, 222, 225
emanationist theory of, 121, 133, 138–139, 222, 225
emergent theory of, 104, 138, 286
Freeman on, 108, 271
Gadamer on, 195, 270
within hermeneutic tradition, 196
and moral values, 238
as necessary aim (Nagel), 111
perspectival view of, 276
pragmatic, 193, 266, 285, 295
and "objective reality," 255, 275
pragmatic relativism, 274, 275
radical postmodern view on, 139
and reality, 104n
as relativized (Guignon), 269
Richardson et al. on, 196, 278, 319
Rorty on, 266, 282, 283
in science (Driver-Linn), 64
as subjective matter (House), 43
and tradition, 155
and transcendence, 282
Woolfolk on, 271
See also at Warrant(s)
Truth claims, of radical postmodernists, 35–38
"Truth in Interpretation" (Guignon), 273–274
Truth-tracking. *See* Realist epistemology
Type-subjective vs. type-objective judgments, 219

Uncertainty theory, 46, 46n17
Universal agreement, about desirable or good consequences, 272
Universal functions, of mind, 229
Universalism, and essentialism, 99n
Universalist/essentialist account, MGTs' rejection of, 217–218
Universality
of argumentative force (Siegel), 334, 344
and particularity

fusion of, 24, 154, 203, 327, 340–346

opposition of (MGTs), 329, 332

in modern and postmodern psychologies (Richardson, Fowers, & Guignon), 84

of rational/imaginative capacity, 202

vs. sociocognitive systems (Nisbett et al.), 339–340

Universals, 153

and agency, 176–180, 362

causal laws as, 292

and causal relation, 314

intuitively grasped (Levinas), 319–320

in "the local and particular" (Harré), 153–154

and MGTs, 153, 192, 342

of mind/rationality, 176–177, 203, 232, 234

and Rescher's circumstantial universality of reason, 245–248, 269

and Siegel, 269, 272

of personhood, 343

and relativism, 199

and Rychlak, 310, 311

and stability, 198–199, 200

and straw man of objectivity, 260, 280, 315, 327, 357

value-laden factors justified by, 289, 290, 291

Universal truths

postmodernists' rejection of, 28

Siegel on, 330

Utility, and theory acceptance, 284

Value-free view from nowhere, 213, 234–251, 268, 330

Value-laden epistemology, 281–285

of MGTs, 317, 356

Value-laden warrant, 272–275, 295

normative thrust of, 287–288

Values, 235–238, 241–244, 260

and "circumstantial universality of reason" (Rescher), 245–248

and epistemic warrant, 183

and human (psychological) sciences, 237–241

and MGTs, 235–236, 237–238, 239, 241

and neutral epistemic standards (Siegel), 248–251

as objective (Richardson et al.), 263

objective knowledge as, 281

subjectified view of, 66

Taylor on, 114

utility of as criterion, 284

and warrant, 282

Vataja, S., 42

Verificationists, Searle on, 110

View from nowhere, 22, 24, 91, 182, 203, 240, 346

and nonrelativist or objectivist epistemology, 270

Siegel on, 330, 331

value-free, 213, 234–251, 260, 268, 330

View from Nowhere, The (Nagel), 62, 111

Virtue and Psychology (Fowers), 6

Warrant(s) (epistemic), 208, 239, 243, 327

constraint on generality of, 328

and culture (Martin & Sugarman), 362

as impersonal (Haack), 244, 245

and neutral epistemic standards (Siegel), 251

as objective though not necessarily transparent, 246

perspectival, 244

political or pragmatic consequences as criteria for, 317

pragmatic views or standards of, 70, 266, 281–285

to psychological knowledge, 237

and radical postmodern view of truth, 139

value-laden, 272–275, 295

normative thrust of, 287–288

and values, 238, 242

Warrant(s) espoused by MGTs, 208, 266, 267

and contexts, 315

critique of, 275

and naturalized epistemology as realist, 286–291

and pragmatic value-laden epistemology as realist, 281–285

and weak relativist epistemology as realist, 275–281

and objective knowledge, 318

standards of

perspectival warrant and fallibilist inquiry/knowing, 267–270

practical reason within a context, 269–270

pragmatic/value-laden warrant, 272–275

weak relativism, 270–271

Ways of Worldmaking (Goodman), 87

Weak relativism, 270–271

Weak relativist epistemology, 275–281

Wegner, Daniel, 46n16, 299n, 354

Wertz, Frederick, 319–320

What's Behind the Research (Slife & Williams), 6

White, S., 34, 38–39, 40, 41

"Why Is Multiculturalism Good?" (Fowers & Richardson), 335

Williams, R.N., 6, 30, 95, 103, 212, 243, 315

Wilson, Timothy, 354

Windschuttle, Keith, 195, 225, 256–257, 258–259

Woolfolk, Robert, 6, 12, 66–67, 86, 95, 133, 145, 187, 196

on emanationist or emergent theory of reality/truth, 138, 220, 271

on forms of psychological inquiry, 357

on generality and particularity, 75

and hermeneutic approach, 210–211, 266, 300

on interpretation, 221

on logical vs. causal dependence, 141

and objectivism, 213

on ontology of flux and flow, 253

on situated knowledge, 224

on value-laden component of knowing, 241

ABOUT THE AUTHOR

Barbara S. Held, PhD, is the Barry N. Wish Professor of Psychology and Social Studies at Bowdoin College in Brunswick, Maine. She is the author of *Back to Reality: A Critique of Postmodern Theory in Psychotherapy* (1995), in which she provides theoretical and philosophical analysis of the postmodern linguistic turn in psychotherapy. Trained as a clinical psychologist, she practiced therapy for many years. Professor Held is the author of numerous scholarly articles and chapters about psychotherapy and is a fellow of the American Psychological Association Divisions 29 (Psychotherapy), 12 (Society of Clinical Psychology), and 24 (Society for Theoretical and Philosophical Psychology). She has a long-standing interest in the philosophy of science, in particular the ontological and epistemological underpinnings of psychological inquiry. In this regard, Professor Held has published in and reviewed for the *Journal of Theoretical and Philosophical Psychology* and *Theory & Psychology*. In her popular book *Stop Smiling, Start Kvetching: A 5-Step Guide to Creative Complaining* (2001) and in subsequent scholarly articles, she has challenged what she calls the "tyranny of the positive attitude in America" and as a result has become a leading critic of the positive psychology movement. This work has led to extensive worldwide media attention, including features in *The New York Times* and *People* magazine as well as appearances on the *Today* show, National Public Radio's *Talk of the Nation*, and the BBC. She lives with her husband on the coast of Maine.